COMMUNICOLOGY

Communicology
An Introduction to the Study of Communication
Second Edition

Joseph A. DeVito

Queens College,
City University of New York

1817

HARPER & ROW, PUBLISHERS, New York

Cambridge, Philadelphia, San Francisco,
London, Mexico City, São Paulo, Sydney

This symbol and the word *communicology* are components of a registered Service Mark of J. G. Lowder and Communication Architects of Lynnwood, Washington. This Service Mark is used by Communication Architects in connection with its consulting services in the field of communications.

Photograph Credits

The following are the pages on which photographs appear.

Page 2, Leo de Wys, Inc.; 8, Karales, Peter Arnold; 21, Fishman, de Wys; 26, Leo de Wys, Inc.; 35, © Shelton, © Peter Arnold; 41, Tony Velez; 49, Shelton, Monkmeyer; 61, Tony Velez; 72, © Seitz, 1978, Woodfin Camp; 75, Hoops, de Wys; 85, Culver; 101, © Shelton, Peter Arnold; 106, Shelton, © Peter Arnold; 118, Karales, © Peter Arnold; 123, Reininger, de Wys; 130, Leo de Wys, Inc.; 136, Leo de Wys, Inc.; 146, Vannucci, de Wys; 152, Pfeffer, © Peter Arnold; 157, Felsenthal, de Wys; 174, Tony Velez; 184, Photo Trends; 191, Photo Trends; 197, © Johnson, 1980, Woodfin Camp; 209, Grossman, de Wys; 216, Lyon, Magnum; 228, Berman, de Wys; 236, Wasinski, de Wys; 244, Tony Velez; 250, Leo de Wys, Inc.; 263, Tony Velez; 267, Culver; 275, Culver; 281, Kiedrowski, Peter Arnold; 284, Corry, de Wys; 297, UPI; 305, © Chih, 1978, © Peter Arnold; 322, Tony Velez; 338, © Chih, 1978, © Peter Arnold; 352, UPI; 357, Tony Velez; 361, Johnson, de Wys; 372, Erwitt, Magnum; 377, Syndication International, Photo Trends; 394, Culver; 408, Culver; 415, Tony Velez; 422, Berman, de Wys; 436, Evans/Contact, de Wys; 440, © Shelton, © Peter Arnold; 470, Tony Velez; 480, Tony Velez; 502, Photo Trends; 507, Photo Trends; 524, Photo Trends; 533, UPI; 540, © Karales, © Peter Arnold; 550, Shelton, © Peter Arnold.

Sponsoring Editor: George A. Middendorf
Supervisor of Editing: Karla Billups Philip
Designer: T. R. Funderburk
Production Manager: Marion A. Palen
Photo Researcher: Mira Schnache
Compositor: Progressive Typographers
Printer and Binder: Halliday Lithograph Corporation
Art Studio: Vantage Art, Inc.
Cover Art: Charles K. Lassiter

COMMUNICOLOGY: An Introduction to the Study of Communication, Second Edition

Copyright © 1982 by Joseph A. DeVito

Library of Congress Cataloging in Publication Data

DeVito, Joseph A., 1938—
  Communicology: an introduction to the study of communication.

  Includes bibliographies and index.
  1. Communication. I. Title.
P90.D48 1982   001.51   81-6864
ISBN 0-06-041652-1   AACR2

THE TITLE

Communicology is the study of the art and science of communication, particularly that subsection concerned with communication by and among human beings. *Communicologist* refers to the communication student-researcher-theorist. Franklin H. Knower, one of the founders of the International Communication Association, and Wendell Johnson, a leading theorist-researcher in semantics and in the speech and hearing sciences, have long advocated the use of these terms.

The study of communication is still young and still embroiled in the laborious process of defining itself. Until now, the term *communication* has been used as a catch-all to refer to three different areas of study: (1) the process or act of communication, (2) the actual message or messages communicated, and (3) the study of the process of communicating. *Communicology* is a far more specific and accurate term to describe the focus of this book. It is not a mere piece of jargon; rather it represents an attempt to refine the language that relates to the field as a whole in order to pinpoint and clarify the broad areas of study within it.

Joseph A. DeVito

Contents

Contents in Detail

Preface

The second edition of *Communicology* has enabled me to retain those features from the first edition that proved useful and effective and to correct or revise those features that needed change. The purpose of the book, however, remains the same: to present a comprehensive overview of communication that will enable students to understand, control, and analyze communication behaviors and events. As in the first edition, I have assumed that the student-communicator has at least a three-part responsibility—as a communication source, a communication receiver, and a communication analyst. Attention is devoted to all three of these functions.

The major changes in this second edition are the inclusion of preliminary units for each of the eight major sections of the text; a more focused practical orientation to the forms of communication, particularly public communication and small group communication; and the integration of intercultural research and theory in the units on verbal messages, nonverbal messages, and conflict. This second edition also includes updated research findings, a more effective integration of contemporary research and theory, new examples and illustrative materials to clarify difficult or abstract concepts further, and new and revised Experiential Vehicles.

Communicology is divided into 30 short units rather than into long chapters—the unit approach makes the book easier and more pleasant to read. Because the units are self-contained, they can be studied in any pattern that suits the needs of a particular course or group of students. The major advantage of this approach is that it will enable the units to be read at almost any time—during a break between classes, before dinner, during lunch, on a bus or train, or anywhere else you get the chance to read. We learn most effectively when we learn in small doses, and so I recommend that no more than one unit be read at any one sitting. It will prove best to read a unit and then spend some time thinking about its contents and about how it relates to your own communication behaviors.

The 30 units are divided into eight major parts. Part One, "Communication," contains four introductory units on the nature and function of communication and the self. Part Two, "Message Reception," focuses on how messages are received and on the two major areas of message reception: perception and listening. Part Three, "Verbal Messages," provides a thorough consideration of the nature of verbal behavior, language in society, and the principles of and barriers to verbal interaction. Part Four focuses on nonverbal behavior and covers the forms of nonverbal communication—for example, facial and body movements, eye contact, space, touch, and paralanguage (the vocal but nonverbal dimension of communication). Parts Five through Eight are devoted to the major forms of communication: interpersonal communication, small group communication, public communication, and mass communication. The objectives here are both theoretical and practical: to provide you with insight into the nature and function of these forms of communication as well as practical guidance in improving your interpersonal, small group, public, and mass communication behaviors as a source, a receiver, and a communication analyst.

Each of these eight parts begins with an overview unit detailing the essential "preliminaries." These "preliminaries" should provide readers with the background information needed to tackle the more detailed material contained in the remaining units and will also ensure that all members of the class begin the study of each topic with similar or comparable backgrounds. The remaining units in each part then cover specific dimensions or aspects of these eight major topics.

Each unit begins with a set of Learning Goals. These will help you focus on the major concepts. Read these goals before beginning the unit to fix in your mind these essential concepts. After reading the unit, return to these goals to see if you are, in fact, able to achieve the goals. If you are not, reread the unit.

At the end of each unit are Sources, which include both the references I used in preparing the text and the references I would suggest for further reading. I realize that most students do not do "further reading," especially in an introductory course. These suggestions are included in the hope that both this text and this course will be different—they are about you and your communication behavior, and perhaps you will be more motivated to study yourself than you are to memorize mathematical formulas or historical data.

A significant part of the text is devoted to Experiential Vehicles. These are exercises designed to enable you to *experience* the concepts and principles discussed in the units rather than to learn them on a purely intellectual level. In fact, some instructors will prefer to devote all of the class time to the Experiential Vehicles and have students do the reading independently. Other instructors will prefer to devote some time to the vehicles and some to an explanation or elaboration of textual material. In either case, the Experiential Vehicles will make the concepts more interesting and enjoyable to learn and the material learned more meaningful and personal.

The boxes sprinkled throughout the text are designed to provide what I consider useful and interesting sidelights on the concepts discussed in the units. The visual materials were carefully chosen to illustrate these concepts as well.

At the end of the text is a glossary of significant terms used in the study of communication. These brief definitions should give you a better understanding of the concepts and processes discussed in the book and should prove useful in review.

I want to thank the many people who helped me in the writing and production of this book. I owe a great deal to those colleagues who reviewed the first and this second edition of the manuscript and who gave freely of their insights, criticisms, and suggestions for improvement: Roy M. Berko of Lorain County Community College; Nancy Wood Bliese of Queens College; Bernard J. Brommel of Northeastern Illinois University; Jerry Butler of the University of Arkansas at Little Rock; Gil Clardy of Washburn University; Pamela Cooper of Northwestern University; William A. Donohue of Michigan State University; Catherine Konsky of Illinois State University; Jo Sprague of San José State University; and, Sanford B. Weinberg of St. Joseph's University. My own students at Queens College helped greatly by providing a willing and receptive audience and by giving me important feedback. As always Maggie and Boo provided the emotional support so needed in writing and revising a work such as this and taught me through experience about interpersonal relationships.

The staff at Harper & Row all contributed greatly to the final product. I especially wish to thank Karla Philip who graciously and skillfully supervised the editing and production of the book; the editors who presided over the speech communication discipline during this book's production, now so ably directed by George A. Middendorf; T. R. Funderburk for the attractive and functional design, and, Mira Schachne for selecting the wide variety of relevant photographs.

Joseph A. DeVito

COMMUNICOLOGY

Part One

Communication

Unit 1

Preliminaries to Communication

PRELIMINARIES TO COMMUNICATION

The Nature of Communication
Communication Components
Some Summary Propositions
   1.1 Communication Components
   1.2 Specific Models of Communication

LEARNING GOALS

After completing this unit, you should be able to:

1. discuss the nature of the universals of communication
2. define the following terms: *communication context, sources-receivers, messages, competence* and *performance, encoding-decoding, noise, feedback, field of experience, communication effect,* and *ethics*
3. explain the transactional nature of communication
4. diagram the model of the universals of communication presented in this unit, labeling all its parts
5. diagram and explain the relationship between competence and performance
6. construct an original model of communication that incorporates the following: context, source-receiver, message, encoding-decoding, noise, feedback, and field of experience
7. identify at least six summary propositions about the nature of communication

This book is about communication, and a definition seems a good place to begin. *Communication* refers to the act, by one or more persons, of sending and receiving messages that are distorted by noise, occur within a context, have some effect, and provide some opportunity for feedback. The communication act, then, would include the following components: *context, source(s)-receiver(s), messages, noise, sending* or *encoding processes, receiving* or *decoding processes, feedback,* and *effect.* These elements seem the most essential in any consideration of the communication act. They are what we might call the *universals of communication* — the elements that are present in every communication act, regardless of whether it is *intrapersonal* (with oneself), *interpersonal* (with one or two others), *small group, public speaking,* or *mass communication.*

Universals may be treated as existing on a number of different levels. At the most general level, the universals of communication would include, for example, source-receiver, message, context, noise, and effect. We might also discuss universals of communication at more specific levels; we might consider those universals included in each of the general universals. For example, the universals included in the *general* universal of source-receiver would include self-awareness, self-disclosure, credibility, attitudes, and so on. The general universals of communication are illustrated in Figure 1.1. The entire unit is devoted to a description and explanation of these universal components.

THE NATURE OF COMMUNICATION

Communication is a transactional process. By *transaction* I mean to specify a number of different characteristics of communication. First, I mean to specify that communication is a process; communication is an act, an event, an activity, an ongoing process. Although we may talk about communication as if it were something static and at rest, it is never so; it is always an ongoing process. Consequently, everything in communication is in a state of constant change. We are constantly changing, the people we are communicating with are changing, our environment is changing. Sometimes these changes go unnoticed; sometimes they intrude in obvious ways. But always the changes are occurring; nothing in communication ever remains static.

Second, in any transactional process, each element is integrally related to every other element; the elements of the communication act are interdependent (never independent); each exists in relation to the others. For example, there can be no source without a receiver; there can be no message without a source; there can be no feedback without a receiver. Each aspect of the communication act (although we may talk about them individually and as if they were separate and distinct parts) is intimately connected with each other element.

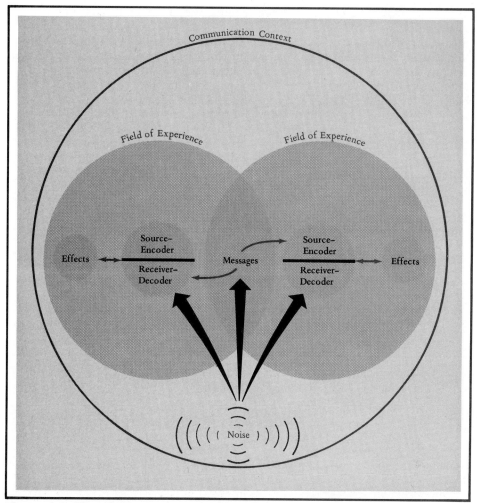

Figure 1.1   The universals of communication.

Third, and closely related to this interdependency, is that a change in any one element of the communication process produces changes in the other elements. For example, you are talking with a group of your friends and your mother enters the group. This change in "audience" will lead to a number of other changes—perhaps in the style of the communications, perhaps in the content of what is said, perhaps in the frequency with which certain people talk, and so on. Regardless of what change is introduced, other changes will be produced as a result of this initial change. Fourth, and perhaps most important, is that each person involved in the communication process acts and reacts as a whole. We are designed—for good or ill—to act as whole beings. One cannot react, for example, solely on an intellectual level or solely on an emotional level; we are not so compartmentalized. Rather, we respond emotionally and intellectually; we respond physically and cognitively; we respond with body and mind. Perhaps the most important corollary of this characteristic is that our actions and reactions in communication are determined not only by what is said but by our interpretation of what is said. Our responses to a movie, for example, are not solely dependent on the words and pictures in the movie but on our entire being—on our previous experiences, our present emotions, our knowledge, our physical well-being or ill health, and a host of other factors. Thus, two people listening to the same message will often derive two very different meanings. Although the words and symbols might have been the same, they will be interpreted very differently by different people. Each individual's interpretation of any communication will be unique; each interpretation will be different from every other interpretation. This transactional nature of communication is well illustrated by one researcher in the form of a spiral, presented in Figure 1.2. This spiral emphasizes that communication has no clear observable beginning and no clear observable end; the spiral continues indefinitely. No communication transaction may be said to have fixed boundaries. Each transaction is, in part, a function of previous communications, and each transaction in turn influences future communications.

COMMUNICATION COMPONENTS

Now that the general structure of the communication process has been outlined, we need to explore the specific components of the communication act in greater depth.

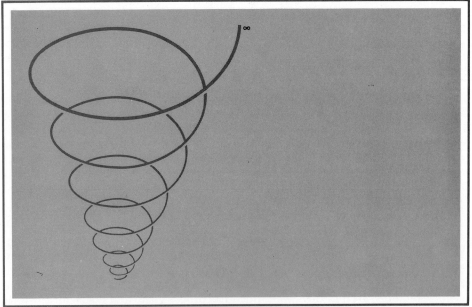

Figure 1.2   Dance's helical spiral. *Source:* Frank E. X. Dance, "Toward a Theory of Human Communication," in F. E. X. Dance, ed., *Human Communication Theory: Original Essays* (New York: Holt, Rinehart and Winston, 1957), p. 296.

COMMUNICATION CONTEXT

Communication always takes place within a *context*. At times this context is subtle and unobtrusive; it seems to be so natural that it is ignored, like background music. At other times, the context stands out boldly, and the ways in which it restricts or stimulates our communications are obvious. Compare, for example, the differences in communicating in a funeral home, a football stadium, or a quiet restaurant.

The context of communication has at least four dimensions: physical, social, psychological, and temporal. The room or hallway or park—that is, the tangible or concrete environment—in which communication takes place is the *physical context*. This physical context, whatever it is, exerts some influence on the content as well as the form of our messages. The *social dimension* of context includes, for example, the status relationships among the participants, the roles and the games that people play, and the norms and cultural mores of the society in which they are communicating. The *psychological context* consists of such aspects as the friendliness or unfriendliness of the situation, the formality or informality, and the seriousness or humorousness of the situation. Communications are permitted at a graduation party that would not be permitted at a funeral or in a hospital. The *temporal dimension* includes the time of day as well as the time in history in which the communication act takes place. For many people the morning is not a time for communication; for others, the morning is ideal. Time in history would be particularly important for the communication researcher, because messages—their appropriateness, their importance, their impact, their insightfulness—depend in great part on the times in which they were uttered. Consider how difficult it would be to evaluate messages on racial, sexual, or religious attitudes and values if we did not know the time in which these messages were communicated. Henry Miller's *Tropic of Cancer*, D. H. Lawrence's *Lady Chatterley's Lover*, and Vladimir Nabokov's *Lolita* were all at one time banned from publication and distribution; now they are frequently found on required reading lists in colleges across the country and throughout the world.

These four dimensions of context interact with one another; each influences and is influenced by the others. If, for example, the temperature in a room becomes extremely hot (a physical change), it would probably lead to changes in the social and psychological dimensions as well. General discomfort seems to make people friendlier, as many have witnessed when a train or bus gets stuck. Change in the context, then, may be brought about in any of three general ways: (1) from outside influences, for example, a train failure; (2) from a change in one of the basic dimensions, for example, time or temperature change; or, (3) from the interaction among the dimensions, for example, friendliness increasing as a result of a train breakdown.

SOURCES-RECEIVERS

In the model of communication presented in Figure 1.1, communication is illustrated as taking place between two persons. If we wanted the diagram to illustrate *intra*personal communication, we would view the two "participants" as two roles or functions of the same person.

But regardless of whether there is one person (as in intrapersonal commu-

All communication transactions take place in a physical-social-psychological-temporal context.

nication), two persons (as in interpersonal communication), or a mass of people (as in mass communication), communication, by definition, demands that someone send signals and someone receive them. One person, of course, might send and receive his or her own signals, as in talking to yourself. But note that each individual is depicted as performing two functions—sending and receiving; each person is both a sender of messages and a receiver of messages. Hence, we use the hyphenated *sources-receivers* to emphasize this dual function. We send messages in speaking, writing, gesturing, smiling and we receive messages in listening, reading, smelling, tasting, and so on. As you are speaking, you are also receiving messages. You are receiving your own messages (you hear yourself, you feel your own movements, you see many of your own gestures) and you are receiving the messages of the other person, sometimes visually, sometimes auditorily, sometimes through touch or smell. Notice that as you speak to anyone you are constantly looking at the other person for responses

—for approval, for understanding, for sympathy, for agreement, and so on. As you read these nonverbal signals, you are performing receiving functions.

Who people are, what they know, what they believe in, what they value, what they want, what they are told, how intelligent they are, what their attitudes are, and so on all influence what they say and how they say it, what messages they receive and how they receive them. A rich, pampered, well-educated child and a poor, neglected, uneducated child do not talk about the same things or in the same way. Nor, of course, will they receive messages of the same content in the same way or in the same form or style.

ENCODING–DECODING

In communicology the processes of speaking or writing and understanding or comprehending are referred to as *encoding* and *decoding*. The act of producing messages—for example, speaking or writing—is termed *encoding*. By putting our ideas into sound waves we are putting these ideas into a code, hence *en*coding. By translating sound waves into ideas we are taking them out of the code they are in, hence *de*coding. Thus we may refer to speakers or writers as encoders and to listeners or readers as decoders.

If further discrimination among the various communicative components is necessary, the idea-generating aspect (that is, the brain) and the message-producing aspect (such as the vocal mechanism) may be distinguished. The idea-generating component would be referred to as the source, while the signal- or message-producing aspect would be referred to as the encoder. If one were talking on a telephone, the source would be the speaker and the vocal mechanism (and the telephone mouthpiece) would be the encoder. Conversely, in listening the brain would be the receiver while the auditory mechanism would be the decoder. The listener in a telephone conversation would be the receiver and the auditory mechanism (and the earpiece of the telephone) would be the decoder. As with *source-receiver*, I have hyphenated *encoding-decoding* to emphasize that the functions are performed *simultaneously*; as we are speaking (encoding), we are also deciphering the response messages of the other individual (decoding).

Essential to an understanding of encoding-decoding are the concepts of language competence and performance and of communicative competence and performance. Let us focus first on language competence and performance. Consider the "simple" act of speaking. Verbal messages are formed with no real problems; we open our mouths and certain things are said without any difficulty. At times we make an error and perhaps say what we did not want to say, but for the most part the vocal mechanism seems obedient. Similarly, when we listen to the words of others, we usually have no difficulty understanding them.

We are able to perform these language feats without any problems because we have, among other things, what is called *language competence*. We know the rules of the language (competence) and therefore can formulate and understand sentences (performance) (Figure 1.3). We are able to produce and understand sentences because we have a set of linguistic rules to tell us that these sounds, structured together in this way, mean something specific. This set of linguistic rules—which we know but cannot necessarily verbalize—is our language competence. When we recognize an error in grammar, for example, we do this by

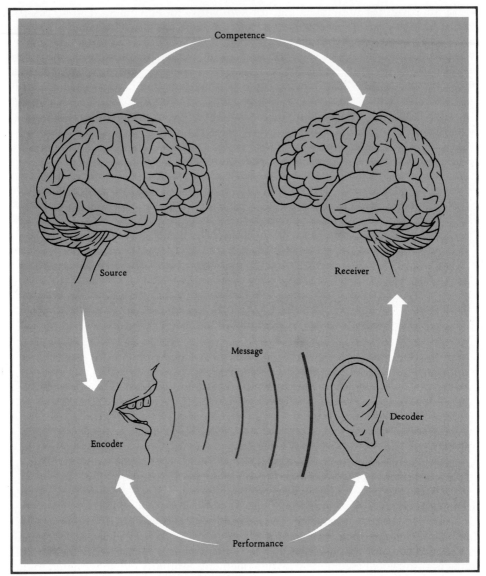

Figure 1.3   Competence and performance.

matching up what was said with a rule that is part of our competence. We know, for example, that the sentence *The teacher graded their own examinations* is ungrammatical because it does not conform to a grammatical rule we have as part of our linguistic competence which states that a singular pronoun must be used to refer to a singular subject. Our actual speaking and comprehending are performance aspects of language.

BOX 1.1
Teaching Chimps to Talk

The human urge to communicate is seen, perhaps in its most blatant form, in our effort to communicate with the lower animals, particularly the chimpanzees.

W. N. and Louise Kellogg were perhaps the first to record their efforts to teach Gua, a $7\frac{1}{2}$-month-old chimp, a human language. The Kelloggs raised Gua along with their son Donald, two months Gua's senior. Gua was treated in almost every way like a human child and like the human child no special effort was made to teach her language. Although there was some success, for the most part the experiment ended in failure. Gua did learn to produce different sounds to mean different things, but these were relatively few. She did manage to understand numerous different sentences (approximately 70, it was reported) and even surpassed Donald in her apparent comprehension of language. But the interesting thing was that even though Gua at one time surpassed Donald in comprehension, she could not be made to respond appropriately to novel utterances—that is, to sentences she had not been explicitly taught.

Improving somewhat on the procedures used with Gua, Keith and Cathy Hayes began seeing their chimp almost immediately after birth and took her into their house when she was only six weeks of age. The Hayeses treated their chimp, Viki, like a retarded child and gave her specific instructions in language. According to the Hayeses, Viki learned to say three words, though not terribly distinctly, and responded to a number of different utterances. She is reported to have responded appropriately to novel utterances, but the extent of this ability does not seem clear.

Some researchers have reasoned that chimps have failed to learn human language not so much because they are incapable intellectually but rather that they are physiologically incapable of producing the sounds. Since the speech signals are not essential to language, recent attempts have focused on teaching chimps human language but through a means that is natural to their species. Allen and Beatrice Gardner of the University of Nevada attempted to teach Washoe sign language, the language of the deaf. Washoe learned a number of words and simple sentences, but it was not always clear if she was also learning the rules for sentence construction. She was able to respond appropriately to many novel utterances and learned to use approximately 300 two-word sentences, but Washoe soon became too difficult to handle and other smaller chimps, that were easier to handle, were substituted.

Sarah, under the direction of psychologist David Premack, is reported to have learned language with remarkable rapidity. Premack created a language for Sarah consisting of plastic pieces that adhere to a magnetic board. Each plastic piece corresponded to a word. In learning the language Sarah had to place the appropriate pieces on the magnetic board. Thus, if she was shown a banana and wanted it she had to first select the plastic piece that meant banana and place it on the board. In one report Sarah was said to have learned 8 names of people, 21 verbs, 6 colors, 21 food names, and 27 concepts—for example, key, table, shoe, dress. Sarah was also able to create and respond appropriately to sentences as complex as "Sarah, insert apple red dish, apple banana green dish." But perhaps the most remarkable feat Sarah is reported to have learned is the concept "name of." When teaching Sarah a new concept she is shown the object and the word (plastic piece) and the relationship term "name of" and apparently has been able in this way to quickly learn the terms for new concepts. The implications of this single accomplishment are vast. Conceivably—and apparently this is one of the main motives of the study—Sarah, after mastering the language fully, might well be able to teach it to her offspring who in turn might teach it to theirs, and so on. The days of *Planet of the Apes* are perhaps far away but chimps and human beings communicating might not be.

Lucy, raised at the Yerkes Laboratory, was taught to communicate by pressing buttons on a computer to indicate her wants. Each request would have to be phrased in a "sentence" complete with a period. If the "sentence" was well formed, Lucy would be granted her request for candy, banana, or open window.

Herb Terrace raised still another chimp, Nim Chimsky. Elaborate socialization procedures were instituted, and Nim apparently lived life much as a human child would. At the beginning of this experiment Nim seemed to have been functioning at a relatively high level, but recently Terrace has claimed that not only has Nim failed to learn language but that the other chimps have not mastered language in any meaningful sense either. Terrace, along with Noam Chomsky, now argues that language seems impossible for any animal to master and that the observed responses of animals which at first appear to be "language" are simply conditioned responses emitted without any awareness of what they are doing.

Competence and performance differ in an important way. Competence is knowledge of language, which is uninfluenced by any psychological or physical processes. Performance, on the other hand, is influenced not only by competence but also by such factors as fatigue, anxiety, boredom, attention span, and interest. When we fail to understand what someone says, it may be due to a competence deficiency. More likely, however, it is due to our failing to attend to what was said or perhaps to our lack of interest—that is, to performance.

This language competence pertains basically to the formation and understanding of sentences—clearly an important aspect of our total communication ability and certainly one that is a prerequisite to the development of any other abilities. But there is another—and, for the study of interpersonal communication, more important—type of competence: namely, communicative competence. *Communicative competence* refers to our knowledge of the more social aspects of communication. It includes such "knowledges" as the role the context plays in determining the substance and form of communication messages—for example, that in certain contexts and with certain auditors some topics are appropriate and some topics are inappropriate.

A knowledge of the role of silence in communication would be another aspect of communication competence—specifically, a knowledge concerning when to speak and when to remain silent, when silence is uncomfortable and when it is welcomed. A knowledge concerning the rules of nonverbal behavior—for example, the appropriateness of touching, of vocal volume, and of physical closeness—would also be part of our communication competence.

We learn communication competence much as we learn how to eat with a knife and fork—by observing others, by explicit instruction, by trial and error, and so on. Some have learned better than others, though, and these are generally the ones we find both interesting and comfortable to talk with; they are the ones who seem to know what to do and how and when to do it. One of the major goals of this text and this course is to spell out the nature of communication competence, to increase your own communication competence, and ultimately to enable you to improve your communication performance.

MESSAGES

The *messages* that are sent and received in communication may be of any form; they may be sent and received through any one or combination of sensory organs. Although we customarily think of communication messages as being verbal (oral or written), these are not the only kinds of messages that communicate. We also communicate nonverbally (without words). For example, the clothes we wear communicate something to other people and, in fact, probably communicate to us as well. The way we walk communicates, as does the way we shake hands or the way we cock our heads or the way we comb our hair or the way we sit or the way we smile or frown. In fact, everything about us communicates. All of this information constitutes our communication messages. And this is true whether it is our intention to communicate or not. Thus, a slip of the tongue or an overheard whisper communicate just as does a carefully prepared speech. All this information (verbal and nonverbal, intentional and unintentional) constitutes our communication messages.

We may think of the communication *channel* as the medium through which the messages pass. Communication rarely takes place over only one channel; rather, two, three, or four different channels are used simultaneously. Thus, for example, in face-to-face interactions we speak and listen (vocal-auditory channel), but we also gesture and receive these signals visually (gestural-visual channel) and we emit odors and smell them (chemical-olfactory channel). Often we touch one another, and this too communicates (cutaneous-tactile channel).

A type of message that should be highlighted is *feedback*. When we send a message—say, in speaking to another person—we also hear ourselves. We get feedback from our own messages—we hear what we say, we feel the way we move, we see what we write, and so on. On the basis of this information we may correct ourselves, rephrase something, or perhaps smile at the clever turn of phrase. In addition to this self-feedback, there is the feedback we get from others. In speaking with another individual, not only are we constantly sending messages, we are also constantly receiving messages. Both parties are sending and receiving messages at the same time. The receiver's messages (sent in response to the source's messages) are termed *feedback*. This feedback, like other messages, can be in many forms: auditory, tactile, visual, gustatory, or olfactory. A frown or a smile, a yea or a nay, a pat on the back or a shot in the mouth are all feedback. In the diagram of the universals of communication (Figure 1.1), the arrows from source-receiver to effect and from one source-receiver to the other source-receiver are drawn going in both directions. This is designed to illustrate the notion of feedback. We perceive our own messages and we perceive the responses and reactions of the other communicator to our own messages.

Feedback may be positive or negative. Positive feedback tells the source that everything is fine and that one should continue as one has been going. Negative feedback tells the source that all is not well and that a reassessment of one's communication behavior is necessary. Negative feedback serves a corrective function by informing the communicator that something needs changing, something needs adjustment. Effectiveness in communication seems largely due to the ability of the communicator to respond appropriately to feedback. Teaching effectiveness may also be seen in the same way. Effective teachers seem to be those who can decode the responses of their students accurately and adjust their own messages accordingly. Ineffective teachers seem oblivious to how students are responding and just continue to communicate as always.

NOISE

In the early development of communication theory, noise was viewed as a disturbance in the channel—as in the telephone cables connecting speaker and hearer. But there are many other kinds of disturbances that need to be identified and analyzed, and it has become convenient to refer to any such communication interference as noise. Noise, in this extended sense, then, may enter into any communication system and is anything that distorts or interferes with the message. Noise is present in a communication system to the extent that the message sent differs from the message received. The screeching of passing cars, the hum of an air conditioner, the lisp of the speaker, the sunglasses a person wears, may all be regarded as noise since they interfere with the effective and efficient transmission of messages from sender to receiver. Noise is also present in written communication. Such noise would include blurred type, the print that shows through from the back page, creases in the paper, poor grammar—anything that prevents a reader from getting the message sent by the writer.

The concept of noise might also refer to psychological interference and would include biases and prejudices in senders and receivers that lead to distortions in processing information. Closed-mindedness is perhaps the classic example of psychological noise.

FIELD OF EXPERIENCE

The overlapping circles in Figure 1.1 refer to what is called a *field of experience*. The assumption here is that communication can only take place to the extent that the participants share the same experiences. Communication is ineffective or impossible to the extent that the participants have not shared the same experiences. Parents have difficulty communicating with their children, in this view, because the children cannot share the parental experience and because the parents have forgotten what it is like to be a child or do not know what it is like to be a child today. When management forgets what it is like to be labor and when labor does not share any of management's experiences, communication becomes extremely difficult, if not impossible. Differences among people serve to make communication more and more difficult; the larger the differences, the more difficult communication becomes. Although many differences cannot be eliminated, communication is still not hopeless. While we cannot, for example, share the actual experiences of our parents, we can perhaps attempt to role-play what it is like being a parent and perhaps in that way better extend the field of experience.

COMMUNICATION EFFECT

Communication *always* has some effect on one or more persons. For every communication act there is some consequence. The effect may be on either one of the participants or on both. When communication affects the environment or context, this is done through people. The effects of communication are, then, first on people; they are always personal. Even when we cannot observe an effect (which is perhaps most of the time), we assume that for every communication act there is an effect. As students of communicology, part of our task is to determine what these effects are. But that, as we shall see, is a very difficult, though extremely important, undertaking.

To the degree that communication has an effect, it also has an *ethical dimension*. Because communication has consequences, there is a rightness-wrongness aspect to any communication act. Unlike principles of effective communication, principles of ethical communication are difficult if not impossible to formulate. Often we can observe the effect of communication and on the basis of the observations formulate principles of effective communication. But we cannot observe the rightness or wrongness of a communication act. The ethical dimension of communication is further complicated by the fact that it is so interwoven with one's personal philosophy of life that it is difficult to propose universal guidelines.

Given these difficulties, we nevertheless include ethical considerations as being integral to any communication act. The decisions that we make concerning communication must be guided by considerations of ethics as well as effectiveness.

15

SOME SUMMARY PROPOSITIONS

As a kind of summary, note the following assumptions about communication.

1. Communication consists of several different elements in constant transaction with one another. The elements most frequently mentioned are source-receiver, encoder-decoder, feedback, message, noise, context, and effect.
2. Each element in communication may be further broken down into more specific elements or components.
3. Communication has no clear observable beginning or end; communication transactions do not have fixed boundaries.
4. Communication is transactional; each element influences every other element.
5. Communication messages may be verbal as well as nonverbal. Communication takes place when we squint as well as when we speak.
6. Communication takes place in a context.
7. Communication is inevitable. All behavior communicates.
8. Each communication event is unique. No two communication acts are ever identical or repetitive.
9. Each communication act influences future transactions and is influenced by past transactions.
10. Noise is inevitable in any communication transaction.
11. Communication is dynamic; communication is not a static event but rather one in constant process.
12. Communication is complex.
13. Communication takes place through the continual encoding and decoding of signals—a process whereby signals transmitted in one code are received and translated into another code.
14. Encoders and decoders are interchangeable. Each party continually encodes and decodes. This characteristic is inherent in any transactional conception of communication.
15. Feedback messages come from the source as well as from the receiver and provide the source with information as to the relative effectiveness of various messages.

SOURCES

Communication concepts are considered in most of the available texts in communication. My reader, *Communication: Concepts and Processes*, 3d ed. (Englewood Cliffs, N.J.: Prentice-Hall, 1981), would be a good starting place. A brief introduction to the entire area is provided by David L. Swanson and Jesse G. Delia, *The Nature of Human Communication* (Palo Alto, Cal.: SRA, 1976). An excellent introduction to communication terminology is provided by Wilbur Schramm in his *Men, Messages, and Media: A Look at Human Communication* (New York: Harper & Row, 1973), and by Reed H. Blake and Edwin O. Haroldsen, *A Taxonomy of Concepts in Communication* (New York: Hastings House,

1975). James C. McCroskey and Lawrence R. Wheeless' *Introduction to Human Communication* (Boston: Allyn & Bacon, 1976) provides an introduction to the various elements and processes of communication. For a more thorough discussion of competence and performance, see Helen S. Cairns and Charles E. Cairns, *Psycholinguistics: A Cognitive View of Language* (New York: Holt, Rinehart & Winston, 1976). For communication models see the summaries by Joseph A. DeVito, *The Psychology of Speech and Language: An Introduction to Psycholinguistics* (New York: Random House, 1970); David Mortensen, *Communication: The Study of Human Interaction* (New York: McGraw-Hill, 1972); Ron Smith's article "Theories and Models of Communication Processes," in Larry L. Barker and Robert J. Kibler, eds., *Speech Communication Behavior: Perspectives and Principles* (Englewood Cliffs, N.J.: Prentice-Hall, 1971). More sophisticated treatments of the theory and models of communication are presented by Leonard C. Hawes in "Elements of a Model for Communication Processes," *Quarterly Journal of Speech* 59 (1973) and *Pragmatics of Analoguing: Theory and Model Construction in Communication* (Reading, Mass.: Addison-Wesley, 1975) and Ernest G. Bormann, *Communication Theory* (New York: Holt, Rinehart and Winston, 1980). A useful overview is provided by Philip Emmert and William C. Donaghy, *Human Communication: Elements and Contexts* (Reading, Mass.: Addison-Wesley, 1981).

Experiential Vehicles

1.1   Communication Components

The purpose of this experiential vehicle is to enable you to explore some of the elements and processes involved in the act of communicating. Examine the following diagram of the communication process and respond to the questions with reference to this diagram.

THE COMMUNICATION PROCESS DIAGRAMMED

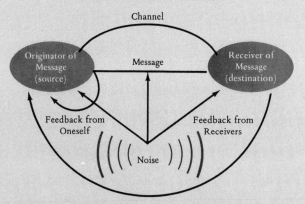

1. Who or what might be designated as a *source* of communication? Identify as many different types of communication sources as you can.
2. Who or what might be designated by the term *destination?* Identify as many different types of communication destinations as you can.
3. What forms might noise take? That is, what types of noise might enter or interfere with a communication system? From what sources might noise originate?
4. How can noise be reduced? Might a communication system ever be noise-free? Explain.
5. What kinds of information can be fed back from the destination to the source?

18

6. Of what value to the source is information fed back from the destination?
7. What kinds of information might the source receive from his or her own communications?
8. Of what value is information fed back that the source receives from his or her own communications?
9. What forms can a message take? That is, what signals can be used to communicate information?
10. Over what channels might a message be communicated? That is, what senses can be utilized by the source and by the receiver in sending and receiving information? What advantages and limitations do each of the senses have in terms of communication?
11. What are the dimensions or significant aspects of the context of the communication act? That is, in analyzing the context of communication, what factors would have to be investigated?
12. How might *interpersonal communication, small group communication, public communication,* and *mass communication* be defined and distinguished from one another on the basis of the elements noted in the preceding diagram?

1.2   Specific Models of Communication

In groups of five or six construct a diagrammatic model of the essential elements and processes involved in one of the following communication situations. This model's primary function should be to describe what elements are involved and what processes are operative in the specific situation chosen. (It may be useful to define the situation chosen in more detail before constructing the model.)

1. Sitting silently on a bus
2. Thinking
3. Asking for a date on the phone
4. Conversing with a very close friend
5. Talking with three or four acquaintances
6. Delivering a lecture to a class
7. Watching television
8. Participating in a formal group discussion
9. Writing a speech for a political candidate
10. Reading a newspaper
11. Performing in a movie
12. Acting a role in a play
13. Arguing with your instructor
14. Selling insurance door-to-door
15. Persuading an angry crowd to disband

Each group should share their models with the rest of the class. Discussion might center on the following:

1. How adequately do the models explain the processes they are supposed to represent? Do they incorporate all the essential elements and processes? Are the relationships among the elements and processes clear?

2. What insight into the actual processes of communication do these models provide? What new ideas or information may be found in these models?
3. What elements and processes included here might also be included in the general models of communication discussed in the unit?
4. What functions do these models serve? Explain.

Unit 2

Communication Postulates

COMMUNICATION POSTULATES

The Impossibility of Not Communicating
Content and Relationship Aspects of Communication
Punctuation of Communication Sequences
Symmetrical and Complementary Interactions
    2.1 Analyzing an Interaction

LEARNING GOALS

After completing this unit, you should be able to:

1. explain the importance of the statement "we cannot *not* communicate"
2. identify the alternatives available when one does not wish to communicate but another person does
3. distinguish between the content and the relationship dimension of communication
4. distinguish among *confirmation, rejection,* and *disconfirmation* in communication
5. explain the concept of punctuation in communication
6. distinguish between *symmetrical* and *complementary* interactions

In *Pragmatics of Human Communication: A Study of Interactional Patterns, Pathologies, and Paradoxes*, Paul Watzlawick, Janet Beavin, and Don Jackson present an analysis of the behavioral effects of communication derived from the study of behavior disorders. Perhaps the most essential part of their analysis of human communication is the postulates, or axioms, of communication—propositions that are essential to an understanding of communication in all its forms and functions. These postulates are universals of communication; they are descriptive of communication in all its forms and functions.

In preview, these postulates state that: (1) In an interaction situation, one cannot *not* communicate; communication is inevitable. (2) In any interpersonal interaction there is a content dimension (the topic or subject of the communications) and a relationship dimension (the relationships that exist between the people communicating); both are important to the eventual outcome of the interaction. (3) Communication sequences are broken up (punctuated) into stimuli and responses in different ways by different people. (4) An interpersonal interaction may be viewed as symmetrical (where each person mirrors the other's behaviors) or complementary (where one person's behavior stimulates the complementary behavior in the other). Each of these four postulates may now be considered in depth.

THE IMPOSSIBILITY OF NOT COMMUNICATING

Often we think of communication as being intentional, purposeful, and consciously motivated. In many instances it is. But in other instances we are communicating even though we might not think we are or might not even want to communicate. Take, for example, the student sitting in the back of the room with an expressionless face, perhaps staring at the front of the room, perhaps staring out the window. Although the student might say that he or she is not communicating with the teacher or with the other students, that student is obviously communicating a great deal—perhaps lack of interest, perhaps boredom, perhaps a concern for something else, perhaps a desire for the class to be over with as soon as possible. In any event, the student is communicating whether he or she wishes to or not. We cannot not communicate. Further, when we are in an interactional situation with this seemingly uncommunicative person, we must respond in some way. Even if we do not actively or overtly respond, that lack of response is itself a response and communicates. Like the student's silence, our silence in response also communicates.

Watzlawick, Beavin, and Jackson give the example of two strangers on a plane; one wishes to talk but the other does not. When we do not wish to interact we have four general alternatives:

BOX 2.1
Phatic Communion

No discussion of communication postulates can omit phatic communion —the small talk that precedes the big talk, the talk that opens the channels of communication so that the important and significant issues may be discussed.

In terms of content, phatic communion is trivial—"Hello," "How are you?" "Fine weather, isn't it?" "Have a nice day," and the like. But in terms of establishing and maintaining relationships, phatic talk is extremely important. For one thing, phatic communication assures us that the social customs are in effect; the general rules of communication that we expect to operate will operate here also. The teacher who says, "Turn to Chapter Three" before saying "Hello" clues us into a situation in which the normal rules seem not to operate.

In first encounters, phatic communion enables us to reveal something of ourselves and at the same time to gain some preliminary information about the other person. Even if it is only to hear the tone or quality of voice, something is gained. Sometimes the important benefit is that phatic talk allows us time to look each other over and to decide on our next move. Phatic communion also shows us that the other person is willing to communicate, that in fact the channels of communication are open, that there is some willingness to pursue the interaction.

Phatic communion, by its nature and because of the purposes it serves, is noncontroversial; with phatic talk there is little chance for conflict or fighting. Similarly, the topics considered are unemotional and hence not ego-involving. They are not intellectually demanding, nor are they too personal. In phatic talk the parties avoid extreme positions; rather, they seem to engage in what appears to be rather bland chatter. But we need to see that what on the surface is shallow is actually a foundation for later and more significant communication.

All of the ways of making verbal contact may well sound trite, but they are for the most part examples of phatic communion. They are messages whose importance and usefulness should not be measured by their originality or their profundity; they should rather be taken simply as attempts to establish some kind of verbal contact.

The person who says, "Haven't I seen you here before?" is probably asking not if you have been here before but rather "Would you like to talk with me?" To answer the literal question and fail to respond to the underlying and more significant question is a clear example of miscommunication.

1. We may simply and explicitly state the desire not to communicate. We may do this nonverbally, which is perhaps the less socially offensive way, or we may do it verbally. The expression of not wishing to communicate, whether verbal or nonverbal, obviously does not follow communication etiquette. De-

spite the fact that the person next to us is a complete bore and that we might just want to daydream, we are under social pressure not to ignore anyone. Yet the option to say we do not wish to communicate is still open to us. Even if we do state this desire not to communicate, communication itself will not cease but rather will simply take place on another level or in a different form. For example, communication may become restricted to the nonverbal channels. Greater physical distance may be established between the two persons. There may be abnormally little eye contact. If verbalization becomes essential, it may be cold and formal or punctuated by vocalized expressions of annoyance.

2. We may simply give in and communicate. This, it seems, is the alternative that many people take, and it seems to be the road of least effort. In fact, it may take more psychic energy to tell this person that you do not wish to communicate than to communicate. And we can still hope that the person will soon tire and go away.

3. We may disqualify our communications in various ways. For example, we may contradict ourselves, speak in incomplete sentences, or change the subject without any apparent motivation. In all of these cases the intent is to get the other person bored or confused so that he or she will stop communicating. Of course it often happens that the person becomes all the more interested in figuring us out and consequently seems to stay with us for what seems like forever.

4. Perhaps the most ingenious way is to pretend to want to talk but to also pretend that something is preventing us from doing so. For example, we might say that we would like to talk but we are just so sleepy that we cannot keep our eyes open and then doze off. Or perhaps we feign a toothache that makes speaking difficult. Or we might pretend to be drunk or sick or deaf. At times, of course, the other person is aware that we are pretending. Yet this is often perceived as a more socially acceptable manner of getting out of talking than honestly stating that we do not want to communicate.

Regardless of what we do or do not do, we are still communicating. All behavior is communication; all behavior has message value.

CONTENT AND RELATIONSHIP ASPECTS OF COMMUNICATION

Communications, to a certain extent at least, refer to the real world or to something external to both speaker and hearer. At the same time, however, communications also refer to the relationships between the parties. For example, a teacher may say to a student, "See me after class." This simple message has a *content aspect*, which refers to the behavioral responses expected—namely, that the student see the teacher after class—and a *relationship aspect,* which tells us how the communication is to be dealt with. Even the use of the simple command states that there is a status difference between the two parties such that the teacher can command the student. This is perhaps seen most clearly when we visualize this command being made by the student to the teacher. It appears awkward and out of place simply because it violates the normal relationship between teacher and student.

    In any communication the content dimension may be the same but the relationship aspect different or the relationship aspect may be the same with the content different. For example, the teacher could say to the student, "You had better see me after class," or he or she could say, "May I please see you after class?" In each case the content is essentially the same; that is, the message being communicated about the behavioral responses expected is about the same in both cases. But the relationship dimension is very different. In the first it signifies a very definite superior-inferior relationship and even a put-down of the student, but in the second a more equal relationship is signaled and a respect for the student is shown. Similarly, at times the content may be different but the relationship essentially the same. For example, a child might say to his or her parents, "May I go away this weekend?" and "May I use the car tonight?" The content is clearly very different in each case and yet the relationship dimension is essentially the same. It is clearly a superior-inferior relationship where permission to do certain things must be secured.

    Thus on the relationship level we communicate, not about the outside world of content, but about the relationship between the communicators. In such communications we offer a definition of ourselves. When we offer this definition of self, the other person may make any of three general responses, according to Watzlawick, Beavin, and Jackson. In *confirmation* the other person verifies the individual's self-definition. The student who responds to the teacher's "You had better see me after class" with "Yes, Professor Perrotta"

All communication transactions have both a content and a relationship dimension.

confirms the teacher's definition of himself or herself. In *rejection* the other person rejects the individual's self-view. Such rejection may be constructive, as when a therapist rejects a patient's self-definition. The student who responds to the teacher's "You had better see me after class," with "No, I don't feel like it" is rejecting the teacher's definition of self. Lastly, in *disconfirmation* the other person ignores or denies the right of the individual to even define himself or herself. The student who ignores the teacher's command is disconfirming the teacher's definition of self.

Many problems between people are caused by the failure to recognize the distinction between the content and the relationship levels of communication. For example, consider the engaged couple arguing over the fact that the woman made plans to study during the weekend with her friends without first asking her boyfriend if that would be all right. Probably both would have agreed that to study over the weekend was the right choice to make; thus the argument is not at all related to the content level. The argument centers on the relationship level; the man expected to be consulted about plans for the weekend whereas the woman, in not doing this, rejected this definition or relationship. Similar situations exist among married couples when one person will buy something or make dinner plans or invite a guest to dinner, as in an example given by Watzlawick, Beavin, and Jackson, without asking the other person first. Even though the other person would have agreed with the decision made, they argue over it because of the message communicated on the relationship level.

Let me give you a personal example. My mother came up to stay for a week at a summer place I had. On the first day she swept the kitchen floor six times though I had repeatedly told her that it did not need sweeping and that I would be tracking in dirt and mud from outside and so all this effort was just wasted. But she persisted in sweeping, saying that the floor was dirty and should be swept. On the content level, we were talking about the value of sweeping the kitchen floor. But on the relationship level we were talking about something quite different. We were each saying, "This is my house." When I realized this (though only after considerable argument), I stopped complaining about the relative usefulness of sweeping a floor that did not need sweeping.

This is not to say that the relationship level is often discussed or even that it should be explicitly discussed by both parties. In fact, Watzlawick, Beavin, and Jackson argue the contrary: "It seems that the more spontaneous and 'healthy' a relationship, the more the relationship aspect of communication recedes into the background. Conversely, 'sick' relationships are characterized by a constant struggle about the nature of the relationship, with the content aspect of communication becoming less and less important." This is not to say that people who discuss their relationships are involved in "unhealthy" or "sick" relationships. In fact, some of the healthiest and most productive relationships involve explicit discussion of various dimensions of the relational bonds. It is, instead, to emphasize that many relationships between people are not productive and not accepted by one or both parties, and consequently an enormous amount of energy is spent struggling over the relationship itself, with the result that too little energy is left for the positive aspects of the relationship. Similarly, this is not to say that people who do not explicitly discuss relational aspects are involved in healthy relationships. Often, the nature of an individual's relationship is unhealthy, unpleasant, and, by most definitions, "sick," and yet there may be no discussion of it. It may be repressed or otherwise hidden from consciousness, or the relationship may be so unpleasant that one or both parties may simply chose to live with the unpleasantness rather than to discuss it explicitly.

We might also note that arguments over the content dimension are relatively easy to resolve. Generally, we may look something up in a book or ask someone what actually took place or perhaps see the movie again. It is relatively easy to verify facts that are disputed. Arguments on the relationship level, however, are much more difficult to resolve, in part because we seldom recognize that the argument is in fact a relationship one.

PUNCTUATION OF COMMUNICATION SEQUENCES

Communication events are continuous transactions. They are broken up into short sequences only for purposes of convenience. What is stimulus and what is response is not very easy to determine when we, as analysts of communication, enter after the communication transaction is under way.

This tendency to divide up the various communication transactions into sequences of stimuli and responses is referred to by Watzlawick, Beavin, and Jackson as the punctuation of the sequences of events. They do not argue that punctuation is wrong; obviously, it is a very useful technique in providing some organization for thinking about and talking about communication transactions. At the same time, because we each see things differently, we each punctuate events differently. To the extent that these differences are significant, the possibility for a communication breakdown exists.

Consider, for example, the following incident. A couple is at a party. The wife is flirting with the other men and the husband is drinking; both are scowling at each other and are obviously in a deep nonverbal argument with each other. In explaining the situation the wife might recall the events by observing that the husband drank and so she flirted with the sober men. The more he drank the more she flirted. The only reason for her behavior was her anger over his drinking. Notice that she sees her behavior as the response to his behavior; his behavior came first and was the cause of her behavior.

In recalling the "same" incident the husband might say that he drank when she started flirting. The more she flirted the more he drank. He had no intention of drinking until she started flirting. To him, her behavior was the stimulus and his was the response; she caused his behavior. Thus she sees the behavior as going from drinking to flirting, and he sees it as going from flirting to drinking.

Consider another and perhaps more familiar example: the students are apathetic, the teacher does not prepare for classes. Figure 2.1A illustrates the sequence of events; there is no absolute beginning and no absolute end. Each action (the student apathy and the lack of teacher preparation) stimulates the other; each serves as the stimulus for the other but there is no initial stimulus or cause. In describing this situation, the teacher might explain the relationships as in Figure 2.1B. In this view, we have the same sequence of events, but they are "punctuated" from the point of view of the teacher. The teacher sees

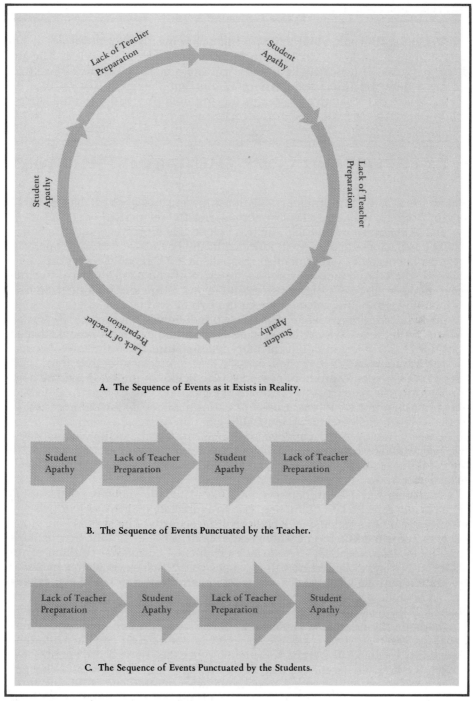

A. The Sequence of Events as it Exists in Reality.

B. The Sequence of Events Punctuated by the Teacher.

C. The Sequence of Events Punctuated by the Students.

Figure 2.1 The sequence of events.

the student apathy as the stimulus for his or her own lack of preparation. The lack of preparation is the response to the student apathy in this view. The students, on the other hand, might describe the situation as in Figure 2.1C. Again, we have here the same sequence of events but "punctuated" so that the teacher's lack of preparation is seen as the stimulus (or cause) and the student apathy is seen as the response (or effect).

SYMMETRICAL AND COMPLEMENTARY INTERACTIONS

Symmetrical and complementary relationships are not good or bad in themselves. Both are usually present in normal, healthy relationships.

In a *symmetrical relationship* the two individuals mirror each other's behavior. The behavior of one party is reflected in the behavior of the other party. If one member nags, the other member responds in kind. If one member expresses jealousy, the other member expresses jealousy. If one member is passive, the other member is passive. The relationship is one of equality with the emphasis on minimizing the differences between the two individuals.

In a *complementary relationship* the two individuals engage in different behaviors, with the behavior of one serving as the stimulus for the complementary behavior in the other. In complementary relationships the differences between the parties are maximized. It is necessary in a complementary relationship for both parties to occupy different positions, one being the superior and one being the inferior, one being passive and one being active, one being strong and one being weak. At times such relationships are established by the culture—as, for example, the complementary relationship existing between teacher and student or between employer and employee. Perhaps the classic complementary relationship would be between the sadist and the masochist, where the sadistic behavior of the sadist serves to stimulate the masochistic behavior of the masochist and vice versa.

Problems may arise in both symmetrical and complementary relationships. In the symmetrical relationship it is easy to appreciate that two individuals who mirror each other's jealousy will find very little security. The jealous behavior is likely to escalate to the point where one or both parties will quit from exhaustion. As Watzlawick, Beavin, and Jackson put it, "In marital conflict, for instance, it is easy to observe how the spouses go through an escalation pattern of frustration until they eventually stop from sheer physical or emotional exhaustion and maintain an uneasy truce until they have recovered enough for the next round."

Perhaps the classic example of problems created in complementary relationships, familiar to many college students, is that of rigid complementarity—an inability to change the type of relationship between oneself and another even though the individuals, the context, and a host of other variables have changed. Whereas the complementary relationship between mother and child was at one time vital and essential to the life of the child, that same relationship when the child is older "becomes a severe handicap for his further development, if adequate change is not allowed to take place in the relationship."

These postulates, as set forth by Watzlawick, Beavin, and Jackson, seem essential to any introductory or advanced analysis of communication. They provide us with insight into the nature and function of human communication as well as into the intricacies of human relationships and interactions.

SOURCES

For this unit I relied on Paul Watzlawick, Janet Helmick Beavin, and Don D. Jackson, *Pragmatics of Human Communication: A Study of Interactional Patterns, Pathologies, and Paradoxes* (New York: Norton, 1967). Another useful work in this area is Jurgen Ruesch and Gregory Bateson, *Communication: The Social Matrix of Psychiatry* (New York: Norton, 1951). Many of the ideas set forth in *Pragmatics* may be found in the work of Bateson. For a useful collection of Bateson's writings, see *Steps to an Ecology of Mind* (New York: Ballantine, 1972). For an insightful application of many of these principles to the therapeutic process see Paul Watzlawick, *The Language of Change: Elements of Therapeutic Communication* (New York: Basic Books, 1978). A useful collection of articles dealing with these concepts is provided by Paul Watzlawick, *How Real is Real? Confusion, Disinformation, Communication: An Anecdotal Introduction to Communications Theory* (New York: Vintage Books, 1977). An overview of research and many of the relevant concepts is provided by Carol Wilder, "The Palo Alto Group: Difficulties and Directions of the Transactional View for Human Communication Research," *Human Communication Research* 5 (winter 1979): 171–186.

Experiential Vehicle

2.1 Analyzing an Interaction

The four postulates of human communication proposed by Watzlawick, Beavin, and Jackson and discussed in this unit should prove useful in analyzing any communication interaction. To understand these postulates better and to obtain some practice in applying them to an actual interaction, a summary of Tennessee Williams' *Cat on a Hot Tin Roof* is presented. Ideally, all students would read the entire play or see the movie and then apply the four postulates to the interactions that take place. The brief summary is presented, then, more in the nature of a "mental refresher." (Note that the original play, as it has been published, differs from the film, particularly in the last act. The film version of the play is somewhat more positive. The summary presented here is from the original stage play, the version Williams prefers.)

Big Daddy and Big Mama Pollitt, owners of a huge estate, have two sons: Brick (married to Maggie, the cat), an ex-football player who has now turned to drink; and Gooper (married to Mae), a lawyer and father of five children with one on the way. All are gathered together to celebrate Big Daddy's sixty-fifth birthday. The occasion is marred by news that Big Daddy may have cancer for which there is no hope of a cure. A false report is given to Big Mama and Big Daddy stating that the test proved negative and that all that is wrong is a spastic colon—a sometimes painful but not fatal illness. It appears, to Maggie and perhaps to others as well, that Gooper and Mae are really here to claim their share of the inheritance.

The desire to assume control of Big Daddy's fortune (estimated at some $10 million and 28,000 acres "of the richest land this side of the valley Nile") has created considerable conflict between Gooper and Mae on the one hand and Maggie on the other. Brick, it appears, does not care about his possible inheritance.

Throughout the play there is conflict between Brick and Maggie. Brick refuses to go to bed with Maggie although Maggie desperately wants him. This fact is known by everyone, since Mae and Gooper have the adjoining room and hear everything that goes on between Brick and Maggie. The cause of this conflict between Brick and Maggie goes back to Brick's relations with Skipper, his best friend. Brick and Skipper were football players on the same team and did just about everything together. So close were they that rumors about their love for each other began to spread. While Brick is in the hospital with a football injury

Maggie confronts Skipper and begs that he either stop loving Brick or tell him of his love. In an attempt to prove Maggie wrong Skipper goes to bed with her but fails and as a result takes to drinking and drugs. Maggie repeatedly attempts to thrash this out with Brick, but he refuses to talk about it or even to listen to Maggie. All he wants to do is drink—waiting for the little click in his head that tells him he can stop.

In a confrontation with Big Daddy, Brick talks of his disgust with lying and his using liquor to forget all the lies around him. Under pressure from Big Daddy, Brick admits that Skipper called to make a drunken confession after his attempted relationship with Maggie but that Brick hung up and refused to listen. It was then that Skipper committed suicide. And this, it appears, is what Brick uses alcohol to forget. In his anger Brick tells Big Daddy that he is dying of cancer.

Gooper and Mae confront Big Mama with the news that Big Daddy has cancer and attempt to get Big Mama to sign some papers concerning the disposition of the property now that Big Daddy has not much longer to live. Perhaps Gooper and Mae's major argument is that they are responsible (as shown by their five children), while Brick and Maggie are not responsible (as shown by Brick's drinking and by his refusal to sleep with Maggie and have a child, something Big Daddy wants very much). At this point Maggie announces that she is pregnant. Big Mama is overjoyed and seems to be the only one who believes her. This, Big Mama reasons, will solve all problems, even the problem of Brick's drinking. Brick of course knows that Maggie is lying but says nothing to betray her.

In the final scene Maggie locks up all the liquor and pressures Brick into going to bed with her in order to make the lie about her pregnancy become truth. Afterwards she promises to unlock the liquor so that they may both get drunk. She sobs that she really loves Brick, while Brick thinks if only that were true.*

After reading the play or viewing the film, identify instances of and explain the importance of:

1. the impossibility of not communicating
   a. What alternatives does Brick use in attempting to avoid communicating with Maggie?
   b. What alternatives does Brick use in attempting to avoid communicating with Big Daddy?
2. the content and relationship aspects of communication
   a. How does Brick deal with the self-definitions of Maggie and Big Daddy?
   b. How does Big Daddy deal with Big Mama's definition of herself?
   c. Are any problems caused by the failure to recognize the distinction between the content and the relationship levels of communication?

* An interesting discussion of *Cat on a Hot Tin Roof* in terms of communication problems is provided by Philip C. Kolin, "Obstacles to Communication in *Cat on a Hot Tin Roof*," *Western Speech Communication* 39 (spring 1975): 74–80. For alternative views of Maggie, Kolin recommends the following articles, both of which should prove useful in analyzing the role of Maggie and in understanding the communication dimension of the play as a whole: James Ray Blackwelder, "The Human Extremities of Emotion in *Cat on a Hot Tin Roof*," *Research Studies* 38 (1970): 13–21, and Paul J. Hurley, "Tennessee Williams: The Playwright as Social Critic," *Theatre Annual* 21 (1964): 40–56.

3. the punctuation of communication sequences
   a. How do Maggie and Brick differ in their punctuation of the events?
   b. Why do they punctuate the sequences differently?
4. the symmetrical and complementary interactions
   a. What type of relationship existed between Brick and Maggie, Gooper and Mae, Big Daddy and Big Mama, Big Daddy and Brick, Big Daddy and Gooper, Maggie and Mae?

As an alternative to analyzing *Cat on a Hot Tin Roof,* the entire class may watch a situation comedy show, television drama, or film and explore these four communication postulates in these presentations. The questions used in this exercise should prove useful in formulating parallel questions for the television program or film. Another way of approaching this topic is to have all students watch the same television programs for an entire evening and have groups of students focus on the operation of different postulates. Thus, one group would focus on examples and illustrations of the impossibility of not communicating, one group on the content and relationship dimensions of messages, and so on. Each group can then report back their findings and insights to the entire class.

Unit 3

Communication and the Self

COMMUNICATION AND THE SELF

The Open Self
The Blind Self
The Hidden Self
The Unknown Self
   3.1 I'd Prefer to Be
   3.2 Satisfaction with Self

LEARNING GOALS

After completing this unit, you should be able to:

1. explain the structure and general function of the Johari Window
2. define the *open*, *blind*, *hidden*, and *unknown selves*
3. provide examples of information that might be contained in each of the four selves
4. explain some of the ways in which self-awareness might be increased

If we had to list some of the qualities we wanted to possess, self-awareness would surely rank high. We all wish to know ourselves better. The reason is that we are in control of our thoughts and our behaviors only to the extent that we understand ourselves, only to the extent that we are aware of ourselves.

This concept of self-awareness is basic to all forms and functions of communication and is best explained by the Johari Window, presented in Figure 3.1. (The name *Johari* was derived from the first names of the two persons who developed the model: Joseph Luft and Harry Ingham.) The window is broken up into four basic areas or quadrants, each of which contains a somewhat different self.

THE OPEN SELF

The *open self*, the first quadrant, represents all the information, behaviors, attitudes, feelings, desires, motivations, ideas, and so on that are known to the self and also known to others. The type of information included here might vary from one's name, skin color, and sex to one's age, political and religious affiliation, and batting average. Each individual's open self will vary in size depending on

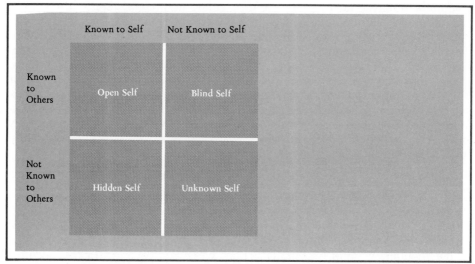

Figure 3.1 The Johari Window. *Source:* Joseph Luft, *Group Processes: An Introduction to Group Dynamics* (Palo Alto, Cal.: Mayfield, 1970), p. 11.

the time and on the individuals he or she is dealing with. At some times we are more likely to open ourselves up than at other times. If, for example, we opened ourselves and got hurt because of it, we might then close up a bit more than usual. Similarly, some people make us feel comfortable and support us; to them, we open ourselves wide, but to others we prefer to leave most of ourselves closed.

In some instances the size of the open self seems directly related to the degree of closeness with the individual: We might reveal most to those we are closest to and least to those we are least close to. It seems that some of our most important desires or motivations often concern the people we are closest to, thus we might not want them to learn such information. Should our need to open ourselves become too strong we might disclose our feelings to a stranger or relative stranger or at least to someone not closely involved with our daily life—for example, a religious counselor or a therapist of some sort. Sometimes a student will select a teacher or an athletic coach to confide in. Despite this variation each person has a "modal area," a kind of average that defines how open one will generally be.

The size of the open self also varies greatly from one individual to another (Figure 3.2). Some people are prone to reveal their innermost desires and feelings, whereas others prefer to remain silent about both the significant and the insignificant things in their lives. Most of us, however, open ourselves to some people about some things at some times.

"The smaller the first quadrant," says Luft, "the poorer the communication." Communication is dependent on the degree to which we open ourselves to others and to ourselves. If we do not allow others to know us (that is, if we keep the open self small), communication between them and us becomes extremely difficult if not impossible. We can communicate meaningfully only to the extent that we know one another and to the extent that we know ourselves. To improve communication, we have to work first on enlarging the open self.

We should also note that a change in the open area—in any of the quadrants—will bring about a change in the other quadrants. We might visualize the window as a whole as being of constant size but with each pane of glass variable, sometimes small, sometimes large. As one pane becomes smaller, one or more of the others must become larger. Similarly, as one pane becomes larger, one or more of the others must become smaller. For example, if we enlarge the open self this will shrink the hidden self. Further, this disclosure in turn will function to lead others to decrease the size of the blind self by revealing to us what they know and we do not know. Thus these several selves are not separate and distinct selves but interacting selves, each one dependent on the others.

THE BLIND SELF

The *blind self* represents all those things about ourselves that others know but of which we are ignorant. This may vary from the relatively insignificant habit of saying "you know" or of rubbing your nose when you get angry or of a peculiar body odor, to something as significant as defense mechanisms or fight strategies or repressed past experiences.

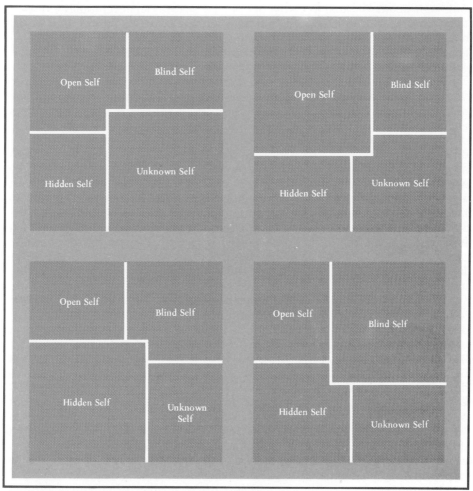

Figure 3.2   Johari Windows of varied structure.

Some people have a very large blind self and seem to be totally oblivious to their own faults and sometimes (though not as often) their own virtues. Others seem overconcerned with having a small blind self. They seek therapy at every turn and join every encounter group. Some are even convinced that they know everything there is to know about themselves, that they have reduced the blind self to zero. Still others only pretend to want to reduce the size of the blind self. Verbally they profess a total willingness to hear all about themselves, but when they are confronted with the first negative feature the defenses and denials go up with amazing speed. In between these extremes lie most of us.

Communication depends in great part on both parties sharing the same basic information about each other. To the extent that blind areas exist, communication will be made difficult. Yet blind areas will always exist for each of us.

Although we may be able to shrink our blind areas we can never totally eliminate them. If, however, we recognize that we do in fact have blind areas, that we can never know everything that others know about us, this recognition will help greatly in dealing with this most difficult and elusive self and with our other selves as well.

The only way to decrease the size of the blind self is to seek out information that others have and we do not have. In everyday interactions, we influence how much of the blind area will be made open by others. This need not be done directly, although at times it is, as when we ask someone's honest opinion about our appearance or our speech or our home. Most often, however, it is done indirectly; in fact, it is a consequence of everything we do. In any interaction with another person we invariably reveal how much of ourselves we want to know about, how much we prefer not to know, which aspects we want to know about, and which aspects we prefer to leave hidden. We also reveal in these interactions how we will react to such revelations. In some contexts we would react defensively, in other contexts openly. Throughout our interactions we give cues as to how we will react in future situations, and we in effect enable others to predict our future behaviors. Generally, if we are open about ourselves and reveal our inner selves to others, others in turn will reveal what is contained in the blind area more readily than they would if we did not engage in any self-disclosure.

Sometimes more active information seeking is necessary. To want such information to be revealed but to do nothing about securing it—which many people do—is simply ineffective; it does not work. We need not be so blatant as to say, "Tell me about myself," or "What do you think of me?" But we can utilize some of the situations that arise every day to gain self-information. It would be perfectly legitimate to say to a friend, for example, "Do you think I came down too hard on the instructor today?" or "Do you think I was assertive enough when asking for the raise?" or "Do you think I'll be thought too forward or pushy if I invite myself over to their house for dinner?" I am not implying that we should seek this information constantly; our friends would then surely and quickly find others with whom to interact. And yet, we can make use of some situations—perhaps those in which we are particularly unsure of what to do or of how we appear—to increase self-awareness.

In our interactions with others we monitor or regulate what kind of information and how much information we want others to reveal about ourselves to ourselves. If, for example, someone tells us about some negative trait he or she feels we possess, and if we in turn become defensive or hurt or respond by cataloguing that person's negative traits, we are in effect saying that we do not want our blind self revealed and we effectively cut off one of the best avenues for increasing self-awareness. This, I admit, is a difficult suggestion to follow, and yet it is essential that we learn to respond openly and nondefensively so that we will be given the information we need to increase self-awareness.

Although communication and interpersonal relations are generally enhanced as the blind area becomes smaller, it should not be assumed that people should, therefore, be forced to see themselves as we see them or to find out everything we know about them. Forcing people to see what we see may cause serious trauma. Such a revelation might cause a breakdown in defenses; it might force people to see their own masochism or jealousy or prejudice when they are not psychologically ready to deal with such information. It is important to recognize that such revelations, since they may cause problems, might best be dealt with in the company of trained personnel. Further, it seems reasonable to inquire into the motivations (if not the ethics) of those who consistently reveal things to people from their blind selves, claiming they are doing this for the person's "own good."

THE HIDDEN SELF

The *hidden self* contains all that you know of yourself and of others but keep to yourself. This area includes all your successfully kept secrets about yourself and others. In any interaction this area includes what is relevant or irrelevant to the conversation but is not something you want to reveal.

At the extremes we have the overdisclosers and the underdisclosers. The overdisclosers tell all. They keep nothing hidden about themselves or others. They will tell you their family history, their sexual problems, their marital difficulties, their children's problems, their financial status, their strategies for rising to the top, their goals, their failures and successes, and just about everything

We all hide ourselves to some people, to some degree.

else. For them the hidden self is very small, and had they sufficient time and others sufficient patience it would be reduced to near zero. The problem with these overdisclosers is that they do not discriminate. They do not distinguish between those to whom such information should be disclosed and those to whom it should not be disclosed. Nor do they distinguish among the various types of information that should be disclosed and should not be disclosed. To discuss one's wife's or husband's psychological problems with coworkers might not be the wisest thing to do, and yet they do it.

The underdisclosers tell nothing. You get the feeling that they know a great deal about themselves but simply refuse to say anything. They will talk about you but not about themselves. Depending upon one's relationship with these underdisclosers we might feel that they are afraid to tell anyone anything for fear of being laughed at or rejected. Or we may feel somewhat rejected for their refusal to trust us. Never to reveal anything about yourself comments on what you think of the people with whom you are interacting. On one level, at least, it is saying, "I don't trust you enough to reveal myself to you."

The vast majority of us are somewhere between these two extremes. We keep certain things hidden and we disclose certain things. We disclose to some people and we do not disclose to others. We are, in effect, selective disclosers.

We must carefully weigh the pros and cons of self-disclosure because the consequences are often great. Consider, for example, the sociology professor. She is married with three school-age children. She recently received her Ph.D., had her first book published, and is now teaching a course in criminology. In discussing drugs and present laws, part of her wants to disclose that as a graduate student she was busted on drug charges and served two years in jail. But the other part of her, the practical part, wants to remain silent for fear of losing her job and therefore causing problems for her family. This is not at all a rare situation. In fact, such a decision-making process seems to occur with amazing frequency. All of us, it seems, hide something. But this takes energy— a fact that we probably do not appreciate as fully as we should. We are forced to expend great amounts of energy to keep parts of ourselves hidden. Hiding some aspects of ourselves is not a passive but an active process at which we must constantly work if we are to succeed. This principle seems to have been recently recognized by many homosexuals who have found that keeping their homosexuality hidden cost them a great deal in psychic energy and that once they moved this information from the hidden to the open area they have felt less burdened.

Although it is comforting to tell ourselves that the information we disclose to others will be treated confidentially, we cannot always be sure that it will. The teacher who confidentially tells her class about her criminal record may have a very sympathetic audience that day. But after a rough midterm she may lose some of her "friends" who may no longer wish to be "burdened" by this "secret."

As potential disclosers we should also recognize that we impose a burden on the person to whom we disclose. In disclosing anything significant we are in effect saying, "I know you will be supportive and not reveal this to anyone else." But at times people cannot be supportive and at times people cannot or simply do not remember that this bit of information is to be classified as secret.

When dealing with our feelings, especially our present feelings, self-disclosure is useful, helpful, and conducive to meaningful dialogue. A few years ago, for example, on the first day of an interpersonal communication course I was teaching I became extremely nervous. I was not sure of the reason, but I was nervous. At that point I had three basic options open to me. One was to withdraw from the situation—for example, by saying I was not feeling well or that I had forgotten something—and just walk out. Second, I could have attempted to hide the nervousness, hoping that it would subside as the class progressed. The third option and the one I chose (although I did not go through these options consciously at the time) was simply to tell the class that I was nervous and did not understand why. The class was most supportive, telling me I had nothing to be nervous about and that I should not worry. They revealed that they were the ones who felt anxious; for many, this was their first college class. I, in turn, assured them that they should not be nervous. After this very simple exchange, all of which happened without any conscious planning or strategy, as an expression of what our feelings were at the time, we worked together closely and warmly for the rest of the semester. This incident was not in itself responsible for the success of the course, yet it helped greatly to set the tone for an open and supportive atmosphere.

The extent to which we reveal ourselves to others, the degree to which we increase our open self, will influence at least three dimensions of self-awareness. First, when we reveal ourselves to others, we reveal ourselves to ourselves at the same time. At the very least we bring into consciousness or into clearer focus what we may have had buried within us. As we discuss ourselves we may see connections that we had previously missed, and with the aid of feedback from others we may gain still more insight. All this helps us to increase our self-awareness. Second, by increasing the open self we increase the likelihood that a meaningful and intimate relationship will develop, and it is through these interactions that we best get to know ourselves. Third, we get to know ourselves, in part, through the perceptions, responses, and reactions of others. If we keep a great deal hidden, we prevent ourselves from securing this feedback and from learning more about ourselves.

It should not be thought, however, that there are only rewards and no risks involved in revealing one's hidden self; clearly there are risks, and there are a number of cautions to be observed. Some of these have already been noted; they will be explored in more detail in Unit 16, "Self-Disclosure in Interpersonal Communication."

THE UNKNOWN SELF

The *unknown self* represents all that exists but which neither we nor others know about. One could legitimately argue that if neither we nor anyone else knows what is in this area, we cannot know that it exists at all. Actually, we do not *know* that it exists but rather we *infer* that it exists. We assume that there are some aspects of ourselves that we are not aware of consciously. We assume that some aspects of ourselves are confined to our subconscious and are therefore unknown to ourselves as well as to others.

We may gain appreciation of the unknown self from a number of different sources. Sometimes this area is revealed to us through temporary changes brought about by drug experiences or through special experimental conditions such as hypnosis or sensory deprivation. Sometimes this area is revealed by various projective tests or dreams. There seem to be sufficient instances of such revelations to justify our including this unknown area as part of the self. The exploration of the unknown self through open, honest, and empathic interpersonal interaction with trusted and trusting others—parents, friends, counselors, children, lovers—is one of the most effective ways of gaining insight into this unknown self.

Although we cannot easily manipulate this area, we should recognize that it does exist and that there are things about ourselves and about others that we simply do not and will not know. And perhaps this is the most important step in increasing self-awareness. A clear recognition that our knowledge of self is incomplete and a determination to increase that knowledge are essential prerequisites to increasing self-awareness.

SOURCES

The Johari model is most thoroughly discussed in the works of Joseph Luft, particularly *Group Processes: An Introduction to Group Dynamics*, 2d ed. (Palo Alto, Cal.: Mayfield Publishing Company, 1970), and *Of Human Interaction* (Palo Alto, Cal.: Mayfield Publishing Company, 1969). Ronald B. Levy's books cover this area but in a more elementary fashion: *Self Revelation Through Relationships* (Englewood Cliffs, N.J.: Prentice-Hall, 1972) and *I Can Only Touch You Now* (Englewood Cliffs, N.J.: Prentice-Hall, 1973). John Powell's *Why Am I Afraid to Tell You Who I Am?* (Niles, Ill.: Argus Communications, 1969), *Why Am I Afraid to Love?* (Niles, Ill.: Argus Communications, 1972), and *The Secret of Staying in Love* (Niles, Ill.: Argus Communications, 1974) are three of the most interesting and perceptive works in this area. They are deceptively simple so do not dismiss them if they appear too elementary. Nathaniel Branden's *The Psychology of Self-Esteem* (New York: Bantam, 1969) and *The Disowned Self* (New York: Bantam, 1971) and Henry Clay Lindgren's *How to Live With Yourself and Like It* (Greenwich, Conn.: Fawcett, 1953) are useful for understanding ourselves. Patricia Niles Middlebrook, in her *Social Psychology and Modern Life* (New York: Knopf, 1974), provides a thorough overview of the social-psychological dimensions of the self. For a relatively detailed discussion of the self in communication, see Kenneth L. Villard and Leland J. Whipple, *Beginnings in Relational Communication* (New York: Wiley, 1976). On satisfaction, see Michael L. Hecht, "The Conceptualization and Measurement of Interpersonal Communication Satisfaction," *Human Communication Research* 4 (spring 1978): 253–264, and "Toward a Conceptualization of Communication Satisfaction," *Quarterly Journal of Speech* 64 (February 1978): 47–62. A thorough overview of research and theory in self-awareness is provided by Chris L. Kleinke, *Self-Perception: The Psychology of Personal Awareness* (San Francisco, California: W. H. Freeman and Company, 1978).

Experiential Vehicles

3.1 I'd Prefer To Be

This exercise should enable members of the class to get to know one another better and at the same time get to know themselves better. The questions asked here should encourage each individual to think and increase awareness of some facet(s) of his or her thoughts or behaviors.

Rules of the Game

The "I'd Prefer To Be" game is played in a group of four to six people, using the following category listing. General procedure is as follows:

1. Each member individually rank-orders each of the 15 groups, using 1 for the most-preferred and 3 for the least-preferred choice.
2. The group then considers each of the 15 categories in turn, with each member giving his or her rank order.
3. Members may refuse to reveal their rankings for any category by saying, "I pass." The group is not permitted to question the reasons for any member's passing.
4. When a member has revealed his or her rankings for a category, the group members may ask questions relevant to that category. These questions may be asked after any individual member's account or may be reserved until all members have given their rankings for a particular category.
5. In addition to these general procedures, the group may establish any additional rules it wishes—appointing a leader, establishing time limits, and so forth.

"I'D PREFER TO BE"

1. _____ intelligent   _____ successful
   _____ wealthy   businessperson
   _____ physically attractive 3. _____ blind
2. _____ movie star   _____ deaf
   _____ senator   _____ mute

45

4. _____ on a date

_____ reading a book

_____ watching television

5. _____ loved

_____ feared

_____ respected

6. _____ alone

_____ with a group of people

_____ with one person

7. _____ brave

_____ reliable

_____ insightful

8. _____ communicating by phone

_____ communicating by letter

_____ communicating face to face

9. _____ traitor to a friend

_____ traitor to one's country

_____ traitor to oneself

10. _____ bisexual

_____ heterosexual

_____ homosexual

11. _____ the loved

_____ the lover

_____ the good friend

12. _____ introvert

_____ extrovert

_____ ambivert

13. _____ a tree

_____ a rock

_____ a flower

14. _____ a leader

_____ a follower

_____ a loner

15. (Ten years from now)

_____ married

_____ single

_____ living with someone but unmarried

Areas for Discussion

Some of the areas for discussion that might prove of value are:

1. What are the reasons for the individual choices? Note that the reasons for the least-preferred choice may often be as important or even more important than the reasons for the most-preferred choice.
2. What do the choices reveal about the individual? Can persons be differentiated on the basis of their choices to these and similar alternatives?
3. What is the homogeneity/heterogeneity of the group as a whole? Do the members evidence relatively similar choices or wide differences? What does this mean in terms of the members' ability to communicate with one another?
4. Do the members accept/reject the choices of other members? Are some members disturbed by the choices other members make? If so, why? Are some apathetic? Why? Did hearing the choices of one or more members make you want to get to know them better?

5. Did any of the choices make you aware of preferences you were not aware of before?
6. Are members reluctant to share their preferences with the group? Why?

3.2 Satisfaction with Self

Probably no one is completely satisfied with himself or herself. Very likely each of us thinks that some aspects could be improved. Similarly, no one seems com-

	Very satisfied	Fairly satisfied	Neither satisfied nor dissatisfied	Fairly dissatisfied	Very dissatisfied
1. My face					
2. My body					
3. My intelligence					
4. My economic status					
5. My popularity among my peers					
6. My general personality					
7. My work and study habits					
8. My status among persons I am romantically interested in					
9. My goals					
10. My sports abilities					
11. My communication abilities					
12. My sensitivity to others					
13. My life up to now					
14. My prospects for the future					
15. My general "style"					

pletely dissatisfied. Satisfaction-dissatisfaction undoubtedly exists in degrees, from very satisfied to very dissatisfied. Further, the degree of our own satisfaction-dissatisfaction will vary, depending on the particular dimension of self being considered. Thus, one may be very satisfied with one's intelligence but very dissatisfied with one's economic status, and so on.

In this experiential vehicle, you are asked to indicate the degree of satisfaction-dissatisfaction you feel for 15 aspects of your self; some aspects are physical, some are cognitive, some are interpersonal. For each of the 15 aspects, indicate in the appropriate space your degree of satisfaction-dissatisfaction. After you have completed this for all 15 items, consider some or all of the following questions, individually, with one other person, or in small groups of five, six, or seven.

1. Are there areas of the self with which you are generally satisfied? Generally dissatisfied?
2. How is your present satisfaction-dissatisfaction influenced by your own history of conditioning? Were you taught—explicitly or implicitly—to feel satisfaction-dissatisfaction over certain aspects of the self? Can you reconstruct this conditioning history? What implications does this history (and its awareness) have for you now?
3. What specific changes can you make in your self to decrease your level of dissatisfaction? Identify as many specific changes as you can think of. How will you go about instituting these changes? Again, be as specific as possible.
4. How does your level of satisfaction-dissatisfaction influence your behaviors? That is, how does your satisfaction-dissatisfaction with your face and body influence your behavior? How does your satisfaction-dissatisfaction with your economic status influence your behavior? How would you behave differently if you were more satisfied with each of the 15 items?
5. In what ways do you communicate your level of satisfaction-dissatisfaction to others? Try to identify specific behaviors and specific verbalizations. How accurately do you think others perceive your satisfaction-dissatisfaction? On what basis do you say this?

Unit 4

Communication and Ethics

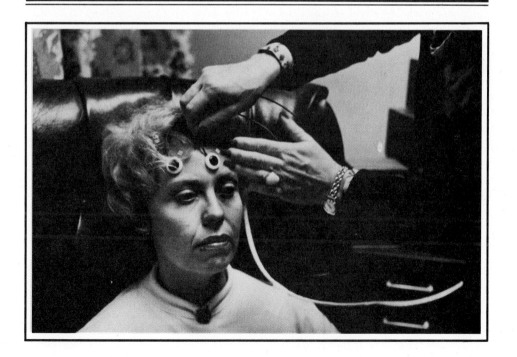

COMMUNICATION AND ETHICS

Repression
Conditioning—As Persuasion, As Therapy
Ghostwriting
Censorship

LEARNING GOALS

After completing this unit, you should be able to:

1. state some of the arguments relating to repression, conditioning, ghostwriting, and censorship
2. explain repression as a question of ethics
3. identify examples from your own experience that illustrate the operation of conditioning principles
4. define conditioning, positive reinforcement, negative reinforcement, and punishment
5. make predictions as to the state of repression, conditioning, ghostwriting, and censorship in the next 50 to 60 years
6. take a tentative stand on the ethical issues involved in repression, conditioning, ghostwriting, and censorship

All communicators, regardless of their specific purposes and regardless of the specific form of communication utilized, need to take into consideration questions of ethics. Every communication act has consequences, whether for one person or for an entire culture, and, therefore, has an ethical dimension, a rightness and a wrongness dimension. Put differently, we live our lives in relationships with other people, and the decisions made by one person will invariably affect others. Your decisions will affect those persons with whom you interact, and their decisions will affect you—sometimes positively, sometimes negatively. Because of this interrelationship among all of us, communications—through which relationships are created, maintained, strengthened, weakened, and destroyed—have a moral dimension. This moral dimension of communication is extremely broad and encompasses literally hundreds of issues.

There are a number of approaches that we might take in the consideration of ethics. For example, we might moralize and urge you to develop a specific set of values. Essentially this takes the form of urging you to adopt the beliefs, attitudes, and values that I have—as author, parent, teacher, minister, or whatever. A very different approach is to omit ethics entirely. This laissez-faire approach assumes that since each person will (and should) develop his or her own set of values, there is no need for its inclusion in any text or course.

The approach I take here, which has recently come to be called the values-clarification method, avoids either of these rather ineffective and extreme methods of dealing with this important issue. There are numerous varieties of values clarification. The one I use here and have used for the last 15 years of teaching is not designed to instill in you any particular set of values or beliefs or ethical system, nor is it content to omit the topic entirely. Rather, its purpose is to bring to heightened awareness the values, attitudes, and beliefs that influence the choices you make. In all your decisions, whether cognitive or behavioral, you are confronted by choices—to do this or that, to buy or sell, to study or not to study, to speak in favor of the senator or against, to write the book or not, and so on. The values that you have will influence these choices. Our function in this discussion is to bring to consciousness these values and the ways in which they influence your decisions and choices. In this way the consistencies and the inconsistencies between the values on the one hand and the choices on the other may be explored. A second purpose of this values-clarification approach is to present alternative values and modes of behavior for your consideration. Instead of one system of values, different approaches are presented so that you may consider the implications and usefulness of each approach for your own lives. A third function is to relate these ethical issues to communication—to spell out the ways in which communication decisions and choices involve ethical considerations.

Our consideration of ethics is presented in two parts: one textual and one experiential. In the textual part, some of the communication problems that involve ethical issues are considered, and an attempt is made to pose alternative modes of viewing these various issues. In the experiential part various issues are presented and you are asked to make decisions and to consider the implications of your decisions. Further, you are asked to consider these several decisions as a whole and to formulate a tentative theory of the ethics of communication. We select here four such issues—issues that are communication-centered and in which the question of ethics is both intellectually and socially relevant. (1) In "Repression" the focus is on the ethical dimension of restrictions on human interactions. (2) In "Conditioning—As Persuasion, as Therapy" the moral implications of the principles of behavioral control to strengthen or change an individual's behavior are considered. (3) In "Ghostwriting" the issues center on utilizing the messages of other people as our own, whether in political speeches or in term papers. (4) Last, in "Censorship," the concern is with the moral implications of preventing certain messages from being made public or at least from getting to those who may wish to hear or read them. All four of these issues are relevant to all four forms of communication examined later in the text. Since all forms of communication are intimately related and overlap considerably, all ethical issues will bear on all communication forms.

REPRESSION

As used here *repression* refers to acts or attitudes that prevent or make extremely difficult various interactions among persons. These behaviors and attitudes, sometimes even written into the law, limit freedom of interaction. Among the most obvious are those that prohibit interracial marriage and homosexual relations. These societal rules make it extremely difficult for certain groups of persons to interact in the manner in which they wish. If an interracial couple wishes to get married, there are actually few places where they will be treated with fairness and equality. Interracial couples will run into difficulty in finding housing, employment, and, most significant, acceptance into a community. Likewise, homosexual men and lesbians will have difficulty in much the same way, and consequently many of them are forced to live "straight" lives on the surface.

If you run a business, for example, should you refuse a job to a person because that person is married to an individual of another race or because that person prefers to interact sexually with persons of the same sex? And if you do have the right to choose your employees on the basis of such preferences, do you still retain the rights to protection of the law, which the society as a whole has granted to everyone?

Homosexuals are currently prevented from holding jobs as teachers, police officers, firefighters, and so forth in most states. These discriminatory laws are not terribly effective. But this is not the issue. The relative ineffectiveness of such prohibitions should not blind us to the social realities that these laws incorporate. What should be considered is that the homosexual cannot function in these jobs as a homosexual but only as a heterosexual. The person is permitted to work only if he or she—at least on the surface—denies the fact of his or her homosexuality and behaves as a heterosexual. We do not ask that a black teacher act white—although society once did demand this in often subtle ways. We do not ask a Jew to act like a Christian or a Christian to act like a Jew if he or she wants a job—although, again, some persons do ask for this concealment or denial of one's identity. Yet, we do ask homosexuals that they not reveal their true identity. These persons are accepted only if they act as the majority does. But are we being fair when we ask for such concealment of identity?

Repression as an ethical issue is, of course, not limited to interracial marriage or homosexuality. These are merely the more obvious and perhaps dramatic manifestations. More generally, repression involves making it difficult for those persons we have some influence over to interact with others as they wish. Repression as an ethical issue preventing interaction pervades our entire social network. It involves parents restricting their children's interaction to those having parental approval. In many cases this involves preventing children from associating with those who are different from themselves—different in nationality, race, or religion. It involves husbands who prevent their wives from having close male friends and wives who prevent their husbands from having close female friends. Here the "prevention" does not come in the form of "don't do that" as with children but rather in more subtle forms of jealous responses, sullenness, and withdrawal. It involves college students who restrict the friendships their own friends may legitimately have by bad-mouthing certain persons or groups. "How can you hang out with her? Everybody knows she's a lesbian." "Why are you with him so much? He's so ugly." "What were you doing with that creep?" It involves the college professor who makes it difficult for students to disagree with him or her and the college dean or president who makes it difficult for the professor to disagree.

There are, of course, many other and different issues that repression raises. But I think the central issue it raises is whether any one group—however large and however sanctioned by state or church—has the right to set down rules of behavior for others and to literally prevent them from their own self-actualization. It is no wonder that so many relationships break up and that so many people are unhappy. Is society fostering discontent and unhappiness by preventing people from being themselves, from interacting as they wish, from presenting themselves to others as they feel they really are? Lest we all ease our consciences too easily, let us recognize that it is we who constitute this "society," and it is we who give it the power it has—the very power we may deplore as we sit comfortably reading about the repressive behaviors of "others."

CONDITIONING—AS PERSUASION, AS THERAPY

In one of the most widely read, condemned, praised, and generally discussed books of this century, *Beyond Freedom and Dignity*, B. F. Skinner sets forth the case for conditioning—a psychological technique for controlling behavior.

According to Skinner, all learned behavior is learned through a process of conditioning, a process governed by rewards and punishments. Put generally, the "theory" of conditioning states that we will learn and repeat those behaviors that have been rewarded in the past, and we will not learn or not repeat those behaviors that have been unrewarded or punished. Behavior may be rewarded through either of two basic means. *Positive reinforcement* involves the presentation of some kind of reward after some bit of behavior has been emitted. The result is that this type of behavior is strengthened in frequency and will be more likely to occur in the future under similar circumstances. *Negative reinforcement,* on the other hand, involves the removal of an aversive or painful stimulus (for example, an unpleasant sound) after some bit of behavior has been emitted. This, too, results in the behavior being strengthened and in its being more likely to occur under similar circumstances in the future. Behavior that is not reinforced, or that is punished, will not be learned—or, if already learned, will be extinguished or weakened.

According to Skinner all learned human behavior can be explained in essentially this way, although there are rather complex types of conditioning schedules to account for the learning of different types of behaviors. But the essence of conditioning is that we learn according to the principles or laws of reinforcement.

Skinner's argument in *Beyond Freedom and Dignity* did not receive so much attention from all segments of the population because it presented a new psychological theory; actually Skinner had presented the same theory decades ago and it can be found in practically every basic psychology textbook. The reason this particular book received so much attention was simply that here Skinner applied the results of laboratory studies to society and denied the existence of what we normally call freedom of choice. We act and behave, according to Skinner, not because we are free to choose but because of the way in which we have been conditioned. In this work, as well as in his novel *Walden Two,* Skinner portrayed and advocated a society organized on the basis of the principles of conditioning.

This thesis proved particularly disturbing to many people. Skinner's critics argued that society should not be based on such principles and that we would be morally unjustified in establishing a society where certain people were granted the right to reward and punish and thus control the behaviors of its people. Skinner's argument, however, is that we do not have a choice in whether or not we wish to be controlled by conditioning. According to Skinner, we *are* so controlled; that is simply in the nature of being human. And the question then becomes, Do we want to organize this process or do we want to leave it unorganized, as it is now?

Admittedly, this is a rather disturbing notion. We all want to be free, to think we are free, and to act as if we are free. Yet, Skinner's arguments and evidence are not easy to dismiss. If we accept Skinner's basic assumptions about conditioning, then we are left with two basic choices. Either we accept the present system in which our behaviors are controlled by rewards and punishments, although in a very inconsistent and often illogical manner, or we establish a society in which these rewards and punishments are organized so that the behaviors of the individuals within the society are controlled for the good of the whole. Naturally, there are intermediate positions; but according to Skinner, we do not have the choice of whether or not we want to be controlled by conditioning. We are human and because of that we learn and we behave according to the principles of reinforcement.

It now seems clear that we are influenced greatly (perhaps even "controlled") by conditioning. The questions we should ask concern the use to which such conditioning principles should be put. We are all, according to Skinner, both objects of conditioning and agents of conditioning. Our behavior is controlled by the reinforcements of others and we, in turn, control the behaviors of others by the reinforcements we apply.

In Anthony Burgess' *A Clockwork Orange* we see the protagonist conditioned to the point where he becomes extremely ill when presented with scenes of violence—scenes in which he would have eagerly participated before this conditioning. So thorough is his conditioning that he is powerless to defend himself when attacked. This is perhaps conditioning in its extreme but we need to examine similar situations and attempt to ferret out the significant issues they raise.

In mental institutions, conditioning is widely applied as a means of behavior control. For example, disruptive and self-destructive behavior may be severely punished in order to reduce it or perhaps eliminate it fully. Small children are at times so self-destructive that they will literally chew huge hunks of flesh out of their arms and legs. Presented with such extreme cases, we may be willing to accept the application of conditioning principles to control such behavior. But would we be willing to accept its application in other situations?

One type of conditioning receiving a great deal of attention is *aversive conditioning.* In this procedure the individual goes through the particular behaviors the therapist wishes to eliminate and is administered some aversive stimulus (for example, an electric shock) while engaging in these behaviors. In relatively short order such behaviors are weakened or eliminated. In one widely publicized case a small child would not keep food in his system. Whatever he was fed, he would throw up. In this case conditioning was used. The infant was wired in such a way so that he would receive a severe electric shock whenever any muscular movements were made in the direction of throwing up after he was fed. Within a matter of days the child stopped throwing up his food and apparently is a healthy young boy today. This same general procedure is used on those who exhibit behavior that society has chosen to condemn. At times these individuals will put themselves under the care of such a conditioning therapist, and with this we would probably not wish to quarrel. Clearly they have a right to attempt to change their behavior should they wish to. But at times no choice is given. In mental hospitals or prisons, people are sometimes forced to submit to such conditioning. And it is not really pertinent to the issues involved here whether they are conditioned by a trained psychologist or by an ignorant prison guard. Both are probably effective in altering the behavior. But the question is whether such persons should be in the position of administering such conditioning without the consent of the individual.

We might argue that such rights are granted to society for its own well-being and, in fact, preservation. This license to alter behavior is then granted for the good of the general population. This argument or reasoning may sound convincing until we recall that in the not so distant past this same argument was used for sterilization of "undesirables" and for the elimination of millions. True, the conditions and times are different now. But are they sufficiently different to risk allocating such great power to a relatively small group?

GHOSTWRITING

One of the perennial topics raised in any discussion of communication is that of ghostwriting. Ghostwriting, broadly conceived, refers to the practice of employing professional writers to prepare one's speeches or articles and then presenting them as if they were one's own.

The most familiar example of this practice is among politicians, who sometimes employ a staff of writers to prepare their speeches. But the practice is much more widespread and certainly is not limited to politics and politicians. Broadly viewed, ghostwriting would include, for example, (1) the student who turns in a term paper or delivers a speech obtained from the fraternity file, from *Reader's Digest*, or from some agency that specializes in preparing such compositions for college students; (2) the student who pays to have his or her thesis or dissertation written by a professional writer; (3) the college teacher who "demands" or "accepts" coauthorship for an article or book actually written and researched by a graduate student; (4) the news reporter who reads the news copy prepared by another individual; and, of course; (5) the politician who presents a speech written by a speech staff. Clearly there are differences among these several examples of ghostwriting; yet each of them raises significant questions.

We might sympathize with the politician on any number of bases. There is not enough time for the politician to prepare all the speeches, especially when campaigning throughout the country. The speeches, if they are to be at all effective, must be individualized for perhaps hundreds of different audiences and must resemble interpersonal communications as much as possible. No one person could possibly have the time necessary for such a monumental undertaking. Certainly the president does not have the time to prepare relatively polished speeches to present over television or at various conferences and conventions. We might further argue that since everyone knows that the politicians are not writing their own speeches, no one is really deceived by the practice. Should one politician attempt to write his or her own speeches, such speeches would surely not be as effective as those of the opponent. Thus by not employing such writers one is, in effect, practically giving up all chances for election.

We might also note that numerous politicians—Franklin D. Roosevelt and Adlai Stevenson are perhaps the clearest examples—guided the speechwriting process of their ghostwriters very carefully. On this basis we might argue, as many have done, that these were really their speeches and not those of their staff.

These are at least some of the familiar arguments used to show that ghostwriting—at least among politicians—should be accepted. But are we or should we be willing to accept this practice? Does practical necessity make a practice acceptable?

When we are attempting to make up our minds regarding the qualifications of several opposing political candidates, is it fair that none of the candidates is actually delivering campaign speeches which he or she has written? Is it fair that politicians would have us listen to a humorous and enlightening speech on, for example, educational reform, when they in fact know nothing about educa-

BOX 4.1
Ethics and Ghostwriting
David D. Draves

A Prevalence of Ghosts

What follows is not a defense of ghostwritten and plagiarized student papers but a partial explanation of why students feel at ease in using ghostwriters to help them to earn college credits:

1. When I prepare for what my civics teacher tells me is my highest political responsibility as a commonplace citizen, voting intelligently in a public election, I must base my decisions on candidate speeches which have been created by a stable of ghostwriters.

2. When I read a professor's research article, I am never sure whether the writer did all the background grubbing or used the labors of ghost graduate students.

3. When my term paper or examination paper is evaluated for a large college lecture course, it generally is read by a ghost graduate student.

4. When I enroll in an introductory college English course, or French course, or mathematics course, very likely I will be instructed by a ghost graduate student—a Miss Zagano—who is teaching me so that the famous person whose reputation helped to bring me to that campus can do more important things.

5. When I enjoy Audrey Hepburn in yet another TV rerun of *My Fair Lady*, I hear a ghost's voice sing the songs of Eliza Doolittle.

6. When I end the day half-listening to Johnny Carson, I hear not the wit of Carson but that of a coterie of ghostwriters.

7. When I relax with an autobiography of a contemporary athlete or movie star, more likely than not I am reading the words of an "as-told-to" or "with" ghost.

Ghosts are all around me, accepted, and, when not graduate students, highly paid. Why should not I employ a ghostwriter to help me accomplish one task for a course which represents less than 3 percent of my college work?

Source: The New York Times Magazine, July 6, 1975. Reprinted by permission of *The New York Times* and David D. Draves.

tional reform and are themselves totally humorless? Does the fact that a practice is universal mean we should accept it? Does the fact that everyone is doing it make it right and justified?

Consider the case of the student handing in a term paper or delivering a speech as his or her own when in fact it was obtained from someone else—perhaps a friend, a magazine, or a professional agency. If the student gets caught, there is little that can save the student from failing the course or at least the assignment. Most instructors would state without reservation that the student's behavior is unethical.

Yet consider the case of the college instructor who is pressured to publish scholarly articles. A bright graduate student comes along and produces a term paper worthy of publication. This much the instructor knows. So a few suggestions for improvement are made along with some stylistic suggestions, and the instructor offers to have it published with the student as coauthor. The assumption when two names appear on an article or a book is that both persons shared in producing the work, but it seems that this instructor did little—certainly not half. And yet the professor's name appears on the article as coauthor. If this instructor gets enough good graduate students he or she may become widely known on the basis of a number of articles with which he or she actually had little to do. Students may even enroll in this instructor's classes or attend the school at which the instructor is teaching because of this reputation. Yet, in fact, this instructor may know very little and may not have had anything significant to do with the publications responsible for this wide reputation. (This situation, I should add, is actually not at all exaggerated. There are many instructors in all disciplines who make this type of thing a common practice.)

We might argue that the instructor has provided the stimulation necessary for this kind of work and that the value of this stimulation is surely half the work. Further, the student would not have known enough about procedures to get the article published alone. Also, the instructor did make some changes in the paper, and who can say that these changes were not the very thing that led to the paper's acceptance for publication? Are these arguments sufficient to justify this widespread practice?

Take the case in which the graduate student, pleased with the guidance received from the instructor, asks the instructor to coauthor the paper. Is the instructor justified in accepting this? Has the instructor a right to pose to the academic world as an expert on a topic he or she may know very little about? And again, is the widespread nature of this practice sufficient to justify it? Like the busy politician who must prepare and present several speeches a week, the college instructor must publish—otherwise the instructor does not get promoted and is not granted tenure. But is need enough to justify practice?

This system is similar to that of news reporters who do not prepare their own news reports. A staff of reporters assemble the facts, professional writers write up the copy, and "news reporters" simply present it to the public. Their qualifications may be nothing more than a pleasant voice and a handsome face. Surely we would rather look at a handsome face than an ugly one and would want to hear a pleasant voice rather than a harsh and rasping one. Who would turn on the news to listen to an unpleasant individual? The ratings would drop to near zero and advertisers would cancel. And so the practice is justified for purely economic reasons. The problem with this is that, like instructors who gain reputations for being experts in fields they know nothing about, these attractive people with pleasant voices get reputations for being authorities on world events when in fact they may know nothing and care less about the politics of the world. The character of Ted Baxter on "The Mary Tyler Moore Show" is perhaps the classic example. But it seems there are "Ted Baxters" all over the channels.

Because these several practices are so widespread, there is an increasing need not for passive acceptance but for active and thorough evaluation. We need to ask if we are doing ourselves an injustice and if we are actually fostering deception by accepting such practices.

CENSORSHIP

In 1973, in *Miller* v. *California*, the Supreme Court ruled in favor of a very rigid censorship law. Essentially, this ruling holds that the individual communities and local governments have the right to determine when an article, book, film, play, or other public communication appeals to "prurient interests" and should therefore be censored.

This decision has raised a number of important issues relative to free speech and, more generally, to the human right to information. Shortly after the decision was made, numerous movies were banned by local communities—not only the X-rated films, such as *Deep Throat* or *The Devil in Miss Jones,* but also films such as *Carnal Knowledge* and *Paper Moon.* The reasons given for banning such movies have generally centered on the claim that these films offend community standards of morality.

Some people would agree that the community as a whole should have the right to determine what comes into the community, specifically what movies are shown in the local theaters, what programs appear on television, what books are made available at the local libraries or assigned in schools, and what magazines are sold. Still more people would agree to grant these rights to the community if that community was unanimous in its decisions. If every citizen in the community did not wish to have a picture shown in the local movie house, then a strong argument could be made for its not being shown—that is, for it being banned. But what about decisions made by fewer than all the people? Clearly these would include all the decisions or at least 99 percent of the decisions normally made on such issues. We might extend the argument and ask, What if only one person wanted to read a particular book? Should the library make the book available? What if 10 percent of the people wanted to read it? Twenty percent? Forty-nine percent?

One of the many paradoxes that censorship laws have created concerns "the public will." It is argued that the local community should set the standards for what is pornographic and that the local community has the right to censor whatever it considers pornographic. Given this situation, we are compelled to wonder how theaters that show films considered to be pornographic by the "community"—and therefore subject to censorship—can manage to make a profit. Any theater owner interested in making a profit would be a fool to schedule films that the members of the community are not going to see. But, of course, the theater owner does make a profit; members of the community clearly do want to see such films. Yet throughout the country films are being ruled pornographic and banned on the basis of the argument that the community does not want to see them.

In early 1977 Larry Flynt, the publisher of *Hustler* magazine, was arrested, bond refused, sentenced to 7 to 25 years in prison, and fined $11,000. The charge was that Flynt published an obscene magazine and engaged in organized crime. "Engaging in organized crime," according to Ohio law, consists of five or more persons conspiring to commit a crime; Flynt was charged with working with his staff (of more than five persons) to publish *Hustler* magazine, which was defined as obscene and hence a crime to publish. One of the many issues this case raises is that this charge of "organized crime" can be used against any

---

BOX 4.2
Newspaper Vending Machines

The New York Times reported on November 16, 1980, that the Gannett Company placed a number of newspaper vending machines throughout certain counties in New York and Connecticut. The machines, the residents protested, were aesthetically offensive; they were painted peach and their slogan was "reach for the peach." In addition they were chained to sign posts and trees which, the residents claimed, detracted from the beauty of their towns and streets. The Gannett Company argued that the First Amendment to the Constitution guaranteed them the right not only to publish but to distribute their newspapers as well. *The New York Times* and the *New York Daily News* filed papers supporting Gannett's position.

If you were a judge hearing this case, how would you rule? What are the implications of your decision on, for example, the distribution of pornographic newspapers and magazines, television tapes, and the use of public streets by other types of vendors?

---

publisher. Hence we may ask, to what extent any publisher is (or should be) free from government interference? Further, if *Hustler* magazine is read by 3 million people—as it claims—then we must recognize that such a situation not only deprives the publisher from publishing the magazine but it also deprives 3 million people of reading the magazine. And would it matter if only 10 people read it or if 50 million people read it?

It is relatively easy to go back into history and find numerous works of literature that were at one time banned as pornographic. Where once people could not read *Lady Chatterley's Lover*, today many students are required to read it as part of some college course in English. Should we wonder if *Deep Throat* will become required viewing in film courses 10 or 20 years from now? Will the writings of Linda Lovelace or Xaveria Hollander become required reading in sex education courses? Such a situation probably seems absurd. But then so did the idea that the works of D. H. Lawrence might one day be required reading seem absurd not so many years ago.

We must recognize that morality and definitions of pornography are time-bound as well as culture-bound (at least according to most systems of ethics). What is considered pornographic in one culture and at one time may not be considered pornographic in another culture or at another time. However, the changing definitions that we have witnessed over time do not seem to be governed by any logic; they appear totally unpredictable.

Still another issue in regard to pornography and its regulation is that it is taken as an axiom that it is the obligation of those who would attempt to depict sexual activities to prove that such depictions are worthy of redeeming social significance. Underlying this notion seems to be the assumption that somehow sex is evil and is therefore to be hidden from public view. Most people do not object to depictions of theft, murder, and war, and yet they do object to depictions of sexual activity.

In an age of mass communication, it becomes increasingly difficult for individuals to make public statements that have broad influence.

Closely related is the controversy over sex education in the schools. For example, the *New York Times* (June 12, 1980) reported that the State Board of

61

Education of New Jersey "bowed to strong pressure from the Legislature and vocal community groups and retreated from its order mandating specific sex education courses at all grade levels in the schools, beginning with kindergarten." Here is a perfect example of contemporary censorship; the adult community censors the sex-related information that school-aged children are exposed to. The censorship pertains to what the teacher may cover in class as well as to what the student may receive as listener and reader.

It somehow seems to be assumed, though the line of reasoning seems a bit tenuous, that sexually oriented communications have undesirable effects on the persons receiving them. Although there seems little evidence to support this, it is nevertheless an empirical question and one that should be answered by evidence. Yet it is paradoxical that in the absence of such evidence the filmmaker, teacher, photographer, and writer must prove their innocence—contrary to the normal system where innocence is assumed and guilt must be proven. In fact, the little evidence that is available seems to suggest that the effects of such exposure are actually beneficial.

Another assumption underlying these provisions seems to be that the effects of such communications can be predicted with a fair degree of accuracy. But this hardly seems the case. When *West Side Story* was shown on television some years ago, it apparently helped to reactivate gangs and gang wars in New York City and perhaps elsewhere as well. Should *West Side Story* have been banned?

There are other issues that we need to consider under the heading of censorship. As citizens we all have the right to make our voices heard. Each of us has the Constitutional right (some would say the obligation) to voice our opinions and our beliefs when they do not endanger the lives or safety of others. Clearly we do not have the right to ruin someone's reputation with lies or yell "fire" in a theater, since this might endanger the lives of others. Yet, we do have the right to speak out for or against a particular way of life or political philosophy or economic policy. But as average citizens how can we do this? To speak and to have our voices heard today is an extremely expensive undertaking. The communications systems throughout the country and the world are too expensive for us to engage for even a single minute. If we wished, for example, to advertise in favor of one of our political views or in support of something we wish to defend, rather like the large corporations do, and we chose to run this ad in *Playboy*, it would cost us at least a few years' salary. It is interesting (yet frightening), for example, to reflect on the fact that Bell Telephone can use our money to advertise to millions of people how hard they are working to bring us the best service at the least possible cost but we, who use the phones every day, cannot advertise to tell these same people of the difficulties we encounter in dealing with them. Of course, this problem is not limited to Bell Telephone, nor was it created by them. Could we purchase one minute of the "Tonight" show to air our views? Clearly we could not, and yet this is exactly what we would have to do if we were to have an effective voice in influencing public opinion. The days of individuals in their basements with old printing presses, cranking out handbills to distribute in front of the local church, are gone forever. Such a procedure today would be ineffective at best.

BOX 4.3
Calvin, Brooke, and Television Standards

One of the most effective television advertisements has been the Calvin Klein commercial for designer jeans featuring Brooke Shields, who played the nymphet in the movie *Pretty Baby*. Although there were many protests that the ads were too suggestive, they apparently were quite effective in increasing sales. In fact, Calvin Klein extended the advertising campaign beyond its originally planned schedule.

In November 1980 the commercial was killed. The stations refused to broadcast it, noting that it fell below their minimal standards. Among the lines of Ms. Shields that apparently led the stations to refuse to air the commercial were "If my Calvins could talk, I'd be ruined" and "What comes between me and my Calvins? Nothing." In addition to such remarks, the television stations apparently objected to the way in which the camera focused too suggestively on certain parts of Ms. Shields' Calvins.

Do you think the stations were justified in refusing to air this commercial? What standards (if any) should a commercial have to meet to be broadcast over the public airways? What ethical issues are raised in this case? Specifically, what issues concerning pornography, censorship, and free speech might be involved in this case and others that this case might raise bring to the fore? If you were asked to rule on this controversy, what would you say? Why?

Are we not effectively censored from communicating our views because we are not millionaires and have access only to interpersonal communication channels? Although there have been some efforts made to require television stations to allot a certain amount of time to the presentation of opposing views, it seems clear that the size of one's voice and hence influence are largely determined by the size of one's bank account.

This problem of expense has been discussed perhaps most often in connection with political campaigning. Without a substantial financial backing it seems impossible to get elected to any high public office. A potential candidate without any money would not be able to advertise, would not be able to buy air time, would not be able to travel to deliver speeches, would not be able to have posters printed and circulated, and so on. And so (if one is at all serious about running for political office) one must obtain this financial backing. And we are well aware that one does not obtain this substantial financial backing without giving something in return. This "something in return" is often given at the expense of the very people who will eventually elect the candidate.

At the same time that we may see dangers in censorship it seems equally clear that some restrictions may be helpful and useful. Most would probably agree that people with access to military information should not be allowed to reveal facts that might prove damaging to national security. We might also agree that restrictions on the basis of age might be legitimate. Perhaps certain information, on subjects such as alcohol and cigarettes, should be restricted to "adults," however we might define that term. And so while we might agree that certain lines may be useful to draw, we seem far from agreeing on exactly where the lines should be.

SOURCES

On communication and ethics see Thomas R. Nilsen, *Ethics of Speech Communication*, 2d ed. (Indianapolis: Bobbs-Merrill, 1974), Richard L. Johannesen, *Ethics in Human Communication* (Columbus, Ohio: Charles E. Merrill, 1975), and R. Johannesen, ed., *Ethics and Persuasion: Selected Readings* (New York: Random, 1967). For ghostwriting, see especially Ernest G. Bormann, "Ethics of Ghostwritten Speeches," *Quarterly Journal of Speech* 47 (1961): 262–267. The discussion in this unit owes much to this Bormann article. Franklyn S. Haiman's "Democratic Ethics and the Hidden Persuaders," *Quarterly Journal of Speech* 44 (1958): 385–393, is particularly relevant to this unit. An interesting and relevant discussion of academic freedom is presented in David Rubin's *The Rights of Teachers* (New York: Avon, 1972). For a discussion of ethics as related to efficiency see Robert T. Oliver, "Ethics and Efficiency in Persuasion," *Southern Speech Journal* 26 (1960): 10–15. Ethical considerations and how they relate to language are covered in Jane Blankenship, *A Sense of Style* (Belmont, Cal.: Dickenson, 1968). Also see Franklyn S. Haiman's "The Rhetoric of the Streets: Some Legal and Ethical Considerations," *Quarterly Journal of Speech* 53 (1967): 99–114. Patricia Niles Middlebrook (*Social Psychology and Modern Life* [New York: Knopf, 1974]), in her discussion of the emotional approach to changing attitudes and her thorough treatment of intensive indoctrination, provides a clear analysis of the effectiveness of these techniques. You may wish to read these two discussions with the issues of ethics we raised here in mind. Wayne C. Minnick provides an interesting discussion of the means-versus-the-ends argument in ethics. See his "A New Look at the Ethics of Persuasion," *Southern Speech Communication Journal* 45 (summer 1980): 352–362. The *Journal of Communication* 30 (spring 1980) contains a number of interesting articles on deception strategies in communication relevant to this discussion of ethics. Mark L. Knapp and Mark E. Comadena, "Telling It Like It Isn't: A Review of Theory and Research on Deceptive Communications," *Human Communication Research* 5 (spring 1979): 270–285, provide a thorough review on deceptive communications. On lying see Dale Hample, "Purposes and Effects of Lying," *Southern Speech Communication Journal* 46 (fall 1980): 33–47.

Experiential Vehicles

4.1 Ethical Principles

Complete the following statements as you would have them read for an ideal society.

1. Parents and society generally should prevent interactions between or among . . . , under the following circumstances: . . .
2. Conditioning should be utilized by social institutions when . . .
3. Ghostwriting should be considered justified when . . .
4. Censorship should be instituted under the following conditions: . . .

After each student has completed these four statements a number of different procedures may be followed. One procedure is to divide up into small groups of five or six and discuss the various completions. The groups might then attempt to construct a compromise statement for each of the four areas in a manner not unlike that which would be followed by government committees. Another procedure is simply to discuss the statements with the class as a whole, again attempting to formulate some general statements that everyone can live with. A third procedure is to collect the various statements (without names on them) and read them aloud to the entire class. The problems and/or advantages of each statement or each type of statement may then be considered.

4.2 Some Questions of Ethics

This exercise is designed to raise only a few of the many questions that could be raised concerning the ethics of communication, and to encourage you to think in concrete terms about some of the relevant issues. The purpose is not to persuade you to adopt a particular point of view but rather to encourage you to formulate your own point of view.

The exercises consist of a series of cases, each raising somewhat different ethical questions. These exercises will probably work best if you respond to each of the cases individually and then discuss your decisions and the implications in groups of five or six. In these small groups simply discuss those cases that you found most interesting. The most interesting cases for small group discussion will probably be those that were the most difficult for you to respond to, that is, those that involved the most internal conflict. A general discussion in which the various groups share their decisions and insights may conclude the session.

Guidelines

1. Carefully read each of the following cases and write down your responses. As you write your decisions, many issues that may be unclear will come to the surface and may then be used as a basis for discussion.
2. Your responses will not be made public, these papers will not be collected, and your decisions will be revealed only if you wish to reveal them. If individuals wish not to reveal their decisions, do not attempt to apply any social pressure to get them to make these decisions public.
3. Do not attempt to avoid the issues presented in the various cases by saying, for example, "I'd try other means." For purposes of these exercises "other means" are ruled out.
4. In the small group discussions focus some attention on the origin of the various values implicit in your decisions. You might, as a starting point, consider how your parents would respond to these cases. Would their decisions be similar or different from yours? Do not settle for "conditioning" as an answer. If you wish to discuss the development of these values in terms of conditioning, focus on specific reinforcement contingencies, the rewards and punishments received that may have led to the development of these various values.
5. Devote some attention to the concept of change. Would you have responded in similar fashion five years ago? If not, what has led to the change? Would you predict similar responses five or ten years from now? Why? Why not? This concept of change is also significant in another respect. Focus attention on the changes or possible changes that might occur as a result of your acting in accordance with any of the decisions. That is, is the student who sells drugs the same individual he or she was before doing this? Can this student ever be the same individual again? How is the student different? If we accept the notion, even in part, that how we act or behave influences what we are, how does this relate to the decisions we make on these issues?
6. Consider the concept of acceptance. How willing is each group member to accept the decisions of others? Are you accepting of your own decisions? Why? Why not? Would you be pleased if your children would respond in the same way you did?
7. Note that there are three questions posed after each case: "What should you do?" asks you to consider your own ethical system and identify the decision that you think is consistent with this system. What is the right decision to make? The "What would you do?" question asks you to consider what probable response you would make should you be confronted with such a decision. What are you most likely to do in this situation? The third question, "What general principle of ethics influences this decision?," asks that you consider the bases for your decision. I assume here that every individual decision will be made—in part—in accordance with or as a result of some general principle, belief, or value. This question asks you to identify that general ethical principle.

GHOSTING

You are a capable and proficient writer and speaker and have, for the past three years, worked full-time for a large political organization as a ghostwriter. During these three years you have prepared papers for publication and speeches to be delivered by the various officers of the organization. Throughout this time you have been firmly committed to the aims and methods of the organization. Consequently, no problem arose. You were serving your political party by making their appeals and policies more persuasive, in addition to earning an extremely high salary as a ghostwriter. Recently, however, the party has decided to endorse a bill that you feel would not be in the public interest. On this issue your attitudes are diametrically opposed to those of the party. As ghostwriter for the organization you are asked to speak in favor of this bill. These informal talks are to be held throughout the state. You realize that if you do not comply you will lose your job. At the same time, however, you wonder if you can ethically give persuasive force to a proposal you feel should not be supported. Not being effective in these interpersonal encounters will not work, since you would be fired after one such interaction.

1. What should you do?
2. What would you do?
3. What general principle of ethics influences this decision?

MANAGING A RADIO STATION

You are the manager of a college radio station and are in charge of all aspects of production. All decisions are made by you—the type of music to be played, the news to be reported, the commercials to be presented. The American Nazi Party asks to buy radio time to announce the formation of a local chapter of the ANP in your community and to ask for contributions to its cause. You personally disagree with the aims and policies of the American Nazi Party, but you wonder if it would be unfair (and unethical) to deny them the right of free speech.

1. What should you do?
2. What would you do?
3. What general principle of ethics influences this decision?

BORROWING A TERM PAPER

In your Communication Theory course an extensive term paper is required. If you were to earn a high enough grade on this paper (at least an A −), you would receive an A in the course. You want this A because it will help a great deal in getting you into graduate school and perhaps even in getting you a fellowship of some kind. Your problem is that you are too pressed for time to do justice to this paper. Your friend, who took a similar course at another university, has completed such a paper and earned an A. Your instructor is sure to evaluate it the same way. Your friend offers you the paper; all you would have to do is have it retyped.

1. What should you do?
2. What would you do?
3. What general principle of ethics influences this decision?

SCHOLARSHIP COMPETITION

You are competing with a fellow student for a full scholarship to law school. Both of you need the scholarship and both of you seem to deserve it equally—your grades, service to the school and community, law board scores, and so on are about the same. Unfortunately, there is only one scholarship to be awarded. The committee charged with selecting the winner is a conservative group and would vote against candidates should they find out anything about their personal lives of which they would disapprove. You have recently learned that your competitor is an ex-convict. You could easily leak this information to the committee, in which case you would surely get the scholarship. No one (not even the members of the committee) would know that you were the source of this information.

1. What should you do?
2. What would you do?
3. What general principle of ethics influences this decision?

FREE LUNCH

> You have been asked by a local organization concerned with the elderly
> to raise money for a free lunch program for the elderly in your commu-
> nity. You consider inviting the local townspeople to a community board
> meeting and then having a few particularly moving elderly persons de-
> liver impassioned speeches on how desperately they need this free
> lunch program. The elderly would stress how many of them would have
> to go without lunch if this program were not instituted. You are certain
> that the townspeople would donate if appealed to in this way and that
> other means of persuasion would have no chance of working. You want
> to institute this free lunch program and the elderly need it, and yet you
> wonder if you are justified in using emotional rather than logical ap-
> peals.

1. What should you do?
2. What would you do?
3. What general principle of ethics influences this decision?

4.3   A Tentative Theory of Communication Ethics

Formulate here what might be called, "My Tentative Theory of the Ethics of
Communication." Formulate a theory that you feel is reasonable, justified, in-
ternally consistent, and consonant with your own system of values. Construct
your theory so that it incorporates at least all the situations presented in the previous exercise—that is, so that another person, given this statement of ethical
principles, should be able to accurately predict how you would behave in each of
the situations presented in the cases in Experiential Vehicle 4.2.

Part Two

Message Reception

Unit 5

Preliminaries to Message Reception

PRELIMINARIES TO MESSAGE RECEPTION

Messages Are Received Actively
Messages Are Received Through Multiple Channels
Messages Are Received Subjectively
Messages Are Received According to the Law of Least Effort
Messages Are Received in Cumulative Style
Messages Are Received in Limited and Partial Form
    5.1 A Stranger

LEARNING GOALS

After completing this unit, you should be able to:

1. explain the active nature of message reception
2. explain the role of reinforcement in message reception
3. explain the multichanneled nature of message reception
4. explain the subjective nature of message reception
5. define and explain the law of least effort and how it operates in message reception
6. explain the cumulative nature of message reception
7. explain the partial and limited nature of message reception
8. provide at least one example from your personal experience to illustrate each of the characteristics of message reception identified in this unit

essage reception is not a simple, solitary act but rather a complex process consisting of a number of different but interrelated activities. After the message, whether verbal or nonverbal, intentional or unintentional, is sent, it is perceived in some way; the message is seen, felt, tasted, smelled, or heard. In Unit 6 we will focus on the processes and principles of perception. Because of the importance of verbal messages in interpersonal communication, listening as one type of message reception is singled out for special consideration in Unit 7.

But before examining the specifics of perception and listening, we need to look at some of the universals of message reception—that is, those characteristics that are common to all aspects of message reception, those qualities that define all the processes of message reception.

MESSAGES ARE RECEIVED ACTIVELY

Message reception is an active rather than a passive process. People are not containers into which information may be poured as you would pour water into a glass. Rather they are active participants in the reception process. We work actively with the messages that we receive, altering them in ways that may better suit our expectations or our individual needs at the time.

We actively select the messages to which we will attend. The Republican will listen to Republican messages, and the Democrat will listen to Democratic messages. We also determine in part the effects that messages will have on us—for example, who we will believe and who we will not believe, those whom we will allow to influence us significantly and those we will not allow to influence us. Graffiti provides an interesting case study in the nature of active message reception.

This is not to say that all message reception is consciously controlled; much of it is subconscious. We may not even be aware of some messages we receive—at least not at the time of reception. But some time later, perhaps years later, they may surface and may be found to have exerted considerable influence on our lives.

Perhaps the principle that seems best capable of explaining the basis one would use in actively seeking certain messages and actively avoiding others is that of reinforcement. The messages we receive and the ways in which we allow ourselves to receive them are greatly influenced by our history of reinforcement and by our present needs and wants. We receive messages, and in fact actively seek out messages, that will reinforce us. We seek out messages that will provide us with some kind of reward. If we are in need of peer approval, we will actively seek out peer-approval messages. If we have a need to be put down, as many do, then we will seek out those messages that put us down.

BOX 5.1
Graffiti

Norman Mailer once characterized graffiti—the scrawlings on toilet walls, fences, and subway trains and stations—as "some of the best prose in America." And the widely syndicated columnist Norton Mockridge in his *The Scrawl of the Wild* notes that "a great deal of the finest, keenest, and most satirical and witty writing being done today is not necessarily in books, magazines, and newspapers—but on fences and walls!" Graffiti seems firmly established; whitewash and cleanser may remove some of it some of the time but as a form of communication it seems here to stay, firmly etched on American edifices as on the American psyche.

    Graffiti comes from the Italian verb *graffiare*, meaning "to scratch," and its noun form, *graffio*, meaning "scratch." *Graffito* is the diminutive form, meaning "little scratch"; the English word *graffiti* is simply the plural form. Its meaning has been generalized to refer to the scratches, scrawlings, and writings in public places—toilets, subway cars, billboards, buildings, fences, rocks, and just about any place where one can write and another can read.

    Some would argue that graffiti is an aggressive act. Richard Freeman,

for example, in his book *Graffiti*, argued that writing graffiti evidenced aggressiveness in at least two ways. First, and perhaps most obvious, is that with most graffiti there is a defacement involved; the wall is smeared with paint, the toilet stall is scratched with a nail, or the train is attacked with a marking pen. The second way graffiti evidences aggressiveness is that the writer—in the very act of writing the graffiti—is saying something that he or she would not normally say, usually something aggressive.

Others would argue that the graffiti writer is psychologically unbalanced. The graffiti writer, in this view, is someone who cannot deal with reality, cannot be assertive on an interpersonal level, and therefore retreats to anonymous writing on subway walls or toilet stalls.

And of course many would claim that the graffiti writer represents a cross section of the general public, that the graffiti writer is no different from anyone else, and that he or she merely chooses to express some thoughts, sometimes, through graffiti. One of the difficult aspects of exploring graffiti in depth is that although there are many samples of it all around us, it is relatively difficult to find people who admit to having written graffiti. And—to complicate matters even further—those who do admit it are probably not typical of those who write it. Just as difficult as finding people who admit to writing graffiti is finding people who do not read it. Almost universally, it seems to me, people read graffiti.

Graffiti serves a number of important communicative functions. Perhaps the most obvious function is that it establishes the identity of someone in a visible and relatively permanent way. Note how many scrawlings on subway cars, on billboards, and on walls merely contain the individual's name, sometimes accompanied by a "was here" or "will return" notation. But the name itself is probably the most important part of such graffiti. Often this identification function is served by noting a romantic connection between oneself and another person. This "Pat loves Chris" type of graffiti is especially prevalent where young people congregate. This is not to deny that many times the name signed is not that of the writer but of some "friend" or enemy or perhaps well-known person.

Another function is to comment on some political, social, religious, or economic issue—perhaps to show off one's knowledge, perhaps to communicate something without the threat of being refuted, perhaps to assist one in thinking out his or her own thoughts, perhaps to serve as a persuasive message to influence the thinking and behaving of others. "Black Power" and "Gay Power" slogans are perhaps the clearest examples of such writings, but the numerous antiwar, antidraft, anti–big business writings serve similar functions.

An additional function—almost always restricted to toilets—is that of sexual solicitation. Such solicitations leave little to the imagination. They state what the writer wants in no uncertain terms. These solicitations come in two basic forms—the "I am looking for" and the "I am available" types. Both serve essentially the same basic function of bringing together persons who want to be brought together. Actually, such solicitations probably result in relatively few such interpersonal meetings. The most important outcome of such writing is probably the fantasies of such interpersonal encounters by their writers and readers. Still another function of graffiti is to tell a story, usually a sexual one. In college toilets, however, many of these stories concern themselves with academic issues—the problems of registering, in getting a fair grade, in being treated as an individual rather than as a computer number.

This graffiti communication, although condemned by many as neurotic, was a logical expression of the writer's feelings at the time. The popular writer has a ready outlet in his or her articles and books, but the average graffiti writer has only the walls in the local toilet. Fortunately, the walls are read by the very audience he or she wishes to attract, and perhaps in that the graffiti writer is more fortunate than other writers.

Similarly, we will avoid messages that will cause pain or discomfort or otherwise punish us. This may take the form of avoiding people who are usually negative toward us or avoiding advertisements extolling the pleasures of smoking after we have decided to quit or avoiding articles about smoking causing cancer when we smoke two packs a day.

In this respect message reception behavior is much like behavior in general. We seek out the rewards and we avoid the punishments, we approach what will reinforce us and we avoid what will punish us. We are no fools.

MESSAGES ARE RECEIVED THROUGH MULTIPLE CHANNELS

Message reception is multichanneled; that is, messages are received simultaneously through a number of different channels. For example, in talking face-to-face with one other person, we receive the auditory messages through our sense of hearing. At the same time, we receive gestural, facial, and eye messages through our sense of vision, tactile messages through our sense of touch, olfactory messages through our sense of smell, and gustatory messages through our sense of taste. Even when we are speaking on the telephone we are still receiving nonauditory messages, this time from our own immediate surroundings. We are constantly taking in visual messages from our immediate physical context, olfactory messages from the coffee on the stove, gustatory messages from the cake we are eating, and so on. In fact, we would have to construct a highly artificial communication situation if we wished to create single-channel message reception. In real-life interaction, single-channel message reception does not seem to exist.

The important implication of the multichanneled nature of message reception is that the messages coming in through the different channels may reinforce one another, contradict one another, or present us with simultaneous but unrelated information. Usually, the messages coming through the different channels reinforce one another; the verbal greeting, for example, is accompanied by a gestural greeting, a smile, or a handshake. At times, however, the messages contradict one another, as when the verbal greeting is accompanied by a pained expression, a sense of uneasiness, or a lack of direct eye contact. At still other times messages received at the same time may be unrelated, as when we are listening to what one person is saying but at the same time admiring the room or listening to still another conversation. Often we are busy receiving our own messages, as when we rehearse what we are going to say next or when we are preoccupied with some problem or some decision we must make or when we are concentrating on a toothache, hunger, or thirst. All of these messages may be unrelated to the message being received from the person with whom we are interacting, but they nevertheless interfere to some extent with our reception of this "primary" message.

MESSAGES ARE RECEIVED SUBJECTIVELY

The message that occurs in the outside world is not the message that we receive. What we receive is actually a function of what occurs outside of us and what occurs inside our skin. Message reception is not an objective process; it is in fact a highly subjective process. The same message (that is, the same message in the outside world) received by two different people is actually two different messages. Similarly, the same message received at two different times is actually two different messages, since we have changed and what went on inside our skins last year is not what is going on now.

Each of these propositions is verified in numerous ways every day of our lives. Consider, for example, going to a movie with a friend. You each see the same movie, but the reception is extremely different; one may find it exciting and entertaining and the other dull and boring. A colleague told me that *All That Jazz* was one of the best movies of all time and that I should be sure to see it. I saw it and had to struggle to stay awake and, in fact, actually fell asleep. The stimulus (the movie) was the same for both of us, but we were very different people with different things going on inside our heads; consequently, the messages received were, for all practical purposes, very different. The difference in perception caused by time is no less striking. Movies that I thought sensational a few years ago I may now view as trite and uninsightful. The movie itself has not changed; what has changed is what is going on inside my skin.

Message reception is often subjective because it is heavily influenced by our individual and unique expectations. If we expect a course to be dull and uninteresting, we will probably find it to be just that. On the other hand, if we expect it to be insightful and exciting, we are likely to find it to be just that. My friends who go to singles bars invariably have their expectations confirmed regardless of what these expectations are. The messages that are sent are probably similar, but when they expect to receive positive messages they seem to perceive the messages as positive, and when they expect to receive negative messages they seem to perceive the messages as negative.

MESSAGES ARE RECEIVED ACCORDING TO THE LAW OF LEAST EFFORT

George Kingsley Zipf formulated a principle called "the law of least effort." Zipf's concern was actually with describing the ways in which language changes; his assumption was that language changes always followed the law of least effort. Pronunciation changes, for example, were always in the direction of less effort, as were changes in word meanings and in syntactic patterns. The principle, however, was applicable to a variety of issues in daily living and was soon applied widely, sometimes without adequate analysis.

I am not sure if the principle of least effort should be applied to as many issues as it has been, but I think it is applicable to message reception. Here it would refer to the practice of receiving those messages that require little effort and avoiding those messages that require us to expend much energy and effort. Probably the easiest messages for us to receive come from television. Physically, all we have to do is turn the knob. We do not have to dress, wait on line for tickets, or travel by car, bus, or train to get to the movie or theater. Psychologically, we can relax while watching television; little (if any) intellectual energy need be expended to watch 98 percent of the shows. This law of least effort is probably not the only reason that television is so popular, but it does seem to be one of the reasons why people spend a great deal more time watching television than they do going to the theater, concerts (even free ones), or even reading.

Messages that are complicated and thus take a great deal of energy to decipher are less popular than are messages that require little effort. Newspapers— even the *New York Times* and the *Wall Street Journal*—make a great effort to simplify in order to enable a reader to go through the newspaper without expending much effort. Picture magazines like *People* and *Us* have become extremely popular largely because they require very little effort to go through. *Reader's Digest* and *Book Digest* are popular in part for the same reason; they require less effort to read than the original articles or books.

One example we might relate to easily is this very book. I wrote it in units so that it would require less effort to get through than would longer chapters. My assumption was that you would be more apt to pick up the book if you could get through a unit in a relatively short period of time. When we face a chapter of 50 or 60 pages of tough prose, we are more likely to put it off until an examination forces us to face it.

Other things being equal, then, we seem to select those messages that require the least effort and the least expenditure of energy.

MESSAGES ARE RECEIVED IN CUMULATIVE STYLE

Message reception is a cumulative process. When we receive messages, they are not simply taken in and stored in isolated compartments in our short-term and long-term memory systems. Rather, the messages that we receive today interact with the messages that we received yesterday, which in turn interacted with the messages received the day before, and so on. And, of course, the messages—the data, the information, the concepts, the ideas, the theories, the beliefs, the attitudes, and so on—that we have stored in our memories up until now will influence the way in which all future messages will be received, remembered, and stored.

If, for example, you receive a message about your best friend, that message will be combined with all the other information that you have about your best friend, about the nature of friendship, and about various other related topics. The way in which it is evaluated, the extent to which you believe it to be true or false, the importance you assign to it, the way it makes you feel, the action you will base on it, and a host of other thoughts and behaviors will depend on how this new message relates to all the other information you have on this and related subjects.

This rather obvious characteristic of message reception has several not-so-obvious implications. First, the very same message received by two different people or by the same person at two different times will be functionally two different messages. This has to be so because the stored information of two people or of the same person at two different times is inevitably different. Second, because we can never know fully how the new message will interact with all previous messages, we can never fully predict the effect that any given message will have. The very same message may have diametrically opposed effects on two different people or on the same person at two different times. This is because the message's effect is dependent on the ways in which it interacts with previously stored messages, and these stored messages cannot be fully known and their interactions cannot be accurately predicted. Third, even though we cannot predict with complete accuracy the way in which a specific message will be received and responded to, the accuracy of our predictions will increase as our knowledge of the individual message receiver increases. If we know a great deal about a person, if we know the kinds of messages this person has, we will be in a somewhat better position to predict how any given message will be received and responded to.

MESSAGES ARE RECEIVED IN LIMITED AND PARTIAL FORM

There are an infinite number of possible messages occurring right now in the outside world. The verbal messages alone usually number in the hundreds, to say nothing of the visual messages, olfactory messages, and so on. And yet out of this tremendous number we receive relatively few.

Clearly there are limits to our capacity to receive messages and to process information, both in terms of its quantity and in terms of its complexity. We can only deal with so much information; when that amount is exceeded, we ignore the rest or simply go through the motions of receiving it when actually nothing is happening. For example, at a disco people will often go through the motions of hearing and responding to verbal messages when in fact they actually cannot make out what is being said. But apparently they get enough cues to know when a smile is appropriate, when a shake of the head is suitable, or when a look of intense concern is expected. Similarly, when messages get too complex, we may receive only the surface elements and ignore the rest. We may understand the words, for example, but their significance may go over our heads. This is seen quite clearly in someone who knows little about art or music when she or he views a painting or listens to a piece of music. Very little beyond the line and color, the words and arrangement may be received.

In part, the limitations are imposed by our mental capacities. We have just so much ability to deal with messages and simply cannot push it beyond its limits. In part, our limitations are imposed by our own prejudices—our relative closed-mindedness or open-mindedness. A person who is extremely prejudiced against Martians, for example, will have difficulty receiving favorable messages about Martians. Instead, the messages may not be received or they may be distorted to the point where they become totally opposite to what the source may have intended.

SOURCES

One of the best sources on message reception is Wilbur Schramm, *Men, Messages, and Media: A Look at Human Communication* (New York: Harper & Row, 1973). The principle of least effort may be found in two works by George Kingsley Zipf, *The Psycho-Biology of Language: An Introduction to Dynamic Philology* (Boston: Houghton Mifflin, 1935) and *Human Behavior and the Principle of Least Effort* (Cambridge: Harvard University Press, 1949). More recent treatments may be found in Phillip Emmert and William C. Donaghy, *Human Communication: Elements and Contexts* (Reading, Mass.: Addison-Wesley, 1981), and Ernest G. Bormann, *Communication Theory* (New York: Holt, Rinehart and Winston, 1980). On the encoding and retrieving of information see Roberta L. Klatzky, *Human Memory: Structures and Processes*, 2d ed. (San Francisco, California: W. H. Freeman, 1980).

Experiential Vehicle

5.1 A Stranger

The purpose of this exercise is to explore the bases you use in dealing with messages and judging people you see for the first time.* Since we all make judgments of people upon seeing them, we need to investigate the ways and means we use in making these judgments.

A stranger (someone you have not seen before) will be brought into class. Look the stranger over and answer the questions that follow. For this phase of the exercise no interaction between you and the stranger should take place. Use the number "1" to indicate your answers.

After this you will be able to interact with the stranger for five or ten minutes. Ask him or her any questions you wish, though none can be directly related to the exercise questions. The stranger should answer any questions posed as fully as he or she thinks necessary. The stranger should not, however, answer any questions that relate directly to the questions posed in the exercise. After this interaction, again answer the questions, this time using "2" to mark your answers.

After the answers have been recorded, the stranger or the instructor will go over each of the questions, specifying which answers the stranger thinks are most appropriate.

Instructions

Before interaction with the stranger answer the questions by placing the number "1" in the appropriate space. After interaction answer the questions by placing the number "2" in the appropriate space.

The stranger would most likely:

1. read

    _____ *The Best of Mad*

    _____ *War and Peace*

    _____ *The Sensuous Man/Woman*

    _____ *I Ching*

    _____ a James Bond novel

2. participate in

    _____ football

* This exercise, though in a somewhat different form, was suggested by James C. McCroskey, Carl E. Larsen, and Mark L. Knapp in their *Teacher's Manual* for *An Introduction to Interpersonal Communication* (Englewood Cliffs, N.J.: Prentice-Hall, 1971).

_____ tennis

_____ golf

_____ skiing

_____ none of these

3. listen to

_____ classical music

_____ rock music

_____ country western music

_____ popular music

_____ disco

4. watch on television

_____ a situation comedy

_____ the news

_____ an educational show

_____ a detective show

_____ sports

_____ a soap opera

5. prefer to be

_____ alone

_____ in a crowd with friends and acquaintances

_____ with one person

_____ with family

6. go to

_____ a rock concert

_____ an art museum

_____ a sports event

_____ an opera

_____ a play

_____ a movie

_____ a disco

7. look for in a mate

_____ intelligence

_____ looks

_____ personality

_____ money

_____ status

_____ sense of humor

8. subscribe to

_____ *Playboy/Playgirl*

_____ *National Geographic*

_____ *Time/Newsweek*

_____ *Popular Mechanics*

_____ *Good Housekeeping*

_____ *Modern Bride*

9. behave

_____ as an extrovert

_____ an an introvert

_____ as an ambivert

10. be

_____ very energetic

_____ very lazy

_____ fairly energetic

_____ fairly lazy

11. behave in most situations

_____ very emotionally

_____ very rationally

_____ fairly emotionally

_____ fairly rationally

12. be generally

_____ very happy

_____ very unhappy

_____ fairly happy

_____ fairly unhappy

13. Also, what is the stranger's:
    Age
    Occupation
    Highest educational level reached
    Marital status
    Financial status
14. Describe the stranger's personality in two, three, or four adjectives.
15. How does the stranger feel now? Explain.

Discussion should focus on at least the following:

1. How do your conclusions support the notion that messages are received actively rather than passively?
2. Through which channels did you receive information about the stranger? Which channels were the most important in your initial decisions? In your later decisions?
3. How might the subjectivity of message reception be demonstrated from your conclusions about the stranger? Could any of your conclusions be said to be objective?
4. Did the law of least effort operate here? How? If it did not operate here, why didn't it? How does this situation differ from those you encounter every day?
5. How did the cumulative nature of message reception operate here?
6. In what ways might the partial and limited nature of message reception be demonstrated from this experience?

Unit 6

Perception

PERCEPTION

LEARNING GOALS

After completing this unit, you should be able to:

1. define *perception*
2. explain the three stages in the perception process
3. distinguish between *static* and *dynamic judgments*
4. define and supply at least one example of each of the three bases for judgment
5. recognize the bases for our own judgments of people
6. define *primacy* and *recency*
7. explain the influence of primacy-recency on perception
8. define the *self-fulfilling prophecy*
9. explain the influence of the self-fullfilling prophecy on perception
10. define *perceptual accentuation*
11. explain the influence of perceptual accentuation on perception
12. define an *implicit personality theory*
13. state at least three propositions that are part of your own implicit personality theory
14. explain the influence of an implicit personality theory on perception
15. define *consistency*
16. explain the influence of consistency on perception
17. define *stereotype*
18. explain the influence of stereotyping on perception
19. recognize the different ways in which you perceive and are perceived by others

Perception is the process by which we become aware of objects and events in the external world through our various senses: sight, smell, taste, touch, and hearing. Perception is an active rather than a passive process. Our perceptions are only in part a function of the outside world; in large measure they are a function of our own past experiences, our desires, our needs and wants, our loves and hatreds. Hans Toch and Malcolm MacLean express the essence of this transactional view of perception most clearly. "Each percept [that which is perceived]," note Toch and MacLean, "from the simplest to the most complex, is the product of a creative act. . . . We can never encounter a stimulus before some meaning has been assigned to it by some perceiver. . . . Therefore, each perception is the beneficiary of all previous perceptions; in turn, each new perception leaves its make on the common pool. A percept is thus a link between the past which gives it its meaning and the future which it helps to interpret."

In communication we are particularly concerned with that area of perception that focuses on people, often called people perception or interpersonal perception, and the judgments we make about them.

STAGES IN THE PERCEPTION PROCESS

Before we explain people perception, some understanding of the general nature of the process of perception is essential. For convenience, we might consider the process of perception as occurring in three stages or steps. These stages are not discrete and separate, as the discussion might imply; in reality they are continuous and blend into one another. See Figure 6.1.

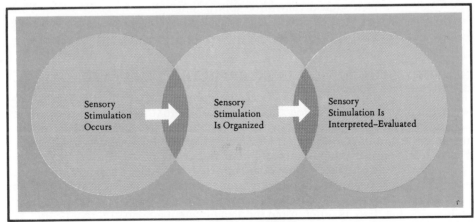

Figure 6.1 The stages in the perception process.

87

SENSORY STIMULATION OCCURS

At this first stage the sense organs are stimulated—we hear Blondie's latest recording, we see someone we have not seen for years, we smell perfume on the person next to us, we taste a slice of pizza, we feel a sweaty palm as we shake hands.

We all have different abilities to hear, see, smell, taste, and feel. Some people can hear very high-pitched sounds, whereas others cannot. Similarly, some can see great distances, whereas others have trouble seeing 10 feet away.

Even when we have the sensory ability to perceive stimuli, we do not always do so. For example, when you are daydreaming in class, you do not hear what the teacher is saying until your own name is called. Then you wake up. You know your name was called, but you do not know why. This is a clear and perhaps too frequent example of our perceiving what is meaningful to us and not perceiving what is not meaningful (or at least what we now judge to be not meaningful).

An obvious implication of this is that what we do perceive is only a very small portion of what could be perceived. Much as we have limits on how far we can see, we also have limits on the quantity of stimulation that we can take in at any given time. When we walk down a street we see a great number of things, but we fail to see even more. Similarly, we hear the teacher calling our name but fail to hear the birds sing, the student next to us chewing gum, the folding of papers, the tapping of a foot, the whispers of the student behind us, the sound of the chalk on the board (unless it squeaks), and so on. One of the goals of education should be to train us to perceive more of what exists, whether it be art, politics, music, communication, social problems, or any other conceivable source of sensory stimulation.

SENSORY STIMULATION IS ORGANIZED

At the second stage the sensory stimulations are organized in some way and according to some principles. Exactly how our sensory stimulations are organized and what principles such organization follow is not always agreed upon. What we do know is that what is perceived is organized into a pattern that is meaningful *to the perceiver*.

SENSORY STIMULATION IS INTERPRETED-EVALUATED

The third step in the perceptual process is interpretation-evaluation, terms that we hyphenate and consider together to emphasize that in reality they cannot be separated. This third step is inevitably a subjective process involving evaluations on the part of the perceiver. Our interpretations-evaluations, then, are not based solely on the external stimulus but rather are greatly influenced by our past experiences, our needs, our wants, our value systems, our beliefs about the way things are or should be, our physical or emotional states at the time, our expectations, and so on. It should be clear from even this very incomplete list of influences that there is much room for disagreement among different people. Although we may all be exposed to the same external stimulus, the way it is inter-preted-evaluated will differ with each person and from one time to another for the same person. We may both hear Blondie, but one person may say they are terrible and the other says they are great.

The sight of someone we have not seen for years may bring joy to one person and anxiety to another. The smell of perfume may be pleasant to one person and repulsive to another. The taste of a slice of pizza may make one person feel great and the other person choke. A sweaty palm may be perceived by one person to indicate nervousness and by another to indicate excitement.

BOX 6.1
Interpersonal Perception—Some Random Research Findings

1. Nursery school children judged by adults as physically unattractive are less well liked by their classmates and are thought to misbehave more than other children.
2. Teachers judge attractive children as having higher intelligence, being more popular, and being more likely to go on to college than less attractive children.
3. Men with lots of body hair are seen as more virile, potent, and active than are men with less body hair.
4. Men with beards were perceived as more potent than men without beards.
5. Blond women are perceived as more beautiful, entertaining, and feminine, whereas dark-haired women are seen as more intelligent, sincere, dependable, and strong.
6. Dark men were seen as more ambitious, rugged, intelligent, and masculine than blond or redheaded men.
7. Women who were very attractive when in college were less happy, less satisfied, and less well adjusted in their forties and fifties than those women who were less attractive when in college.
8. Although college students claim that they look for friendliness, sincerity, and intelligence in their dates, it appears that physical attractiveness is actually the most important variable.
9. Men who are extremely thin or extremely fat are perceived as dependent, shy, and withdrawn, whereas muscular men are perceived as active, dominant, and energetic.
10. People with short noses and low foreheads were perceived as generous, happy, and youthful; those with narrow mouths were perceived as more intelligent than those with wide mouths.

Source: These and numerous other findings are discussed by Patricia Miles Middlebrook, *Social Psychology and Modern Life* (New York: Knopf, 1974): 369–417.

PERCEPTUAL JUDGMENTS

TYPES OF JUDGMENTS

Static judgments refer to those characteristics of another person that are relatively unchanging. Judgments of such characteristics as race, occupation, age, or nationality would be examples of static judgments, since these characteristics are relatively enduring. We often also make judgments about an individual's habitual response to specific situations. For example, such statements as "He's a soft touch when anyone needs help" or "She drives carefully" or "He eats well" represent static judgments. Similarly, we make judgments concerning an individual's general behavior without regard to specific situations. Examples include the statement that an individual is quick-tempered, that he or she is extroverted, or that he or she is mercenary. We also make numerous general *sociometric judgments*. These are judgments concerning relations among people— for example, "He loves her," "She hates her brother," or "The children are afraid of their father." All of these are static judgments since they refer to lasting or habitual characteristics.

Dynamic judgments, on the other hand, refer to the characteristics of other people that change more rapidly. One type of dynamic judgment would concern the specific response of an individual, for example, "He wants to leave the party," "She is having a good time," or "He is tired." These are judgments concerning a specific situation at a specific time. Judgments of affect would also be of the dynamic type. We can, for example, judge the moods of different people ("He is afraid," "She is happy," "He is in love"). A final type is what Mark Cook calls *regulation judgments*. These judgments refer to the behavior of people in social situations. For example, when we are in a group we do not usually talk when someone else is talking. When that person has finished we may make a regulation judgment that it is proper for us to talk now. We also make regulation judgments about the type of social situation we are in. Consequently, we regulate the topics and the language that might be appropriate or inappropriate. At a family dinner we would probably not talk about the same things or speak in the same way as we would in a locker room. This social type of judgment allows us to regulate appropriate behavior.

BASES FOR JUDGMENTS

The judgments that we make about other people are based on behaviors (or appearance) of the individual and some rule or rules that link that behavior with some type of judgment. For example, we see a person with thick glasses and conclude that he or she is studious. To make that judgment, however, we must have, somewhere in our perceptual system, a rule that goes something like this: "People who wear thick glasses are studious."

The question we need to ask now is how we acquire the rules we have— that is, how do the rules develop? Generally such rules are derived from experience, analogy, and/or authority (Figure 6.2).

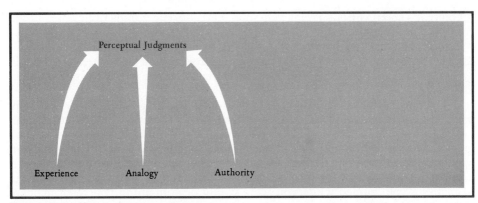

Figure 6.2   The bases for judgments.

Experience

Perhaps the most obvious ways to formulate rules about people and their characteristics is from experience. This experience may be derived from our own personal interactions or it may be from the interactions of others that we observe either in reality or in fiction (radio, television, movies, novels). Thus, for example, from our own experience we may formulate such rules as "All college athletes are stupid," "All members of street gangs engage in violence," or "All doctors are mercenary." Or we may formulate rules on the basis of what we observe in the media and conclude that all convicts are good-hearted, all nurses are dedicated, and all unmarried men are swingers.

Analogy

Another way of formulating rules is on the basis of analogy. We assume that person X will respond in a particular way because person Y, who is similar to person X, has responded in this way. Such analogies are perhaps most often formed on the basis of one's own behavior but are also formed on the basis of the behavior of one's friends, one's family, and one's heroes.

Thus, for example, if I as a teacher were to assume the role of mediator with a group of arguing students, I might then infer that another teacher would also assume the role of mediator given a similar situation. My implicit rule might be something like: "Teachers, when with a group of arguing students, will assume mediator roles." Very often when we are trying to predict how another individual will react, we attempt to reason by analogy and ask, "What would I do in this situation?" The assumption here is that other people act as we do.

Authority

When we were growing up we learned a great many rules from our parents about other people and about the ways in which they behave. Depending on the orientation of the family, these rules might have been in the form of traditional stereotypes about various racial, religious, and national groups or perhaps in the form of suggested modes of behavior. For example, we might have learned that "all foreigners are untrustworthy," "all Americans are materialistic," "all Italians are religious," and so on. Or we might have learned such rules as "People who study hard will achieve success" or "Honest people will come out ahead in the long run."

In many instances (and probably in most), our judgments are drawn from some complex system of rules derived from all three bases—experience, analogy, and authority—rather than from just one. Thus, for example, you may see a person from your home town and make some kind of judgment. That judgment would be based on rules derived from your experience with home town people, from an analogy with your own behavior or general response tendency, or from something you learned when you were young or something you read or heard from an authoritative source.

It is not possible to examine a judgment and discover the specific basis for the rules that were used to formulate that judgment. But by being aware of the ways in which such rules are formed, we are in a better position to examine the judgments we make, and to evaluate and perhaps revise them.

The bases for the judgments we make about people—experience, analogy, and authority—provide us, then, with insight into where we get the data we use in formulating these interpersonal judgments. The perceptual processes, examined next, give us insight into the laws we abide by or the rules we follow in formulating these judgments about people.

PERCEPTUAL PROCESSES

People, or interpersonal, perception is an extremely complex affair. Perhaps the best way to explain some of these complexities is to examine at least some of the psychological processes involved in people perception (Figure 6.3).

PRIMACY–RECENCY

Assume for a moment that you were enrolled in a course in which half the classes were extremely dull and half the classes were extremely exciting. At the end of the semester you are to evaluate the course and the instructor. Would the evaluation be more favorable if the dull classes constituted the first half of the semester and the exciting classes constituted the second half of the semester or if the order were reversed? If what comes first exerts the most influence, we have what is called a *primacy effect*. If what comes last (or is the most recent) exerts the most influence, we have a *recency effect*.

In an early study on the effects of primacy-recency in people perception, Solomon Asch read a list of adjectives describing a person to a group of subjects and found that the effects of order were significant. A person described as "intelligent, industrious, impulsive, critical, stubborn, and envious" was evaluated as more positive than a person described as "envious, stubborn, critical, impulsive, industrious, and intelligent." The implication here is that we utilize early

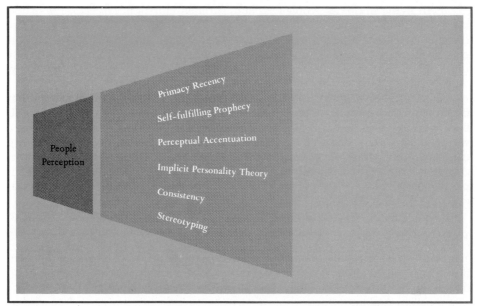

Figure 6.3   Some psychological processes involved in people perception.

information to provide us with a general idea as to what a person is like, and we utilize the later information to make this general idea or impression more specific. Numerous other studies have provided evidence for the effect of first impressions. For example, in one study subjects observed a student (actually a confederate of the experimenter) taking a test. The task of the subject was to estimate the number of questions the student got right and to predict how well the student would do on a second trial. The confederate followed two different orders. In one order, the descending order, the correct answers were all in the beginning. In the ascending order, the correct answers were toward the end. In each case, there were the same number correct and incorrect. Subjects judged the descending order to contain more correct responses. They also estimated that students in the descending order would do better on a second trial and judged them to be more intelligent.

SELF-FULFILLING PROPHECY

Perhaps the most widely known example of the self-fulfilling prophecy is the *Pygmalion Effect,* now widely popularized. Basically, teachers were told that certain pupils were expected to do exceptionally well—that they were late bloomers. However, the names of these students were selected at random by the experimenters. The results were not random. Those students whose names were given to the teachers actually did perform at a higher level than did the other students. In fact, these students even improved in IQ scores more than did the other students.

Eric Berne in *Games People Play* and Thomas Harris in *I'm O.K., You're O.K.* both point out the same type of effect but in a somewhat different context. These transactional psychologists argue that we live by scripts given to us by our parents and that we essentially act in the way in which we are told to act. Much like the children who were expected to do well, we all, according to transactional psychology, live by the scripts given to us as children.

Consider, for example, people who enter a group situation convinced that the other members will dislike them. Almost invariably they are proven right; the other members do dislike them. What they may be doing is acting in such a way as to encourage people to respond negatively. Or similarly, when we enter a classroom and prophesize that it will be a dull class, it turns out, more often than not, to be a dull class. Now it might be that it was in fact a dull class. But it might also be that we defined it as dull and hence made it dull; we made a prophecy and then fulfilled it.

PERCEPTUAL ACCENTUATION

"Any port in a storm" is a common enough phrase that, in its variants, appears throughout our communications. To many, even an ugly date is better than no date at all. Spinach may taste horrible but when you are starving, it can taste like filet mignon. And so it goes.

In what may be the classic study on need influencing perception, poor and rich children were shown pictures of coins and later asked to estimate their size. The poor children estimated the size as much greater than did the rich children. Similarly, hungry people perceive food objects and food terms at lower recognition thresholds (needing fewer physical cues) than people who are not hungry.

In terms of people perception, this process, called *perceptual accentuation*, leads us to see what we expect to see and what we want to see. We see people we like as being better-looking than people we do not like; we see people we like as being smarter than people we do not like. The obvious counterargument to this is that we actually prefer good-looking and smart people—not that people whom we like are seen as being handsome and smart. But perhaps that is not the entire story.

As social psychologist Zick Rubin describes it, male undergraduates participated in what they thought were two separate and unrelated studies; it was actually two parts of a single experiment. In the first part each subject read a passage; half the subjects were given an arousing sexual seduction scene to read, and half were given a passage about seagulls and herring gulls. In the second part of the experiment, subjects were asked to rate a female student on the basis of her photograph and a self-description. As might be expected, the subjects who read the arousing scene rated the woman as significantly more attractive than did the other group. Further, the subjects who expected to go on a blind date with this woman rated her more sexually receptive than did the subjects who were told that they had been assigned to date someone else. How can we account for such findings?

Although this experiment was a particularly dramatic demonstration of perceptual accentuation, this same general process occurs every day. We magnify or accentuate that which will satisfy our needs and wants. The thirsty person sees a mirage of water, the sexually deprived person sees a mirage of sexual satisfaction, and only very rarely do they get mixed up.

IMPLICIT PERSONALITY THEORY

We each have a theory of personality, complete with rules or systems, although we may not be able to verbalize it. More specifically, we have a system of rules that tells us which characteristics of an individual go with which other characteristics. Consider, for example, the following brief statements. Note the characteristic in parentheses that best seems to complete the sentence:

> John is energetic, eager, and (intelligent, stupid).
> Joe is bright, lively, and (thin, fat).
> Jim is handsome, tall, and (flabby, muscular).
> Jane is attractive, intelligent, and (likable, unlikable).
> Mary is bold, defiant, and (extroverted, introverted).
> Susan is cheerful, positive, and (attractive, unattractive).

It is not important which words you selected. And certainly there are no right or wrong answers. What should be observed, however, is that certain of the words "seemed right" and others "seemed wrong." What made some seem right was our implicit personality theory, the system of rules that tells us which characteristics go with which other characteristics. The theory tells us that a person who is energetic and eager is also intelligent, not stupid, although there is no logical reason why a stupid person could not be energetic and eager.

CONSISTENCY

There is a rather strong tendency to maintain balance or consistency among our perceptions. As so many of the current theories of attitude change demonstrate, we strive to maintain balance among our attitudes; we expect certain things to go together and other things not to go together. On a purely intuitive basis, for example, respond to the following sentences by noting the expected response.

1. I expect a person I like to (like, dislike) me.
2. I expect a person I dislike to (like, dislike) me.
3. I expect my friend to (like, dislike) my friend.
4. I expect my friend to (like, dislike) my enemy.
5. I expect my enemy to (like, dislike) my friend.
6. I expect my enemy to (like, dislike) my enemy.

According to most consistency theories, our expectations would be as follows: We would expect a person we liked to like us (1) and a person we disliked to dislike us (2). We would expect a friend to like a friend (3) and to dislike an enemy (4). We would expect our enemy to dislike our friend (5) and to like our other enemy (6). All of these—with the possible exception of the last one— should be intuitively satisfying. With some reflection even the last (6) should seem logical. Note, too, that when we formulate our implicit personality theories, as noted above, we strive to formulate theories that possess a high degree of consistency.

Further, we would expect someone we liked to possess those characteristics that we liked or admired. And we would expect our enemies not to possess those characteristics that we liked or admired. Conversely, we would expect people we liked to lack unpleasant characteristics and people we disliked to possess unpleasant characteristics.

In terms of people perception this tendency for balance and consistency may influence the way in which we see one another. It is easy to see our friends as being possessed of fine qualities and our enemies as being possessed of unpleasant qualities. Donating money to the poor, for example, can be perceived as an act of charity (if from a friend) or as an act of pomposity (if from an enemy). We would probably laugh harder at a joke told by a well-liked comedian than at that very same joke if told by a disliked comedian.

STEREOTYPING

One of the most frequently used shortcuts in people perception is that of *stereotyping*. Originally, "stereotype" was a printing term that referred to the plate that printed the same image over and over again. A sociological or psychological stereotype, then, is a fixed impression of a group of people. We all have stereotypes whether they be of national groups, religious groups, or racial groups, or perhaps of criminals, prostitutes, teachers, plumbers, or artists.

When we have these fixed impressions we will often, upon meeting someone of a particular group, see that person primarily as a member of that group. Then all the characteristics we have in our minds for members of that group are applied to this individual. If we meet someone who is a prostitute, for example, we have a host of characteristics for prostitutes that we are ready to apply to this one person. To further complicate matters, we will often see in this person's behavior the manifestation of various characteristics that we would not see if we did not know that this person was a prostitute. Stereotypes distort our ability to perceive people accurately. They prevent us from seeing an individual as an individual; instead the individual is seen only as a member of a group.

Forming impressions from stereotypes and from implicit personality theories are somewhat similar processes. The main difference is that stereotypes are organized around national, religious, ethnic, and similar groups; we reason that since an individual is a member of a particular group then he or she must possess these various characteristics. Implicit personality theories, on the other hand, are organized in terms of clusters of characteristics; we reason from two or three known characteristics to the inference that this other, unknown characteristic is also a part of this individual. For example, with stereotypes we reason that since these people are Venusians they are also energetic, courageous, and intelligent. With an implicit personality theory we reason that since these people are energetic and courageous, they are also intelligent (since intelligence, in our hypothetical theory, goes with energy and courage). As can be appreciated, both stereotypes and implicit personality theory rely heavily on our desire or need for consistency. It is psychologically comfortable for us to see an unknown Venusian as conforming to our stereotype of all Venusians. Similarly it is psychologically comfortable for us to see an energetic and courageous person as intelligent, since this conforms to our expectations.

SOURCES

An excellent introduction to perception and communication is provided by Hans Toch and Malcolm S. MacLean, Jr., "Perception and Communication: A Transactional View," *Audio Visual Communication Review* 10(1967): 55–77. Also see Thomas M. Steinfatt, *Human Communication: An Interpersonal Introduction* (Indianapolis: Bobbs-Merrill, 1977) for a general overview. A thorough summary of this area is contained in Mark Cook's *Interpersonal Perception* (Baltimore: Penguin, 1971), on which I relied heavily for the entire unit. A more thorough and scholarly presentation of this area is by Renato Tagiuri, "Person Perception," in G. Lindzey and E. Aronson, eds., *The Handbook of Social Psychology*, 2d ed. (Reading, Mass.: Addison-Wesley, 1969) 3:395–449. Standard reference works in this area include Michael Argyle, *Social Interaction* (London: Methuen, 1969), and Renato Tagiuri and Luigi Petrullo, eds., *Person Perception and Interpersonal Behavior* (Stanford, Cal.: Stanford University Press, 1958). A brief but insightful account of people perception is provided by Albert Hastorf, David Schneider, and Judith Polefka in *Person Perception* (Reading, Mass.: Addison-Wesley, 1970). I also found Zick Rubin's *Liking and Loving: An Invitation to Social Psychology* (New York: Holt, 1973) a useful source. Much of the discussion of the perceptual processes is based on the insights provided by Rubin. The cited study by Solomon Asch is "Forming Impressions of Personality," *Journal of Abnormal and Social Psychology*, 41 (1946): 258–290. The cited study on forming impressions of exam-taking students was conducted by Edward E. Jones, Leslie Rock, Kelley G. Shaver, and Lawrence M. Ward: "Pattern of Performance and Ability Attribution: An Unexpected Primacy Effect," *Journal of Personality and Social Psychology* 10 (1968): 317–340. Both studies are discussed by Rubin. A brief overview is provided by Robert A. Baron and Donn Byrne, *Social Psychology: Understanding Human Interaction*, 3d ed. (Boston, Mass.: Allyn & Bacon, 1981) and a more thorough review by Chris L. Kleinke, *Self-Perception: The Psychology of Personal Awareness* (San Francisco, California: W. H. Freeman, 1978).

Experiential Vehicles

6.1   Perceiving My Selves

The purposes of this experiential vehicle are to get us to understand better how we perceive ourselves, how others perceive us, and how we would like to perceive ourselves. In some instances and for some people these three perceptions will be the same; in most cases and for most people, however, they will be different.

Following this brief introduction are nine lists of items (animals, colors, communications media, dogs, drinks, food, music, sports, and transportation). Read over each list carefully, attempting to look past the purely physical existence of the objects to their "personality" or "psychological meaning."

1. First, for each of the nine lists indicate the one item that best represents how you perceive yourself—not your physical self but your psychological-philosophical self. Mark these items *MM* (Myself to Me).

2. Second, for each of the nine lists select the one item that best represents how you feel others see you. By "others" is meant acquaintances—neither passing strangers nor close friends but people you meet and talk with for some time—for example, people in this class. Mark these items *MO* (Myself to Others).

3. Third, for each of the nine lists select the one item that best represents how you would like to be. Put differently, what items would your ideal self select? Mark these items *MI* (Myself as Ideal).

After all nine lists are marked three times, discuss your choices in groups of five or six persons in any way you feel is meaningful. Your objective is to get a better perspective on how your self-perception compares with your perception by others and your ideal perception. In discussions you should try to state as clearly as possible why you selected the items you did and specifically what each selected item means to you at this time. You should also welcome any suggestions from the group members as to why they think you selected the items you did. You might also wish to integrate consideration of some or all of the following questions into your discussion.

1. How different are the items marked *MM* from *MO*? Why do you suppose this is so? Which is the more positive? Why?
2. How different are the items marked *MM* from *MI*? Why do you suppose this is so?

3. What does the amount of or the number of differences between the items marked *MM* and the items marked *MI* mean for personal happiness?
4. How accurate were you in the items you marked *MO*? Ask members of the group which items they would have selected for you.
5. Which of the three perceptions (*MM*, *MO*, *MI*) is easiest to respond to? Which are you surest of?
6. Would you show these forms to your best same-sex friend? Your best opposite-sex friend? Your parents? Your children? Explain.

ANIMALS

_____bear

_____cobra

_____deer

_____fox

_____hyena

_____lion

_____monkey

_____rabbit

_____squirrel

_____turtle

COLORS

_____black

_____blue

_____brown

_____green

_____gray

_____pink

_____purple

_____red

_____white

_____yellow

COMMUNICATIONS MEDIA

_____body language

_____book

_____film

_____fourth-class mail

_____gossip

_____radio

_____smoke signals

_____special delivery letter

_____telephone

_____television

DOGS

_____afghan

_____boxer

_____chihuahua

_____dalmation

_____German shepherd

_____greyhound

_____husky

_____mutt

_____poodle

_____St. Bernard

DRINKS

_____beer

_____champagne

_____coffee

_____milk

_____orange juice

_____prune juice

_____scotch

_____sherry

_____water

_____wine

FOOD

_____apple pie

_____Big Mac

_____caviar

_____filet mignon

_____french fries

_____gum drops

_____ice cream sundae

_____jello

_____peanut butter

_____tossed salad

MUSIC	SPORTS	TRANSPORTATION
_____broadway/film	_____auto racing	_____bicycle
_____country western	_____baseball	_____bus
_____disco	_____boxing	_____jet plane
_____folk	_____bullfighting	_____horse and wagon
_____hymns	_____chess	_____kiddy car
_____jazz	_____fishing	_____motorcycle
_____opera	_____ice skating	_____Rolls-Royce
_____popular	_____skydiving	_____skateboard
_____rock	_____tennis	_____van
_____new wave	_____yachting	_____Volkswagen

6.2   Perceiving Others

List the name of the person in this class with whom you would most like to:

1. have a date
2. go into business
3. have dinner
4. go to your family gathering
5. discuss your inner feelings
6. work on a class project
7. attend a party
8. travel
9. fix a car
10. room
11. drive cross-country
12. be happy
13. be sad
14. be locked in a jail cell
15. go camping

Class members should discuss their results as a whole. Specifically, consider the following:

1. What cues did the people give you that led you to feel as you did about them?
2. What quality of the person named led you to select him or her for that purpose?
3. Think of (but do not verbalize) the persons with whom you would least like to do the 15 things listed. Why? That is, what cues did these people give that led you to feel as you did about them?
4. For which purposes do you think other people would select you? What qualities do people see in you that would lead them to select you for one or more of these 15 items?

Unit 7

Listening

LISTENING

LEARNING GOALS

After completing this unit, you should be able to:

1. define *listening*
2. explain the importance of feedback to listening
3. explain the five characteristics of effective feedback
4. explain the role of feedback in communication accuracy
5. list and explain the five obstacles to effective listening
6. list and explain the five guides to effective listening
7. identify and explain the three basic processes in sequential communication

There can be little doubt that we listen a great deal. Upon awakening we listen to the radio. On the way to school we listen to friends, to people around us, and perhaps to screeching cars, singing birds, or falling rain. In school our listening day starts in earnest and we sit in class after class listening to the teacher, to comments by other students, and sometimes even to ourselves. We listen to friends at lunch and return to class to listen to more teachers. We arrive home and again listen to our family and friends. Perhaps we then listen to records, radio, or television. All in all we listen for a good part of our waking day.

THE NATURE AND IMPORTANCE OF LISTENING

Numerous studies have been conducted to determine the percentage of our communication time devoted to listening as compared with speaking, reading, and writing. In one study, for example, it was found that adults in a variety of occupations spent approximately 70 percent of their day in one of the four communications activities. Of that time, approximately 42 percent was spent in listening, 32 percent in talking, 15 percent in reading, and 11 percent in writing. Listening percentages for students are even higher.

That we listen a great deal of the time, then, can hardly be denied. Whether we listen effectively or efficiently, however, is another matter. Although we might occasionally complain about having to study writing in elementary school, in high school, and again in college, we would probably not deny its usefulness. Despite occasional problems in such courses, most people would admit that improvement in writing is both necessary and possible. With listening, however, our attitudes are different. For some reason we do not feel that it is necessary to improve our listening or that it is even possible. If you search through your college catalog, you will find numerous courses designed to improve writing skills. And, of course, you will even find courses designed to improve your tennis, golf, and fencing abilities. Yet you will probably not find a single course in listening, despite its importance and its pervasiveness. The one exception to this general rule is found in music departments, where courses in listening to music will be offered. If it is useful to teach "music listening," would not a similar concern for language and speech be logical? It seems to be assumed that because we listen without a great deal of effort, we open our ears something like we open a drain. But this view, as we shall see, is far from accurate.

In actual practice most of us are relatively poor listeners, and our listening behavior could be made more effective. Given the amount of time we engage in listening, the improvement of that skill would seem well worth the required effort. And it does take effort. Listening is not an easy matter; it takes time and energy to listen effectively.

KNOWING HOW TO LISTEN COULD DOUBLE THE EFFICIENCY OF AMERICAN BUSINESS.
DID YOU HEAR THAT?

Business today is held together by its communication system.

And listening is undoubtedly its weakest link.

Most of us spend about half our business hours listening. Listening poorly. Research studies show that on the average we listen at a 25% level of efficiency.

A statistic that is not only surprisingly low, but terribly costly.

With more than 100 million workers in America, a simple ten dollar listening mistake by each of them would cost a billion dollars.

Letters have to be retyped; appointments rescheduled; shipments reshipped.

And when people in large corporations fail to listen to one another, the results are even costlier.

Ideas get distorted by as much as 80% as they travel through the unwieldy chain of command.

Employees feel more and more distant, and ultimately alienated from top management.

Well, as one of the world's largest corporations —with 87,000 employees and five divisions—we at Sperry simply can't afford to pay the price of poor listening.

So we've set up extensive listening programs that Sperry personnel throughout the world can take part in. From sales representatives to computer engineers to the Chairman of the Board.

These programs are making us a lot better at listening to each other. And when you do business with Sperry Univac, or any of our other divisions, you'll discover that they're making us a lot better at listening to you.

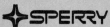

✦ SPERRY

We understand how important it is to listen.

Sperry is Sperry Univac computers, Sperry New Holland farm equipment, Sperry Vickers fluid power systems, and guidance and control equipment from Sperry division and Sperry Flight Systems.

How efficient a listener are you?
Write to Sperry, Dept. 4C, 1290 Avenue of the Americas, New York, New York 10019 for a listening quiz that's both fun and a little surprising.

By listening we mean *an active process of receiving aural stimuli.* Contrary to popular conception, listening is an *active* rather than a passive process. Listening does not just happen; we must make it happen. Listening takes energy and a commitment to engage in often difficult labor.

Listening involves *receiving* stimuli and is thus distinguished from hearing as a physiological process. The word "receiving" is used here to imply that stimuli are taken in by the organism and are in some way processed or utilized. For at least some amount of time, the signals received are retained.

Listening involves *aural* stimuli—that is, signals (sound waves) received by the ear. Listening therefore is not limited to verbal signals but encompasses all signals sent by means of fluctuations in air—noises as well as words, music as well as prose.

Make special note of the fact that there is nothing in this definition that implies that listening as a skill is limited to formal speaking situations, such as when a public speaker addresses a large audience. Listening is a skill that is of crucial importance in interpersonal and in small group communication, as well as in public speaking and mass communication.

Jesse S. Nirenberg, in his *Getting Through to People*, distinguishes three levels of listening. First, there is the level of *nonhearing.* Here the individual does not listen at all; rather, he or she looks at the speaker and may even utter remarks that seem to imply attention such as "O.K.," "yes," and "mm," but there is really no listening. Nothing is getting through. The second level is the level of *hearing.* Here the person hears what is being said and even remembers it but does not allow any of the ideas to penetrate beyond the level of memory. Third is the level of *thinking,* where the listener not only hears what the speaker is saying but also thinks about it. The listener here evaluates and analyzes what is being said. It is this third level, the level of *listening-thinking,* that we are defining as listening.

LISTENING AND FEEDBACK

The concept of *feedback* is crucial to an understanding of listening as an active process. *Feedback* refers to those messages sent from listeners and received by speakers which enable speakers to gauge their effects on their receivers. If speakers are to learn the effects of their messages and if they are to adapt their messages more effectively, then listeners must be trained to send these messages of feedback to speakers. Here are some guides for effective use of the feedback mechanism in communication. Effective feedback is immediate, honest, appropriate, clear, and informative.

IMMEDIATE FEEDBACK

The most effective feedback is that which is most immediate. Ideally, feedback is sent immediately after the message is received. Feedback, like reinforcement, loses its effectiveness with time; the longer we wait to praise or punish, for example, the less effect it will have. To say to children that they will get punished when Daddy comes home probably does little to eliminate the undesirable be-

Feedback tells us that someone is listening and it helps to guide our subsequent communications.

havior, simply because the punishment or feedback comes so long after the behavior.

HONEST FEEDBACK

Feedback should be honest. To say this is not to provide license for overt hostility or cruelty. It is to say, however, that feedback should not merely be a series of messages that the speaker wants to hear and that will build up his or her ego. Feedback should be an honest reaction to a communication.

Feedback concerning one's understanding of the message as well as one's agreement with the message should be honest. We should not be ashamed or afraid to admit that we did not understand a message, nor should we hesitate to assert our disagreement.

We can, of course, consistently give speakers the feedback they want. You can shake your head, indicating understanding, as the teacher pours forth some incomprehensible drivel and nod agreement with his or her equally incomprehensible theories. This may make the teacher feel that you are intelligent and clever. But note the effect that this kind of behavior has: It reinforces the behavior of the teacher. It will lead that teacher to continue addressing classes with this same incomprehensible drivel. In effect, you have told the teacher that he or she is doing a good job by your positive feedback. The same is true with any speaker in any type of communication situation.

The quality of teaching and in fact of all the communicative arts is in large part a reflection of the listeners; we are the ones who keep the levels of communication where they are.

APPROPRIATE FEEDBACK

Feedback should be appropriate to the general communication situation. For the most part we have learned what is appropriate and what is not appropriate from observing others as we grew up. And so there is no need for spelling out what is and what is not appropriate. We should recognize, however, that appropriateness is a learned concept; consequently, what is appropriate for our culture is not necessarily appropriate for another culture. Thus for students to stamp their feet when a teacher walks in might signal approval or respect in one culture, as it did in Germany in the early twentieth century, but might signal hostility in another, as it would in the United States in the 1980s.

We should also note that feedback to the message should be kept distinct from feedback to the speaker. We need to make clear, in disagreeing with speakers, for example, that we are disagreeing with what they are saying and not necessarily rejecting them as people. We may dislike what a person says but like the person saying it. When students say that a class session is boring, they are not saying that they dislike the teacher personally, but merely that they disliked the class session. When a public speaking instructor negatively evaluates the speech of a particular student, it does not imply personal dislike for the student. Such feedback should be seen as descriptive of the message and not of the individual. This is not to imply that listeners do not or should not make evaluations of the speakers themselves; we all do this. Rather, this is to emphasize that these kinds of feedback—that directed at the source and that directed at the message—should be kept distinct in the minds of both speaker and listener-critic.

CLEAR FEEDBACK

Feedback should be clear on at least two counts. It should be clear enough so that speakers can perceive that it is feedback to the message and not just a reflection of something you ate that did not agree with you. Second, the feedback should be clear in meaning; if it is to signal understanding, then it should be clear to the speaker that that is what you are signaling. If you are disagreeing, then that, too, should be clear.

INFORMATIVE FEEDBACK

The feedback you send to speakers should convey useful information; it should tell them something that will prove helpful in their attempt to communicate.

In any classroom there are always some students who sit with the same expression on their faces regardless of what is going on. You could lecture on the physics of sound or you could show a stag film and their expression would remain unchanged—or at least relatively so. These people communicate no information and serve only to confuse the speaker. Similarly, to always respond in the same way conveys no useful information. To communicate useful information, responses must be, in part at least, unpredictable. If speakers are able to completely predict how you will respond to something they say, then your response does not serve any useful feedback function.

It is useful in this connection to recall the postulate explained earlier (Unit 2), namely that we cannot not communicate. All feedback, from a motionless stare to vigorous applause, communicates. What we need to be concerned with is providing speakers with feedback that will prove useful and helpful in their task of adjusting and improving their message transmission.

The importance of listening can hardly be denied. We spend most of our communication time in listening, and we probably learn more from listening than from anything else. In any form of communication, listening and feedback are so closely related that we cannot be said to listen effectively if immediate, honest, appropriate, clear, and informative feedback is not given.

OBSTACLES TO EFFECTIVE LISTENING

Listening is at best a difficult matter. Yet it may be made easier, more pleasant, and more efficient if some of the obstacles or barriers to effective listening are eliminated. Although there are many that could be identified, five general classes of obstacles are considered here.

PREJUDGING THE COMMUNICATION

Whether in a lecture auditorium or in a small group of people, there is a strong tendency to prejudge the communications of others as uninteresting or irrelevant to our own needs or to the task at hand. Often we compare these communications with something we might say or with something that we might be doing instead of "just listening." Generally, listening to others comes in a poor second.

By prejudging a communication as uninteresting we are in effect lifting the burden of listening from our shoulders. So we just tune out the speaker and let our minds recapture last Saturday night.

All communications are, at least potentially, interesting and relevant. If we prejudge them and tune them out we will never be proved wrong. At the same time, however, we close ourselves off from potentially useful information. Most important, perhaps, is that we do not give the person a fair hearing.

REHEARSING A RESPONSE

For the most part we are, as Wendell Johnson, the semanticist and language pathologist, put it, our own most enchanted listeners. No one speaks as well or on such interesting topics as we do. If we could listen just to ourselves, listening would be no problem.

Particularly in small group situations but also in larger settings the speaker may say something with which we disagree; for the remainder of that speaker's time we rehearse our response or rebuttal or question. We then imagine his or her reply to our response and then our response to his or her response and so on and on. Meanwhile, we have missed whatever else the speaker had to say—perhaps even the part that would make our question unnecessary or something that might raise other and more significant questions.

If the situation is a public speaking one, and the speech is a relatively long one, then perhaps it is best to jot down the point at issue and go back to listening. If the situation is a small group one, then it is best to simply make mental note of what you want to say and perhaps keep this in mind by relating it to the remainder of what the individual is saying. In either event the important point is to get back to listening.

FILTERING OUT MESSAGES

I once had a teacher who claimed that whatever he could not immediately understand was not worth reading or listening to; if it had to be worked at, it was not worth the effort. I often wonder how he managed to learn, how he was intellectually stimulated, if indeed he was. Depending on our own intellectual equipment, many of the messages that we confront will need careful consideration and in-depth scrutiny. Listening will be difficult, but the alternative—to miss out on what is said—seems even less pleasant than stretching and straining our minds a bit.

Perhaps more serious than filtering out difficult messages is filtering out unpleasant ones. None of us wants to be told that something we believe in is untrue, that people we care for are unpleasant, or that ideals we hold are self-destructive. And yet these are the very messages we need to listen to with great care. These are the very messages that will lead us to examine and reexamine our unconscious assumptions. If we filter out this kind of information we will be left with a host of unstated and unexamined assumptions that will influence us without our influencing them.

INEFFICIENTLY USING THE THOUGHT–SPEECH TIME DIFFERENTIAL

It should be obvious that we can think much more quickly than a speaker can speak. Consequently, in listening to someone our minds can process the information much more quickly than the speaker can give it out. At conventions it was especially interesting to listen to Ralph Nichols, a nationally known expert on listening. Unlike most speakers, Nichols would speak very rapidly. At first, his speech sounded peculiar because it was so rapid. Yet it was extremely easy to understand; our minds did not wander as often as they did when listening to someone who spoke at a normal speed. I would not recommend that we all speak more rapidly, since there are various side effects that are difficult to control. But it is important to realize that in listening there is a great deal of time left over; only a portion of our time is used in listening to the information in the messages.

Although the normal rate of speaking is about 160 to 170 words per minute, we can listen with relative ease at the rate of around 500 words per minute.

When someone is speaking at a normal rate, we are left with a number of possibilities—from letting our mind wander back to that great Saturday night to utilizing the time for understanding and learning the message. Obviously, the latter would be the more efficient course of action. With this extra time, then, we might review concepts already made by the speaker, search for additional meanings, attempt to predict what the speaker will say next, and so on. The important point is that we stay on the topic with the speaker and not let our thoughts wander to distant places.

FOCUSING ATTENTION ON LANGUAGE OR DELIVERY

It is often difficult not to concentrate on the stylistic peculiarities of an individual. In hearing a clever phrase or sentence, for example, it is difficult to resist the temptation to dwell on it and analyze it. Similarly, it is difficult for many to ignore various gestures or particular aspects of voice. Focusing on these dimensions of communication only diverts time and energy away from the message itself. This is not to say that such behaviors are not important, but only that we can fall into the trap of devoting too much attention to the way the message is packaged and not enough to the message itself.

GUIDES TO EFFECTIVE LISTENING

Listening ability—like speaking, reading, and writing abilities—can be improved. As in the case of these other abilities, there are no easy rules or simple formulas. There are, however, some guidelines that should be of considerable value if followed.

LISTEN ACTIVELY

Perhaps the first step to listening improvement is the recognition that it is not a passive activity; it is not a process that will happen if we simply do nothing to stop it. We may hear without effort, but we cannot listen without effort.

Listening is a difficult process; in many ways it is more demanding than speaking. In speaking we are in control of the situation; we can talk about what we like in the way we like. In listening, however, we are forced to follow the pace, the content, and the language set by the speaker.

Perhaps the best preparation for active listening is to act like an active listener, physically and mentally. This may seem trivial and redundant. In practice, however, it may be the most often abused rule of effective listening. Students often, for example, come into class, put their feet up on a nearby desk, nod their head to the side, and expect to listen effectively. It just does not happen that way. Recall, for example, how your body almost automatically reacts to important news. Almost immediately you assume an upright posture, cock your head to the speaker, and remain relatively still and quiet. We do this almost reflexively because this is how we listen most effectively. This is not to say that we should be tense and uncomfortable but only that our bodies should reflect our active minds. Even more important than this physical alertness is a mental alertness, an active listening attitude. As listeners we need to enter the communication interaction—whether interpersonal, small group, or public speaking—as coequal partners with the speakers, as persons emotionally and intellectually ready to engage in the mutual sharing of meaning.

LISTEN FOR TOTAL MEANING

In listening to another individual we need to learn to listen for total meaning. The total meaning of any communication act is extremely complex, and we can be sure that we will never get it all. However, the total meaning is not only in the words used. The meaning is also in the nonverbal behavior of the speaker. Sweating hands and shaking knees communicate just as surely as do words and phrases.

Along with the verbal and nonverbal behaviors we should also recognize that the meaning of a communication act lies also in what is omitted. The speaker who talks about racism solely in the abstract, for example, and who never once mentions a specific group, is communicating something quite different from the speaker who talks in specifics.

LISTEN WITH EMPATHY

It is relatively easy to learn to listen for understanding or for comprehension. But this is only a part of communication. We also need to *feel* what the speaker feels; we need to empathize with the speaker.

To empathize with others is to feel with them, to see the world as they see it, to feel what they feel. Only when we achieve this will we be able to understand another's meaning fully.

There is no fast method for achieving empathy with another individual. But it is something we should work toward. It is important that we see the teacher's point of view, not from that of our own, but from that of the teacher. And equally it is important for the teacher to see the student's point of view from that of the student. If students turn in late papers, teachers should attempt to put themselves in the role of the students to begin to understand the possible reasons for the lateness. Similarly, if teachers fail papers because they are late, students should attempt to put themselves in the role of teachers and attempt to understand the reason for the failure.

So often we witness behavior that seems foolish and ridiculous. We see, for example, a child cry because he or she lost money. From our point of view the amount lost is insignificant and it therefore seems foolish to cry over it. What we need to do, however, is to see the situation from the point of view of the child—to realize that the amount of money is not insignificant to the child and that perhaps the consequences of losing the money are extremely serious. Popular college students might intellectually understand the reasons for the depression of

111

the unpopular student, but that will not enable them to understand emotionally the feelings of depression. What popular students need to do is to put themselves in the position of the unpopular student, to role-play a bit, and begin to feel his or her feelings and think his or her thoughts. Then these students will be in a somewhat better position to "really understand," to empathize.

William V. Pietsch, in his imaginative *Human BE-ing*, makes the point that most of our education has been concerned with objective facts to the almost total neglect of subjective feelings. We need to recognize that understanding and problem solving cannot be achieved solely with reference to the intellect; the emotions as well need to be examined. "Real listening," says Pietsch, "means 'tuning in' to what the other person is *feeling* so that we *listen to emotions*, not simply to 'ideas.'"

LISTEN WITH AN OPEN MIND

Listening with an open mind is an extremely difficult thing to do. It is not easy for us, for example, to listen to arguments against some cherished belief. It is not easy to listen to statements condemning what we so fervently believe. It is not easy to listen to criticisms of what we think is just great.

In counseling students one of the most difficult tasks is to make them realize that even though they may dislike a particular teacher they can still learn something from him or her. For some reason many people will attempt to punish the people they dislike by not listening to them. Of course, if the situation is that of teacher and student, then it is only the student who suffers by losing out on significant material.

We also need to learn to continue listening fairly, even though some signal has gone up in the form of an out-of-place expression or a hostile remark. Listening often stops when such a remark is made. Admittedly, to continue listening with an open mind is a difficult matter, yet here it is particularly important that listening does continue.

LISTEN CRITICALLY

Although we need to emphasize that we should listen with an open mind and with empathy, it should not be assumed that we should listen uncritically. Quite the contrary. We need to listen fairly but critically if meaningful communication is to take place. Listening with an open mind will help us to understand the messages better; listening with a critical mind will help us to analyze that understanding and to evaluate the messages judiciously. As intelligent and educated citizens, it is our responsibility to evaluate critically what we hear. This is especially true in the college environment. While it is very easy to simply listen to a teacher and take down what is said, it is extremely important that what is said is evaluated and critically analyzed. Teachers have biases too; at times consciously and at times unconsciously these biases creep into scholarly discussions. They need to be identified and brought to the surface by the critical listener. Contrary to what most students will argue, the vast majority of teachers will appreciate the responses of critical listeners. It demonstrates that someone is listening.

SOURCES

On the nature of listening and for numerous studies see Robert O. Hirsch, *Listening: A Way to Process Information Aurally* (Dubuque, Iowa: Gorsuch Scarisbrick, 1979); C. William Colburn and Sanford B. Weinberg, *An Orientation to Listening and Audience Analysis* (Palo Alto, Cal.: SRA, 1976); Larry L. Barker, *Listening Behavior* (Englewood Cliffs, N.J.: Prentice-Hall, 1971); and Carl Weaver, *Human Listening: Processes and Behavior* (Indianapolis: Bobbs-Merrill, 1972). Perhaps the classic in the area is Ralph Nichols and Leonard Stevens, *Are You Listening?* (New York: McGraw-Hill, 1957). On listening and feedback the chapter by Kathy J. Wahlers in Barker's *Listening Behavior* was most helpful. Listening from the point of view of auditory attention is covered in Neville Moray's *Listening and Attention* (Baltimore: Penguin, 1969). Ella Erway's *Listening: A Programmed Approach*, 2d ed. (New York: McGraw-Hill, 1979) covers the nature of listening, its importance, and the ways in which it can be improved.

The obstacles to effective listening covered here are also covered in a number of books on listening such as those listed above. Similarly, the guides to effective listening presented here are also considered in other texts in different ways. A useful overview is Ralph Nichols' "Do We Know How to Listen? Practical Helps in a Modern Age," *Communication Education* 10 (1961): 118–124. This article contains ten suggestions for improving listening. Most of the suggestions for improving listening, such as those presented here as well as those presented in other texts, owe their formulation to the work of Ralph Nichols. Another useful and informative source is Wendell Johnson's *Verbal Man* (New York: Colliers, 1969). For serial (or sequential) communication, read William V. Haney, "Serial Communication of Information in Organizations," in Joseph A. DeVito, ed., *Communication: Concepts and Processes*, 3d ed. (Englewood Cliffs, N.J.: Prentice-Hall, 1981) and Haney's *Communication and Organizational Behavior: Text and Cases*, 3d ed. (Homewood, Ill.: Irwin, 1973). Barrie Hopson and Charlotte Hopson's *Intimate Feedback: A Lovers' Guide to Getting in Touch with Each Other* (New York: New American Library, 1976) contains much that is relevant to effective listening. The theories and experimental research bearing on the issues of attention, memory, and comprehension—all relevant to listening and listening effectiveness—are well surveyed in David H. Dodd and Raymond M. White, Jr., *Cognition: Mental Structures and Processes* (Boston, Mass.: Allyn and Bacon, 1980).

Experiential Vehicles

7.1 Sequential Communication

This exercise is designed to illustrate some of the processes involved in what might be called "sequential communication"—that is, communication that is passed on from one individual to another.

This exercise consists of both a nonverbal (visual) and a verbal part; both are performed in essentially the same manner. In the visual communication, six subjects are selected to participate. Five of these leave the room while the first subject is shown the visual communication. The first subject is told to try to remember as much as possible in order to reproduce it in as much detail as possible. After studying the diagram, the first subject reproduces it on the board. The second subject then enters the room and studies the diagram. The first diagram is then erased and the second subject draws his or her version. The process is continued until all subjects have drawn the diagram. The last reproduction and the original drawing are then compared on the basis of the processes listed below.

The verbal portion is performed in basically the same way. Here the first subject is read the statement once or twice or even three times; the subject should feel comfortable that he or she has grasped it fully. The second subject then enters the room and listens carefully to the first subject's restatement of the communication. The second subject then attempts to repeat it to the third subject and so on until all subjects have restated the communication. Again, the last restatement and the original are compared on the basis of the processes listed below.

Members of the class not serving as subjects should be provided with copies of both the visual and the verbal communications and should record the changes made in the various reproductions and restatements.

Special attention should be given to the following basic processes in sequential communication.

1. *Omissions.* What kinds of information are omitted? At what point in the chain of communication are such omissions introduced? Do the omissions follow any pattern?
2. *Additions.* What kinds of information are added? When? Can patterns be discerned here or are the additions totally random?
3. *Distortions.* What kinds of information are distorted? When? Are there any

patterns? Can the types of distortions be classified in any way? Are the distortions in the directions of increased simplicity? Increased complexity? Can the sources or reasons for the distortions be identified?

Nonverbal (Visual) Communication

Verbal Communication

Millie is a particularly bright and energetic chimp. She lives at the Queens Zoo, one of the country's most famous attractions. Frequently, Millie has been discovered throwing bananas at passers-by when she thinks no one is looking. The keeper has punished her by taking away her food but she persists. And in fact she has been found teaching her two babies to do the same thing. If this continues, the authorities may have to get rid of her or confine her to the indoors.

7.2   Feedback in Communication

The purpose of this exercise is to illustrate the importance of feedback in communication. The procedure is to have a listener at the blackboard and a speaker prepared to communicate under various different conditions.

The object of the interactions is for the speaker to communicate to the listener instructions for reproducing a diagram. Sample diagrams appear in the *Instructor's Manual*, although any diagram with five or six parts in different relationships to one another will be suitable. The different conditions under which this task is attempted should enable you to investigate the importance of feedback in communication.

First Condition

The speaker is given a diagram that is neither too complex nor too simple. With his or her back to the listener, the speaker must communicate instructions for reproducing the diagram. The listener is not allowed to speak.

Second Condition

The speaker is given another diagram and must tell the listener how to reproduce it. This time the speaker may observe what the listener is doing and may comment on it. The listener is not allowed to speak.

Third Condition

The speaker is given a third diagram and must tell the listener how to reproduce it. The speaker may again observe what the listener is doing and may comment on it. This time, however, the listener may ask any questions he or she wishes of the speaker. Members of the class should see the diagrams.

Discussion should center on the accuracy of the drawings and the confidence the listeners had in their attempts at reproducing the diagrams. Which is the most accurate? Which is the least accurate? To what extent did the feedback, first visual and then both visual and auditory, help the listener reproduce the diagram?

In the following conditions, how would the lack of feedback influence the communication interactions?

1. A trial lawyer addressing a jury
2. A teacher lecturing to a class of students
3. A used car salesperson trying to sell a car
4. An amorous lover with the loved one
5. A typist typing a letter

Part Three

Verbal Messages

Unit 8

Preliminaries to Verbal Messages

PRELIMINARIES TO VERBAL MESSAGES

Language as a Symbol System
Language as Meaning
  8.1 Word Coinage

LEARNING GOALS

After completing this unit, you should be able to:

1. define the following terms: *specialization, productivity, displacement, rapid fading, arbitrariness,* and *cultural transmission*
2. identify those features that make human language superior to animal communication systems
3. define denotation and connotation
4. explain the Pollyanna Hypothesis

In this unit we explore the concept of verbal messages by focusing on some essential preliminaries. First, the nature of the human language system (the system of words and grammatical rules that governs the creation of our verbal messages) is explained, and its essential characteristics are identified and defined. Once the nature of language in general is understood, we then focus on meaning and examine denotative and connotative meaning.

LANGUAGE AS A SYMBOL SYSTEM

Language may be thought of as the code, the system of symbols, utilized in the construction of verbal messages. Language may be defined as a specialized, productive system capable of displacement and composed of rapidly fading, arbitrary, culturally transmitted symbols. Contained in this definition are six characteristics of the principal human verbal message system: specialization, productivity, displacement, rapid fading, arbitrariness, and cultural transmission. Each of these characteristics will be discussed in turn.

SPECIALIZATION

A specialized communication system, according to Charles Hockett, is one whose "direct energetic consequences are biologically irrelevant." Human language serves only one major purpose—to communicate. It does not aid any biological functions. On the other hand, while a panting dog communicates information about its presence and perhaps about its internal state, the panting serves first and foremost the biological function of temperature regulation. The fact that communication accompanies or results from this behavior is only incidental.

PRODUCTIVITY

Human verbal messages evidence productivity—sometimes referred to as openness or creativity. That is, our verbal messages are novel utterances; each utterance is generated anew. There are exceptions to this general rule, but these seem few and trivial. For example, sentences such as "How are you?," "What's new?," and "Good luck" do not evidence productivity; they are not newly created each time they are uttered. Except for sentences such as these, all other verbal messages are created at the time of utterance. When you speak, you are not repeating memorized sentences but creating your own sentences. Similarly, your understanding of verbal messages evidences productivity in that you can understand new utterances as they are uttered. Your ability to comprehend verbal messages is not limited to previously heard and learned utterances.

The rules of grammar have imposed some restrictions on the way in which sentences may be generated, and so complete productivity, in regard to form at least, does not exist. For example, we do not utter such sentences as, "The rock thinks quietly," or "The tulip attacked the poor old turtle." Our language has built-in restrictions that, to stick with these examples, require that a "human" or "animal" noun (rather than an "inanimate" noun such as *rock* or *tulip*) serve as the subject of such verbs as *thinks* or *attacked*. The poet, of course, may and frequently does violate such rules.

Some animal systems also evidence productivity. For example, bees can communicate about new sources of food and new home sites, and so their system is productive in this sense. And yet it is a very limited productivity; it seems restricted to such topics as food, housing, and the general maintenance of the hive and colony. Human message systems, on the other hand, evidence an almost unlimited productivity, which enables us to talk about millions of topics in millions of different ways.

Another dimension of productivity is that human message systems allow the introduction of new words. When something is discovered or invented, we can create new words to describe it. When new ideas or new theoretical concepts are developed, we can create words to describe them. And it does not seem to matter whether we create the new word by joining together old words or parts of old words or create it from scratch. What does matter is that the language system is open to expansion—a feature that seems absent from just about all known animal communication systems.

DISPLACEMENT

Human language can be used to talk about things that are remote in both time and space; one can talk about the past and the future as easily as the present. And one can talk about things that one has never seen and will never see—about mermaids and unicorns, about supernatural beings from other planets, about talking animals. One can talk about the unreal as well as the real, the imaginary as well as the actual. Displacement also refers to the fact that messages may have effects or consequences that are independent of their context. Thus, for example, statements uttered in one place today may have effects elsewhere tomorrow. That is, both the referents (what is talked about) and the effects of messages may be displaced.

Displacement is an important capability of human verbal-message systems because it is absent from most animal communication systems. For example, birds do not emit danger calls unless danger is actually present. Dogs do not bark or growl unless there is a disturbance in the immediate environment. These systems lack the ability for displacement references. On the other hand, bee language does evidence displacement. When forager bees locate a food supply, they return to the hive and perform an intricate dance that indicates how much food has been found, how far away the food is, and in which direction the bees must fly to reach the food. Similarly, when scout bees locate a new home site, they return and perform a dance that communicates its distance from available food supplies, its distance from other beehives, the protection it affords from wind and rain, and similar issues relevant to the suitability of a new home. The bee communication system, then, evidences displacement, because its members may communicate about things that are not physically present in their immediate environment.

Displacement, together with productivity, also makes possible the ability to lie. Humans are able to lie because they are able to form new utterances (productivity) and because their utterances are not limited to what is in one's immediate environment (displacement). Thus, for example, we may say, "I found a sunken treasure off the coast of Manhattan, and for a mere $27.50 I'll give you a map that will make you a millionaire," without this sentence's ever having been uttered before and without any concern for what is or is not actually present in one's environment.

In other words, there are no linguistic limitations that restrict our utterances to accurate descriptions of reality. Although animal lovers are fond of telling stories about pets trying to fool them, it appears that lying is extremely rare, if not totally absent, in animal communication. Bees, for example, seem incapable of lying; at least there have been no reports of bees communicating false information concerning food supplies or home sites.

RAPID FADING

Speech sounds fade rapidly; they are evanescent. They must be received immediately after they are emitted or else they will not be received at all. Although mechanical devices now enable sound to be preserved much as writing is preserved, this is not a characteristic of human language. Rather, these are extralinguistic means of storing information and aiding memory. Of course, all signals fade; written symbols and even symbols carved in rock are not permanent. In relative terms, however, speech signals are probably the least permanent of all communicative media.

ARBITRARINESS

Language signals are arbitrary; they do not possess any of the physical properties or characteristics of the things for which they stand. The word *wine* is no more tasty than the word *sand*, nor is the latter any less wet.

Opposed to arbitrariness is *iconicity*. Iconic signals do bear a resemblance to their referents. A line drawing of a person is iconic in representing the body parts in proper relation to one another. But it is arbitrary in representing the texture and thickness of the anatomical structures.

Both arbitrariness and iconicity are relative. For example, a line drawing is more arbitrary than a black-and-white photograph, which is more arbitrary than a color photograph. Paralinguistic features (volume, rate, rhythm) are more iconic than the features normally classified as belonging to language. Rate, for example, may vary directly with emotional arousal and hence would be iconic. But the sound of the word *fast* is not actually fast.

Names are arbitrary in large part; there is no real relationship between the name and the individual. And yet, names are not totally arbitrary; many names indicate the ethnic group to which an individual belongs and usually indicate sex.

CULTURAL TRANSMISSION

The form of any particular human language is culturally or traditionally transmitted. The child raised by English speakers learns English as a native speaker, regardless of the language of his or her biological parents. The genetic endowment pertains to human language in general rather than to any specific human language.

One of the consequences of cultural transmission is that any human language can be learned by any normal human being. All human languages—English, Chinese, Italian, Russian, Bantu, or any of the other approximately 3000 languages—are equally learnable; no one language should present any greater difficulty for a child than any other language. It should be added, however, that this ability to learn any language is true only at particular times in the life of the individual. One generally cannot learn to speak a language as fluently as a native after passing a certain age, usually around puberty.

These six features do not, of course, exhaust the characteristics of language. Taken together, however, they should serve to clarify how human language is made up and some of its dimensions and should enable you to better distinguish human language from all other communication systems—whether

Meaning is created by the interaction of speaker and listener.

these be animal systems, such as the language of the bee, or invented languages, such as the language of semaphore or mathematics.

LANGUAGE AS MEANING

If it were not for the desire of one person to communicate a meaning to another person, language would probably not exist. Of all the functions of language, the communication of one person's meaning to another is surely the most significant. Consequently, meaning must be placed at the center of any attempt to explain language.

A PROCESS VIEW OF MEANING

Meaning is an active process created in cooperation between source and receiver, speaker and listener, writer and reader. This is illustrated in the model developed by Wendell Johnson, one of the leading semanticists, and depicted here in Figure 8.1. Although it may seem complex, the model is actually rather simple when compared to the truly complex process of transferring meaning from one person to another. The surrounding rectangle indicates that communication takes place in a context that is external to both speaker and listener and to

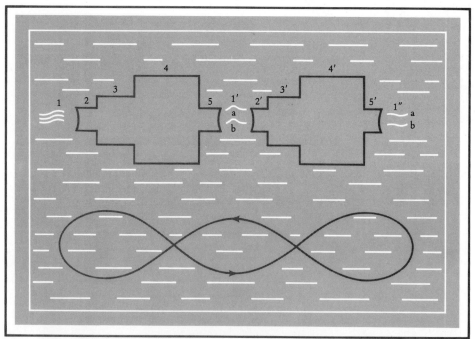

Figure 8.1 Johnson's model of communication. *Source:* Wendell Johnson, "The Spoken Word and the Great Unsaid," *Quarterly Journal of Speech* 37 (1951): 421.

the communication process as well. The twisted loop indicates that the various stages of communication are actually interrelated and interdependent.

The actual process begins at 1, which represents the occurrence of an event —anything that can be perceived. This event is the stimulus. At stage 2 the observer is stimulated through one or more sensory channels. The opening at 2 is purposely illustrated as being relatively small to emphasize that out of all the possible stimuli in the world, only a small part of these actually stimulate the observer. At stage 3 organismic evaluations occur. Nerve impulses travel from the sense organs to the brain, causing certain bodily changes, for example, in muscular tension. At 4 the feelings aroused at 3 are beginning to be translated into words—a process that takes place in accordance with the individual's unique language habits. At stage 5, from all the possible linguistic symbols, certain ones are selected and arranged into some pattern.

At 1' the words that the speaker utters, by means of sound waves, or the words that are written, by means of light waves, serve as stimulation for the hearer, much as the outside event at 1 served as stimulation for the speaker. At 2' the hearer is stimulated, at 3' there are organismic evaluations, at 4' feelings are beginning to be translated into words, at 5' certain of these symbols are selected and arranged, and at 1″ these symbols, in the form of sound and/or light waves, are emitted and serve as stimulation for another hearer. The process is a continuous one.

A few of the implications this model has for meaning should be noted here. First, it should be clear that meaning is a function not only of messages (whether verbal, nonverbal, or both) but of the interaction of these messages and the receiver's own nervous system. We do not "receive" meaning; rather, we create meaning. Words do not mean; people mean. Meanings are not in words but in people.

One of the best examples of the confusion that can result when this relatively simple fact is not taken into consideration is provided by Laing, Phillipson, and Lee in *Interpersonal Perception* and analyzed with insight by Paul Watzlawick in *How Real Is Real?* A couple on the second night of their honeymoon was sitting at a hotel bar. The woman struck up a conversation with the couple next to her. The husband refused to communicate with the couple and became antagonistic to his wife as well as to the couple. The wife then became angry because he created such an awkward and unpleasant situation. Each became increasingly disturbed, and the evening ended in a bitter conflict in which each was convinced of the other's lack of consideration. Eight years later they analyzed this argument. Apparently "honeymoon" had meant very different things to each of them; to the husband it had meant a "golden opportunity to ignore the rest of the world and simply explore each other." His wife's interaction with the other couple implied to him that there was something lacking in him to make her seek out additional people with whom to interact. To the wife "honeymoon" had meant an opportunity to try out her new role as wife. "I had never had a conversation with another couple as a wife before," she said. "Previous to this I had always been a 'girl friend' or 'fiancée' or 'daughter' or 'sister.'"

The second implication is that although not all communication occurs in reference to some external stimulus, communication makes sense, Johnson argues, only when it does in some way relate to the external world. This quality, it might be added, is often used to distinguish healthy from unhealthy communications and normal from "non-normal" persons.

Third, the words selected to communicate are a relatively small sample of all possible words. Consequently, messages created by different people are going to be different. Similarly, messages created by the same person on different occasions are going to be different as well.

Fourth, the meaning we derive from an event is formed on the basis of only a small sample of stimuli. Out of the infinite number of stimuli that are present in the external world, only a small sample reach the individual. These stimuli will differ from one person to another and for the same person from one time to another. Thus, the meaning we derive from an event is a unique as well as a limited or partial meaning.

DENOTATION AND CONNOTATION

Although a variety of types of meaning may be identified, two general types are essential to identify in communication; these are denotation and connotation. In order to explain these two types of meaning, let us take as an example the word *death*. To a doctor this word might simply mean, or denote, the time when the heart stops. Thus to the doctor this word may be an objective description of a particular event. On the other hand, to the dead person's mother (upon being informed of her son's death) the word means much more than the time when the heart stops. It recalls to her the son's youth, his ambitions, his family, his illness, and so on. To her it is a highly emotional word, a highly subjective word, a highly personal word. These emotional or subjective or personal reactions are the word's connotative meaning. The *denotation* of a word is its objective definition. The *connotation* of a word is its subjective or emotional meaning.

Some words are primarily and perhaps even completely denotative. Words like *the*, *of*, and *a*, are perhaps purely denotative; no one seems to have emotional reactions to such words. Other words are primarily denotative, such as *perpendicular*, *parallel*, *cosine*, *adjacent*, and the like. Of course, even these words might have strong connotative meanings for some people. Words such as *geometry*, *north* and *south*, *up* and *down*, and *east* and *west* — words that denote rather specific directions or areas — often produce strong emotional reactions from some people. For example, the student who failed geometry might have a very strong emotional reaction to the word even though to most people it seems a rather unemotional, objective kind of word. Other words, such as derogatory racial names and curse words, are primarily connotative and often have little denotative meaning. The very simple point is that words may vary from highly denotative to highly connotative. A good way to determine the word's connotative meaning is to ask where it would fall on a good-bad scale. If "good" and "bad" do not seem to apply to the word, then it has little, if any, connotative meaning for you. If, however, the term can be placed on the good-bad scale with some degree of conviction, then it has connotative meaning for you.

Another distinction between the two types of meaning has already been implied. The denotative meaning of a word is more general or universal — that is, most people agree with the denotative meanings of words and have similar definitions. Connotative meanings, however, are extremely personal, and few people

BOX 8.1
The Pollyanna Hypothesis

One of the most interesting hypotheses about language usage to be advanced is that of the Pollyanna Hypothesis. The Pollyanna Hypothesis states that "there is a universal human tendency to use evaluatively positive (E+) words more frequently, diversely, and facilely than evaluatively negative (E−) words." Put differently, we all tend to say the positive rather than the negative thing more often, in more different situations, and with greater ease. Some examples of the kind of evidence used to formulate this hypothesis might make this clearer still. In one situation the experimenters gave 100 high school boys in 13 different language communities a list of 100 culture-common nouns. The boys were instructed to write down the first qualifier that occurred to them for each of the 100 nouns. In 12 of the 13 language communities, more E+ words were supplied than E− words.

In the language of children this Pollyanna effect is also present. When the vocabularies of children are analyzed it is found that the frequency and diversity of the usage of E+ terms is much higher than that of E− terms. Although this difference gets smaller as the child grows older, E+ words are still more frequently and more diversely used in adult language.

Numerous studies have shown that E+ words are easier to learn than E− words. E+ words can be learned in less time and with fewer errors than can E− words. Also, it has been demonstrated repeatedly that E+ words can be recognized at lower recognition thresholds than can E− words. That is, the stimulus has to be more intense (brighter, louder) for E− words to be recognized than for E+ words.

Two major theories have been advanced to account for this effect. One position argues that the positive evaluation leads to the high frequency of usage. That is, the words are used more frequently because they are of positive evaluation. The other position argues that the high frequency leads to positive evaluation. That is, the words that are used most frequently become more positive in evaluation. This position is also known as the "mere exposure" hypothesis, and although at first it may appear totally inaccurate and illogical, there is much experimental support in its favor. In terms of language usage, however, the first position seems the more accurate.*

*For more information see Jerry Boucher and Charles E. Osgood, "The Pollyanna Hypothesis," *Journal of Verbal Learning and Verbal Behavior* 8 (1969): 1–8.

would agree on the precise connotative meaning of a word. If this does not seem correct, try to get a group of people to agree on the connotative meaning for words such as *religion, God, democracy, wealth,* and *freedom.* Chances are very good that it will be impossible to get agreement on such words.

The denotative meaning of a term can be learned from a good dictionary. When we consult a dictionary it is the denotative meaning we are seeking. The dictionary would tell us, for example, that *south* means "a cardinal point of the compass directly opposite to the north, the direction in which this point lies" and so on. Connotative meaning, on the other hand, cannot be found in a dictionary. Instead it must be found in the person's reactions or associations to the word. To some people, for example, *south* might mean poverty, to others it might mean wealth and good land investment, to still others it might recall the Civil War or perhaps warmth and friendliness. Obviously, no dictionary could be compiled for connotative meanings, simply because each person's meaning for a word is different.

Denotative meaning differs from connotative meaning in yet another way. Denotative meanings are relatively unchanging and static. Although definitions of all words change through time, denotative meanings generally change very slowly. The word *south*, for example, meant (denotatively) the same thing a thousand years ago that it does now. But the connotative meaning changes rapidly. A single favorable experience in the south, for example, might change completely one's connotative meaning for the word. With denotative meaning, of course, such changes would not occur.

SOURCES

For universal characteristics of language I relied on the work of Charles F. Hockett, particularly "The Problem of Universals in Language," in J. H. Greenberg, ed., *Universals of Language* (Cambridge, Mass.: MIT Press, 1963), and "The Origin of Speech," *Scientific American* 203 (1960): 89–96. The concepts of language universals are thoroughly surveyed in Greenberg's *Universals of Language*. Most of the material, however, presumes a rather thorough knowledge of linguistics.

Portions of the material in this unit were adapted from my *The Psychology of Speech and Language: An Introduction to Psycholinguistics* (New York: Random House, 1970). On language universals, see also Jean Aitchison, *The Articulate Mammal* (New York: McGraw-Hill, 1977). On these universals and the ways in which human communication differs from animal communication, see A. Akmajian, R. A. Demers, and R. M. Harnish, *Linguistics: An Introduction to Language and Communication* (Cambridge, Mass.: MIT Press, 1979). A thorough and sophisticated introduction to language may be found in Janice Moulton and George M. Robinson, *The Organization of Language* (Cambridge: Cambridge University Press, 1981). This treatment presupposes some knowledge of language and linguistics. A more popular introduction to language from the point of view of the studies conducted on teaching language to the apes may be found in Herbert S. Terrace, *Nim: A Chimpanzee Who Learned Sign Language* (New York: Washington Square Press, 1981).

Experiential
Vehicle

8.1   Word Coinage

Although language and culture are closely related, and although the language closely reflects the culture, there often seem to be concepts important to a culture or a subculture for which the language does not provide a convenient one-word label.

Sometimes slang or "substandard" forms fill this void—for example, *youse* or *you all* for "you" (plural) or *screw* for "prison guard." Sometimes words are created because of some social issue—for example, *Ms.* for a form of address for women regardless of marital status.

In order to gain greater insight into the relationship between language and culture/subculture and to become more familiar with the dimensions and functions of words, perform the following exercise in groups of five or six.

1. Create a new word for some concept that is important to the culture or to a particular subculture and for which a single-word label does not exist.
2. Define this word as it would be defined in a dictionary and identify its part(s) of speech.
3. List its various inflectional forms and definitions.
4. Provide two or three sentences in which the word is used.
5. Justify the coinage of this new word, considering, for example, why this word is needed, what void it fills, what it clarifies, what its importance is, what its effect might be should it be used widely, and so forth.

Unit 9

Language in Society

LANGUAGE IN SOCIETY

Sublanguages
Language Racism and Sexism
   9.1 Some Sublanguages

LEARNING GOALS

After completing this unit, you should be able to:

1. define *sublanguage, subculture, codifiability, cant, jargon, argot,* and *slang*
2. explain the functions of sublanguages
3. explain the relationship between the frequency of synonyms for a concept and the importance of that concept to a culture or subculture
4. identify how sociological variables influence the forms of address used
5. explain the concept of language racism and sexism

Language is a social institution; it exists because human beings interact in society. As a social institution language both reflects and influences the society of which it is a part. In this unit, language as a social institution is examined. First, we explore the nature of sublanguage, languages used by various subcultures for intragroup communication, their functions, and some of the different types of sublanguages. Second, with the notion of sublanguages as a base, we explore language racism and sexism in an attempt to suggest just a few of the ways in which language both reflects and influences the social group.

SUBLANGUAGES

One of the common features shared by all human languages is the existence within the language of *sublanguages*—languages used by subcultures or subgroups for communication among their members. In order to explore the concept of sublanguages in depth, the nature of language as a social institution must first be understood.

LANGUAGE AS A SOCIAL INSTITUTION

Language is a social institution designed, modified, and extended (some purists might even say distorted) to meet the ever-changing needs of the culture or subculture. As such, language differs greatly from one culture to another and, equally important though perhaps less obvious, from one subculture to another.

Subcultures are cultures within a larger culture and may be formed on the basis of religion, geographical area, occupation, sexual orientation, race, nationality, living conditions, interests, needs, and so on. Catholics, Protestants, and Jews; New Yorkers, Californians, and mountain folk; teachers, plumbers, and musicians; homosexuals and lesbians; blacks, Chinese, and American Indians; Germans, Italians, and Mexicans; prisoners, suburbanites, and ghetto dwellers; bibliophiles, drug addicts, and bird watchers; diabetics, the blind, and ex-convicts may all be viewed as subcultures, depending, of course, on the context on which we focus. In New York, for example, New Yorkers would obviously not constitute a subculture, but throughout the rest of the world they would. In the United States as a whole, Protestants would not constitute a subculture (though Catholics and Jews would). In New York City, on the other hand, Protestants would constitute a subculture. Blacks and Chinese would be subcultures only outside of Africa and China. As these examples illustrate, the majority generally constitutes the culture, and the various minorities generally constitute the subcultures. Yet this is not always the case. Women, although the majority in our culture, may be viewed as a subculture primarily because society as a whole is male-oriented. Whether a group should be regarded as a subculture or a culture, then, depends on the context being considered and the orientation of the society of which these groups are a part.

Each individual belongs to several subcultures. At the very least he or she belongs to a national, a religious, and an occupational subculture. The importance of the subcultural affiliation will vary greatly from one individual to another, from one context to another, from one time or circumstance to another. For example, to some people in some contexts an individual's religious affiliation may be inconsequential and his or her membership in this subculture hardly thought of. When, on the other hand, the individual wishes to marry into a particular family, this once inconsequential membership may take on vast significance.

Because of the common interests, needs, or conditions of individuals constituting a subculture, sublanguages come into being. Like language in general, sublanguages exist to enable members of the group to communicate with one another. And, again like language in general, there are various regional variations, changes over time, and other variations. There are, however, other functions that sublanguages serve, and these functions constitute their reason for existence. If they did not serve these several functions, they would soon disappear. It should not be assumed, of course, that all sublanguages must serve all the functions noted.

FUNCTIONS OF SUBLANGUAGES

One of the most obvious facts about language and its relation to culture is that concepts that are important to a given culture are given a large number of terms. For example, in our culture money is extremely important; consequently, we have numerous terms for it: *finances, funds, capital, assets, cash, pocket money, spending money, pin money, change, bread, loot, swag,* and various others. Transportation and communication are other concepts for which numerous terms exist in our language. Without knowing anything about a given culture, we could probably make some pretty good guesses as to the important concepts in that culture simply by examining one of its dictionaries or thesauruses. With sublanguages, the same principle holds. Concepts that are of special importance to a particular subculture are given a large number of terms. Thus one function of sublanguages is to provide the subculture with convenient synonyms for those concepts that are of great importance and hence are spoken about frequently. To prisoners, for example, a prison guard—clearly a significant concept and one spoken about a great deal—may be denoted by *screw, roach, hack, slave driver, shield, holligan,* and various other terms. Heroin, in the drug subculture, may be called *H, Harry, smack, Carga, joy powder, skag, stuff,* or just plain *shit.*

A related function of sublanguages is to provide the subculture with convenient distinctions that are important to the subculture but generally not to the culture at large—and thus distinctions that the general language does not make. For example, the general culture has no need for making distinctions among various drugs—all may be conveniently labeled *drugs.* But to members of the drug subculture it is essential to make distinctions that to outsiders may seem unimportant or even trivial. The general culture, for example, does not distinguish between "getting stoned" and "on a high." Yet to the members of the drug sub-culture these are two different states that need to be distinguished.

This function is also clearly seen in the technical jargon of the academic world. Whereas to most people it is sufficient to distinguish between statements and questions, for example, the linguist and psycholinguist find these distinctions too gross. Consequently, they distinguish for questions between active and passive, tag and nontag, open and yes/no, and numerous others. Whereas the term *learning* may be sufficient for the general population, the psychologist needs to distinguish between classical and instrumental learning, incidental and instructed learning, response and stimulus learning, and so on. In the field of communication, instead of the general term *message* we distinguish between digital and analogic messages, verbal and nonverbal messages, content and relational messages, content and metamessages, and so on. These distinctions are all helpful in conceptualizing and communicating the data and theories of a discipline.

Sublanguages serve to increase the *codifiability* of the general language. Codifiability refers to the ease with which certain concepts may be expressed in a language. Short terms are of high codifiability; long expressions are of low codifiability. All languages and sublanguages seem to move in the direction of increasing codifiability. As a concept becomes important in a culture or subculture, the term denoting it is shortened or some other simpler expression is adopted to denote it; thus *television* becomes *TV*, *motion picture* becomes *movie*, and *lysergic acid diethylamide* becomes *LSD* or simply *acid*. The expression "turn on" is the drug subculture's highly codifiable term for the general culture's low-codifiable expression "to take a drug or participate in some experience that alters one's awareness." Similarly, it is much easier to say "lid" than "an ounce of marijuana" and "dex" than "dextroamphetamine capsules."

Sublanguages also serve as means of identification. By using a particular sublanguage, speakers identify themselves to hearers as members of that subculture—assuming, of course, that hearers know the language being used. Individuals belonging to various nationality-based subcultures will frequently drop a foreign word or phrase in the conversation to identify themselves to their hearers. Similarly, homosexuals and ex-convicts will at times identify themselves by using the sublanguage of their subculture. When the subcultural membership is one that is normally hidden, as in the case of homosexuals and ex-convicts, the clues to self-identification are subtle. Generally, they are only given after the individuals themselves receive some kind of positive feedback that leads them to suspect that the hearer also belongs to the subculture in question or that the hearer is at least sympathetic. In a similar vein, the use of sublanguages also functions to express to others one's felt identification with that subculture. For example, blacks may address each other as brother and sister when meeting for the first time. The use of these terms by blacks as well as the frequent use of foreign expressions by members of various national groups communicate to others that the speaker feels a strong identification with the group.

Sublanguages also enable members of the subculture to communicate with one another while in the presence of nonmembers without having their conversation completely understood. A common example of this, which many of us may have heard but been unaware of, occurs in stores that attempt to take unfair advantage of customers. Salespersons will describe arriving customers as "J.L." (just looking), "skank" (cheap individual), "T.O." (turn over to an experienced salesperson), or "palooka" (one who is on a buying binge). In certain situations, of course, the sublanguage may mark the individual as a member of a particular subculture, and so he or she would refrain from using the sublanguage. This is often the case among criminals when in a noncriminal environment. At other times, however, the use of a sublanguage does not lead to an individual's identification as a subculture member, and the sublanguage serves the useful purpose of excluding nonmembers from the class of decoders.

One of the less noble functions of sublanguages—capitalized on by numerous professionals—is to impress and at times confuse outsiders. The two functions, I think, often go hand in hand; many people are impressed in direct proportion to their confusion. Insurance policies and legal documents are perhaps the best examples. I suspect that in many instances this technical language is used to impress and confuse people. Then, when there is doubt about something, the insurance adjuster and the lawyer begin with an advantage—they understand the language whereas you and I do not. Similarly, in evaluating and eventually in signing such documents, we are unable even to ask the right questions, because there is so much we do not understand. Fortunately, as *Time* magazine has reported, "the forces of hereinafter, *res ipsa loquitur* and party of the first part are now clearly on the defensive." The Federal Trade Commission and the Department of Health, Education and Welfare once enlisted the aid of communication experts to rewrite much of their incomprehensible prose.

Physicians and many academics also need to be put into this class. We are easily impressed by the physician's facile use of technical terms and are more apt to pay for the services of those who—like the witch doctors of primitive societies—know the language. To talk of a "singultus spasm" or "bilateral periorbital hematoma" instead of hiccups or a black eye does little to aid meaningful communication. From an analysis of this "medicalese," sociolinguist Joyce Hertzler notes (and I fully agree): "The conclusion must be that the effort is being made to mystify the public with respect to the highly technical and esoteric nature of their knowledge and performance, and to create an aura about their profession." And often, I fear, the academics' use of the technical language of their particular disciplines functions more to impress and confuse than to illuminate and clarify.

A less obvious function of sublanguages, though an important one, is that they serve to provide the group with a kind of identity and a sense of fraternity. Because ex-convicts all over the country know the same sublanguage, they are, in a sense, bound together. Obviously, the more the subculture has a need to band together, the greater the importance of a specialized language.

KINDS OF SUBLANGUAGES

Sublanguage has been used here as a general term to denote a variation from the general language that is used by a particular group or subculture existing within the broader, more general culture. But there are different kinds of sublanguages.

Cant is the specialized vocabulary of some disreputable or underworld subculture. It is the sublanguage of pickpockets, murderers, dope peddlers, and

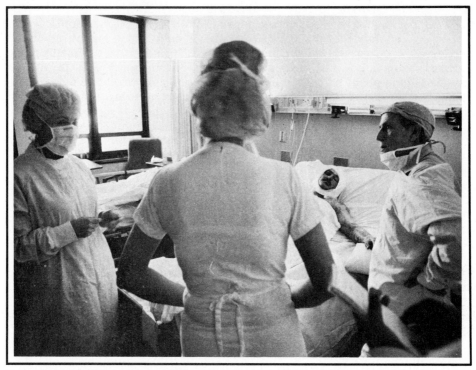

Some jargon facilitates meaningful communication while other jargon can hinder it.

prostitutes. Expressions such as *college* (meaning prison), *stretch* (jail sentence), *to mouse* (to escape from prison), and *lifeboat* (a pardon) are examples of cant. In its true form cant is not understood by outsiders. Today, with television and movies so much a part of our lives, it is difficult for any group, however specialized and "underground," to hide its specialized language. Consequently, many know some of these expressions, as well as those presented in the experiential vehicle following this unit.

Argot designates the specialized vocabulary of any nonprofessional (usually noncriminal) group and would include, for example, the specialized sublanguage of the taxi driver, the truck driver, the CB operator, and the soldier. As is the case with cant, these vocabularies would ideally not be understood by nonmembers were it not for television and film. Expressions such as *dog* (meaning a motor vehicle inspector), *kidney buster* (hard-riding truck), and *sweatshop* (bulletproof cab with poor ventilation) are examples of argot.

Jargon is the technical language of a professional class—for example, college professors, writers, medical doctors, and lawyers. Terms such as *perceptual accentuation, inflationary spiral*, and *behavioral objectives* are examples of professional academic jargon, as are the writer's technical terms for proofreading and editing, the doctor's terms for diseases and medications, and the lawyer's terms for legal documents and criminal offenses.

Slang is the most general of the terms and designates those words in our vocabulary that are derived from cant and argot particularly, and that are understood by most people but not often used in "polite society" or in formal written communications. Terms such as *skirt* (meaning woman), *skiddoo* (leave fast), *goo-goo eyes, hush money, booze, brass* (impudence), and *to knock off* (to quit working) are examples of slang. Usually slang is fairly short-lived; terms such as *skirt, skiddoo,* and *goo-goo eyes* are rarely used today and when used conjure up an image of a person who is out-of-touch with reality. There are, of course, exceptions to this short life; some slang terms have been around for some time and remain classified as slang. For example, according to the famous lexicographer H. L. Mencken, *booze* dates back to the fourth century, *brass* to 1594, and *to knock off* to 1662.

With the passage of time and increased frequency of usage, slang terms enter the general language as socially acceptable expressions. When this happens, new terms are needed and are coined by the subcultures. The old terms are then dropped from the sublanguage, since they now serve none of the functions for which they were originally developed.

This is just one of the ways in which new words enter the language and in which sublanguages are kept distinct from the general language.

LANGUAGE RACISM AND SEXISM

No discussion of sublanguages would be complete without consideration of the terms and phrases used to denigrate various subcultures. These are not themselves sublanguages but are linguistic devices (terms and phrases) used to refer to the various subcultures, usually negatively. Perhaps the most obvious examples are those that refer to a person's race. We all know these terms, and listing them here would serve no purpose. In fact, I suspect that part of the reason these terms persist is because academics and the media use them to illustrate how "liberal" they are and feel that in doing so they are really putting down such prejudice. I think that the use of such terms, for example, on "All in the Family," does not work against their increased popular use but rather seems to make them appear more acceptable and more harmless than they really are. We do not have to tell a racist joke to illustrate how racist jokes foster racial prejudice.

These derogatory terms are used by the principal culture to disparage subcultural members, their customs, or their accomplishments. Every subgroup has such negative terms, whose main function is to separate the majority from the minority group and to create a sociological and linguistic hierarchy, with the majority members on the top and the minority members on the bottom. The social consequences of such hierarchies in terms of employment, education, and housing opportunities and general community acceptance seem well known.

One of the qualifications frequently made in this connection is that it is permissible for members of the subculture to refer to themselves with these negative terms without any problems being created. That is, Italians may use the negative terms referring to Italians, blacks may use the negative terms referring to blacks, and so on. The reasoning seems to be that groups should be able to laugh at themselves. I am not sure we should accept this position. In fact, it

BOX 9.1
Names
Harry Edwards

What's in a name? For blacks, slavery. Edwards tells why his daughter's name is Tazamisha Imara.

Names have always been of great importance to people. Mohammed admonished his followers to "Name your children with good names"; Proverbs 22:1 advises that "A good name is rather to be chosen than great riches." Then there's the statement "Things, animals and slaves are named by their owners and masters; if a people are to be free they must name themselves." That was said to me a few years back by the Honorable Jamel Abdul Almen (formerly H. Rap Brown).

Today increasing numbers of blacks have divested themselves of their slavery-generated property labels by changing their names. The reason for these changes has nothing to do with attempting to become more acceptable to the American mainstream, or to impede identification or to sound professionally "flashy." Rather, the reason is the attempt to develop a more honest self-image and to initiate a more realistic perspective on relations between black and white America. Some blacks have changed their names as part of adopting a religious philosophy. Thus we have had to accustom ourselves to looking at Muhammad Ali without seeing Cassius Clay; to watching Kareem Abdul-Jabbar play basketball without remarking that Lew Alcindor was a great college player. Other blacks, especially young blacks, have adopted names native to black African tribes and nations. Whether as a result of religious conversion or cultural identification, however, discarding Anglo-American names and taking on African or Muslim names—even if the name is only an "X"—constitute a step toward a new self-awareness and social and political perspective.

After all, the names borne by most black people are obvious insignia of a lack of common identity and unique sense of peoplehood. During slavery, blacks were deprived of their African names and ultimately all knowledge of them. Often a black slave would be given the last name of his slave master. After emancipation, many ex-slaves, not knowing any other names, chose Anglo-American names. Many voluntarily took the last names of their former slave masters and of certain white slavers whom they had been taught to regard as heroes. To this day, therefore, black people in America bear such names as George Washington Jackson and Thomas Jefferson Jones, these names having passed down through the generations from parents to children with dignity and pride. But you can't make chicken pie out of chicken shit. While these names are appropriate for whites and their descendants, the fact remains that black people have been for generations naming their progeny in a style derived from the very people who enslaved their ancestors and reduced them to chattel, and who oppress and discriminate against them today.

The children of any people hold in sacred trust the heritage of that people. They are the buds from which new life springs; they insure a people's immortality. In recognition of these facts, my wife and I are not going to pass on to our children a name that labels them as property and that glorifies the oppressors of both our ancestors and us. We have chosen Swahili names instead. We chose Imara as the family name because it means "strength"—black people must be strong to spirit, in mind, and in dedication if we are to survive America. We decided to name our first girl child Tazamisha, which means "attractive," because the beauty of any people is most readily apparent in its women. And we chose as her middle name Heshima, which means "dignity," because the dignity of any people is no greater than that exhibited by its women. All of our children will have the last name of Imara and African first names.

By the time Tazamisha is in school she will have heard us explain hundreds of times the significance of her name. Some people may laugh at her name or ridicule her about it. But we will teach her to be patient with and considerate of other people's attitudes toward her name and the fact that it is different from that of her parents. If they are willing to listen, she can explain it to them. Afterward, she can ask them to explain the significance of their own names. What, for instance, is the meaning of "Margie Sue Hickenson," "Bubba Joe Johnson," "Cornbread Smith," "Jefferson Davis Williams," "Bolivar Q. Shagnesty," and the like? And after they have answered this question, they and Tazamisha can all sit down and have a good laugh together. Tazamisha may marry a Jones or a Smith, but she doesn't have to take his name. Yet, it is not *just* the name but the initiation of a political and cultural education that will go on through the years.

But why give our daughter an African name and not change our own? Because our goal is to educate our daughter politically and culturally and at the same time to minimize the risk of launching her on a pseudocultural trip. My wife and I will eventually change our names. And we will make a big family occasion of it. But this will only be *after* we have raised our children. If one or both of us should die before that time, we have chosen our African names and we will be buried under them. For the present, however, the political condition of black people in America and our love and concern for our children demand that we retain the names we have. They will grow up hearing us explain time and time again the significance of this unconventional situation. This will provide a means of constantly reinforcing their understanding of themselves, their knowledge of the relationship they share with other black people, and the nature of their condition in American society. This is the first step in the development of a more realistic perspective that will allow them to see the steamroller of racism before it has rolled over them.

Beginning with their names, we will dispense with all the little "white lies" that blacks have become accustomed to telling themselves and each other, because every lie, every delusion, weakens our ability to deal intelligently with reality as it affects us. In an increasingly bureaucratic society, the simple fact that our name is different from our children's will provide invaluable opportunities for their political and cultural education. And the lessons will not be whispered in some closet or alleyway but spoken boldly with pride and conviction. When friends ask us what our daughter's name is, we will explain; when we enroll her in school, we will explain; whenever the question arises, we will explain—patiently, thoroughly, and not so much for the benefit of the listener as for our daughter, Tazamisha Heshima Imara. And she will be there—listening, learning, understanding.

Source: Reprinted by permission of the author.

seems likely that such personal usage is even more damaging, because the negative connotations of these terms feed back to the individual and may well function to reinforce the negative stereotypes that society has already assigned this group. The use of such terms in effect tells the individual that her or his subcultural affiliation is somehow not as good as that of the majority culture.

This is seen clearly when gay men and lesbians use the negative terms of heterosexual society to refer to themselves. By using these terms they seem to be in effect confirming, at least in part and perhaps subconsciously, the connotations that the heterosexual culture has included in these terms. This is not to imply that the connotations in the minds of the subculture member and the majority member will be the same but only to suggest that the connotations both persons have may have negative aspects that may not necessarily or always be conscious.

Consider some of the language used to refer to the subculture of women. A woman loses her last name when she marries and in certain instances loses her first name as well. She changes from "Ann Smith" to "Mrs. John Jones." (It is only in rare instances that this procedure is not followed; Mrs. John Warner will no doubt continue to be known as Elizabeth Taylor. Although even here there are exceptions. On a recent talk show, Gary Morton, for example, noted that when his wife, Lucille Ball, comes home from work, she becomes "Mrs. Morton.")

We say a woman "marries into" a man's family and that a family "dies out" if there are no male children. We do not speak of a man marrying into a woman's family (unless that family is extremely prestigious or wealthy or members of royalty), and a family can still "die out" even if there are ten female children. In the marriage ceremony we hear "I now pronounce you man and wife," not "man and woman" or "husband and wife." The man retains his status as man, but the woman changes hers from woman to wife.

Many of the terms used for women are used to define her sexually. Consider, for example, the once parallel terms *master* and *mistress*. These terms at one time designated people who had power and privilege over others. Now, however, *master* refers not to a man who has power over other people but to a man who has power over things, as in, for example, "He is the master of his fate," "He is a master craftsman," or "He is a master teacher." But note that *mistress* did not develop in a parallel way; the term now denotes a sexual relationship and particularly a sexual relationship in which the woman is possessed by and subordinated to the man, as in "She is the senator's mistress." The term *professional*, when applied to a man, refers to his high-status occupation. When applied to a woman, it often has a sexual connotation. The same is true for the phrase "in business."

Another interesting lack of parallelism between the sexes is found in the terms *bachelor* and *spinster*. *Bachelor* varies from neutral to positive in connotation, but *spinster* is always negative. We would say, "Margaret is dating an eligible bachelor," but would not say, "Joe is dating an eligible spinster." The term *spinster* seems to preclude eligibility. Even when the terms are used metaphorically, this same lack of parallelism can be seen. When we say that "Joe is a regular bachelor," we imply that he is free and is living an exciting and sexually fulfilling life. But when we say, "Margaret is a regular spinster," we imply that she is living an uninteresting and sexually unfulfilling life.

The use of *man* to designate "human being" and the use of the masculine pronoun to refer to any individual regardless of sex further illustrate the extent of linguistic sexism. There seems to me no legitimate reason why the feminine pronoun could not alternate with the masculine pronoun in referring to hypothetical individuals or why such terms as *he and she* or *her and him* could not be used instead of just *he* or *him*.

SOURCES

On sublanguages, see H. L. Mencken, *The American Language* (New York: Knopf, 1971). Mencken's chapter entitled "American Slang" is a classic work and a very interesting one. I relied heavily on Mencken for the discussion of sublanguages and for the examples of the various sublanguages presented in the experiential vehicle. Much interesting research relevant to sublanguages is reported in the various works on sociolinguistics; for example, Joshua A. Fishman, *The Sociology of Language* (Rowley, Mass.: Newbury House, 1972), and Dell Hymes, *Foundations in Sociolinguistics: An Ethnographic Approach* (Philadelphia: University of Pennsylvania Press, 1974). One of the most insightful essays is Paul Goodman, "Sublanguages," in *Speaking and Language: Defence of Poetry* (New York: Random House, 1971). The theory and research on forms of address are thoroughly covered in Roger Brown, *Social Psychology* (New York: Free Press, 1965). Many of the insights and examples concerning language sexism came from Casey Miller and Kate Swift, *Words and Women: New Language in New Times* (Garden City, N.Y.: Doubleday, 1976), and Robin Lakoff, *Language and Woman's Place* (New York: Harper & Row, 1975). I recommend both of these books highly. In this connection, see also Cheris Kramer, "Women's Speech: Separate but Unequal?" *Quarterly Journal of Speech* 60 (February 1974): 14–24. The broad area of sex differences in communication is surveyed in Barbara Eakins and R. Gene Eakins, *Sex Differences in Communication* (Boston: Houghton Mifflin, 1978). A sublanguage of a somewhat different type, the language of intimacy used by couples, is explored by Robert Hooper, Mark L. Knapp, and Lorel Scott, "Couples' Personal Idioms: Exploring Intimate Talk," *Journal of Communication* 31 (winter 1981): 23–33.

141

Experiential
Vehicle

9.1 Some Sublanguages

Presented below are a few brief lexicons of some sublanguages. Note how these terms serve the functions discussed in this unit and how many of them are in the process of passing into the general language.

These lexicons are presented as matching quizzes so that you can test your knowledge of the various sublanguages. Write the number of the sublanguage term (left column) next to the letter of the corresponding general-language term (right column).

CRIMINAL TALK

1. maker, designer, scratcher, connection
2. paper, scrip, stiff
3. jug stiff, cert
4. beat, sting, come-off
5. buttons, shamus, fuzz
6. mark, hoosier, chump, yap
7. poke, leather, hide
8. cold poke, dead skin
9. gun, cannon, whiz
10. booster
11. booster box
12. bug
13. dinah, noise
14. double
15. gopher
16. hack
17. soup, pete
18. jug heavy
19. stiff
20. heavy racket

a. bank burglar
b. false key
c. racket involving violence
d. forger
e. wallet
f. a parcel with a trap inside for hiding stolen merchandise
g. burglar alarm
h. iron safe
i. forged check
j. pickpocket
k. dynamite
l. forged bank check
m. shoplifter
n. watchman
o. policeman
p. negotiable security
q. pickpocket victim
r. nitroglycerine
s. empty wallet
t. picking a pocket

CB TALK

1.	green stamps	a.	unmarked police car
2.	good buddy	b.	other CB owners/operators
3.	seat covers	c.	state police
4.	X-ray machine	d.	overnight stop
5.	plain wrapper	e.	radar unit ahead
6.	ranch	f.	diner
7.	bear cave	g.	FCC (Federal Communications
8.	cut some Z's		Commission)
9.	clean	h.	fog
10.	ground clouds	i.	money
11.	boy scouts	j.	toll ahead
12.	handle	k.	low overhead
13.	bean store	l.	get some sleep
14.	green stamp road	m.	traffic tickets
15.	keep your nose between the ditches and smokey out of your britches	n.	passengers
		o.	drive safely; watch for speed traps
16.	mama bear	p.	no police in sight
17.	big daddy	q.	CB transmission
18.	invitations	r.	police station
19.	haircut palace	s.	police radar
20.	brush your teeth and comb your hair	t.	policewoman

CARNIVAL TALK

1.	paleface	a.	tattooed man
2.	frog	b.	bareback rider
3.	tents	c.	owner of the show
4.	kinker	d.	freak
5.	Bible	e.	palmist
6.	picture gallery	f.	musician
7.	mitt reader	g.	zebra
8.	bump reader	h.	eating stand
9.	rosinback	i.	clown
10.	jenny	j.	newcomer to the carnival
11.	governor	k.	program for the show
12.	convict	l.	elephant handler
13.	geek	m.	contortionist
14.	grab joint	n.	phrenologist
15.	windjammer	o.	any performer
16.	pretty boy	p.	tops
17.	shanty	q.	head electrician
18.	first-of-May	r.	ferris wheel
19.	hoister	s.	bouncer
20.	bull man	t.	merry-go-round

MOUNTAIN TALK

1.	a-fixin'	a.	hard rain
2.	doin's	b.	bag
3.	fetch	c.	look at
4.	put out	d.	getting ready to do something
5.	aim	e.	get rid of
6.	smart	f.	hurt
7.	book read	g.	clean up
8.	lollygag	h.	function or event
9.	crick	i.	loaf or loiter
10.	biggety	j.	nervous
11.	plumb	k.	bring
12.	shed of	l.	stiffness
13.	poke	m.	a great distance
14.	red	n.	angry
15.	skittish	o.	geographical area
16.	gander	p.	intend, plan
17.	parts	q.	exactly, on the dot
18.	smack-dab	r.	completely
19.	fur piece	s.	educated
20.	gully-washer	t.	snobbish, stuck-up

GAY TALK

1.	auntie	a.	burlesque of one's own homosexuality
2.	bring out	b.	to introduce someone to homosexuality
3.	dyke	c.	one who wears the clothes of the opposite sex
4.	butch	d.	to let others know that one is homosexual
5.	camp	e.	one who engages in homosexual activity but does not consider himself homosexual
6.	chicken	f.	homosexual
7.	closet queen	g.	to enter the gay life
8.	come out	h.	masculine homosexual woman
9.	cruise	i.	old homosexual, generally effeminate
10.	drag queen	j.	effeminate male homosexual
11.	fag hag	k.	to be undecided between homosexuality and heterosexuality
12.	to be on the fence	l.	masculine-appearing homosexual, male or female
13.	to drop one's pins		
14.	leather bars	m.	to search for a sexual partner
15.	mother	n.	a young boy
16.	gay	o.	one who introduces another to the gay life
17.	number	p.	a promiscuous homosexual
18.	queen	q.	homosexual bars whose customers dress in leather
19.	trade	r.	a casual sexual partner
20.	whore		

(Continued)

s.   a male homosexual who does not actively
     participate in the gay social life
t.   a heterosexual who prefers to socialize with
     gays

COMMUNICATION TALK

1. argot
2. codifiability
3. credibility
4. paralanguage
5. batons
6. immanent reference
7. endomorphy
8. empathy
9. homophily
10. ideographs
11. elementalism
12. intensional orientation
13. Machiavellianism
14. metacommunication
15. phatic communion
16. proxemics
17. redundancy
18. emblems
19. specialization
20. stereotype

a.   the characteristic of communication by
     which it always refers to the immediate
     situation
b.   the degree of similarity among individuals
c.   the fatty dimension of a body
d.   vocal but nonverbal dimension of
     communication
e.   a kind of sublanguage, generally of a
     criminal class
f.   the process of dividing verbally what
     cannot be divided nonverbally (in reality)
g.   the degree to which a message is
     predictable
h.   techniques by which control is exerted by
     one person over another
i.   a perspective in which primary attention
     is given to labels
j.   communication that is primarily social;
     communication that opens the channels of
     communication
k.   communication about communication
l.   nonverbal behaviors that directly translate
     words or phrases
m.   body movements that sketch the path or
     direction of a thought
n.   the fixed impression of a group through
     which one then perceives specific
     individuals
o.   body movements that accent or emphasize
     a specific word or phrase
p.   the feature of language that refers to the
     fact that human language serves no
     purpose other than communication
q.   the study of how space communicates
r.   feeling as another feels
s.   believability
t.   the ease with which certain concepts may
     be expressed in a given language

Unit 10

Principles of
Verbal Interaction

PRINCIPLES OF VERBAL INTERACTION

Immanent Reference
Determinism
Recurrence
Relativity of Signal and Noise
Reinforcement/Packaging
Adjustment
The Priority of Interaction
The Forest and the Trees
   10.1 Forms of Address

LEARNING GOALS

After completing this unit, you should be able to:

1. distinguish between *immanent reference* and *displacement*
2. define and explain the principle of determinism
3. define recurrence in verbal interaction
4. explain the relativity of signal and noise
5. explain reinforcement/packaging
6. explain the way the principle of adjustment operates in communication
7. explain the principle of the forest and the trees as it applies to the analysis of communication interactions
8. identify the operation of the universals of verbal interaction in the verbal interactions of others
9. identify at least three or four instances of your own behavior in which these universals were operative

Perhaps the most common and the most sophisticated means of communication is that of verbal interaction: talking and listening. The best way to approach this area is to focus on those characteristics or features that are present in all verbal interactions regardless of their specific purpose, their particular context, or their unique participants. Rather than being limited to specific kinds or types of verbal interactions, these characteristics or principles are universal. They are, in effect, generalizations applicable to any and all verbal interactions.

Universals such as these are significant for at least two major reasons. First, they provide a rather convenient summary of essential principles of verbal interaction. In effect, they define what constitutes a verbal interaction: what is its nature, and what are its essential aspects. Second, these universals provide us with a set of principles for analyzing verbal interactions. These principles should prove useful for analyzing any interaction that is primarily or even partially linguistic. They provide us with a set of questions to ask about any verbal interaction.

The principles, or universals, are taken from one of the most interesting research studies in the entire area of language. Three researchers (Robert Pittenger, Charles Hockett, and John Danehy) pooled their talents to analyze in depth the first five minutes of a psychiatric interview. Each word, phrase, and sentence; each intonation, pause, and cough were subjected to an incredibly detailed analysis. At the conclusion of this research the authors proposed various principles that they felt would be of value to students and researchers attempting to understand and analyze verbal interactions.

IMMANENT REFERENCE

It is true that human beings have the ability to use what linguists Leonard Bloomfield called "displaced speech" and Charles Hockett labeled "displacement": Human language may make reference to the past as well as to the future; human beings can talk about what is not here and what is not now. Nevertheless, all verbalization makes some reference to the present, to the specific context, to the speaker, and to the listener. All verbal interactions, in other words, contain *immanent references*.

All communications are comments on the immediate circumstances, on the present context, on the speaker and/or listener. Although, for example, we talk about a movie seen two weeks ago, the fact that we are choosing to talk about this movie at this time says something about our present feelings. Although we may criticize a friend or former friend for something done years ago, the fact that we are talking about this now says something about our present—perhaps about

BOX 10.1
Forms of Address

Roger Brown and his associates, in their investigation of the pronouns of address in European languages (Brown and Gilman, 1960) and of the forms of address in English (Brown and Ford, 1961), provide excellent examples of the relationship between speech and source-receiver relationships. In many European languages there are two pronouns of address where English has only one, *you*. One pronoun would be used by a subordinate to a superior; for example, in French the servant speaking to his master would say *vous*, in Spanish *Usted*, in Italian *Lei*, and in German *Sie*. The other pronoun would be used by the superior addressing his subordinate; in French, Spanish, and Italian he would say *tu*, in German *du*. Following Brown, V may be used to symbolize the pronoun of address used by a subordinate to a superior (upward communication) and T to symbolize the form used by a superior to a subordinate (downward communication) on the basis of the Latin *vos* and *tu* from which many of the modern forms derive. When equals are communicating both use the same pronoun—that is, there is reciprocal usage. If they have much in common or are very friendly T is used; if they have little in common or are strangers both use V. During the Middle Ages, however, status determined which form would be used. Reciprocal V was used by the nobility while reciprocal T was used by the lower classes.

There are two basic dimensions of social relationships: power versus equality (that is, status) and solidarity versus nonsolidarity (that is, friendship or intimacy). Power relationships are established on the basis of a number of different criteria. Age, wealth, social position, and occupation are probably the most obvious determinants. Those who are older, richer, of higher social status, or in higher occupations use T in addressing those who are younger, poorer, lower in social status, or in lower occupations. These latter persons in turn use V in addressing members of the former groups. Similarly, solidarity relationships are established in a number of ways. When, for example, persons work at the same job, have the same parents, attend the same school, or play on the same team, their relationship is one of solidarity and they would use T in addressing each other. In the situations described there is no conflict; there is no doubt as to the correct pronoun to use. There are situations, however, in which there is doubt as to the correct pronoun of address. These conflicts appear in situations in which both power and solidarity and nonsolidarity exist. For example, in the case of a younger brother addressing his older brother both power and solidarity are present, and each dictates a different form. The power relationship requires that the younger brother use V but the solidarity relationship requires T. The conflict does not exist for the older brother, since both power and solidarity dictate T. In the other situation the conflict centers on the form to be used by the more powerful member.

For example, in the army the soldier says V to his officer since both power and nonsolidarity demand this form. However, what does the officer say to his subordinate? His superiority dictates T, but his nonsolidarity relationship dictates V.

According to Brown and Gilman, these conflicts were resolved, at least up to the middle of the nineteenth century, on the basis of power. Thus in the above examples the younger brother would have given V in addressing his older brother and the officer would have given T in addressing the soldier. More recently, however, solidarity has become the more significant, as judged from questionnaire results obtained from native speakers of various European languages. Today the younger brother says T and the officer V—the forms dictated by their solidarity and nonsolidarity relationships. This is not to say that power is no longer influential. In fact, as Brown and Gilman point out, power determines who may initially introduce reciprocal T. The suggestion to use reciprocal T or its first use cannot come from the less powerful; it can only come from the more powerful.

Use of the pronouns of power and solidarity has an interesting parallel in English. Similar social relationships are reflected in the use of the first name (FN) or a title plus the last name (TLN). Even more so than in the case of pronouns, the form of address used in English is not predictable from a knowledge of the addressor or addressee, however detailed that knowledge may be. The forms used can only be predicted from knowledge of the relationship existing between the two parties involved in the communication act.

Source: From *The Psychology of Speech and Language: An Introduction to Psycholinguistics*, by Joseph A. DeVito, Copyright © 1970 by Random House, Inc. Reprinted by permission of the publisher.

our present feelings for our former friend, perhaps about our present attitudes toward lying or fraud or whatever led to our negative attitude toward this person. Although we may talk about the future—in, say, making plans for a career after graduation—we assume by the principle of immanent reference that these plans represent significant comments on our present view of ourselves, our capabilities, our values, our desires. Notice that in the form of address we use in addressing another individual we are not only noting the individual's name or title but we are also saying something about our own relationship with that person and are often indicating something about our own status. See, for example, Box 10.1, "Forms of Address."

In attempting to understand verbal interaction, then, it is always legitimate to ask such questions as "To what extent does this communication refer to this particular situation?" "To what extent does this communication refer to the speaker?" "In what ways is the speaker commenting on the listener?"

The answers to such questions may not be obvious. In many instances, in fact, the answers may never be found. Yet these questions are potentially answerable and thus always worth asking.

DETERMINISM

All verbalizations are to some extent determined; all verbalizations are to some extent purposeful. Whenever something is said, there is a reason. Similarly, when nothing is said in an interactional situation there is a reason. Words, of course, communicate, and there are reasons why the words used are used. But silence also communicates, and there are reasons why silence is used. Watzlawick, Jackson, and Beavin, in their *Pragmatics of Human Communication*, put it this way: one cannot *not* communicate. Whenever we are in an interactional situation, regardless of what we do or say or don't do or say, we communicate. Words and silence alike have message value; they communicate something to other people, who in turn cannot *not* respond and are, therefore, also communicating.

Consequently, it is always legitimate in analyzing interactions to ask the reasons for the words as well as the reasons for the silence. Each communicates and each is governed by some reason or reasons; all messages are determined.

RECURRENCE

In our interactions individuals will tell us—not once but many times and not in one way but in many ways—about themselves: who they are, how they perceive themselves, what they like, what they dislike, what they want, what they avoid, and so on.

Whatever is perceived as important or significant to an individual will recur in that person's verbal interactions; he or she will tell us in many different ways and on many different occasions what these things are. Of course, they will rarely be communicated in an obvious manner. People who find themselves in need of approval do not directly ask others for approval. Rather, they go about obtaining approval responses in more subtle ways, perhaps asking how others like their new outfit, perhaps talking about their grades on an examination, perhaps talking about how they never betray a confidence.

RELATIVITY OF SIGNAL AND NOISE

What is a signal and what is noise in any given communication is relative rather than absolute. If we are interested in hearing a particular story and the speaker, in narrating it, breaks it up by coughing, we might become annoyed because the coughing (noise) is disturbing our reception of the story (signal). But suppose this individual seeks some form of medication and in his or her interactions with the doctor coughs in a similar way. To the doctor this coughing might be the signal; the coughing might communicate an important message to the doctor. Similarly, when listening to a stutterer tell a story we may focus on the story, which would be the signal. The stuttering would be the noise interfering with our reception of the signal. But to the speech pathologist the stutters are the signals to which he or she attends and the story might be the noise.

The point is simply this: What is signal to one person and in one context might be noise to another person in another context.

REINFORCEMENT/PACKAGING

In most interactions messages are transmitted simultaneously through a number of different channels. We utter sounds with our vocal mechanism but we also utilize our body posture and our spatial relationships at the same time to reinforce our message. We say no and at the same time pound our fist on the table. One channel reinforces the other. The message is presented as a "package."

The extent to which two simultaneous messages reinforce each other or contradict each other, then, is extremely important in understanding human communication. The same verbal message when accompanied by different non-verbal messages is not the same message and cannot be responded to in the same way.

The reinforcement of one communication channel with another usually occurs without conscious awareness.

ADJUSTMENT

Communication may take place only to the extent that the parties communicating share the same system of signals. This is obvious when dealing with speakers of two different languages; one will not be able to communicate with the other to the extent that their language systems differ.

This principle takes on particular relevance, however, when we realize that no two persons share identical signal systems. Parents and children, for example, not only have different vocabularies to a very great extent but, even more important, have different denotative and especially different connotative meanings for the terms they have in common. Different cultures and subcultures, even when they share a common language, often have greatly differing nonverbal communication systems. To the extent that these systems differ, and unless a language adjustment is made, communication will not take place.

THE PRIORITY OF INTERACTION

This principle simply states that in understanding and in analyzing verbal interactions we must begin with the interaction itself, with the actual behavior. Only when we begin here can we effectively go on to deal with such questions as purpose, motivation, and mental processes.

This does not mean that questions of purpose and motivation are meaningless or even that they are of less importance than questions focusing on more objective areas. However, we first need to analyze fully the actual interaction behavior and only then can we legitimately deal with the various mental concepts.

THE FOREST AND THE TREES

This last principle is included as a warning, as a cautionary note. The previous principles have mostly focused attention on microscopic analysis—that is, on a detailed dissection of the verbal interaction. And certainly this is a valid way of approaching verbal language.

Yet it must not be forgotten that any interaction is *more* than the sum of its parts. It is a whole that cannot be fully understood from an analysis only of its parts, much as the forest is more than the individual trees. There is a possible danger, then, of missing the forest while concentrating solely on the individual trees—this principle calls this to our attention.

SOURCES

The universals of verbal interaction are taken from Robert E. Pittenger, Charles F. Hockett, and John J. Danehy's *The First Five Minutes: A Sample of Microscopic Interview Analysis* (Ithaca, N.Y.: Paul Martineau, 1960). Also in this area see Eric H. Lenneberg, "Review of *The First Five Minutes*," *Language* 38 (1962): 69–73. For additional material on expressive language see Robert E. Pittenger and

Henry Lee Smith, Jr., "A Basis for Some Contributions of Linguistics to Psychiatry," *Psychiatry* 20 (1957): 61–78, and Norman A. McQuown, "Linguistic Transcription and Specification of Psychiatric Interview Material," *Psychiatry* 20 (1957): 79–86. On methods of analysis see Frederick Williams, "Analysis of Verbal Behavior," and Mervin D. Lynch, "Stylistic Analysis," in Philip Emmert and William D. Brooks, eds., *Methods of Research in Communication* (New York: Houghton Mifflin, 1970). Alternative approaches to the analysis of verbal interactions are discussed in Gerald R. Miller and Henry E. Nicholson, *Communication Inquiry: A Perspective on a Process* (Reading, Mass.: Addison-Wesley, 1976), Michael T. Motley, *Orientations to Language and Communication* (Chicago: Science Research Associates, 1978), and William D. Brooks, Marla G. Scafe, and Ina C. Siler, *Verbal Language and Communication* (Dubuque, Iowa: Gorsuch Scarisbrick, 1980).

Experiential Vehicle

10.1 Forms of Address

For each of the following persons indicate the form of address you would use in speaking to them *and* the form of address you would expect them to use in speaking to you.

Use the following shorthand:

TLN —title plus last name
FN   —first name
TFN —title plus first name
T   —title

	You to Them	Them to You
1. Your college professor	_____	_____
2. A fellow student	_____	_____
3. A younger child	_____	_____
4. Your doctor or dentist	_____	_____
5. Your employer	_____	_____
6. Your employee	_____	_____
7. Your high school teacher	_____	_____
8. Your uncle or aunt	_____	_____
9. Your nephew or niece	_____	_____
10. Your state senator	_____	_____
11. Your college president	_____	_____
12. Your minister, priest, or rabbi	_____	_____
13. John Travolta or Bo Derek	_____	_____
14. A street bum	_____	_____
15. A millionaire	_____	_____

In groups of five or six or in a general class discussion, consider some or all of the following questions:

1. What sociological variables influenced your decisions? That is, what led you to select the forms of address you selected?
2. How do the forms of address used communicate something about the speaker? That is, in what ways do they illustrate immanent reference?
3. Do the forms of address illustrate determinism in any way? How?
4. How might the forms of address illustrate recurrence? Can you see this operating in the college classroom?
5. Might the forms of address constitute noise? Signal? On what basis would you distinguish the situations in which the forms of address are signals from those in which they are noise?
6. How might the forms of address you used reinforce other verbal behaviors and/or nonverbal behaviors? Try to be as specific as possible in identifying these other verbal and nonverbal behaviors.
7. In what ways do the forms of address used illustrate adjustment or the lack of it? What effects does reciprocal usage have on the interpersonal interaction? What effects does nonreciprocal usage have?

Unit 11

Barriers to Verbal Interaction

BARRIERS TO VERBAL INTERACTION

Polarization
Intensional Orientation
Fact-Inference Confusion
Allness
Static Evaluation
Indiscrimination
   11.1 E-Prime
   11.2 Facts and Inferences
   11.3 Poetry Evaluation

LEARNING GOALS

After completing this unit, you should be able to:

1. define *polarization, intensional orientation, fact-inference confusion, allness, static evaluation,* and *indiscrimination*
2. identify examples of these six misevaluations in the media
3. identify examples of these six misevaluations in your own communications

Although communication may break down at any point in the process from sender to receiver, perhaps the most obvious site of breakdown is in the actual message. Breakdown, of course, may occur in any form of communication, and the breakdowns noted here are applicable to all forms of communication.

Six barriers to verbal interaction are considered in this unit:

1. *Polarization:* The tendency to divide reality into two unrealistic extremes.
2. *Intensional orientation:* The tendency to respond to the way things are talked about or labeled rather than to the reality.
3. *Fact-inference confusion:* The tendency to respond to inferences as if they were facts.
4. *Allness:* The tendency to assume that one knows all there is to know or that what has been said is all that there is to say.
5. *Static evaluation:* The tendency to ignore change and to assume that reality is static and unchanging.
6. *Indiscrimination:* The tendency to group unlike things together and to assume that because they have the same label, they are all alike.

POLARIZATION

Polarization refers to the tendency to look at the world in terms of opposites and to describe it in terms of extremes — good or bad, positive or negative, healthy or sick, intelligent or stupid, rich or poor, and so on. It is often referred to as the "fallacy of either-or" or "black and white." Although it is true that magnetic poles may be described as positive or negative and that certain people are extremely rich and others are extremely poor, the vast majority of cases are clearly in the middle, between these two extremes. Most people exist somewhere between the extremes of good or bad, healthy or sick, intelligent or stupid, rich or poor. Yet there seems to be a strong tendency to view only the extremes and to categorize people, objects, and events in terms of these polar opposites.

This tendency may be easily illustrated by attempting to fill in the polar opposites for such words as the following:

$$\text{hot} \longrightarrow \underline{\hspace{2cm}}$$

$$\text{high} \longrightarrow \underline{\hspace{2cm}}$$

$$\text{good} \longrightarrow \underline{\hspace{2cm}}$$

$$\text{popular} \longrightarrow \underline{\hspace{2cm}}$$

$$\text{sad} \longrightarrow \underline{\hspace{2cm}}$$

Filling in these opposites should have been relatively easy and quick. The words should also have been fairly short. Further, if a number of people supplied opposites, we would find a high degree of agreement among them.

Now, however, attempt to fill in the middle positions with words meaning, for example, "midway between high and low," "midway between hot and cold," and so on. These midway responses (compared to the opposites) were probably more difficult to think of and took more time. The words should also have been fairly long or phrases of two, three, four, or more words. Further, we would probably find rather low agreement among different people completing this same task.

It might be helpful to visualize the familiar bell-shaped curve. Few items exist at either of the two extremes, but as we move closer to the center, more and more items are included. This is true of any random sample. If we selected a hundred people at random we would find that their intelligence, height, weight, income, age, health, and so on would, if plotted, fall into a bell-shaped or "normal" distribution. Yet our tendency seems to be to concentrate on the extremes, on the ends of this curve, and ignore the middle, which contains the vast majority of cases.

With certain statements it is legitimate to phrase them in terms of two absolutes. For example, this thing that you are holding is either a book or it is not. Clearly the classes of Book and Not Book include all possibilities. And so there is no problem with this kind of statement. Similarly, we may say that the student will either pass this course or will not pass it, these two categories including all possibilities.

We create problems, however, when we use this basic form in situations in which it is inappropriate—for example, "the politician is either for us or against us." Note that these two possibilities do not include all possibilities; the politician may be for us in some things and against us in other things, or he or she may be neutral. During the Vietnam War there was a tendency to categorize people as either hawk or dove, but clearly there were many people who were neither and many who were probably both—hawks on certain issues and doves on others.

What we need to beware of is implying and believing that two extreme classes include all possible classes, that an individual must be a hawk or a dove and that there are no other alternatives. "Life is either a daring adventure or nothing," said Helen Keller. But for most people it is neither a daring adventure nor nothing but rather something somewhere in between these two extremes.

INTENSIONAL ORIENTATION

Intensional orientation (the *s* in intensional is intentional) refers to the tendency to view people, objects, and events in terms of the way in which they are talked about or labeled rather than in terms of the way they actually exist and operate.

Extensional orientation, on the other hand, is the tendency to look first to the actual people, objects, and events and only after this to their labels. It is the tendency to be guided by what we see happening rather than by the label used for what is happening.

Intensional orientation is seen when we act as if the words and labels are more important than the things they represent, when we act as if the map is more important than the territory. In its extreme form intensional orientation is seen in the person who, afraid of dogs, begins to sweat when shown a picture of a dog or when hearing people talk about dogs. Here the person is responding to the labels, to the maps, as if they were the actual thing or territory.

Intensional orientation may be seen clearly in the results of the numerous studies on prestige suggestion. Basically, these studies demonstrate that we are influenced more when we assume that the message comes from a prestigious personality than when it comes from an average individual. Such studies have shown that if given a painting, we will evaluate it highly if we think it was painted by a famous artist. But we will give it a low evaluation if we think it was produced by a little-known artist. Other studies have focused on our agreement with dogmatic statements, our judgments of literary merit, our perception of musical ability, and so on. In all of these studies the influencing factor is not the message itself—that is, the painting, the piece of literature, the music—but the name attached to it. Advertisers, of course, have long known the value of this type of appeal and have capitalized on it quite profitably.

One of the most ingenious examples of intensional orientation requires that you role-play for a minute and picture yourselves seated with a packet of photographs before you. Each of the photographs is of a person you have never seen. You are asked to scratch out the eyes in each photograph. You are further told that this is simply an experiment and that the individuals whose pictures you have will not be aware of anything that has happened here. As you are scratching out the eyes, you come upon a photograph of your mother. What do you do? Are you able to scratch out the eyes as you have done with the pictures of the strangers or have you somehow lost your ability to scratch out eyes? If, as many others, you are unable to scratch out the eyes, you are responding intensionally. You are, in effect, responding to the map (in this case the picture) as if it were the territory (your own mother).

In a study conducted not long ago psychologist Philip Goldberg claimed that women and men were prejudiced against women. Specifically, he found that women and men felt that articles written by men were more authoritative and more valuable than identical articles with feminine bylines. This result was found for messages in "traditionally masculine fields," such as law and city planning, as well as in "traditionally feminine fields," such as elementary school teaching and dietetics. Again this is a clear example of intensional orientation, of our tendency to look at the label (in this case the byline) and to evaluate the territory (in this case the actual article) only through the label.

In a letter addressed to Ann Landers a young lady wrote that she was distressed because her parents reacted so negatively to the idea of her fiancé becoming a nurse. Ann Landers offered some comfort but added, "But I do feel that they ought to call male nurses something else." This is a rather classic example of intensional orientation.

An experiment conducted with stutterers should further illustrate this notion of intensional orientation. Early research has found that stutterers will stutter more when talking with people in authority than with subordinates. Stutterers will stutter very little when talking with children or when addressing

BOX 11.1
The Name of the Situation as Affecting Behavior

B. L. Whorf

In the course of my professional work for a fire insurance company, in which I undertook the task of analyzing many hundreds of reports of circumstances surrounding the start of fires . . . it became evident that not only a physical situation . . . but the meaning of that situation to people, was sometimes a factor, through the behavior of the people, in the start of the fire. . . .

Thus around a storage of what are called "gasoline drums," behavior will tend to a certain type, that is, great care will be exercised; while around a storage of what are called "empty gasoline drums" it will tend to be different—careless, with little repression of smoking or of tossing cigarette stubs about. Yet the "empty" drums are perhaps the more dangerous, since they contain explosive vapor. Physically the situation is hazardous, but the linguistic analysis according to regular analogy must employ the word "empty," which inevitably suggests lack of hazard. . . .

In a wood distillation plant the metal stills were insulated with a composition prepared from limestone and called at the plant "spun limestone." No attempt was made to protect this covering from excessive heat or the contact of flame. After a period of use the fire below one of the stills spread to the "limestone," which to everyone's great surprise burned vigorously. Exposure to acetic acid fumes from the stills had converted part of the limestone (calcium carbonate) to calcium acetate. This when heated in a fire decomposes, forming inflammable acetone. Behavior that tolerated fire close to the covering was induced by use of the name "limestone," which because it ends in "stone" implies noncombustibility. . . .

A tannery discharged waste water containing animal matter in an outdoor settling basin partly roofed with wood and partly open. This situation is one that ordinarily would be verbalized as "pool of water." A workman had occasion to light a blow-torch nearby, and threw his match into the water. But the decomposing waste matter was evolving gas under the wood cover, so that the setup was the reverse of "watery." An instant flare of flame ignited the woodwork, and the fire quickly spread into the adjoining building. . . .

Beside a coal-fired melting pot for lead reclaiming was dumped a pile of "scrap lead"—a misleading verbalization, for it consisted of the lead sheets of old radio condensers, which still had paraffin paper between them. Soon the paraffin blazed up and fired the roof, half of which was burned off.

Such examples, which could be greatly multiplied, will suffice to show how the cue to a certain line of behavior is often given by the analogies of the linguistic formula in which the situation is spoken of, and by which to some degree it is analyzed, classified, and allotted its place in that world which is "to a large extent unconsciously built up on the language habits of the group." And we always assume that the linguistic analysis made by our group reflects reality better than it does.

Source: From "The Relation of Habitual Thought and Behavior to Language," in *Language, Culture, and Personality, Essays in Memory of Edward Sapir,* edited by Leslie Spier, A. Irving Hallowell, and Stanley S. Newman, reprint ed. (Menasha, Wis.: Sapir Memorial Fund, University of Utah Press, 1941), pp. 75–77. Reprinted by permission.

animals, for example, but when it comes to teachers or employers they stutter a great deal. Another finding on stuttering is that of adaptation. This refers to the fact that as a stutterer reads a particular passage he or she will stutter less and less on each successive reading. In this experiment the researcher obtained from the stutterers the names of the persons to whom they had most difficulty speaking. At a later date the researchers had each stutterer read a passage five times. As predicted, the stuttering decreased on each reading to the point where it was almost entirely absent on the fifth reading. Before the sixth reading the experimenter placed in front of the stutterer a photograph of the person the stutterer had named as most difficult to speak to, and on the sixth reading the stuttering increased approximately to the level during the first reading of the passage. Again, the individual was responding to the photograph, the label, the map, as if it were something more, as if it were the actual thing.

Labels are certainly helpful guides, but they are not the things for which they are the symbols and should not be confused with them.

FACT-INFERENCE CONFUSION

We can make statements about the world that we observe, and we can make statements about what we have not observed. In form or structure these statements are similar and could not be distinguished from each other by any grammatical analysis. For example, we can say, "She is wearing a blue jacket," as well as "He is harboring an illogical hatred." If we diagrammed these sentences they would yield identical structures, and yet we know quite clearly that they are very different types of statements. In the first one we can observe the jacket and the blue color. But how do we observe "illogical hatred"? Obviously, this is not a descriptive statement but an inferential statement. It is a statement that we make not only on the basis of what we observe but also on the basis of what we observe plus our own conclusions.

There is no problem with making inferential statements; we must make them if we are to talk about much that is meaningful to us. The problem arises, then, not in making inferential statements but in acting as if those inferential statements are factual statements.

Consider, for example, the following anecdote: A woman went for a walk one day and met her friend, whom she had not seen, or heard from, or heard of, in 10 years. After an exchange of greetings, the woman said, "Is this your little

163

boy?" and her friend replied, "Yes, I got married about six years ago." The woman then asked the child, "What is your name?" and the little boy replied, "Same as my father's." "Oh," said the woman, "then it must be Peter."

The question, of course, is how did the woman know the boy's father's name if she had not seen or heard from or heard of her friend in the last 10 years? The answer, of course, is obvious. But it is obvious only after we recognize that in reading this short passage we have made an inference which, although we are not aware of our having made an inference, is preventing us from answering a simple question. Specifically, we have made the inference that the woman's friend is a woman. Actually, the friend is a man named Peter.

This is very similar to the example used to illustrate sexism in the language. One version goes something like this: A boy and his father are in an accident. The father is killed and the little boy is rushed to the hospital to be operated on. The surgeon is called in, looks at the boy, and says, "I can't operate on this boy; he's my son." The question is, how could the boy be the surgeon's son if his father was killed in the accident? Of course, the surgeon is the boy's mother. This is a particularly good example for illustrating our expectations in regard to male and female occupations. Because of our prior conditioning we almost feel compelled to qualify the term surgeon if the surgeon is female but not if the surgeon is male. Similarly, we speak of women lawyers and women doctors but of male nurses.

Perhaps the classic example of this type of fact-inference confusion concerns the case of the "empty" gun that unfortunately proves to be loaded. With amazing frequency we find in the newspapers examples of people being so sure that the guns are empty that they point them at another individual and fire. Many times, of course, they are empty. But, unfortunately, many times they are not. Here one makes an inference (that the gun is empty) but acts on the inference as if it is a fact and fires the gun.

Some of the essential differences between factual and inferential statements are summarized in Table 11.1.

Distinguishing between these two types of statements does not mean to

Table 11.1   Differences Between Factual and Inferential Statements

Factual statements	Inferential statements
1. may be made only after observation	1. may be made at any time
2. are limited to what has been observed	2. go beyond what has been observed
3. may be made only by the observer	3. may be made by anyone
4. may only be about the past or the present	4. may be about any time—past, present, or future
5. approach certainty	5. involve varying degrees of probability
6. are subject to verifiable standards	6. are not subject to verifiable standards

imply that one type is better than another type. Neither is better than the other. We need both types of statements; both are useful, both are important.

The problem arises when we treat one type of statement as if it were another type. Specifically, the problem arises when we treat an inferential statement as if it were a factual statement.

Inferential statements need to be accompanied by tentativeness. We need to recognize that such statements may prove to be wrong, and we should be aware of that possibility. Inferential statements should leave open the possibility of other alternatives. If, for example, we treat the statement "The United States should enforce the blockade" as if it were a factual statement, we eliminate the possibility of other alternatives. When making inferential statements we should be psychologically prepared to be proved wrong. This requires a great deal of effort but probably effort well spent. If we are psychologically prepared to be proved wrong we will be less hurt if and when we are shown to be incorrect.

ALLNESS

The world is infinitely complex and because of this we can never know all or say all about anything—at least we cannot logically say all about anything. And this is particularly true in dealing with people. We may *think* we know all there is to know about individuals or about why they did what they did, yet clearly we do not know all. We can never know all the reasons we ourselves do something, and yet we often think that we know all the reasons why our parents or our friends or our enemies did something. And because we are so convinced that we know all the reasons, we are quick to judge and evaluate the actions of others with great confidence that what we are doing is justified.

We may, for example, be assigned a textbook to read and because previous texts have been dull and perhaps because the first chapter was dull we infer that all the rest will likewise be dull. Of course, it often turns out that the rest of the book is even worse than the beginning. Yet it could be that the rest of the book would have proved exciting had it been read with an open mind. The problem here is that we run the risk of defining the entire text (on the basis of previous texts and perhaps the first chapter) in such a way as to preclude any other possibilities. If we tell ourselves that the book is dull it probably will appear dull. If we say a course will be useless ("all required courses are useless"), it will be extremely difficult for that instructor to make the course anything but what we have defined it to be. Only occasionally do we allow ourselves to be proved wrong; for the most part we resist rather fiercely.

The parable of the six blind men and the elephant is an excellent example of an allness orientation and its attendant problems. You may recall from elementary school that the poem by John Saxe concerns six blind men of Indostan who came to examine an elephant, an animal they had only heard about. The first blind man touched the elephant's side and concluded that the elephant was like a wall. The second felt the tusk and said the elephant must be like a spear. The third held the trunk and concluded that the elephant was much like a snake. The fourth touched the knee and knew the elephant was like a tree. The fifth felt the ear and said the elephant was like a fan. And the sixth grabbed the tail and concluded that the elephant was like a rope. Each of these learned men reached his own conclusion regarding what this marvelous beast, the elephant, was really like. Each argued that he was correct and that the others were wrong. Each, of course, was correct; but at the same time each was wrong. The point this poem illustrates is that we are all in the position of the six blind men. We never see all of something; we never experience anything fully. We see part of an object, an event, a person—and on that limited basis conclude what the whole is like. This procedure is a relatively universal one; we have to do this since it is impossible to observe everything. And yet we must recognize that when we make judgments of the whole based only on a part we are actually making inferences that can later be proved wrong. If we assume that we know all of anything we are into the pattern of misevaluation called *allness*.

Students who walk into a class convinced that they cannot learn anything will probably not learn anything. And while it may be that the teacher was not very effective, it may also be that the students have closed their minds to the possibility of learning anything. Disraeli once said that "to be conscious that you are ignorant is a great step toward knowledge." That observation is an excellent example of a nonallness attitude. If we recognize that there is more to learn, more to see, more to hear, we will leave ourselves open to this additional information and will be better prepared to assimilate it into our existing structures. An implicit or explicit *etc.* should end every sentence.

STATIC EVALUATION

In order to gain a better understanding of the concept of static evaluation, try to write down a statement or two that makes no reference to time—that is, we must not be able to tell whether the statement refers to the past, present, or future. Write this statement down before reading on. Next, attempt to date the following quotation. Approximately when was it written?

> Those states are likely to be well administered in which the middle class is large, and larger if possible than both the other classes or at any rate than either singly; for the addition of the middle class turns the scale and prevents either of the extremes from being dominant.

These two brief exercises should illustrate an interesting dimension of the English language. It was probably extremely difficult, if not impossible, to produce a sentence that made no reference to time whatsoever. Time, in English, is an obligatory category, which means that all sentences must contain some reference to past, present, or future. Our verb system is constructed in such a way that it is impossible to produce a sentence without including a reference to time in the verb. This is not true in all languages. Second, in dating the quotation, most people would find themselves missing the actual date by at least a few hundred years. The statement was actually written by Aristotle in his *Politics* approximately 2300 years ago.

Thus while it is impossible to make statements without reference to past, present, or future, it is almost impossible to tell when statements were produced. These, of course, are obvious statements about language. Yet their consequences are not often obvious.

Often when we form an abstraction of something or someone—when we formulate a verbal statement about an event or person—that abstraction, that statement, has a tendency to remain static and unchanging while the object or person to whom it originally referred may have changed enormously. Alfred Korzybski, the founder of the study of language called General Semantics, used an interesting illustration in this connection: In a tank we have a large fish and many small fish, which are the natural food for the large fish. Given freedom in the tank, the large fish will eat the small fish. After some time we partition the tank with the large fish on one side and the small fish on the other, divided only by a clear piece of glass. For a considerable time the large fish will attempt to eat the small fish but will fail each time; each time it will knock into the glass partition. After some time it will "learn" that attempting to eat the small fish means difficulty and will no longer go after them. Now, however, we remove the partition and the little fish swim all around the big fish. But the big fish does not eat them and in fact will die of starvation while its natural food swims all around. The large fish has learned a pattern of behavior and even though the actual territory has changed, the map remains static.

While we would probably all agree that everything is in a constant state of flux, the relevant question is whether we act as if we know this. Put differently, do we act in accordance with the notion of change, instead of just accepting it intellectually? Do we realize, for example, that because we have failed at something once we need not fail again? Do we realize that if someone does something to hurt us that they too are in a constant state of change? Our evaluations of ourselves and of others must keep pace with the rapidly changing real world; otherwise we will be left with attitudes about and beliefs in a world that no longer exists.

T. S. Eliot, in *The Cocktail Party,* said that "what we know of other people is only our memory of the moments during which we knew them. And they have changed since then . . . at every meeting we are meeting a stranger."

INDISCRIMINATION

Nature seems to abhor sameness at least as much as vacuums, for nowhere in the universe can we find two things that are identical. Everything is unique— everything is unlike everything else.

Our language, however, provides us with common nouns, such as *teacher, student, friend, enemy, war, politician,* and *liberal,* which lead us to focus on similarities. Such nouns lead us to group all teachers together, all students together, and all friends together and perhaps divert attention away from the uniqueness of each individual, each object, each event.

The misevaluation of *indiscrimination,* then, is one in which we focus on classes of individuals or objects or events and fail to see that each is unique, each is different, and each needs to be looked at individually.

This misevaluation is at the heart of the common practice of stereotyping

Table 11.2   Barriers to Verbal Interaction

Be careful of:	Be conscious of:
1. Polarization; either-or thinking	1. Multivalued orientation; many-sided perspective
2. Intensional orientation	2. Extensional orientation; the word is not the thing
3. Fact-inference confusion	3. Facts are NOT inferences; inferences are NOT facts
4. Allness	4. Nonallness; the word is not ALL the thing; use the *etc.*
5. Static evaluation	5. Process evaluation; date all statements
6. Indiscrimination	6. Nondiscrimination; index all nouns

national, racial, and religious groups. A stereotype is a relatively fixed mental picture of some group that is applied to each individual of the group without regard to his or her unique qualities. It is important to note that although stereotypes are usually thought of as negative they may also be positive. We can, for example, consider certain national groups as lazy or superstitious or mercenary or criminal but we can also consider them as intelligent, progressive, honest, hard-working, and so on. Regardless of whether such stereotypes are positive or negative, however, the problem they create is the same. They provide us with shortcuts that are often inappropriate. For example, when we meet a particular individual our first reaction may be to pigeonhole him or her into some category —perhaps a religious one, perhaps a national one, perhaps an academic one. Regardless of the type of category we attempt to fit him or her into, we invariably fail to devote sufficient attention to the unique characteristics of the individual before us. As college students you may resent being stereotyped by other students, whether the stereotype is based on your nationality, your religion, your race, or your actual or imagined behavior, such as egotist, jock, cheapskate, apple polisher. Each group seems to stereotype the others quite readily while just as rapidly deploring the unfair stereotyping that goes on in a supposedly academic community.

It should be emphasized that there is nothing wrong with classifying. No one would argue that classifying is unhealthy or immoral. It is, on the contrary, an extremely useful method of dealing with any complex matter. Classifying helps us to deal with complexity; it puts order into our thinking. The problem arises not from classifying itself. It arises from our classifying, then applying some evaluative label to that class, and then utilizing that evaluative label as an "adequate" map for each individual in the group. Put differently, indiscrimination is a denial of another's uniqueness.

A summary of the "do's" and "don't's" of verbal interaction appears in Table 11.2.

SOURCES

The barriers to verbal interaction owe their formulation to the work of the General Semanticists. I would especially recommend the following for beginners:

John C. Condon, Jr., *Semantics and Communication*, 2d ed. (New York: Macmillan, 1975); William V. Haney, *Communication and Organizational Behavior: Text and Cases*, 3d ed. (Homewood, Ill.: Richard D. Irwin, 1973); S. I. Hayakawa, *Language in Thought and Action*, 3d ed. (New York: Harcourt Brace Jovanovich, 1972).

The nature of E-prime, explained in Experiential Vehicle 11.1, is discussed in detail in D. David Bourland, Jr., "A Linguistic Note: Writing in E-Prime," *General Semantics Bulletin*, nos. 32 and 33, 1965/1966.

Much that appears in this unit appears in more detail in my *General Semantics: Guide and Workbook*, rev. ed. (DeLand, Florida: Everett/Edwards, 1974). A number of the exercises are taken from this book as well. My cassette tape series *General Semantics: Nine Lectures* (DeLand, Florida: Everett/Edwards, 1971) also covers this material. For somewhat different points of view see Gerard Nierenberg and Henry Calero, *Meta-Talk: Guide to Hidden Meanings in Conversations* (New York: Simon and Schuster, 1973) and John C. Condon, Jr., *Interpersonal Communication* (New York: Macmillan, 1977). An excellent application of the principles discussed here may be found in Anatol Rapoport, "Verbal Maps and Global Politics," *et cetera* 37 (winter 1980): 297–313.

Experiential Vehicles

11.1 E-Prime

E-prime is normal English minus the verb to be. The term E' refers to the mathematical equation, $E - e = E'$, where E = the English language and e = the verb *to be*. E', therefore, refers to normal English without the verb *to be*.

D. David Bourland, Jr., suggests that if we wrote and spoke without the verb *to be* we would more accurately describe the event. The verb *to be* often suggests that qualities are in the person or thing rather than in the observer making the statement. We often forget that these statements are evaluative rather than purely descriptive sentences. For example, we say "Johnny is a failure" and imply that failure is somehow *in* Johnny instead of in someone's evaluation of Johnny. This type of thinking is especially important in making statements about ourselves. We say, for example, "I can't learn mathematics," or "I'm unpopular," or "I'm lazy" and imply that these qualities (the inability to learn mathematics, the unpopularity, and the laziness) are *in* us. But these are simply evaluations that may be incorrect or, if at least partly accurate, may change. The verb *to be* implies a permanence which simply is not true of the world we live in. Consider how different these statements would be if phrased without the verb *to be*. We might say, for example, "I have failed two mathematics courses" or "My mathematics instructor gave me a D in calculus." Or we might say, "No one asked me out this weekend," or "The neighbors did not invite me to the party." Or we might say, "I don't enjoy working on this term paper," or "I overslept and missed my last two appointments." Notice how these "rewrites" center on concrete events and leave open the possibility of change.

To further appreciate the difference between statements that use the verb *to be* and those that do not, try to rewrite the following sentences without using the verb *to be* in any of its forms —that is, *is, are, am, was,* or any other variants.

1. I'm ugly.
2. He is unhappy.
3. What is love?
4. Is this helpful?
5. This exam was unfair.
6. Hate is a useless emotion.
7. Is life meaningful?
8. Was the book good?

9. This course is difficult.
10. This class is the best in the school.

11.2   Facts and Inferences

Carefully read the following report and the observations based on it.* Indicate whether you think the observations are true, false, or doubtful on the basis of the information presented in the report. Circle T if the observation is definitely true, circle F if the observation is definitely false, and circle ? if the observation may be either true or false. Judge each observation in order. Do not reread the observations after you have indicated your judgment and do not change any of your answers.

A well-liked college teacher had just completed making up the final examinations and had turned off the lights in the office. Just then a tall, dark, broad figure appeared and demanded the examination. The professor opened the drawer. Everything in the drawer was picked up and the individual ran down the corridor. The dean was notified immediately.

---

1. The thief was tall, dark, and broad.   T F ?
2. The professor turned off the lights.   T F ?
3. A tall figure demanded the examination.   T F ?
4. The examination was picked up by someone.   T F ?
5. The examination was picked up by the professor.   T F ?
6. A tall, dark figure appeared after the professor turned.
   off the lights in the office.   T F ?
7. The man who opened the drawer was the professor.   T F ?
8. The professor ran down the corridor.   T F ?
9. The drawer was never actually opened.   T F ?
10. In this report three persons are referred to.   T F ?

11.3   Poetry Evaluation

Following are three poems. Please read each poem carefully.

1. Write a brief evaluation of each poem. Use any criteria you wish in evaluating these poems—that is, meaningfulness, universality, depth of insight, communicativeness, relevance, and so on.
2. In the upper right-hand corner of the poem rank the poem in order of merit: 1 = the best of the three; 2 = the second best; and, 3 = the worst of the three.

---

* This experiential vehicle is taken from Joseph A. DeVito, *General Semantics: Guide and Workbook,* rev. ed. (Deland, Florida: Everett/Edwards, Inc., 1974), p. 55, and is modeled on those developed by William V. Haney.

3. Please do NOT talk while doing these evaluations.

At the round earth's imagined corners, blow
Forty years back, when much had place
Your trumpets, angels, and arise, arise
That since has perished out of mind.
Of souls, and to your scattered bodies go,
He spoke as one afoot will wind
All whom the flood did, and fire shall o'erthrow,
A morning horn ere men awake;
All whom war, dearth, age, agues, tyrannies,
His note was trenchant, turning kind.

Solemn and gray, the immense clouds of even
Despair, law, chance, hath slain, and you whose eyes
Pass on their towering unperturbed way
Shall behold God, and never taste death's woe.
Through the vast whiteness of the rain-swept heaven,
But let them sleep, Lord, and me mourn a space,
The moving pageants of the waning day;
The counterfeits that Time will break,
Brooding with sullen and Titanic crests
Teach me how to repent; for that's as good.
  —John Donne, *Prelude to God, VII*

Rank: _____

The forests were old and black,
  the clouds are heavy and brown.
But the world is red and gold,
  and its people pink and blue.

The heavens are pale and timid,
  the skies are still and cold.
But the water is pure and clear,
  and its people pink and blue.

The dogs are lonely and sad,
  the cats are crying and still.
But the streets are joyful and gay,
  and its people pink and blue.
  —Alexander Pope, *Elegy for Pink and Blue*

Rank: _____

How doth the little crocodile
  Improve his shining tail,
And pour the waters of the Nile
  On every shining scale!

How cheerfully he seems to grin,
  How neatly spreads his claws,
And welcomes little fishes in
  with gently smiling jaws.
  —Grace Whitherspoon, *The Crocodile*

Rank: _____

After all three poems are evaluated and ranked, your instructor will provide you
with some background material on these poems. Keep this material in mind and
refer back to your evaluations as you read the unit. What conclusions are you
willing to come to as a result of this experience?

Part Four

Nonverbal Messages

Unit 12

Preliminaries to Nonverbal Messages

PRELIMINARIES TO NONVERBAL MESSAGES

Communicative
Determined
Contextual
Believable
Rule-Governed
Packaged
Metacommunicational
    12.1 Breaking Nonverbal Rules

LEARNING GOALS

After completing this unit, you should be able to:

1. explain the principle that holds that nonverbal communication occurs in a context
2. explain the reasons why nonverbal behaviors in an interactional situation always communicate
3. explain the concept of "tells"
4. explain how time communicates
5. explain the determined nature of nonverbal communication
6. identify the reasons for assuming that nonverbal communication is highly believable
7. explain the *rule-governed* nature of nonverbal communication
8. explain the *packaged* nature of nonverbal communication
9. define *metacommunication*
10. provide at least three examples of the ways in which nonverbal behavior is frequently metacommunicational
11. cite at least three examples of unwritten nonverbal rules of behavior

Today there is great interest in nonverbal communication, or what is more popularly called "body language." The gimmick used in selling the books or articles about nonverbal communication is the promise that we will learn to decipher what other people are thinking simply by observing their "body language," The cover of Julius Fast's *Body Language*, for example, shows the picture of a woman sitting in a chair with her arms folded and her legs crossed. Surrounding the woman are such questions as "Does her body say that she's a loose woman?," "Does your body say that you're hung up?," "Does his body say that he's a manipulator?," and so on. Who could resist learning this kind of information? It would be indispensable at parties and all sorts of social gatherings. Success in one's business and social life would be almost assured should one just learn to read body language.

But as anyone who has read such works knows, such significant insight is not so easy to attain. Perhaps the primary reason is simply that we do not know enough about nonverbal communication to enable the layperson to make instant and accurate readings of the inner workings of the mind. And yet we have — especially in the last 10 years — learned a great deal about this nonverbal communication business.

By "nonverbal communication" we mean behavior that does not involve words. In the units to follow we cover a large part of this nonverbal area. A preview of the material to be covered will help to further define and clarify "nonverbal communication." In Unit 13 we take a broad view of kinesics and include there movements of the body (for example, gestures of the hands, gross bodily movements, walking styles) and general body type; movements of the face (for example, smiling, frowning); and eye movements. In Unit 14, "Proxemics," we consider the messages communicated by varying distances between people; the communicative function of touch; territoriality (that ownership-like response that one makes to a particular space or object); and the use of color to communicate. Under "Paralanguage and Silence," in Unit 15, we focus on the vocal dimension of communication (for example, rate and volume) and the absence of verbalization and its communicative functions.

In the present unit we identify a few characteristics of nonverbal communication that seem valid and useful. These characteristics should provide a kind of framework through which we might better view the specifics of nonverbal communication (Figure 12.1). The goal of this discussion is not to provide the means for personality diagnosis or for dating success or for determining when someone is bluffing in a poker game. The purposes are instead (1) to enable us to understand ourselves better, (2) to enable us to understand others better, and (3) to enable us to communicate more effectively.

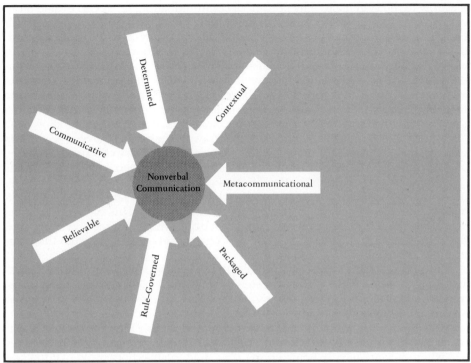

Figure 12.1   The characteristics of nonverbal communication.

COMMUNICATIVE

Nonverbal behavior in an interactional situation always communicates. This observation is true of all forms of communication, but it seems particularly true of nonverbal communication. All behavior in an interactional situation is communicative. It is impossible not to behave, and consequently, it is impossible not to communicate. Regardless of what one does or does not do, regardless of whether it is intentional or unintentional, one's nonverbal behavior communicates something to someone (assuming that there is an interactional setting). Further, these messages may be received consciously or subconsciously; we need not be consciously aware that we are receiving messages for them to communicate meaning to us.

Sitting silently in a corner and reading a book communicates to the other people in the room just as surely as would verbalization. Staring out the window during class communicates something to the teacher just as surely as would your saying, "I'm bored." Notice, however, an important difference between the nonverbal and the verbal statements. The student looking out the window, when confronted by the teacher's "Why are you bored?" can always claim to be just momentarily distracted by something outside. Saying, "I'm bored," however, prevents the student from backing off and giving a more socially acceptable meaning to the statement. The nonverbal communication, however, is also more convenient from the point of view of the teacher. The teacher, if confronted with the student's "I'm bored," must act on that in some way. Some of the possibilities include saying, "See me after class," "I'm just as bored as you are," "Who cares?," "Why are you bored?," and so on. All of them, however, are confrontations of a kind. The teacher is in a sense forced to do something even though he or she might prefer to ignore it. The nonverbal staring out the window allows the teacher to ignore it. This does not mean that the teacher is not aware of it or that the staring is not communicating. Rather, nonverbal communication allows the "listener" an opportunity to feign a lack of awareness. And, of course, this is exactly what so many teachers do when confronted by a class of students looking out the window, reading the newspaper, talking among themselves, and so on.

There are, however, exceptions to this general rule. Consider, for example, if the student, instead of looking out the window, gave the teacher some unmistakable nonverbal signal such as a thumb pointing down. This type of nonverbal communication is not so easy to feign ignorance of. Here the teacher must confront this comment just as surely as he or she would have to confront the comment "I'm bored."

Even the less obvious and less easily observed behaviors communicate. The smaller movements of the eyes, hands, facial muscles, and so on also communicate just as do the gross movements of gesturing, sitting in a corner, or staring out a window.

These small movements are extremely important in interpersonal relationships. We can often tell, for example, when two people genuinely like each other and when they are merely being polite. If we had to state how we know this, we would probably have considerable difficulty. These inferences, many of which are correct, are based primarily on these small nonverbal behaviors of the participants, the muscles around the eyes, the degree of eye contact, the way in which the individuals face each other, and so on. All nonverbal behavior, however small or transitory, is significant—each has a meaning, each communicates. Another means often used to infer whether two individuals like each other is that of behavioral synchrony, which refers to the situation in which two people behave nonverbally in the same way. This synchrony may be a result of one person imitating the nonverbal behaviors of the other or it may be simply that the two people behave "spontaneously" in the same way. Although we normally think of behavioral synchrony in connection with general bodily movements and hand gestures, nonverbal synchrony is also evidenced in posture (for example, one's way of standing, sitting, or crossing of legs) and in voice (for example, one's rate of speaking, loudness, or pausing patterns). Generally, behavioral synchrony is an index of mutual liking.

As can easily be appreciated, in poker playing the communicative significance of the nonverbal messages is particularly important—they often reveal the type of hand another player is holding. Nonverbal messages that reveal the type of hand a player holds are called "tells." Derived from the word *telegraph*, *tells* refers to telegraphing the hand held. You may remember that in the movie *Mister Cory* Tony Curtis rubbed his nose when he was bluffing. His nose rubbing was a "tell" and told the more observant players that he was in fact bluffing. Some players tell their good hand by excessive movement in their chairs or by rubbing

BOX 12.1
Time Talks

Significant messages are often communicated by our use of time, an area of nonverbal communication referred to as *chronemics*. Three types of time are often distinguished.

Technical or *scientific* time is that used when precise measurement is essential. Perhaps the most common example is the scientist's millisecond (one-thousandth of a second). The radio and television advertiser also uses technical time when talking of 15-second and 30-second commercials, in which each second may cost thousands of dollars.

A second type of time is *formal* time. Here the customary temporal units of hour, day, week, month, and so on are used.

The third and perhaps the most interesting type is *informal* time. Here time is measured with such general terms as soon, right away, anytime, later, when you get ready, as soon as I can, when I finish this, and so on. It is this area of informal time that presents the most difficulties in communication since the meanings assigned to these general temporal units vary greatly from one person to another and from one culture or subculture to another. Regardless of how time is evaluated or what type of time we refer to, time communicates just as surely and sometimes more forcefully than words and gestures.

Consider, for example, some students who constantly arrive late for biology class. Their previous class is next door, and so difficulty in getting to the class is not the problem. Yet they consistently come late. (Consider what you would think if the biology teacher were always late for class.) For some reason they find themselves engaged in something else which invariably consumes more time than anticipated. These same students, however, are always early for their communication class. Regardless of the reasons for being late and early, they communicate something to the instructors of both courses. To the biology teacher it might be that the students hate the class, that they are somehow disorganized, or that they have weak kidneys. To the communication teacher it might mean that they are anxious to get better acquainted with the other students, that they are interested in the course, or perhaps that they have nothing else to do.

Within our culture, for example, consider what arriving or leaving early or late at a party might mean. On one level the time of arrival and departure might communicate something about interest or enjoyment. But such messages also communicate something about our willingness to socialize, our concern for the host, our level of frustration tolerance, our need to make a grand entrance or exit, and so on. Some people seem particularly sensitive to the appropriateness of time, while others seem totally oblivious. Some people consistently arrive late for dinner, for example, and then wonder why they are seldom invited back. Some seem totally unaware of when to leave. Although we may look at our watch several times, yawn three or four times at strategic places in the conversation, mention that there is a full day of work ahead of us tomorrow, and give any number of other cues, there seems to be no awareness of time with some people.

Time is especially linked to status considerations. For example, the importance of being on time varies directly with the status of the individual. If the person is extremely important, we had better be there on time; in fact, we had better be there early just in case he or she is able to see us before schedule. As an individual's status decreases, it is less important for us to be on time. Students, for example, must be on time for conferences with teachers, but it is more important to be on time for deans and still more important to be on time for the president. Teachers, on the other hand, may be late for conferences with students but not for conferences with deans or the president of the college. Deans, in turn, may be late for teachers but not for the president. Within any given hierarchy, similar unwritten rules seem to be followed in dealing with time. This is not to imply that these "rules" are just or fair. It is only to point out that they exist. Surely teachers should not be late for appointments with students, nor should deans be late for appointments with teachers. These "rules" merely state the general cultural attitude toward such violations of schedules. Even the time of dinner and the time from the arrival of guests to eating varies on the basis of status. Among lower-status individuals dinner is served relatively early, and if there are guests, they eat soon after they arrive. For higher-status people dinner is relatively late, and a longer period of time elapses between arrival and eating—usually the time it takes to consume two cocktails.

Promptness or lateness in responding to letters, in acknowledging gifts, and in returning invitations all communicate significant messages to other individuals. Such messages may be indexed on such scales as interest-lack of interest, organized-disorganized, considerate-inconsiderate, sociable-unsociable, and so on. If, in asking for a date, the call is made the night before or even the same night as the expected date, it may communicate any number of things. Say, Chris calls Pat Saturday afternoon for a date that evening. Calling at that particular time may communicate, for example, that Chris had another date who canceled, or that Chris knew that Pat would be free and so there was no need to give notice, or that Chris was such a catch that Pat would welcome Chris regardless of the time called, and so on. In turn Pat's response or answer communicates significant meaning to Chris. Pat's acceptance might confirm Chris's expectation that Pat was free or that Pat would welcome Chris's call at any time. Pat's rejection, depending on the kind of ego Chris had, might communicate that Pat really wanted to date Chris but could not appear too eager or that Pat didn't really want to date Chris and only used the short notice as an excuse.

the top of their cards with their thumb or by squinting their eyes. So important are these tells and the attempts to cover them up that the art of poker playing may well be said to rest on the ability to send false messages and to decode the false messages of others. For the poker players among the readers I should add that tells may also be verbal, for example, excessive talking, the asking of questions to which the person already knows the answers ("Whose turn is it?" "What is the betting limit?"), and talking about matters that are totally irrelevant in the context of the game ("What are we going to do tomorrow night?" "Did you see that game yesterday?").

Although we concentrated here on behaviors, we should not assume that all nonverbal communication takes place behaviorally. There are numerous nonverbal messages that are communicated—by our clothing and other artifacts such as jewelry, makeup, buttons, the car you drive, the home you live in, the furniture you have and its arrangement, and, in fact, just about every object with which you associate yourself. Your association with an Alfa Romeo, Fendi leather, and Missoni woolen sweaters says something quite different from what your association with a Volkswagen, vinyl, and Acrilan would say. A Rolex and a Timex may both give you the correct time, but each communicates differently something about you. Whatever you wear (or do not wear) and whatever you are associated with (or are not associated with) will communicate to whomever you interact with.

DETERMINED

In Unit 9 it was pointed out that verbal messages evidence the quality of determinism—that is, all verbalizations are motivated in some way. This same quality of determinism is true for nonverbal messages as well. The smile or frown, the forward or backward glance, the strong or mild hug, the long or short kiss—all are motivated in different ways. Much as the smile and the frown, for example, will communicate different meanings to receivers, they will also be reflections of different meanings in the source. Smiling seems obviously motivated by a different set of factors than does frowning. From this rather weak claim, many will make the further assumption that we can therefore learn a person's motives (or subconscious desires or repressed fears or strengths and weaknesses) by analyzing her or his nonverbal behaviors. As we noted above, such significant insight into a person's personality and motivation does not come so easily. We cannot tell what is going on inside a person's skin by focusing solely on what is going on nonverbally.

This is illustrated in an experiment in which analysts looked for various nonverbal cues in videotapes of happily and unhappily married couples who were experiencing considerable interpersonal conflict. It was found that the happy couples sat closer together, looked more frequently into each other's eyes, and touched each other more than they touched themselves. The unhappy couples, on the other hand, crossed their arms and legs, made less direct eye contact with each other, and touched themselves more than they touched each other. Clearly, then, happy and unhappy couples behave differently nonverbally. But this is not the same as saying that couples who touch themselves more than they touch each other are unhappy or are experiencing interpersonal conflict.

Their touching means something, but exactly what it means for the person him-self or herself cannot be accurately determined from the nonverbal behavior alone.

Our analysis of nonverbal behaviors and our assumption of determinism may assist us in suggesting possible hypotheses about what is going on inside the person. But that is about as far as we can legitimately go with our present level of knowledge of nonverbal communication. One of the reasons for this is simply that people are different; one person's smile may mean "I'm happy," whereas another person's smile may cover up seething hostility. Also, there are contextual factors that influence nonverbal behaviors; a smile with one person in one place may mean something totally different from a smile with someone else in another place. Social and cultural factors also influence what a person means when he or she engages in various nonverbal behaviors; whereas one culture may encourage direct eye contact in interpersonal interaction, another culture may discourage it. These are just a few of the many influencing factors that should caution us against postulating specific meanings for specific nonverbal behaviors.

CONTEXTUAL

Like verbal communication, nonverbal communication exists in a context, and that context helps to determine to a large extent the meanings of any nonverbal behaviors. The same nonverbal behavior may have a totally different meaning when it occurs in another context. A wink of the eye to a beautiful person on a bus means something completely different from the wink of the eye that signi-fies a put-on or a lie. Similarly, the meaning of a given bit of nonverbal behavior will differ depending on the verbal behavior it accompanies or is close to in time. Pounding the fist on the table during a speech in support of a particular politi-cian means something quite different from that same fist pounding in response to news about someone's death.

It is the differing cultural contexts that seem to provide the most provoca-tive examples of the ways in which nonverbal behaviors may differ in meaning. Weston La Barre, the cultural anthropologist, provides a number of fascinating examples. Spitting in most Western cultures is a sign of disgust and displea-sure. However, for the Masai of Africa it is a sign of affection, and for the Amer-ican Indian it may be an act of kindness when, for example, the medicine man spits on the sick in order to cure them. In certain Eastern European Yiddish cultures, a person spits three times after a compliment in order to ward off bad luck. Sticking out the tongue to Westerners is an insult; to the Chinese of the Sung dynasty it served as a symbol to mock terror or to make fun of the anger of another individual; and to the modern South Chinese it serves to express embar-rassment over some social mistake. Mediterranean peoples have a number of hand gestures that communicate quite specific meanings. For example, kissing the fingers means approval, stroking the fingers on the chin signifies a lack of knowledge and concern over a particular event or statement, and forward movement of the hand with the palm downward means "don't worry," "take it slow." For other peoples these gestures have no meanings. Since there is no real relationship between the gestures and the meanings they signify, the meanings cannot be deduced simply by observing the behaviors.

When divorced from the context it is impossible to tell what any given bit of nonverbal behavior may mean. Of course, even if we know the context in detail we still might not be able to decipher the meaning of the nonverbal behavior. In attempting to understand and analyze nonverbal communication, however, it is essential that full recognition be taken of the context.

BELIEVABLE

For some reasons, not all of which are clear to researchers in nonverbal communication, we are quick to believe nonverbal behaviors even when these behaviors contradict the verbal behavior. Consider, for example, a conversation between a teacher and a student. The student is attempting to get a higher grade for the course and is in the process of telling the teacher how much hard work was put into the classes and how much enjoyment was derived from them. Throughout the discussion, however, the student betrays his or her real intentions with various small muscle movements, inconsistent smiles, a lack of direct eye contact, and so on. Somehow, the teacher goes away with the feeling, based on the nonverbal behavior, that the student really hated the class. For the most part, research has shown that when the verbal and the nonverbal messages differ, we will believe the nonverbal. In fact, nonverbal researcher Albert Mehrabian argues that the total impact of a message is a function of the following formula: *Total Impact = .07 verbal + .38 vocal + .55 facial*. This formula leaves very little influence for verbal messages. Only one-third of the impact is vocal (that is, paralanguage, rate, pitch, rhythm), and over half of the message is communicated by the face. Caution should be exercised in using this formula. It was developed by Mehrabian and his colleagues from their studies on connotative meaning, or the emotional impact, of a message and is not applicable to all messages, as is sometimes implied by writers in nonverbal communication. Although it is intriguing to speculate on what percentage of message impact is due to nonverbal elements, the truth is that we simply do not yet have a valid and reliable answer.

But we do seem to believe the nonverbal over the verbal. Exactly why this is so is not entirely clear. It may be that we feel verbal messages are easier to fake. Consequently, when there is a conflict, we distrust the verbal and accept the nonverbal. Or it may be that the nonverbal messages are perceived without conscious awareness. We learned them without being aware of any such learning and we perceive them without conscious awareness. Thus when such a conflict arises we somehow get this "feeling" from the nonverbal. Since we cannot isolate its source, we assume that it is somehow correct. Of course, a belief in the nonverbal message may simply result from our being reinforced for conclusions consistent with nonverbal behavior; consequently, we tend to repeat that kind of judgment. Perhaps in the past we have been correct in basing judgments on nonverbal cues and so continue to rely on them rather than on verbal ones.

RULE-GOVERNED

The characteristic of rule-governed behavior is easily appreciated when applied to verbal communication. In fact, the entire field of linguistics is devoted to explaining the rule-governed nature of language. The formulation of rules governing the sound, meaning, and structural systems of language occupies the bulk of the contemporary linguist's time. These are the rules that native speakers of the language follow in producing and in understanding sentences — rules that they may be unable to state explicitly.

Nonverbal communication is also rule-governed. We learned both the ways to communicate nonverbally *and* the rules of appropriateness at the same time from observing the behaviors of the adult community. For example, we learned how to express sympathy along with the rules that our culture has established for appropriately communicating sympathy. We learned that touch is permissible under certain circumstances but not under others, and we learned which type

The communicative, determined, contextually bound, believable, rule-governed, packaged, and metacommunicational dimensions of nonverbal communication are all evidenced in this scene from *The Sting*, as they are in all nonverbal transactions.

184

of touching is permissible and which is not. That is, we learned the rules governing touch behavior. Some of these rules, stated rather informally, would hold that lower-status persons may not initiate touching behavior with higher-status persons, but higher-status persons may initiate touching with lower-status persons. Thus, the teacher may put her or his arm around the student's shoulder, but the student may not do this to the teacher—at least not at first. We learned that women may touch each other in public; for example, they may hold hands, walk arm in arm, engage in prolonged hugging, and even dance together. Men may not do this, at least not without social criticism. And perhaps most obviously we learned that there are certain parts of the body that may not be touched and certain parts that may. As the relationship changes, so do the rules of touching. Generally, as we become more and more intimate, the rules for touching become less and less restrictive.

Another clear example is the rules governing eye contact. In our culture we are permitted to gaze at a stranger on a train or a bus for only a very short time, and then we are supposed to turn away. If we do not follow this rule, our intentions are questioned. We learned rules for sitting and walking behavior. Boys sit with their legs open and girls sit with their legs closed. Men take big steps when they walk; women take small steps. Men sit with their arms stretched out; women sit with their arms close to their bodies.

As can readily be appreciated even from these brief illustrations, these rules will vary from one culture to another. Different cultures often have very different rules governing the nonverbal behavior of their members. The very same behavior may be thought polite and considerate in one culture and aggressive and impolite in another. Further, as this short list should also have illustrated, many of the rules are sex-specific. Men and women do not learn the same rules, although they know the appropriate rules for each other and will frequently criticize each other for not following the appropriate rules for their sex. *Sissy* and *tomboy* are two of the milder designations for those who do not follow these rules. As boys and girls get older, the name calling gets more vicious.

Like the nonverbal behaviors themselves these rules are learned without conscious awareness. We learn them largely from observing others. The rules are only brought to our attention, to conscious awareness, in formal discussions of nonverbal communication, such as this one, and when the rules are violated and the violations are called to our attention—either directly by some tactless snob or indirectly through the examples of others. While linguists are attempting to formulate the rules for verbal messages, nonverbal researchers are attempting to formulate the rules for nonverbal messages—rules that native communicators know and utilize every day but cannot necessarily verbalize. A major function of the following units on nonverbal communication is to bring to consciousness some of these implicit rules and the meanings and implications behind their appropriate and inappropriate usage.

PACKAGED

Nonverbal behaviors—whether of the hands, the eyes, or the muscle tone of the entire body—are normally accompanied by other nonverbal behaviors that reinforce or support one another. The nonverbals occur in packaged forms. We do not express fear in our eyes, for example, while the rest of our body relaxes as if sleeping. We do not express anger through our posture while our face smiles. Rather, the entire body expresses the emotion. For purposes of analysis we may wish to focus primarily on the eyes or the facial muscles or the hand movements, but we need to recognize that these do not occur apart from other nonverbal behaviors. In fact, it is physically difficult to express an intense emotion with only one part of the body. Try to express an emotion with, say, your face while ignoring the rest of the body. You will probably find that the rest of the body takes on the qualities of that emotion as well. You will probably experience considerable difficulty if you attempt to restrict the expression of this emotion to only one part of the body.

It is even more difficult to express widely different or contradictory emotions with different parts of your body. For example, when you are afraid of something and your body tenses up, it becomes very difficult to relax your facial muscles and smile.

In any form of communication—whether interpersonal, small group, public speaking, or mass media—we generally do not pay much attention to the packaged nature of nonverbal communication. It is so expected that it goes unnoticed. But when there is an incongruity, when the weak handshake belies the smile, when the nervous posture belies the focused stare, when the constant preening belies the relaxed whistling or humming, we take notice. Invariably we are led to question the credibility, the sincerity, the honesty of the individual. And research tells us that our instincts serve us well in this type of situation. When nonverbal behaviors contradict one another, there seems good reason to question the believability of the communicator.

METACOMMUNICATIONAL

All behavior, verbal as well as nonverbal, can be metacommunicational. Any given bit of behavior can make reference to communication. We can say, "This statement is false," or, "Do you understand what I am trying to communicate to you?" In each case these statements have made references to communication and are therefore called *metacommunicational statements.*

Nonverbal behavior is very often metacommunicational. That is why this principle or assumption is noted here specifically. Nonverbal behaviors frequently function to make a statement about some verbal statement. The most obvious example, of course, is the crossing of the fingers behind one's back when telling a lie. We observe frequently someone making a statement and winking. The wink functions as a comment on the statement. These are obvious examples. Consider more subtle metacommunication. Take the first day of class as an example. The teacher walks in and says something to the effect that he or she is the instructor for the course and might then say how the course will be conducted, what will be required, what the goals of the course will be, and so on. But notice that much metacommunication is also going on. Notice that the clothes the teacher wears and how he or she wears them, the length and style of hair, the general physical appearance, the way he or she walks, the tone of voice, and so on all communicate about the communication—as well as, of course, communicating in and of themselves. These nonverbal messages function to comment on the verbal messages the instructor is trying to communicate. On the basis of these cues, students will come to various conclusions. They might conclude that this teacher is going to be easy even though a long reading list was given or that the class is going to be enjoyable or boring or too advanced or irrelevant.

The metacommunicational function of nonverbal communication is not limited to its role as an adjunct to verbal communication; nonverbal communication may also comment on other nonverbal communication. This is actually a very common type of situation. For example, the individual who, when meeting a stranger, both smiles and presents a totally lifeless hand for shaking is a good example of how one nonverbal behavior may refer to another nonverbal behavior. Here the lifeless handshake belies the enthusiastic smile.

Most often, when nonverbal behavior is metacommunicational it functions to reinforce (rather than contradict) other verbal or nonverbal behavior. You may literally roll up your sleeves when talking about cleaning up this room, or smile when greeting someone, or run to meet someone you say you are anxious to see, or arrive early for a party you verbally express pleasure in attending. On the negative, though still consistent side, you may arrive late for a dental appointment (presumably with a less than pleasant facial expression) or grind your teeth while telling off your boss. The point is simply that much nonverbal communication is metacommunicational. This does not mean that nonverbal communication may not refer to people, events, things, relationships, and so on (that is, be *object* communication), nor does it mean that verbal communication may not be metacommunication. We merely stress here the role of nonverbal communication as metacommunication because of its frequent use in this role.

These characteristics of communicative, determined, contextual, believable, rule-governed, packaged, and metacommunicational are not necessarily the only characteristics that might be noted. Yet, taken together, they should provide a firm foundation for approaching the more specific aspects of nonverbal communication considered in the units to follow. These characteristics, it should be emphasized, apply to all forms of nonverbal communication—body communication, spatial communication, vocal communication, and even silence.

SOURCES

General introductions to nonverbal communication are plentiful. Mele Koneya and Alton Barbour, *Louder Than Words . . . Nonverbal Communication* (Columbus, Ohio: Charles Merrill, 1976), William C. Donaghy, *Our Silent Language: An Introduction to Nonverbal Communication* (Dubuque, Iowa: Gorsuch Scarisbrick, 1980), and Thomas W. Benson and Kenneth D. Frandsen, *An Orientation to Nonverbal Communication* (Chicago: Science Research Associates, 1976), are brief introductions to the various areas of nonverbal communication. Mark Knapp's *Nonverbal Communication in Human Interaction*, 2d ed. (New York: Holt, Rinehart and Winston, 1980) surveys the same area but in greater detail and with more attention to the numerous experimental and descriptive studies. Similar coverage is provided by Dale G. Leathers, *Nonverbal Communication Systems* (Boston: Allyn & Bacon, 1976). A brief collection of readings has been edited by Haig A. Bosmajian, *The Rhetoric of Nonverbal Communication: Readings* (Glenview, Ill.: Scott, Foresman, 1971). Albert Mehrabian provides a brief but insightful overview in his "Communication Without Words," *Psychology Today* 2 (September 1968). A section by Mehrabian, "Nonverbal Communication," in C. David Mortensen and Kenneth K. Sereno, eds., *Advances in Communication Research* (New York: Harper & Row, 1973), provides an excellent review of significant literature and presents four experimental studies on various aspects of nonverbal communication. For a discussion of Mehrabian's formula for the relative impact of verbal and nonverbal elements, see Timothy G. Hegstrom, "Message Impact: What Percentage is Nonverbal?," *Western Journal of Speech Communication* 43 (spring 1979): 134–142. Flora Davis's *Inside Intuition* (New York: Signet, 1973) provides an excellent popular review of nonverbal communication. An interesting collection of articles and original essays on all aspects of nonverbal communication is provided by Lawrence Rosenfeld and Jean Civikly, *With Words Unspoken* (New York: Holt, Rinehart and Winston, 1976). On the concept of "tells," see David Hayano, "Poker Lies and Tells," *Human Behavior* 8 (March 1979): 16–22, and "Communicative Competency Among Poker Players," *Journal of Communication* 30 (spring 1980): 113–120. On behavioral synchrony see M. LaFrance and C. Mayo, *Moving Bodies: Nonverbal Communication in Social Relationships* (Monterey, Cal.: Brooks/Cole, 1978).

Judee Burgoon, "Nonverbal Communication Research in the 1970s: An Overview," in Dan Nimmo, ed., *Communication Yearbook 4* (New Brunswick, N.J.: Transaction Books, 1980), pp. 179–197, provides an excellent review of the central issues and research in the area. This article is particularly useful for its discussion of the functions of nonverbal communication. On metacommunication see William W. Wilmot, "Metacommunication: A Re-examination and Extension," in Dan Nimmo, ed., *Communication Yearbook 4* (New Brunswick, N.J.: Transaction Books, 1980), pp. 61–69.

Experiential Vehicle

12.1 Breaking Nonverbal Rules

The general objective of this exercise is to become better acquainted with some of the "rules" of nonverbal communication and to analyze some of the effects of breaking such rules.[1]

Much as we learn verbal language (that is, without explicit teaching), we also learn nonverbal language—the rules for interacting nonverbally. Among such rules we have learned might be some like the following:

1. Upon entering an elevator, turn to the door and stare at it or at the numbers indicating where the elevator is until your floor is reached.
2. When sitting down in a cafeteria, take a seat that is as far away from the next person as possible.
3. When sitting next to other people (or in the general area), do not invade their private space with your body or your belongings.
4. When sitting directly across from people, do not stare at them (that is, directly at their eyes) for more than a second or two.
5. Members of the opposite sex should not stare at the various sexual parts of the other person's body while that person is watching you.
6. When strangers are talking, do not enter their group.
7. When talking with someone, do not stand too close or to far away. You may move closer when talking about intimate topics. Never stand close enough so that you can smell the other person's body odor. This rule may be broken only under certain conditions—for example, when the individuals involved are physically attracted to each other or when one individual is consoling another or when engaged in some game where the rules require this close contact.
8. When talking in an otherwise occupied area, lower your voice so that other people are not disturbed by your conversation.
9. When talking with others, look at their eyes and facial area only occasionally. Neither stare at them nor avoid their glance completely.
10. When talking with people, do not touch them more than absolutely necessary. This is especially important when the parties do not know each other. Some touching is permitted when the parties are well acquainted. Touching

---

[1] This exercise was suggested to me by Professor Jean Civikly.

is more permissible for women than it is for men—that is, it is more permissible for women to touch men than for men to touch women and more permissible for women to touch women than for men to touch men.

Procedure

The procedures are relatively simple. Groups of two students are formed; one student is designated as rule breaker and one is designated as observer.

The task of the rule breaker is simply to enter some situation where one or more rules of nonverbal communication would normally be operative and break one or more rules. The task of the observer is to record mentally (or in writing if possible) what happens as a result of the rule breaking.

Each group should then return after a specified amount of time and report back to the entire class on what transpired.

Again, remember to observe the rights of others; do not engage in any experience that will embarrass or endanger another person.

Unit 13

Kinesics

KINESICS

Body Movements
Facial Movements
Eye Movements

LEARNING GOALS

After completing this unit, you should be able to:

1. provide two or three examples of nonverbal behaviors meaning different things in different cultures
2. define and provide at least two examples of *emblems, illustrators, affect displays, regulators,* and *adaptors*
3. identify instances of the five types of movements in the behaviors of others and in your own behaviors
4. identify the types of information communicated by the face
5. identify at least two problems in determining the accuracy of judgments about the communication of facial expressions
6. explain how context and culture influence facial expressions and their decoding
7. explain micromomentary expressions
8. identify at least three functions of eye movements
9. explain the types of information communicated by pupil dilation and constriction

The term *kinesics* has been given a wide variety of definitions. Some researchers prefer to restrict the term to gestures of the hands and movements of the body. Others prefer a broader perspective and include not only hand gestures and body movements but facial expressions, eye movements, and foot and leg movements. Here kinesics is defined broadly to include that area of nonverbal communication concerned with body, facial, and eye movements.

BODY MOVEMENTS

In dealing with movements of the body, a classification offered by Paul Ekman and Wallace V. Friesen seems the most useful. These researchers distinguish five classes of nonverbal movements based on the origins, functions, and coding of the behavior: emblems, illustrators, affect displays, regulators, and adaptors (Figure 13.1).

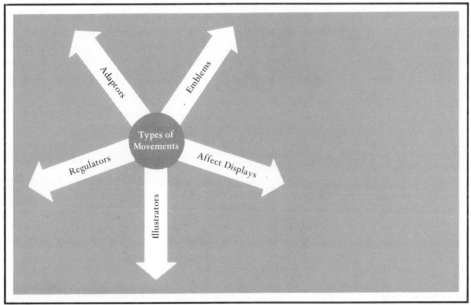

Figure 13.1 Types of movements.

EMBLEMS

Emblems are nonverbal behaviors that rather directly translate words or phrases. Emblems include, for example, the O.K. sign, the peace sign, the come here sign, the hitchhiker's sign, the "up yours" sign, and so on. Emblems are nonverbal substitutes for specific words or phrases and are probably learned in essentially the same way as are specific words and phrases—without conscious awareness or explicit teaching and largely through a process of imitation.

Although emblems seem rather natural to us and almost inherently meaningful, they are as arbitrary as any word in any language. Consequently, our present culture's emblems are not necessarily the same as the emblems of 300 years ago or the same as the emblems of other cultures.

Emblems are often used to supplement the verbal message or as a kind of reinforcement. At times they are used in place of verbalization—for example, when there is a considerable distance between the individuals and shouting would be inappropriate or when we wish to "say" something behind someone's back.

ILLUSTRATORS

Illustrators are nonverbal behaviors that accompany and literally "illustrate" the verbal messages. In saying, "Let's go up," for example, there will be movements of the head and perhaps hands going in an upward direction. In describing a circle or a square you are more than likely to make circular or square movements with your hands. So well learned are these movements that it is physically difficult to reverse them or to employ inappropriate ones.

In using illustrators we are aware of them only part of the time; at times they may have to be brought to our attention and our awareness. Illustrators seem more natural and less arbitrary than emblems. They are partly a function of learning and partly innate. Illustrators are more universal; they are more common throughout the world and throughout time than are emblems. Consequently, it is likely that there is some innate component to illustrators, contrary to what many researchers might argue.

AFFECT DISPLAYS

Affect displays are more independent of verbal messages than are illustrators and are less under conscious control than are emblems or illustrators.

Affect displays are the movements of the facial area that convey emotional meaning; these are the facial expressions that show anger and fear, happiness and surprise, eagerness and fatigue. They are the facial expressions that "give us away" when we attempt to present a false image and that lead people to say, "You look angry today, what's wrong?" We can, however, also consciously control affect displays, as actors do whenever they play a role.

Affect displays may be unintentional—as when they give us away—but they may also be intentional. We may want to show anger or love or hate or surprise and, for the most part, we do a creditable job. Actors are often rated by the public for their ability to accurately portray affect by movements of their facial

BOX 13.1
Body Type

One can communicate through body type as well as through body movement.

We can probably describe some of the major characteristics of physique in males, and to a lesser extent in females, under three general headings: (1) endomorphy, the fatty dimension; (2) mesomorphy, the muscular dimension; and (3) ectomorphy, the skinny dimension. We might then attempt to classify any given body in terms of the degree to which it possessed each of these three dimensions. Each body would be described by a three-digit number, with each digit a number from 1 to 7. The first number would describe the endomorphic dimension, the second the mesomorphic dimension, and the third the ectomorphic dimension. An extremely fat individual, for example, the fat man or woman of the circus, would be described as 7-1-1 indicating that he or she is high on endomorphy but low on the other two dimensions. Mr. America, Hercules, and Atlas would be described as 1-7-1—all muscle. The thin man or woman of the circus would be 1-1-7—just skin and bones. Of course few people are at these extremes. We might attempt to illustrate this by estimating the body types of persons who most of us have seen. Johnny Carson, for example, might be described as 2-5-4, whereas Merv Griffin might be described as 3-4-2. Joe Namath might be described as 3-6-1 and Mick Jagger as 1-3-6. These, of course, are simply estimates that illustrate the concept; they are not accurate measurements. These three-digit numbers, then, represent one's *somatotype,* or the degree to which a person is fat, muscular, and skinny. Male examples are used here because these body types were formulated on the basis of studies of the male body.

Try to picture the following individuals as they are described; try to see their physical characteristics or, better still, attempt to draw them.

Person 1. This man is dominant, confident, impetuous, domineering, enterprising, adventurous, competitive, determined, and hot-tempered.

Person 2. This man is dependent, contented, sluggish, placid, affable, tolerant, forgiving, sociable, generous, soft-hearted.

Person 3. This man is tense, anxious, withdrawn, cautious, serious, introspective, suspicious, cool, precise.

If your responses were consistent with those of others to whom similar tests were given, you probably pictured Person 1 as high on mesomorphy, as having a rather muscular build. Person 2 was probably pictured as high in endomorphy, as rather short and fat. Person 3 was probably pictured as high in ectomorphy, as relatively tall and thin.

There is considerable debate over the relationship between personality characteristics, such as those listed above, and somatotype. Some research does seem to indicate a rather strong relationship between body build and personality. A further question is what this relationship can be ascribed to. Is it genetic? Are people born with tall skinny bodies also born with certain personality traits, such as tenseness, withdrawnness, and so on? Is the relationship cultural? Are heavy people expected to be affable, sluggish, tolerant, forgiving, and so on, and do they therefore take on these characteristics, which everyone seems to think they possess anyway? This question has not been settled. What is clear is that people have certain reactions to different body types; the body types communicate something to us. We expect the heavy person to be sociable, generous, and affable. We expect the muscular individual to be dominant, confident, impetuous, and hot-tempered. We expect the thin person to be tense, precise, cool, and suspicious. At least in general we seem to have these expectations. Whether or not our judgments are well founded, we do seem to make inferences about people's personality from merely looking at their body build. And just as we have expectations of others based on their body build, they will have expectations of us based on our body build. Further, if these stereotypes are strong enough—and in many cases they seem to be—we will have expectations about ourselves based on our body build. The fact that these characteristics, these stereotypes, are so common across large sections of the population attests to the importance of body build in nonverbal communication.

It should also be noted that because of these different perceptions we will also have different perceptions of the same actions when they are performed by persons of different body build. For example, if a man at a dance sits in the corner with his head down and his arms clasped in front of him we would probably read different things into it if he were heavy, muscular, or thin.

muscles. And we are familiar with the awkward attempt of the would-be lover to seem seductive only to appear ludicrous.

REGULATORS

Regulators are nonverbal behaviors that "regulate," monitor, maintain, or control the speaking of another individual. When we are listening to another, we are not passive; rather, we nod our heads, purse our lips, adjust our eye focus, and make various paralinguistic sounds such as "mm-mm" or "tsk." Regulators are clearly culture-bound and are not universal.

Regulators in effect tell speakers what we expect or want them to do as they are talking—"Keep going," "What else happened?," "I don't believe that," "Speed up," "Slow down," and any number of other speech directions. Speakers in turn receive these nonverbal behaviors without being consciously aware of them. Depending on their degree of sensitivity, they modify their speaking behavior in line with the directions supplied by the regulators.

Regulators would also include such gross movements as turning one's head, leaning forward in one's chair, and even walking away.

ADAPTORS

Adaptors are nonverbal behaviors that when emitted in private—or in public but without being seen—serve some kind of need and occur in their entirety. For example, when you are alone you might scratch your head until the itch is put to rest. Or you might pick your nose until satisfied. In public, when people are watching us, we perform these adaptors, but only partially. And so you might put your fingers to your head and move them around a bit but you probably would not scratch enough to totally eliminate the itch. Similarly, you might touch your nose but probably would not pursue this simple act to completion.

In observing this kind of nonverbal behavior it is difficult to tell what the partial behavior was intending to accomplish. For example, in observing someone's finger near the nose we cannot be certain that this behavior was intended to pick the nose, scratch it, or whatever. These reduced adaptors are emitted without conscious awareness.

Three types of adaptors are generally distinguished. *Self-adaptors* are not intended to communicate information to others but rather serve some personal need—for example, grooming, cleaning, excretory, and autoerotic activity.

Object adaptors are nonverbal behaviors that make use of some kind of prop —a pencil, a tie, a styrofoam cup, a cigarette or pipe—but in which the prop does not serve any instrumental function. Object adaptors would not include writing with a pencil or tying a tie or smoking a cigarette; rather, they include banging the desk with the pencil or chewing on it or playing with one's tie or

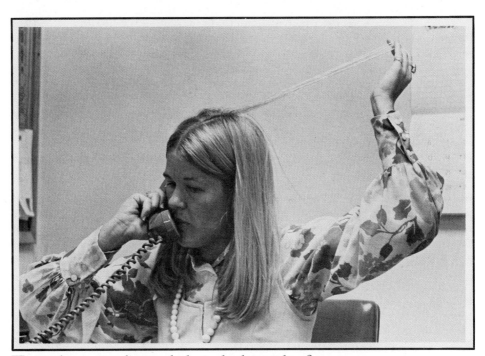

What is this woman doing and why is she doing it here?

197

chewing on a pipe. Object adaptors are thought by some theorists to release excess energy and seem to occur most often when the individual is anxious or nervous.

Alter adaptors include the movements learned in the manipulation of material things — in fixing a car, in changing a tire, in sewing a dress, in licking an envelope. They include movements that were (and are) necessary for protecting ourselves from attack or for attacking others, for establishing intimacy, or for withdrawing from an interpersonal interaction. When they are used as adaptors they are usually performed in abbreviated form and in circumstances that are emotionally related to their original purposes. In many of the more popularized versions of nonverbal behavior it is to adaptors that most attention is given. Here the authors talk about people crossing their legs in a way that is supposed to indicate sexual invitation, crossed in a way that indicates introversion, or crossed in a way that indicates aggressiveness, and so on. The attempt here is to identify nonverbal behaviors that are performed without conscious awareness and that reveal some kind of inner desires or tendencies.

FACIAL MOVEMENTS

The popularity of books on nonverbal communication is due in no small part to the interest people have in the type of information that such messages may communicate. Generally, research has found that facial messages communicate types of emotions as well as selected qualities or dimensions of emotion. Although researchers are not unanimous in their agreement, most agree with Paul Ekman, Wallace V. Friesen, and Phoebe Ellsworth, who claim that facial messages may communicate at least the following "emotion categories": happiness, surprise, fear, anger, sadness, and disgust/contempt. Nonverbal researcher Dale Leathers has proposed that facial movements may also communicate bewilderment and determination.

The communication of the six emotions identified by Ekman and his colleagues are generally referred to as primary affect displays. That is, these are relatively pure, single emotions. Other emotional states and other facial displays are combinations of these various primary emotions and are referred to as *blends*. Approximately 33 affect blends have been identified and seem to be fairly consistently recognized by trained nonverbal analysts. These affect blends may be communicated by different parts of the face. Thus, for example, you may experience both fear and disgust at the same time. Your fear may be signaled by your eyes and eyelids, whereas your disgust may be signaled by movements of the nose, cheek, and mouth area. Sometimes different emotions are displayed within the same area; for example, one eyebrow may communicate one emotion, whereas the other eyebrow may communicate a different emotion.

The accuracy with which people express emotions facially and the accuracy with which receivers decode these expressions have been the object of considerable research. One problem is that it is difficult to separate the ability of the encoder from the ability of the decoder. Thus, an individual may be quite adept at communicating emotions, but the receiver may prove to be insensitive. On the other hand, the receiver may be quite good at deciphering emotions, but the sender may be inept. And, of course, there are tremendous differences between one person and another as well as with the same person at different times. A second problem is that accuracy seems to vary with the method of the research. In some cases still photographs are used and people are asked to judge the emotions the people pictured are experiencing. Some research uses live models or actors and actresses who have been trained to communicate the different emotions. Still others use more spontaneous methods. For example, an individual judge views a person who is himself or herself viewing and reacting to a film. The judge, without seeing the film, has to decode the emotion the viewer is experiencing. As can be appreciated, each method yields somewhat different results. Accuracy also varies with the emotions themselves. Some emotions are easier to communicate and to decode than others. Ekman, Friesen, and Carlsmith, for example, report that happiness is judged with an accuracy ranging from 55 to 100 percent, surprise from 38 to 86 percent, and sadness from 19 to 88 percent. All this is not to say that the results of these studies are of no value; rather, it is merely to inject a note of caution in dealing with "conclusions" from nonverbal research.

Try to communicate surprise using only facial movements. Do this in front of a mirror and attempt to describe in as much detail as possible the specific movements of the face that make up surprise. If you signal surprise like most people, you probably employ raised and curved eyebrows, long horizontal forehead wrinkles, wide-open eyes, a dropped-open mouth, and lips parted with no tension. Even if there were differences—and clearly there would be from one person to another—you could probably recognize the movements listed here as indicative of surprise. Paul Ekman has developed what he calls FAST—the Facial Affect Scoring Technique. With this technique the face is broken up into three main parts: eyebrows and forehead, eyes and eyelids, and the lower face from the bridge of the nose down. Judges then attempt to identify various emotions by observing the different parts of the face and writing descriptions similar to the one for surprise given above for the various emotions. As can easily be appreciated, different areas of the face seem best suited to communicating different emotions. For example, fear seems to be most clearly communicated by the eyes and eyelids while disgust seems most clearly communicated by the nose, cheek, and mouth area.

In Unit 1 we noted that the context greatly influences the other aspects of communication. Communication by facial expression is no exception. It has been found repeatedly that the same facial expressions are perceived differently if people are supplied with different contexts. For example, in a study by Cline it was found that when a smiling face was presented looking at a glum face, the smiling face was judged to be vicious and taunting, but when the same smiling face was presented looking at a frowning face, it was judged to be peaceful and friendly. This is similar to the experiments done by the Russian filmmaker Kuleshev in the 1920s, who first used "montage"—a technique of film editing—by juxtaposing a "reaction shot" of a man's face with various different events. To the viewer, the face seemed to register different emotions depending on what scene it followed.

The culture also influences communication by facial expression. It appears from cross-cultural studies that facial expressions, at least of the six primary

BOX 13.2
Smiling

Smiling begins soon after birth. It is a kind of smiling that is indiscriminate, undifferentiated, unfocused, and apparently without communicative significance, at least in the mind of the child. It does seem to occur more often when the child has eaten and is ready to sleep and so is probably an expression of the child's satisfaction. Around the fifth week of life, this undifferentiated smiling is replaced by a focused smiling that fixes on specific objects and persons. From this point on, the smile serves numerous and varied communicative functions.

We may smile, for example, to demonstrate nonaggressive intentions as when we step on someone's foot or bump into someone on the street or in a bus. Here we offer a faint smile to indicate that we did not mean anything aggressive in our actions. Obviously, we smile to indicate pleasure and satisfaction. And we seem to do this even when alone; we seem to be telling ourselves that we are pleased and satisfied. We smile to indicate embarrassment or even acceptance of a not-so-favored alternative. A hooker will smile to communicate her intentions to a john; a mother will smile to indicate approval for her child's actions; and a poker player will smile to hide a bluff.

And, of course, the very same smile will vary in meaning from one situation to another. Take, for example, a woman smiling and then place her in such contexts as: (1) a crowded singles bar in New York while talking with her girlfriend but looking at a man at the bar; (2) in a classroom after a professor returns the term papers; (3) at a tennis match after just winning the last point; (4) sitting in a chair all alone in a state mental hospital.

Smiling behavior, of course, does not occur in isolation but rather accompanies a number of other nonverbal gestures as well. The eyes generally change, usually getting wider, the pupils dilate, and the body seems more relaxed and at ease.

A number of persons have investigated the differences in smiling behavior. For example, when approaching strangers women have a tendency to smile more frequently than do men. It has been reported that smiling is most frequent among those living in the Southeast of the United States and those who smile the least live in the Great Lakes area. There are even age differences. Benjamin Spock, for example, claims that older persons smile almost automatically at people they interact with, while the younger generation does not.

Charles Darwin argued that smiling was innate—a universal human expression of pleasure. Contemporary nonverbal researchers such as Paul Ekman have argued this same universality. In his *The Face of Man* Ekman proposes that smiling is taken as a sign of pleasure throughout the world, which would lead us to assume that smiling is an innate reaction to pleasure. Others, such as Ray Birdwhistell and Erving Goffman, for example, believe that smiling and in fact most nonverbal behavior is the result of learning and that great differences exist from one culture to another.

Source: For this box I relied on many of the insights provided by Bernard Feder and Elaine Feder, "Smiles," *Human Behavior* 7 (December 1978): 43–45.

emotions, have a somewhat universal nature. For example, people in Borneo and New Guinea who have had little contact with Western cultures were able to match accurately emotions with pictures of facial expressions. Further, their own facial expressions, posed to communicate various emotions, were later accurately decoded by Americans. Studies such as these seem to point to a universality among some facial gestures. Other researchers, however, point out that gestures are learned and that they vary from one culture to another. It would appear that there are, in fact, wide variations in facial communication but that these variations are not so much in judging the different emotions as in what is permissible and what is not permissible to do in one culture as compared with another. For example, in some cultures it is permissible openly and publicly to show contempt or disgust, but in others people are taught to hide such emotions in public and to display them only in private. It appears that the cultural differences are greatest in terms of what is or is not communicated rather than in what can or cannot be encoded or decoded or in the specific movements that go into expressing the emotions.

A frequently asked question in this regard concerns whether these emotions can really be hidden or whether they somehow manifest themselves below the level of conscious awareness. Is our contempt encoded facially without our being aware of it or even without observers being aware of it? Although we do not have a complete answer to this question, some indication that we do, in fact, communicate these emotions without awareness comes from research on micromomentary expressions. Haggard and Isaacs conducted studies in which they showed films of therapy patients in slow motion. They noted that often the patient's expression would change dramatically. For example, a frown would change to a smile and then quickly back to a frown. If the film was played at normal speed, the change to the smile would go unnoticed. Only when the film was played at slow speed was it apparent that the patient smiled in between frowning. Generally, if a facial expression is of less than two-fifths of a second's duration, the expression goes unnoticed unless it is filmed and then played back at reduced speed. These extremely brief movements are called *micromomentary expressions*, and it has been proposed that these are indicative of an individual's real emotional state and that our conditioning leads us to repress such expressions. A related question would be whether we receive such micromomentary expressions without being aware of it.

EYE MOVEMENTS

From Ben Jonson's poetic observation "Drink to me only with thine eyes, and I will pledge with mine" to the scientific observations of contemporary researchers, the eyes are regarded as the most important nonverbal message system.

The messages communicated by the eyes vary depending on the duration, direction, and quality of the eye behavior. For example, in every culture there are rather strict, though unstated, rules for the appropriate duration for eye contact. When eye contact falls short of this amount, we may think the person is uninterested, shy, or preoccupied, for example. When the appropriate amount of time is exceeded we generally perceive this as indicating unusually high interest. The direction of our eye gazing also communicates. Our cultural norm in communicating with another person is that we glance alternatively at the other person's face, then away, then again at the face, and so on. When these directional norms are broken, different meanings are communicated—perhaps one of abnormally high or low interest, perhaps a self-consciousness, perhaps a nervousness over the interaction, and so on. The quality, how wide or how small our eyes get during the interaction, also communicates meaning—especially, it seems, concerning interest level and such emotions as surprise, fear, and disgust.

Mark Knapp as well as various other researchers note four major functions of eye communication. One is to use the eyes to seek feedback from the other person. In talking with someone, we look at him or her intently, as if to say, "Well, what do you think?" or "React to what I've just said."

A second and related function is to inform the other person that the channel of communication is open and that he or she should now speak. The clearest example of this is seen in the college classroom, where the instructor asks a question and then locks eyes with a student. Without saying anything else it is assumed and presumed that the student should answer the question. Instructors who learn the names of their students do not have to use eye contact to identify student-respondents. But whether names or eyes are used, the function is essentially the same; it is a cue to speak.

A third function is to signal the nature of the relationship between two people, for example, one of positive or negative regard. We may attempt to hide our feelings, and here we would avoid eye contact. We may also signal status relationships with our eyes. This is particularly interesting, because the same movements of the eyes may signal either subordination or superiority. The superior individual, for example, may stare at the subordinate or may glance away. Similarly, the subordinate may look directly at the superior or perhaps to the floor. Power is often signaled by what is called visual dominance behavior. The average speaker maintains a high level of eye contact while listening and a lower level while speaking. When powerful individuals want to signal dominance, they will tend to reverse this "normal" pattern and will maintain a high level of eye contact while talking but a much lower level while listening. Eye movements may also signal whether the relationship between two people is an amorous one, a hostile one, or one of indifference. Because some of the eye movements expressing these different relationships are so similar, we often utilize information from other areas, particularly the face, to decode the message before making any final judgments.

Last, eye movements are often used to compensate for increased physical distance. By making eye contact we overcome psychologically the physical distance between us. When we catch someone's eye at a party, for example, we become psychologically close even though we may be separated by a considerable physical distance. Eye contact and other expressions of psychological closeness, such as self-disclosure and degree of intimacy, have been found to vary in proportion to each other.

In addition to eye movements, considerable research has been done on pupil dilation, or pupillometrics, largely as a result of the impetus given by psychologist Ekhard Hess of the University of Chicago. In the fifteenth and sixteenth centuries in Italy, women used to put drops of belladonna (which literally means "beautiful woman") into their eyes to dilate the pupils so that they would look more attractive. Generally, contemporary research seems to support the logic of these women; dilated pupils are in fact judged to be more attractive than constricted pupils. Pupil size is also indicative of one's interest and level of emotional arousal. One's pupils enlarge when one is interested in something or when one is emotionally aroused. When homosexuals and heterosexuals were shown pictures of nude bodies, the homosexuals' pupils dilated more when viewing same-sex bodies, while the heterosexuals' pupils dilated more when viewing opposite-sex bodies. Perhaps we judge dilated pupils as more attractive because we judge the individual's dilated pupils to be indicative of an interest in us. The dilation of the pupils also seems to vary depending on the degree of agreement one has with political figures. For example, it has been found that when shown slides of Martin Luther King the pupils of black liberals dilated but constricted when shown slides of George Wallace. The pupils of white conservative students responded in the opposite way. More generally, Ekhard Hess has argued —with, it seems, both experimental and intuitive support—that pupils dilate in response to positively evaluated attitudes and objects and constrict in response to negatively evaluated attitudes and objects.

SOURCES

Perhaps the most authoritative source for body communication is Ray L. Birdwhistell's *Kinesics and Context: Essays on Body Motion Communication* (New York: Ballantine Books, 1970). This paperback contains 28 articles by Birdwhistell on body communication plus a most complete bibliography of research and theory in this area. Another interesting source is *Approaches to Semiotics*, edited by Thomas A. Sebeok, Alfred S. Hayes, and Mary Catherine Bateson (The Hague: Mouton, 1964). This volume also contains an excellent study by Weston La-Barre, "Paralinguistics, Kinesics, and Cultural Anthropology," and articles by Alfred S. Hayes and Margaret Mead that are particularly useful for the study of kinesics. The discussion and classification of "types of body movements" is from P. Ekman and W. V. Friesen, "The Repertoire of Nonverbal Behavior: Categories, Origins, Usage, and Coding," *Semiotica* 1 (1969): 49–98. Two works by Albert E. Scheflen will be found both interesting and informative: *Body Language and the Social Order* (Englewood Cliffs, N.J.: Prentice-Hall, 1972) and *How Behavior Means* (Garden City, N.Y.: Anchor Press, 1974). Portions of the discussion of the areas of kinesics were taken from my "Kinesics—Other Codes, Other Channels," *Communication Quarterly* 16 (April 1968): 29–32. Good general introductions include Flora Davis, *Inside Intuition* (New York: New

American Library, 1973), and Gerald Nierenberg and Henry Calero, *How To Read a Person Like a Book* (New York: Pocket Books, 1971).

An interesting study on the nonverbal behavior of assault victims may be found in Betty Grayson and Morris I. Stein, "Attracting Assault: Victims' Nonverbal Cues," *Journal of Communication* 31 (winter 1981): 68–75.

The studies referred to in the discussion of facial and eye communication are as follows: Paul Ekman, Wallace V. Friesen, and Phoebe Ellsworth, *Emotion in the Human Face: Guidelines for Research and an Integration of Findings* (New York: Pergamon Press, 1972), Paul Ekman, W. V. Friesen, and S. S. Tomkins, "Facial Affect Scoring Technique: A First Validity Study," *Semiotica* 3 (1971): 37–58, M. G. Cline, "The Influence of Social Context on the Perception of Faces," *Journal of Personality* 2 (1956): 142–185, E. A. Haggard and K. S. Isaacs, "Micromomentary Facial Expressions as Indicators of Ego Mechanisms in Psychotherapy," in *Methods of Research in Psychotherapy*, ed. L. A. Gottschalk and A. H. Auerbach (Englewood Cliffs, N.J.: Prentice-Hall, 1966). The Ekman, Friesen, and Carlsmith study may be found in *Emotions in the Human Face*.

The discussion of body type is based on the famous and much criticized work of William H. Sheldon. See, for example, *The Varieties of Human Physique* (New York: Harper & Row, 1940), and W. H. Sheldon and S. S. Stevens, *The Varieties of Temperament* (New York: Harper & Row, 1942). The studies referred to on stereotyped images are Richard M. Lerner, "The Development of Stereotyped Expectancies of Body Build Behavior Relations," *Child Development* 40 (1969): 137–141, and J. R. Staffieri, "A Study of Social Stereotype of Body Image in Children," *Journal of Personality and Social Psychology* 7 (1967): 101–104. These are just two of the many examples that could have been cited. The exercise on body type comes from J. B. Cortes and F. M. Gatti, "Physique and Self-Description of Temperament," *Journal of Consulting Psychology* 29 (1965): 408–414.

On eye movements see, for a brief introduction, Ekhard H. Hess, "The Role of Pupil Size in Communication," *Scientific American* 233 (November 1975): 110–112, 116–119. For a more detailed account, see Ekhard H. Hess, *The Tell-Tale Eye* (New York: Van Nostrand Reinhold, 1975). For a discussion of visual dominance behavior, see R. V. Exline, S. L. Ellyson, and B. Long, "Visual Behavior as an Aspect of Power Role Relationships," in P. Pliner, L. Krames, and T. Alloway, eds., *Nonverbal Communication of Aggression* (New York: Plenum, 1975).

In addition to these works, the works of Knapp and Leathers, cited in the previous unit, were very helpful and should prove useful to anyone interested in the areas of body, facial, and eye movements.

Experiential Vehicles

13.1 Instructing Nonverbally

The purpose of this exercise is to heighten your awareness of nonverbal communication, particularly communication with one's body.[1]

In this exercise the class is broken up into groups of five or six. One member from each group leaves the room for approximately a minute. When these subjects are out of the room, each group is given an instruction that they must communicate to the subject, and the nonverbal cue or cues to which they are restricted. All groups, of course, should be given the same instruction and be limited to the same nonverbal cue or cues so that the task will be equally difficult for all groups.

The first group to get the subject to comply with their instruction wins the round and gets 10 points. After the instruction is complied with, the process is repeated, this time with another subject chosen from the group, another instruction, and different nonverbal cue or cues. The exercise is completed when one group wins 50 points, when time is up, or when some other point is reached.

Some sample instructions and types of nonverbal cues follow. Instructors may wish to compile their own list of instructions to be sure they have not been seen by any member of the class.

Sample Instructions

leave the room
give the teacher a pat on the back
shake hands with each member of the group
open (close) all the windows
open (close) the door
bring into the class someone who is not a member of the class
write the time on the board
find a red pen
raise your hand
clap hands
sit on the floor

[1] This exercise was adapted from one developed by my students in interpersonal communication.

put your shoes on the wrong feet
get a drink of water
hold up a notebook with the name of the school on it
comb your hair

Nonverbal Cues

vocal (but nonverbal) cues
hand and arm movements
eye movements (but not head movements)
head movements
the entire body
tactile cues
manipulation of the objects in the room
leg movements (including feet movements)

13.2   Body Type

Instructions

Fill in each blank in statements 1 through 5 with a word from the list of 12 words following it. (A word that fits you exactly may not be in the list, but select the word that seems to fit you most closely.) Then answer question 6.

1. I feel_____, _____, and _____ most of the time.
   calm, anxious, cheerful, contented, relaxed, confident, tense, impetuous, complacent, reticent, energetic, self-conscious
2. When I study or work, I seem to be_____, _____, and _____.
   efficient, enthusiastic, reflective, placid, sluggish, competitive, leisurely, meticulous, precise, determined, thoughtful, cooperative
3. Socially, I am _____, _____, and _____.
   outgoing, affable, tolerant, gentle-tempered, considerate, awkward, affected, soft-tempered, argumentative, shy, talkative, hot-tempered
4. I am rather _____, _____, and _____.
   active, warm, domineering, introspective, forgiving, courageous, suspicious, cool, sympathetic, serious, softhearted, enterprising
5. Other people consider me rather _____, _____, and _____.
   generous, adventurous, withdrawn, dominant, optimistic, affectionate, reckless, detached, sensitive, kind, cautious, dependent
6. Underline the *one* word out of the three in each of the following lines that most closely describes the way you are:
   a. assertive, relaxed, tense
   b. hot-tempered, cool, warm
   c. withdrawn, sociable, active
   d. confident, tactful, kind
   e. dependent, dominant, detached
   f. enterprising, affable, anxious

Do *not* read any further until you have completed all six questions.

The assumption of this test is that people of a particular body type behave in a certain way—a way that is significantly different from the ways people with other body types behave. Three major body types are distinguished: endomorphy, or heavy and generally short; mesomorphy, or muscular; and ectomorphy, or skinny and generally tall. The scoring for this test is done as follows: Match each word that you selected on the test with its corresponding body type, as indicated in the list below. The heading on the list from which the greatest number of words were chosen should indicate the body type of the person who chose them. The tendency toward the other two body types should also be indicated by the number of terms selected from each of the other two lists.

ENDOMORPHY	MESOMORPHY	ECTOMORPHY
affable	active	anxious
affected	adventurous	awkward
affectionate	argumentative	cautious
calm	assertive	considerate
complacent	cheerful	cool
contented	competitive	detached
cooperative	confident	gentle-tempered
dependent	courageous	introspective
forgiving	determined	meticulous
generous	dominant	precise
kind	domineering	reflective
leisurely	efficient	reticent
placid	energetic	self-conscious
relaxed	enterprising	sensitive
sluggish	enthusiastic	serious
sociable	hot-tempered	shy
softhearted	impetuous	suspicious
soft-tempered	optimistic	tactful
sympathetic	outgoing	tense
tolerant	reckless	thoughtful
warm	talkative	withdrawn

Note Carefully

The research on which this test is based has been criticized from a number of different points of view. The purpose of this exercise is not to illustrate that these body types are associated with the various personality characteristics (in very many instances they are not), but rather to demonstrate that we seem to expect people of certain body types to be associated with certain personality characteristics. We seem to expect the thin person to be tense, the fat person to be jolly, and the muscular person to be assertive. Often we are wrong, and yet we do have various expectations. The major purpose of this experiential vehicle is to provide an opportunity for examining our expectations.

It should be added that this test has been based on results obtained largely from heterosexual males. The relationships between body type and personality characteristics for women and for homosexual males may be very different from that postulated here.

Unit 14

Proxemics

PROXEMICS

Proxemic Dimensions
Proxemic Distances
Factors Influencing Proxemic Distance
    14.1 Spatial Relationships and Communication Functions
    14.2 Spatial Relationships and Communication Interactions

LEARNING GOALS

After completing this unit, you should be able to:

1. define *proxemics*
2. define the following: *postural-sex identifiers, sociofugal-sociopetal orientation, kinesthetic factors, touch, vision, thermal factors, smell,* and *loudness* as proxemic dimensions
3. identify and explain the four proxemic distances
4. give examples of the kinds of communications that would take place in each of the four proxemic distances
5. explain at least three functions frequently served by touch communication
6. define *territoriality*
7. given examples of the operation of territoriality from your own experiences
8. identify and explain the operation of at least three factors influencing proxemic distance
9. explain at least five messages that may be communicated by different seating arrangements

Edward T. Hall, in the study he calls "proxemics," has provided much new and significant insight into nonverbal communication by demonstrating how messages from different channels may be analyzed by relating them to the spatial dimensions of communication. More formally, in "A System for the Notation of Proxemic Behavior," Hall has defined *proxemics* as the "study of how man unconsciously structures microspace—the distance between men in the conduct of their daily transactions, the organization of space in his houses and buildings, and ultimately the layout of his towns."

Like verbal behavior, proxemic behavior communicates; space speaks just as surely and just as loudly as do words. Speakers who stand close to their listener, with their hands on the listener's shoulders and their eyes focused directly on those of the listener, clearly communicate something very different from the speaker who sits crouched in a corner with arms folded and eyes to the floor.

Like verbal and kinesic behavior, proxemic behavior is learned without any conscious or direct teaching by the adult community. Children are merely exposed to certain spatial relations, which they internalize unconsciously, much as children seem to acquire the particular codes of speech or body motion.

PROXEMIC DIMENSIONS

The best way to explain proxemics is to present briefly the eight general classes of proxemic behaviors and their more specific categories, as systematized by Hall.

> *Postural-sex identifiers* refer to the posture and sex of the communication source and receiver. Hall has divided this class into six possible categories: man prone, woman prone, man sitting or squatting, woman sitting or squatting, man standing, woman standing.
>
> *Sociofugal-sociopetal orientation,* referring to the physical directness of the communication, specifies the relationship of one person's shoulders to the other person's shoulders. These positions are categorized on a nine-point scale, ranging from face-to-face communication, in which the shoulders of both parties are parallel, through the situation in which the shoulders of the two parties form a straight line, to the situation in which there is back-to-back communication and the shoulders are again parallel. The nine positions are: parallel face-to-face, 45° angle, 90°, 135°, 180°, 225°, 270°, 315°, and parallel back-to-back communication.
>
> *Kinesthetic factors* refer to the closeness of the two persons involved in communication and the potential that exists for the holding, grasping, or

touching of each other. The four major categories are: within body-contact distance, within touching distance with the forearm extended, within touching distance with the arm extended, and within touching distance by reaching. More specific degrees of closeness lying between any two of these four major classes—for example, just outside body-contact distance—might also be recorded.

Touch, referring to the amount and type of physical contact between the two parties, is quantified along a seven-point scale: caressing and holding, caressing and feeling, extended holding, holding, spot touching, brushing or accidental touching, and no contact.

Vision, the extent of visual contact between the two persons, is divided into four categories: sharp, focused looking at the other person's eyes; clear, focused looking at the person's face or head; peripheral, looking at the person in general but not focused on the head; and no visual contact.

Thermal factors, the amount of body heat of one person perceived by the other, are categorized into four types: detection of conducted heat, detection of radiant heat, probable detection of some kind of heat, and no detection of heat.

Loudness, or vocal volume, is described on a seven-point scale: silent, very soft, soft, normal, somewhat above normal, and very loud.

Smell is categorized into five types: detection of differentiated body odor, detection of undifferentiated odor, detection of breath odor, probable detection of some odor, and no detection.

These categories may appear at first to be somewhat rigid or too finely delineated. In analyzing proxemic behavior, however, adjacent categories can be combined to form more general ones or, if additional distinctions are needed, the categories may be further divided. Hall has presented this system as a *tentative* strategy for analyzing proxemic behaviors.

PROXEMIC DISTANCES

One of the earliest references to space as communication occurs in the Gospel according to Luke (14:7–11):

> When thou are invited to a wedding feast, do not recline in the first place, lest perhaps one more distinguished than thou have been invited by him. And he who invited thee and him, come and say to thee, "Make room for this man"; and then thou begin with shame to take the last place. But when thou art invited, go and recline in the last place; that when he who invited thee comes in, he may say to thee, "Friend, go up higher!" Then thou wilt be honored in the presence of all who are at table with thee. For everyone who exalts himself shall be humbled, and he who humbles himself shall be exalted.

This brief passage illustrates one of the concepts or meanings that space communicates—namely, status. We know, for example, that in a large organization, status is the basis for determining how large an office one receives, whether that office has a window or not, how high up the office is (that is, on what floor of the building), and how close one's office is to that of the president or chairperson.

In communication space is especially important, although we seldom think about it or even consider the possibility that it might serve a communicative function. Edward Hall, for example, distinguishes four distances that he claims define the type of relationship permitted. Each of these four distances has a close phase and a far phase, giving us a total of eight clearly identifiable distances. The four distances, corresponding to the four major types of relationships, are: intimate, personal, social, and public (Figure 14.1).

INTIMATE DISTANCE

In *intimate distance*, ranging from the close phase of actual touching to the far phase of 6 to 18 inches, the presence of the other individual is unmistakable. Each individual experiences the sound, smell, and feel of the other's breath. The *close phase* is used for lovemaking and wrestling, for comforting and protecting. In the close phase the muscles and the skin communicate while actual verbalizations play a minor role. In this close phase whispering, says Hall, has the effect of increasing the psychological distance between the two individuals. The *far phase* allows us to touch each other by extending our hands. The distance is so close that it is not considered proper in public, and because of the feeling of inappropriateness and discomfort (at least for Americans) the eyes seldom meet but remain fixed on some remote object.

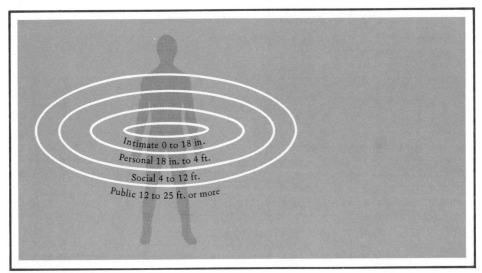

Figure 14.1 Proxemic distances.

213

BOX 14.1
Touch

Touch is perhaps the most primitive form of communication. In terms of sense development, it is probably the first to be utilized; even in the womb the child is stimulated by touch. Soon after birth the child is fondled, caressed, patted, and stroked by the parents and by any other relative who happens to be around. The whole world wants to touch the new infant. Touch becomes for the child a pleasant pastime, and so he or she begins to touch. Everything is picked up, thoroughly fingered, and put into the mouth in an attempt to touch it as closely as possible. The child's favorite toys seem to be tactile ones—cuddly teddy bears, teething rings, and even pieces of blankets. Much in the same way as children touch objects in the environment, they also touch themselves; children play with toes and fingers, nose and lips, and ears and genitals. At some point, children are stopped from picking their noses and playing with their genitals. No reason is given other than the admonition, "Don't do that," or a gentle slap on the hands. As children mature and become sociable, they begin to explore others through touch, though again there are certain parts that are forbidden to touch or have touched by others.

Touching as a form of communication can serve any number of functions. In fact, one would be hard-pressed to name a general function or communication that could not be served by tactile communication. Special note, however, should be made of two major functions normally served by tactile communications.

Perhaps the most obvious is a sexual one. Touch seems to be the primary form of sexual interaction. From fondling one's genitals as a child, to kissing, to fondling another individual, to sexual intercourse, touch plays a primary role. Men shave or grow beards, women shave their legs and underarms, and both use body oils and creams to keep their skin smooth in conscious or subconscious awareness of the powerful role of touch as a form of communication.

Touch also serves a primary role in consoling another individual. For example, we put our arms around people, hold their heads in our hands, hold their hands, or hug them in an attempt to empathize with them more fully. It seems like an attempt to feel what other people are feeling by becoming one with them—perhaps the ideal in empathic understanding. Try to console someone, even in role playing when you are not allowed to touch, and you will see how unnatural it seems and how difficult it is to say the appropriate words.

Touching implies a commitment to the other individual; where and how we touch seems to determine the extent of that commitment. To shake someone's hand, for example, involves a very minor commitment. Our culture has, in effect, defined hand shaking as a minor social affair.

But to caress someone's neck or to kiss someone's mouth implies a commitment of much greater magnitude.

The location, amount, and intensity of tactile communication is also culturally determined, at least in part. For example, southern Europeans will touch each other a great deal more than will northern Europeans or Americans. Women seem to be allowed to touch more and to be touched more than men. For example, it has been shown that women are touched more often than are men by same-sex friends, different-sex friends, mothers, and fathers. This seems true even for infants; girls between 14 and 24 months, for example, are touched more than boys of the same age. Similarly, mothers touch both male and female children more than do fathers, who, in fact, hardly touch more than the hands of their children.

Touching ourselves, of course, also communicates. Lily Tomlin, in her role as Ernestine the telephone operator, touches herself a great deal in an attempt to communicate a certain egocentric personality that, together with the power of the telephone company, can even call on the president and make trouble. In real life we are all familiar with the individual who is constantly fixing his or her hair—to the point where we feel like screaming and perhaps do.

PERSONAL DISTANCE

Each of us, says Hall, carries around with us a protective bubble defining our *personal distance*, which allows us to stay protected and untouched by others. In the *close phase* of personal distance (from 1.5 to 2.5 feet) we can still hold or grasp each other but only by extending our arms. We can then take into our protective bubble certain individuals—for example, loved ones. In the *far phase* (from 2.5 to 4 feet) two people can only touch each other if they both extend their arms. One person can touch the other by extending his or her arms fully to the point where the two people can touch only if both extend their arms. This far phase is the extent to which we can physically get our hands on things, and hence it defines, in one sense, the limits of our physical control over others.

Even at this distance we can see many of the fine details of an individual—the gray hairs, teeth stains, clothing lint, and so on. However, we can no longer detect body heat. At times we may detect breath odor but generally at this distance etiquette demands that we direct our breath to some neutral corner so as not to offend (as the television commercials warn us we might do).

This distance is particularly interesting from the point of view of the body odor and the colognes designed to hide it. At this distance we cannot perceive normal cologne or perfume. Thus it has been proposed that the cologne has two functions: First, it serves to disguise the body odor or hide it; and second, it serves to make clear the limits of the protective bubble around the individual. The bubble, defined by the perfume, simply says, You may not enter to the point where you can smell me.

BOX 14.2
Space, Death, and Violence

Traditionally, spatial relationships are studied in terms of the ways in which different people treat space and its effects on interpersonal and public interactions. Space, however, has implications for much more. We have long known that animals, when placed in crowded environments, will engage in bizarre behavior; they will become aggressive, will attack those they would live with peacefully under uncrowded conditions, will no longer engage in behavior directed at the care and feeding of the young, and so on. Experimental situations like these can hardly be performed on human beings, and yet certain "natural" situations do exist where the effects of space on human beings can be investigated. For example, researchers investigated a prison system and a maximum security psychiatric hospital and measured the death rates for various years. Somewhere between 20,000 and 30,000 people were included in the survey. In the prison system it was found, for inmates 45 years or older, that their death rate was "conservatively two to one higher" during the times when the prisons were crowded. Similarly, blood pressure levels were found to be higher for inmates in three-person and six-person cells, where each inmate's space averaged 19 square feet, than for inmates in two-person cells, where the inmate space averaged 29 square feet. Similar findings were derived from the investigation of the psychiatric hospital.

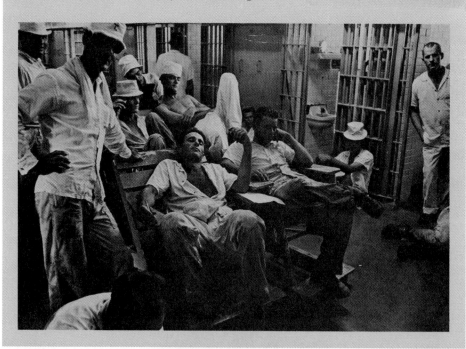

In another study the effects of space violations among violent and nonviolent prison inmates were investigated. Inmates were wired with electrodes to monitor their galvanic skin responses, responses that are taken as measures of their emotional arousal. The subject inmates were approached by a young man who moved slowly toward the inmate first from the front and then from the left, the right, and the back. The young man moved in until the inmate told him to stop. From both the verbal commands and the galvanic skin responses, it was clearly shown that the violent inmates preferred (or had need of) greater distances than the nonviolent inmates. All prisoners were more apprehensive when the young man approached from the rear than when he approached from the front or the sides. Some clinical workers have claimed that violent prisoners can be trained to become less apprehensive over physical closeness, which in turn decreases their violent tendencies.

It seems clear from these and numerous other similar findings that these data should be incorporated into the design and construction of prison and hospital (and even school) facilities. Exactly how this will be done remains to be seen.

Source: The studies cited here are reported in *Human Behavior* 7 (November 1978): 59–60.

When personal space is invaded we often become uncomfortable and tense. When people stand too close to us, our speech may become disrupted, unsteady, jerky, and staccato. We may have difficulty maintaining eye contact and may frequently look away from the person talking with us. This discomfort may also be manifested in excessive body movement. At other times we do not seem to mind the invasion of personal space and in fact would not even define it as invasion. For example, when at a crowded party, others enter our personal space bubble but there is no tension or discomfort; in fact, we seem to enjoy this physical closeness. Similarly, it has been shown that when people we like enter our personal space we perceive the situation as being less crowded than when less liked people enter the very same space. That is, psychologically people we like crowd us less than people we do not like even though physically the situations are identical. It has also been shown that our tolerance for physical closeness depends in part on our learning histories. For example, in one experiment subjects were "interviewed" under crowded conditions three times; in each "interview" the subject's personal space was invaded. In only the first interview, however, did the subject display the tension characteristic of personal space invasion. Apparently the subjects learned to tolerate this type of closeness. Similarly, people living in cultures or working in occupations where crowding is considered "normal" or expected do not seem to display the discomfort that is characteristic of personal space invasions.

BOX 14.3
Territoriality

One of the most interesting concepts in ethology (the study of animals in their natural surroundings) is *territoriality*. For example, male animals will stake out a particular territory and consider it their own. They will allow prospective mates to enter but will defend it against entrance by others, especially other males of the same species. Among deer, for example, the size of the territory signifies the power of the buck, which in turn determines how many females he will mate with. Less powerful bucks will be able to hold on to only small parcels of land and consequently will mate with only one or two females. This is a particularly adaptive measure since it ensures that the stronger members of the society will produce most of the offspring. When the "landowner" takes possession of an area—either because it is vacant or because he gains it through battle—he marks it, for example, by urinating around the boundaries.

These same general patterns are felt by many to be integral parts of human behavior. Some researchers claim that this form of behavior is innate and is a symptom of the innate aggressiveness of humans. Others claim that territoriality is learned behavior and is culturally based. Most, however, seem to agree that a great deal of human behavior can be understood and described as territoriality regardless of its possible origin or development.

If we look around at our homes, we would probably find certain territories that different people have staked out and where invasions are cause for at least mildly defensive action. This is perhaps seen most clearly with siblings who each have (or "own") a specific chair, room, radio, and so on. Father has his chair and mother has her chair. Archie and Edith Bunker always sit in the same chairs, and great uproars occur when Archie's territory is invaded. Similarly, the rooms of the house may be divided among members of the family. The kitchen, traditionally at least, has been the mother's territory. Invasions from other family members may be tolerated but are often not welcomed, and at times they are resisted. Invasions by members not of the immediate family, from a sister-in-law, mother-in-law, or neighbor, for example, are generally resented much more.

In the classroom, where seats are not assigned, territoriality can also be observed. When a student sits in a seat that has normally been occupied by another student, the regular occupant will often become disturbed and resentful and might even say something about it being his or her seat.

Like animals, human beings also mark their territory (though generally not with urine). In a library, for example, you may mark your territory with a jacket or some books when you leave the room. You expect this marker to function to keep others away from your seat and table area. Most of the time it works. When it does not work, there is cause for conflict.

Similarly, mild conflict is seen when an individual takes a seat very close to someone else in a place that is not crowded and where a more distant seat would be possible. We seem to resent this invasion of our privacy, of our territory. In driving a car, tailgating is resented not only because it is dangerous but also, it seems, because it represents an invasion of one's territory; somehow we feel that the area 10 or 15 feet behind us is ours and other cars should not encroach upon it.

The territory of human beings (like that of animals) communicates status in various ways. Clearly the size and location of the territory indicates something about status. A townhouse on Manhattan's East Side, for example, is perhaps the highest-status territory for home living in the country; it is large and at the same time located on the world's most expensive real estate. Status is also signaled by the unwritten law granting the right of invasion. High-status individuals have a right (or at least more of a right) to invade the territory of others than vice versa. The boss of a large company, for example, can invade the territory of a junior executive by barging into her or his office, but the reverse would be unthinkable. Similarly, a teacher may invade the personal space of a student by looking over his or her shoulder as the student writes. But the student cannot do the same in return.

SOCIAL DISTANCE

At the *social distance* we lose the visual detail we had in the personal distance. The *close phase* (from 4 to 7 feet) is the distance at which we conduct impersonal business, the distance at which we interact at a social gathering. The *far phase* (from 7 to 12 feet) is the distance we stand at when someone says, "Stand away so I can look at you." At this level business transactions have a more formal tone than when conducted in the close phase. In offices of high officials the desks are positioned so that the individual is assured of at least this distance when dealing with clients. Unlike the intimate distance, where eye contact is awkward, the far phase of the social distance makes eye contact essential—otherwise communication is lost. The voice is generally louder than normal at this level but shouting or raising the voice has the effect of reducing the social distance to a personal distance. It is at this distance that we can work with people and yet both not constantly interact with them and not appear rude. At certain distances, of course, one cannot ignore the presence of another individual. At other distances, however, we can ignore the other individual and keep to our own business.

This social distance requires that a certain amount of space be available. In many instances, however, such distances are not available; yet it is necessary to keep a social distance, at least psychologically if not physically. For this we attempt different arrangements with the furniture. In small offices in colleges for example, professors sharing an office might have their desks facing in different directions so that each may keep separate from the other. Or they may position their desks against a wall so that each will feel psychologically alone in the office and thus be able to maintain a social rather than a personal distance.

BOX 14.4
Colors

When we are in debt we speak of being "in the red"; when we make a profit we are "in the black." When we are sad we are "blue," when we are healthy we are "in the pink," when we are jealous we are "green with envy," and when we are happy we are "tickled pink." To be a coward is to be "yellow" and to be inexperienced is to be "green." When we talk a great deal we talk "a blue streak," and when we talk to no avail we talk until we are "blue in the face." When we go out on the town we "paint it red," and when we are angry we "see red." Our language, especially as revealed through these time-worn clichés, abounds in color symbolism.

Henry Dreyfuss, in his *Symbol Sourcebook*, reminds us of some of the positive and negative meanings associated with various colors. Some of these are presented in Table B.1. Dreyfuss also notes some cultural comparisons for some of these colors. For example, red in China is a color for joyous and festive occasions, whereas in Japan it is used to signify anger and danger. Blue for the Cherokee Indian signifies defeat, but for the Egyptian it signifies virtue and truth. In the Japanese theater blue is the color

Table B.1   Some Positive and Negative Messages of Colors

Color	Positive Messages	Negative Messages
red	warmth passion life liberty patriotism	death war revolution devil danger
blue	religious feeling devotion truth justice	doubt discouragements
yellow	intuition wisdom divinity	cowardice malevolence impure love
green	nature hope freshness prosperity	envy jealousy opposition disgrace
purple	power royalty love of truth nostalgia	mourning regret penitence resignation

Source: Adapted from Henry Dreyfuss, *Symbol Sourcebook* (New York: McGraw-Hill, 1971).

for villains. Yellow signifies happiness and prosperity in Egypt, but in tenth-century France yellow colored the doors of criminals. Green communicates femininity to certain American Indians, fertility and strength to Egyptians, and youth and energy to Japanese. Purple signifies virtue and faith in Egypt, but grace and nobility in Japan.

In English it has been demonstrated that our connotative meanings for colors vary considerably. In Table B.2 five color terms are presented with their average ratings on evaluation (for example, the good-bad, positive-negative dimension of language), potency (for example, the strong-weak, large-small dimension of language), and activity (for example, the active-passive, fast-slow dimension of language). The numbers are based on a 7-point scale ranging from +3 for the good, strong, and active sides of the scales through 0, which is the neutral position, to −3 for the bad, weak, and passive sides of the scale. As can be seen, red and blue are the most positive in terms of evaluation, and gray is the most negative. Red is the most potent, and gray is the least potent. Red was judged as the most active and gray as the least active.

There is also some scientific evidence that colors affect us physiologically. For example, it has been found that respiratory movements increase with red light and decrease with blue light. Similarly, the frequency of eye blinks increases when eyes are exposed to red light and decrease when exposed to blue light. This seems consistent with our intuitive feelings about blue being more soothing and red being more active and also with the ratings noted in Table B.2. And remember the difficult time that Bette Davis gave everyone in *Jezebel* because she insisted on wearing a red dress to a particularly staid ball. Had she insisted on a white or a blue dress, there would have been less of a problem, and probably even less of a story. In *Gone With the Wind*, Rhett Butler, upon hearing of Scarlett O'Hara's indiscretion with Ashley Wilkes, and knowing that everyone at the upcoming ball would be talking about Scarlett's behavior, makes her wear a red dress—a color symbolic of her supposedly shameless and immoral behavior. Even the name "Scarlett" foretells something of her tem-

Table B.2 Evaluation, Potency, and Activity Ratings for Five Color Terms

	Evaluation	Potency	Activity
yellow	.544	.212	−.637
red	1.256	1.012	−.050
green	.969	.706	−.619
gray	−.200	−.394	−1.362
blue	1.225	.812	−.375

Source: Adapted from James Snider and Charles E. Osgood, eds., "Semantic Atlas for 550 Concepts," in *Semantic Differential Technique: A Sourcebook* (Chicago: Aldine, 1969), pp. 625–636.

perament and her future behavior. And in Nathaniel Hawthorne's *The Scarlet Letter*, Hester Prynne is forced to wear the letter "A" for "adultress," and it is no accident that the "A" is red.

Perhaps the most talked about (but least documented) communicative function of color is its supposed reflection of personality. Faber Birren, in his *Color in Your World*, argues that if you like red, your life is directed outward and you are impulsive, active, aggressive, vigorous, sympathetic, quick to judge people, impatient, optimistic, and strongly driven by sex. If, on the other hand, you dislike red, you also dislike the qualities in those people who like red, such as aggressiveness, optimism, and the like. You feel that others have gotten the better deal in life and you never feel really secure. Sexually, you are unsatisfied.

The messages that colors communicate about a culture are easily determined, while the personality traits that colors supposedly reveal are quite difficult and perhaps impossible to determine. As is true of so many aspects of nonverbal communication, we should be particularly cautious in drawing conclusions about people on the basis of their preferences for different colors.

PUBLIC DISTANCE

In the *close phase* of *public distance* (from 12 to 15 feet) an individual seems protected by space. At this distance one is able to take defensive action should one be threatened. On a public bus or train, for example, we might keep at least this distance from a drunkard so that should anything come up (literally or figuratively) we could get away in time. Although at this distance we lose any fine details of the face and eyes, we are still close enough to see what is happening should we need to take defensive action.

At the *far phase* (more than 25 feet) we see individuals not as separate individuals but as part of the whole setting. We automatically set approximately 30 feet around public figures who are of considerable importance, and we seem to do this whether or not there are guards preventing us from entering this distance. This far phase is of course the distance from which actors perform on stage; consequently, their actions and voice have to be somewhat exaggerated.

FACTORS INFLUENCING PROXEMIC DISTANCE

There are numerous variables that have been demonstrated to have a significant effect on our treatment of space in communication situations. And although not all research findings are in agreement, a few generalizations seem warranted. One of the most obvious factors influencing our treatment of space is that of the status of the individuals. People of equal status will generally maintain a closer distance between themselves than will people of unequal status. As noted in the discussion of territoriality, when the status is unequal, the higher-status person may approach the lower-status person more closely than the lower-status may approach the higher-status person. This is similar to the situation in which the higher-status person may invade the territory of the lower-status person but not vice versa.

There are a number of cultural differences as well. Americans generally stand fairly far apart when conversing, at least when compared with certain European and Middle Eastern cultures. Arabs, for example, will stand much closer to each other than will Americans. Italians and Spaniards will likewise maintain less distance in their interactions than will many northern Europeans. At times these space differences create intercultural difficulties. One group may be perceived as cold and psychologically distant, whereas another group may be perceived as pushy and too forward, all because of their differential treatment of space. As might be expected, the cultures that keep substantial distances between themselves also engage in relatively little interpersonal touching.

The physical context also influences the space we maintain between us. Generally, the larger the physical space we are in, the smaller the interpersonal space. Thus, for example, the space between two people conversing will be smaller if those people are in the street than if they are in an apartment. The space will be smaller if they are in a large room than if they are in a smaller room. The larger the space, the more we seem to have a need to close it off and make the immediate communication context manageable.

The purpose or subject matter of the communication will also influence the amount of space we employ. For example, if we talk about personal matters or share secrets, we maintain a close distance; when we talk about impersonal general matters, the space is generally larger. Psychologically, it seems we are attempting to exclude others from hearing even though physically there may be no one within earshot. We maintain a closer distance if we are being praised than if we are being blamed. It would seem that we want to move in closer to the praise lest it fall on someone else and that we want to remove ourselves (physically) from the blame. Our proxemic behavior seems to reflect this quite clearly.

There are a number of studies that have pointed out sex and age differences. Generally, it seems that women stand closer to one another than do men. Opposite sex pairs seem to stand the farthest apart. Similarly, women are allowed to touch each other more than men are and more than unacquainted opposite-sex pairs. Children generally stand closer to each other than do adults, indicating that the distances we maintain are learned rather than innately or biologically determined.

We stand farther apart from enemies than from friends, from authority figures and higher-status persons than from peers, from those who are physically handicapped than from the nonhandicapped, and from those of a different racial group than from our own.

We maintain more distance between ourselves and people we may subconciously evaluate negatively. For example, in one study students were interviewed by persons supposedly working on theses. Some of these "interviewers" wore "Gay and Proud" buttons and mentioned that they were members of the Association of Gay Psychologists. The other half wore no such buttons and mentioned no such association. Without the student's knowledge, measures were taken of the distance they placed their chair from the "interviewer." When the interviewer was of the same sex, the students established almost a foot more distance between themselves and the gay interviewer, even though the students verbally expressed tolerant and generally favorable attitudes toward gay people.

SOURCES

For spatial communication the work of Edward T. Hall is perhaps the most well known and the most insightful. The discussion of proxemic dimensions comes from his "A System for the Notation of Proxemic Behavior," *American Anthropologist* 65 (1963): 1003–1026. The discussion of proxemic distances comes from his *The Hidden Dimension* (New York: Doubleday, 1966). Hall's first popular work on spatial communication and perhaps still one of the most famous is *The Silent Language* (New York: Doubleday, 1959). Robert Sommer also deals with spatial communication but from a somewhat different point of view. Particularly interesting are his *Personal Space: The Behavioral Basis of Design* (Englewood Cliffs, N.J.: Prentice-Hall, 1969); *Design Awareness* (San Francisco: Rinehart Press, 1972); and *Tight Spaces: Hard Architecture and How to Humanize It* (Englewood Cliffs, N.J.: Prentice-Hall, 1974). The Experiential Vehicles on seating positions (14.1 and 14.2) are based on the work of Sommer summarized in *Personal Space*.

For body touching, see Ashley Montague, *Touching: The Human Significance of the skin* (New York: Harper & Row, 1971). For Jourard's studies on touching, see Sidney M. Jourard, *Disclosing Man to Himself* (New York: Van Nostrand Reinhold, 1968), and *Self-Disclosure* (New York: Wiley, 1971). Marc Hollender and Alexander Mercer conducted the study on holding, discussed in "Wish to Be Held and Wish to Hold in Men and Women," *Archives of General Psychiatry* 33 (January 1976): 49–51. On the role of touching in status and power relationships, see Nancy M. Henley, *Body Politics: Power, Sex, and Nonverbal Communication* (Englewood Cliffs, N.J.: Prentice-Hall, 1977).

The study on spatial relationships with homosexual interviewers was conducted by Stephen Morin et al., "Gay Is Beautiful—at a Distance," paper presented to the American Psychological Association (Chicago, 1975), and is reported in Mark Snyder, "The Many Me's of the Self Monitor," *Psychology Today* 13 (March 1980): 33–40, 92. On crowding, see Paul M. Insel and Henry Clay Lindgren, *Too Close for Comfort: The Psychology of Crowding Behavior* (Englewood Cliffs, N.J.: Prentice-Hall, 1978) and "Too Close for Comfort: When One Person's Company Is Another's Crowd," *Psychology Today* 10 (December 1977): 98–106. *The Lüscher Color Test*, I. A. Scott, ed. and trans. (New York: Pocket Books, 1971), and Faber Birren, *Color in Your World* (New York: Collier Books, 1962), are interesting attempts to relate color and personality and are useful for raising rather than answering questions.

Experiential
Vehicles

14.1   Spatial Relationships and Communication Functions[1]

Below are presented diagrams of tables and chairs. Imagine that the situation is the school cafeteria and that each is the only table not occupied. For each of the eight diagrams, place an X where you and a friend of the same sex would seat yourselves for each of the four conditions noted.

1. Conversing, to talk for a few minutes before class

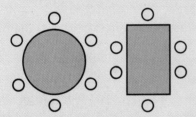

2. Cooperating to study together for the same exam or to work out a math problem

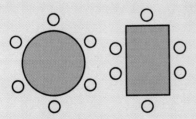

---

[1] This exercise and the one following are based on studies conducted by Robert Sommer and reported in *Personal Space: The Behavioral Basis of Design* (Englewood Cliffs, N.J.: Prentice-Hall, 1969).

3. Co-acting to study for different exams

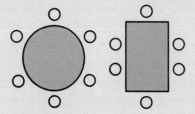

4. Competing against each other in order to see who would be the first to solve a series of puzzles

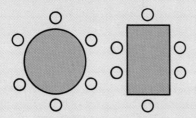

For Discussion

1. Why did you select the positions you did?
2. Explain the differences in opportunity for nonverbal interaction that the different positions allow.
3. How do these different positions relate to verbal communication?
4. Would you have chosen the same positions if the other person were of the opposite sex? Explain.
5. Compare your responses with the responses of others. How do you account for the differences in seating preferences?
6. Are there significant differences in choices between the round and the rectangular tables? Explain.

14.2   Spatial Relationships and Communication Interactions

Below are presented diagrams of tables and chairs. Imagine that the situation is the school cafeteria and that this is the only table not occupied. In the space marked X is seated the person described above the diagram. Indicate by placing an X in the appropriate circle where you would sit.

1. A young man/woman to whom you are physically attracted and whom you would like to date but to whom you have never spoken

2. A person whom you find physically unattractive and to whom you have never spoken

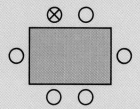

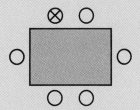

3. A person you dated once and had a miserable time with and whom you would never date again

4. A person you have dated a few times and would like to date again

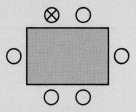

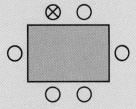

5. An instructor who gave you an "F" in a course last semester (which you did not deserve) and whom you dislike intensely

6. Your favorite instructor, whom you would like to get to know better

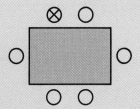

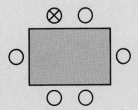

For Discussion

1. Why did you select the positions you did? For example, how does the position you selected enable you to achieve your purpose better?
2. Assume that you were already seated in the position marked X. Do you think that the person described would sit where you indicated you would (assuming the feelings and motives are generally the same)? Why? Are there significant sex differences? Significant status differences? Explain.
3. What does the position you selected communicate to the person already seated? In what ways might this nonverbal message be misinterpreted? How would your subsequent nonverbal (and perhaps verbal) behavior reinforce your intended message? That is, what would you do to ensure that the message you intend to communicate is in fact the message communicated and received?

Unit 15

Paralanguage and Silence

PARALANGUAGE AND SILENCE

LEARNING GOALS

After completing this unit, you should be able to:

1. define *paralanguage*
2. identify three or four major classes of paralinguistic phenomena
3. explain at least three messages that variations in paralinguistic phenomena might communicate
4. identify at least three functions of silence
5. explain some of the cross-cultural differences regarding silence

An old exercise to increase the student's ability to express different emotions, feelings, and attitudes was to have the student say the following sentences while accenting or stressing different words: "Is this the face that launched a thousand ships?" Significant differences in meaning are easily communicated depending on where the stress is placed. Consider, for example, the following variations:

1. IS this the face that launched a thousand ships?
2. Is THIS the face that launched a thousand ships?
3. Is this the FACE that launched a thousand ships?
4. Is this the face that LAUNCHED a thousand ships?
5. Is this the face that launched a THOUSAND SHIPS?

PARALANGUAGE

Each of the five sentences communicates something different. Each, in fact, asks a totally different question even though the words used are identical. All that distinguishes the sentences is stress, one of the aspects of what is called *paralanguage*. Paralanguage may be defined as the vocal (but nonverbal) dimension of speech. It refers to the manner in which something is said rather than to what is said.

THE STRUCTURE OF PARALANGUAGE

An outline of a classification offered by George L. Trager is presented in Table 15.1. More important than the specifics of this table is that paralanguage encompasses a great deal of vocal expression and can be classified and analyzed rather precisely for various different purposes. Although in outline form the breakdown of paralinguistic phenomena is as shown, the four major classes are: *voice qualities, vocal characterizers, vocal qualifiers,* and *vocal segregates.*

If we assume the validity of the proposition that nothing never happens, that all behavior serves a communicative function, then we must further assume that each of these paralinguistic features also communicates meaning. Thus the speaker who speaks quickly communicates something different from the one who speaks slowly. Even though the words might be the same, if the speed differs, the meaning we receive will also differ. And we may derive different meanings from "fast talk" depending on the speaker. Perhaps in one person we might perceive fear, feeling that he or she is hurrying to get the statement over with. In another we might perceive annoyance or lack of concern, inferring that he or she speaks rapidly so that not too much time is wasted. In still another we might

Table 15.1   Paralanguage: A Classification

I. Voice Qualities
  A. Pitch Range
      1. Spread
          a. Upward
          b. Downward
      2. Narrowed
          a. From above
          b. From below
  B. Vocal Lip Control
      1. Rasp
      2. Openness
  C. Glottis Control
      1. Sharp transitions
      2. Smooth transitions
  D. Pitch Control
  E. Articulation Control
      1. Forceful (precise)
      2. Relaxed (slurred)
  F. Rhythm Control
      1. Smooth
      2. Jerky
  G. Resonance
      1. Resonant
      2. Thin
  H. Tempo
      1. Increased from norm
      2. Decreased from norm

II. Vocalizations
  A. Vocal Characterizers
      1. Laughing/crying
      2. Yelling/whispering
      3. Moaning/groaning
      4. Whining/breaking

      5. Belching/yawning
  B. Vocal Qualifiers
      1. Intensity
          a. Overloud
              1. somewhat
              2. considerably
              3. very much
          b. Oversoft
              1. somewhat
              2. considerably
              3. very much
      2. Pitch Height
          a. Overhigh
              1. slightly
              2. appreciably
              3. greatly
          b. Overflow
              1. slightly
              2. appreciably
              3. greatly
      3. Extent
          a. Drawl
              1. slight
              2. noticeable
              3. extreme
          b. Clipping
              1. slight
              2. noticeable
              3. extreme
  C. Vocal Segregates
      1. Uh-uh
      2. Uh-huh
      3. Sh
      4. (Pause)

Source: George L. Trager, "Paralanguage: A First Approximation," *Studies in Linguistics* 13 (1958): 1–12; George L. Trager, "The Typology of Paralanguage," *Anthropological Linguistics* 3 (1961): 17–21; and Robert E. Pittenger and Henry Smith, Jr., "A Basis for Some Contributions of Linguistics to Psychiatry," *Psychiatry* 20 (1957): 61–78.

perceive extreme interest, feeling that the person is speaking quickly so that he or she can get to the punch line and hear our reaction.

JUDGMENTS BASED ON PARALANGUAGE

From the various paralinguistic cues, often combined with other information that we have about the situation and from other nonverbal and verbal cues, we make a variety of judgments. Most important among these judgments are judgments about people and judgments about conversational turns.

Judgments About People

We are a diagnostically oriented people, quick to make judgments about another's personality based on various paralinguistic cues. At times our judgments turn out to be correct, at other times incorrect. But the number of times correct and incorrect does not seem to influence the frequency with which we make such judgments. We may, for example, conclude that speakers who speak so softly that we can hardly hear them seem to have some kind of problem. Perhaps they feel inferior—they "know" that no one really wants to listen, "know" that nothing they say is significant, and so speak softly. Other speakers will speak at an extremely loud volume, perhaps because of an overinflated ego and the belief that everyone in the world wants to hear them, that what they have to say is so valuable that they cannot risk our not hearing every word. Speakers who speak with no variation, in a complete monotone, seem uninterested in what they are saying and seem to encourage a similar disinterest from the listeners—if any are still around. We might perceive such people as having a lack of interest in life in general, as being rather bland individuals. All of these conclusions are, at best, based on little evidence. Yet this does not stop us from making such conclusions.

It is important for us to inquire into the relationship between paralanguage and impression formation. It does seem that certain voices are symptomatic of certain personality types, of certain problems, and specifically that the personality orientation leads to the vocal qualities. When listening to people speak—regardless of what they are saying—we form impressions based on their paralanguage as to what kind of people they are. Our impressions seem to consist of physical impressions (about body type perhaps and certainly about sex and age), personality impressions (they seem outgoing, they sound shy, they appear aggressive), and evaluative impressions (they sound like good people, they sound evil and menacing, they sound lovable, they have vicious laughs).

Much research has been directed to the question of the accuracy of these judgments—that is, how accurately may we judge a person on the basis of voice alone. One of the earliest studies on this question was conducted by T. H. Pear. Pear used nine speakers and had over 4000 listeners make guesses about these nine speakers. The sex and age of the speaker appeared to be guessed with considerable accuracy. However, the listeners were only able to guess accurately the occupations of the clergymen and the actor.

Other studies, perhaps taking their cue from Pear, pursued the relationship between vocal characteristics and personal characteristics. Most studies suggest, in agreement with Pear, that sex and age can be guessed accurately on the basis of the voice alone. This is not to say that complete accuracy is possible with age, but it does seem possible to guess age within relatively small ranges.

Among the most interesting findings on voice and personal characteristics is one showing that listeners can accurately judge the status (whether high, middle, or low) of speakers from hearing a 60-second voice sample. In fact, many listeners reported that they made their judgments in less than 15 seconds. It has also been found that the speakers judged to be of high status were rated as being of higher credibility than those speakers rated middle and low in status.

There is much greater agreement in the literature when we consider the question of identifying the emotional states of listeners from their vocal expression. Generally, in these studies the content of the speech is nonexistent or is held constant. Thus in a content-free situation the speaker would attempt to communicate anxiety, for example, by saying the alphabet or perhaps by reciting numbers. In the situation where the content is held constant, the speakers say the same sentences (generally rather unemotional ones) for all the emotions they are to communicate.

It has been found that speakers can communicate or encode emotions through content-free speech or through content that is unrelated to the emotions, and listeners are able to decode these emotions. A typical study would involve speakers using numbers to communicate different emotions. Listeners would have to select the emotions being communicated from a list of 10 emotions that they were given. In situations like this listeners are generally effective in guessing the emotions.

Listeners vary in their ability to decode the emotions, speakers vary in their ability to encode the emotions, and the accuracy with which emotions are guessed depends on the emotions themselves. For example, while it may be easy to distinguish between hate and sympathy, it may not be so easy to distinguish between fear and anxiety. This type of study is used as the basis for the exercise at the end of this unit.

Judgments About Conversational Turns

Paralinguistic cues are widely used to signal conversational turns, the changing (or maintaining) of the speaker or listener role during the conversation. Perhaps the most obvious way in which paralinguistic cues are used in conversational turns is when the speaker uses them to maintain his or her speaking position. Thus, the speaker may in the course of conversation pause while vocalizing -em, -er, and the like. These vocalized pauses are insurance that no one else will jump in and take over the role of speaker; they announce to others in the conversation that this speaker is not finished but has more to say. In a somewhat more oblique way we may also note that paralinguistic cues are used to maintain one's role as listener. This would take the form of vocalizing some reinforcing or approving type of sound while someone else is talking. This kind of positive feedback in effect tells the speaker to keep on going, to say more, and, perhaps most important, that this listener approves of what is being said.

One of the most important conversational functions paralinguistic cues serve is to announce to the others in the conversation that the speaker has finished and that it is now someone else's turn to speak. So, for example, the speaker may at the end of a statement add some paralinguistic cue such as *eh?*, which asks the others in the conversation to speak now. But notice that such paralinguistic cues do not give the new speaker carte blanche but relinquish the speaker's position to another one with specific stipulations. Thus, the speaker who says, "Schmedly gave me the F unfairly, eh?" is actually making three statements with this simple *eh?* First, the speaker is asking the other person to speak. Second, the speaker is asking that the other person speak specifically to the topic of the F grade. And third, the speaker is asking the new speaker to agree that the F was unfair. Of course, not all paralinguistic invitations to speak ask that the listener speak so specifically. Often, speakers will indicate that they have finished speaking by dropping their intonation or by a prolonged silence or by asking some general type of question. In these cases, the new speaker has considerably more freedom.

Still another function of paralinguistic cues is to indicate to the speaker that a listener would like to say something, that the listener would like to take his or her turn as speaker. Sometimes listeners do this by simply saying, "I would like to say something," but often it is done paralinguistically by uttering some vocalized *-er* or *-um* that tells the speaker (at least the sensitive speaker) that someone else would now like to speak. (These vocalizations are in many instances indistinguishable from those the speaker uses to maintain the speaking position.) This request to speak is also often done with facial and mouth gestures. Frequently, a listener will indicate a desire to speak by opening his or her eyes and mouth wide as if to say something or just begin to gesture with a hand.

SILENCE

Don Fabun noted that "the world of silence may be a cold and bitter one; like the deep wastes of the Arctic regions, it is fit for neither man nor beast. Holding one's tongue may be prudent, but it is an act of rejection; silence builds walls — and walls are the symbols of failure." Thomas Mann, in one of the most-often quoted observations on silence, said, "Speech is civilization itself. The word, even the most contradictory word, preserves contact; it is silence which isolates." On the other hand, the philosopher Karl Jaspers observed that "the ultimate in thinking as in communication is silence," and Max Picard noted that "silence is nothing merely negative; it is not the mere absence of speech. It is a positive, a complete world in itself."

All of these are rather extreme statements on the nature and function of silence. Actually, I think all are correct—for some occasions, for some people, and for some times. The one thing on which all observations are clearly in agreement, and that needs to be stressed here, is that silence communicates. As we have seen, one of the universals of nonverbal behaviors is that they always communicate, and this is no less true of silence. Our silence communicates just as surely and just as intensely as anything we might verbalize.

Perhaps the best way to approach silence is to consider some of the functions it might serve or the meanings it may communicate. One of the most frequent functions of silence is to allow the speaker time to think. In some cases, the silence allows the speaker the opportunity to integrate previous communications in order to make the necessary connections before the verbal communications may logically continue. In other instances it gives the speaker or the listener time for the previous messages to sink in; here it is often used to the same effect as the paralinguistic pause—as a kind of emphasis. This is seen most clearly after someone makes what he or she thinks is a profound statement, almost as if to proclaim that this message should not be contaminated by other, less significant, and less insightful messages. At still other times the silence allows the individual to think of his or her future messages. Lecturers will often remain silent for short periods—though they might seem inordinately long to the lecturer as well as to the listeners — in order to think of what is to come next or perhaps to recall some fact or reference. In many instances people remain silent in order to prepare themselves for the intense communications that are to follow. It is rather like the calm before the storm. Before messages of intense conflict, as well as before messages confessing undying love, there is often silence. Again, the silence seems to prepare the receiver for the importance of the future messages.

Some people use silence to hurt others. Silence is used as a weapon, and we often speak of giving someone "the silent treatment." After a conflict, for example, one or both individuals might remain silent as a kind of punishment. Children often imitate their parents in this and refuse to talk to playmates when they are angry with them. Silence to hurt others may also take the form of refusing to acknowledge the presence of another person; here silence is a dramatic demonstration of the total indifference one person feels toward the other. It is a refusal to recognize the person as a person, a refusal to treat him or her any differently than one would treat an inanimate object. Such silence is most often accompanied by blank stares into space, a preoccupation with a magazine or some manual task, or perhaps by feigning resting or sleeping. Here the nonverbal movements reinforce silence as a refusal to acknowledge the individual as a person.

Sometimes silence is used as a response to personal anxiety, shyness, or threats. One might feel anxious or shy among new people and prefer to remain silent. By remaining silent the individual precludes the chance of rejection. It is only when the silence is broken and an attempt to communicate with another person is made that one risks rejection. At other times the silence may be a kind of flight response made to threats by another individual or group of individuals. A street gang that makes remarks as one passes is one example. By remaining silent, by refusing to engage in verbal combat, we attempt to remove ourselves psychologically from the situation.

Silence may be used to prevent the verbal communication of certain messages. For example, in conflict situations silence is sometimes used to prevent certain topics from surfacing and to prevent one or both parties from sticking their proverbial feet into their proverbial big mouths. We made the point earlier that verbal expressions can never be reversed; once said, something cannot be unsaid. In conflict situations silence often allows us time to cool off before uttering expressions of hatred, severe criticism, or personal attacks, and here it serves us to good advantage.

Like the eyes or face or hands, silence can also be used to communicate varied emotional responses. Sometimes silence communicates one's determination to be uncooperative or one's defiance; by refusing to engage in verbal communication we defy the authority or the legitimacy of the other person's position. In many religious ceremonies reverence is signaled by silence. Often the congregation remains silent throughout a religious ritual or verbalizes only responses. Silence is often used to communicate annoyance, usually coupled with a pouting expression, arms crossed in front of the chest, and nostrils flared. In some of these situations silence is used because talk is perceived as superfluous or perhaps as less effective.

Of course, silence is often used when there is simply nothing to say, when nothing occurs to one to say, or when one does not want to say anything. James

In pleasant situations, silence might be used to express affection or love, especially when coupled with long and loving stares into each other's eyes.

Russell Lowell expressed this best, I think: "Blessed are they who have nothing to say, and who cannot be persuaded to say it." Few would probably want to argue with Lowell. Yet, it is not very easy to determine exactly when there is nothing to say. For a radio commentator or announcer to have nothing to say and to remain silent would be unthinkable. Radio, and to only a somewhat lesser extent television, cannot afford to remain silent for anything but the shortest pause: air time is just too expensive. Also, silence on radio or television is so unexpected and seems so out of place that listeners would become annoyed and would probably change the station.

Silence also proves troublesome at parties, where it is taken as a sure sign of failure and even the most banal chatter would be a welcomed alternative. When meeting someone for the first time, when visiting someone at a hospital, or when attending a funeral, silence becomes particularly awkward and speaking particularly difficult. We know we should say something but just then can think of nothing. Even "weather talk" would be welcomed.

The communicative functions of silence in these situations are not universal. The Apache, for example, regard silence very differently. Among the Apache mutual friends will not feel the need to introduce strangers who may be working in the same area or on the same project. The strangers may remain silent for several days. During this time they are looking each other over, attempting to determine if the other person is all right. Only after this period would the individuals talk. During the courting period, especially during the initial stages, Apache individuals remain silent for hours; if they do talk, they generally talk very little. It is only after a couple has been dating for several months that they will have lengthy conversations. These periods of silence by the men are generally attributed to shyness or self-consciousness. The use of silence is explicitly taught to the women, and they are especially discouraged from engaging in long discussions with their dates. Silence during courtship is to many Apache a sign of modesty. When a young woman speaks a great deal, she is thought to be betraying prior experience with men, and in some cases it is seen as a sign of the woman's willingness to engage in sexual relations.

Perhaps the major implication of the study of both paralanguage and silence is that the way in which something is said (or not said) and the silence that accompanies (or does not accompany) any interaction are significant message factors that communicate meaning just as surely as do words and sentences, smiles and frowns.

SOURCES

For a classification and introduction to paralinguistic phenomena, see George L. Trager's "Paralanguage: A First Approximation," *Studies in Linguistics* 13 (1958): 1–12, and "The Typology of Paralanguage," *Anthropological Linguistics* 3 (1961): 17–21. Mark Knapp's *Nonverbal Behavior in Human Interaction*, 2d ed. (New York: Holt, 1978) provides an excellent summary of research findings, as does Dale Leathers' *Nonverbal Communication Systems* (Boston: Allyn & Bacon, 1976). George F. Mahl and Gene Schulze likewise provide a thorough summary of the research and theory in this area. See their "Psychological Research in the Extralinguistic Area," in T. A. Seboek, A. S. Hayes, and M. C. Bateson, eds., *Approaches to Semiotics* (The Hague: Mouton, 1964). For a collection of research studies on paralanguage see Joel R. Davitz, ed., *The Communication of Emotional Meaning* (New York: McGraw-Hill, 1964). For the study by T. H. Pear, see his *Voice and Personality* (London: Chapman and Hall, 1931). For a thorough review of paralanguage see (in addition to the Mahl and Schulze and Knapp) Ernest Kramer, "Judgment of Personal Characteristics and Emotions from Nonverbal Properties," *Psychological Bulletin* 60 (1963), and Albert Mehrabian, *Silent Messages* (Belmont, Cal.: Wadsworth, 1971). On silence, see Max Picard, *The World of Silence* (Chicago: Gateway, 1952) for a philosophical perspective, and Irving J. Lee, "When to 'Keep Still,'" in Joseph A. DeVito, ed., *Language: Concepts and Processes* (Englewood Cliffs, N.J.: Prentice-Hall, 1973), for a communications perspective. On silence among the Apache, see K. H. Basso, "'To Give up on Words': Silence in Western Apache Culture," in Pier Paolo Giglioli, ed., *Language and Social Context* (Baltimore: Penguin Books, 1972). On the need for research in the area of silence see Richard L. Johannesen, "The Functions of Silence: A Plea for Communication Research," *Western Speech* 38 (1974): 25–34. Thomas J. Bruneau, in his "Communicative Silences: Forms and Functions,"

Journal of Communication 23 (March 1973): 17–46 provides a thorough treatment of silence as communication. On the use of silence as a political strategy see Barry Brummett, "Towards a Theory of Silence as a Political Strategy," *Quarterly Journal of Speech* 66 (October 1980): 289–303. Jim Crocker provides useful experiences to teach the various functions and forms of silence in his "Nine Instructional Exercises to Teach Silence," *Communication Education* 29 (January 1980): 72–77.

Experiential Vehicles

15.1 Paralanguage Communication[1]

In this exercise a subject recites the alphabet, attempting to communicate each of the following emotions:

anger
fear
happiness
jealousy
love
nervousness
pride
sadness
satisfaction
sympathy

The subject may begin the alphabet at any point and may omit and repeat sounds, but the subject may use only the names of the letters of the alphabet to communicate these feelings.

The subject should first number the emotions in random order so that he or she will have a set order to follow that is not known to the audience, whose task it will be to guess the emotions expressed.

As a variation, have the subject go through the entire list of emotions, once facing the audience and employing any nonverbal signals desired and once with his or her back to the audience without employing any additional signals. Are there differences in the number of correct guesses, depending on which method is used?

For Discussion and Response

1. What are some of the differences between encoding-decoding "emotional meaning" and "logical meaning"?
2. Davitz and Davitz found the number of correct identifications for these emo-

---

[1] This exercise is based on J. R. Davitz and L. J. Davitz, "The Communication of Feelings by Content-Free Speech," *Journal of Communication* 9 (1959): 6–13.

tions to be as follows: anger (156), nervousness (130), sadness (118), happiness (104), sympathy (93), satisfaction (75), love (60), fear (60), jealousy (69), and pride (50). Do these figures correspond to those obtained in class? What conclusions would you draw relevant to the relative ease-difficulty of expressing the several emotions?

3. Do you think there is a positive relationship between encoding and decoding abilities in situations such as this? Is the person adept at encoding the emotions also adept at decoding them? Explain.
4. What variables might influence encoding ability? Decoding ability?
5. What personality factors seem relevant to the encoding and decoding of emotions?

15.2   Communication Maze

Twenty communication terms are hidden in this communication maze. The terms may read forward, backward, up, down, or diagonally but are always in a straight line. The terms may overlap, and individual letters may be used more than once. The terms are those used in these first 15 units. The definitions of the terms follow.

1. sublanguage of an underworld or criminal class
2. confidence in the existence or truth of something
3. self
4. spatial behavior
5. distortion present in all communication systems
6. credibility or believability
7. knowledge of a language or communication system
8. to extract a message from a code
9. the feeling of another person's feeling
10. the moral dimension of communication and behavior
11. information that tells the source how the message is being received
12. the study of face and body movements
13. the conversational language of a group that is understood only by members of the group
14. overused expression
15. the argot, cant, and jargon of various subcultures that is known by the general public
16. a set of symbols used to translate a message from one form to another
17. the degree of predictability of a message
18. unfair treatment of one of the sexes, usually referring to women
19. faith in the behavior of another person
20. forbidden, culturally censored

MAZE

```
C   A   N   T   R   U   S   T   R   R   S   S

O   R   N   Y   H   T   A   P   M   E   C   A

M   G   S   L   A   N   G   O   X   D   I   X

P   O   C   S   B   K   O   I   H   U   M   P

E   T   I   O   O   B   S   P   K   N   E   H

T   L   S   H   A   M   O   N   C   D   X   I

E   O   E   T   H   I   C   S   A   A   O   F

N   E   N   E   Y   M   E   E   B   N   R   E

C   L   I   C   H   E   S   L   D   C   P   I

E   M   K   O   K   V   I   I   E   Y   S   L

O   V   A   D   E   C   O   D   E   O   G   E

L   T   H   E   E   F   N   O   F   E   X   B
```

Part Five

Interpersonal Communication

Unit 16

Preliminaries to Interpersonal Communication

PRELIMINARIES TO INTERPERSONAL COMMUNICATION

The Purposes of Interpersonal Communication
Effectiveness in Interpersonal Communication
16.1 Me and You: Communicating Interpersonally

LEARNING GOALS

After completing this unit, you should be able to:

1. cite examples of interpersonal communication from your own experiences and observations
2. define *interpersonal communication*
3. explain at least three purposes of interpersonal communication
4. define *empathy* and distinguish it from sympathy
5. define *equality* as it relates to interpersonal communication
6. define *openness* and identify the three aspects of interpersonal communication to which it refers
7. define *supportiveness*
8. explain the role of description, problem orientation, and provisionalism in generating supportiveness
9. define *positiveness* and explain the three aspects of interpersonal communication to which it refers
10. identify the presence of empathy, equality, openness, supportiveness, and positiveness in interpersonal interactions

Interpersonal communication may be defined by noting its major components. Here we would define interpersonal communication as the sending of messages by one person and the receiving of messages by another person, or small group of persons, with some effect and with some opportunity for immediate feedback. These components have already been explained in Unit 1, "Preliminaries to Communication." Another approach to defining interpersonal communication is a developmental one. Here we define interpersonal communication as a kind of progression (or development) from impersonal communication at one extreme to personal communication at the other extreme. This progression from impersonal to personal signals or defines the development of interpersonal communication. I here follow communicologist Gerald Miller's thoughtful analysis.

In the developmental approach communications are viewed as existing on a continuum ranging from impersonal at one end to increasingly interpersonal or intimate at the other end. Interpersonal communication is characterized by, and distinguished from, impersonal communication on the basis of at least three factors. First, interpersonal interactions are characterized by the participants' basing their predictions about each other not on the basis of the other person's membership in a specific group or culture (as would be the case in impersonal communications) but on psychological data—that is, the ways in which this person differs from the members of his or her group. In impersonal encounters we respond to each other according to the class or group to which we belong, for example, we respond to a particular college professor in the way we respond to college professors in general. Similarly, the college professor responds to a particular student in the way professors respond to students generally. As the relationship becomes more and more personal, however, both the professor and the student begin to respond to each other not as members of their groups but as individuals; each begins to respond to the other on the basis of the individual's uniqueness. Another way of putting this would be to say that in impersonal encounters the social or cultural role of the person tells us how to interact, while in personal or interpersonal encounters the psychological role of the person tells us how to interact.

Second, interpersonal interactions are based on *explanatory knowledge* of each other. When we know a particular person, we can predict how that person will react in a variety of situations. In interpersonal situations we cannot only predict how a person will act but we can also advance explanations for the behaviors of the person. The college professor may in an impersonal relationship know that Pat will be five minutes late to class each Friday. That is, the professor is able to predict Pat's behavior. In an interpersonal situation, however, the professor cannot only predict Pat's behavior but can also offer explanations for the behavior—in this case, give reasons why Pat is late.

Third, in impersonal situations the rules of behavioral interaction are set down by social norms. Students and professors behave toward each other—at least in impersonal situations—according to the social norms that have been established by the culture or subculture in which they are operating. However, as the relationship between a student and a professor becomes interpersonal, the rules established by the social norms are no longer the important ones and no longer totally regulate the interaction. The individuals establish rules of their own. To the extent that the individuals establish rules for interacting with each other rather than use the rules set down by the society, the situation is interpersonal.

These three characteristics vary in degree. We respond to one another on the basis of psychological data *to some degree*; we base our predictions of another's behavior *to some degree* on the basis of our explanatory knowledge; and we interact on the basis of mutually established rules rather than on socially established norms *to some degree*. As already noted, a developmental approach to communication implies a continuum ranging from highly impersonal to highly intimate. "Interpersonal communication" occupies a broad area of this continuum, though each person might draw its boundaries a bit differently. Therefore, although this developmental view does not enable us to make universally agreed-upon decisions concerning what is or what is not interpersonal, the three characteristics noted above should give us some added insight into interpersonal communication and how it might be distinguished from formal or impersonal communication.

THE PURPOSES OF INTERPERSONAL COMMUNICATION

All behavior, as already noted, is determined; all behavior has one or more purposes, and although these purposes may not always be obvious, we can be certain that they do exist. More specifically, what are the purposes of interpersonal communication?

Four general purposes, which seem among the most significant, may be noted here. Put differently, interpersonal communications are determined by one or more of the following four purposes (at least generally): personal discovery, discovery of the external world, establishing meaningful relationships, and changing attitudes and behaviors (see Figure 16.1). It should be noted that the purposes of the communication need not be conscious at the time of the interpersonal encounter, nor is it essential that individuals agree that they are in fact communicating for these purposes. Purpose is a most peculiar concept; it may be subconscious as well as conscious, unrecognizable as well as recognizable.

Two major qualifications should be noted here. First, no list of communication purposes can be exhaustive. Obviously there are other purposes for interpersonal communication. The four considered here seem the major ones and, hence, are singled out for discussion. Second, no communication interaction is motivated by one factor. Single causes do not seem to exist in the real world, and

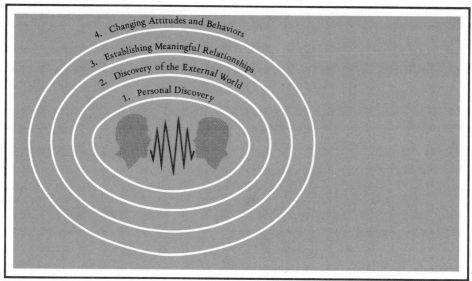

Figure 16.1   The purpose of interpersonal communication.

so any interpersonal communication interaction is probably motivated by a combination of factors rather than only one factor.

Since interpersonal communication involves at least one other person, all four of these purposes affect both the self and other(s). These purposes are motivating factors to varying degrees. They are not all-or-none issues; rather, they motivate participation in varying degrees depending upon the individuals involved, their needs, wants, and histories, the context of the communication, and the numerous other factors we have already noted as being essential to any communication act.

PERSONAL DISCOVERY

One of the major purposes of interpersonal communication which is not shared by public speaking or mass communication is that of personal discovery. When we engage in an interpersonal encounter with another person we learn a great deal about ourselves as well as about the other person. In fact, our self-perceptions are in large part a result of what we have learned about ourselves from others during interpersonal encounters.

Interpersonal communication provides an almost unique opportunity for us to talk about our favorite subject—ourselves. Nothing seems as interesting or exciting or as worthy of discussion as our own feelings, our own thoughts, our own behaviors. By talking about ourselves with another individual we are provided with an excellent source of feedback on our feelings, thoughts, and behaviors. From this type of encounter we learn, for example, that our feelings about ourselves, others, and the world are not so different from someone else's feelings. And the same is true about our behaviors, our fears, our hopes, our desires. This positive reinforcement helps to make us feel "normal."

We also learn how we appear to others, what our strengths and weaknesses are, who likes us and who dislikes us and why. Usually, we choose our interpersonal partners carefully so that most of what we hear is positive or at least more supportive than not. And this helps to build a stronger self-image.

DISCOVERY OF THE EXTERNAL WORLD

Much as interpersonal communication gives us a better understanding of ourselves and the other person with whom we are communicating, it also gives us a better understanding of the external world—the world of objects, events, and other people. Much of the information we now have comes from interpersonal interactions. In fact, our beliefs, attitudes, and values have probably been influenced more by interpersonal encounters than by the mass media. While it is true that a great deal of information comes to us from the media, it is often discussed and ultimately "learned" or internalized through interpersonal interactions.

Recall the meaningful educational experiences that you have had up to this point. Very likely interpersonal encounters with teachers or parents would rank high, certainly higher than would any individual lecture.

ESTABLISHING MEANINGFUL RELATIONSHIPS

One of the greatest desires (some would say "needs") people have is that of establishing and maintaining close relationships with other people. We want to feel loved and liked and in turn we want to love and like others. Much of the time we spend in interpersonal communication is devoted to establishing and maintaining social relationships with others. Recall the times you spotted a friend on campus and felt good about it; you were not concerned with the topic that would be discussed but rather simply with the idea that a relationship would be established. Or, even better, recall your wanting to date someone. It was the relationship between you and this other person that was the important point. The importance of this is probably best seen in our lack of concern for the subject matter of discussion when we are with someone we care for a great deal. It does not matter whether we talk about a movie, about philosophy, about cars, or about people. What does matter is that we are together and that we are relating to each other.

CHANGING ATTITUDES AND BEHAVIORS

Many times we attempt to change the attitudes and behaviors of others in our interpersonal encounters. We may wish them to vote a particular way, try a new diet, buy a particular item, listen to a record, see a movie, read a book, enter a particular field, take a specific course, think in a particular way, believe that something is true or false, value some idea, and so on. The list is endless. We spend a good deal of our time engaged in interpersonal persuasion.

It is interesting to note that the studies that have been done on the effectiveness of the mass media versus interpersonal situations in changing attitudes

The specific behaviors we engage in and the attitudes we hold probably result more from interpersonal communication than from any other form of communication.

and behaviors seem to find that we are more often persuaded through interpersonal communication than through mass media communication.

EFFECTIVENESS IN INTERPERSONAL COMMUNICATION

Interpersonal communication, like any form of behavior, can vary from extremely effective to extremely ineffective. Probably no interpersonal encounter is a total success or a total failure; it could have been better, but it could have been worse. Here we attempt to characterize effective interpersonal communication, recognizing that each communicative act is different and that principles or rules must be applied judiciously with a full recognition of the uniqueness of communication events.

Effective interpersonal communication seems to be characterized by at least the following five qualities: empathy, equality, openness, supportiveness, and positiveness (Figure 16.2).

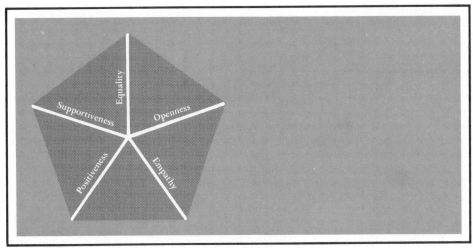

Figure 16.2   Effective interpersonal communication.

EMPATHY

The most difficult of all communication qualities to achieve is perhaps empathy. To empathize with someone is to feel as that person feels, and *empathy* refers to a person's ability to feel what another person is feeling, from that other person's perspective. Empathy is the ability to participate in the experience of another person. To sympathize, on the other hand, is to feel for the individual — to be sorry for the person or to be happy for the person, for example. To empathize is to feel as the individual feels, to be in the same shoes, to feel the same feelings in the same way.

If we are able to empathize with people, we are then in a position to understand where they are coming from, where they are now, and where they are going. Empathy enables one to understand (emotionally and intellectually) what the other person is experiencing. This empathic understanding in turn enables the individual to adjust his or her communications — what is said, how it is to be said, what is to be avoided, if and when silence is to be preferred, if self-disclosures should be made, and so on. In fact, Truax includes one's communication ability as part of the definition of empathy. "Accurate empathy," says Truax, writing from the point of view of the psychotherapist, "involves both the sensitivity to current feelings and the verbal facility to communicate this understanding in a language attuned to the client's own feelings."

More difficult than defining empathy is describing or advancing ways to increase our empathic abilities. Perhaps the first step is to avoid evaluating the other person's behaviors. If we evaluate them as right or wrong, good or bad, we will see these behaviors through these labels and consequently will fail to see a great deal that might not be consistent with these labels. Second, the more we know about a person — his or her desires, experiences, abilities, fears, and so on — the more we will be able to see what that person sees and feel as that person feels. Third, we should try to experience what the other person is feeling from his or her point of view. Playing the role of the other person in our minds (or even out loud) should help us to see the world a little more as he or she does.

EQUALITY

Equality is a peculiar characteristic. In any situation there is probably going to be some inequality. One person will be smarter, richer, better-looking, or a better athlete. Never are two people absolutely equal in all respects. Even identical twins would be unequal in some ways. Despite this inequality, interpersonal communication is generally more effective when the atmosphere is one of equality. This does not mean that unequals cannot communicate. Certainly they can. Yet their communication, if it is to be effective, should recognize the equality of personalities. By this is meant that there should be a tacit recognition that both parties are valuable and worthwhile human beings and that each has something important to contribute.

Equality should also characterize interpersonal communication in terms of speaking versus listening. If one participant speaks all the time while the other listens all the time, effective interpersonal communication becomes difficult if not impossible. There should be an attempt at achieving an equality of sending versus receiving. Depending on the situation, one person will normally speak more than the other person, but this should be a function of the situation and not of the fact that one person is a "talker" and another person is a "listener."

OPENNESS

The quality of *openness* refers to at least three aspects of interpersonal communication. First, and perhaps most obvious, is that effective interpersonal communicators must be willing to open up to the other people with whom they are interacting. This does not mean that we should immediately pour forth our entire life histories. Interesting as they may be, they are not usually very helpful to the communication or interesting to the other individuals. Openness simply means a willingness to self-disclose, to reveal information about oneself that might normally be kept hidden but which is relevant to the interpersonal encounter.

The second aspect of openness refers to the willingness of a communicator to react honestly to incoming stimuli. Silent, uncritical, and immovable psychiatrists may be of some help in a clinical situation, but they are generally boring conversationalists. We want (and have a right to expect) people to react openly to what we say. Nothing seems worse than indifference; even disagreement seems more welcome. Of course there are extremes here too.

The third aspect of openness I take from Arthur Bochner and Clifford Kelly's concept of owning feelings and thoughts. To be open in this sense is to acknowledge that the feelings and thoughts we express are ours and that we bear the responsibility for them. We do not attempt to shift the responsibility for our feelings to others. Bochner and Kelly put it this way: "the person who owns his feelings or ideas makes it clear that he takes responsibility for his own feelings and actions. Owning shows a willingness to accept responsibility for oneself and commitment to others. It is the antithesis of blaming others for the way one feels." Bochner and Kelly advise us not to say, "Isn't this group supposed to listen to people?" but rather, "I feel ignored. I don't think people in this group listen to me."

This difference is interesting from another point of view as well. When we own our feelings and thoughts we say in effect "This is how *I* feel," "This is how *I* see the situation," "This is what *I* think," with the *I* always paramount. And so instead of saying, "This discussion is useless," we would say something like "*I* think this discussion is useless" or "*I'm* bored by this discussion" or "*I* want to talk more about myself" or any other such statement that includes reference to the fact that *I* am making an evaluation and not describing objective reality. By including in such statements what the general semanticists call "to me-ness," we make explicit the fact that our feelings are the result of the interaction between the outside reality and our own preconceptions, attitudes, prejudices, and the like.

SUPPORTIVENESS

An effective interpersonal relationship is one that is *supportive*. Open and empathic interpersonal communication cannot survive in a threatening atmosphere. If participants feel that what they say will be criticized or attacked, for example, they may be reluctant to open up or to reveal themselves in any meaningful way.

In a supportive environment silence, where it is not imposed on the speaker or caused by speaker apprehension, does not take on a negative value. Rather, silence is seen as a positive aspect of communication; an opportunity for relating nonverbally.

In an insightful analysis of supportiveness—and its opposite, defensiveness—Jack Gibb identifies a number of climates or atmospheres that lead to supportiveness and a number that lead to defensiveness. In all, Gibb considers six climates: empathy, equality, spontaneity, description, problem orientation, and provisionalism. The first three (empathy, equality, and spontaneity, or openness) have already been discussed as general characteristics of interpersonal communication effectiveness, and these need not be repeated here. The role of description, problem orientation, and provisionalism in generating supportiveness, however, should be identified.

When a communication is perceived as being a description of some situation or event or as a request for information, we normally do not perceive it as threatening. Contrast this, however, with communications that are perceived as evaluative or judgmental; these communications often lead us to become defensive and to erect some kind of barrier between ourselves and those with whom we are communicating. I do not mean to imply that all communications that are perceived as evaluative encourage defensiveness or that all communications perceived as descriptive encourage supportiveness. But usually messages that are seen as descriptive are more likely to lead to a lowering of defenses and an increased feeling of supportiveness.

In a similar way, communications that are seen as being oriented to the problem, as being addressed to the issue of solving a particular problem—rather than, say, to the controlling of the behavior of the members of the group—encourage supportiveness. Problem-oriented communications will generally be met with openness. Control-oriented communications will generally be met with resistance and defensiveness. According to Jack Gibb, attempts to control our thoughts and our behaviors are met with defensiveness because they challenge the individual's self-concept. "Implicit in all attempts to alter another person," says Gibb, "is the assumption by the change agent that the person to be altered is inadequate. That the speaker secretly views the listener as ignorant, unable to make his own decisions, uninformed, immature, unwise, or possessed of wrong or inadequate attitudes is a subconscious perception which gives the latter a valid base for defensive reactions."

Another characteristic that leads to supportiveness is provisionalism; its counterpart, certainty, leads to defensiveness. You are probably familiar with teachers who say that they want all their students to think for themselves, to develop inquiring minds, and to explore all sides of the question—to have open minds, to leave room for differences of opinion and new facts, and so on. Most teachers will verbalize some such goals at some time in their classes. Such teachers are encouraging provisionalism among students. Unfortunately, however, these same teachers are often in practice very dogmatic. And when we see this in the teachers' own behavior, we become resentful—and rightly so.

We resist people who "know" everything and who always have a definite answer to any questions. Such people are set in their ways and will tolerate no differences. They have arguments ready for any possible alternative attitude or belief. After a very short time we become defensive with such people, and we hold back our own attitudes rather than subjecting them to attack. But we open up with people who take a more provisional position, who are willing to change their minds should reasonable arguments be presented. With such people we feel equal.

Closed-minded people are heavily dependent on reinforcement for their reactions to information. They will evaluate information on the basis of the rewards and the punishments they receive. We all do this to some extent; the closed-minded person, however, does this to a greater degree than do most people. The open-minded person is better able to resist the reinforcements of other people and outside situations.

All communications contain immanent reference; all communications are to an extent ego-reflexive; all communications say something about the speaker as well as about taxes, crime, pollution, or whatever. In dealing with this inevitable message duality, the "certain" person has difficulty separating the information about the source or speaker from the information about the world. The "provisional" person, on the other hand, can accept or reject the information about the world and either accept or reject the information about the speaker independently of each other.

"Certain" people see the world as generally threatening. Because of this perceived threat, they become anxious and unable to deal with the relevant information independent of the source (as already noted). Consequently, they come to rely very heavily on authority. They do not evaluate information themselves but allow some authority to evaluate it for them. Then all they must do is accept the authority's conclusions. Open-minded people, on the other hand, see the world as nonthreatening, even friendly. They are not anxious and hence may evaluate information calmly and rationally. Although they do not ignore authority, they do not accept what an authority says uncritically.

In terms of interpersonal relationships, "certain," or closed-minded, people will evaluate others according to the similarity-dissimilarity of others' belief systems with their own. They evaluate positively those people who have similar belief systems and negatively those people who have dissimilar belief systems. Some research shows that closed-minded people become friends with people who are of the same religion, same race, and same political persuasion. "Provisional," or open-minded, individuals do not use similarity of belief systems or homophily as the measure of interpersonal relationships. The "certain," or closed-minded, and the "provisional," or open-minded, individual are extreme types. Few people are completely closed or completely open. The vast majority exist somewhere in between these two extremes. What is most important to understand is that to the extent that we act "certain" and closed-minded, we encourage defensive behavior in the listener. To the extent that we act in a provisional manner, with an open mind, with a full recognition that we might be wrong and that we might revise our attitudes and opinions, we encourage supportiveness.

POSITIVENESS

Positiveness in interpersonal communication refers to at least three different aspects or elements. First, interpersonal communication is fostered if there is a certain positive regard for the self. The persons who feel negative about themselves will invariably communicate these feelings to others, who in turn will probably develop similar negative feelings. On the other hand, people who feel positive about themselves will convey this feeling for themselves to others, who in turn are likely to return the positive regard.

Second, interpersonal communication will be fostered if a positive feeling for the other person is communicated. This obviously will make the other person feel better and will encourage more active participation on a more meaningful level. One will, for example, be more likely to self-disclose.

Third, a positive feeling for the general communication situation is important for effective interaction. Nothing is more unpleasant than communicating with someone who does not enjoy the exchange or does not respond favorably to the situation or context. A negative response to the situation makes one feel almost as if one is intruding and communication seems sure to break down quickly.

A NOTE ON HOMOPHILY–HETEROPHILY

These five characteristics of effective interpersonal communication (empathy, equality, openness, supportiveness, and positiveness) are qualities that can be learned, and so it seems important that they be singled out for discussion. We should, however, make note here of the concepts of homophily and heterophily, which, although not learned behaviors, greatly influence interpersonal communication effectiveness. *Homophily* refers to the degree of similarity between the parties engaged in interpersonal communication and *heterophily* to the degree of difference between the parties. The similarity and difference may refer to just about any characteristic—age, religion, political leaning, financial status, educational level, and so forth. If you prefer to avoid the communication jargon, read *homophily* as *similarity* and *heterophily* as *dissimilarity*.

Generally, research has shown that interpersonal communication is more effective when the parties are homophilous. James McCroskey, Carl Larson, and Mark Knapp, for example, state: "More effective communication occurs when source and receiver are homophilous. The more nearly alike the people in a communication transaction, the more likely they will share meanings." We will, according to this principle, communicate best with people who are most like ourselves. Butchers will communicate best with butchers, Texans will communicate best with Texans, and college students will communicate best with college students.

Because of the contribution that homophily-heterophily makes to the study of interpersonal communication, it needs to be discussed in relation to the five characteristics of effective interpersonal communication. The more homophilous individuals are, the more open they will be with each other. This seems to follow, since we seem to be most comfortable with those who are like us. Consequently, we are more apt to reveal ourselves and to self-disclose to people like ourselves. We feel perhaps that they would reveal themselves and disclose to us. And so by being open we do not risk as much as we would in a heterophilous situation.

Empathy is greatest when people are homophilous and least when people are heterophilous. We can more easily feel as other people do (which is the essence of empathy) when we are like them to begin with. There is little distance to travel in order to empathize when we are similar to the individuals, but much distance when they are not like us. Consider the difficulty a poor person would have empathizing with the disappointment of a rich one because he or she must give up the second car, or the difficulty a rich person would have in empathizing with a poor person's hunger.

It seems that we all want to support people who are like us more than people who are very different from us. By supporting homophilous people we are in effect supporting ourselves. People like us, we may feel, will be supportive to us, and so we respond in kind and support them. We can be silent with people who are like us and not be uncomfortable. We do not feel we have to impress them with our knowledge or intelligence.

When we are with people who are homophilous we feel more positive toward ourselves, because we are not made to feel inferior as we might be made to feel if we were with heterophilous people. We generally enjoy the act of communicating in a homophilous situation more than we would in a heterophilous one. Of course, we generally like people who are like us more than we like people who are unlike us. In a sense, being with homophilous individuals provides a kind of confirmation of self.

Perhaps the most obvious relationship that exists with homophilous people is that of equality. By definition, homophilous people are equal to us, neither inferior nor superior. Hence there is more likely to be an atmosphere of equality, a free give and take of ideas, and an awareness that both participants have something to contribute.

Although communication is most effective when the individuals are homophilous, we should note that change is often brought about when the parties involved are "optimally heterophilous" in regard to the subject under discussion. According to McCroskey, Larson, and Knapp, if the two people are homophilous in regard to the subject matter, then neither will be competent enough to change the attitudes, beliefs, or behaviors of the other. Also, when the individuals are too far apart in their competence on a subject, the more competent one will obviously not be changed by the less competent one, and the less competent one will probably have difficulty in understanding the other. Consequently, no change will take place here either. But when one party is optimally heterophilous, optimally more competent than the other, he or she will be better able to effect change in the other. Although "optimal heterophily" lies somewhere between total similarity and total difference, exactly where it lies on this similarity-difference continuum and when it may be expected to occur cannot be identified very precisely.

SOURCES

For the discussion of effectiveness I relied (sometimes consciously and at times subconsciously) on the work of Jack Gibb, particularly his very insightful "Defensive Communication," *Journal of Communication* 11 (1961): 141–148. For a more popular and detailed account see Theodora Wells, *Keeping Your Cool Under Fire: Communicating Non-Defensively* (New York: McGraw-Hill, 1980).

For empathy, see R. Schafer, "Generative Empathy in the Treatment Situation," *Psychoanalytic Quarterly* 38 (1959): 342–373, R. Greenson, "Empathy and Its Vicissitudes," *International Journal of Psychoanalysis* 41 (1960): 418–424, and C. Truax, "A Scale for the Measurement of Accurate Empathy," Wisconsin Psychiatric Institute Discussion Paper no. 20 (Madison, 1961). These and various other contributions to the study of empathy are discussed by Henry M. Backrach, "Empathy," *Archives of General Psychiatry* 33 (1976): 35–38.

For an overview of homophily and heterophily, see James C. McCroskey, Carl E. Larson, and Mark L. Knapp, *An Introduction to Interpersonal Communication* (Englewood Cliffs, N.J.: Prentice-Hall, 1971). For a more extensive treatment see E. M. Rogers and F. F. Shoemaker, *Communication of Innovations* (New York: Free Press, 1971). See Mark I. Alpert and W. Thomas Anderson, Jr., "Optimal Heterophily and Communication Effectiveness: Some Empirical Findings," *Journal of Communication* 23 (September 1973): 328–343, for a review of relevant findings and an example of an experimental study on this question. Some of the variables influencing exposure to information are explored in Elizabeth C. Hirschman, "Social and Cognitive Influences on Information Exposure: A Path Analysis," *Journal of Communication* 31 (winter 1981): 76–87.

A book that provides an excellent transition between the characteristics of effective interpersonal communication and the self is Edmond G. Addeo and Robert E. Burger, *Egospeak: Why No One Listens to You* (New York: Bantam, 1973). See Murray S. Davis, *Intimate Relations* (New York: Free Press, 1973), for a look at interpersonal communication from the point of view of the sociologist and Kurt Danziger, *Interpersonal Communication* (New York: Pergamon, 1976), for the point of view of the psychologist. These two works are excellent complements to the work by communicologists emphasized here. The concept of owning feelings and thoughts comes from Arthur P. Bochner and Clifford W. Kelly, "Interpersonal Competence: Rationale, Philosophy, and Implementation of a Conceptual Framework," *Communication Education* 23 (November 1974): 279–301.

Experiential
Vehicles

16.1 Me and You: Communicating Interpersonally

The purpose of this experience is to enable you to participate in an interpersonal communication encounter in which: (1) there will be relatively immediate feedback, (2) you will be able to explore some of your own feelings about yourself, (3) you will have the opportunity to self-disclose as much or as little as you like, and (4) you will be able to explore some of the ways others form impressions of you and you form impressions of others.

Instructions

Dyads are formed with persons who do not know each other well. In the first phase one person (A) reads the following list of words to the other person (B) one at a time. B responds aloud to each of the words with a sentence or two in which he or she attempts to relate the word or concept to himself or herself. The process is continued for all 10 words. In the second phase, the process is repeated with person B reading the words to person A, who likewise responds to each of the words.

After each person has responded to all 10 words, write a short paragraph about your impressions of the other person. Ideally, these paragraphs should be based solely on the interactions that just took place. Inevitably, however, they will be influenced by previous interactions. The paragraphs are to be written from the point of view of how this person appears to you, not from the point of view of "what this person really is" (assuming that that question could ever be answered). After the paragraphs are completed, exchange and discuss them in any way that seems meaningful to you.

Stimulus Words*

love	the future
death	school
your family	war
occupation	God
yourself	sex

* Other stimulus words may be used, of course; however, the same words should be used for both participants.

16.2   Effective Interpersonal Interaction

In order to see the characteristics of effective interpersonal communication in actual operation, the following role-playing situations have been designed. The procedure is as follows:

1. Participants should be selected (preferably from volunteers) to role-play the characters in the situations described below.
2. Participants should act out the parts, developing their roles and the interactions as seems logical at the time.
3. In these role-playing situations the participants will either closely follow the characteristics of effective interpersonal communication or clearly violate the characteristics as they are instructed by the group leader or instructor.
4. The remainder of the class should monitor the role playing, observing how closely the participants are following or violating the characteristics of effective interpersonal communication. Two general procedures have been found useful for this monitoring:
   a. The observers may stop the role-playing session as soon as any member fails to follow his or her instructions. The person who stops the role playing should naturally explain why he or she felt that the participants were not following instructions. After essential discussion the role playing should resume, to be stopped again when any role player fails to follow instructions. *Note:* If this procedure is used, it is best not to stop the role playing during the first three minutes. This will allow the members an opportunity to begin to feel the characters they are playing.
   b. The observers may take notes during the role playing, reserving all discussion of the characteristics of effective interpersonal communication until the role-playing session is completed. If this procedure is followed, it is generally useful to ask the role players how closely they felt they were following the instructions.

Role-Playing Situations

Any or all of the following situations may be used to illustrate (1) following the characteristics of effective interpersonal communication or (2) violating the characteristics. It is recommended that at least one of the situations be used to illustrate following and one violating the characteristics, so that the differences between the two interactions may be more easily noted.

1. *Participants:*
   Joan Davis (college sophomore)
   Homer Davis (Joan's father)
   Ann Davis (Joan's mother)

   Situation:
   Joan wants to go away for the weekend with her boyfriend and use the family car. Homer and Ann are totally against this. First, they thoroughly detest Joan's boyfriend. Second, they disapprove of unmarried couples spending weekends together. Third, they want to use the car themselves.

2. *Participants:*
   Chris Martin (Diane's husband)
   Diane Martin (Chris' wife)
   Marlene Jason (Diane's mother)

   Situation:
   Diane and her mother have just gone to purchase new furniture for the Martins' home. They have picked out extremely expensive furniture, which Chris and Diane cannot afford. Upon hearing of this, Chris becomes angry and demands that different furniture be selected. Marlene says that she will pay for the furniture since she wants her daughter to have the best. Chris argues that what comes into the house should be bought by Diane and himself and that they should not accept such gifts, since there will inevitably be strings attached as there have been in the past.

3. *Participants:*
   James and Thelma (married couple)
   Frank and Carol (married couple)

   Situation:
   James and Frank want to go bowling alone. Thelma and Carol want to go to dinner and the movies with their husbands. The husbands feel that this is their one day out a week and that their desire to spend it bowling is not unreasonable. The wives argue that this, too, is their only chance to go out and that they have a right to this outing.

4. *Participants:*
   Dr. Mary James (professor)
   Michell Russo (student)
   Daniel Miller (student)
   Ronald Kennedy (student)

   Situation:
   Michell, Daniel, and Ronald have just received their grades for their Introduction to Communication course and have gone to complain to Dr. Mary James. Michell received a C+, Daniel received an F, and Ronald received a D. All three students feel that they deserved better grades. Dr. James feels that the grades the students received—based on their class performance and their examination scores—were fair.

5. *Participants:*
   Dr. Michael Craeman (professor)
   Joan Mitchell (student)
   Danny Santos (student)
   Molly McCoy (student)
   Dr. Joseph Bartlett (professor)

Situation:

Joan, Danny, and Molly have written a letter of complaint against Dr. Michael Craeman and submitted it to Dr. Bartlett, chairperson of the Sociology Department. The students claim that Dr. Craeman's classes are dull, that he is often late to class, that his tests are impossible to pass, and that they are not learning anything.

Unit 17

Interpersonal Relationships:
Development and Deterioration

INTERPERSONAL RELATIONSHIPS: DEVELOPMENT AND DETERIORATION

Relationship Development
Relationship Deterioration

LEARNING GOALS

Upon completion of this unit, you should be able to:

1. identify some of the contact substitutes our culture has established
2. identify at least four reasons for the development of interpersonal relationships
3. explain at least three guides and obstacles to relational development
4. explain the nature of relational deterioration
5. explain how changes in the factors accounting for relational development may lead to relational deterioration
6. explain how psychological, behavioral, and contextual changes might account for relational deterioration
7. explain how relationship changes may alter the relationship between two persons
8. identify the characteristics that figure into relational deterioration management

In this unit we focus on the development and the deterioration of interpersonal relationships. Specifically we consider the reasons we seek relationships and the guidelines and obstacles to relationship development, the nature and causes of relational deterioration, and some of the ways in which relational deterioration may be most effectively managed. There is probably nothing as important to you or me or indeed to anyone as contact with another human being. So important is contact with another person that when this is absent for prolonged periods of time, depression sets in, self-doubt surfaces, and one finds it difficult to conduct even the very basics of daily living. Desmond Morris, in *Intimate Behaviour*, notes that contact with other human beings is so important that our culture has established all sorts of substitutes so that when human contact is absent, all may not be totally lost. There are, according to Morris, professional contact persons like doctors, nurses, and masseurs who are often seen not because of some physical ailment but because of the need for contact.

RELATIONSHIP DEVELOPMENT

REASONS FOR RELATIONAL DEVELOPMENT

Each person pursues a relationship or desires contact for unique and individual reasons; no two relationships are pursued for exactly the same reason. Consequently, there are millions of reasons for seeking contact. Here we consider just a few.

One reason that comes to mind easily is that contact with another human being helps to alleviate loneliness. At times we experience loneliness because we are physically alone, although being alone does not necessarily produce loneliness. Many can experience closeness with others though separated by long distances. At other times we are lonely because we have a need for close contact—sometimes physical, sometimes emotional, and most often both—which is, at least at the time, unfulfilled. From a different perspective, Chester Bennett makes a similar observation: "Psychological studies of ship-wrecked sailors and prisoners in solitary confinement, experimental investigations of people who are closeted with their own thoughts for relatively brief periods of time, show how difficult it is for most of us to cope with isolation. We like solitude in small doses—if we can find a place to be alone in today's world. But mostly we seek companionship. We want to share experiences, even the private ones, with someone."

We want to feel that someone cares, that someone likes us, that someone will protect us, that someone ultimately will love us. And perhaps close relationships with another person assure us that someone does care, does like us, and will just be there when we need human contact.

Some people, in an attempt to alleviate loneliness, seek always to surround themselves with numerous acquaintances. Sometimes this helps; often it only serves to make the loneliness all the more real. One close relationship usually works a lot better. Most of us know this, and that is why we seek to establish relationships.

Human beings, not unlike experimental monkeys and rats, need stimulation; if they are not stimulated, they withdraw; sometimes they die. Human contact is one of the best ways—though clearly not the only way—to be stimulated. We are composites of many different dimensions, and all our dimensions need stimulation. We are intellectual creatures, and so we need intellectual stimulation. We talk with people about ideas, we attend classes, we argue about different interpretations of a film or novel. We thus exercise our reasoning, our analytical, and our interpretative abilities. In so doing we improve, sharpen, and expand them.

But we are also physical creatures and need physical stimulation as well. We need to touch and be touched; we need to hold and be held; we need to look at people and have them look at us—not through us or around us or at our new jacket, but at *us*. Perhaps we need to be assured that we are physical beings. College classrooms have consistently failed to take into consideration the physical stimulation needed for growth and development. A hand on our shoulder, a tight hug, or a warm handshake may help us more than being told our interpretation of Kant was correct.

We are also emotional creatures and need emotional stimulation. We need to laugh and to cry. We need to feel hope and surprise, to experience warmth and affection. We need exercise for our emotions as well as for our intellectual capacities. In our culture men have been taught that it is wrong to cry or to be fearful. And women have been taught that it is wrong to be aggressive or to feel sexual. Both sexes need to be retaught—each also needs the emotions at one time assigned only to the other sex.

We need contact with other human beings because through them we learn about ourselves; we acquire that essential knowledge of self largely through interaction with others. In the discussion of self-awareness in Unit 3, I tried to make the point that we see ourselves in part through the eyes of others. If our friends see us as warm and generous, for example, we will probably also see ourselves as warm and generous. Our self-perceptions are greatly influenced by what we think others think of us, and so contact with others enables us to see ourselves in a somewhat different way, from a somewhat different perspective.

We seek contact with other people because we find them attractive (see Box 17.1). Sometimes it is physical attractiveness, sometimes it is personality, sometimes it is intellectual or athletic ability that we find attractive.

The most general reason why we establish relationships, and one that could include all the others, is that we seek human contact so that our pleasures may be maximized and our pains minimized. We seem to have a need to share our good fortune with other people—perhaps to earn their praise, perhaps to assure us that we are in fact fortunate, perhaps to participate with us in enjoying the new-found pleasures. We also have a need to seek out relationships when we are

Relationships are of great value at all times but especially so when we want someone to share our pleasure or lessen our pain.

in emotional or physical pain. Perhaps this goes back to when we were children and ran to mother so that she could kiss our wounds or tell us everything was all right. We now find it difficult to run to mother, and so we go to others, generally to friends who will provide us with the same kind of consolation that mother did.

GUIDES AND OBSTACLES TO RELATIONAL DEVELOPMENT

Initial encounters fail or succeed largely for the same reasons that well-established relationships fail or succeed. And so perhaps the best answer to the question of what makes some attempts successes and others failures is contained in this book. After all, interpersonal communication is interpersonal communication. In Unit 16 we considered positiveness, openness, equality, empathy, and supportiveness as the five characteristics of effective interpersonal communication. These same five qualities will go a long way in making first encounters successful as well. But there are also other factors more specific to initial encounters, and these will be considered here. These characteristics should be looked at as additions to those postulated for effectiveness in interpersonal communication generally.

In this discussion the guides are considered together with the obstacles because they seem here to be opposite ends of the same qualities.

BOX 17.1
Interpersonal Attraction

We are all attracted to some people and not attracted to others. In a similar way, some people are attracted to us and some people are not. This seems to be the universal human condition. If we were to examine the people we are attracted to and the people we are not attracted to we would probably be able to see patterns in the decisions or judgments we make. Even though many of these decisions seem subconsciously motivated, we can nevertheless discern patterns in the interpersonal choices we make.

We are all probably attracted to "a type" of person or to "types" of people. This ideal type (which differs for each person) can probably be found, in varying degrees, in each of the people we are attracted to and its opposite, in varying degrees, in each of the people to whom we are not attracted. It has been found that most people are interpersonally attracted to others on the basis of five major variables: *attractiveness, proximity, reinforcement, similarity,* and *complementarity.*

1. *Attractiveness* comes in at least two forms. When we say, "I find that person attractive," we probably mean either (1) that we find the person physically attractive or (2) that we find that person's personality or ways of behaving attractive. For the most part we tend to like physically attractive people rather than physically ugly people, and we tend to like people who possess a pleasant personality rather than an unpleasant personality.

2. If we look around at the people we find attractive, we probably find that they are the people who live or work in close *proximity* to us. This is perhaps the one finding that emerges most frequently from the research on interpersonal attraction. In one of the most famous studies, Festinger, Schachter, and Black studied friendships in a student housing development. They found that the development of friendships was greatly influenced by the distance between the units in which the people lived and by the direction in which the units faced. The closer the students' rooms were to each other the better the chances were that they would become friends. It was also found that the students living in units that faced the courtyard had more friends than the students who lived in units facing the street. The people who became friends were the people who had the greater opportunity to interact with one another. We might add that the vast majority of marriages are between people who have lived very close to each other physically.

3. Perhaps the most obvious statement anyone could make about interpersonal attraction and the reasons we like or dislike people is that we like those who like us and dislike those who dislike us. Naturally there are exceptions; there are some who love people who do not love them and there are those who hate those who love them. For most of

us, for most of the time, however, we like those who like us. Put in more behavioral terms, we tend to like those who reward or reinforce us. The reward or *reinforcement* may be social, as in the form of compliments or praise of one sort or another, or it may be material, as in the case of the suitor whose gifts eventually win the hand of the beloved.

4. If people could construct their mates, their mates would look, act, and think very much like themselves. By being attracted to people like ourselves we are in effect validating ourselves, saying to ourselves that we are worthy of being liked, that we are attractive. Generally, although there are exceptions, we like people who are similar to ourselves in color, race, ability, physical characteristics, intelligence, and so on. We are often attracted to mirror images of ourselves. *Similarity* is especially important when it comes to attitudes. We are particularly attracted to people who have attitudes similar to our own, who like what we like, and who dislike what we dislike. This similarity is most important when dealing with salient or significant attitudes. For example, it would not make much difference if the attitudes of two people toward food or furniture differed (though even these can at times be significant), but it would be of great significance if their attitudes toward children or religion or politics were very disparate. Marriages between people with great and salient dissimilarities are more likely to end in divorce than are marriages between people who are a lot alike.

5. Although many people would argue that "birds of a feather flock together," others would argue that "opposites attract." That opposites attract is the principle of *complementarity*. Take, for example, the individual who is extremely dogmatic. Would he or she be attracted to others who are high in dogmatism or would he or she be attracted to those who are low in dogmatism? The similarity principle would predict that this person would be attracted to those who were like him or her (that is, high in dogmatism), while the complementarity principle would predict that this person would be attracted to those who were unlike him or her (that is, low in dogmatism). From your own observations and experiences, you know that at times the similarity and at times the complementarity principle operates. Research studies find the same; sometimes it is similarity, sometimes it is complementarity.

Perceived Interest and Lack of Interest

All of us want to be thought of as being of interest to someone. We want to be told, verbally as well as nonverbally, that someone is interested in us. How this is told to us does not seem to matter as much as the fact that we are told in one way or another. And we want to be told that someone is interested in us for ourselves—not for what he or she can get out of us, whether it be a job, money, sex, or whatever. And surely when someone attempts to make contact, he or she almost inevitably demonstrates some kind of interest; otherwise, why would the person want to make contact? This sounds logical until we begin to observe initial encounters and are forced to come to the conclusion that many people simply do not know how to demonstrate interest in another person. Perhaps it is because they are not genuinely interested in the first place. But perhaps they are interested and simply do not know how to express this interest.

A clear example of this occurs frequently at crowded singles bars or discos. One person may go up to another and begin a conversation, but he or she continues to look around and fails to maintain the eye contact that says, "I am interested in you," and fails psychologically and physically to exclude the others in the bar. Instead you get the feeling that the person is engaged in this conversation but still on the lookout for someone better to come along.

Interest and lack of interest can be demonstrated in many different ways. Direct eye contact and the exclusion of others, already mentioned, are obvious examples. But our general body posture also says a great deal about our interest in another person. The individual who keeps his or her body at a 90 degree angle to the body of the other person seems to be demonstrating a decided lack of interest. Similarly, the totally passive individual seems to be saying, "I'm here, but I'm not really interested—at least not enough to get really involved." The failure to listen to what the other person is saying—perhaps because we want to hear the conversation of the party next to us or the music—seems almost too obvious to mention, yet it seems to occur with extremely high frequency.

Self Versus Other Orientation

People who are preoccupied with themselves usually wind up staying by themselves. Except to themselves, they are bores. Each of us wants to feel that the other person wants to hear about us, wants to listen to what we have to say. I suspect that the time spent listening versus talking and the time spent talking about oneself versus talking about the other person would provide us with reasonably good indications of the success or failure of the initial encounter. The person who talks only about himself or herself impresses nobody. A reasonable balance between talk and listening, between self and other orientation, is needed.

There is a danger in going to the other extreme, however, and concentrating so much on the other person that we do not reveal anything about ourselves. And although the other person may conclude that we are mysterious and fascinating, he or she may also conclude that we are shallow, having nothing to contribute, and live a very dull existence. Or more realistically, he or she may conclude—more often subconsciously than consciously—that we do not want to give of ourselves and do not want to share anything about ourselves with anyone.

Acceptance and Nonacceptance

In the discussion of supportiveness, we pointed out that evaluative statements increase defensiveness. To the extent that a person feels evaluated and tested, he or she will become defensive. In initial encounters this same kind of situation manifests itself. The concepts of acceptance and nonacceptance, however, seem more appropriate here. We want to feel that we are being accepted as a unique and significant individual. We want to feel that our attitudes, our values, and our opinions are accepted. We want to know that our feelings are accepted as valid expressions of what we are experiencing. We want to be accepted as equals.

This is not to say that we expect the other person to believe as we do, to hold the same values and opinions as we do, or to feel as we feel. Rather, we expect the other individual to recognize our right to believe as we do, to feel as we feel. Thus, I can disagree with your opinions or I can feel totally different about the same incident or person; yet I should still be able to see that your opinions and your feelings are valid for you.

To the extent that we feel accepted rather than challenged or rejected, we feel free to express ourselves. And perhaps this is what we really look for in a relationship—an opportunity to express ourselves as we wish without fear of rejection, without fear that love will be withdrawn, without fear that we will be punished.

Need Fulfillment Versus Need Nonfulfillment

We began this unit with some of the reasons why we seek contact and relationships with other people. One of the major reasons noted in a number of different contexts was that interpersonal contact fulfills needs—to alleviate loneliness, to be stimulated, to gain knowledge of the self, and so on. Even in the initial phases those needs are paramount, and to the extent that they are fulfilled, or at least to the extent that there seems some promise that they might be fulfilled, the interpersonal encounter will be developed and maintained. To the extent that these needs are not fulfilled or are thwarted, the interpersonal encounter will not be pursued or will be terminated if it is already developed.

Naturally, not everything is so clear-cut. It would be foolhardy to assume that a logical analysis such as this actually goes on in the minds of the individuals engaged in the interpersonal interaction. Far from it. Rather, one probably senses in some vague and general way the extent to which the interaction is enjoyable or unenjoyable, and it is on this basis that relationships are continued or terminated. The perceived enjoyment or unenjoyment is in turn related closely to the extent to which the interaction is fulfilling of our significant needs.

RELATIONSHIP DETERIORATION

THE NATURE OF RELATIONAL DETERIORATION

By relational deterioration I mean the weakening of the bonds holding people together. At times the relationship may be weakened only mildly. Although such relationships may appear normal to outsiders, to the participants it is clear that the relationship has weakened. The obvious extreme of relational deterioration is the complete termination of the relationship. In between these two extremes are an infinite number of variations. Relational deterioration, then, exists on a continuum from just a little bit less than intimate to total separation and total dissolution.

The process of deterioration may be gradual or sudden. Murray Davis, in *Intimate Relations,* uses the terms "passing away" to designate gradual deterioration and "sudden death" to designate immediate or sudden deterioration. An example of "passing away" is when one of the parties in a relationship develops close ties with a new intimate and this new relationship gradually pushes out the old intimate. An example of "sudden death" is when one or both of the parties break a rule that was essential to the relationship (for example, the rule of complete fidelity), and both realize that since the rule has been broken, the relationship cannot be sustained and, in fact, must be terminated immediately.

The deterioration or termination of a relationship may be the primary responsibility of both parties, one of the parties, or neither party—a possibility that we often fail to consider. In the first case, both parties may wish to go their separate ways, perhaps each with a new intimate or perhaps alone. In either case they both agree that separation is the best choice. In the second case, one of the parties wants to leave while the other party wants to remain in the relationship. These are the types of relationships movies and romantic novels are made of—the struggle to hold together a family, a marriage, or a friendship. In the third case, neither party wants the relationship to deteriorate, but perhaps one of the parties says or does something that is so detrimental to the other person and to the relationship, to use Murray Davis's example, that it becomes apparent that the relationship cannot survive. An act of infidelity is perhaps the clearest example. Say one of the individuals has an affair that the other person cannot accept or even tolerate. The relationship may deteriorate even though neither party really wants to see it end. The deterioration or termination of the relationship is brought about by the combination of the infidelity and the inability to accept or tolerate such an act.

All relationships are different; what pulls one relationship apart may well hold another together. The death of a child, for example, will at times function to destroy a marriage and at other times will solidify it. Outside threats usually strengthen a relationship, though at times they have the effect of tearing it apart. Yet for all its variations, relational deterioration does have some characteristics that can be observed, predicted, and at times corrected in time to save the relationship. But it should not be assumed that all relationships should be retained as they are or even that all relationships should be retained at all. Not all breakups are bad, and few, if any, bad breakups are all bad. While in the midst of a breakup this may be difficult to appreciate, but in retrospect it seems almost always to be true.

At times a relationship may be unproductive for one or both parties, and a breakup is often the best thing that could happen. Such a termination may provide a period for the individuals to regain their independence and to again become self-reliant. Some relationships are so absorbing that there is little time available for reflection on oneself, on others, and on the relationship itself. Some distance often helps.

One of the major problems with some relationships is that they prevent one or both parties from developing new relationships, from becoming involved with new intimates, from developing new friends and associations. A termination of such a relationship provides the individuals with opportunities to develop these new associations and to explore different types of relationships with different types of people.

These are obviously not the only redeeming characteristics of terminating a relationship that might be mentioned; each relationship is different, and each individual is different. What one finds a benefit, another may find a burden. The freedom to explore new relationships may be viewed by one person as a challenging and exciting opportunity; to another person it may be threatening and frightening. And so it would be foolhardy to specify with any degree of authority what the specific benefits may be to specific people in specific relationships. The only point I want to make here is that relational deterioration does not have to have only negative consequences. For the most part, it is up to the individual to draw out of any decaying relationship some good, some positive characteristics, some learning that can be used later on.

SOME CAUSES OF RELATIONAL DETERIORATION

In all interpersonal interactions, the causes are as numerous as the individuals involved, and so it is with considerable modesty that I even attempt to identify some of the causes of relational deterioration. In reviewing these it is important to recognize that each relationship is different, each follows a different pattern, and each responds differently to different influences. Having offered this qualification, perhaps the best place to start is to look at some of the reasons why relationships are developed and see how changes in these factors may lead to deterioration.

Earlier I noted some factors that are important in establishing relationships. When these are no longer operative or when they are changed drastically, it may be a cause of relational deterioration. For example, one of the major reasons why people seek relationships is to alleviate loneliness. When loneliness is no longer lessened by the relationship, when one or both of the individuals experience loneliness for prolonged or frequent periods, the relationship may well be on the road to decay. The same is true when the relationship no longer fulfills the needs for stimulation (intellectual, physical, and emotional) and contact and no longer maximizes pleasures and minimizes pains.

In addition to those factors that in one form help to establish a relationship and in another form help to dissolve it, there are a number of other factors that might be mentioned as causes of relational deterioration. Psychological change in one or both parties may contribute to relational deterioration. Prominent among psychological changes would be the development of incompatible attitudes and values, vastly different intellectual interests and abilities, major goal changes, and the discovery of previously unknown differences. To the extent that these are incompatible with those of the other individual, the relationship will be shaky. This does not mean that one person cannot be a Democrat and the other a Republican. It does mean that a staunch atheist and a devout fundamentalist are going to have some problems. When one party in a marriage believes in open marriage and the other does not, they are probably heading for some difficulty.

Behavioral change, like psychological change, is also significant. For exam-

273

ple, the individual who once devoted much time to the other person and to the development of the relationship and who then becomes totally absorbed in business or in school and devotes all free time to business activities or studying is going to find significant repercussions from this change. The individual who becomes addicted to drugs or alcohol will likewise present the relationship with a serious problem.

Contextual changes may also exert considerable influence on the relationship. Some relationships cannot survive separation by long distances as when, for example, one of the parties is forced to move far away. When I moved to Illinois from New York to pursue graduate work, my primary relationship survived two years of long-distance separation because it was particularly strong and because it continued to serve many of the needs already mentioned. But I witnessed many other relationships decay and terminate because the individuals were not able to surmount the physical distance barriers. This is a particularly difficult problem for people in the military. The physical separation is too important for many people, and many such relationships deteriorate, as stereotyped in the "Dear John" letters of war years. Long incarceration in prison or long hospital confinement are also context changes that may lead to severe trouble for a relationship.

When there are significant changes in the status relationship between two people or between one member and a third party, the relationship may undergo considerable change and possibly relational deterioration. This type of situation is seen, for instance, when students and teachers develop a romantic relationship. The relationship develops as a student-teacher relationship and is maintained for some time as that. But as the student matures and perhaps becomes a teacher too or otherwise assumes a position equal to or superior in status to that of the teacher, their relationship undergoes considerable change; frequently, this results in some kind of deterioration. In F. Scott Fitzgerald's *Tender Is the Night* we see the same kind of situation, though here it is between a young psychiatrist, Dick Diver, and a wealthy and beautiful patient, Nicole Warren. While Nicole is mentally ill and in need of Dick's care, the relationship flourishes for both; each apparently serves the needs of the other. But as Nicole gets stronger, Dick gets weaker; the relationship changes drastically and ultimately deteriorates.

Sometimes the relationship changes because of the development of another relationship with some third party. At times this may be a romantic interest; at other times it may be a parent; frequently it is a child. When an individual's needs for affection were once supplied by the other party in the primary relationship and are now supplied by a child, the primary relationship is in for considerable alteration and sometimes termination.

An important factor influencing the course of deterioration is the degree of commitment the individuals have toward each other and toward the relationship itself. All our relationships are held together in part by our degree of commitment. And the strength of the relationship, including its resistance to possible deterioration, is often directly related to the degree of commitment of the individuals. When relationships show signs of deterioration and yet there is still a strong commitment to the relationship—a strong desire to keep the relationship together—the individuals may well surmount the obstacles and reverse the pro-

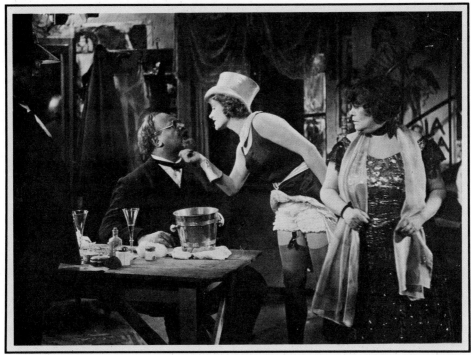

In *The Blue Angel*—the famous German film with Marlene Dietrich and Emil Jannings—we see a relationship between a sophisticated and well-respected schoolteacher, Professor Immanuel Rath, and a low-class cabaret entertainer, Lola Frohlich. Their relationship prospers as long as she is able to look up to him and respect him. When their relationship changes and he becomes her servant, a willing victim of Lola's humiliation and abuse, their relationship becomes a mockery and dies.

cess of deterioration. When that commitment is weak and the individuals doubt that there are good reasons for staying together, relational deterioration seems to come faster and stronger.

Sometimes commitment is conceived in terms of material considerations; people may feel committed because they have invested all their money together, because they have established a business together, or because they own real estate together. At other times the commitment is based on time considerations. People may feel that since they have lived together for these past 10 or 15 years, there is too much time that would be lost if the relationship were terminated. College students who have dated the same person for three or four years often feel that the time investment has been so great that they might as well continue the relationship, and often they allow it to progress to a permanent relationship, perhaps marriage. Although much could be said for this attitude, it seems to me that time is never wasted if something is learned from it or, more important, if we have lived in the present and enjoyed the relationship for its day-to-day value rather than for what it will mean 10 or 20 years from now.

It is far better to terminate a four-year-old relationship that is unsatisfactory than to continue it for the rest of one's life. Unfortunately, only to those who are not now or who have never been in such a relationship will this seem obvious. Sometimes the commitment is based on emotional investment; so much emotional energy may have been spent on the relationship that the individuals find it difficult even to consider dissolving it. Or people may feel committed because they care for each other and for the relationship and feel that for all its problems and difficulties, the relationship is more good than bad, more productive than destructive, more pleasurable than painful. And this, it seems to me, is the kind of commitment that will function to stem and perhaps reverse relational deterioration. Other bases for commitment (materialism, time, emotional investment) may function to preserve the surface features of the relationship but will probably have little influence on preserving its meaning and intimacy.

All these "causes" of relational deterioration are also effects of our responses to relational deterioration. For example, just as contextual changes may influence the deterioration of a relationship, they may also be an effect of the relational deterioration. Thus, when things start to get bad, the individuals may remove themselves physically from one another in response to the deterioration. This physical separation in turn functions as a cause of further deterioration by driving the individuals further apart emotionally and psychologically. Similarly, the degree of commitment that the individuals have for each other may lessen as other signs of deterioration manifest themselves, but in turn the lack of commitment may also function as a cause of deterioration in, for example, lessening the need the individuals may feel to resolve conflicts or to leave the channels of communication open.

RELATIONAL DETERIORATION MANAGEMENT

When relationships go bad, there are three basic alternatives: (1) to keep it as it is, and make no change, (2) to dissolve the relationship, and (3) to change one or more of the elements—that is, to attempt to make the relationship better. Of these three possibilities, I reject only the first one as illogical; the second and third are both candidates for serious consideration. I, therefore, offer here suggestions not for keeping a relationship intact but rather for managing deterioration, whether that entails an attempt to save the relationship or an attempt to terminate it as quickly and with as little pain as possible.

Perhaps flexibility, a willingness to bend and to change, is the major quality in successful relational management, whether we are talking about the development or the deterioration of a relationship. If one or both of the parties lose flexibility, the problems confronting the individuals stand little chance of being dealt with effectively. This flexibility includes a willingness to be open to the other person's feelings, to recognize one's own subjectivity in viewing the situation, and to listen openly to alternative points of view and always with a willingness to change if the situation calls for it.

One of the characteristics of language noted earlier is that it is a great deal easier to change when extreme positions are avoided. When positions are stated as absolutes, it is psychologically difficult for an individual to retract what has been said. "I could never love you again," "I can't bear to touch you," and "I always hated your mother" are statements that will prove at best difficult to retract.

Similarly, it should be recognized that decisions are not necessarily absolute or final or permanent; they can be changed and should be changed if the situation seems to warrant it. To assume that decisions are permanent and unalterable prevents one from exploring other possible decisions and from recognizing that a mistake may have been made and that now a better decision might be instituted.

One of the major failures in communication is to close the channels of communications, to refuse further interaction. There must always be a willingness to communicate, because the only way relational deterioration is going to be dealt with is through communication. This is not to say that the parties should continue to communicate at all costs. At times it may be necessary, even helpful, to separate, to be with one's own thoughts and to cool off by oneself or with another person. The willingness to continue communication at a later time, however, must always be there.

We need to recognize that in all aspects of relationships, but especially in relational deterioration, we have an obligation not only to our partner but also to ourselves and various other people. Sometimes we tend to stay in a relationship even though it is unproductive and causes only grief, for fear of hurting the other person. But this only causes us to hurt ourselves instead. This is a foolish kind of deception. Even though one of the two people may be content to live with this kind of relationship, often it would be better to terminate it. I would venture to say that if one party is unhappy in a relationship, then the other party is probably unhappy as well.

Closely related to the obligation to self is honesty. Some people are so desirous of saving a relationship that they never express their dissatisfactions, fears, and unfulfilled ambitions. They rest content with the surface signs of a relationship. When a relationship is deteriorating we need to be honest enough with ourselves and with the other person to confront the sources of the difficulty—to look honestly at ourselves, at the other person, and at the relationship itself and to analyze what has gone wrong and what would have to be changed if the relationship is to survive. And, more important, we need to ask ourselves if the survival of the relationship is in the best interests of the parties involved. It may be, and it may not be. Both possibilities need to be considered. That there are tremendous difficulties in breaking up should not blind us to the very real difficulties that may be faced in staying together.

SOURCES

Murray S. Davis, *Intimate Relations* (New York: Free Press, 1973), and Mark L. Knapp, *Social Intercourse: From Greeting to Goodbye* (Boston: Allyn & Bacon, 1978), are both useful on relational development and deterioration. Also see Chester C. Bennett, "Secrets Are for Sharing," *Psychology Today* 2 (February 1969): 31–34. Textbooks in interpersonal communication also cover relational development and deterioration. See, for example, Kenneth L. Villard and Leland J. Whipple, *Beginnings in Relational Communication* (New York: Wiley, 1976), and Michael D. Scott and William G. Powers, *Interpersonal Communication: A Question of Needs* (Boston: Houghton Mifflin, 1978). A series of research studies on intimate communication has been edited by George Levinger and Harold L. Raush, *Close Relationships: Perspectives on the Meaning of Intimacy* (Amherst: University of Massachusetts Press, 1977). Two excellent summaries of research on intimate relationships are Glenn Wilson and David Nias, *The Mystery of Love* (New York: Quadrangle/The New York Times Book Co., 1976) and Elaine Walster and G. William Walster, *A New Look at Love* (Reading, Mass.: Addison-Wesley, 1978).

Experiential Vehicles

17.1 Heroes

This exercise consists of the names of 100 noted personalities currently in the news. Some of these people you will recognize and will probably know a great deal about. Others, however, may seem totally unfamiliar. Your task is to select the five persons you would nominate for your personal hall of fame. That is, select the five people you feel could serve as your personal heroes.

HEROES

Bella Abzug
Muhammad Ali
Neil Armstrong
Joan Baez
F. Lee Bailey
Pearl Bailey
James Baldwin
Christiaan Barnard
Ingmar Bergman
Julian Bond
Marlon Brando
Leonid Brezhnev
Helen Gurley Brown
Carol Burnett
Truman Capote
Johnny Carson
Jimmy Carter
Cesar Chavez
Julia Child
Shirley Chisholm
Noam Chomsky
Salvador Dali
Angela Davis
Sammy Davis, Jr.
Doris Day

Jean Dixon
Queen Elizabeth II
Werner Erhard
Jane Fonda
Betty Friedan
Indira Gandhi
Nikki Giovanni
Billy Graham
Edith Head
Patty Hearst
Katharine Hepburn
Xaviera Hollander
Lauren Hutton
Mick Jagger
Elton John
Pope John Paul II
Erica Jong
Barbara Jordan
Ted Kennedy
Billie Jean King
Coretta King
Henry Kissinger
Louise Lasser
Sophia Loren
Shirley MacLaine

Mary McCarthy
Paul McCartney
Mary McGrory
Rod McKuen
Marshall McLuhan
Maharishi Mahesh Yogi
Steve Martin
Liza Minnelli
Sun Myung Moon
Mary Tyler Moore
Patricia Murphy
Ralph Nader
Louise Nevelson
Richard Nixon
Joyce Carol Oates
Jacqueline Kennedy Onassis
Dolly Parton
Norman Vincent Peale
Sylvia Porter
Ronald Reagan
Robert Redford
Vanessa Redgrave
Harry Reems
Burt Reynolds
David Rockefeller

Jonas Salk
Arnold Schwarzenegger
Neil Sedaka
Bobby Seale
Tom Seaver
Carly Simon
O. J. Simpson
Frank Sinatra
B. F. Skinner

Margaret Chase Smith
Alexander Solzhenitsyn
Elizabeth Taylor
Shirley Temple
Mother Teresa
Margaret Thatcher
Pauline Trigère
Margaret Truman

Gloria Vanderbilt
Abigail van Buren
Gore Vidal
Barbara Walters
Lina Wertmüller
Roy Wilkins
Tennessee Williams
Stevie Wonder

17.2   Positive Words*

This exercise is performed by the entire class. One person is "it" and takes a seat in the front of the room or in the center of the circle. (It is possible, though not desirable, for the person to stay where he or she normally sits.) Going around in a circle or from left to right, each person says something positive about the person who is "it."

Note: For this exercise only volunteers should be chosen. Students may be encouraged but should not be forced to participate. Although this exercise is perhaps more appropriate to the content of the earlier units, it is best done when the students know each other fairly well. For this reason, it is put here.

Students must tell the truth—that is, they are not allowed to say anything about the person that they do not believe. At the same time, however, all statements must be positive. Only positive words are allowed during this exercise. Persons may, however, "pass" and say nothing. No one may ask why something was said or why something was not said. The positive words may refer to the person's looks, behavior, intelligence, clothes, mannerisms, and so on. One may also say, "I don't know you very well but you seem friendly" or "You seem honest" or whatever. These statements, too, must be believed to be true. After everyone has said something, another person becomes "it."

After all volunteers have been "it" respond to the following questions individually:

1. Describe your feelings when thinking about becoming "it."
2. How did you feel while people were saying positive words?
3. What comments were the most significant to you?
4. Would you be willing to be "it" again?
5. How do you feel now that the exercise is over? Did it make you feel better? Why do you suppose it had the effect it did?
6. What implications may be drawn from this exercise for application to everyday living?
7. Will this exercise change your behavior in any way?

After you have completed all these questions, share with the entire class whatever comments you would like to.

* This exercise was suggested by Diane Shore Gonzales.

Unit 18

Self-Disclosure in Interpersonal Communication

SELF-DISCLOSURE IN INTERPERSONAL COMMUNICATION

The Rewards of Self-Disclosure
Sources of Resistance to Self-Disclosure
Dangers of Self-Disclosure
Contexts for Self-Disclosure

LEARNING GOALS

After completing this unit, you should be able to:

1. define *self-disclosure*
2. distinguish between *history* and *story*
3. explain at least three rewards of self-disclosure
4. explain at least three sources of resistance to self-disclosure
5. explain the contexts of self-disclosure
6. explain the differences in self-disclosure in terms of topic, sex, and age

Along with the recent interest in encounter groups, integrity groups, and intra- and interpersonal communication generally has come great interest in the concept of *self-disclosure*. In terms of the Johari Window discussed in Unit 3, self-disclosure consists of revealing information about yourself that is in the hidden area—that is, it is a process of moving information from the hidden area to the open area. More formally, we may define self-disclosure as a type of communication in which information about the self is communicated to another person. Special note should be taken of several aspects of this elementary definition.

Self-disclosure is a type of communication. Thus overt statements pertaining to the self as well as slips of the tongue, unconscious nonverbal movements, and public confessions would all be classified as self-disclosing communications.

Self-disclosure is information, in the information theory sense, meaning something previously unknown by the receiver. Information is new knowledge. To tell someone something he or she already knew would not be self-disclosure; in order to be self-disclosure some new knowledge would have to be communicated.

Self-disclosure involves at least one other individual. In order to self-disclose, the communication act must involve at least two persons; it cannot be an *intra*personal communication act. Nor can we, as some people attempt, "disclose" in a manner that makes it impossible for another person to understand. This is not a disclosure at all. Nor can we write in diaries that no one reads and call this self-disclosure. To be self-disclosure the information must be received and understood by another individual.

Gerard Egan, in *Encounter*, makes another distinction that may prove useful. He distinguishes between "history," which he calls "the mode of noninvolvement," and "story," which he calls "the mode of involvement." *History* is a manner of revealing the self that is only pseudo self-disclosure. It is an approach that details some facts of the individual's life but does not really invite involvement from listeners. From a person's history we may learn what the individual did or what happened to him or her throughout that person's life, but somehow we really do not get to know the person, to know how the person feels or thinks.

Story, on the other hand, is authentic self-disclosure. In story individuals communicate their inner selves to others and look for some human response rather than just simple feedback. The speaker takes a risk, puts himself or herself on the line, and reveals something significant about who he or she is and not merely what he or she has done. From story we learn the inner feelings of the individual—the fears, desires, and ambitions, for example.

BOX 18.1
Secrets

Webster's Third New International Dictionary defines secret as "something kept hidden, something kept from the knowledge of others, concealed as one's private knowledge, or shared only confidentially with a few persons; information entrusted to one in confidence." Telling secrets differs from self-disclosure in that in self-disclosure there are only two persons involved: one person tells another person something about himself or herself. In telling secrets one person tells a second person something about a third person. Thus, there are in telling secrets a source, a receiver, and a subject of the secret. In comparison with self-disclosure, little is known about the communication of secrets. We have learned a few things, however.

Most secrets, though clearly not all, are negative. Approximately 50 percent of all secrets involve something that would be considered negative. Often the secret concerns something that some third party did that would normally be considered illegal, immoral, or unconventional. Such secrets would involve, for example, cheating on an examination, being involved in an illegal abortion, alcoholism, drug addiction, the termination of a relationship, and feelings of depression, helplessness, and loneliness. Some secrets are positive and would involve, for example, plans for a surprise party or perhaps a secret engagement, going-steady commitment, or some

such similar issue. Approximately 25 percent of the secrets are of this type. And an equal amount are neutral and would be difficult to classify as either negative or positive.

Two general effects are seen from the sharing of secrets. Perhaps the most obvious effect is that the teller and the listener develop a more positive feeling for each other. Telling a secret is a way of demonstrating closeness and intimacy and it usually works. The second type of effect is that the listener generally develops a more negative feeling for the subject of the secret. This follows logically from the fact that most secrets involve negative behaviors and feelings.

Even when anonymous questionnaires were used, people were more willing to admit to having heard secrets than to having told them. College students, for example, noted that they heard an average of 4.2 secrets during the week but that they only told an average of 2.7. The differences were greater for men than for women. Men, for example, said that they heard an average of 2.4 secrets but only told an average of 0.9. Women, on the other hand, admitted to having heard 3.2 secrets but told an average of 2.6.

Assuming a fair sample, the number of secrets told must equal the number of secrets heard, and yet there are wide differences in the reports of what was heard and what was revealed, especially among the men. Exactly why this is so cannot be determined from the currently available studies. There is greater pressure on men to not reveal secrets (the stereotype of the strong and silent man still dominates the popular mind). But whether this pressure leads men to in fact not reveal secrets or simply to not admit to their revealing secrets is another issue.

We do not tell secrets randomly. Rather, our secrets are told to certain persons and not to others. Our secrets concerning sex, for example, are told to those persons to whom we talk about sex; our secrets about drugs are told to those to whom we normally talk about drugs. And so, like self-disclosure, the telling of secrets is selective, has the effect of bringing the relationship between the source and receiver closer, and is significantly different for men and women.

Source: These thoughts are based largely on the research of W. A. Hillix, Herbert Harari, and Deborah A. Mohr, "Secrets," *Psychology Today* (September 1979): 71–76.

THE REWARDS OF SELF-DISCLOSURE

The obvious question when the topic of self-disclosure arises is, *Why?* Why should anyone self-disclose to anyone else? What is it about this type of communication that merits its being singled out and discussed at length? There is no clear-cut answer to these very legitimate questions. There is no great body of statistical research findings that attests to the usefulness or importance of self-disclosure. Yet there is evidence in the form of testimony, observational reports, and the like that has led a number of researchers and theorists to argue that self-disclosure is perhaps the most important form of communication in which anyone could engage.

One argument is that we cannot know ourselves as fully as possible if we do not self-disclose to at least one other individual. It is assumed that by self-disclosing to another we gain a new perspective on ourselves, a deeper understanding of our own behavior. In therapy, for example, very often the insight does not come directly from the therapist; while the individual is self-disclosing, he or she realizes some facet of behavior or some relationship that had not been known before. Through self-disclosure, then, we may come to understand ourselves more thoroughly. Sidney M. Jourard, in his *The Transparent Self*, notes that self-disclosure is an important factor in counseling and psychotherapy and argues that people may need such help because they have not disclosed significantly to other people.

Closely related is the argument that we will be better able to deal with our problems, especially our guilt, through self-disclosure. One of the great fears that many people have is that they will not be accepted because of some deep dark secret, because of something they have done, or because of some feeling or attitude they might have. Because we feel these things are a basis for rejection, we develop guilt. If, for example, you do not love—or perhaps you hate—one of your parents, you might fear being rejected if you were to self-disclose such a feeling; thus a sense of guilt develops over this. By self-disclosing such a feeling, and by being supported rather than rejected, we are better prepared to deal with the guilt and perhaps reduce or even eliminate it. Even self-acceptance is difficult without self-disclosure. We accept ourselves largely through the eyes of others. If we feel that others would reject us, we are apt to reject ourselves as well. Through self-disclosure and subsequent support we are in a better position to see the positive responses to us and are more likely to respond by developing a positive self-concept.

Keeping our various secrets to ourselves and not revealing who we are to others takes a great deal of energy and leaves us with that much less energy for other things. We must be constantly on guard, for example, lest someone see in our behavior what we consider to be a deviant orientation, or attitude, or behavior pattern. We might avoid certain people for fear that they will be able to tell this awful thing about us, or avoid situations or places because if we are seen there others will know how terrible we really are. By self-disclosing we rid ourselves of the false masks that otherwise must be worn. Jourard puts this most clearly:

> Every maladjusted person is a person who has not made himself known to another human being and in consequence does not know himself. Nor can he be himself. More than that, he struggles actively to avoid becoming known by another human being. He works at it ceaselessly, twenty-four hours daily, and it is work! In the effort to avoid becoming known, a person provides for himself a cancerous kind of stress which is subtle and unrecognized, but none the less effective in producing not only the assorted patterns of unhealthy personality which psychiatry talks about, but also the wide array of physical ills that have come to be recognized as the province of psychosomatic medicine.

Self-disclosure is also helpful in improving communication efficiency. It seems reasonable to assume that we understand the messages of others largely to the extent that we understand the other individuals—that is, we can understand what an individual says better if we know the individual well. We can tell what certain nuances mean, when the person is serious and when joking, when the person is being sarcastic out of fear and when out of resentment, and so on. Self-disclosure is an essential condition for getting to know another individual. You might study a person's behavior or even live together for years, but if that person never self-discloses, you are far from understanding that individual as a complete person.

Perhaps the main reason why self-disclosure is important is that it is necessary if a meaningful relationship is to be established between two people. Without self-disclosure meaningful relationships seem impossible to develop. There are, it is true, relationships that have lasted for 10, 20, 30, and 40 years without self-disclosure. Many married couples would fall into this category, as would colleagues working in the same office or factory or people living in the same neighborhood or apartment house. Without self-disclosure, however, these relationships are probably not terribly meaningful, or at least they are not as meaningful as they might be. By self-disclosing we are in effect saying to other individuals that we trust them, that we respect them, that we care enough about them and about our relationship to reveal ourselves to them. This leads the other individual to self-disclose in return. This is at least the start of a meaningful relationship, a relationship that is honest and open and one that goes beyond the surface trivialities.

SOURCES OF RESISTANCE TO SELF-DISCLOSURE

For all its advantages and importance, self-disclosure is a form of communication that is often fiercely resisted. Some of the possible reasons for its resistance should be examined so that we may better understand our own reluctance to enter into this type of communication experience.

Perhaps the most obvious reason—and some would argue the only reason—for our reluctance to self-disclose, according to Gerard Egan, is that there is a societal bias against it, and we have internalized this bias. We have been conditioned against self-disclosure by the society in which we live. The hero in American folklore is strong but also silent; he bears responsibilities, burdens, and problems without letting others even be aware of them. He is self-reliant and does not need the assistance of anyone. Males have internalized this folk hero, it seems, at least to some extent. Women are a bit more fortunate than men. They are allowed the luxury of self-disclosure; they are allowed to tell their troubles to someone, to pour out their feelings, to talk about themselves. Men are more restricted. Women are allowed greater freedom in expressing emotions, to verbalize love and affection; men are somehow conditioned to avoid such expressions, which men have been taught are signs of weakness rather than strength.

Although it is difficult to admit, many people resist self-disclosing because of a fear of punishment, generally, rejection. We may vividly picture other people laughing at us or whispering about us or condemning us if we self-disclose. These mental pictures help to convince us that self-disclosure is not the most expedient course of action. We rationalize and say it is not necessary to tell anyone anything about ourselves. We are fine as we are, or so we tell ourselves.

We may also fear punishment in the form of tangible or concrete manifestations, such as the loss of a job, the loss of some office, or of some "friends." At times this does happen. The ex-convict who self-discloses his or her past record may find himself or herself without a job or out of political office. Generally, however, these fears are overblown. They are often in the nature of excuses that allow us to rest content without self-disclosing.

Gerard Egan, in *Encounter*, points out that this fear of rejection operates like a reverse halo effect. A *halo effect* refers to the generalizing of virtue from one area to another. For example, your communication teacher may know a great deal about communication and may be perceived as highly credible in that field. The halo effect operates to generalize that perceived credibility to other fields as well, and so when she or he talks about politics or economics or psychology we are more apt to see her or him as credible and knowledgeable in these areas too. The *reverse halo effect* operates in a similar manner. We wrongly assume that if we tell others something negative about ourselves their negative responses will generalize to other aspects of our behavior and they will see us as generally negative, much as we may see the teacher of one field as competent in other fields.

Another possible reason why we resist self-disclosure is what Egan calls *fear of self-knowledge.* We may have built up a beautiful, rationalized picture of ourselves—emphasizing the positive and eliminating or minimizing the negative aspects. Self-disclosure often allows us to see through the rationalizations. We see those positive aspects for what they are, and we see the negative aspects that were previously hidden.

DANGERS OF SELF-DISCLOSURE

Undoubtedly there are numerous advantages to be gained from self-disclosure. Yet these should not blind us to the fact that self-disclosure often involves very real risks—to one's job, to one's professional advancement, to one's social and family life, and to just about any and every aspect of one's life. Politicians who disclose that they have been seeing a psychiatrist may later find their own political party no longer supporting their candidacy and voters unwilling to risk having someone who needed analysis in a position of power. Men and women in law enforcement agencies, such as city or state police officers or FBI agents, who disclose that they are homosexuals or lesbians may soon find themselves confined to desk jobs at some isolated precinct, prevented from further advancement, or charged with criminal behavior and fired. Teachers who disclose their former or present drug behavior or that they are living with one of their students may find themselves denied tenure, teaching the undesirable courses at the undesirable hours, and eventually being victims of "budget cuts." And the teachers or students who find a supportive atmosphere in their interpersonal communication course and who disclose about their sex lives, their financial conditions, or their self-doubts, anxieties, or fantasies may find that some of the less-sympathetic hearers may later use that information to the self-discloser's detriment.

All communication revolves around questions of choice, an observation I have made repeatedly. With self-disclosure, the choices are particularly difficult to make, largely because the advantages and the disadvantages are so significant and cannot be easily predicted. To one person, self-disclosures may bring only rewards; to another, the same self-disclosures may bring only punishments. One may receive a promotion for demonstrating self-confidence; the other may be fired for unbecoming behavior.

In attempting to make your choice between disclosing and not disclosing, it is important to keep in mind—in addition to the advantages and dangers already noted—the irreversible nature of communication. Regardless of how many times we may attempt to qualify something, "take it back," or deny it, once something is said, it cannot be withdrawn. We cannot erase the conclusions and inferences listeners have made on the basis of our disclosures. I am not advocating that you therefore refrain from self-disclosing but only reminding you to consider the irreversible nature of communication as one additional factor involved in your choices.

CONTEXTS FOR SELF-DISCLOSURE

As a particular form of communication, self-disclosure occurs more readily under certain circumstances than under others. Generally, self-disclosure is reciprocal. In any interaction self-disclosure by A is more likely to take place if B engages in self-disclosure than if B does not. This seems obvious and predictable. Yet its consequences are interesting. It implies that a kind of spiral effect operates here, with each person's self-disclosure serving as the stimulus for additional self-disclosure by the other person, which in turn serves as the stimulus for self-disclosure by the other person and on and on.

Self-disclosure, perhaps because of the numerous fears we have about revealing ourselves, is more likely to occur in small groups than in large groups. Dyads are perhaps the most frequent situations in which self-disclosure seems to take place. This seems true for any number of reasons. A dyad seems more suitable because it is easier for the self-discloser to deal with one person's reactions and responses than with the reactions of a group of three, four, or five. The self-discloser can attend to the responses quite carefully and on the basis of the support or lack of support monitor the disclosures, continuing if the situation is supportive and stopping if it is not supportive. With more than one listener such monitoring is impossible, since the responses are sure to vary among the listeners. Another possible reason is that when the group is larger than two, the self-disclosure takes on aspects of public exhibition. It is no longer a confidential matter; now it is one about which many people know. From a more practical point of view it is often difficult to assemble in one place at one time only those people to whom we would want to self-disclose.

Research has not been able to identify fully the kind of person with whom self-disclosure is likely to take place. There seems a great deal of individual variation here. Some studies have found that we disclose more often to those people who are close to us—for example, our spouses, our family, our close friends. Other studies claim that we disclose to people we like and do not disclose to people we dislike, regardless of how close they are to us. Thus an indi-

BOX 18.2
Sex Differences in Self-Disclosure

It has generally been reported that men disclose less than women do, although some studies found that males disclosed more while still other studies found no differences. Judy Pearson's research, on the other hand, has shown that sex role was a significant variable and that "masculine women" self-disclosed to a greater extent than women who scored low on masculinity scales. "Feminine men" self-disclosed to a greater extent than did men who scored low on femininity scales. Other research findings show that females are more likely to disclose positive statements than are males but that both males and females are similar in disclosing negative statements. Commenting on the male reluctance to self-disclose that most researchers have found, Patricia Middlebrook notes that "part of the male role in our society may involve not discussing the self, which, in turn, may add to the level of stress experienced by males and to their early death." Although we may not wish to accept so extreme a relationship as Middlebrook suggests, it does seem that the need or pressure to not self-disclose creates stress and discomfort for males. It has also been found that generally females disclose earlier in the relationship than do males, although some recent research suggests that males disclose earlier.

It is interesting to note that men and women give different reasons for avoiding self-disclosure. The main reason for avoiding self-disclosure, however, is common to both men and women and it is: "If I disclose, I might project an image I do not want to project." In a society where one's image is so important—where one's image is often the basis for success or failure—this reason for avoiding self-disclosure is expected. Other reasons for avoiding self-disclosure, however, are unique for men and women. For men the reasons reported are: "If I self-disclose, I might give information that makes me appear inconsistent," "If I self-disclose, I might lose control over the other person," and "Self-disclosure might threaten relationships I have with people other than close acquaintances." Lawrence Rosenfeld sums up the male reasons for self-disclosure avoidance as: "If I disclose to you, I might project an image I do not want to project, which could make me look bad and cause me to lose control over you. This might go so far as to affect relationships I have with people other than you." The principal objective of men is to avoid self-disclosure so that control can be maintained.

In addition to fearing the projection of an unfavorable image, women avoid self-disclosure for the following reasons: "Self-disclosure would give the other person information that he or she might use against me at some time," "Self-disclosure is a sign of some emotional disturbance," and "Self-disclosure might hurt our relationship." The general reason, then, that women avoid self-disclosure, says Rosenfeld, is: "If I disclose to you I might project an image I do not want to project, such as my being emotionally ill, which you might use against me and which might hurt our relationship." The principal objective for avoiding self-disclosure for women is "to avoid personal hurt and problems with the relationship."

Since self-disclosure depends so greatly on the roles that our culture dictates for both men and women and since these roles are changing so rapidly, we should be seeing significant changes in male and female self-disclosure patterns during these years.

Rosenfeld summarizes the results of his investigation by observing: "The stereotyped male role—independent, competitive, and unsympathetic—and the stereotyped female role—dependent, nonaggressive, and interpersonally oriented—were evident in the reasons indicated for avoiding self-disclosure. Seeking different rewards from their interpersonal relationships, many males and females go about the business of self-disclosing, and *not* self-disclosing, differently." You might wish to test some of these findings yourself by talking with your peers about the reasons they avoid self-disclosure and about the reasons for their reasons. That is, why do men and women have different reasons for avoiding self-disclosure? What is there in the learning histories of the two sexes that might account for such differences?

vidual may disclose to a well-liked teacher even though they are not particularly close and yet not disclose to a brother or sister with whom he or she is close but who is not liked very much. Other studies claim that a lasting relationship between people increases the likelihood of self-disclosure, while still others claim that self-disclosure is more likely to occur in temporary relationships, for example, between prostitute and client or even between strangers on a train.

In their excellent review of research McCroskey and Wheeless discuss a number of correlates of self-disclosure. Among the major correlates noted are reciprocal self-disclosure, competence, trustworthiness, personality, anxiety, and liking-loving.

We tend to self-disclose when the person we are with also self-discloses. This probably leads us to feel more secure and, in fact, reinforces our own self-disclosing behavior. Competent people, it has been found, will engage in self-disclosure more than will people judged less competent. "It may very well be," note McCroskey and Wheeless, "that people who are more competent also perceive themselves to be more competent, and thus have the self-confidence necessary to take more chances with self-disclosure. Or, even more likely, competent people may simply have more positive things about themselves to disclose than less competent people."

Mutual trust seems to be a prerequisite to self-disclosing behaviors. Generally, the more we trust a person the more likely it is that we will self-disclose to him or her. Trust, however, is not a sufficient condition for self-disclosure; we do not self-disclose to everyone we trust. People who are highly sociable and extroverted generally self-disclose more than those who are less sociable and introverted.

Self-disclosure is strangely related to anxiety. Anxiety in general, or anxiety about some particular situation, seems to have the effect of increasing self-disclosure significantly or reducing it to a minimum. Perhaps the relationship between self-disclosure and liking and loving is the easiest to appreciate intuitively. Usually, the more we like or love someone the more likely we will self-disclose to that person. Although this is not always the case, it seems more true than false.

According to Jourard there are topic, sex, and age differences in self-disclosure communications. Certain areas are more likely to be self-disclosed than others. For example, we would be more likely to self-disclose information about our jobs or hobbies than about our sex lives or about our financial situation. Male college students are more likely to disclose to a close friend than to either of their parents, but college women will disclose about equally to their mothers and to their best girlfriends and will not disclose very much to their fathers or to their boyfriends. There are even differences in the amount of self-disclosure in different age groups. Self-disclosure to a spouse or to an opposite-sex friend increases from the age of about 17 to about 50 and then drops off. As might be expected, husbands and wives self-disclose to each other more than they do to any other person or group of persons. "This confirms the view," says Jourard in *The Transparent Self*, "that marriage is the 'closest' relationship one can enter, and it may help us the better to understand why some people avoid it like the plague. Anyone who is reluctant to be known by another person and to know another person—sexually and cognitively—will find the prospective intimacy of marriage somewhat terrifying."

SOURCES

On self-disclosure, see Sidney M. Jourard, *Disclosing Man to Himself* (New York: Van Nostrand Reinhold, 1968), and *The Transparent Self*, rev. ed. (New York: Van Nostrand Reinhold, 1971). In writing this unit I relied heavily on the insights of Gerard Egan; see especially his *Encounter: Group Processes for Interpersonal Growth* (Belmont, Calif.: Brooks/Cole, 1970), or, if you prefer a shorter version, *Face to Face: The Small-Group Experience and Interpersonal Growth* (Belmont, Calif.: Brooks/Cole, 1973). An overview of self-disclosure in communication is provided by W. Barnett Pearce and Stewart M. Sharp, "Self-Disclosing Communication," *Journal of Communication* 23 (December 1973): 409–425. This article also provides an excellent review of the research on self-disclosure and communication. Another excellent review is by Paul Cozby, "Self-Disclosure: A Literature Review," *Psychological Bulletin* 79 (1973): 73–91. Sam Keen and Anne Valley Fox, *Telling Your Story: A Guide to Who You Are and Who You Can Be* (New York: New American Library, 1973), provide some interesting insights on self-disclosure.

A great deal of research is currently being conducted on self-disclosure. For example, for the five dimensions of self-disclosure, see Lawrence R. Wheeless and Janis Grotz, "Conceptualization and Measurement of Reported Self-Disclosure," *Human Communication Research* 2 (summer 1976): 338–346. On sex differences see Shirley J. Gilbert and Gale G. Whiteneck, "Toward a Multidimensional Approach to the Study of Self-Disclosure," *Human Communication Research* 2 (summer 1976): 347–355. On valence, see Shirley J. Gilbert and David Horenstein, "The Communication of Self-Disclosure: Level Versus Valence," *Human Communication Research* 1 (summer 1975): 316–322. On the relationship between trust and self-disclosure, see Lawrence R. Wheeless and Janis Grotz, "The Measurement of Trust and Its Relationship to Self-Disclosure," *Human Communication Research* 3 (spring 1977): 250–257. For the study on self-disclosure avoidance, see Lawrence Rosenfeld, "Self-Disclosure Avoidance: Why I Am Afraid to Tell You Who I Am," *Communication Monographs* 46 (March 1979): 63–74. On sex roles and self-disclosure, see Judy C. Pearson, "Sex Roles and Self-Disclosure," *Psychological Reports* 47 (1980): 640.

Experiential
Vehicles

18.1 Self-Disclosure Questionnaire

Complete the accompanying questionnaire by indicating in the appropriate spaces your willingness-unwillingness to self-disclose these matters to members of a group of students chosen at random from this class.

In a group of five or six persons discuss the questionnaires, self-disclosing what you wish to self-disclose and not disclosing what you do not wish to disclose. Consider at least the following:

1. Are there any discrepancies between what you indicated you would self-disclose and what you were actually willing to self-disclose?
2. What areas were people most unwilling to self-disclose? Why? Discuss these reasons in terms of conditioning.
3. After the group got going and a number of people self-disclosed, did you feel more willing to self-disclose? Explain your feelings.
4. Were negative qualities (or perceived negative qualities) more likely to remain undisclosed? Why?
5. How would the results of your questionnaire have differed if this information was to be disclosed to your parents, a stranger you would never see again, a counselor, and a best friend? Would the results differ depending on the sex of the individual to whom the disclosures were to be made? Explain the reasons why.

SELF-DISCLOSURE QUESTIONNAIRE

	Would definitely self-disclose	Would probably self-disclose	Don't know	Would probably not self-disclose	Would definitely not self-disclose
1. My religious beliefs					
2. My attitudes toward other religions					
3. My attitudes toward different nationalities and races					
4. My political beliefs					
5. My economic status					
6. My views on abortion					
7. My views on pornography					
8. My views on premarital relations					
9. My major pastime					
10. My parents' attitudes toward other religions					
11. My parents' attitudes toward different nationalities and races					
12. My parents' political beliefs					
13. My parents' economic status					
14. My relationship with my parents					
15. My sexual fantasies					
16. My past sexual experiences					
17. My perceived sexual attractiveness					
18. My desired physical attractiveness					
19. My most negative physical attribute					
20. My physical condition or health					
21. My ideal mate					

SELF-DISCLOSURE QUESTIONNAIRE (*Continued*)

22. My drinking behavior					
23. My drug behavior					
24. My gambling behavior					
25. My personal goals					
26. My most embarrassing moment					
27. My unfulfilled desires					
28. My major weaknesses					
29. My major worry					
30. My major strengths					
31. My present happiness-unhappiness					
32. My major mistakes					
33. My general attractiveness					
34. My general self-concept					
35. My general adequacy					

18.2   Self-Disclosure

On an index card write a statement of information that is currently in the hidden self. Do not put your names on these cards; the statements are to be dealt with anonymously. These cards will be collected and read aloud to the entire group.[1]

Discussion of Statements and Model

1. Classify the statements into categories — for example, sexual problems, attitudes toward family, self-doubts, and so forth.
2. Why do you suppose this type of information is kept to the hidden self? What advantages might hiding this information have? What disadvantages?
3. How would you react to people who disclosed such statements to you? For example, what difference, if any, would it make in your relationship?
4. What type of person is likely to have a large hidden self and a small open self? A large open self and a small hidden self?
5. In relation to the other group members, would your open self be larger? Smaller? The same size? Would your hidden self be larger? Smaller? The same size?

[1] The general idea for this exercise comes from Gerard Egan, *Encounter* (Belmont, Cal.: Brooks/Cole, 1970).

Unit 19

Conflict

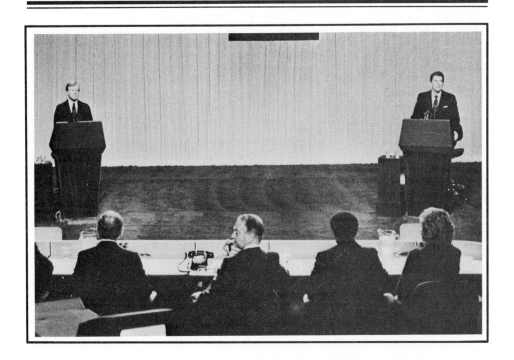

CONFLICT

The Nature of Conflict
Conflict and Communication
Some Specific Interpersonal Conflicts
Conflict Resolution
    19.1 Male and Female
    19.2 Values and Communication
    19.3 Win as Much as You Can

LEARNING GOALS

After completing this unit, you should be able to:

1. define *conflict*
2. provide at least three examples of conflict situations
3. state at least three conditions under which conflict is likely to occur
4. explain some of the effects that conflict has on communication
5. identify at least two sources of communication problems between males and females
6. identify at least two sources of communication problems among gay males, lesbians, and straights
7. identify at least two sources of communication problems between the races
8. identify at least two sources of communication problems between teachers and students
9. explain the role of the media in maintaining the differences between the sexes, gays/lesbians and straights, and the races
10. explain some of the principles of communication that are relevant to conflict and its resolution
11. explain at least four pseudomethods of conflict resolution
12. explain the five stages in conflict resolution

In this unit we examine conflict from a number of different perspectives. First, we inquire into the nature of conflict, the ways in which it is manifested, and some of the problems, as well as some of the values, to be derived from conflict. Second, we inquire into the relationship between conflict and communication, considering the effect of conflict on communication and of communication on conflict. Third, we consider some specific conflicts that occur frequently in our culture. The insights provided here into the general nature of conflict and conflict resolution should provide a useful base for examining these more specific conflicts. Last, we look at conflict resolution, both the pseudomethods of resolution and the stages that might go into a model for resolving conflicts.

THE NATURE OF CONFLICT

Conflict exists in many forms, and its effects may range from extremely productive and healthy to extremely destructive and unhealthy. In its most insidious form, conflict is war between individuals or nations. The object of the game is to bring the enemy to surrender. To accomplish this, anything goes. In sports, boxing perhaps comes closest to real conflict. Although disguised as competition and supported as analogous to baseball or football, the object of boxing is to harm your opponent to the point where he will surrender or to the point where he is rendered incapacitated for 10 seconds. The greater the harm a fighter inflicts on his opponent the closer he is to winning the bout and being proclaimed a hero. Verbally abusing one another would be conflict as well. It is a kind of verbal version of the boxing ring, as, for example, in slander or libel.

In its less extreme form conflict may be seen as competition. Perhaps the most familiar example of competition is professional or amateur sports. Baseball, football, horse racing, chess, and in fact most activities in which someone wins and someone loses are clear examples of competition. Another unambiguous example of competition is the auction sale where two or more people are bidding for the same object; one will win and the others will lose. Competition is more relevant to interpersonal interactions when, for example, two or more people are vying for the affection of another or perhaps vying to marry a particular person. Here one will win and the others will lose. In a similar way siblings compete for the attention and rewards of their parents and relatives.

Conflict in interpersonal relationships, then, may best be viewed as referring to situations in which there exists competition for specific goals. Notice that although many of our preconceived notions about conflict point to its negative qualities and although many conflicts do in fact have negative consequences, there is nothing inherently negative in conflict. As will be illustrated repeatedly, conflict may actually be quite productive, exciting, and helpful in our interpersonal relationships.

Conflict is likely to occur when both parties want or perhaps need the same thing—a particular river, grazing land, a protective mountain, a desirable job, an important promotion—and the only way to secure the desired object is to compete with any other person or group intent on taking it from you. Conflict is also likely to occur when one or more parties are threatened. Perhaps the classic version of this is in the fighting of young boys where one of the boys is threatened to the point where he cannot extricate himself in a socially acceptable manner without actually fighting and so delivers the first blow. In more mature versions the same basic pattern is followed, only the threats are more subtle and more sophisticated and the consequences more lethal. Even among nations the same general pattern is followed. First, the threats are verbal; then they are physical—for example, blockading ships, shooting down a plane, or war.

Naturally, conflict is more likely to occur among persons who dislike or hate each other, though there is also much conflict in marriage and among lovers. And this suggests another condition under which conflict is likely to occur—namely, when one party has been hurt. When this happens, he or she is often likely to hurt back. If, for example, the husband hurts the wife by not responding favorably to her advances, she in turn may attempt to hurt him. As a result he in turn may attempt to hurt her. As a result she may retaliate and hurt him and he again may respond in kind. The process of conflict often spirals with one response serving as the stimulus for another response and so on. Each attack becomes more and more deadly.

Although the usual view is that conflict is negative, as the examples above may suggest, there are also a number of values or benefits to be derived from conflict, and explicit note should be made of these. Alan Filley in his *Interpersonal Conflict Resolution* considers four major values. (1) Many conflict situations have the effect of diffusing more serious conflicts. This is especially the case when the conflicts (perhaps more accurately described as competitive exchanges) are played out according to a system of rules. The disagreements that result often reduce the probability of more significant conflicts arising. (2) Conflict situations lead us to acquire new information, new ways of looking at things. They energize our creativity and force us to explore new ideas and new ways of behaving. (3) When the conflict is an intergroup one then conflict functions to increase group cohesiveness. One of the most powerful ways to encourage members of a group to interact cooperatively and efficiently is to put the group into conflict with another group. (4) Last, Filley notes that conflict provides an opportunity for individuals or groups to measure their power, strength, or ability, since it is in conflict situations that such qualities are mobilized to their peak.

When there is conflict within an interpersonal relationship and when we attempt to resolve that conflict, we are saying in effect that the relationship is worth the effort. To confront such a conflict we must care, at least to some degree, about the relationship, otherwise we would walk away from it. Although there may be exceptions, as when we confront conflict to save face or to gratify some ego need, it seems generally true that confronting a conflict indicates a degree of concern, of commitment, of desire to preserve the relationship.

CONFLICT AND COMMUNICATION

As already noted, the generation and the resolution of conflict are essentially communication processes. Consequently, there are two general areas concerning conflict and communication that need to be explored. The first concerns the effects that conflict has on communications. The second concerns the principles of communication that may be relevant to conflict resolution or, put differently, the effects that communication has on conflict. Each of these areas will be explored in turn.

Conflict frequently leads us to change our evaluative reactions to the individual or group with whom we are in conflict. At times this results in increased negative regard, as it frequently does among warring nations, tribes, or gangs. Seldom do warring nations emerge from battle with increased positiveness toward each other. Each side is generally viewed more negatively after the battles than before. In part this seems due to our psychological need to justify our own hostility and in some cases cruelty. At times conflict results in increased positive regard, as it frequently does when, for example, family members conflict over such issues as individual rights or family obligations and when intellectuals argue over philosophical, political, and economic issues. Here we frequently come out of the conflict with greater understanding for the other person's position and increased respect for the person's standing up for his or her rights, beliefs, and values.

Conflict frequently leads to a drastic change in our openness or lack of it with our competitor. Often of course it leads us to close ourselves off from the other individual, since it is often disadvantageous to reveal our weaknesses to a person who is attempting to achieve the same goal we are. Thus, to tell a person with whom we are competing for a particular job that we lied about having been graduated from college might create a serious and obvious problem. At other times, however, conflict leads us to become more open. Especially when the conflict involves a relationship that we care a great deal about, we may increase our openness and honesty about our feelings, our past history, our weaknesses, and the like in an attempt to bring about a sharing of our "real" selves. The hope is frequently that the other person will behave in a like fashion and through this mutual self-disclosure the difficulties and differences that generated the conflict will be resolved.

Our major goal in communicology, however, should be to provide insight into how conflict might be resolved through the application of principles of effective communication. In an earlier discussion (Unit 16) five characteristics of effective interpersonal communication were considered: (1) openness, (2) empathy, (3) supportiveness, (4) positiveness, and (5) equality of both parties. These five principles might well be repeated here as guides to effective conflict management, but there are other principles that might be advanced that are perhaps more unique to conflict situations and their resolution.

Perhaps the most important point to recognize is that conflict is not synonymous with the elimination of differences. There will always be differences, even disagreements among people. These are as natural as they are inevitable. In conflict resolution we wish to lessen the destructive and unproductive fighting, not to eliminate difference and diversity.

A special attempt should be made in conflict situations to focus on the issues rather than on the personalities involved. Although we can never communicate objectively about the world without communicating about ourselves, we need to make a special effort in conflict to distinguish between these communications, since there is such a strong tendency to blame someone for the conflict and to refocus the conflict onto this other person.

In any conflict there are areas and issues of agreement. In any discussion of conflict we need to capitalize on these agreements and perhaps use them as a basis to approach disagreements and conflicts gradually. Little is accomplished by emphasizing disagreement and minimizing agreement. In some instances we may have to journey far from the actual field of conflict to find such areas of agreement. In most cases, however, we will find them in the midst of the actual conflict.

We must also recognize that flexibility and a willingness to compromise are especially important in conflict situations. If we wish to resolve a conflict and yet approach it with the idea that things must be seen our way, then there will be little hope of agreement; instead there is a good chance that conflict will escalate. A willingness to change, to bend, to give seems essential in any attempt at conflict resolution.

Conflict cannot be resolved unless the communication channels are kept open. To walk out on conflict situations or to refuse to confront the issues may create more problems than it solves. This is not to say that we should constantly verbalize or that periodic moratoriums are not helpful. Rather, it is to emphasize that we need to be willing to communicate—to say what is on our minds and to *listen* to what the other party is saying.

SOME SPECIFIC INTERPERSONAL CONFLICTS

In any culture that is reasonably large, various smaller groups will inevitably come into conflict with one another. No culture is totally homogeneous, and the heterogeneity that exists often gives rise to conflicts and assorted communication problems—interpersonal, public, or mass. Here we consider only a few of these possible conflicts: namely those between males and females, homosexuals and heterosexuals (gays, lesbians, and straights), and whites and blacks. In the brief discussions to follow we attempt to focus on some of the causes for the failure of these groups to communicate as effectively as they might. At this point, however, we are more concerned with asking questions than with providing answers. In reading about the conflicts presented here we should attempt to focus on at least the following issues raised in our previous consideration of conflict: (1) the problems as well as the benefits to be derived from conflict and especially from attempts at conflict resolution and (2) the influences that conflict has on communication and communication has on conflict.

MALES AND FEMALES

Despite the numerical superiority of women, our culture is largely male-dominated and male-oriented. Men control the major businesses, politics, and education and even make the more important decisions in the home. Men get paid more for the same job, are more quickly hired, and are promoted faster than women. And although there have been attempts to change this situation, the changes have been slow. It is extremely difficult to alter that which has been with us for so long.

But perhaps more important than male control of business or politics are the cultural roles that are defined for men and for women. The role of a woman, as defined in everything from elementary school readers to television advertisements, is that of a domestic, a person whose major task is to have children, raise them properly, and make a comfortable home for her husband and family. These roles are particularly apparent in the old movies where Loretta Young gives up her political aspirations for those of Robert Preston, where Nora Charles is an assistant to Nick Charles in their pursuit of justice, and where James Bond does the important jobs while the women are for decoration and for the pleasure of Agent 007.

That this situation has not changed drastically is supported by the numerous studies conducted on the role of women in the media. Helen Franzwa, for example, concluded that "the images of women portrayed in the media and in school are limited to the role of housewife and mother." And in a study on women's roles in advertising, Alice Courtney and Thomas Whipple found that

> the typical female product representative is a young housewife, pictured in the home, using the advertised product in the kitchen or bathroom. The world for women in the ads is a domestic one, where women are housewives who worry about cleanliness and food preparation and serve their husbands and children. . . . Men are portrayed as the voices of authority. They are ten times more likely to be used as the voice over and twice as often seen as the product representative during the evening programming hours. . . . Men are shown in a wide range of occupations and roles in both their out-of-home working and leisure lives. . . . Men are portrayed as the dominant sex in the promotion of most products and services which are significant to the family and where the decision-making process is at all extensive.

Males and females in our society have clearly defined permissible and nonpermissible communication behaviors. And although this, too, is changing, it seems to be changing at an extremely slow rate. For example, college women in my classes tell me that they cannot call a man up for a date, they cannot approach a man in a singles bar but must wait until he approaches them, and must not, under any circumstances, appear overly interested or overly anxious with a date. Although women may verbalize an agreement with the general idea that they should be able to do these things, they also seem to be in agreement that the actual practice of doing these things is quite different.

All this is not to say that there are no real differences between men and women beyond the rather obvious anatomical differences. Corrinne Hutt in her *Males and Females* offers an excellent summary of some of the essential differences:

> The male is physically stronger but less resilient, he is more ambitious and competitive, he has greater spatial, numerical and mechanical ability, he is more

likely to construe the world in terms of objects, ideas and theories. The female at the outset possesses those sensory capacities which facilitate interpersonal communion; physically and psychologically she matures more rapidly, her verbal skills are precocious and proficient, she is more nurturant, affiliative, more consistent, and is likely to construe the world in personal, moral and aesthetic terms.

At the present time it seems impossible to determine the relative influence of biological versus social factors. What does seem clear, however, is that there are many instances in which males and females are discriminated against because of their sexual differences rather than because of any differences in ability, behavior, or attitude. Too often individuals are not permitted to engage in certain behaviors or entertain certain thoughts or hold certain beliefs and attitudes because of their sexual identity and not because of their competence. Cases abound in which communication barriers are erected between men and women because of each other's sex.

In large part such barriers are due to the roles and the rules we expect and teach males and females to follow. For example, males are not supposed to disclose a great deal of personal information about themselves whereas women are encouraged to do so. Males are permitted to talk freely about sex with males and to a lesser degree with females; women are not supposed to talk openly about sex with anyone but especially not with males. Women are supposed to be more tactful in their speech and more indirect; men are encouraged to be direct, even blunt. Women are allowed to express greater emotionality than are males. Women are allowed to touch each other while communicating; men are discouraged from touching each other. Women are permitted to be excited by various crises; males are only permitted to be excited by major crises and even then in relatively controlled ways. Women are allowed to be concerned about their appearance and are even permitted to exhibit a degree of conceit; males are supposed to appear in the rough and to shun any conceit over physical appearance. Males are supposed to be thick-skinned and not easily hurt; women are supposed to be soft and easily hurt. Males are supposed to be aggressive and authoritative; women are supposed to be submissive. Such a list might be continued for several pages. But the point here is that the communications of males and females are different in great part because of our expectations and our differential training. For example, we reward aggressiveness in men and punish it in women; we reward emotionality in women and punish it in men. To the extent that restrictions are placed on communicating our true feelings (if women must hide "toughness" and males must hide "softness," for example), communication between males and females will be unproductive, dishonest, and unsatisfying.

Before leaving this topic, two points should be made explicit. First, the points presented here about males and females obviously do not apply to all males and females. Rather, the intention was to characterize some of the stereotypes under which both sexes in at least some parts of our culture operate. Certainly patterns of behaviors, expectations of males and females, and other variables that influence male and female communication are constantly changing and so what was true yesterday is not necessarily true today and (hopefully, at

The fight for women's rights, begun relatively recently, has brought about great changes on the one hand, but considerable resentment in those (both male and female) who would prefer to maintain the *status quo.*

least) what is true today will not be true tomorrow. Second, it should be clear that the discrimination expressed, the restrictions imposed, and the barriers erected are not only the work of male against female or of female against male but also of male against male and of female against female.

GAYS/LESBIANS AND STRAIGHTS

The situation of homosexuals is unlike the situation of males and females or of blacks and whites in that we cannot tell who is gay or lesbian (homosexual) and who is straight (heterosexual) just by looking at them. Contrary to the popular myth, no one—not straights and not gays or lesbians—can tell by looking at someone whether the person is straight or gay/lesbian. This seems at once an advantage and a disadvantage. It is an advantage to lesbians and gays in that it enables them to appear straight and thus secure jobs and move in any social group they wish without anyone knowing their affectional preference. But this has worked as a disadvantage also. It has enabled the straight majority to force lesbians and gays into a closet and to hide their "gayness" or "lesbianness." We cannot ask that a black appear white or that a white appear black, but we do ask that a gay appear straight.

Because of the diversity of the discriminatory laws and social reactions, gays and lesbians must be homosexual in secret. It would be difficult at best for

305

a family doctor, a community lawyer, a local politician, or a carpenter to admit openly that he or she is gay or lesbian. Clearly they would have to be prepared to lose a great deal. But it is claimed by many that they would gain a great deal also: they would gain in self-respect and they would finally come to terms with their own homosexuality—an essential part of their personalities.

Because of discrimination and the resulting inability of many gays and lesbians to live openly gay or lesbian lives, they are usually portrayed as extremely unhappy individuals. One character in *Boys in the Band* echoes this popular image, saying, "Show me a happy homosexual and I'll show you a gay corpse." Some people argue that the unhappiness is caused by the inner conflicts over one's sexual preference while others would argue that the unhappiness is caused by the society making life difficult for the gay or lesbian. Interestingly enough, however, a recent *Psychology Today* survey on happiness found on the basis of over 52,000 responses that "happiness is not a matter of sexual preference." "Homosexuals in the sample," concluded the researchers, "are neither more nor less happy than heterosexuals." Perhaps lesbians and gays are unhappy only in the minds of straights.

The discriminatory laws and even more important the public hostility toward homosexuality have forced many to marry, have children, and to lead, on the surface, lives that are straight. It has been estimated that one out of every six males is gay and that only slightly fewer women are lesbian. If this figure is at all accurate, then a large number of our relatives, our friends, our fellow students, our teachers, and our neighbors are gay and lesbian.

Because of the need to hide their affectional orientation, gays and lesbians have developed a sublanguage that is generally unknown to the straight world or at least to the large majority of the straight world. This sublanguage, like all sublanguages, enables the group members to communicate among themselves without others being aware of what is going on and at the same time provides the group members with a group identity, a feeling of belonging to some larger whole.

Gays, lesbians, and straights will approach many topics from an entirely different perspective; marriage, children, family, divorce, sex, dating, and the like, topics that are significant to most college students, will be treated very differently by gays, lesbians, and straights. Contrary to popular stereotypes, gay men and lesbians are not against marriage, children, and family. In fact, many gay men and lesbians are currently married to persons of the opposite sex, many have children, and many are devoted to large and close families. Many other gay men and lesbians are involved in relationships that are in many ways similar to what straight society would call marriage and consider their unions just as much a family as would any straight couple—the unions are long-lasting, exclusive, loving, and productive. Similarly, many gay men and lesbians have their children living with them whether they are single, in conventional marriages, or in gay or lesbian unions. It should be easily appreciated, then, that both gay men and lesbians and straights will view significant concepts differently. It is not that one group evaluates them positively and another negatively or that to one group they are meaningful concepts and to the other they are meaningless. Rather, there are differences as a result of one's affectional preference and also a result of the individual's unique history, present outlook, and a host of extra-affectional variables.

At the same time that there are these differences, it should also be noted that lesbians and straight women, for example, are all women and as such have been taught the values and attitudes that society has determined are appropriate for women. Consequently, lesbians and straight women are probably more similar in their attitudes and values toward significant issues than are lesbians and gay men or than are straight women and straight men. The same is true for gay men; they are in many respects more similar to straight men than they are to lesbians. At least this seems to be the case now. I suspect, however, that as the lesbian and gay communities become more cohesive there will emerge a greater degree of similarity among lesbians, among gay men, and among homosexuals in general.

The ability of any group to empathize with the other group is limited. Generally, gays and lesbians will understand straights better than the other way around simply because straight society is more accessible to inspection. The same is true with blacks and whites. Blacks will understand whites better than whites will understand blacks simply because the white culture has been portrayed more often and in more different types of situations than has the black culture.

Of all the intercultural conflicts, the media seem most reluctant to deal with that involving gay/lesbian and straight. The more elitist media—books and intellectual magazines, for example—have dealt with homosexuality on at least a semiregular basis. But the more popular media, particularly movies and television, have done very little to alter the image of the gay male and lesbian or to present anything that would facilitate communication and understanding between gay and straight. In such movies as *Reflections in a Golden Eye*, *Midnight Cowboy*, *Boys in the Band*, *Cruising*, and *La Cage aux Folles*, for example, homosexuals are portrayed as mentally unbalanced and it is made clear that it is the homosexuality that causes the imbalance. There have been some notable exceptions—*Sunday, Bloody Sunday* and *The Man Who Fell to Earth*—but these have been few.

The television image is not much better. On the now defunct "Nancy Walker Show" her secretary was a gay male, or as he put it, he was "g-a-y." For the most part he was to be laughed at rather than laughed with and was probably more harmful than helpful to mutual understanding. In *That Certain Summer* we find probably the first sympathetic portrayal of homosexual males played by Hal Holbrook and Martin Sheen. Yet, on closer inspection, we note that the only physical contact allowed these two was holding hands, and their discussions of homosexuality indicated that it was a negative rather than a positive or neutral experience. In *Alexander: The Other Side of Dawn* we again note that physical contact between two homosexuals was never shown, although that between female and male prostitute was shown in relatively graphic detail. Perhaps the most antihomosexual aspect of this television film was its implication that Alexander's problems were all going to be solved now that he was back with his girlfriend Dawn and removed from gay society.

We seem to have few comparable depictions of lesbianism. *Glitter Palace* dealt with the issue of lesbianism, as did the more effective *A Question of Love*, in which Gena Rowlands and Jane Alexander play lesbian lovers who fight for, but lose, the custody of one woman's child. Based on a real case, this show was one of the few examples in which the media portrayed lesbians in a positive light.

News and talk shows have been a bit more progressive and are now giving some time to discussions of male and female homosexuality—interviews with lesbian mothers and gay athletes are becoming more and more frequent and seem to be having some good effect. At least some of the mystique has been dispelled. Perhaps most important is that people are beginning to realize that bringing homosexuality "out of the closet" does not create any catastrophes—no great numbers of people have had heart attacks, gays and lesbians have not taken over politics or sports, and marriage and heterosexual dating are still popular.

BLACKS AND WHITES

Perhaps the most thoroughly discussed of all the conflicts among people are the racial conflicts. In our society the conflicts between blacks and whites are perhaps the most significant. Controversy over busing to achieve school balance among the races, the quotas demanded by racial groups to achieve a balance in various occupations, and the changes argued for in local laws discriminating against the nonwhite minority are common enough in our daily newspapers.

On a more interpersonal level there are problems because of different world views, different expectations, and different interactions permitted and not permitted by family, friends, or the general population.

Each of us views the world differently, yet those of the same race have a great deal in common. Many common values—history, religion, ethical principles, politics—are shared by members of the same racial or ethnic group. Consequently, there is a greater similarity in the world view of members of the same racial group than in members of different racial groups. Time is the classic example, and has been noted briefly in our discussion of nonverbal communication. White culture demands promptness; to be late for a class or an appointment is a serious offense. Black culture asks only for a general promptness. Black students who are late to class generally do not think there has been any serious infraction of the rules; white students do. And when the teachers are white—as most teachers are—this small difference can create serious problems. Even the values that the groups place on literature, history, and economics will vary drastically. Put differently, the shared field of experience is much more limited when we are communicating with a different race.

We should recognize that there are actually many subcultures within any large culture: there are many black subcultures within the general black culture, as there are many white subcultures within the general white subculture. What is true for members of one subculture may not be true for members of another subculture, despite the fact that they are both black or both white. And so, although there are similarities throughout the culture, there are also significant differences. As communicologists it is important for us to appreciate both the similarities and the differences.

Similarly, we all have different expectations of ourselves as well as of others. That is, we have various prejudices and stereotypes which, in effect, tell us what to expect of the members of other races. Thus we may expect the black male to be a super athlete or very strong. We can expect the Italian to have a good voice and to be popular sexually. We expect the German to be intellectual and organized. We expect the Spaniard to be religious and loyal to family. And these are only the positive expectations. For these groups as well as for any other group we also have negative expectations, and these cause even greater problems.

Jon Blubaugh and Dorthy Pennington, in their *Crossing Difference . . . Interracial Communication,* identify a number of assumptions one group makes about the other group that impede effective interpersonal communication. These assumptions lead us to expect certain behaviors and attitudes and to not expect others. Some of the assumptions that whites make about blacks that are potentially damaging in interpersonal communication include: blacks try to use whites, blacks are all alike in their behaviors and attitudes, blacks are oversensitive and are embarrassed by open recognition of color, and—perhaps most damaging—white society is superior to black society. The assumptions blacks make about whites are equally damaging and would include: whites are all alike, are all deceptive and do not try to understand black society, whites try to use blacks, and, the most extreme, all whites are racists.

Assumptions such as these are not confined to blacks and whites but are repeated, in perhaps slightly different form, by each racial or national group about other racial or national groups. To the extent that these stereotypes persist, meaningful interpersonal communication between the races will be impossible. The communication that does occur is likely to be superficial and, at least in part, dishonest. We might illustrate—as have Blubaugh and Pennington—that each of these stereotypes is logically false. But most of us probably know that already. Assumptions such as these, it seems, must be challenged and proved false through our own actual experiences. An intellectual awareness of the illogic of such assumptions provides a necessary first step, but this must be followed by more visceral experiences and ultimately an emotional awareness of and rejection of such stereotypes.

Along with our expectations of the different racial groups we also have ideas as to what interactions are permissible and what interactions are not permissible with members of the different racial groups. For example, it may be permissible for a white male to go bowling or to a ball game with black males, but it may not be permissible for that same white male to go on a date with a black female. Or the more liberal will allow that dating may take place but it may not progress beyond that, and certainly marriage would be ruled out in many cases. Similarly, we may find it permissible to work with members of different racial groups but we may find it totally nonpermissible for them to live in our neighborhood or in the same apartment house as we do. Or we might find it permissible for them to attend the same school as we do but not the same church or the same social club. And it should be noted, the strictures against such interactions come from both blacks and whites. All three of these areas (world view, expectations, and permissible and nonpermissible interactions) will stand as obstacles to meaningful interracial communication.

The media present further problems in any attempt to achieve meaningful interracial communication. Most often blacks and Chicanos and Indians and in fact most persons who are not of the white Anglo-Saxon Protestant majority are portrayed as members of a racial group rather than simply as people who incidently happened to be members of a particular racial group. For example, "Sanford" plays on the fact that Sanford is black rather than white, and we laugh at Fred's prejudices against whites and Chicanos, but we never are allowed to forget that he is black. Similarly with "Good Times" and "The Jeffersons," their blackness is written into the script as a major plot. On "Diff'rent Strokes" and "Benson," the blackness of the characters is also one of the major plots. Notice, however, that throughout the years of "The Mary Tyler Moore Show," Mary Richards made very little of her being a Protestant or being white. This is true with most of the programs: to be white is incidental but to be nonwhite is essential to the plot. This state of affairs is particularly unfortunate because it prevents the viewing of the nonwhite minorities as people first and as members of the various racial groups second. Not all persons feel that it is unfortunate, however. Many members of minority groups feel that, for example, the blackness of a character should be emphasized. But it would seem that while this might have been true in the beginning, it does not have to be true now. Gregg Morris was black, on "Mission Impossible," but he was first a person and second an engineer, and the color of his skin happened to be black. The same was true, though to a lesser extent, on Bill Cosby's show. More recently we saw Billy Dee Williams as Lando Calrissian in *The Empire Strikes Back*; first, he was his character, a political leader, and second, he happened to be black.

We seem to have come full circle over the past several decades. At one point in history no one was supposed to notice the race of any other person. When a boxing match was telecast years ago when everyone had a black-and-white set, it always amazed me that the announcers would attempt to distinguish the fighters not by saying the black or the white but by noting that one fighter had a purple stripe on his trunks whereas the other fighter had a blue stripe. We were in effect afraid to notice color, or for that matter religion or nationality. Some years ago with the rise of black consciousness we were asked to take notice of the race, religion, and nationality of the people. And we were asked not to forget it. People became justifiably proud of being whatever they were, and so we were asked to take notice of specific characteristics. But we may now have passed that stage and perhaps what we should now notice is that this one person has done X, Y, and Z and that this other person has done A, B, and C and not that one person's ancestors were born in Algeria and another person's ancestors were born in Syria or in Russia or in Greece or in Zambia.

These three examples of conflicting groups are certainly not exhaustive; numerous other groups could have been cited. Perhaps the most significant is that between young and old, but there are many others. Gay men and lesbians, for example, are often in conflict, as are labor and management, members of a religious group or church and the hierarchy of that group or church, and farmers and industrialists. The groups used in the previous discussion, however, seemed among the most important for our purposes of understanding both communication and conflict. With these specific conflicts in mind, we now explore conflict resolution—both the pseudo means and the legitimate and productive means of conflict resolution.

CONFLICT RESOLUTION

There are a wide variety of ways to deal with conflict. Some of these are productive in the sense that they enable us to deal honestly and meaningfully with the conflict and to offer some promise of its ultimate resolution. Some of these ways (open communication, focusing on issues) were discussed under "Conflict and Communication." An alternative way of approaching conflict resolution is to focus on the various stages one would normally go through in resolving conflict. Before examining these stages, it will be beneficial to look first at those methods that, on the surface, appear to deal with conflict but in reality do not, what we call "pseudomethods" of conflict resolution.

PSEUDOMETHODS OF RESOLUTION

Although many such pseudomethods might be identified, we concentrate here on the five that seem the most important. One of the values of going through some of these pseudomethods for resolving conflict is to enable us to identify such strategies better in the behaviors of others and ultimately in our own behaviors as well. This latter ability is not an easy one to develop; but its importance makes the effort worthwhile.

Avoidance or Redefinition

One of the most frequently employed methods of conflict "resolution" is to avoid the conflict. This may take the form of actual physical flight, where the individual may leave the scene of the conflict or perhaps fall asleep and just mentally withdraw. Or it may take the form of emotional or intellectual avoidance where the individual leaves the conflict psychologically by not dealing with any of the arguments or problems raised. A similar method is to redefine the conflict so that it becomes no conflict at all or so that it becomes irrelevant to the individuals and hence unnecessary to deal with.

Force

Perhaps the most common picture of a pseudomethod of conflict resolution is that involving physical force. When confronted with a conflict, many prefer not to deal with the issues but rather to simply force their decision or way of thinking or behaving on the other by physically overpowering the other individual, or at least by the threat of such physical force. At other times, the force used is more emotional than physical. In either case, however, the issues are avoided, and the individual who "wins" is the individual who exerts the most force. This is the technique of warring nations and spouses.

Minimization

Sometimes we deal with conflict by making light of it, by saying and perhaps believing that the conflict, its causes, and its consequences are really not important. We might argue that if left alone time will resolve it. But time does absolutely nothing; over time *we* may do something, but time itself never acts one way or the other. Sometimes we minimize the conflict with humor and may literally laugh at the conflict. Sometimes it is obvious that our laughter is prompted by fear or embarrassment or personal inadequacy in dealing with the conflict situation. But in many instances the humor seems logical enough; it eases the tension and, at least for a time, makes for more effective interpersonal relations. The problem is that the laughter did nothing to get at the root of the problem and when the laughter dies the conflict is still very much alive.

Blame

Sometimes conflict is caused by the actions of one of the individuals; sometimes it is caused by clearly identifiable outside forces. Most of the time, however, it is caused by such a wide variety of factors that any attempt to single out one or two factors is doomed to failure. And yet, a frequently employed fight strategy is to avoid dealing with the conflict by blaming someone for it. In some instances we blame ourselves. This may be the result of a realistic appraisal of the situation or it may be an attempt to evoke sympathy or to gain pity from the other individual. More often, however, we blame the other person. If a couple has a conflict over a child's getting into trouble with the police, for example, the parents may—instead of dealing with the conflict itself—start blaming each other for the child's troubles. As can easily be appreciated (when we are not parties to the conflict), such blaming solves nothing other than temporarily relieving a degree of intrapersonal guilt.

Silencers

One of the most unfair but one of the most popular fight strategies is the use of silencers. By "silencers" I mean a wide variety of fighting techniques that literally silence the other individual. One frequently used silencer is crying. When confronted by a conflict and unable to deal with it or when winning seems unlikely, the individual cries and thus silences the other person. Another technique is to hurt the other individual to the extent that he or she is silenced. This might involve bringing up some embarrassing inadequacy or some physical or personality problem. "You should be put back in the mental hospital" or "How can you talk when you can't even get a job and support your family" may be totally irrelevant to the specific conflict but may go a long way toward silencing the other person.

STAGES IN CONFLICT RESOLUTION

Any conflict situation may be approached as would a problem requiring a decision. The methods suggested for dealing with conflict are very similar to the methods of reflective thinking long taught as educational techniques and in small group communication classes. We here distinguish five principal stages in conflict resolution. A diagram of these essential stages is presented in Figure 19.1.

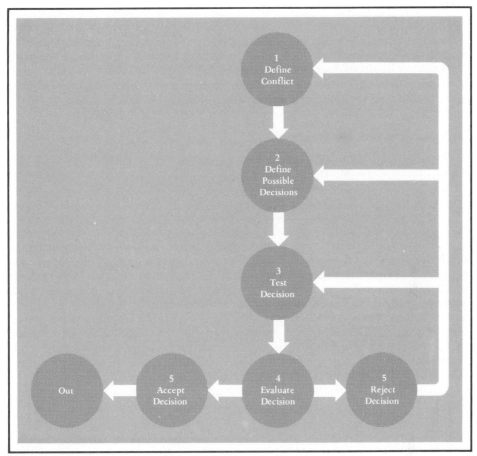

Figure 19.1   Stages in conflict resolution.

1. Define the Conflict

This step is perhaps the most essential, and yet many attempts at conflict resolution omit this stage entirely. We need to ask ourselves what the specific nature of the conflict is and why the conflict exists. It is at this stage that we should collect as many relevant data and opinions as we possibly can. Special care should be taken to ensure that we collect data and opinions that may undermine our position as well as those that are more supportive.

In defining the conflict we should attempt to operationalize it as much as possible. Conflict defined in the abstract is difficult to deal with and resolve. There should be an attempt to deal with conflicts in behavioral terms if possible. Thus, it is one thing for a husband to say that his wife is "cold and unfeeling" and quite another to say she does not call him at the office or kiss him when he comes home or hold his hand when they are at a party. The latter behaviors can be dealt with, whereas the abstract "cold and unfeeling" will be difficult to han-

313

dle. Further, it is useful to operationalize our conflicts because it forces us to be specific and to spell out exactly what we are fighting about. For a wife to say that her husband does not make her feel attractive but then fails to provide concrete examples of such behaviors is saying something quite different from the wife who says her husband does not make her feel attractive and who can easily rattle off 20 recent specific situations in which he criticized her appearance, laughed at her clothes, and whistled at other women.

2. Define Possible Decisions

For any conflict there are a number of possible decisions that can be made. In some instances a number of possible decisions would resolve the conflict; in other cases only one possible decision would work. But in all cases we need to analyze all possible alternatives first.

The word *decision* is used deliberately instead of the more common *solution*. To say that we will find a solution to a conflict assumes that we will eliminate the conflict. Very probably this is not what will happen—we actually strive to lessen the conflict. To imply that we will actually solve a conflict like we solve a mathematical equation is assuming too simplistic a view of human behavior and human interpersonal relationships. More likely we are attempting to make a decision so that future interactions may be undertaken in a somewhat more productive setting. For example, if a husband discovers that his wife is having an affair with a neighbor and they move to another city or neighborhood, they have not "solved" the problem; rather, they have made a decision so that future interactions may take place in a more productive atmosphere. In short, the word *decision* seems more descriptive of what actually goes on in conflict resolution.

In analyzing the possible decisions to the conflict we should attempt to predict the consequences of each of them. This is impossible to do with complete accuracy, and yet some attempt should be made in this direction. We should guard against any tendency to dismiss possible decisions before we give them a fair hearing. Many excellent decisions are never put into operation because they at first seem strange, incorrect, or too difficult to implement.

3. Test Decision

The true test of any decision can only be made when the decision is put into operation. And so we play the odds—we select that decision that seems the most logical and try it out. Although each decision put into operation should be given a fair chance, we should recognize that if a particular decision does not work, another decision should be operationalized in its place. Putting a decision into operation with the idea that if this does not work that conflict resolution is impossible is destructive.

4. Evaluate the Decision

When the decision is in operation we need to evaluate it, examining the ways in which it helps to resolve (or aggravate) the conflict. Does it feel right? Does it make for improved interpersonal communication? Does it significantly lessen the conflict? Is it a practical decision? Will it prove desirable to all parties involved? Will it prove a durable decision or will it only work for a short time? The questions that we ask in evaluating any decision will vary with the nature of the problem. After we evaluate the decision, we move to Step 5.

5. Accept or Reject the Decision

If the decision is evaluated positively, we move to accept the decision and then to *OUT* in our diagram (Figure 19.1). If the decision does not prove satisfactory, then we can do one of three things. First, we might attempt to test another decision; perhaps the decision we ranked as number two will prove more satisfactory. And again we try it out. A second possibility is to redefine the various decisions and then test one of them. The third course of action is to go back and reanalyze and redefine the conflict itself. That is, we can reenter the conflict resolution process at any of the previous stages. In any case, another decision must eventually be put into operation. Perhaps it will work better than the previous one. And perhaps we will have learned something from the last decision-making process that will prove useful in subsequent conflict resolution attempts.

SOURCES

An excellent overview of conflict is provided by David Dressler, *Sociology: The Study of Human Interaction* (New York: Knopf, 1969). A more detailed overview is Alan C. Filley's *Interpersonal Conflict Resolution* (Glenview, Ill.: Scott, Foresman, 1975). Two works relating conflict and communication should be noted: Fred E. Jandt's *Conflict Resolution Through Communication* (New York: Harper & Row, 1973) is a collection of 16 articles, many of which are helpful in conceptualizing the role of conflict in communication and the role of communication in conflict. *Perspectives on Communication in Social Conflict* (Englewood Cliffs, N.J.: Prentice-Hall, 1974), edited by Gerald R. Miller and Herbert W. Simons, contains eight thorough and perceptive articles on communication and conflict. This work also contains a bibliography of over 500 items.

George R. Bach and Peter Wyden's *The Intimate Enemy* (New York: Avon, 1968) is a popular, well-written, and insightful account of conflict and productive and unproductive ways of fighting.

Much is currently being written on sexism. Particularly relevant works from the point of view of communication include Robin Lakoff's *Language and Women's Place* (New York: Harper & Row, 1975); Cheris Kramer, "Women's Speech: Separate but Unequal," *Quarterly Journal of Speech* 60 (February 1974): 14–24; Casey Miller and Kate Swift, "One Small Step for Genkind," in Joseph DeVito, ed., *Language: Concepts and Processes* (Englewood Cliffs, N.J.: Prentice-Hall, 1973); and *Words and Women: New Language in New Times* (New York: Doubleday, 1976). An excellent overview is provided by Bobby R. Patton and Bonnie Ritter Patton, *Living Together . . . Female/Male Communication* (Columbus, Ohio: Charles E. Merrill, 1976). A most comprehensive source is Barbara Eakins and R. Gene Eakins, *Sex Differences in Communication* (Boston: Houghton Mifflin, 1978).

The studies cited on the role of women in the media are: Helen H. Franzwa, "Working Women in Fact and Fiction," *Journal of Communication* 24 (spring 1974): 104–109, and Alice E. Courtney and Thomas W. Whipple, "Women in TV Commercials," *Journal of Communication* 24 (spring 1974): 110–118. The spring 1974 issue of the *Journal of Communication* carried an entire series of articles on women in the media.

On the gay-straight issue there is again much that is currently being written. See, for example, James W. Chesebro and Caroline D. Hamsher, *Orientations to Public Communication* (Palo Alto, Cal.: Science Research Associates, 1976). An excellent collection, useful for raising the consciousness of both gays and straights, is *Out of the Closets: Voices of Gay Liberation* (New York: Douglas, 1972). The results of the happiness survey may be found in Philip Shaver and Jonathan Friedman, "Your Pursuit of Happiness," *Psychology Today* 10 (August 1976): 26–32, 75. A collection of papers by communicologists has been edited by James Chesebro, *Gayspeak* (New York: Pilgrim Press, 1982).

On racism see Andrea Rich, *Interracial Communication* (New York: Harper & Row, 1974); Arthur Smith, *Transracial Communication* (Englewood Cliffs, N.J.: Prentice-Hall, 1973); and Jon A. Blubaugh and Dorthy L. Pennington, *Crossing Difference . . . Interracial Communication* (Columbus, Ohio: Charles E. Merrill, 1976). On both racism and sexism see N. J. Demerath and Gerald Marwell, *Sociology: Perspectives and Applications* (New York: Harper & Row, 1976).

An overview of conflict between the races, sexes, and generations is provided by William D. Brooks and Philip Emmert, *Interpersonal Communication* (Dubuque, Iowa: Wm. C. Brown, 1976).

For a provocative study on conflict in intimate relationships see Mary Anne Fitzpatrick and Jeff Winke, "You Always Hurt the One You Love: Strategies and Tactics in Interpersonal Conflict," *Communication Quarterly* 27 (winter 1979): 3–11.

Experiential Vehicles

19.1 Male and Female

This exercise is designed to increase awareness of some matters that may prevent meaningful interpersonal communication between the sexes. It is also designed to encourage meaningful dialogue among class members.

The women and the men are separated; one group goes into another classroom and one group stays in the original room. The task of each group is to write on the board all the things that they dislike having the other sex think, believe, do, and/or say about them. The women should write on the board all the unpleasant things that men think, believe, say, or do in reference to women— things that prevent meaningful interpersonal communication from taking place. The men do likewise.

After this is completed, the groups change rooms. The men go into the room in which the women have written their dislikes and the women go into the room in which the men have written their dislikes. The men discuss what the women have written and the women discuss what the men have written. After satisfactory discussion has taken place the groups should get together in the original room. Discussion might center on the following:

1. Were there any surprises?
2. Were there any disagreements? That is, did the men (or women) write anything that the women (or men) argued they do not believe, think, do, or say, or that they did not believe was negative?
3. How do you suppose the ideas about the other sex started?
4. Is there any reliable evidence in support of the beliefs of the men about the women or the women about the men?
5. What is the basis for the things that are disliked? Put differently, why was each statement written on the blackboard?
6. What kind of education or training program (if any) do you feel is needed to eliminate these problems?
7. Specifically in what ways do these beliefs, thoughts, actions, and statements prevent meaningful interpersonal communication?
8. How do you feel now that these matters have been discussed?

19.2   Values and Communication

The class is divided into groups of approximately five or six members each. Each group is charged with the same basic task, but each discharges its task from a different perspective. The general task is to select those objects that best reflect American values.

By "values" we mean those objects or ideas that people regard as positive or negative, beautiful or ugly, clean or dirty, pleasant or unpleasant, valuable or worthless, moral or immoral, just or unjust, true or false, and so forth and those objects or ideas that influence the judgments and decisions people make.

The only limitations or restrictions are that (1) five objects be selected—no more and no less; size, weight, and cost are of no consequence and should not influence your decisions, and that (2) the objects be in existence at the present time in the same form they will be in when chosen; that is, you may not construct objects specifically for selection nor combine several objects and count them as one.

Each group is to select objects representing American values as seen from the point of view of one of the following groups:

1. the previous generation
2. the current generation
3. the next generation
4. males
5. females
6. the poor
7. the rich
8. the middle class
9. gay men
10. lesbians
11. heterosexuals
12. professors
13. college students
14. blacks
15. whites
16. American Indians

Each group then reports to the entire class the selections made and the specific values each selection represents. Discussion may then focus on any number of communication related issues such as:

1. the accuracy with which each group represented the values of the group it was assigned
2. the difficulty of communication across generations, sex, economic class, race, and so forth
3. the degrees of stereotyping evidenced by the objects and values selected
4. the degree to which the members' own values influenced their selections of values for the group assigned
5. the role of values in influencing communication generally and of divergent values in hindering communication

6. the ways in which communication might be facilitated when basic values differ

19.3   Win as Much as You Can*

This exercise is designed to explore some of the concepts of cooperation and competition considered in this unit. "Clusters" of eight persons are formed. Each cluster consists of four teams of two members each. Visualizing the area as a clock, the four teams are placed at 12, 3, 6, and 9 o'clock. The teams should be far enough apart from each other so that they can communicate without the other teams' hearing them.

The game consists of 10 rounds. In each round each team selects "X" or "Y." The selection is made on the basis of each team's prediction of what the other teams will select and the itemized "payoffs" as presented in the following "Payoff Table." For each round each team must select either "X" or "Y." Both team members must agree on which letter to select.

The sequence of events should follow the "Score Sheet" (presented following the Payoff Table). For each round the teams are allowed a certain amount of time (listed in the column headed "Time") in which to make their selection of "X" or "Y." After they reach their decision, the "X" or "Y" is recorded in the column headed "Choice." Only after each team has recorded its choices are the choices revealed. When the choices are revealed, refer to the Payoff Table to determine how many points were won or lost. For example, if two teams selected "X" and two teams selected "Y," then according to the Payoff Table the teams selecting X would each win 2 points and the teams selecting "Y" would each lose 2 points. Another example: if one team selected "Y" and three teams selected "X," the team that selected "Y" would lose 3 points and the teams that selected "X" would win 1 point each.

The amount won or lost for each round should be noted in the appropriate column, and a balance should be noted in the column headed "Balance."

Note that for rounds 5, 8, and 10 the game is played a bit differently. Before conferring with one's partner, all teams in the cluster confer for three minutes. Here the teams may talk about anything they wish, but they may not mark their choices at this time. They can only mark their choices after private consultations with their partners, which take place immediately after the cluster conferences. Note also that these three rounds are bonus rounds; the amount won or lost in that round is multiplied by 3 in round 5, by 5 in round 8, and by 10 in round 10.

Only consider the following questions *after* you have played the game.

1. How would you describe the behavior of the members of the cluster? How would you describe your own behavior?

* This exercise owes its formulation to an exercise by William Gellerman in J. William Pfeiffer and John E. Jones, eds., *A Handbook of Structured Experiences for Human Relations Training*, vol. 2 (La-Jolla, Calif.: University Associates, 1974).

PAYOFF TABLE

4 X's	lose 1 point each
3 X's 1 Y	win 1 point each lose 3 points
2 X's 2 Y's	win 2 points each lose 2 points each
1 X 3 Y's	win 3 points each lose 1 point each
4 Y's	win 1 point each

SCORE SHEET

Round	Time	Conference	Choice	Points won	Points lost	Balance
1	2 min.	partner				
2	1 min.	partner				
3	1 min.	partner				
4	1 min.	partner				
5	3 min. 1 min.	cluster partner		× 3 =	× 3 =	
6	1 min.	partner				
7	1 min.	partner				
8	3 min. 1 min.	cluster partner		× 5 =	× 5 =	
9	1 min.	partner				
10	3 min. 1 min.	cluster partner		× 10 =	× 10 =	Total =

2. Is this behavior typical? That is, did you behave here as you would in a real-life situation?

3. How do you feel about the way you played the game? Are you pleased? Disappointed? Sorry? Guilty? Explain the basis for your feelings.

4. If you were playing for points on an examination or even for points toward your final grade in the course, would you have played differently? Explain. What if you were playing for money—say, one dollar per point?

5. Were you surprised at the way in which other members of your cluster played? Explain.

Part Six

Small Group Communication

Unit 20

Preliminaries to Small Group Communication

PRELIMINARIES TO SMALL GROUP COMMUNICATION

The Small Group
Types of Small Groups
    20.1 Individual and Group Decisions
    20.2 Small Group Communication Patterns

LEARNING GOALS

After completing this unit, you should be able to:

1. define the nature of a small group
2. identify the essential steps that should be followed in problem-solving discussions
3. explain the four principles of brainstorming
4. identify the two ways in which therapeutic groups may be health-producing
5. explain one set of procedures that may be followed in therapy or consciousness-raising groups
6. explain the distinction between the problem-solving and the educational or learning group

We are all members of various small groups. The family is the most obvious example, but we also function as members of a team, a class, a collection of friends, and so on. Some of our most important and most personally satisfying communications take place within the small group context.

In this unit we first inquire into the nature of the small group and identify its characteristics. With this as a foundation we next examine four major types of small groups and the procedures that discussants may follow in participating in such group communications. The four types of groups to be examined are the problem-solving group, the idea-generation group, the therapy or personal growth group, and the educational or learning group.

THE SMALL GROUP

For our purposes a *group* is best defined as a collection of individuals, few enough in number so that all members may communicate with relative ease as both senders and receivers, who are related to each other by some common purpose and with some degree of organization or structure among them. Each of these characteristics needs to be explained a bit.

A group is first of all a collection of individuals few enough so that all members may communicate with relative ease as both senders and receivers. This part of the definition touches on one of the most essential aspects of the small group—the number of individuals. Generally, a small group consists of approximately 5 to 12 people. The important point to keep in mind is that each member should be able to function as both source and receiver with relative ease. If the group gets much larger than twelve, this becomes difficult if not impossible.

The members of a group must be related to one another in some way. People in a movie house would not constitute a group, since there is no relationship among the various individuals. With individuals constituting a small group the behavior of one member is significant for the other members, whereas for individuals not constituting a small group the behavior of one member may not even be noticed by the other members.

There must be some common purpose among the members for them to constitute a group. This does not mean that all members must have exactly the same purpose in mind. Actually, this would be impossible. But generally there must be some similarity in the reasons for the individuals to interact.

The people must be connected by some organization or structure. Individuals not constituting a group have no such structure; the behaviors of the various individuals do not constitute any system; there is no pattern to their behaviors. In a small group there is pattern. At times the structure is a very rigid one—as in groups operating under parliamentary procedure, where each comment must follow prescribed rules. At other times, the structure is very loose, as in a social gathering, dinner, or card game. And yet in both groups there is some organization, some structure: two people do not speak at the same time, comments or questions by one member are responded to by others rather than ignored, and so on.

Another characteristic that is frequently included in other definitions of the small group is proximity. It is often held that the members must be face to face for them to constitute a small group. This is usually the case; however, with conference telephones becoming more and more popular, we should recognize that the characteristic of proximity is only included because it is usually, but not always, present. Individuals on a conference call fulfill all the characteristics of a small group and should be recognized as such.

The area of small group communication, then, is concerned with the interaction process that occurs within small group settings. Alvin Goldberg and Carl Larson define the area more formally: "Group communication is an area of study, research and application that focuses not on group process in general, but on the communication behavior of individuals in small face-to-face discussion groups." If we eliminate the "face-to-face" characteristic, the definition seems a suitable one.

TYPES OF SMALL GROUPS

Each of four major types (the problem-solving group, the idea-generation group, the therapy group, and the educational or learning group) is discussed according to its general nature and the procedures that members would follow in participating in such groups.

The Problem-Solving Group

Perhaps the type of group most familiar to us when we think of small group communication is the problem-solving group. Here we have a group of individuals meeting to solve a particular problem or to at least reach a decision that may be a preface to the problem solving itself.

In one sense this is the most exacting kind of group to participate in, since it requires not only a knowledge of small group communication techniques but a thorough knowledge of the particular problem and usually a rather faithful adherence to a somewhat rigid set of procedural rules.

In a problem-solving discussion it is useful to identify approximately eight steps that should be followed (see Figure 20.1). These steps are designed to make problem solving more efficient and more effective. Although some of the initial steps may at first seem unnecessary and there may be a temptation to short-circuit this process, it has been found repeatedly that this does not in fact save time; rather it wastes time. Many discussants will, for example, attempt to state the solutions as soon as the discussion starts, but this frequently creates additional problems and often generates unnecessary conflict.

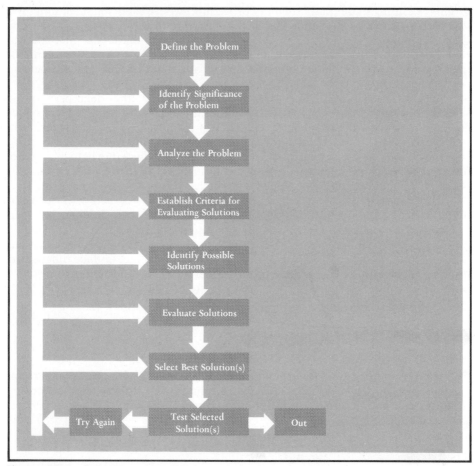

Figure 20.1   Steps in problem-solving discussion.

1. Define the Problem

In many instances the nature of the problem is clearly specified, and everyone in the group knows exactly what the problem is, for example, what color the new soap package should be or what the name for the new candy bar should be. In other instances, however, the problem may be vague, and it remains for the group to define it in concrete, unambiguous, specific terms. Thus, for example, the general problem may be poor campus communications. But such a vague and general topic is difficult to tackle in a problem-solving discussion, and so it is helpful to specify the problem clearly for purposes of this discussion—for example, "How can we improve the school newspaper?" Generally, it is best to define the problem as an open-ended question ("How can we improve the student newspaper?") rather than as a statement ("The student newspaper needs to be improved") or a yes/no question ("Does the student newspaper need improvement?"). The open-ended question allows for greater freedom of exploration and does not restrict the ways in which the problem may be approached. Further, the statement of the problem should not suggest possible solutions, as would, for example, "How can faculty supervision improve the student newspaper?" Here we are stating that faculty supervision is the solution to the problem of improving the student newspaper rather than leaving the solutions open for the discussants to identify and evaluate.

The problem should also be limited in some way so that it identifies a manageable area for discussion. Thus, to state as a discussion problem "How can we improve the university?" seems too broad, and although it may be a useful question it is probably too general for most problem-solving discussions. Rather, it would be more effective to limit the problem and to identify one subdivision of the university on which the group might focus, for example, the student newspaper, student-faculty relationships, registration, examination scheduling, or student advisement.

2. Identify the Significance of the Problem

In many groups all the participants will be aware of the importance or significance of the problem. In other groups it may be helpful for the significance of the problem to be stressed. Sometimes the importance of an issue is recognized only in the abstract, and it may be helpful for its importance to be made more concrete. Sometimes it is recognized that the problem is important for others, and it remains to be pointed out how the problem affects the members of the group themselves. Group members need to be aware of what the implications of the problem are, how this problem may lead to other problems, in what ways this problem blocks goals that group members value, how this problem impinges on the lives of group members, and so on. The more important the problem is perceived to be by the group members, the more importance they will give to the problem-solving process and the more energy they will be willing to expend in dealing with the problem.

3. Analyze the Problem

In the analysis of the problem the group members seek to identify the ramifications of the problem. Given a general problem, we seek in this analysis stage to identify its particular dimensions. Although there are no prescribed questions to ask of all problems, appropriate questions (for most problems) seem to revolve around the following issues. (1) *Duration.* How long has the problem existed? Is it likely that it will continue to exist in the future? What is the predicted course of the problem? For example, will it grow or lessen in influence? (2) *Causes.* What are the major causes of the problem? How certain may we be that these are the actual causes? (3) *Effects.* What are the effects of the problem? How significant are these effects? Who is affected by this problem? How significantly are they affected by the problem? Is this problem causing other problems? How important are these other problems?

Applied to our newspaper example, the specific questions we might ask in the analysis stage might look something like this. Under "duration" we might ask, "How long has there been a problem with the student newspaper?" "Will the problem continue in the future?" "Does it look as though it will grow or lessen in importance?" Under "causes" we might ask, "What seems to be causing the newspaper problem?" "Are there specific people (an editor, a faculty adviser, for example) who might be causing the problem?" "Are there specific policies (editorial, advertising, design) that might be causing the problem?" "How sure are we that these 'causes' are the actual or real causes of the problem?" Under "effects" we might ask, "What effects is this problem producing?" "How significant are these effects?" "Who is affected—students? alumni? faculty?" "Are there people within or outside the college community who are not benefiting as they should be from the student newspaper?"

4. Establish Criteria for Evaluating the Solutions

Before any solutions are proposed, the group members should identify the standards that will be employed in evaluating the possible solutions, the criteria that will be used in selecting one solution over another. This is a particularly difficult aspect of problem solving but an essential one. Generally two types of criteria need to be considered. First, there are the practical criteria—for example, that the solutions must not increase the budget (assuming that there is a limited amount of money to be spent on the newspaper); the size of the newspaper cannot be increased (if this is tied to the budget); the number of issues per semester may not be increased. The solution must be such that it enables the staff of the paper to be drawn from all volunteers regardless of their qualifications, must lead to an increase in the number of advertisers, the readership must increase by at least 10 percent, and so on. Second, there are the value criteria, and these clearly are much more difficult to identify and to determine. These might include, for example, that the newspaper must be a learning experience for all those who work on the paper or that it must reflect the attitudes of the board of trustees, of the faculty, or of the students.

After the solutions are identified (see step 5), the members go back to these standards to make certain that the new solution does meet these criteria.

5. Identify Possible Solutions

At this brainstorming stage the members attempt to identify as many solutions as possible. It is best to focus on quantity rather than quality. Try to identify as many solutions as possible. Brainstorming may be particularly useful at this point. In this case such solutions might include incorporating reviews of faculty publications; student evaluations of specific courses; reviews of restaurants in the campus area; outlines for new courses; student, faculty, and administration profiles; and employment information.

6. Evaluate Solutions

After all the solutions have been proposed, the members go back and evaluate each of them according to the criteria for evaluating solutions established in step 4. For example, to what extent does incorporating reviews of area restaurants meet the criteria for evaluating solutions? Would it increase the budget? Would it lead to an increase in advertising revenue? Each solution should be matched against the criteria for evaluating solutions.

7. Select the Best Solution(s)

At this stage the best solution or solutions are selected and put into operation. Thus, for example, we might incorporate in the next issues reviews of faculty publications and outlines for new courses, assuming that these two possible solutions best met the criteria for evaluating solutions.

8. Test Selected Solutions

After we put the solution(s) into operation, we attempt to test their effectiveness. We might, for example, poll the students in terms of their responses to the new newspaper, or we might examine the number of copies purchased (if the students buy individual copies), or we might analyze the advertising revenue or determine whether the readership did increase 10 percent.

If these solutions prove ineffective, then it is necessary to go back to one of the previous stages and go through part of the process again. Often this takes the form of selecting other solutions to test, but it may involve going further back to, for example, a reanalysis of the problem, an identification of other solutions, or a restatement of criteria.

These eight steps may seem at first to be rather rigidly prescribed, and for beginning problem-solving discussions it would probably not be a bad idea to follow the pattern with some precision. When discussants become more adept at the problem-solving process, the steps may be approached with greater flexibility, where participants go back and forth and may skip a step and come back to it after a normally later step has been covered. Even with such flexibility, however, the problem-solving process is generally fairly clearly prescribed. In contrast, the structure for the idea-generation discussion, to be considered next, is fairly loose.

THE IDEA-GENERATION GROUP

Many small groups exist solely for the purpose of generating ideas, whether they are involved in advertising, politics, education, or, in fact, any field where ideas are needed, and that would include all fields. Although members may get together and simply generate ideas, a formula is usually followed, particularly that formula called brainstorming.

Brainstorming is a technique for literally bombarding a problem and generating as many ideas as possible. In this system the group members meet in two periods: the first is the brainstorming period proper and the second is the evaluation period. The procedure is relatively simple. A problem is selected that is amenable to many possible solutions or ideas. Group members are informed of the problem to be brainstormed before the actual session so that some prior thinking on the topic is done. When the group meets, each person contributes as many ideas as he or she can think of. Ideas should be recorded either in writing or on tape. During this idea-generating session four general rules are followed.

1. No Negative Criticism Is Allowed

All ideas are treated in exactly the same way; they are written down by a secretary. They are not evaluated in this phase, nor are they even discussed. Any negative criticism—whether verbal or nonverbal—is itself criticized by either the leader or the members.

2. Quantity Is Desired

The assumption made here is that the more ideas the better; somewhere in a large pile of ideas will be one or two good ones that may be used. The more ideas generated, the more effective the brainstorming session.

3. Combinations and Extensions Are Desired

While we may not criticize a particular idea, we may extend it or combine it in some way. The value of a particular idea, it should be noted, may well be in the way it stimulates another member to combine or extend it.

4. Freewheeling Is Wanted

By this is meant that the wilder the idea the better. Here the assumption is that it is easier and generally more profitable to tone an idea down rather than to spice it up. A wild idea can easily be tempered, but it is not so easy to elaborate on a simple or conservative idea.

After all the ideas are generated, a period that takes no longer than 15 or 20 minutes, the entire list of ideas is evaluated, and the ones that are unworkable are thrown out while the ones that show promise are retained and evaluated. Here, of course, negative criticism is allowed.

THE PERSONAL GROWTH GROUP

Personal growth groups exist in a variety of forms and serve a variety of functions. Some groups are designed to enable members to cope with particular problems better, even though the problem may be "external" to the member—for example, having an overactive child, a promiscuous spouse, or an alcoholic parent. Other groups are more clearly therapeutic and are designed to change significant aspects of one's personality or behavior. There are so many varieties of personal growth groups that a catalog of all of them would be impossible. Instead, a few of the more popular will be briefly identified, and the procedures used in one of these will be considered in depth.

The *encounter group* seeks to provide an interpersonal and small group atmosphere that facilitates personal growth and the ability to deal effectively with other people. One of its assumptions is that the members will be more effective psychologically and socially if they get to know themselves better (particularly their feelings but also their failures, vices, virtues, and the like) and get to like themselves better (despite the recognized faults). Consequently, the atmosphere of the encounter group is one of acceptance, where freedom to express one's inner thoughts, fears, and doubts is stressed.

The *assertiveness training group* is designed to increase the ability of its members to act more assertively in a wide variety of situations. These groups are extremely popular right now and seem to be having considerable success in getting people to stand up for their rights.

The *psychodrama group* is most clearly therapeutic in function. Unlike the encounter group, the assertiveness training group, and the consciousness-raising group (to be discussed next), the psychodrama group assumes that the member has a problem and that this problem has to be dealt with through acceptance (that one's father is dead, that one's child is retarded, that one's most intimate relationship has deteriorated) or through some attitudinal or behavioral change (to stop drinking or taking drugs, to become less rigid, to diet). As its name implies the group members participate in or act out a psychological drama. The acting out—together with the feedback from other group members, from the leader, and from oneself—is effective in helping the member better understand the problem, accept the problem situation as it is, or change some attitude, belief, or behavior.

eg. Five day Plan

The *consciousness-raising group* grew out of the women's movement and was originally designed to help women cope with the problems society confronts them with and with the rapid changes in attitudes and behaviors taking place throughout all levels of society. The members of a consciousness-raising group all have one characteristic in common (for example, they are all women, all unwed mothers, all gay fathers, or all ex-priests) and it is this commonality that leads the members to get together and assist one another in dealing with themselves as well as others. Notice that in the consciousness-raising group the assumption is that similar people are best equipped to assist in one's personal growth.

As already illustrated, each type of personal growth group differs from each other type. Even within each type there are wide variations; no two encounter or consciousness-raising groups are the same. Yet, there are enough similarities to justify our describing one type of personal growth group, a consciousness-raising group, to provide further insight into this important type of small group communication situation.

This consciousness-raising group is leaderless; all members (usually ranging from 6 to 12 in number) are equal in their control of the group and in their presumed knowledge.

A topic is selected by majority vote of the group. At times this topic is drawn from a prepared list of topics and at other times it is suggested by one of the group members. If this group is concerned with, say, women's liberation, then the topics are naturally related to this general issue of women's liberation. But regardless of what topic is selected, it is always discussed from the point of view of the larger topic that brings these particular people together—in this case women's liberation. Thus, whether the topic is "men" or "employment" or "family," the topic is pursued in light of the issues and problems of the liberation of women. The topics may be more completely phrased as "men and the liberated woman" or "the liberated woman and employment" or "the liberated woman and the family."

After a topic is selected, a starting point is established through some random procedure. For example, a pencil might be spun, with the discussion beginning with the member at which the pencil points. Each member speaks for up to 10 minutes about his or her feelings, experiences, thoughts. The focus is always on oneself. No interruptions are allowed. After the member has finished the other group members may ask questions of clarification. Challenges, arguments, and disagreements are not permitted. Should a member argue or challenge the speaker, any member of the group may call that person out of order. The feedback from other members is to be totally supportive. After the questions of clarification have been answered, the next member speaks; generally proceeding in a clockwise direction. The same procedure is followed until all members have spoken. After the last member has spoken a general discussion follows, during which time members may attempt to relate different aspects of their experience to the experiences of others or tell the group how they feel about certain issues.

After this discussion period (usually around 20 to 60 minutes) the group disbands to meet again at a prearranged time and place.

With this procedure one's consciousness is raised by the individual formulating and verbalizing his or her thoughts on a particular topic, hearing how others feel and think about the same topic and how they have dealt with the issue involved, and formulating and answering questions of clarification. The procedure is not without problems, and it is not presented as a model to follow but merely as one pattern that many consciousness-raising groups do follow.

THE EDUCATIONAL OR LEARNING GROUP

In *educational* or *learning groups* the purpose is to acquire new information or skill through a mutual sharing of knowledge or insight. At times one person, say a teacher, will have the information, and the group exists simply as a means for disseminating the information the teacher possesses. But this function is just as well, if not more effectively, served by a lecture. In most small group learning situations all members have something to teach and something to learn, and the members pool their knowledge to the mutual benefit of all.

In the educational or learning group, members may follow a variety of discussion patterns. For example, a historical topic might be developed chronologically, with the discussion progressing from the past into the present and perhaps predicting the future. Issues in developmental psychology—for example, language development in the child or physical maturity—might also be discussed chronologically. Many topics lend themselves to spatial development, where the discussion follows a left-to-right or a north-to-south pattern—for example, the development of the United States might take a spatial pattern going from east to west or a chronological pattern going from 1776 to the present. Other suitable patterns, depending on the nature of the topic and the needs of the discussants, might be developed in terms of causes and effects, problems and solutions, structures and functions.

Perhaps the most popular pattern is the topical pattern, in which the main topic is divided into its subdivisions without regard for time or space considerations, for example. A group might discuss the functions of the legal profession by itemizing each of the major functions and discussing these without regard for any additional system of ordering. The structure of a corporation might also be considered in terms of its major divisions. As can be appreciated, each of these two topics may be further systematized by, say, ordering the functions of the legal profession in terms of importance or complexity and ordering the major structures of the corporation in terms of decision-making power.

These patterns, it should be noted, are essentially the same patterns that we consider under the structures of public speaking; they are actually patterns for organizing all sorts of communications.

What is most important for the discussants and the leader to recognize is that some pattern, some prearranged agenda, must be developed if the discussion is to progress productively and if each of the major topics is to be given adequate time.

SOURCES

Introductions to the area of small group communication are plentiful and generally excellent. A particularly useful collection is that of Robert S. Cathcart and Larry A. Samovar, eds., *Small Group Communication: A Reader*, 3d ed. (Dubuque, Iowa: Brown, 1979). Other useful works include Dennis S. Gouran, *Discussion: The Process of Group Decision-Making* (New York: Harper & Row, 1974); B. Aubrey Fisher, *Small Group Decision Making: Communication and the Group Process*, 2d ed. (New York: McGraw-Hill, 1980); and Alvin A. Goldberg and Carl E. Larson, *Group Communication: Discussion Processes and Applications* (Englewood Cliffs, N.J.: Prentice-Hall, 1975). On personal growth groups see Charles M. Rossiter, Jr., "Defining 'Therapeutic Communication,'" *Journal of Communication* 25 (summer 1975): 127–130. For interesting discussions of consciousness-raising discussions see James W. Chesebro, J. F. Cragen, and P. McCullough, "The Small Group Technique of the Radical Revolutionary: A Synthetic Study of Consciousness-Raising," *Communication Monographs* 40 (1973): 136–146, and Edith Folb, "The Conscious-Raising Group: An Alternative Structure," in Cathcart and Samovar, *Small Group Communication*, pp. 182–197. A number of interesting case studies as well as a thorough overview of small group communication are provided by John F. Cragan and David W. Wright, *Communication in Small Group Discussions: A Case Study Approach* (St. Paul, Minn.: West, 1980). A summary and critique of 114 studies in small group communication are provided by John F. Cragan and David W. Wright, "Small Group Communication Research of the 1970's: A Synthesis and Critique," *Central States Speech Journal* 31 (fall 1980): 197–213. Also see Ernest G. Bormann, "The Paradox and Promise of Small Group Communication Revisited," *Central States Speech Journal* 31 (fall 1980): 214–20 and Samuel L. Becker, "Directions of Small Group Research for the 1980's," *Central States Speech Journal* 31 (fall 1980): 221–24.

Experiential Vehicles

20.1 Individual and Group Decisions

The purpose of this experience is to explore the differences between individual and group decisions. The exercise is completed in two parts.

First, each individual should rank the 20 persons presented in the order in which they became president, using 1 for the person who was the earliest president, 2 for the person who was the next earliest, down to 20 for the person who was the most recent president. The 20 presidents listed are the 20 most recent.

Second, after each member has completed his or her ranking, groups of five or six should be formed. Each group should then construct its own ranking, again using 1 for the earliest president down to 20 for the most recent president.

After the group rankings are completed, the correct answers will be announced and each member should compute his or her own error score. In addition, the error score of the group should be computed. Error scores are computed as follows: Subtract the ranking you gave each president from the correct ranking without regard to + or − signs. For example, if you gave Harding a ranking of 13 and he was actually 16 then you would have 3 error points for this entry. Similarly, you would have 3 error points if you had ranked Harding 19. Compute your individual error score by subtracting your rankings from the correct rankings for all 20 presidents and adding up the error points. This sum constitutes your error score. Compute the error score of the group in the same way. A low score is good (i.e., accurate) and a high score is bad (i.e., inaccurate).

Compare the error score of each individual member with the error score of the group. Did anyone achieve a better individual (i.e., lower) error score than the group? If so, why did this happen? For example, what did this person say when the group was constructing its ranking? Explain in detail.

This brief exercise should illustrate that, generally, group decisions, especially when dealing with questions of fact, are likely to be more accurate than individual decisions.

TWENTY UNITED STATES PRESIDENTS

_____ Jimmy Carter

_____ Harry S Truman

_____ Grover Cleveland

——————— Lyndon B. Johnson

——————— Calvin Coolidge

——————— Theodore Roosevelt

——————— James A. Garfield

——————— Warren G. Harding

——————— John F. Kennedy

——————— Gerald R. Ford

——————— William McKinley

——————— Chester A. Arthur

——————— Benjamin Harrison

——————— Richard M. Nixon

——————— Dwight D. Eisenhower

——————— Franklin D. Roosevelt

——————— William H. Taft

——————— Herbert C. Hoover

——————— Woodrow Wilson

——————— Ronald Reagan

20.2   Small Group Communication Patterns

In this exercise we attempt to explore the efficiency and satisfaction of communication. Five groups of equal numbers are formed according to the following patterns:

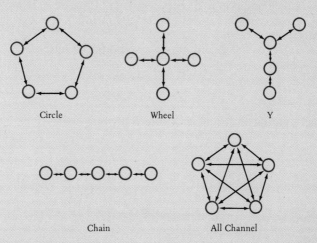

Circle   Wheel   Y

Chain   All Channel

Arrows connecting two individuals indicate that communication may take place between them. Individuals not connected by arrows may communicate not directly but only indirectly through the individual(s) with whom they are connected.

The problem is the same for all groups. Each group is to reach *unanimous* agreement on how many squares are contained in the following diagram:

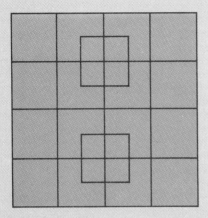

All messages are to be written on individual pieces of paper. Members may pass to other members only those messages that they themselves have written. Thus, if members receive a message they wish to pass on to another member, they must rewrite the message.

Efficiency and Satisfaction Indexes

The efficiency of the groups should be indexed in at least two ways. First, the time necessary for completion should be carefully noted. Second, the messages sent should be saved and counted. Efficiency will thus be indexed by the time it took to arrive at the correct answer and by the number of messages needed for communicating.

The satisfaction of the group members should be indexed by responses on the following scales:

Task Participation

Rate your participation in the task on the following scales:

interesting ____: ____: ____: ____: ____: ____: ____ boring

enjoyable ____: ____: ____: ____: ____: ____: ____ unenjoyable

dynamic ____: ____: ____: ____: ____: ____: ____ static

useful ____: ____: ____: ____: ____: ____: ____ useless

good ____: ____: ____: ____: ____: ____: ____ bad

Compute your mean score for these scales as follows: (1) number the scales from 7 to 1 from left to right, (2) total the scores from all five scales (this number should range from 5 to 35), and (3) divide by five to get your mean score.

Each group should then compute the group mean score by totaling the individual mean scores and dividing the sum by the number of participants.

Efficiency and Satisfaction Scores

Channel Patterns	Efficiency		Satisfaction
	Time	Number of Messages	Group Mean Scores
Circle	____	____	____
Wheel	____	____	____
Y	____	____	____
Chain	____	____	____
All channel	____	____	____

For Discussion

1. Which patterns are most effective in ensuring rapid and accurate communication? Which patterns are least effective? Would this be true with all problems? With what types of problems would it be different? Why?
2. Which patterns result in the greatest degree of member satisfaction? Which patterns result in least satisfaction? How is this related to the leader's role in the group?
3. Are there realistic counterparts to these five communication structures? Do we find these communication structures and patterns in the "real world"? Where? What are some of the consequences of these various communication patterns?
4. How does structure influence function? Examine your own group situation and consider how the structure of the group (the positioning of the members for example) influenced the functions the members played. Does this have a realistic counterpart? In what ways do you function differently as a result of the structure in which you find yourself?
5. What implications would you be willing to draw from this experience for improved communication in the classroom?

Unit 21

Members and Leaders in Small Group Communication

MEMBERS AND LEADERS IN SMALL GROUP COMMUNICATION

Members in Small Group Communication
Leaders in Small Group Communication
21.1 Analyzing Leadership Styles

LEARNING GOALS

After completing this unit, you should be able to:

1. identify and define the three major types of member roles
2. provide at least two examples of each of the three major types of member roles
3. identify and explain at least four functions of leaders in small group communication
4. identify and define the three leadership styles
5. state at least one occasion under which each of the three leadership styles would be appropriate

In this unit, we consider the roles or functions of small group members and leaders. Each person may well serve all these roles throughout his or her membership in various groups. More often, however, people fall into particular roles that they fulfill in every group in which they participate whether they wish to or not, whether the roles are productive or not. By gaining insight into the various roles of both members and leaders we will be in a better position to analyze our own small group behavior and to change it if we wish.

MEMBERS IN SMALL GROUP COMMUNICATION

To function as a member (rather than as a leader) in a small group communication situation seems so natural that some considerations of the small group fail to devote any attention to members even though considerable time is spent on leaders and leadership. But obviously the members' roles are by far the more important. Furthermore, members and leaders are not so different from each other; members serve many of the functions normally considered to be in the province of leaders, and leaders serve many of the functions normally considered the province of members. In this section we present a consideration of the major roles that members may serve in small group communication and offer some suggestions for more effective and enjoyable member participation.

MEMBER ROLES IN SMALL GROUP COMMUNICATION

Kenneth Benne and Paul Sheats (1948) proposed a classification of the roles of members in small group communication that seems to serve as the best overview of this important topic even though it is some 30 years old. Benne and Sheats classify member roles or functions in three general classes: group task roles, group building and maintenance roles, and individual roles. Each of these general functions may be served by different specific roles. These roles are, of course, frequently served by leaders as well.

Group Task Roles

Group task roles are roles that enable the group to focus more specifically on the achievement of its goal or goals. In the performance of any of these roles, the individual does not act as an isolated individual but rather as a member of a larger whole. The individual's behavior is governed by the immediate and long-range needs and goals of the group. The effective group member will generally serve a number of these functions, perhaps all of them, although it is often observed that certain people lock into very few and very specific roles. Thus, for example, one person may almost always seek the opinions of others, another may concentrate on elaborating details, still another on evaluating, and so on. Usually, this singular focus is counterproductive; it is generally better for the roles to be spread more evenly among the members so that each member may serve many group task roles.

Twelve specific roles are distinguished as group task roles. The *initiator-contributor* presents new ideas or new perspectives on old ideas. He or she may suggest new goals, a new definition of the problem, or perhaps new procedures or organizational strategies. The *information seeker* asks for facts and opinions; this person attempts to secure clarification of the issues being discussed. The *opinion seeker* attempts to discover the values underlying the group's task. The *information giver* presents facts and opinions to the group members, while the *opinion giver* presents values and opinions and attempts to spell out what the values of the group should be. The *elaborator* gives examples and tries to work out possible solutions, trying to build on what others have said. The *coordinator* spells out relationships among ideas and suggested solutions. The coordinator also coordinates the activities of the different members. The individual serving the *orienter* function summarizes what has been said and addresses himself or herself to the direction the group is taking as well as to the digressions of the group members. He or she attempts to provide the group members with a clear picture of where they are going. The *evaluator-critic* evaluates the group's decisions or proposed solutions. This person questions the logic or the practicality of the suggestions and thus provides the group with both positive and negative feedback on their various decisions and solutions. The *energizer* stimulates the group to greater activity while the *procedural-technician* takes care of the various mechanical duties such as distributing group materials and arranging the seating. Last, the *recorder* writes down the activities of the group, their suggestions, and their decisions. The recorder serves as the memory of the group.

Group-Building and Maintenance Roles

No individual and no group can be task-oriented in all matters at all times. The group is a unit of varied interpersonal relationships among its members, and these interpersonal relationships need to be built up and maintained if the group is to function effectively—if the group members are to be both satisfied and productive. When these functions are not served, it is frequently observed that the group members tire of the group quickly, become irritable when the group process gets bogged down, engage in frequent conflicts with one another, and find the small group communication process unsatisfying on a personal or social level. The group and its members need the same kind of interpersonal support that individuals need. The group-building and maintenance roles serve this general function.

Group-building and maintenance roles are broken down into seven specific roles. The *encourager* supplies members with positive reinforcement in terms of social approval or praise for its ideas. This person provides the group with understanding and acceptance. The *harmonizer* mediates the various differences between group members. The *compromiser* attempts to resolve conflict between

BOX 21.1
Risky-Shift Phenomenon

Many of our everyday decisions involve some degree of risk. Given two alternatives, one usually involves more risk than the other, and the amount of risk we are willing to take will play some part in our decision-making process. An interesting phenomenon concerning risk has emerged from research on small group communication and has come to be called the *risky-shift* phenomenon. Generally, it has been found that decisions reached after discussion are riskier than decisions reached before discussion. Thus, if we have to choose between two alternatives, we would be more apt to choose the riskier alternative after discussion than before. It has also been found that decisions are more risky in group-centered rather than in leader-centered groups.

Although the procedures to investigate the risky shift have varied greatly from one researcher to another, the general procedure is to present participants with a number of cases involving a decision between a safe but relatively unattractive alternative and a risky but relatively attractive alternative. For example, M. A. Wallach, N. Kogan, and D. J. Bem (1962, p. 77) used the following case: "An electrical engineer may stick with his present job at a modest but adequate salary, or may take a new job offering considerably more money but no long-term security." The subjects would then indicate their decisions individually and then discuss the case in a small group. After the discussion each subject would indicate his or her decision a second time. In terms of our example, before discussion the engineer would be advised to stick with his present job but after discussion to take the job offering the higher salary but less security.

Research has indicated that the risky-shift phenomenon seems to hold for both sexes, for all subject areas, and for both hypothetical and real situations. The inevitable question that arises is, Why does this happen?

Some possibilities are: (1) risk is highly valued in certain roles; (2) taking risks is a cultural (American?) value and people raise their status by taking risks; (3) the risky individual is the most influential member of a group and therefore succeeds in influencing other group members in the direction of greater risk taking; and (4) individual responsibility is diffused in a group, whereas when one is alone the responsibility is one's own.

his or her ideas and those of others. The compromiser will offer a compromise by either changing his or her position half way or even by giving up his or her initial position. The *gatekeeper-expediter* keeps the channels of communication open by reinforcing the efforts of others. The gatekeeper-expediter may propose to hear from a member who has not yet spoken or propose to limit the length or frequency of the contributions from the members. The *standard setter*, or *ego ideal*, sets or proposes standards pertaining to the functioning of the group or to solutions. The *group observer and commentator* keeps a record of the group proceedings and uses this in the group's evaluation of itself. Last, the *follower* goes along with the members of the group. He or she passively accepts the ideas of others and functions more as an audience for the other members than as an active member. This last role is not one that is generally recommended, and yet in some instances—for example, when the group is under considerable stress or when there has been a great deal of interpersonal conflict—it may be productive and may help preserve group cohesiveness.

Individual Roles

In contrast to the group task and the group-building and maintenance roles that are productive, aid the group in achieving its goal, and are group-oriented, the roles noted here are counterproductive, hinder the group in achieving its goal, and are individual-oriented. These individual roles, often termed *dysfunctional*, hinder the group's effectiveness in terms of both productivity and in terms of personal satisfaction.

Eight specific types are considered under individual roles. The *aggressor* expresses negative evaluation of the actions or feelings of the group members. The aggressor attacks the group or the problem being considered. The *blocker* provides negative feedback, is disagreeable, and opposes other members or suggestions regardless of whether he or she has reasonable grounds for doing so or not. The *recognition seeker* attempts to have attention focused on himself or herself and achieves this by boasting and talking about his or her own accomplishments rather than the task at hand. The *self-confessor* expresses his or her own feelings and personal perspectives rather than focusing on the group. The *playboy* and *playgirl* possess all the negative features we think of when we talk of playboys and playgirls. This person is cynical and plays around without any regard for the group process. The *dominator* tries to run the group or the group members. This person may attempt to achieve this by pulling status, by flattering members of the group, or simply by acting the role of the boss. The *help seeker* expresses insecurity or confusion or deprecates himself or herself and thereby attempts to make the other members sympathetic toward him or her. Lastly, the *special interest pleader* disregards the specific goals of the group and pleads the case of some special group, whether it is labor or management, students or faculty, miners or farmers, or some minority group. To this person all problems are seen as opportunities to plead for a special interest.

MEMBER PARTICIPATION IN SMALL GROUP COMMUNICATION

Here are several guidelines that will help make the participation of members in small group communication both more effective and more enjoyable. These suggestions are offered as a kind of elaboration and extension of the basic characteristics of effective interpersonal communication identified in Unit 16—namely, openness, empathy, supportiveness, positiveness, and equality.

Be Group-Oriented

Perhaps the most general and the most important suggestion to keep in mind is that in the small group communication situation you are a member of a

BOX 21.2
Groupthink

After examining the decisions and the decision-making processes of large government organizations—the catastrophic decisions of the Bay of Pigs and Pearl Harbor, the decision processes that went into the development of the Marshall Plan, and President Kennedy's handling of the Cuban missile crisis—Irving Janis developed a theory he calls "groupthink." Groupthink, according to Janis (1971, p. 43), may be defined as "the mode of thinking that persons engage in when *concurrence seeking* becomes so dominant in a cohesive ingroup that it tends to override realistic appraisal of alternative courses of action." The term itself is meant to signal a "deterioration in mental efficiency, reality testing, and moral judgments as a result of group pressures."

There are many specific behaviors of the group members that may be singled out as characteristic of groupthink. One of the most significant behaviors is that the group limits its discussion of possible alternatives to only a small range. It generally does not consider other possibilities as alternatives. Once the group has made a decision, it does not reexamine its decisions even when there are indications of possible dangers. Little time is spent in discussing the reasons why certain of the initial alternatives were in fact rejected. For example, if high cost led the group to reject a certain alternative, the group members will devote little time, if any, to the ways in which the cost may be reduced. Similarly, the group members make little effort to obtain expert information even from people within their own organization.

The group members are extremely selective in the information they consider seriously. Facts and opinions contrary to the position of the group are generally ignored, while those facts and opinions that support the position of the group are welcomed. The group members generally limit themselves to the one decision or one plan. They fail to discuss alternative decisions or plans in the event that their initial decision fails or encounters problems on the way to implementation.

The following symptoms should help in recognizing the existence of groupthink in the groups we observe or in which we participate.

1. Group members think the group and its members are invulnerable to dangers.
2. Members create rationalizations to avoid dealing directly with warnings or threats.
3. Group members believe their group is moral.
4. Those opposed to the group are perceived in simplistic stereotyped ways.
5. Group pressure is put on any member who expresses doubts or questions the group's arguments or proposals.
6. Group members censor their own doubts.

7. Group members believe all members are in unanimous agreement, whether such agreement is stated or not.
8. Group members emerge whose function it is to guard the information that gets to other members of the group especially when such information may create diversity of opinion.

group, a member of some larger whole. Your participation is of value to the extent that it advances the goals of the group with effectiveness and with member satisfaction. Your responsibility is toward the group rather than to any one individual. The effective participant is one who cooperates with others to achieve some mutually satisfying goal. In the small group situation your task is to pool your talents, knowledge, and insight so that a solution may be arrived at that is more effective than a solution that could have been reached by any one individual.

Persons who attempt to parade their intelligence or individual knowledge, for example, are personally oriented rather than group-oriented, and their solo performances hinder rather than advance the goals of the group.

Part of this group orientation involves a recognition that each person in the group is of value and is equal to each other person. Therefore, in making a comment or advancing a proposal, do so with a clear understanding that there are a number of people in the group who should be addressed equally. This simple suggestion is often violated, especially in groups where there is a powerful leader or perhaps where there is one lone but vocal dissenter. In these groups it often happens that members address their comments to these individuals rather than to the group as a whole in an attempt to impress the leader or to convince or silence the dissenter. This type of behavior spirals—an increased focus on the leader or on the dissenter leads to a further increased focus on the leader or the dissenter, which in turn leads to a still further increased focus, and so on.

The receiving end of this issue is that members should be responsive to the comments of all members and, in fact, should facilitate the contributions of all members rather than being responsive to only those members they like or those they wish to impress. All members have the potential for making valuable contributions, and it is unfair to give any member less than full attention. Further, indicate your responsiveness verbally and nonverbally. Make the person know—with what you say and what you do with your body—that you are listening, understanding, and taking into consideration what he or she is saying.

This call for group orientation is not to be taken as a suggestion for abandoning one's individuality or giving up one's personal values or beliefs for the sake of the group. This is clearly an undesirable extreme but one seen frequently in many contemporary cults and small groups (see Box 21.2). Individuality with a group orientation is what is advocated here.

Center Conflict on Issues

Conflict in small group communication situations is inevitable. If some form of conflict does not occur, the group is probably irrelevant or the members are so bored they do not care what is going on. Conflict is a natural part of the exchange of ideas; it is not something that should be feared or ignored. Conflict should be recognized as a natural part of the small group communication process, but it should be centered on issues rather than on personalities. Conflict creates problems in small group communication when it is person-centered rather than issue-centered.

When you disagree with what someone has said, make it clear that your disagreement, your conflict, is with the proposal advanced, the solution suggested, the ideas expressed, and not with the person herself or himself. Similarly, when someone disagrees with what you say, do not take this as a personal attack but rather as an opportunity to discuss issues from an alternative point of view.

Often conflict does center on personalities, and when this happens members of the group have a responsibility to redirect that conflict to the significant issues and should try to get the conflicting individuals to see that the goals of the group will be better advanced if the conflict is pursued only insofar as it relates to the issues under consideration. For example, right before Chris and Pat come to blows one might say, "Then, Chris, you disagree with Pat's proposal mainly because it ignores the needs of the handicapped, right?" and go on to suggest that perhaps the group might focus on how the proposal might be enlarged or altered to deal with the needs of the handicapped. At other times a more direct approach may be necessary, and you may need to say, for example, "Let's stick to the issues" or "Can we get back to the proposal" or perhaps "Let's hear from a third point of view."

Be Critically Open-Minded

One of the most detrimental developments in a small group occurs when members come to the group with their minds already made up. When this happens, the small group process degenerates into a series of individual debates, each person arguing for his or her own position. As noted repeatedly, the small group process is a cooperative venture where each member contributes something to the whole and where the resultant decision or solution emerges from the deliberations of all members. Each member therefore should come to the group equipped with relevant information—facts, figures, and ideas that will be useful to the discussion—but should not have decided on the solution or conclusion they will accept. Thus, any solutions or conclusions that are advanced should be done so with tentativeness rather than definiteness. Discussants should be willing to alter their suggestions and revise them in the light of the discussion.

Similarly, the information and conclusions that anyone advances in a small group communication situation should be offered with a recognition that what is said may be proved wrong. There are few things (if any) that we can be so sure of that we can advance them as facts. Instead we should offer what we have with a clear recognition that perhaps it may not be quite as factual as we would like to think it is. After all, the source we got our information from might be wrong, the information may have been revised by a later survey or report, or our memory may have failed us.

On the receiving end this suggestion advises us to listen openly but critically to the comments, the information, the conclusions of others. We should not come to the discussion prepared to listen openly to some people but not to others, nor should we come prepared to accept everything some people say without critically evaluating it. If we regard the information that we advance with tentativeness, then we should respond in kind to the information advanced by others. This is not to say that we need to ask the source and check the references of everything anyone says but rather that uncritical acceptance is just as dangerous as closed-mindedness. We need to be judiciously open-minded, judiciously critical with our own contributions as well as with the contributions of others.

Ensure Understanding

Most discussions that go wrong probably do so because of a failure to understand. We need to make sure that our ideas and our information are understood by all participants. If something is worth saying, it is worth making sure that it is clearly understood. And so when in doubt, ask the members if what you are saying is clear—not with "Can you understand that bit of complex reasoning?" but rather with "Is that clear?" or "Did I explain that clearly?"

Make sure too that you understand fully the contributions of the other members, especially before you take issue with them. In fact, it is often wise to preface any extended disagreement with some kind of statement such as "As I understand you, you want to exclude Martians from playing on the football team, and if that is correct then I want to say why I think that would be a mistake." Then you would go on to state your objections. In this way you give the other person the opportunity to clarify, deny, or otherwise alter what was said and thus frequently save yourself a long argument and the group's time and energy.

LEADERS IN SMALL GROUP COMMUNICATION

In many—though not all—small group communication situations, one person may serve as leader; sometimes leadership may be shared by several persons. This person may be appointed or may simply emerge during the progress of the group communication. In considering leaders and leadership, we need to focus on three main dimensions. First, we need to consider some definitional aspects and ask what a leader is and how a leader might be distinguished from a nonleader in a small group communication situation. What characteristics does a leader possess that distinguish this person from nonleaders? Second, we need to identify the roles or functions that leaders perform and how leaders might best go about serving these important functions. Third, we should identify the general styles that leadership may take and the ways these leadership functions may be exercised.

DISTINGUISHING THE LEADER

In some instances, it is easy to identify who is the leader and who are the followers. In other instances the distinction seems blurred—at times one person seems the leader, at other times it is someone else. Unfortunately, we have no universally accepted system for identifying the leader of a small group communication situation. Rather, we have different definitions or approaches that vary in their usefulness depending on the specifics of the situation. These several approaches—even from a brief enumeration—when taken together, will provide you with considerable insight into what a leader is and how a leader may be distinguished from a nonleader.

For example, one approach identifies the leader as the person who is the focus of the members' behaviors; the leader is the one to whom the group's messages are addressed, the one who is given the greatest attention by members of the group. While this approach accurately identifies, for example, the teacher as the leader of a classroom situation or the presiding officer as the leader at a meeting, it forces us into the trap of identifying the class clown (who may be getting a great deal of attention and to whom most messages may be directed) as the leader of a class or the lone ill-behaved, screaming child as the leader in a group of adults trying to discuss the world's problems.

Another approach would be to consider the leader the one who leads the group to some specific goals, whether these are the goals of the group or the goals of the leader. Here the leader is defined as the one who can lead the group members to some conclusion or in some direction. Still another approach would simply define the leader as the one whom the group members regard as the leader. To find out who the leader is by this approach, we would simply ask the group members. It often happens, however, that while the group members may identify one person as the leader, another person might actually be having greater influence and may be more effectively serving the various leadership functions than this supposed leader.

The leader may also be identified as the one who occupies the titular position of leadership. Thus, for example, the president of a corporation is the leader of the corporation, the principal is the leader of the school, the captain is the leader of the team. It can easily be appreciated that in some situations the person in the leadership position does not perform leadership functions but rather merely occupies this position while some lower-ranking individual wields the real power to influence other members of the group.

Still another approach and the one that seems most useful is to define a leader as the one who performs the functions that we consider part of leadership. That is, the leader is the one who engages in leadership behaviors; put simply, the leader is the one who leads. (These leader behaviors or roles are identified in detail in the next section.)

Closely related to the leader's functions are the characteristics or traits the leader possesses and how these traits distinguish this person from the nonleaders in the group. Generally, the research seems to show that leaders differ from nonleaders in three general areas: in ability, in sociability, and in motivation.

The leader has abilities that members do not have or has these abilities to a greater degree than nonleaders. More specifically, some studies indicate that leaders are more intelligent whereas others find that leaders are a compromise between the brightest and the dullest. Leaders are generally more knowledgeable about specific issues and have more ready answers. In short, they know more things and let others know they know more things. Leaders also have greater insight into problems and into people than do nonleaders. In terms of sociability, leaders seem more popular among their members and more cooperative. Leaders are more dependable and participate more actively in the small group interactions than do nonleaders. Concerning motivational factors, leaders have greater initiative; they will initiate projects, solutions, and suggestions more often than will nonleaders. Leaders also have greater persistence and determination than do nonleaders. These traits seem intuitively satisfying; none of them seems unexpected, and very likely your own experience would confirm the findings of these experimental researchers.

LEADERS' FUNCTIONS

In the relatively formal small group situations such as politicians planning a campaign strategy, advertisers discussing a campaign, or teachers considering educational methods, the leader has a number of specific functions.

These functions are not the exclusive property of the leader; rather they are functions that when performed are performed by a person serving a leadership role. Put differently, it is more important that these functions be served than who serves them. In situations where a specific leader is appointed or exists by virtue of some position or prior agreement, these functions are generally expected to be performed by him or her. It is important to note that leadership functions are performed best when they are performed unobtrusively—when they are performed in a nonobvious, natural manner. Leaders carry out six major functions.

1. Activate the Group Interaction

In many situations the group needs no encouragement to interact. Certainly this is true of most groups with definite goals and an urgency about their mission. On the other hand, there are many groups which for one reason or another need some prodding, some stimulation to interact. Perhaps the group is newly formed and the members feel a bit uneasy with one another. Here the leader serves an important function by stimulating the members to interact. It is also important to note that this function needs to be served when the individuals of a group are acting as individuals rather than as a group. This is often the case in classroom situations when some members of a class know each other from other classes or perhaps when they graduated from the same high school. These students may stick together and function as subgroups rather than as equal members of the large groups. In this case the leader must do something to make the members recognize that they are part of a group rather than of a subgroup or pair.

2. Maintain Effective Interaction Throughout

Even after the group is stimulated to group interaction, it is necessary for the leader to see that the members maintain effective interaction throughout the discussion and throughout the membership. Discussions have a way of dragging after the preliminaries are over and before the meat of the problem is gotten to. When this happens it is necessary for the leader to again prod the group to effective interaction. Also, interaction is seldom shared by all members equally, but this in itself does not create problems. Problems are created, however, when this disproportionate participation is extreme or when members feel an uneasiness about entering the group interaction.

3. Keep Members on the Track

The leader should recognize that most individuals are relatively egocentric and have interests and concerns that are unique to them. Because of this, each individual will tend to wander off the track a bit. It is the leader's task to keep all members on the track—perhaps by asking relevant questions, by interjecting internal summaries as the group goes along, or perhaps by providing suitable transitions so that the relationship of an issue just discussed to one about to be considered is made clear. In some problem-solving and educational groups a formal agenda may be used to assist in this function.

4. Ensure Member Satisfaction

The leader should recognize that all members have different psychological needs and wants and many people enter groups because of these needs and wants. Even though a group may, for example, deal with political issues, the various members may have come together for reasons that are more psychological than political or intellectual. If a group such as this is to be effective, it must not only meet the surface purposes of the group (in this case political) but also the underlying or psychological purposes that motivated many of the members to come together in the first place.

One sure way to ignore these needs is for the leader to insist that the group members do nothing that is not directly related to the surface purposes of the group. Digressions, assuming that they are not extremely frequent or overly long, are significant parts of the small group communication process and should be recognized as such.

5. Encourage Ongoing Evaluation and Improvement

All groups will encounter obstacles as they attempt to solve a problem, reach a decision, or generate ideas. No group is totally effective. All groups have room for improvement. This, of course, is an obvious statement. What is not so obvious is that it is the responsibility of the group members (encouraged by the leader) to seek out these obstacles and to attempt to improve the process of group interaction. This is an extremely important but an extremely difficult task for any individual or group to undertake. People do not like to confront their shortcomings or be told that they are not functioning as effectively as they might. And yet, if the group is to improve it must focus some attention on itself, and along with attempting to solve some external problem must attempt to solve its own internal problems as well.

6. Prepare the Group Members for the Discussion

Groups form gradually and need to be eased into any discussion that is meaningful. It is the function of the leader to prepare the group members for the discussion, and this involves preparing the members for the small group interaction as well as for the discussion of a specific issue or problem.

Diverse members should not be expected to just sit down and discuss a problem without becoming familiar with each other at least superficially. Similarly, if the members are to discuss a specific problem, it is necessary that a proper briefing be introduced. Perhaps materials need to be distributed to group members before the actual discussion, or perhaps members need to be instructed to read certain materials or view a particular film or television show. Whatever the prediscussion preparations, it should be organized and coordinated by the leader.

These are just a few functions generally considered to be the responsibility of the leader. Obviously there are additional tasks of the leader that are unique to each individual situation. These tasks will become apparent as the group interacts and as the members develop greater skill in the process of small group interaction. The few functions presented here should provide some initial guidance in conducting and leading an effective small group discussion.

LEADERSHIP STYLES

The six functions of the leader may be served in various different ways or under different leadership styles. Generally three types of leadership are distinguished: laissez-faire, democratic, and authoritarian. Each type actually designates a class of leadership within which there is considerable variation; these leadership styles exist on a continuum. The laissez-faire and the democratic leaders are at times difficult to distinguish, as are the democratic and the autocratic. And yet, there is enough difference among the styles—at least in their pure forms—to warrant our considering them as different approaches to leadership. In the real world these three styles inevitably appear in varied forms.

Laissez-Faire

The laissez-faire leader allows the group to develop and progress on its own and even allows it to make its own mistakes. This leader gives up or denies any real leadership authority, and so this type may well be called a nonleadership style rather than a leadership style. The laissez-faire "leader" does answer questions or provide relevant information, but he or she does this only when specifically asked. This leader gives little if any reinforcement to the group members; at the same time this leader does not punish either and so is nonthreatening. He or she takes no initiative in directing or suggesting alternative courses of action.

Democratic Leader

The democratic leader provides direction but allows the group to develop and progress the way the members wish. The group members are encouraged to

The military probably provides the best examples of authoritarian leaders.

determine group goals and group procedures. The democratic leader stimulates self-direction and self-actualization of the group members. Unlike the laissez-faire leader the democratic leader does give the members reinforcement and does contribute suggestions for direction and alternative courses of action. Always, however, this leader allows the group to make its own decisions.

Authoritarian Leader

The authoritarian leader is the opposite of the laissez-faire leader. This leader determines the group policies or makes decisions without consulting or securing agreement from the group members. This leader is impersonal, and communication goes to the leader and from the leader but rarely from member to member. This leader attempts to minimize intragroup communication. In this way the leader's role becomes even more important.

The authoritarian leader assumes the greatest responsibility for the progress of the group and wants no interference from group members. This person is concerned with getting the group to accept his or her decisions. It should be noted that this leader often satisfies the group's psychological needs; he or she rewards and punishes the group much like a parent does. And like a parent the leader concentrates responsibility on himself or herself.

A number of important studies have been conducted to examine the relative effectiveness of these various leadership styles. In one study (Ralph White and Ronald Lippett) groups of boys were led by the three different styles. It was found that in the laissez-faire group, the discussion was member-centered but the boys were inefficient. In the democratic group, cohesiveness was greatest, as was member satisfaction. The work completed was less than that produced by the authoritarian group, but it was judged to be of higher quality. In the authoritarian group the boys were most productive and efficient. However, the morale and satisfaction were lower than in the democratic group. Marvin Shaw found that a group led by an authoritarian leader made fewer errors, took less time, and communicated with fewer messages in solving mathematical problems than the democratic group.

Cecil Gibb (1969, p. 259), in summarizing the results of a series of studies on democratic as opposed to authoritarian leadership, notes that the authoritarian (compared to the democratic) group produced "(1) a greater quantity of work, but (2) less work motivation and (3) less originality in work; (4) a greater amount of aggressiveness expressed both toward the leader and other group members; (5) more suppressed discontent; (6) more dependent and submissive behavior; (7) less friendliness in the group; and (8) less 'group mindedness.'"

Each of these leadership styles has its place, and we should not consider one style superior to the others. Each is appropriate for a different purpose. In a social group at a friend's house any leadership other than laissez-faire would be difficult to tolerate. But as Cecil Gibb notes, when speed and efficiency are paramount, authoritarian leadership seems the most appropriate. It also seems appropriate when the group members continue to show lack of motivation toward the task despite repeated democratic efforts to move them. When all members are about equal in their knowledge of the topic or when the members are very concerned with their individual rights, then the democratic leader seems the most appropriate.

SOURCES

On members' roles see Kenneth D. Benne and Paul Sheats, "Functional Roles of Group Members," *Journal of Social Issues* 4 (1948): 41–49. On leadership roles see any of the references noted in Unit 19. For the definitional aspects of leadership I relied on the reviews by L. F. Carter, "On Defining Leadership," in M. Sherif and M. O. Wilson, eds., *Group Relations at the Crossroads* (New York: Harper & Row, 1953): 262–265, and Marvin Shaw, *Group Dynamics: The Psychology of Small Group Behavior*, 3d ed. (New York: McGraw-Hill, 1981). On styles of leadership see the seminal study by Ralph White and Ronald Lippitt, *Autocracy and Democracy* (New York: Harper & Row, 1960). Also see Marvin E. Shaw, "A Comparison of Two Types of Leadership in Various Communication Nets," *Journal of Abnormal and Social Psychology* 50 (1955): 127–134, and J. F. Sargent and G. R. Miller, "Some Differences in Certain Communication Behaviors of Autocratic and Democratic Leaders," *Journal of Communication* 21 (1971): 233–252. Perhaps the single best source on leadership is Cecil A. Gibb's "Leadership," in G. Lindsey and E. Aronson, eds., *The Handbook of Social Psychology*, 2d ed., vol. 4 (Reading, Mass.: Addison-Wesley, 1969), pp. 205–282.

For groupthink see the works of Irving Janis. A useful overview is provided in his "Groupthink," *Psychology Today* 5 (November 1971): 43–46, 74–76. A more detailed account is presented in Janis' "Groupthink Among Policy Makers," in *Sanctions for Evil*, N. Sanford and C. Comstock, eds. (San Francisco: Jossey-Bass, 1971). Janis's *Victims of Groupthink: A Psychological Study of Foreign Policy Decisions and Fiascoes* (Boston: Houghton Mifflin, 1972) presents the most thorough discussion.

For the risky-shift phenomenon see Marvin Shaw, *Group Dynamics: The Psychology of Small Group Behavior*, for a general overview, and Roger Brown, *Social Psychology* (New York: Free Press, 1965) for some interesting insights into this phenomenon. The study cited by M. A. Wallach, N. Kogan, and D. J. Bem was titled "Group Influence on Individual Risk Taking," *Journal of Abnormal and Social Psychology* 65 (1962): 75–86. D. Cartwright, "Determinants of Scientific Progress: The Case of Research on the Risky Shift," *American Psychologist* 28 (1973): 222–231, provides an excellent analysis of the area.

Experiential Vehicle

21.1 Analyzing Leadership Styles

Divide the class into six groups of equal size. Two groups should be assigned a laissez-faire leader, two groups an authoritarian leader, and two groups a democratic leader. All groups should be given the same three problems presented below. The groups should discuss the problems in the order given and should complete the first problem before going on to the next one.

Each group should discuss the problem and attempt to reach a decision regarding the solution. When any group has arrived at a unanimous solution they should raise their hands and the instructor will tell them only if their answer is correct or incorrect. If the answer is correct, then the time it took to arrive at that answer should be recorded and the group should go on to the next problem. Be sure to note starting time so that total time for completion may be accurately recorded. If the answer is incorrect the group should be so informed, and they should continue discussing the problem until they reach the correct solution. The times for completion should be recorded on the Time Chart. In addition, general discussion should center on the questions following the Time Chart.

Problem 1

A man bought a horse for $70 and sold it for $80. He then bought the horse back for $90 but soon sold it again for $100. How much money did the man make or lose or did he break even in his horse trading?

Problem 2

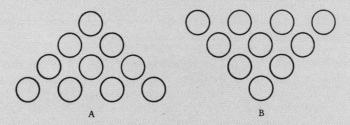

A   B

Construct Figure B from Figure A by moving no more than three circles.

Problem 3

Draw four straight lines without removing pencil from page and without crossing over or retracing lines to connect all nine dots.

. . .

. . .

. . .

TIME CHART

	Laissez-faire Leader		Authoritarian Leader		Democratic Leader	
	Group 1	Group 2	Group 1	Group 2	Group 1	Group 2
Problem 1						
Problem 2						
Problem 3						

For Discussion

1. Did the leaders perform according to those characteristics noted in the text? How might their performances have been improved? Be as specific as possible.
2. Describe any differences in time among the three types of leadership. Among which types of leadership were the differences greatest? Would these same differences manifest themselves in real-life small group communication situations? Explain.
3. What are the implications of the differences in the time it took the groups to solve the problems? How do you account for these differences?
4. Would these same time differences manifest themselves if the problems did not have a definite answer—for example, if they had been ethical issues requiring group agreement? Explain.
5. How did the members of the different groups enjoy the task? That is, was there a difference in the degree of satisfaction with the task among the members of the different groups? How do you account for the differences?
6. How did the leaders of the different groups enjoy the task? Were there differences in the degree of satisfaction with the task among the leaders of the different groups? If so, how do you account for the differences?

Unit 22

Small Group Analysis and Evaluation

SMALL GROUP ANALYSIS AND EVALUATION

The Need for Evaluation and Analysis
Guidelines for Evaluation and Analysis
Methods for Evaluation and Analysis
    22.1 Analyzing Small Group Interaction

LEARNING GOALS

After completing this unit, you should be able to:

1. explain three benefits to be derived from the evaluation and analysis of small group communication situations
2. explain and give examples of at least four guidelines suggested for the evaluation and analysis of small group interaction
3. explain the function(s) of interaction process analysis
4. identify the four main categories for messages in interaction process analysis
5. utilize interaction process analysis to analyze the group's messages
6. identify the purposes of interaction diagrams
7. identify at least two ways that messages can be recorded using interaction diagrams
8. utilize interaction diagrams to analyze group processes
9. construct an original rating scale to evaluate some aspect of group process
10. utilize a rating scale to evaluate a group's performance
11. construct an original satisfaction scale to evaluate the satisfaction of the group members
12. utilize a productivity index to evaluate the group's end product

As already illustrated, small group communication is an extremely complex process. And one of the best ways to further our insight into this process is to stand back a bit and attempt to analyze and evaluate it.

THE NEED FOR EVALUATION AND ANALYSIS

There are a number of benefits to be derived from this evaluative process. First, by analyzing and evaluating small group interaction we are in a better position to understand the various principles of effective and ineffective small group communication. By focusing on the small group interactions as a critic, we can come to see more clearly the successful or unsuccessful application of the various principles of effective communication.

Second, as critics and as analysts we can help to guide group members into more effective patterns of small group interaction by providing them with useful and appropriate feedback. Often, it is difficult for an individual to see himself or herself objectively or for the group as a whole to see itself objectively; the analyst can help the participants and the group to achieve at least some measure of objectivity and can point out ways in which the communications may have been made more effective. For example, from inspecting one of the interaction diagrams explained below, in which the number of contributions of each member are recorded, it is relatively easy to see that one individual dominates or monopolizes the discussion or that another individual might suffer from communication apprehension or shyness and contributes little if anything. These individuals need to be shown in concrete terms the patterns of their interactions (or lack of them) as a first step toward guiding them to more effective and more productive communication patterns. Without such an objective measure it is often difficult to make individuals realize how much or how little they have talked. Since leaders are often those who talk the most and to whom the other members address their comments, it is easier to see the leadership patterns in a small group with the aid of these quantitative measures of amount and direction of talk. Through some methods we can see quite clearly the roles that various individuals come to assume. For example, one individual may serve the social-emotional role of demonstrating solidarity, another may concentrate on giving opinions, while still another on asking for information. When these roles are played to the exclusion of other roles, when individual members begin to show little or no flexibility, it is important that some reorientation be suggested. Such reorientation or feedback is most effective, it seems, when it is based on the descriptive information provided by these analysis methods.

Third, the analyst-critic contributes to the development of critical standards for the evaluation of small group interaction and sets higher and higher standards for small group participants. That is, the critic does not merely analyze how effectively or ineffectively the small group members utilized certain principles, but actually formulates—at least in some instances—critical standards (standards of excellence) that group members may measure themselves against. In this function, the critic stands with the theorist in formulating principles for effective small group communication.

Because analysis and evaluation is such a vital part of the entire small group communication process, this entire unit is devoted to analyzing and evaluating small group interaction. More specifically, presented are some general guidelines to follow in offering evaluation and analysis of small group communication as well as some general approaches to or methods for the analysis of small group interaction.

GUIDELINES FOR EVALUATION AND ANALYSIS

In offering an analysis or an evaluation of any individual small group member or of the group as a whole, there are a number of guidelines that will be helpful. The few suggested here should prove intuitively satisfying; none are terribly controversial. I mention them here because they are so often abused, with the result that critical evaluations lose much of their effectiveness.

First, be positive. All participants and all groups have undoubtedly done something right; mention this. If you have trouble finding something positive to say, look again; it's there. This does not mean that negative aspects should not be stated but only that something positive should also be said. Generally it will be helpful if you state the positive first and reserve the negative for second position.

Second, try to be descriptive before being evaluative. Describe what you think happened in the group and then offer your evaluation of why you think this aspect should be viewed positively or negatively. Instead of saying, for example, that effective leadership was not exercised, start by noting that the group seemed to go off the track a number of times and that no one directed the group back to its main task. Instead of saying that there was a lack of interest among the members, say that three of the six members never said anything during the entire group interaction and that this led you to feel that some members might not have been interested in the topic or in the way in which the group was progressing. In this way, you will be stating in clear terms the basis for your evaluation and the reasoning you used in arriving at your critical conclusion. By stating description first you also force yourself to anchor your critical comments to the specifics of the group rather than to some abstract or general feeling.

Third, try to be as specific as you can in offering any critical comment. Instead of saying that the leadership was poorly exercised, state exactly what aspect of leadership was poorly exercised. Was it that the leader failed to provide an effective definition of the problem? Was it that members argued over who was to be the leader? Was it that the leader was too autocratic? Your reason for thinking that leadership was poorly exercized should be stated in specific terms. Try to focus your critical comments on specific principles of small group communi-

Unlike productivity, group satisfaction is only observable in some groups, some of the time.

cation rather than on generalities. Try to support your statements with specific examples.

Fourth, your critical comments should function in some way to improve the group's performance. Therefore, try to phrase your comments in as constructive a way as possible. If you offer a negative evaluation, try to specify how that could have been avoided or how something could have been improved. For example, instead of saying that participation was not spread evenly among members, you might say that it would have helped if the leader had asked some open-ended questions to draw out the more silent members or that the leader might have provided the more reticent members with an opportunity to express what they thought about various issues or that members might have directed their comments not only at the more talkative members but at the more reticent members as well. With these comments, the group will be able to see what could have been done to spread participation more evenly rather than simply being told that participation was uneven.

Fifth, own your own feelings and thoughts. By this I mean that when stating an opinion, make it clear that that opinion is yours and that it emanates from your perception of the group. It should be clear that your evaluation is *your* evaluation and that what you are saying may not be true in any objective sense. For example, in evaluating a group discussion, you might say (not owning your own thoughts and feelings): "The discussion rambled," "The leadership was ineffective," or "The group members were ill prepared." Or you might say (owning your own thoughts and feelings): "I was bored," "I thought the leader should have done X, Y, and Z instead of A, B, and C," or "I felt the members should have had more specific knowledge of the topic." In the former cases, you imply that boredom, ineffective leadership, and lack of preparation were somehow in the group. Actually, these are in your perceptions. And these comments are valuable precisely because they are the perceptions of one careful analyst—namely, you. Other critics might have found the discussion exciting, the leader most effective, and the preparation of the members impressive. In all criticism it should be recognized that the evaluations are a function of what went on in the group *and* what went on in the critic's head.

These are not the only guidelines that critics might follow in offering evaluative comments, yet they should prove a suitable foundation. It is especially important that group members recognize that critical analysis is not necessarily negative and that the criticism is offered with a view to making the participants and the group as a whole more effective. So in hearing evaluations try not to be defensive; recognize that the critic is serving an important function and that these comments will ultimately benefit you. Recognize further that the critic is under pressure and that your defensiveness does not help the critic to be open and honest. Yet, it is precisely this openness and honesty that will foster useful and productive criticism.

METHODS FOR EVALUATION AND ANALYSIS

Here we consider four general methods for the analysis of small group communication: interaction process analysis, interaction diagrams, rating scales, and productivity and satisfaction indexes. Each of these methods of analysis provides us with a slightly different perspective on the small group communication act.

INTERACTION PROCESS ANALYSIS

Perhaps the most widely used system of analysis is that proposed by Robert Bales known as interaction process analysis, or IPA. *Interaction process analysis* is a form of content analysis, a method that classifies messages into four general categories: (1) social-emotional positive, (2) social-emotional negative, (3) attempted answers, and (4) questions. Each of these four areas contains three subdivisions, giving us a total of twelve categories. It is assumed that all the messages occurring in small groups may be classified into one of these twelve categories:

Social-Emotional Positive
   to show solidarity
   to show tension release
   to show agreement

Social-Emotional Negative
to show disagreement
to show tension
to show antagonism

Attempted Answers
to give suggestions
to give opinions
to give information

Questions
to ask for suggestions
to ask for opinions
to ask for information

Note that the categories under social-emotional positive are the natural opposites of those under social-emotional negative, and those under attempted answers are the natural opposites of those under questions. With even brief experience in using this system, one can categorize the various messages with relative ease.

Generally, charts are constructed to record the type and frequency of messages communicated in the small group. A typical chart would look something like that presented in Figure 22.1.

	Judy	Helen	Linda	Grace	Rhoda	Diane
Shows Solidarity	/		卌 /			/
Shows Tension Release						
Shows Agreement	///		//			//
Shows Antagonism				卌 //		
Shows Tension		卌		///		
Shows Disagreement	///			卌		
Gives Suggestions				//	///	
Gives Opinions		//				
Gives Information	///			/		
Asks for Suggestions			////			卌
Asks for Opinions			///			
Asks for Information	卌					

Figure 22.1   Interaction process analysis form.

From this chart, which represents the messages communicated in a relatively short period of time, we can already see that certain members are taking on various roles. Grace seems negative; she is high on antagonism, tension, and disagreement. Linda seems particularly positive with numerous messages showing solidarity and asking for suggestions and opinions. Helen, on the other hand, seems particularly tense but does nothing to relieve the tension or to display positive feelings. We can make more significant observations after observing a longer period of interaction.

INTERACTION DIAGRAMS

Interaction diagrams are particularly useful for recording the number of messages addressed to one person from another. They enable us to quantify who speaks to whom. There are various different ways to draw these interaction diagrams. Perhaps the most popular method is to represent each member by a circle and draw arrows from the source to the receiver, as in Figure 22.2. The arrows drawn to "group" indicate that the comments were addressed to all members of the group.

Alternatively we might begin with a model of the group with arrows con-

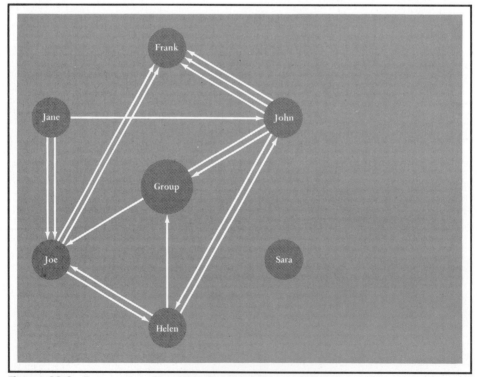

Figure 22.2   Interaction diagram—I.

necting each possible dyad and simply mark off each comment on the appropriate line, as illustrated in Figure 22.3.

In each of these cases we have a record of who spoke to whom and how often. As can be appreciated, the diagrams can become pretty messy if there is much communication or if there are many members. Therefore an interaction diagram of the form presented in Figure 22.4 seems more workable. With slash marks we can easily record the various messages. Viewing the names on the left as the sources and those at the top as receivers, we can easily separate, for example, those messages from Joe to Helen (second column, top row) from those from Helen to Joe (first column, second row). Also included is a slot for those messages addressed to the group as a whole.

This model seems the most practical of the three since it allows for a clear recording of the messages regardless of how many members there are or how many messages are communicated.

RATING SCALES

Rating scales are by far the easiest of all the methods of evaluation. They may be completed by the small group members themselves or by outside observers.

The scales may focus on any of the numerous variables present in small

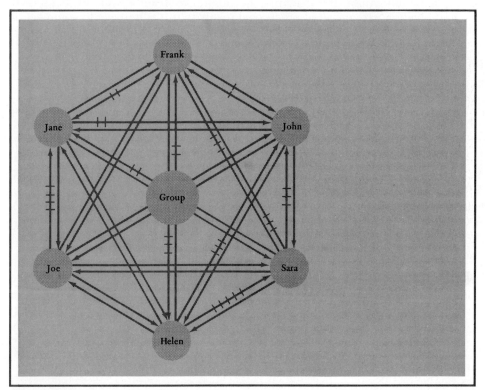

Figure 22.3 Interaction diagram—II.

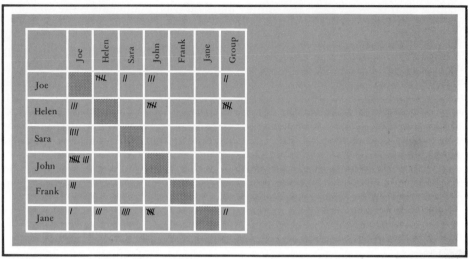

Figure 22.4   Communication matrix for recording interactions.

group communication. For example, we might construct a scale to focus on a communication pattern, an interpersonal relationship, adherence to some set of rules or principles, and any of the numerous aspects of small group process.

One sample of such a scale follows.

This discussion was:

interesting ____: ____: ____: ____: ____: ____: ____ uninteresting

clear ____: ____: ____: ____: ____: ____: ____ unclear

purposeful ____: ____: ____: ____: ____: ____: ____ nonpurposeful

optimistic ____: ____: ____: ____: ____: ____: ____ pessimistic

shared
equally by
all members ____: ____: ____: ____: ____: ____: ____ monopolized by one or a few members

PRODUCTIVITY AND SATISFACTION INDEXES

Productivity and satisfaction indexes may be used to evaluate (1) the quantity and/or quality of the end product of the small group, (2) the time it took the group to reach the solution or end product, and (3) the satisfaction the group members feel as a result of the group process and/or the end product.

It should be recognized that quality, and even some aspects of quantity, are extremely difficult to measure. Further, by focusing on the end product we are deemphasizing the processes that went on among the members to achieve that particular end. Satisfaction presents even further difficulties, especially when we attempt to account for the reasons why members feel satisfied or dissatisfied. A simple satisfaction index follows and is identical to the one we used in the "Small Group Communication Patterns" experiential vehicle (20.2).

I found this discussion:

interesting ____: ____: ____: ____: ____: ____: ____ boring

enjoyable ____: ____: ____: ____: ____: ____: ____ unenjoyable

dynamic ____: ____: ____: ____: ____: ____: ____ static

useful ____: ____: ____: ____: ____: ____: ____ useless

good ____: ____: ____: ____: ____: ____: ____ bad

SOURCES

Most works in small group communication, cited in the previous two units, give some attention to methods of analysis and evaluation. In addition I would particularly recommend the following. Michael Burgoon, Judee K. Heston [Burgoon], and James McCroskey, in their *Small Group Communication: A Functional Approach* (New York: Holt, Rinehart and Winston, 1974), provide an appendix, "Methods of Understanding and Evaluating Interaction in the Small Group," which should prove an excellent supplement to the present unit. Also see John K. Brilhart, *Effective Group discussion*, 2d ed. (Dubuque, Iowa: Brown, 1974), pp. 163–187. Bales system is most thoroughly presented in Robert Bales, *Interaction Process Analysis* (Reading, Mass.: Addison-Wesley, 1967). On satisfaction in communication see Michael L. Hecht, "The Conceptualization and Measurement of Interpersonal Communication Satisfaction," *Human Communication Research* 4 (spring 1978): 253–264, and "Toward a Conceptualization of Communication Satisfaction," *Quarterly Journal of Speech* 64 (February 1978): 47–62. Theoretical approaches relevant to the analysis of small group interaction are thoroughly surveyed by Marvin E. Shaw, *Group Dynamics: The Psychology of Small Group Behavior*, 3d ed. (New York: McGraw-Hill, 1981).

Experiential
Vehicle

22.1   Analyzing Small Group Interaction

The purpose of this experience is to enable you to become more familiar with the methods for analyzing small group interaction.

Six class members should be selected to discuss one of the following topics for approximately 10 minutes.

1. What alternatives are there to the current grading system?
2. What are the major characteristics of an effective teacher?
3. What makes a person educated?
4. What does *love* mean?
5. How might our educational system be improved?

All other members should select a method of analysis and record the group interaction on the Interaction Diagram, the Rating Scale, or the Communication Matrix. After approximately 10 minutes the discussion should be stopped, and the six group discussion members should then complete the Satisfaction Index.

INTERACTION DIAGRAM

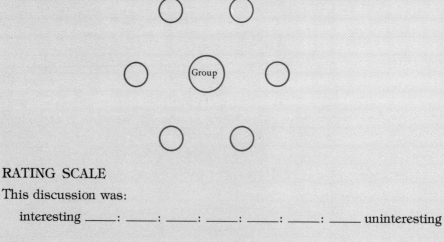

RATING SCALE

This discussion was:

interesting ____ : ____ : ____ : ____ : ____ : ____ : ____ uninteresting unclear _____: _____: _____: _____: _____: _____: _____ clear

purposeful _____: _____: _____: _____: _____: _____: _____ nonpurposeful

pessimistic _____: _____: _____: _____: _____: _____: _____ optimistic

shared
equally by
all members _____: _____: _____: _____: _____: _____: _____ monopolized by
one or a few
members

efficient _____: _____: _____: _____: _____: _____: _____ inefficient

COMMUNICATION MATRIX FOR RECORDING INTERACTIONS

Fill in the appropriate names in all columns and rows.

Names							Group

SATISFACTION INDEX

(To be completed by members of the group discussion.)
In this discussion, I felt:

satisfied _____: _____: _____: _____: _____: _____: _____ dissatisfied

pleased _____: _____: _____: _____: _____: _____: _____ displeased

bored _____: _____: _____: _____: _____: _____: _____ excited

happy _____: _____: _____: _____: _____: _____: _____ sad

After each member has completed at least one analysis form, respond to all questions in connection with the method of analysis you used.

1. What are some of the advantages in using the method of analysis you selected?
2. What are some of the difficulties or disadvantages in using your method of analysis?
3. Does this method help you to describe what happened in the group? Explain.
4. Does this method help you to evaluate the quality of the discussion?
5. What other aspects or dimensions of the group process should be included in the analysis forms? Put differently, what do these analysis methods omit?
6. How reliable are the methods used? Test this by comparing how similar-dissimilar the analyses are when performed by different people.
7. How valid are the methods used? Do they enable you to analyze what they claim to analyze?

Part Seven

Public Communication

Unit 23

Preliminaries
to Public
Communication

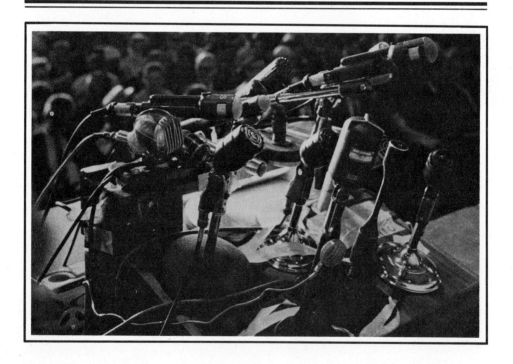

PRELIMINARIES TO PUBLIC COMMUNICATION

The Nature of Public Communication
Purposes of Public Communication
Subjects for Public Communications
Methods of Delivery
   23.1 Some Principles of Public Communication

LEARNING GOALS

After completing this unit, you should be able to:

1. define *public communication*
2. define four major purposes of public communication
3. explain how specific speech purposes are defined in terms of behavioral objectives
4. identify at least three qualities that should govern the selection of subjects of public communications
5. identify and define the four methods of presentation in public speaking

In this unit the topic of public communication is introduced with a consideration of some of its preliminary concepts. First, we look into the nature of public communication, define it, and distinguish it from other forms of communication. Second, both the general and specific purposes that public communication may serve are considered. Third, the subjects or topics of public communication are discussed in terms of the criteria that should govern their selection and some of the ways in which subjects may be narrowed to appropriate dimensions. Also included here is an extensive listing of suggested topics appropriate for public speaking experiences. Fourth, the methods of presentation for public communication (impromptu, manuscript, memorized, and extemporaneous) are analyzed in terms of their advantages and disadvantages.

THE NATURE OF PUBLIC COMMUNICATION

Public communication or public speaking exists when a speaker delivers a relatively prepared, relatively continuous address in a specific setting to a relatively large audience that provides the speaker with relatively little feedback.

First, we should include a note on the word *relatively*. No form of communication can be defined in absolute terms; all forms seem to exist on a continuum. Dyadic communication seems to lead into small group communication, which seems to lead to public speaking, which leads to mass communication, and so on. The word *relatively* is inserted repeatedly to eliminate the inevitable but fruitless questions about how large an audience must be for there to be public speaking, how prepared a speech must be for it to be a public speech, and so on.

More important, we need to consider the essential characteristics of public speaking as noted in the preceding explanation. The notion of a *relatively prepared* speech is included to emphasize the idea that a public speech does not occur because people happen to be in public when they open their mouths but only results from preparation prior to actual utterance. A person can easily speak in public without any preparation, but he or she is not delivering a public speech. A speech, by definition, is a prepared composition, and hence a *public speech* is a prepared composition delivered to a public audience.

A public speech is a *relatively continuous address*. A speech is not broken as is a dialogue or small group communication, with one person speaking and then another. In a public speech the speaker speaks and the audience, one would hope, listens. It should also be noted that the audience members provide the speaker with *relatively little feedback*. The trained speaker will be able to read subtle feedback cues that the members of the audience give off; the novice speaker will let these go unnoticed. Relatively speaking, however, there is little feedback. The speaker has some opportunity to adjust his or her message on the

BOX 23.1
The Gettysburg Address
Abraham Lincoln

Abraham Lincoln (1809–1865) delivered his famous Gettysburg Address in 1863. At the dedication of the National Cemetery at Gettysburg, Edward Everett, an influential Unitarian pastor and popular orator, was invited to deliver the dedication address, which he did. Lincoln also attended and as President was asked to say "a few appropriate remarks." The few remarks were the Gettysburg Address—perhaps the most popular speech in all of American history. Some newspapers ridiculed the speech, some praised it, but only few recognized its greatness at the time.

It is included here because it is a model of stylistic excellence and one of the best examples of "appropriateness."

Fourscore and seven years ago our fathers brought forth on this continent a new nation, conceived in liberty and dedicated to the proposition that all men are created equal. Now we are engaged in a great civil war, testing whether that nation, or any nation so conceived and so dedicated, can long endure. We are met on a great battlefield of that war. We have come to dedicate a portion of that field as a final resting place for those who here gave their lives that that nation might live. It is altogether fitting and proper that we should do this. But, in a larger sense, we cannot dedicate—we cannot consecrate—we cannot hallow—this ground. The brave men, living and dead, who struggled here have consecrated it far above our poor power to add or to detract. The world will little note nor long remember what we say here, but it can never forget what they did here. It is for us, the living, rather to be dedicated here to the unfinished work which they who fought here have thus far so nobly advanced. It is rather for us to be here dedicated to the great task remaining before us—that from these honored dead we take increased devotion to that cause for which they gave the last full measure of devotion; that we here highly resolve that these dead shall not have died in vain; that this nation, under God, shall have a new birth of freedom; and that government of the people, by the people, for the people, shall not perish from the earth.

basis of audience reaction but not as much as would a member of a dyad or small group.

The receiver of the message is a *relatively large audience*. It is larger than a small group but smaller than in a mass communication situation. Generally, the audience is in close proximity with one another, as distinguished from the audience of a mass communication, which is widely scattered. The audience may be homogeneous or heterogeneous. Generally, they are more homogeneous than a mass communication audience but less homogeneous than small group members.

Public speaking also occurs in a *specific setting*. Unlike mass communication, where the audience members are in numerous different settings, the public speaking audience is in a specific, definable context. And in any evaluation of a public speech it is necessary to take that specific setting into account. Students in a large lecture class, for example, are in a clearly different setting from members attending a political rally, who in turn are different from members of a rock concert audience.

PURPOSES OF PUBLIC COMMUNICATION

In considering public communication purposes we need to focus first on the general purposes where we distinguish among the informative speech, the persuasive speech, and the special occasion speech. Second, we focus on specific purposes. These specific purposes are the specific information the speaker wishes the audience to learn, the specific beliefs or attitudes the speaker wants the audience to embrace, the specific behaviors the speaker hopes the audience will engage in.

GENERAL PURPOSES

Three general speech purposes or types of speeches may be distinguished: the informative speech, the persuasive speech, and the special occasion speech. Speeches delivered *to inform* the audience are many and varied and range from the lectures in college classrooms to a newscaster's presentation of some relevant facts to a friend explaining how the internal combustion engine works. It is particularly important to note that a speech to inform must do just that and it must contain information not previously known to the audience or information that is presented in a new or different way. The college teacher who presents information the audience already knows is not giving an informative speech.

Speeches *to persuade* are concerned with reinforcing or changing attitudes, beliefs, or behaviors. Here we are concerned with making the audience think something or do something. The speech to persuade may seek to have us believe that one candidate is better than the other or to get us to contribute to this candidate's campaign fund or to vote for him or her in the next election.

Some theorists make a distinction between speeches designed to reinforce or change attitudes and beliefs on the one hand and speeches designed to alter behavior on the other. The former are designated speeches to convince and the latter, speeches to persuade.

The *special occasion* speech encompasses a mixed collection of those speeches designed for specific audiences on specific occasions. The special occasion speech would include three types of speeches: (1) the speech of introduction, in which the speaker introduces another speaker or group of speakers; (2) the speech of praise or censure, in which the speaker extols the virtues of a particular individual, institution, or group of persons or, alternatively, condemns them; and (3) the speech to secure good will, in which the speaker attempts to establish a more positive view of himself or herself or of some other individual, institution, or perhaps way of life.

No speech is solely an informative speech or a persuasive speech or a special occasion speech. Elements of each type probably exist in all speeches. A lecture on the topic "Career Opportunities" will no doubt communicate new in-

Jane Fonda uniquely combines persuasion with information and entertainment, making her speeches enjoyable, intellectually stimulating, and effective in changing attitudes and behaviors.

formation and hence be in part an informative speech. But it will also function to persuade the audience in some ways; it may, for example, motivate them to take certain courses or to go to a particular school and hence would be in part a persuasive speech. Also, the speech may function to secure good will for the speaker or to praise particular professions or ways of life and hence be a special occasion speech. It is best, therefore, to view speeches in terms of primary purposes rather than exclusive purposes.

SPECIFIC PURPOSES

Just as each speech has a general purpose, each speech also has one or more specific purposes. And, of course, there are various degrees of specificity one might wish to distinguish. For our purposes it is best to distinguish the major issues of any given speech as the specific purposes.

In informative speeches the specific purposes refer to the information the speaker will present to the audience. For example, one specific purpose might be to inform the audience of the five major stages in language development in children, or of the major land purchases of the United States, or of recent experiments in memory.

With speeches to persuade we state in the specific purpose what we hope to persuade the audience to think or do. For example, one specific purpose might be to persuade the audience that Senator Smile should be reelected; another, that New York City should become our 51st state; and another, that the Academy Awards should be abolished. Note that in speeches to persuade it is not necessary that the audience be able to act on the basis of their belief or attitude. For example, we might wish to convince high school students that Senator Smile should be reelected even though they cannot vote themselves. In other types of speeches to persuade we define the specific behavior we wish the audience to engage in. For example, we might attempt to persuade the audience to buy savings bonds, or to read a news magazine, or to buy a Pontiac rather than a Dodge.

Specific Purposes in Terms of Behavioral Objectives

The previous discussion on speech purposes has been, for the most part, based on traditional and contemporary speech communication theory. The theories are useful ones and have certainly stood the test of time. Presented here, however, is another approach to the specific purposes of a speech. Use whichever theory or approach seems the more useful or the easier. The new approach is simply to state the specific purposes of your speech in terms of behavioral objectives—in terms of what you want the audience to be able to do as a result of having heard your speech. Each unit of this text is prefaced in a similar way with behavioral objectives that state what you should be able to do after reading the unit.

In the speech to inform state the information that the audience will learn from the speech and how the audience will be able to demonstrate this learning in behavioral terms. For example, a specific purpose might be phrased as: The

BOX 23.2
Nobel Prize Acceptance Speech
William Faulkner

William Faulkner (1897–1962), one of the leading American writers of the twentieth century, was awarded the Nobel Prize for literature in 1949 and the Pulitzer Prize in 1955. Although Faulkner wrote poems, short stories, movie scripts, and a play, he is best known for his novels—for example, *The Sound and the Fury* (1929) and *The Reivers* (1962). Faulkner delivered the following speech on December 10, 1950, in Stockholm, Sweden, reportedly in his first dress suit and before television cameras for the first time.

The speech is instructive for its clarity of style and purpose, and the universality of its theme.

I feel that this award was not made to me as a man, but to my work—a life's work in the agony and sweat of the human spirit, not for glory and least of all for profit, but to create out of the materials of the human spirit something which did not exist before. So this award is only mine in trust. It will not be difficult to find a dedication for the money part of it commensurate with the purpose and significance of its origin. But I would like to do the same with the acclaim too, by using this moment as a pinnacle from which I might be listened to by the young men and women already dedicated to the same anguish and travail, among whom is already that one who will someday stand here where I am standing.

Our tragedy today is a general and universal physical fear so long sustained by now that we can even bear it. There are no longer problems of the spirit. There is only the question: when will I be blown up? Because of this, the young man or woman writing today has forgotten the problems of the human heart in conflict with itself which alone can make good writing because only that is worth writing about, worth the agony and the sweat.

He must learn them again. He must teach himself that the basest of all things is to be afraid; and, teaching himself that, forget it forever, leaving no room in his workshop for anything but the old verities and truths of the heart, the old universal truths lacking which any story is ephemeral and doomed—love and honor and pity and pride and compassion and sacrifice. Until he does so, he labors under a curse. He writes not of love but of lust, of defeats in which nobody loses anything of value, of victories without hope, and, worst of all, without pity or compassion. His griefs grieve on no universal bones, leaving no scars. He writes not of the heart but of the glands.

Until he relearns these things, he will write as though he stood among and watched the end of man. I decline to accept the end of man. It is easy enough to say that man is immortal simply because he will endure; that when the last ding-dong of doom has clanged and faded from the last worthless rock hanging tideless in the last red and dying evening, that even then there will still be one more sound: that of his puny inexhaustible voice, still talking. I refuse to accept this. I believe that man will not merely endure: he will prevail. He is immortal, not because he alone among creatures has an inexhaustible voice, but because he has a soul, a spirit capable of compassion

> and sacrifice and endurance. The poet's, the writer's, duty is to write about these things. It is his privilege to help man endure by lifting his heart, by reminding him of the courage and honor and hope and pride and compassion and pity and sacrifice which have been the glory of his past. The poet's voice need not merely be the record of man; it can be one of the props, the pillars, to help him endure and prevail.

audience will be able to state the five stages of language development in the child; the audience will be able to list the five major land purchases of the United States in the nineteenth century; or, the audience will be able to summarize the essential methods and findings of three recent experiments in the psychology of memory. Note that in stating the purposes in this way we are stating not only what we want the audience to learn but also how we want them to demonstrate it. These same purposes might have been put in other forms, that is, we might have said that the audience would be able to *recognize* the five major stages in the language development of the child or *define* the five major stages once they know the names of the stages. Put differently, include in the statement of purpose the type of learning that is to be demonstrated. This may be designated by using such terms as *recognize, identify, summarize, list,* and *state.*

In the speech to persuade we may rely on oral or written expressions of agreement or change. We could state, for example, that the audience will state their preference that Senator Smile be reelected, that they will argue in favor of New York City becoming the 51st state, and so on. Or we could use written methods and say, for example, that the audience will change their opinion in favor of Senator Smile on a shift-of-opinion ballot or that in a mock election they would vote for Senator Smile. We might also focus on behavior and state the behavior we wish the audience to exhibit; for example, we might say that the audience will buy savings bonds, read a news magazine, or buy the Pontiac.

The behavioral objectives of the special occasion speech would vary depending on the nature of the speech. If the speech were one to secure good will for the Chrysler Corporation, then the specific purpose might be something like: the audience will verbalize positive responses to Chrysler Corporation or the audience will agree that Chrysler Corporation is a company of high reputation and considerable competence. In the speech of introduction, the specific purpose might be something like: the audience will be able to state the three main qualifications for this speaker speaking on this topic or the audience will be able to present a brief biographical sketch of the speaker.

In using behavioral objectives to state speech purposes we force ourselves to state specifically what we wish the audience to be able to do after hearing our speech. This statement then provides an important reference point against which all other parts of the speech may be checked. For example, for every bit of supporting material we would use we would ask ourselves if this helped the audience to attain the behavioral objectives noted in the purpose. If it does not advance the behavioral objective in some way, then it should not be used.

SUBJECTS FOR PUBLIC COMMUNICATIONS

As should be clear from listening to public speeches, whether on television, at local organizations, or at school, the topics seem to know no boundaries. Every possible topic is appropriate for a public speech. It is impossible to conceive of a topic that would not be appropriate to at least some specific audience, and herein lies the major criterion for evaluating a topic for a public speech—appropriateness to some specific audience. Exactly what constitutes appropriateness will not always be easy to determine but it should be a major consideration of each speaker. Generally, intuition and some good common sense will guide the would-be public speaker away from the inappropriate to the appropriate. Nevertheless, some specific suggestions are advanced.

First, the topic should be considered worthwhile to the audience. The audience members should be able to view the speech and the topic as a worthwhile investment of their time and energy. Whether the purpose is to inform; to persuade; or to introduce, praise, or secure good will, the audience members should feel that their time was well spent. Put differently, the audience members should consider themselves better off for having heard the speech; they should have gained something as a result of hearing it.

Second, the topic of a public speech should be interesting or, more important, must be made interesting by the speaker. Most subjects are potentially interesting, but we should not assume that most subjects are already interesting or are inherently interesting to any audience. In fact, the speaker will probably be better off if he or she assumes that it is the speaker's total obligation to make the subject interesting. At times this is easy and at times it will tax the most imaginative of speakers. It takes little effort to make a speech on increasing teachers' salaries interesting to teachers but much effort to interest the same audience in a speech on Latin vowels or the history of football.

Third, and perhaps most important, is that the topic of a public speech must be limited in scope and purpose. A major problem with beginning speeches is that they attempt to cover everything in five minutes: the history of Egypt, why our tax structure should be changed, the sociology of film, and the like are clearly too broad and attempt to cover too much. The inevitable result is that nothing much gets covered—everything is touched but only on the surface. No depth of insight is achieved with a broad topic, and all that the speaker succeeds in doing is telling the audience what it already knew. Invariably the audience feels cheated, feels that it has gained nothing as a result of listening to this speech.

Perhaps the best way to narrow and limit the topic is to begin with a general topic and divide it into its component parts. Then, take one of these parts and divide it into its component parts. Continue with this general process until the topic seems manageable—one that can reasonably be covered in some depth in the allotted time. For example, take the topic of television programs as the first general topic area. This might then be divided into such subtopics as comedy, children's programs, educational programs, news, movies, soap operas, quiz programs, and sports. We might then take one of these topics, say comedy, and divide it into subtopics. Perhaps we might consider it on a time basis and divide comedy into its significant time periods as presented on television: pre-1950, 1950–1960, 1960–1970, and 1970 to the present. Let us say we are most interested in the current period, 1970 to the present. Divide this into further subtopics such as "major programs"—"Laverne and Shirley," "Three's Company," "The Jeffersons," "Benson," and so on. We might then take some portion of this subtopic and begin to construct a speech around a specific topic. Some such topics might be "Women in Television Comedy," "Race Relations in Situation Comedy," "Comedy Spinoffs," and so on. The important point, regardless of whether you would have subdivided the topics in this way or not, is that the resultant topic is at least beginning to look manageable, whereas "television programs" without some specificity would take a lifetime to cover adequately.

As an aid to narrowing your topic to manageable proportions, you might consider using a tree diagram, similar to that presented in Figure 23.1. We begin with "film," our general topic. One obvious division is into type, broadly conceived: drama, comedy, and musical. Let us say that we are primarily interested

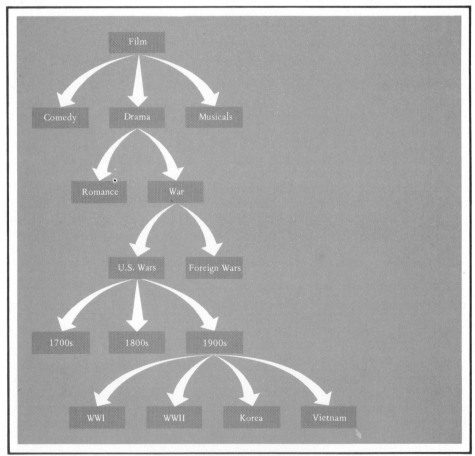

Figure 23.1   Narrowing a topic with a tree diagram.

BOX 23.3
Some Topics for Public Speaking

Art/Music/Theater Topics

Abstract art: meaning of; and emotion; leading artists; Kandinsky; Léger; Mondrian; Picasso; Pollock; contributions of movement; contemporary significance of; values of

Acting: actors; actresses; Actor's Studio; training; fame; styles; film; theater; television; mime

Dance: art of; modern; social aspects of; and theater; of death; disco; ballet

Disco: growth of; and meeting people; music; dancing; and drugs; clothes; current scene

Entertainment: industry; benefits; abuses; tax; functions of; and communication

Movies: censorship; famous; making; producing; directing; acting in; history of; economics of; career training; and communication

Music: festivals; forms; instruments; composition; styles; drama; opera; rock; punk; disco; country-western; popular; symphonic; new wave

Theater: Greek; Roman; commedia dell'arte; American; British; Eastern; Italian; French; performers; styles of; and television; and film; Broadway; and critics

Biological-Physiological Topics

Anesthesia: nature of; types of; uses of; development of; dangers of

Biological: clock; control; warfare; rhythm; sciences

Biorhythm: nature of; predictions from; life cycles; charting

Brain: -washing; damage; genius; intelligence; aphasia

Cloning: nature of; with plants; with human beings; with animals; advances in

Diseases: major diseases of college students; prevention; detection; treatment; recovery

Food: health; preservatives; additives; red dye; and allergies; preparation

Medicine: preventive; forensic; and health insurance; history of; and poisoning; alchemy; industrial

Nutrition: nature of; functions of food; essential requirements; animal; human; and starvation; and diet; vitamins

Transplants: nature of; rejection; donor selection; legal aspects; ethical aspects; religious aspects; future of; advances in

Communication Topics

Advertising: techniques; expenditures; ethical; unethical; subliminal; leading agencies; history of; slogans

BOX 23.3 *(Continued)*

Animal communication: animal-to-animal communication; human-to-animal communication; chimpanzees; dolphins; bees; birds
Censorship: arguments for and against; and violence; and sex; and television; and literature; court decisions on
Freedom of speech: laws protecting; and Constitution; significance of; abuses of; and censorship; and economics
International language: development of; advantages of; problems with; and nationalism; Ido; Esperanto
Languages: artificial; sign; natural; learning of; loss of; pathologies of; sociology of; psychology of
Media: forms of; contributions of; abuses; regulation of; popularity of; influences of; and violence; and censorship; Nielsen ratings
Television: development of; history of; workings of; satellite; cable; commercials; propaganda; and leisure time; programming; economics of; effects of; and violence; and radio; and film; producing; careers in
Translation: computer; missionary impetus; problems in; history of
Writing: styles; forms of; calligraphy; graphology; development of; relationship to speech; picture; syllabic; shorthand

Economic Topics

Business: cycles; associations; law; in performing arts; finance
Capitalism: nature of; economics of; development of; depression and inflation; philosophy; alternatives to
Corporation: law; business; nature of; history; growth of the
Cost of living: index; and inflation; throughout world
Credit: nature of; public; agricultural; card living; unions; bureau
Inflation: and deflation; causes of; effects of; types of
Investment: stocks; gold; real estate; art; restrictions on; bank; allowance
Salaries: minimum wage; professional; white- and blue-collar; racial variation; and unions; and inflation
Sales: advertising; methods; forecasting; and excise taxes
Taxation: alcohol; cigaret; history of; purposes of; historical methods of; types of; without representation; evasion
Treasury Department: monetary system; origin; functions of; subordinate agencies; and counterfeiting
Wealth: economic; distribution of; primitive economic systems; contemporary view of

Philosophical Topics

Astrology: alchemy; influence of; nature of; significance of
Empiricism: radical; nature of; doctrines; opposition to

BOX 23.3 (*Continued*)

Existentialism: meaning of; and choice; history of; leaders in; movement

Numerology: functions of; systems of; accuracy of predictions; contemporary practices in

Occultism: theories of; practices; rituals; astrology; theosophy; witchcraft; divination

Phenomenology: characteristics of; principles of; growth of; development of; and education

Relativism: philosophy; ethical; meaning of; leaders of; influence

Religion: different religions; leaders in; influence of; beliefs; and agnosticism; and atheism; and God; social dimension of; and art

Scientology: religious dimensions; development of; L. Ron Hubbard; and dianetics

Utopianism: nature of; criticisms of; virtues of; Sir Thomas More's *Utopia;* Christian communism; in classical thought; in literature; and socialism; and Skinner's *Walden Two*

Witchcraft: meaning of; white and black; and magic; structure of; functions of; theories of; in primitive societies; in contemporary societies

Zen: meaning of; principles of; historical development of; contemporary interest in; teachings of; influence of

Political Topics

Abolition: movement; slavery; Civil War; leaders; rhetoric

Alien: beings; rights; illegal; deportation

Amnesty: in draft evasion; in criminal law; and pardons; in Civil War; in Vietnam War; conditions of

Communism: development of; theories of; religion and; ideologies

Equal Rights Amendment (*ERA*): origin of; opposition to; future of; implications of

Government: federal; state; city; powers of; abuses of; types of; democracy; socialism; communism

Imperialism: nature of; economics of; problems with; practices; history

League of Nations: nature of; structure; contributions of; problems with; Woodrow Wilson and

Nationalism: nature of; history of; philosophy of; chauvinism; self-determination

Supreme Court: judicial review; decisions; makeup of; chief justices; jurisdiction; and balance of power

United Nations (*UN*): development of; functions of; agencies; and League of Nations; structure of; veto powers; Security Council

War: conduct of; financing; destruction by; causes of; debts; games; casualties; effects of

BOX 23.3 (*Continued*)

Psychological Topics

Aggression: aggressive behavior in animals; in human beings; as innate; as learned; and territoriality

Alcohol: alcoholism; nature of; Alcoholics Anonymous; Al Anon; physical effects of; among the young; treatment of alcoholism

Autism: nature of; treatment for; symptoms; causes

Behaviorism: B. F. Skinner; principles of; controlling own behavior; *Walden Two;* in education; and language

Depression: nature of; and suicide; among college students; dealing with

Guilt: causes of; symptoms of; dealing with; effects of; and suicide; and religion; and self-disclosure

Intelligence: quotient; tests; theories of; cultural differences; measuring

Love: nature of; theories of; romantic; family; and hate; and interpersonal relationships; of self; and materialism

Narcissism: nature of; and Narcissus; Freudian view of; and autoeroticism; and love of others

Personality: development of; measurement of; theories of; disorders

Psychic phenomena: ESP; psychokinesis; reliability of; and frauds; theories of

Subconscious: Freud; development of concept; defense mechanisms

Sociological Topics

Cities: problems of; population patterns; and crime; movement into and out of

Crime: Prevention; types of; and law; and punishment

Discrimination: and prejudice; racial; religious; and nationality

Divorce: rate; throughout world; causes of; advantages of; disadvantages of; proceedings; traumas associated with

Ethnicity: meaning of; and prejudice; theories of; and culture

Feminism: meaning of; implications of; changing concepts of; and chauvinism; and sexism

Gay: rights, lifestyle; laws against; prejudice against; and religion; and lesbian; statistics; relationships

Heroes: nature of; and adolescence; fictional; social role of; real-life

Prison: reform; systems; security; routine; effect on crime; personality; behavior; and sex; and conditioning

Racism: nature of; self-hatred; genetic theory; human rights; education; religious; UN position; in United States

Suicide: causes; among college students; laws regulating; methods; aiding the suicide of another; philosophical implications; religious dimension; male and female differences

> **BOX 23.3** (*Continued*)
>
> *Values:* and attitudes; and communication; economic; changing; religious; axiology; sex differences

in drama, and so we further subdivide drama, perhaps into romance and war. If war is our particular interest, we have to further divide it, say into foreign wars and United States wars. If the latter is our primary interest we further subdivide it; this time our division is a temporal one and we divide it into eighteenth-, nineteenth-, and twentieth-century wars. The twentieth century might further be divided into World War I, World War II, Korea, and Vietnam. Now we are approaching something manageable, and we might develop a speech on some aspect of Vietnam as seen in films; a number of specific topics should come quickly to mind: the image of Americans in Vietnam films, audience response to films about Vietnam, women in films of Vietnam, problems in filming Vietnam movies, and so on. Or we might further divide the Vietnam branch into specific films and deal with one of them—for example, *Coming Home, Deer Hunter, Apocalypse Now.*

METHODS OF DELIVERY

Once the speech is prepared, it is ready to be delivered. Speakers vary widely in their methods of delivery. Some speak "off the cuff," with no apparent preparation, while others read their speeches from manuscript. Some memorize their speeches word for word, while others construct a detailed outline and actualize the speech itself at the moment of delivery. We may distinguish four general methods of delivery, four ways in which the speaker can deliver his or her speech: impromptu, manuscript, memorized, and extemporaneous methods of delivery. Each method has both advantages and disadvantages.

THE IMPROMPTU METHOD OF DELIVERY

The *impromptu method* of delivery involves speaking without any specific preparation for the speech. The speaker and topic meet for the first time and immediately the speech begins. The basic rationale for impromptu speeches is that it will help the speaker to learn poise and various aspects of delivery. Its greatest advantage in a classroom situation is that there is very little pressure for excellence or in fact for anything approaching the standards that would be held to if the speaker had time to research, prepare, and polish the speech.

Perhaps the major disadvantage is that it often makes the public speaking experience one that focuses on appearances. The aim is often only to *appear* to give an effective and well-thought-out speech. Other disadvantages include the inability to attend to style and to organizational matters. Because of the obvious inadequacies with such speeches, the audience is likely to get bored by the experience, and their boredom is likely to show in the form of negative feedback. This, in turn, will make the speaker feel all the more awkward and uncomfortable. The entire situation is apt to degenerate into one which becomes a game rather than an intellectual experience.

Nevertheless, it should be clear that on some occasions impromptu speaking cannot be avoided. In a classroom situation after someone has spoken, you might be asked to comment on the speaker and the speech you just heard and in effect give an impromptu speech. In asking or answering questions in an interview situation you are giving impromptu speeches, albeit extremely short ones. At meetings, persons with particular expertise are often called upon to comment on various issues impromptu.

② THE MANUSCRIPT METHOD OF DELIVERY

In the *manuscript method* the entire speech is written down and is read to the audience. The process is time-consuming and laborious, as you can easily imagine, but for many occasions there is no substitute. For example, where exact timing and wording is required, the manuscript method is perhaps the only method that could be used with "relative" ease and security. It would be disaster if a political leader attempted to speak on sensitive issues and did not speak from manuscript. An ambiguous word, phrase, or sentence that might on more sober reflection prove too insulting, belligerent, conciliatory, or revealing could cause serious problems. With a manuscript speech, an in-depth analysis of style, content, organization, and in fact every element of the speech can be undertaken. In fact, the great advantage of manuscript speeches is that an entire staff of speech experts and advisers can review them, and each can offer suggestions as to what potential problems might arise, how they might be improved, and so on. And so manuscript delivery has the great advantage that the speaker is able to say exactly, word for word, what he or she—or a host of advisers— wish to say.

There is no danger of forgetting, no danger of being unable to find the right word. Everything is there for you on paper. Consequently, a great deal of anxiety is removed, especially for the beginning speaker. Another advantage that becomes more and more important as you go up in status and general importance is that with a manuscript you can deliver the speech and at the same time (or earlier or later, if you prefer) distribute copies to the press.

There are also disadvantages with manuscript delivery. Perhaps the most obvious is that it takes a great deal of time to write out a speech word for word. This is more of a problem for the beginning speaker than it is for the more accomplished speaker, who has had experience and who has learned to compose quickly.

Another disadvantage is that it is difficult to sound natural and nonmechanical when one reads a speech. Reading material from the printed page with liveliness, naturalness, and spontaneity is itself a skill that is difficult to achieve without considerable practice. Audiences seem not to like when people read their speeches, preferring that the speaker speak with them. Consequently, it is difficult to please and ultimately inform or persuade an audience when reading from manuscript.

It is also difficult to take in and respond to feedback from your listeners. With a manuscript you are commited to the speech word for word. What happens when you see on the faces of your audience that your last point was not understood? To stop and amplify—to supply additional examples, to clarify complex terms and relationships, or to spell out the reasoning in more detail— would cause a number of problems. More than likely the speaker would be forced to go on and to ignore these feedback signs.

THE MEMORIZED METHOD OF DELIVERY

The *memorized method* simply involves the writing out of the speech word for word and the committing of it to memory. The speech is then usually "acted out." Like the manuscript method, the memorized method is used when exact timing and exact wording are crucial—for instance, in politically sensitive cases and in cases where the media impose severe restrictions.

The memorized method allows the speaker to devote careful attention to style. As in the manuscript speech, the exact word, phrase, or sentence may be gone over carefully, and any potential problems may be eliminated. One of the reasons the memorized delivery is used is so that the speaker may have all the advantages of the manuscript method but be free to move about and otherwise concentrate on delivery.

The great disadvantage is that there is always the danger of forgetting. Generally, in the way that speeches are learned, each sentence hangs on the previous one and cues the recall of the following one. When one sentence is forgotten, it is likely that the entire speech will be forgotten. And when this danger is coupled with the natural nervousness that accompanies the beginning speaker's efforts, it seems an inadequate method of delivery to select.

The memorized method is even more time-consuming than the manuscript method, since it involves all the time needed in the manuscript method plus the additional time needed for memorizing the speech. When we recognize that we may easily forget the speech, even after spending hours memorizing it, it hardly seems worth it. The memorized method does not allow for ease in adjusting to feedback. In fact, there is less opportunity to adjust to listener feedback than there is in the manuscript method.

Last, we should note that once you have memorized the speech, unless you are an accomplished actor, it will be difficult if not impossible to sound natural. No doubt you will sound memorized, and this is sure to impair your effectiveness.

THE EXTEMPORANEOUS METHOD OF DELIVERY

The *extemporaneous method* of delivery involves thorough preparation, a commitment to memory of the main ideas and the order in which they will appear, and perhaps a commitment to memory of the first few and last few sentences of the speech. But there is here no commitment to exact wording.

389

The extemporaneous method is useful in just about all situations where exact timing and wording are not required. Good college lecturers will use the extemporaneous method; they have prepared thoroughly, have the organization clearly in mind, and know what they want to say and where they want to say it. But they have given no commitment to exact wording.

This method allows greater flexibility for feedback. Should a point need clarification, it may be introduced when it would be most effective without the speaker having to worry that he or she will forget the rest of the speech. With this method it is easy to be natural because you are yourself. It is the method that comes closest to conversation or, as some theorists have put it, "enlarged conversation" because the speaker can move about and interact with the audience.

One of the greatest advantages of extemporaneous speaking is that the time and energy that go into the speech are used to maximal effectiveness. There is no time expended on memorizing the speech or on writing it out. Instead, the time that is spent on the speech is spent in dealing with the ideas and with their structure and style—issues that are worthy of our time and effort.

Although the extemporaneous method is clearly to be preferred, especially in the public speaking classroom situation, it, too, has some disadvantages. Perhaps the major disadvantage is that the speaker may grope for the exact words. Actually, this problem can be minimized if the speech is rehearsed a number of times in advance.

Another disadvantage is that the precise attention to style that the speaker can give the speech in the manuscript and memorized methods cannot be given here. And yet, this disadvantage also can be circumvented by memorizing those phrases you want to say exactly. There is nothing in the extemporaneous method that would preclude your commiting selected phrases to memory. In fact, I would urge you—especially in your early speeches—to memorize the few opening and concluding lines of your speech.

All four methods have something to recommend them. The impromptu method is useful in training certain aspects of public speaking; the manuscript and memorized methods are especially useful when exact timing and wording are essential; and the extemporaneous is most useful when naturalness, responsiveness to feedback, and general flexibility are important. Generally, I would suggest that you build your speeches around the extemporaneous method of delivery and attempt to perfect your ability as a speaker utilizing this method. At the same time you should acquire some familiarity with the other methods in the event that you will have to employ them.

SOURCES

On public speaking there are many excellent works to consult. I would recommend the following. For a thorough review of the research literature on public speaking see James C. McCroskey, *An Introduction to Rhetorical Communication,* 3d ed. (Englewood Cliffs, N.J.: Prentice-Hall, 1978). For a thorough presentation of the relevant theories and principles of effective public speaking see, for example, Joseph A. DeVito. *The Elements of Public Speaking* (New York: Harper & Row, 1981), or Douglas Ehninger, Alan H. Monroe, and Bruce E. Gronbeck, *Principles and Types of Speech Communication*, 8th ed. (Glenview, Ill.: Scott, Foresman, 1978). For a brief presentation see James Byrns, *Speak for Yourself* (New York: Random House, 1981) or Judy Pearson and Paul Nelson, *Confidence in Public Speaking* (Dubuque, Iowa: Brown, 1981).

Experiential
Vehicle

23.1 Some Principles of Public Communication

Respond to the following statements by writing *T* if the statement is generally or usually true and *F* if the statement is generally or usually false.

_____ 1. The most important principle of public speaking is delivery (voice and body actions).

_____ 2. The most effective speeches are written out in their entirety.

_____ 3. A good essay is automatically a good speech and vice versa.

_____ 4. A course in public speaking should enable you to speak with some facility on almost any subject.

_____ 5. Nervousness always hinders one's speaking effectiveness.

_____ 6. A good public speaker uses logic instead of emotion in order to persuade.

_____ 7. The styles of an effective speech and an effective written composition are basically the same.

_____ 8. The effective speaker is born rather than made.

_____ 9. The systematic study of public speaking is a relatively recent development.

_____ 10. The ethical speaker is always an effective speaker.

_____ 11. The speaker should strive to make his or her audience realize that his or her voice and body actions are especially good.

_____ 12. The accomplished speaker has learned, and the beginning speaker should learn, the various gestures and vocal patterns used to express the various emotions.

_____ 13. The speaker should prepare his or her speech so that he or she knows exactly what words will be used.

_____ 14. Effectiveness should be the sole criterion that guides the speaker.

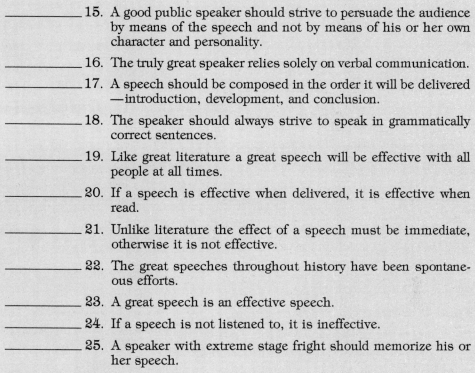

_____ 15. A good public speaker should strive to persuade the audience by means of the speech and not by means of his or her own character and personality.

_____ 16. The truly great speaker relies solely on verbal communication.

_____ 17. A speech should be composed in the order it will be delivered —introduction, development, and conclusion.

_____ 18. The speaker should always strive to speak in grammatically correct sentences.

_____ 19. Like great literature a great speech will be effective with all people at all times.

_____ 20. If a speech is effective when delivered, it is effective when read.

_____ 21. Unlike literature the effect of a speech must be immediate, otherwise it is not effective.

_____ 22. The great speeches throughout history have been spontaneous efforts.

_____ 23. A great speech is an effective speech.

_____ 24. If a speech is not listened to, it is ineffective.

_____ 25. A speaker with extreme stage fright should memorize his or her speech.

Small groups or the class as a whole may then discuss the responses to these statements.

Unit 24

Supporting Materials in Public Communication:
Amplification and Argument

SUPPORTING MATERIALS IN PUBLIC COMMUNICATION: AMPLIFICATION AND ARGUMENT

Supporting the Speech with Amplification
Supporting the Speech with Argument

LEARNING GOALS

After completing this unit, you should be able to:

1. define and explain the nature of examples and illustrations, testimony, definition, statistics, and visual aids in the speech
2. explain the nature of argument in public speaking
3. identify the three general tests for reasoning
4. explain the nature of analogy as a form of reasoning
5. distinguish between the literal and the figurative analogy
6. explain the nature of cause-effect reasoning
7. explain the nature of reasoning by sign
8. explain the nature of specific instances as a type of reasoning
9. explain the nature of reasoning from a generalization to a specific instance

Once the speech topic and purpose are established, you need to develop supporting materials—materials that amplify your main ideas; materials that convince your audience that what you are saying is logical, beneficial, and in their best interests; materials that motivate them to believe as you do; materials that lead them to see you as a responsible and credible advocate. These four types of supporting materials are considered in this and the following unit. Materials devoted to amplification and argument are considered here; materials that are devoted to psychological appeals and speaker credibility are considered in the next unit.

SUPPORTING THE SPEECH WITH AMPLIFICATION

In this section five major forms of supporting materials that amplify are considered: examples and illustrations, testimony, definitions, statistics, and visual aids.

EXAMPLES AND ILLUSTRATIONS

Examples and illustrations are specific instances that are drawn and explained in varying degrees of detail. A relatively brief specific instance is referred to as an example, whereas a longer and more detailed example told in narrative or story-like form is referred to as an illustration.

Examples and illustrations are particularly useful when you wish to make an abstract concept or idea concrete. For example, it is difficult for the audience to see exactly what you would mean by such concepts as "persecution," "denial of freedom," "friendship," and "love," to name just a few, without your providing specific instances—examples and illustrations—of what *you* mean by such concepts. Another advantage of using examples and illustrations in these situations is that you can ensure that the various listeners will develop similar pictures of these concepts—rather than have each listener fill in his or her own definition of "love" or "friendship" and so on.

Here, for example, Ronald Allen, professor of speech at the University of Wisconsin, uses a number of specific instances to make the relatively abstract "different kinds of messages using diverse media" more meaningful and concrete.

> I anticipate that teachers of communication would broaden the focus of language arts study to include a variety of different kinds of messages using diverse media in several communication contexts. A student pondering the expression of love, for example, might study a sonnet by Elizabeth Barrett Browning; Shakespeare's *Romeo and Juliet*; the movie *Love Story*; the historical

novel *Nicholas and Alexandra*; the TV program "Mary Hartman, Mary Hartman"; the popular song "A Little Bit More" by Dr. Hook: and his or her own familial and social experiences with the expression of affection. The expression of feelings, like other important communication functions, deserves study from a number of vantage points.

Another obvious advantage is to make an idea live in the minds of the listeners—to make an idea vivid and real. To talk in general terms about the starvation in various parts of the world might have some effect on the listeners. But very often one specific example or illustration, as of a six-year-old girl who roams the streets eating garbage and being thankful for finding moldy and decaying bread and who wears no clothes even in the winter would make the entire idea of starvation more vivid and real. The same is true with many concepts. In explaining friendship, you might tell a story about the way in which a particular friend acted or in describing love as it is given and received in your own life.

Examples and illustrations may be real or factual on the one hand or hypothetical or imagined on the other. Thus, in explaining friendship you might tell the story of the behavior of an actual friend (and thus have a real or factual example or illustration) or you might formulate a kind of composite or ideal friend and describe how this person would act in such and such a situation (and thus have a hypothetical or imagined example or illustration). Both types are useful; both types are effective.

TESTIMONY

In using testimony for amplification you would generally be concerned with one of two things. First, you may be concerned with the opinions, beliefs, predictions, or values of some authority or expert. You might, for example, be interested in stating an economist's predictions concerning inflation and depression, an art critic's evaluation of a painting or art movement, a media analyst's opinion of television commercials, and so on. Here, for instance, United States Congresswoman Shirley Chisholm addresses the Independent Black Women's Caucus of New York City and uses the testimony of noted psychologist Rollo May to bolster her argument that black women must assume political power rather than wait for it to be given to them.

As Rollo May has put it:

> Power cannot, strictly speaking, be given to another, for then the recipient still owes it to the giver. It must in some sense be assumed, taken, asserted, for unless it can be held *against* opposition, it is not power and will never be experienced as real on the part of the recipient.

And those of us in this room know all too well that whatever is given to us is almost always a trap.

Second, you may be interested in the individual as a witness (in the broad sense) to some event or situation. You might, for example, be concerned with the individual who saw a particular accident, with the person who spent two years in a maximum security prison, in the person who underwent a particular

BOX 24.1
Some Research Sources

The Card Catalog

The *card catalog* contains cards of three types: title cards, subject cards, and author cards. Each card also contains such information as the number of pages in the book; whether or not the book has illustrations, bibliographies, and index; the date of publication; the publisher; and, of course, the identifying number, which tells you where the book can be found in your library

The Vertical File

The *vertical file*, sometimes called the "information file," contains clippings from newspapers and magazines, pamphlets, and other materials such as photographs and letters, organized by topic and arranged in files.

Encyclopedias

> *Encyclopaedia Britannica:* 30 volumes; the most comprehensive and authoritative of all encyclopedias
>
> *Collier's Encyclopedia:* 24 volumes; distinguished by its illustrations and clarity of style
>
> *Encyclopedia Americana:* 30 volumes; especially useful for American things
>
> *Columbia Encyclopedia* and *Random House Encyclopedia:* useful one-volume encyclopedias
>
> *The New Catholic Encyclopedia, Encyclopaedia Judaica, Encyclopedia of Islam, Encyclopedia of Buddhism, McGraw-Hill Encyclopedia of Science and Technology, International Encyclopedia of the Social Sciences:* as their titles imply, these are more specialized works and are representative of the wide variety of available encyclopedias.

Biographical Material

> *Biography Index* contains an index to biographies appearing in numerous and different sources.
>
> *Dictionary of National Biography* (*DNB*) contains articles on famous dead British men and women as does its short edition, *Concise Dictionary of National Biography.*
>
> *Dictionary of American Biography* (*DAB*) contains articles on famous dead Americans as does its short edition, *The Concise Dictionary of American Biography.*

Dictionary of Canadian Biography (*DCB*) contains articles on those who have contributed significantly to Canada.

Current Biography contains articles on living individuals, most with photographs.

Directory of American Scholars, International Who's Who, Who's Who in America, Who's Who (primarily British), *Dictionary of Scientific Biography*, and *American Men and Women of Science* are more specialized and are representative of the numerous biographical sources available.

Newspaper, Magazine, and Journal Indexes

The New York Times Index, published since 1913, indexes articles of all sorts published in *The New York Times*.

Reader's Guide to Periodical Literature, published from 1900, indexes over 100 different popular magazines.

Education Index covers articles from journals and magazines relevant to education.

The Catholic Periodical and Literature Index, The Social Science and Humanities Index, Business Periodicals Index, Art Index, and *Applied Science and Technology Index* are more specialized indexes.

Psychological Abstracts, Sociological Abstracts, Language and Language Behavior Abstracts, and *Communication Abstracts* contain brief summaries of articles in these various areas of study.

Almanacs

The World Almanac & Book of Facts, published since 1868, is the most popular and probably the best of the numerous almanacs, which contain information on the arts, science, governments, population, geography, religion, and just about every other conceivable topic.

Information Please Almanac, Reader's Digest Almanac and Yearbook, and *The New York Times Encyclopedia Almanac* are similar in style and purpose to *The World Almanac & Book of Facts*.

Whitaker's Almanac focuses on Great Britain, and *Canadian Almanac and Directory* focuses on things Canadian.

Statistical Abstracts of the United States summarizes just about any facts and figures you might be interested in.

operation, in the Trappist monk who lived for ten years under a vow of silence, and so on.

Testimony may be presented to the audience in the form of direct quotations or in the form of paraphrase, where you, the speaker, put into your own words what the expert or witness said. Quotations are useful, but at times they become cumbersome; often they are not directly related to the point you are trying to make and their relevance at times gets lost. The quotation may be in technical language that members of the audience will not understand and it then becomes necessary to interject definitions as you go along. Unless the quotation is relatively short, reasonably comprehensible to the audience, and directly related to the point you are trying to make, it would be advisable to use your own words, noting, of course, that the ideas, the predictions, the evaluations, and whatever were developed by, say, Nicely Pendleton.

③ DEFINITION

Definitions are useful as amplifying material when you are attempting to explain difficult or unfamiliar concepts or when you wish to make a concept more vivid or forceful. Hugh Walpole, for example, in his classic *Semantics: The Nature of Words and Their Meanings*, considers 25 ways in which a concept may be defined: by behavior ("a scientist is one who . . ."), by sex ("a rooster is the male of the domestic fowl"), by part relations ("a hand is part of the arm"), and so on. I note here some of the modes of definition most useful to you as a speaker attempting to support a statement or idea.

One of the most useful is to define a term by its etymology, that is, the historical development of the word, or its derivation. For example, in attempting to define the word *communication* you might note that it comes from the Latin *communis*, meaning "common," and thus in "communicating" you seek to establish a commonness, a sameness, a similarity with another individual. And *woman* comes from the Anglo-Saxon *wifman*, which meant literally a "wife man" where the word *man* was applied to both sexes. Through phonetic change *wifman* became *woman*. Most of the larger dictionaries and, of course, the more specialized etymological dictionaries would prove helpful in your search for etymological definitions.

You may also define a term by authority. You might, for example, define *lateral thinking* by authority and say that Edward deBono, who developed lateral thinking in 1966, has noted that "lateral thinking involves moving sideways to look at things in a different way. Instead of fixing on one particular approach and then working forward from that the lateral thinker tries to find other approaches." Or you might use the authority of cynic and satirist Ambrose Bierce and define *love* as nothing but "a temporary insanity curable by marriage" and *friendship* as "a ship big enough to carry two in fair weather, but only one in foul."

Operational definition is perhaps the most important means of definition. Here you define a concept by indicating the operations one would go through in constructing the object. Thus, for example, to operationally define a chocolate cake, you would provide the recipe. The operational definition of stuttering would include an account of how the act of stuttering is to be performed and by what procedures stuttering might be observed.

You might also define a term by noting what that term is not—that is, defining by negation. "A wife," you might say, "is not a cook, a cleaning person, a babysitter, a seamstress, a sex partner. A wife is . . . " "A teacher," you might say, "is not someone who tells you what you should know but rather one who . . ."

You might also define a term by direct symbolization—that is, by showing the actual thing or, if that is not possible, by showing some picture or model of it. This, as can be appreciated, is perhaps the best method for defining observables but would obviously not work with abstract concepts, such as friendship and love, or things that are impossible to perceive, such as molecules and infrared rays.

④ STATISTICS

Statistics are summary numbers. Statistics are organized sets of numbers that help us to see at a glance trends or other important characteristics of an otherwise complex set of numbers. Particularly helpful for the speaker are the measures of central tendency, measures of correlation, and measures of difference.

Measures of central tendency tell you the general pattern of a group of numbers. The *mean* is the arithmetic average of a set of numbers—calculated by adding all the figures and dividing by the number of figures. For example, the mean of 5, 8, and 8 would be 7. The *median* is the middle score; 50 percent of the cases fall above the median and 50 percent below. For example, if the median score on the midterm was 78, it would mean that half the class scored higher than 78 and half scored lower. Lastly, the *mode* is the most frequently occurring score; it is the single score that most people received. If the mode of the midterm was 85, it would mean that more students received 85 than any other single score.

Measures of correlation tell you how closely two or more things are related. You might say, for example, that there is a high correlation between smoking and lung cancer or between poverty and crime or between psychological insight and suicide. It is important that you recognize that high correlations do not mean causation. The fact that two things vary together (are highly correlated) does not mean that one causes the other. Some third factor might be operating. For example, job satisfaction and educational level are highly correlated. The higher the educational level, the higher the job satisfaction. But it would be naive to assume that educational level leads to job satisfaction. Rather, some third factor seems to be operating here—namely, that with higher education, the available jobs become more interesting and more rewarding, and this leads to high job satisfaction. With low educational levels, the available jobs are generally uninteresting and unrewarding, and this leads to low job satisfaction.

Measures of difference tell you the extent to which scores differ from some hypothetical average or from one another. For example, the *range* tells us how far apart the lowest score is from the highest score. The range is computed by subtracting the lowest from the highest score. If the lowest score on the midterm was 76 and the highest was 99, then the range would be 23 points. Generally, a high range indicates great diversity and a low range indicates great similarity.

Percentiles are useful for specifying the percentage of scores that fall below a particular score. For example, if you scored 700 on the College Entrance Examination Board test, you were approximately in the 97th percentile. This means that 97 percent of those taking the test scored lower than 700. Generally, the 25th, 50th, and 75th percentiles (also called respectively, the first, second, and third quartiles) are distinguished. The second quartile or 50th percentile is also the median, since exactly half the scores are above and half are below.

In the following two excerpts the speakers use summary figures (here measures of central tendency) to make their assertions more vivid and more meaningful. Ernest L. Boyer uses the arithmetic mean to demonstrate that children are avid television viewers.

> Young children—2 to 5 years old—now watch television over 4 hours every day, nearly 30 hours a week. That's more than 1,500 hours every year. And by the time a youngster enters first grade he or she has had 6,000 hours of television viewing.

To stress the prevalence of emotional problems and suicide among college students, a student, Patricia Ann Hayes uses statistics effectively.

> Dr. Dana Farnsworth, a leading expert in the field of student mental health, lists some rather ominous nationwide statistics for colleges. He stresses that of each 10,000 students 1,000 will have emotional conflicts severe enough to warrant professional help, 300–400 will have feelings of depression deep enough to impair efficiency, 5–10 will attempt suicide, and 1–3 will succeed in taking his own life. If these statistics are true, my university should encounter 15–45 suicide attempts of which 3–6 will be successful.

VISUAL AIDS

One of the most powerful means of amplification you have as a speaker is that of visual aids. To aid comprehension and to make ideas easier to remember, few forms of amplifying material can serve as well as visual aids. Visual aids may be of various types. They would include the actual objects being discussed as well as replicas and models that would help the listeners see what is being considered. Charts, maps, graphs, and diagrams are also useful in explaining trends, showing relative distance and size, clarifying complex figures, and demonstrating significant relationships. Pictures, slides, and films help listeners to visualize what you are talking about. If you wish to speak on sun poisoning and its dangers, then it would be much more effective if you included some visualization, some pictures of victims of sun poisoning, so that listeners could see how horrible its effects really are. Printed information is often helpful. When you wish to explain, for example, the organizational structure of a particular corporation, you could show a chart detailing the structure and the major functions of each office. In discussing a particular proposal, perhaps a printed statement of the proposal and statements by those persons who have endorsed the proposal would be helpful. After a lecture that might prove complex, I often distribute an outline of the lecture so that the students can combine that outline with their notes in studying. Perhaps the most often used visual aid is the blackboard —a relatively easy-to-use and effective aid.

Audio material is also very helpful. It would be impossible to give a speech on contemporary music, for example, without allowing your audience to hear exactly what you are talking about. Similarly, to talk about television commercials without some audio (and video) would be only covering a small portion of the topic.

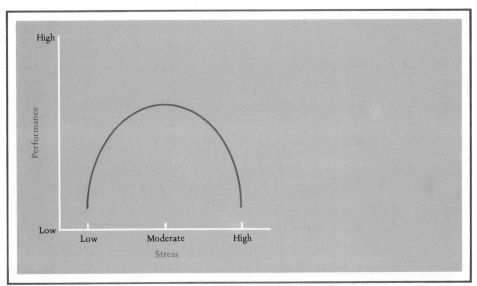

Figure 24.1 A little stress is best. The hypothetical relationship between stress and performance of a learned task. Performance is best at moderate levels of stress. *Source:* Herbert Harari and Robert M. Kaplan, *Psychology: Personal and Social Adjustment* (New York: Harper & Row, 1977), p. 346.

Figures 24.1 and 24.2 are two examples of visual aids. These were professionally prepared, so do not think that your own visual aids must be this professional. Nevertheless, it is not a bad idea to have a high degree of quality in visual aids, as well as in verbal material, as your goal. The graph in Figure 24.1 illustrates the relationship between stress and performance and reinforces the verbal description of this relationship. The stages in mate selection and the mate selection filters, illustrated in Figure 24.2, enable the listener-viewer to see as well as hear how individuals narrow down the field of prospective mates.

SUPPORTING THE SPEECH WITH ARGUMENT

Here Dr. Watson is narrating a conversation he had with Sherlock Holmes:

"How do I know that you have been getting yourself very wet lately, and that you have a more clumsy and careless servant girl?"

"My dear Holmes," said I, "this is too much. . . . It is true that I had a country walk on Thursday and came home in a dreadful mess; but as I have changed my clothes, I can't imagine how you deduce it. As to Mary Jones, she is incorrigible, and my wife has given her notice; but there again I fail to see how you worked it out."

He chuckled to himself and rubbed his long nervous hands together.

"It is simplicity itself," said he; "my eyes tell me that on the inside of your left shoe, just where the firelight strikes it, the leather is scored by six almost

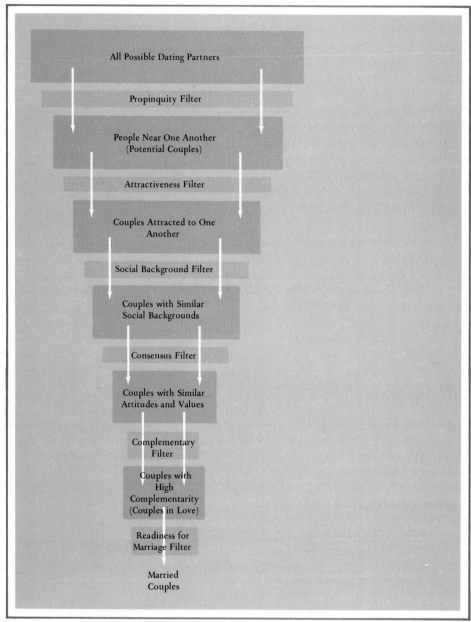

Figure 24.2   Mate selection filters. *Source:* J. Richard Udry, *The Social Context of Marriage* (Philadelphia: Lippincott, 1971).

parallel cuts. Obviously they have been caused by someone who has very carelessly scraped round the edges of the sole in order to remove crusted mud from it. Hence, you see, my double deduction that you had been out in vile weather, and that you had a particularly malignant bootslicking specimen of the London Slavey."

On the basis of various bits and pieces of "evidence," Holmes has drawn a "conclusion." The evidence together with the conclusion constitutes an argument—the substance of this section. More specifically, in this section we continue the discussion of supporting materials, this time focusing on materials that prove or attempt to prove the validity of a proposition or conclusion. First we consider the general nature of argument and reasoning and some general tests of evidence. Next we focus on the major types of argument: reasoning from analogy, reasoning from causes and effects, reasoning from sign, and reasoning from specific instances.

THE NATURE OF ARGUMENT, REASONING, AND SUPPORT

By "argument" I do not mean a disagreement or a dispute, but rather a reason or series of reasons that lead to or support a conclusion. Evidence plus the conclusion that the evidence supports equal an argument. By "reasoning" I mean the process of presenting evidence (or "reasons") for a particular conclusion or claim you wish to make.

When you argue a point in a public speech or attempt to demonstrate the usefulness of a particular way of looking at something or postulate some general principle, you are attempting to prove something to the listeners. That is, your function is a rhetorical one in the sense that you hope to prove the proposition—not in any objective sense but rather in the minds of the listeners. In the vast majority of cases that you would deal with as a public speaker, the issues cannot be proved in any objective sense. Rather, you seek as a speaker to establish the probability of your conclusions in the minds of the listeners. Thus, the process is in part a logical one of demonstrating the postulated relationship, but also a psychological one of convincing or persuading the listeners to accept the conclusions as you have drawn them. Throughout this discussion this dual function should be kept in mind.

Another important factor that must be kept in mind is that what is said here is applicable to the speaker in constructing the speech, to the listener in receiving and responding to the speech, and to the speech critic or analyst in analyzing and evaluating the speech. A poorly reasoned argument, inadequate evidence, and stereotyped thinking, for example, must be avoided by the speaker, recognized and responded to by the listener, and negatively evaluated by the critic.

Before getting to the specific forms of argument or reasoning, there are some general tests of support that are applicable to all forms of argument, and these should be stated at the outset. We state these general tests and in fact all the tests of adequacy in the form of questions so that you may ask yourself these questions as you are evaluating various sources of evidence and thus test the adequacy of the argument and support more easily.

405

Is the Support Recent?

We live in a world of rapid change, and what was true ten years ago is not necessarily true today. Economic strategies that worked for your parents will not necessarily work for you. Whereas, for example, your parents saved money and avoided getting into debt, in times of inflation many economists advise us not to save but to spend and to borrow as much money as possible. As the world changes, so must our strategies for coping with it. And what is true of economic examples is also true of other areas. No area, in fact, is immune to change. Therefore, it is particularly important that your supporting materials be recent. Recency alone, obviously, does not make an effective argument. Yet, other things being equal, the more recent the evidence and support the better.

Is There Corroborative Support?

Very few conditions in this world are simple; most relationships, most issues are complex. Consequently, in reasoning about any issue it is helpful if you can find evidence to support the proposition from different areas, sources, and perspectives. For example, consider receiving advice that you take such-and-such a course of study. It would be helpful if you had evidence from educational authorities attesting to, say, the value of the program. But it would also help if you had evidence from government statistics showing that demands in these areas are going to increase rapidly over the next four years, economic forecasts from industry attesting to the likelihood that such a program of study will adequately prepare you for high-level company positions without the danger of finding that when you enter business your skills will have to be upgraded, and so on. That is, in supporting a thesis, it helps if evidence and argument can be gathered from numerous and diverse sources all pointing to the same conclusion. This will obviously be of value to the speaker, since it will help to convince listeners that the conclusion is a valid one, but, will also go a long way in giving greater credence to what you as a speaker are saying in general.

Are the Sources Unbiased?

We each see the world through our own individual filters; we do not see the world objectively but through our prejudices, biases, preconceptions, and stereotypes. Consequently, it is essential in evaluating evidence to ask if the sources are unbiased or, more realistically, how biased the sources are and the direction of their biases.

You would normally not treat a report on the connection between smoking and lung cancer, conducted by major tobacco companies, with the same credibility that you would give it if it were conducted by some impartial medical research institute. You know that the tobacco companies have an interest to protect, and you would normally be suspicious of research conducted and disseminated by an individual or group of individuals who wish to protect their financial investment and livelihood. This, of course, is an obvious example; few of us would be fooled by such reports. And yet we listen every day to commercials on television reporting the results of research that invariably supports the superiority of one product (their product) over another (someone else's product). And although we may say that such research reports do not influence us, I am inclined to think that advertisers know what they are doing. If they are spending millions of dollars each year on such advertisements, we can be pretty sure that they are making that money back from increased sales. Thus, "three out of four doctors recommend . . ." sounds impressive until you realize that conceivably the "researchers" could have gone to hundreds of groups of four doctors to find one group of four where three doctors recommended their product.

In short, as a speaker and as a listener you have to be particularly careful to recognize bias in your sources. It is always legitimate to ask, then, to what extent might this source be biased? Might this source have a special interest that leads her or him to offer the evidence being offered?

These, then, are some general questions that may be asked of all forms of evidence and argument. We now turn to some of the specific types of argument.

REASONING FROM ANALOGY

In reasoning from analogy you compare like things and conclude that since they are alike in so many respects they are also alike in this heretofore unknown or unexamined respect. Analogies may be literal or figurative. In a literal analogy the items being compared are from the same class—whether cars, people, countries, cities, or whatever. For example, in a literal analogy we might argue that the cities of New York, Philadelphia, London, and Paris are like Los Angeles in all essential respects—they are all large in area, have a few million people, have a central inner city, and so on. These other cities all have profited from low-cost subway transportation. Therefore, Los Angeles would also profit from the construction of a subway system. Here, then, we have taken a number of like items belonging to the same class (large cities), have pointed out a number of similarities (area, population), and then reasoned that the similarity would also apply to the unexamined item (the subway system).

Analogies may also be figurative; here the items being compared come from different classes. These analogies are really more useful for amplification than for reasoning.

In a speech, "The Vital Need for Technology and Jobs," Thomas A. Vanderslice, vice president and group executive of General Electric Company, used a most effective figurative analogy, comparing the human body with the country, to stress the importance of research and improvement.

> I am told that Casey Stengel, on reaching one of his supernumerary birthdays, was asked,—looking back on his long life in baseball, what would he have done differently.
>
> The "Old Perfesser" thought a bit, and said: "If I'd known I was going to live so long, I'd have taken better care of myself."
>
> My remarks today are dedicated to the proposition that this country, and our form of government, will be around for a while yet, and we'd better take good care of what we have.

As this example illustrates the figurative analogy functions to create an image; it

To Holmes, reasoning out a conclusion was always elementary.

does not function to prove anything. Its main purpose is to clarify, and it is particularly useful when you wish to make a complex process or relationship clearly understandable to the audience.

REASONING FROM CAUSES AND EFFECTS

In reasoning from causes and effects you may go in either of two directions. You may reason from cause to effect (from observed cause to unobserved effect) or from effect to cause (from observed effect to unobserved cause).

Causal reasoning would go something like this. You would argue, for example, that X results from Y, and since X is undesirable Y should be eliminated. With actual events substituted, you would have something like this: Cancer (X) results from smoking (Y), and since cancer is bad, smoking should be eliminated. Alternatively, of course, you might argue that X results from Y, and since X is desirable Y should be encouraged. For example, general self-confidence (X) results from positively reinforcing experiences (Y); therefore, to encourage the development of self-confidence, foster positively reinforcing experiences.

REASONING FROM SIGN

About six years ago I went to my doctor because of some minor skin irritation. Instead of looking at my skin the doctor focused on my throat, noticed that it was enlarged, felt around a bit, and began asking me a number of questions. Did I tire easily? Yes. Did I drink lots of liquid? Yes. Did I always feel thirsty? Yes. Did I eat a great deal without gaining any weight? Yes. She then had me stretch out my hand and try to hold it steady. I could not do it. Last, she took a close look at my eyes and asked if I noticed that they had expanded. I had not been aware of it, but when it was pointed out I could see that my eyes had expanded a great deal. All of these indicators were signs of a particular illness. Based on these signs, she made the preliminary diagnosis that I had a hyperthyroid condition. The results from blood and other tests confirmed the preliminary diagnosis. I was promptly treated and the thyroid condition was corrected.

Medical diagnosis is a good example of reasoning by sign. The general procedure is relatively simple. If a sign and an object, event, or condition are repeatedly or frequently paired, then the presence of the sign is taken as evidence or proof of the presence of the object, event, or condition. Thus, the tiredness, the extreme thirst, the overeating, and so on were taken as signs of thyroid, since they frequently accompany thyroid disease. When these signs (or symptoms) disappeared after treatment with radioactive iodine, it was taken as a sign that the thyroid disease had been arrested. Further tests confirmed this as well.

More mundane, but perhaps more meaningful instances of reasoning by sign occur every day. The teacher looks at the class and sees two students in the back reading the newspaper, three students staring out the window, four students engaged in private conversation, one asleep. Any teacher with all faculties intact would reason from these signs to the conclusion that somehow the class was not very interested in the lecture. In a disco, bar, or party, if someone asks you to dance and to buy you a drink, engages you in conversation, and stares longingly into your eyes, you would normally take these as signs that this individual is interested in you and would like to pursue the relationship.

REASONING FROM A SPECIFIC INSTANCE TO A GENERALIZATION AND FROM A GENERALIZATION TO A SPECIFIC INSTANCE

In reasoning from specific instances, you examine several specific instances and then conclude something about the whole. Thus, you taste one piece of spaghetti as it is cooking and conclude something about the whole—for example, that it needs to cook a bit more. With spaghetti, there is little danger in this kind of reasoning; the worst that could happen is that a pound of spaghetti will be served overcooked or undercooked—certainly no great tragedy. Consider, however, the same process when you examine (or meet or interact with) several members of a particular racial or religious group and on that basis conclude something about the entire class.

Reasoning from specific instances is particularly useful when you want to develop a general principle or conclusion but cannot examine the whole. You sample a few communication courses and conclude something about communication courses in general; you visit several Scandinavian cities and conclude something about the whole of Scandinavia. This same general process operates in dealing with one person. You see, for example, a particular person in several situations and conclude something about that person's behavior in general. You date a person a few times or maybe even for a period of several months and on that basis draw a general conclusion about the suitability of that person as a spouse.

You may also argue in the other direction—namely, from a general principle to some specific instance. That is, you begin with some general statement or axiom that is accepted as true by the audience and argue that since this is true of the entire class, it must also be true of this specific instance, which is a member of that class.

Reasoning from general principles—which is actually more a way of presenting your argument than a type of reasoning or argument—is useful when you wish to argue or demonstrate that some unexamined instance has certain characteristics. The general principle and this unexamined item's membership in that class are noted, and the conclusion is drawn that therefore this item also possesses the qualities possessed by the whole. For example, listeners may all accept the notion that Martians are lazy, uncooperative, and dull-witted. This is the general principle or axiom that is accepted. The argument would then take the form of applying this general principle to a specific instance—for example, "Obviously, then, we should not hire Delta X since we would not want a lazy, uncooperative, stupid colleague."

SOURCES

On amplification see, for example, Douglas Ehninger, Alan H. Monroe, and Bruce E. Gronbeck, *Principles and Types of Speech Communication*, 8th ed. (Glenview, Ill.: Scott, Foresman, 1978), and Donald C. Bryant and Karl R. Wallace, *Fundamentals of Public Speaking*, 5th ed. (Englewood Cliffs, N.J.: Prentice-Hall, 1976). The speeches cited in this unit include: Ronald Allen, "Do You Really Want to Know Why Johnny Can't Write or Read, or Speak or Listen?" *Vital Speeches of the Day* 43 (Dec. 15, 1976): 148–150; Shirley Chisholm, "Vote for the Individual, Not the Political Party," *Vital Speeches of the Day* 44 (Aug. 15, 1978): 670–671; Ernest L. Boyer, "Communication: Message Senders and Receivers," *Vital Speeches of the Day* 44 (Mar. 15, 1978): 334–337; Patricia Ann Hayes, "Madame Butterfly and the Collegian," *Winning Orations, 1967* (Detroit: The Interstate Oratorical Association, 1967), pp. 7–10, reprinted in *Contemporary American Speeches*, 2d ed., ed. Wil A. Linkugel, R. R. Allen, and Richard L. Johannesen (Belmont, Cal.: Wadsworth, 1969), pp. 262–266.

For argumentation and logic I would recommend the following: Craig R. Smith and David M. Hunsaker, *The Bases of Argument: Ideas in Conflict* (Indianapolis: Bobbs-Merrill, 1972); Abne M. Eisenberg and Joseph A. Llardo, *Argument: A Guide to Formal and Informal Debate*, 2d ed. (Englewood Cliffs, N.J.: Prentice-Hall, 1980); Douglas Ehninger and Wayne Brockriede, *Decision by Debate*, 2d ed. (New York: Harper & Row, 1978); Nicholas Capaldi, *The Art of Deception* (Buffalo, N.Y.: Prometheus Books, 1971); and Michael A. Gilbert, *How to Win an*

Argument (New York: McGraw-Hill, 1979). Perhaps the best single source is Stephen Toulmin, Richard Rieke, and Allan Janik, *An Introduction to Reasoning* (New York: Macmillan, 1979). A full text of the speech by Vanderslice may be found in Thomas A. Vanderslice, "The Vital Need for Technology and Jobs," *Vital Speeches of the Day* 43 (Dec. 15, 1976): 150–154.

Experiential Vehicles

24.1 Amplification

Here are presented some rather bland, uninteresting statements. Select one of them and amplify it, using at least three different methods of amplification. Identify each method used. Since the purpose of this exercise is to provide you with greater insight into forms and methods of amplification, you may, for this exercise, manufacture, fabricate, or otherwise invent facts, figures, illustrations, examples, and the like. In fact, it may prove even more beneficial if you went to extremes in constructing these forms of support.

1. Significant social and political contributions have been made by college students.
2. The Sears Tower in Chicago is the world's tallest building.
3. Dr. Kirk is a model professor.
4. My grandparents left me a fortune in their will.
5. The college I just visited seems ideal.
6. The writer of this article is a real authority.
7. I knew I was marrying into money as soon as I walked into the house.
8. Considering what that individual did, punishment to the fullest extent of the law would be mild.
9. The fortune-teller told us good news.
10. The athlete lived an interesting life.

24.2 Reasoning Adequacy

Here are, in brief, a few arguments. Read each of them carefully and (1) identify the type of reasoning used, (2) apply the tests of adequacy discussed in this unit, and (3) indicate what could be done to make the reasoning more logical *and* more persuasive.

1. Last year, the three campus theater productions averaged 250 paid admissions. In a college of 12,000 students and with a theater that seats 1,000, the record is not a particularly good one. It seems clear that students are apathetic and simply do not care about theater or about campus activities in general. Something should be done about this—to encourage an appreciation for the arts and support for college-sponsored activities in general.

2. Students are apathetic. This is true of high-school as well as college students, at urban as well as at campus schools. We see it all around us, so why bother to build a new theater? The students are not going to attend the productions. Let's direct that money to something that will be used, something that will be useful to the students and to the community as a whole.

3. Dr. Manchester should be denied tenure for being an ineffective teacher. Two of my friends are in Manchester's statistics course and hate it; they have not learned a thing. Manchester's student evaluation ratings are way below the department and the college average, and the readings Manchester assigns are dull, difficult, and of little relevance to students.

4. The lack of success among the Martians who have settled on Earth is not difficult to explain. They simply have no ambition, no drive, no desire to excel. They're content to live off unemployment, drink cheap wine, and smoke as much grass as they can get their hands on.

5. I went out with three people I met at discos. They were all duds. In the disco they were fine, but once we got outside I couldn't even talk with them. All they knew how to do was wear clothes and dance. So when Pat asked me out I said no. I just decided it would be a big waste of time.

6. College professors are simply not aware of the real world. They teach their courses in an atmosphere that is free of all the problems and complexities of real life. How could they possibly advise me as to how to go about preparing for and finding a job?

7. I took Smith's course in rhetorical theory and it was just great—and easy. In fact, only one test was given and it was simple. Everybody got an A or a B+. We didn't even have a term paper, and the lectures were all really interesting and relevant. This semester I had room for an elective, so I'm taking Smith's psycholinguistics course.

8. One recent sociological report indicates some interesting facts about Theta Three. In Theta Three there are, as most of us know, few restrictions on premarital sexual relations. Unlike in our country, the permissive person is not looked down on. Social taboos in regard to sex are few. Theta Three also has the highest suicide rate per 1000 inhabitants. Suicide is not infrequent among teenagers and young adults. This condition must be changed. But before it is changed, life must be accorded greater meaning and significance. Social, and perhaps legal, restrictions on premarital sexual relations must be instituted if the individual is to come to have self-respect. Only in this way will the suicide rate—Theta Three's principal problem today—be significantly reduced.

9. In 1936 the *Literary Digest* took a poll to predict whether Landon or Roosevelt would win the presidential election. The *Digest* sent pre-election ballots to 10 million people, chosen at random from telephone directories and from lists of registered owners of automobiles. Two million ballots were returned, and the *Digest* concluded that Landon would win the election.

10. Pat and Chris are unhappy and should probably separate. The last time I visited, Pat told me that they just had a big fight and in fact mentioned that they now fight regularly. Chris spends more time with friends than with Pat and frequently goes out after work with people from the office. Often, Chris has told me, they sit for hours without saying one word to each other.

Unit 25

Supporting Materials in Public Communication:
Psychological Appeals and Speaker Credibility

SUPPORTING MATERIALS IN PUBLIC COMMUNICATION: PSYCHOLOGICAL APPEALS AND SPEAKER CREDIBILITY

Supporting the Speech with Psychological Appeals
Supporting the Speech with Speaker Credibility

LEARNING GOALS

After completing this unit, you should be able to:

1. explain the nature of psychological appeals
2. explain Maslow's hierarchy of motives
3. identify at least five principles of motivation
4. explain their relevance to the public speaking transaction
5. explain the operation of at least five motivational appeals
6. explain "psychological balance" and its relation to motivation
7. define *speaker credibility*
8. explain the ways in which credibility impressions may be formed
9. distinguish among initial, derived, and terminal credibility
10. explain the five components of credibility identified here

In this unit we continue the discussion of supporting materials by focusing on *psychological appeals*—their nature, the principles of motivation, and some of the specific motivational appeals that should prove useful in public communication, and *speaker credibility*—its nature, the ways in which credibility impressions are formed, and the specific characteristics that make a person believable.

SUPPORTING THE SPEECH WITH PSYCHOLOGICAL APPEALS

Persuasion is a complex process. What functions to persuade one person may have no effect on another. What persuades one person to vote for censorship may persuade another person to campaign vigorously for the removal of all restrictions on free communication. What persuades one person to act immediately may persuade another to act two months or even two years from now. There are, in effect, differences and variations on all aspects and dimensions of persuasion. Because of this variation, it is difficult to ferret out just those items of information that will prove useful to constructing and presenting a public speech.

But amid all this uncertainty it seems universally agreed that psychological appeals—the appeals to one's needs, desires, and wants—are most powerful in most situations. Because of the importance of psychological appeals, this first part is devoted to explicating their role in public speaking. Specifically, we will focus on four major issues. First, the nature of psychological appeals is discussed. Second, using the theory and research in the psychology of motivation, a set of five principles of motivation as applied to public speaking is developed. Third, we consider specific motivational appeals and how these may be used in public speaking. Fourth, we discuss psychological balance and its relationship to motivation.

THE NATURE OF PSYCHOLOGICAL APPEALS

By psychological appeals I mean those appeals that are directed at an individual's needs, wants, desires, wishes, and so on. Although psychological appeals are never totally separate from rational appeals—appeals that are directed to one's reasoning and logic—they are considered separately here. We are primarily concerned here with motives, with those forces that energize or move or motivate a person to develop, change, or strengthen particular attitudes or ways of behaving. For example, one motive might be the desire for status; this motive might then move the individual to develop certain attitudes about appropriate and inappropriate occupations, the importance or unimportance of saving and investing money, and so on. It may move this person to behave in certain ways — to buy Gucci shoes, a Rolex watch, and a Tiffany diamond. It should be clear from these examples that this same status motive may motivate different persons in different ways. Thus, the status motive may lead one person to enter the poorly paid but respected occupation of nursing and another to enter the well-paid but often disparaged real estate or diamond business.

Abraham Maslow, in one of the most widely employed systems, uses a five-fold classification of motives, presented visually in Figure 25.1. One of the assumptions here is that people seek to fulfill the needs at the lowest levels first and that only when these needs are fulfilled will they be able to concern themselves with the needs at the next highest level. Thus, for example, peo-

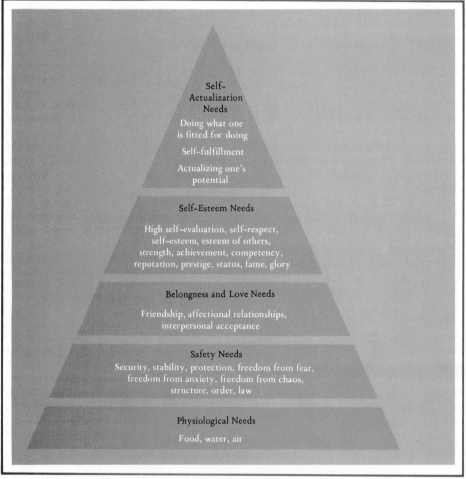

Figure 25.1 Maslow's "hierarchy of needs." *Source:* Based on Abraham Maslow, *Motivation and Personality* (New York: Harper & Row, 1970).

ple do not concern themselves with the need for security or freedom from fear if they are starving (that is, if their food need has not been fulfilled). Similarly, they would not be concerned with friendship or affectional relationship if their need for protection and security has not been fulfilled. I have appropriated the insights of Maslow as well as of various other theorists and researchers in the development of the principles of motivation that follows.

PRINCIPLES OF MOTIVATION

If you are to apply motivational appeals to persuasion effectively and in fact to all forms of public speaking, then you will need to understand some basics of motivation and the ways in which motives operate. Here we study some general principles of motivation as they relate to the public speaking process in general and to persuasion in particular. These principles should prove useful in understanding motivation, in applying motivational appeals in your public speeches, and in listening-evaluating the speeches of others.

1. **Motives function differently with different people.** This is simply a specific application of a more general principle: People are different. No two people are the same. Consequently, the very same motive in different people will be responded to differently. Further, different motives in different people may lead to the same behavior. Thus, three persons may choose to become college professors—one because of the security, another because of its relative freedom, and still another because of its status. The resultant behavior in all three cases is essentially the same, but the motivational histories are very different.

Because of this you need to rely not on the appeal to one motive but on appeals to a number of different motives, and the motives that are appealed to must be appealed to with a clear recognition of the differences among people.

2. **Motives are general classes of needs, desires, and wants.** For example, the achievement motive may include a host of specifics that, when taken together, make up and define achievement for this specific individual. People are not motivated by appeals to abstract and general motives but rather to specific aspects or manifestations of these motives—a simple fact that most works on public speaking and persuasion fail to make clear. Thus, to appeal to status—defined in abstract and general terms—does nothing or at best very little to motivate specific attitudes and behaviors. Rather, you need to appeal to, for example, the desire to be recognized by others on the street, having a job that is respected by family and peers, having a home in an exclusive part of town, going to Europe on a luxury liner and returning on the Concorde, and so on. That is, you need to operationalize the general motive right down to specifics; generally, the more specific, the more effective the appeal. Consider, for example, the difference between the teacher's appeal to read this book because it will help to make you an educated person versus the appeal to read this book because it will help you to pass this course or the next test.

3. **Motives often conflict with one another.** It would be convenient if all our motives energized us in the same direction and for the attainment of the

same goal. But that is not the case, and that is why we experience conflicts. The major types that have been identified, and which you will remember from elementary psychology, are the approach-approach, approach-avoidance, and avoidance-avoidance conflicts. In the approach-approach conflict there are two desirable but mutually exclusive alternatives. You are motivated to approach both but can have only one. For example, you may be offered two excellent jobs: one may offer glamour and the other may offer security; you want both but can have only one. Or, you might want to take two excellent communication courses, but they meet at the same time and you can take only one. In the approach-avoidance conflict you have one alternative which is both desirable and undesirable. One motive leads you to approach it and one motive leads you to avoid it. Exercise is a common example: One motive (good health or an attractive body) may lead you to approach the exercise, but one motive (physical discomfort) may lead you to avoid it. Or, the motive to lose weight, stay on your diet, and remain physically attractive may lead you to say no to the chocolate cake, but the motive to enjoy yourself may lead you to say yes. In the avoidance-avoidance situation there are two alternatives, both undesirable but one of which must be chosen. Thus, to get to San Antonio from New York there are two major alternatives—flying (fear may motivate you to avoid this alternative) and train or bus (time and physical discomfort may motivate you to avoid this alternative). And yet you have to get to San Antonio; one alternative has to be chosen. Or, you might have to choose between giving up your ski weekend to write a term paper or failing the course—two unpleasant alternatives but one of which must be chosen.

4. **Behavior is multiply motivated.** Isolated motives—if such things do exist—do not lead to behavior or attitude change. Rather, motives operate in packages. In some cases the various motives reinforce and supplement one another; in other cases they contradict and conflict with one another. Speakers who appeal to one motive and only one motive fail to recognize that behavior is not a simple matter. Not all the motives are of equal strength, and so it will be to your advantage to concentrate your energies on those that seem most potent. Yet, you should not neglect the fact that motives operate in packages and interact with one another. Thus, it may be helpful for you to appeal not only to one or two or three motives for positive action but also to several motives that seem to be inhibiting the action. For example, if you want an audience to contribute money to fund space research, appeals might be made to such motives as curiosity, loyalty to one's country, and safety. But some time might be wisely spent counteracting the motives that may prevent the audience from opening up their wallets—for example, the need for personal security or financial gain. You would need to show, for example, that the money that is contributed would not militate against any of the needs and desires that the audience has, while it would work positively toward the achievement of their other wants and needs.

5. **Motives change.** Those motives that are crucial to you at this time in your life and that motivate a great deal of your current thinking and behaving may not be operative 10 years from now, two years from now, or even two days

from now. They may fade and others may take their place. Now, for example, attractiveness may be one of the more dominant motives in your life; you have a strong need to be thought attractive to your peers. Later on in life this attractiveness may be replaced by, for example, the desire for security, for financial independence, for power, or for fame. And, of course, the strength of the various motives changes. Whereas certain motives may be extremely strong now, they may only play a secondary role in your later life.

MOTIVATIONAL APPEALS

In employing motivational appeals, there are many specific motives you might address. Naturally each audience will be a bit different, and motives that are appropriately appealed to in one situation might be inappropriate or ineffective in another. Judgment and taste will always have to be exercised. Here just a few of the motives to which appeals may be made are suggested.

Fear

We are motivated in great part by a desire to escape from fear. We fear the loss of all those things that we desire; we fear the loss of money, of family, of friends, of love, of attractiveness, of health, of job, and, in fact, just about everything we now have and value. We fear punishment, rejection, failure. We also fear the unknown, the uncertain, the unpredictable.

The use of fear in persuasion has been studied extensively, and the results seem to indicate that moderate amounts of fear probably work best. With low levels of fear the audience is not motivated sufficiently to do anything, and with high levels of fear they become too frightened to consider the speech at all and simply tune the speaker out.

A good example of the use of fear in persuasion can be seen in the commercials currently being run on television for various legal firms. You are led to believe that if you do not have this firm's legal representation, all sorts of harm will come to you. Another example is the American Express traveler's checks commercial where you are led to believe that if you lose traveler's checks other than American Express they will not be refunded. It was interesting to watch the counteradvertisements that First National City Bank launched protesting this American Express commercial. The later American Express commercials have Karl Malden add that refunds are made by other companies but that most persons prefer American Express. Nevertheless, the fear tactic remains in the main part of the commercial.

Power/Control/Influence

We all want power, control, and influence. First, we want such power over ourselves; we want to be in control of our own destinies, our own fate. We want to be responsible for our own successes and, to a lesser extent, our own failures. As Emerson put it, "Can anything be so elegant as to have few wants, and to serve them one's self?"

We also want control over other persons. We want to be influential. We want

From the time we were children, fear has been a potent motivational appeal.

to be opinion leaders. We want others to come to us for advice, for guidance, for instruction. I think this is why the role of teacher is so appealing to so many people. Similarly, we want to have control over events and things in the world. We want to control our environment. Practically every communication book designed for the popular market (that is, nontextbook) emphasizes how the knowledge of communication will enable you to achieve power and control and influence—whether in sales, in work, or in love.

Affiliation

We want friendship, companionship. We have a desire to be a part of a group, despite our equally potent desires for independence and individuality. Notice that the advertisements for discos, singles bars, dating services, and, in fact, all sorts of places of this nature will emphasize the need for affiliation, for companionship. On this basis alone they successfully gain the attention, interest, and participation of hundreds of thousands. Affiliation seems to assure us that we are in fact worthy creatures. If we have friends and companions, then surely we are people of some merit. In a recent survey of high school seniors entering college in the fall of 1979, "strong friendships" was rated as "extremely important" by 69 percent of the 17,000 students surveyed. "A good marriage and family life"—another example of an affiliative need—was the only life goal ranked higher than strong friendships; it was listed as "extremely important" by 79 percent of those surveyed. Further, when these students were asked what factors would contribute to future job satisfaction, 57 percent noted that a "chance to make friends" was "very important."

Achievement

We want to achieve in whatever we do. As students you want to be successful students; as a teacher-writer, I too want to be successful. Together we want to achieve as friends, as parents, and as lovers, and this is why we read books and listen to speeches that purport to tell us how to be better achievers. Although achievement is in part a personal matter and we want to achieve for ourselves, we also like to have others recognize our achievements, to be reinforced and told that in fact our achievements are really achievements and are valuable achievements at that. "Being successful in my work" was noted as "extremely important" by 63 percent of entering college students.

Financial Gain

Today, as perhaps it was in earlier times, the financial gain motive is extremely potent. To some extent I suspect we are all motivated by the desire for financial gain. Advertisers well know this motive and will frequently get persons interested in their messages by using such key words as "sale," "50 percent off," and "save now." All of these are appeals to the desire for money. Today, many students are choosing their majors and in fact their careers for the money they promise. Accounting is currently enjoying unprecedented popularity on college campuses, largely because there is a reasonably good chance of getting a fairly well-paying job. English, history, and philosophy, on the other hand, are currently experiencing a severe decline. Clearly this up-and-down pattern is related in large part to jobs and to money. Concern for lower taxes, for higher salaries, for fringe benefits are all related to the money motive. Show the audience that what you are saying or advocating will make them money and they will listen with considerable interest, much as they read the current get-rich-quick books that are flooding the bookstalls.

Status

One of the motives that account for a great deal of our behavior—some would argue too much—is our desire for status. In our society status is measured by the occupation and the finances of an individual. Often the job and the money are positively related; at other times they are not. Nevertheless, in most estimates of status, the two are significant. But there are other kinds of status that we might mention. For example, there is the status that comes from competence on the athletic field, from excelling in the classroom, or from superiority on the dance floor. To link your propositions with the desire for status, however conceived by your specific audience, will probably prove most effective. Beginning college students give considerable attention to their future jobs but rank interest and the utilization of skills and abilities as more important than those qualities we normally think of as being part of status. For example, in a recent survey 17,000 students were asked what would make for future job satisfaction. Of those qualities listed as "very important," 93 percent noted "interesting to do" and 74 percent noted "uses skills and abilities." On the side normally considered as qualities of status a "chance to earn a good deal of money" was noted by 47 percent, "a job most people look up to, respect" by 37 percent, and "high status, prestige" by 26 percent. I suspect that these figures change considerably as the person gets older—whether that is for good or for ill—and specifically that they change in the direction of giving greater importance to status in the form of financial gain and societal approval.

PSYCHOLOGICAL BALANCE AND MOTIVATION

Balance theory, also referred to as consistency and homeostasis, offers another approach to motivation. The assumptions of balance theory are simple and intuitively satisfying. The general assumption of all balance theories of motivation (and there are actually numerous variations) is that there is a universal human tendency to maintain balance. *Balance* might be defined as a state of psychological comfort in which your attitudes and the objects and persons about which you have attitudes are related as you would want them to be or as you would psychologically expect them to be. The alternative, *imbalance,* would then be defined as a state of psychological discomfort in which the attitudes and attitude objects are related in ways that are undesirable and psychologically unexpected. Let me make these two states more specific, and the intuitive appeal of this approach will become clear. If you love someone, you expect that person to love you in return. If that love is returned, you are in a state of balance. But if that love is not returned, you are in a state of imbalance or psychological discomfort. You expect your best friend to dislike your worst enemy. If this is the case, you are in a state of psychological comfort, of balance. If, on the other hand, your friend likes your enemy, you are in a state of psychological discomfort or imbalance.

The following three situations are representative of the balanced states:

1. Well-liked Professor Schmedley favors positively evaluated marijuana reform laws ($P + P$).
2. Disliked Senator Millstone favors negatively evaluated capital punishment ($N + N$).
3. Well-liked M. M. Birdfood dislikes disliked W. W. Bigtoe ($P - N$) and vice versa ($N - P$).

In the first example two positively evaluated objects (denoted by P) relate positively ("favors," denoted by $+$). You expect two positively evaluated objects to be positively connected. You expect two of your friends, for example, to like each other: $P + P$. In the second example, two negatively evaluated objects connect positively ("favors"). You expect two negatively evaluated objects to go together, to like each other. You expect two of your enemies to like each other: $N + N$. In the third example a positively evaluated object relates negatively ("dislikes") to a negatively evaluated object. You expect a positively and a negatively evaluated object to be disconnected (or negatively related). You expect your friend to dislike your enemy: $P - N$.

The following three situations represent states of imbalance or psychological discomfort. In such cases, individuals will be motivated to change their attitudes in order to restore balance.

1. Well-liked Professor Schmedley argues against positively evaluated marijuana reform laws $(P - P)$.
2. Disliked Senator Millstone argues against negatively evaluated capital punishment $(N - N)$.
3. Well-liked M. M. Birdfood likes disliked W. W. Bigtoe $(P + N)$ and vice versa $(N + P)$.

In the first example, two positives are negatively related. Since you expect two positives to be positively related, you are psychologically uncomfortable in this situation. In the second example, two negatives are negatively related. Since you expect two negatives to be positively related, you are in a state of psychological discomfort. In the third example, a positive and a negative are positively related. Since you expect a positive and a negative to be negatively related, you are in a state of imbalance.

A state of imbalance creates motivation to change attitudes. Consider the three imbalanced situations. In the first you might restore psychological comfort by changing your attitudes toward Professor Schmedley or toward marijuana reform laws. Or you might even change your perception of the connection between the two positively evaluated objects and say, for example, that the good professor objects publicly but privately favors such laws. Any one of these changes would produce balance states. Note, however, that two changes would only produce another imbalanced state. For example, if you changed your attitude toward both the professor and the reform laws, you would have two negatives negatively connected, $N - N$, another imbalanced state.

In the second example you might change your negative evaluation of the senator to a positive one or your negative attitude toward capital punishment to a positive one or you might perceive the negative connection between the two as somehow not being accurate and come to believe that there is really a positive connection between these two negative objects.

In the third example you can change your evaluation of either one of the elements (either toward Birdfood or toward Bigtoe) or, as in the previous examples, question the connection between the two attitude objects.

Balance theory has a number of significant implications for the public speaker.

1. A person is only motivated to change attitudes and behaviors when she or he is in a state of imbalance. When a person is in a state of balance there is no motivation to change; all is comfortable and there is no reason to change (just as

the satiated individual does not seek food). You will succeed in changing the attitudes of the audience only to the extent that you create a state of imbalance or psychological discomfort and show that acceptance of your propositions will restore balance or psychological comfort.

2. You must thoroughly know the audience's attitudes and the connections they perceive among various attitude objects. It would be impossible to use the credibility of, say, Senator Milktoast without first knowing what attitudes the audience holds toward the senator. Thorough audience analysis must precede any attempt to utilize the principles of balance to motivate attitude and behavior change.

3. You have two basic alternatives to gain acceptance for a proposition or point of view. First, you could associate the proposition positively with some positively evaluated source. That is, you could create a positive bond between an already positively evaluated source and your proposition. Thus, this pattern would be in a state of balance if your proposition were positively evaluated: $P + P$. A second alternative is to associate negatively your proposition with some negatively evaluated source. That is, you would create a negative bond between an already negative source and your proposition. This pattern would be in a state of balance if your proposition were positively evaluated: $N - P$.

If, on the other hand, you are arguing against a particular proposition or point of view—that is, if you want to create a negative attitude toward a certain issue—you again have two alternatives. First, you might create a positive bond between an already negatively evaluated source and your proposition, leading to a state of balance if your issue is negatively evaluated: $N + N$. Second, you might create a negative bond between an already positive source and the issue you wish the audience to feel negatively about. This too would create a balanced state: $P - N$.

You probably utilize these very principles every day when you attempt to persuade someone to think or behave in a certain way. Consider, for example, trying to convince a friend to take a particular course with you. Although the specifics might differ from one person to another and from one situation to another, the general pattern would probably be to create a positive connection between this course and some other positively evaluated attitude objects. And so you might say, for example, that other students rated the course as excellent; this would produce a balanced state if the course were evaluated positively as well: other students (P) rated highly ($+$) this course (P). If you want someone to stay away from a particular person, for example, you might attempt to create a positive connection between this person and some negatively evaluated object— for example, you might argue that this individual has been responsible for the mistreatment of numerous animals or has been bad-mouthing you and your friends. Such an argument would positively connect a negative (mistreatment of animals) with this particular person. The pattern would be in a state of balance if this person were negatively evaluated ($N + N$).

4. If you create imbalance in the minds of the audience, you should seek to provide specific and immediate restoration of balance through the acceptance of your proposition or thesis. The reason you create imbalance in the minds of the audience is so that they will seek balance restoration from you and your proposi-

tion. Some years ago, for example, people were frightened about atomic attacks, radiation, and the like. They were put into a state of imbalance; they and their families (*P*) were positively associated with attack and radiation (all *N*). The balance restorer was the bomb shelter, which functioned to change the positive connection to a negative one. We and our families would not be connected to radiation; the resultant pattern was a balanced one: $P - N$.

We see this same principle operate today in all aspects of persuasion. We are told, for example, that our energy resources are being depleted and that we will in effect soon be positively connected to all sorts of negative consequences. The pattern is that we (*P*) will be positively related (+) to the negatives of high costs of energy and the lack of available energy and, hence, the lack of comfort in the heat and the cold (all *N*). Clearly this is a case of psychological discomfort ($P + N$). The balance restorer is to save energy. In this way the positive connection to all these negatives will be eliminated or changed to a negative ($P - N$). In fact, you could probably find this basic pattern in every effective persuasive speech, regardless of the specific topic, the audience to which it was addressed, when the speech was constructed, or whether or not the speaker consciously understood anything about motivation.

SUPPORTING THE SPEECH WITH SPEAKER CREDIBILITY

We have all probably had the experience of listening to a public speaker and as a result of who the speaker was or what the speaker said or how it was said, believing that person. Similarly, we have probably also had the experience of disbelieving someone after listening to him or her.

THE NATURE OF SPEAKER CREDIBILITY

The question we should now consider is, What leads us to believe some speakers and to disbelieve others? What is there about a speaker that makes him or her believable? This question, generally called *speaker credibility*, is our fourth form of support and has been discussed and investigated for as long a time as speech itself has been investigated. Aristotle, in his *Rhetoric*, said:

> Persuasion is achieved by the speaker's personal character when the speech is so spoken as to make us think him credible. We believe good men more fully and more readily than others; this is true generally whatever the question is, and absolutely true where exact certainty is impossible and opinions are divided.

> There are three things which inspire confidence in the orator's own character—the three, namely, that induce us to believe a thing apart from any proof of it: good sense, good moral character, and good will.

Although Aristotle was writing some 2300 years ago, the characteristics noted as contributing to persuasion—good sense, good moral character, and good will—are essentially the same qualities stressed by modern theorists.

FORMING CREDIBILITY IMPRESSIONS

The credibility that you are perceived to possess is a function of your reputation (or what the audience knows of you prior to your actual public speech) and what you do during the actual speech situation. Most of us would find it difficult to operate with the philosophy of Henry Ford, who observed, "It is all one to me if a man comes from Sing Sing or Harvard. We hire a man, not his history." Most of us—and the results of numerous experimental investigations clearly support this observation—do consider a person's history, weighing it very heavily in the total evaluation, and do combine that information from history with the more immediate information derived from the present interactions. Information from these two sources—from history and from present interactions—interact, and the audience forms some terminal assessment of your credibility.

In your communicology classroom you have probably made a credibility assessment of every other student, especially if the course has been in progress for some time. You may not have verbalized this assessment or even thought about it consciously. Yet, if you do think about it, you will probably realize that you have high credibility for certain of your fellow students and lower credibility for others. This may be because of various experiences. Perhaps you have heard each student give a few speeches and on that basis you have formed some impressions. Or perhaps you have been in other classes with some students and from their performance in these other classes have formed some impression. Or perhaps you have formed an impression from the questions they asked or from the way they dress or from their backgrounds or from the way they look. Or perhaps you have formed impressions on the basis of what others have told you or from your own interactions with them.

The sources from which we draw impressions are limitless. What you need to realize is that in the same way that you have formed impressions of others, others have formed impressions of you. Some of our impressions—and some of theirs—are logical and some emotional.

It is important to recognize not only that others have some impressions concerning your credibility but also to understand what these impressions are. Only by understanding these impressions and evaluations will we be in a position to change them in the direction we wish. And although we may do this throughout our interactions with people, as public speakers we do this largely during our speech. Most often, of course, a public speaker does not know his or her audience as intimately as you know your fellow classmates; consequently, in most situations you will not be able to modify the audience's perceptions of you through personal interactions.

If there is some sort of formal introduction to your speech, you may have some important references integrated into this introduction to help establish your credibility. Thus, for example, if you are to speak on living under wartime conditions, it would be important for the audience to know that you have in fact lived under these conditions, and so you might ask the person introducing you to mention that for three years you lived in Vietnam or Cambodia. When teachers introduce themselves to their classes they often establish their credibility with references to their degrees, where they studied, a textbook that they have written, or some research project on which they are working. At first glance this may seem, at the least, immodest. But note that as long as the references are true, such credibility-establishment references serve the function of allowing the audience to appreciate better the information they will be receiving and to evaluate it in different ways.

During any speech we naturally talk about ourselves, whether explicitly or implicitly. The topics we talk about, the vocal emphasis we give them, our facial expression as we talk about them, the degree of conviction we express, and so on all say something about ourselves. *Derived credibility* is the credibility that a listener perceives based on what takes place during the public speaking encounter. All communication is self-reflexive; all communication says something about the speaker or source. Consequently, all communications relate, directly or indirectly, to the speaker's credibility. Inevitably, in our speeches we convey impressions of our intelligence, our morals, or our good will toward others.

Note, for example, how our impressions change when a person mispronounces a word we think he or she should know or when some kind of grammatical or factual mistake is made. When this happens we tend to think less of the individual's intelligence or competence and perhaps would be less likely to believe what the person is saying. Conversely, if a person is able to cite obscure facts or quote famous philosophers or do complicated mathematical operations, the credibility that person is seen to possess is likely to increase.

In many instances specific and direct attempts are made to exchange the perceived credibility of a particular individual. For example, when politicians are confronted with some wrong they have done or unpopular decision they have made, they quickly attempt to rebuild their credibility by stressing that they did this based on facts and figures not available to the general public (knowledge), that they are good people and would never do anything immoral (high moral character), or that they would only do what is right for the rest of the state or country and that the people's interests were really paramount (good will).

More specifically, we should ask what factors influence the perception of credibility in listeners. That is, what does a speaker do that enhances or detracts from his or her credibility? A great deal of research has been directed at discovering the various means of achieving high derived credibility.

The way in which the message is presented and constructed influences credibility a great deal. If a person communicates haltingly, with poor grammar, with numerous hesitations, and with an uneasiness, we would probably perceive that person to be of low credibility and not readily believe him or her. Conversely, the speaker who speaks with assurance, who speaks in accordance with the rules of grammar, and who appears self-confident seems to have a much better chance of being perceived as credible. Thus the words we choose in speaking, the way in which we arrange those words, the way in which we organize our arguments, questions, or responses influence our credibility.

The fairness with which one presents oneself seems also to influence the perception of credibility. If we feel that people have some kind of ulterior motive, we are less likely to believe them. On the other hand, speakers who present themselves honestly are believed more readily.

Generally, we perceive as believable people who are like ourselves. The more similar people are to our own backgrounds, attitudes and beliefs, goals and ambitions, the more likely it is that they will be perceived as credible. Closely related to this is the issue of "common ground." When people align themselves with what we align ourselves with, they establish common ground with us and are generally perceived as more believable than people who do not establish this common ground. I guess we do not like to think that people who are like us would be anything but knowledgeable, of good character, and of good will.

On the basis of your reputation and what happens during the speech, the audience forms some impression of your terminal credibility. That is, based on the initial credibility and the derived credibility, a terminal credibility image is formed. At times this is higher than the initial credibility, and at times it is lower. But it is always a product of the interaction of the before, or initial, and the during, or derived, credibility. After the job interview, after the teacher and students finish the last discussion of the course, after the speaker sits down there is formed in the mind of each audience member some terminal credibility picture. It is important to emphasize here that credibility is a perception of the speaker that exists in the minds of the audience, and although we may talk of the speaker possessing credibility we always mean *in the minds of the audience.*

THE COMPONENTS OF CREDIBILITY

Speakers of all kinds—regardless of purpose—are concerned with the components or dimensions of credibility. They are concerned with what goes into making a person appear believable or credible. Although various writers put their emphases in different places, most agree with James McCroskey, who defines five major dimensions: *competence, character, intention, personality,* and *dynamism.*

The more intelligent and knowledgeable a speaker is thought to be, the more that speaker will be perceived as credible, and the more likely it is that he or she will be believed. The teacher, for example, is believed to the extent that he or she is thought knowledgeable about the subject. Similarly, the textbook writer is thought credible to the extent that he or she is thought competent.

Competence is logically subject-specific. A person may be competent in one subject and totally incompetent in another subject. However, people often do not make the distinction between areas of competence. Thus a person who is thought competent in politics will often be thought competent in general and will thus be perceived when talking on health or physical education. As a critic or analyst of public speaking you should be particularly sensitive to competence being subject-specific.

We will perceive a speaker as credible if we perceive that speaker as having what Aristotle referred to as a high moral character. Here we would be concerned with the individual's honesty and basic nature. We would want to know if we could trust that person. A speaker who can be trusted is apt to be believed; a speaker who cannot be trusted is apt not to be believed.

An individual's motives or intentions are particularly important in determining credibility. The salesperson who says all the right things about a product is often doubted because his or her intentions are perceived as selfish; credibility is therefore low. The salesperson is less believable than a consumer advocate who evaluates a product with no motives of personal gain. Of course it is extremely difficult to judge whether individuals are concerned with our good or with theirs. But when we can make the distinction, it greatly influences our perception of credibility.

Generally, we perceive as credible or believable speakers we like rather than speakers we do not like. And, it seems, we like speakers who have what we commonly refer to as a "pleasing personality." We believe speakers who are friendly and pleasant rather than speakers who are unfriendly and unpleasant. Positive and forward-looking speakers are seen as more credible than negative and backward-looking speakers. Perhaps we reason that they have gotten themselves together and so are in a better position to know what is right and what is wrong. We would be leery of accepting marital advice from an unhappily married couple, perhaps for a similar reason. If they cannot solve their own problems, we reasonably doubt their ability to help us.

The shy, introverted, soft-spoken individual is generally perceived as less credible than the assertive, extroverted, and forceful individual. The great leaders in history have generally been dynamic people. They were assertive and emphatic. Of course, we may still have the stereotype of the shy, withdrawn college professor who, though not very dynamic, is nevertheless credible. Generally, however, the more dynamic the speaker is, the more credible he or she is perceived to be. Perhaps it is because we feel that the dynamic speaker is open and honest in presenting himself or herself whereas the shy, introverted individual may be seen as hiding something.

In short, the speaker who is seen as competent, of good character, of legitimate intention, of pleasant personality, and dynamic will be perceived as credible. That speaker's credibility will decrease as any one of these five qualities decreases; his or her credibility will increase as any one of these five qualities increases.

Knowing that these five characteristics make up credibility is the first step in the very practical task of making yourself a more credible public speaker. The second step is to implement these components or characteristics.

First and most obviously, attempt to develop and/or strengthen these characteristics as a person and as a speaker. Become competent, of good character, of good intention, personable, and dynamic. I know that this is easy to say but extremely difficult to put into practice. Nevertheless, it is important to have these as goals, for their development is the best insurance that they will function to make us credible in public speaking situations as well as in our everyday interactions.

Second, attempt to demonstrate your possession of the five components of credibility, especially in the introduction (whether you introduce your own speech or whether someone else does it), but also throughout the speech. If you have a broad knowledge of a topic or, say, firsthand experience, then tell the audience of this knowledge and experience.

Third, as with so many things, do what you do in moderation. Be careful that you do not emphasize your competence so much that the audience concludes that you therefore must be incompetent. It's rather like the people who keep telling us that they are telling the truth. They say it so often and so forcefully that we conclude that they must be lying. "Doubt the man," advises Colette, "who swears to his devotion." So, while you should stress your credibility, do so modestly and always truthfully.

As a kind of summary, it may be helpful for you to look at your own credibility from the point of view of the listeners. They might ask, for example, such questions as the following.

1. Are you competent to speak on the issue? How do we know you are competent? What evidence is there attesting to your knowledge and intelligence?
2. Are you honest and of good character? Can you be trusted to present the evidence and argument fairly and fully? What evidence is there for concluding that you are fair, honest, and of good character?
3. Are your intentions selfish or are they to help the audience? Do you have ulterior motives for arguing the position you are advocating? If so, how does this influence what you are saying and what you want the audience to do? What evidence is there for your good intentions?
4. Are you personable? Are you optimistic? Do you seem to have yourself together? What evidence is there for us to conclude that you are in fact together?
5. Are you dynamic? Are you assertive and emphatic? Or are you withdrawn, hesitant, and nonassertive? What evidence is there for your dynamism?

Notice that in each set of questions there is one question that asks, "What evidence is there . . . ?" If a speaker is to be perceived as competent, for example, then we should be able to point to specific parts of the speech where this is established or to specific behaviors of the speaker where this is demonstrated.

SOURCES

Patricia Niles Middlebrook's *Social Psychology and Modern Life* (New York: Knopf, 1974) covers motivational appeals most thoroughly and provides an excellent summary of contemporary research. For the system proposed by Abraham Maslow, see his *Motivation and Personality* (New York: Harper & Row, 1970). Herbert Simons provides a useful summary and analysis of motivational theories in his "Psychological Theories of Persuasion," *Quarterly Journal of Speech* 57 (December 1971): 383–392. Wayne N. Thompson, in his *The Process of Persuasion: Principles and Readings* (New York: Harper & Row, 1975), reprints some seminal works on motivation and persuasion and provides a useful analysis of these and current research.

Generally, for psychological appeals, works on persuasion will prove more helpful than most public speaking or psychology texts. See, for example, Erwin P. Bettinghaus, *Persuasive Communication*, 3d ed. (New York: Holt, Rinehart and Winston, 1980), and Raymond S. Ross and Mark G. Ross, *Understanding Persuasion* (Englewood Cliffs, N.J.: Prentice-Hall, 1981). For the study on student values see Jerald G. Bachman and Lloyd D. Johnston, "The Freshmen, 1979," *Psychology Today* 13 (September 1979): 79–87.

Credibility is a variable that has always been a major part of the study of public speaking, has been the subject of numerous experimental studies, and is considered in most of the available texts. A summary of early research is contained in Kenneth Andersen and Theodore Clevenger, "A Summary of Experimental Research in *Ethos*," *Communication Monographs* 30 (1963): 59–78. Also useful are James C. McCroskey, "Scales for the Measurement of Ethos," *Communication Monographs* 33 (1966): 65–73, and Jack L. Whitehead, "Factors of Source Credibility," *Quarterly Journal of Speech* 54 (February 1968): 59–63. Wayne N. Thompson, *The Process of Persuasion: Principles and Readings* (New York: Harper & Row, 1975), provides an excellent analysis together with selected readings. Perhaps the best single source is James C. McCroskey, *An Introduction to Rhetorical Communication*, 3d ed. (Englewood Cliffs, N.J.: Prentice-Hall, 1978).

Experiential
Vehicles

25.1 Motivational Analysis and the Advertisement

This exercise is designed to provide you with an opportunity to gain greater insight into the nature and function of motivational appeals. Here the focus is on analyzing the motivational appeals in advertisements, and in the next exercise the focus is on motivational appeals in the speech.

Each student should select (and bring to class) an advertisement from a recent magazine or newspaper that relies heavily on motivational appeals and explain to the class—in an informal talk of about five minutes—the operation of psychological appeals in the advertisement. More specifically, analyze the advertisement in terms of the principles of motivation and the specific appeals. The following questions are presented as guidelines for your analysis, though you need not (and should not) restrict yourself to these questions.

1. To what specific audience is the advertisement addressed? On what do you base your assumption? Can you point to specific messages (verbal and/or nonverbal) in the advertisement that lead you to make the assumption you did?
2. What is (are) the specific purpose(s) of the advertisement? (Observe carefully: few advertisements have just one purpose.) How is this purpose stated? Verbally? Nonverbally? Directly? Indirectly?
3. What motivational appeals are used and how are they used? Fear? Power/control/influence? Affiliation? Achievement? Financial gain? Status? Any others?
4. Have the advertisers attempted to appeal to the need for balance? Is there any evidence of the advertiser attempting to create an inconsistency or imbalance and then attempting to restore balance by the advertised product or service?

25.2 Motivational Analysis and the Speech

This exercise is similar to the previous one except that it focuses on the use of motivational appeals in a public speech rather than in an advertisement. The general purpose of this experience is the same, however—to provide you with an opportunity to gain greater insight into the structure and function of motivational appeals.

434

Select a speech from those included in the boxes in this text, from a recent newspaper, or from *Vital Speeches of the Day,* and explain to the class in an informal talk of about five minutes the operation of psychological appeals in the speech.

The following questions may help to provide some structure to your analysis.

1. What is the primary audience for this speech? Is there a secondary audience? What specific message elements lead you to your conclusions?
2. What is the primary purpose of the speech? Is there a secondary or tertiary purpose? What specific message elements lead you to your conclusion?
3. What motivational appeals did the speaker use? Fear? Power/control/influence? Affiliation? Achievement? Financial gain? Status?
4. Did the speaker make any attempt to create an imbalance and to restore balance? Explain.

25.3 Credibility and the Famous Person

Listed here are some 20 famous people. For each person identify the subject matter area(s) in which each person would be perceived as credible and give at least one reason why you think so. Use your class as the target audience.

1. Edward Kennedy
2. Francis Ford Coppola
3. Elizabeth Taylor
4. Rona Barrett
5. Mario Puzo
6. Paul McCartney
7. Bella Abzug
8. James Baldwin
9. David Brinkley
10. Bob Guccione
11. John Ehrlichman
12. S. I. Hayakawa
13. Coretta King
14. Henry Kissinger
15. Linus Pauling
16. Ronald Reagan
17. Truman Capote
18. Abigail Van Buren
19. Julian Bond
20. Fidel Castro

After completing this exercise, discuss your responses with others, either in small groups or in the class as a whole. From an analysis of these responses, the following should be clear and may also serve as springboards for further discussion:

1. Each individual will be perceived in a somewhat different way by each other individual.
2. Each person—regardless of "expertise" or "sophistication"—will be perceived as credible on some topics by some audiences.
3. Credibility exists in the preception of the audience rather than in the person-speaker.

Unit 26

Structure and Style in Public Communication

STRUCTURE AND STYLE IN PUBLIC COMMUNICATION

Structure in Public Communication
Stylistic Considerations

LEARNING GOALS

After completing this unit, you should be able to:

1. identify and define at least five patterns of organization for a public speech
2. identify the three functions of an introduction
3. identify the three functions of a conclusion
4. identify at least two functions that outlines may serve
5. identify two major types of outlines
6. identify at least four suggestions made here concerning the mechanics of outlining
7. identify at least six principles of style

In this unit, we consider the structure and style of the public speech — the organizational patterns for arranging the main points of the speech, the ways of developing introductions and conclusions, and the prescriptions and proscriptions of wording the speech.

STRUCTURE IN PUBLIC COMMUNICATION

All speeches are difficult to understand. The audience hears a speech but once and must instantly make sense of this complex mass of verbiage. Often an audience will simply tune out the speaker if the difficulty of understanding becomes too great. Because of this the speaker must aid the listeners in any way possible. Perhaps the best way to aid comprehension is to organize what is to be said in a clear and unambiguous manner.

A speech consists of a body — the main assertions, propositions, or issues and their supporting materials — an introduction, and a conclusion. In organizing a speech, careful consideration must be given to each of these divisions. Here we first consider the body of the speech and the appropriate organizational patterns that may be used. Second, we focus on the introduction and specify the functions that the introduction is to serve and some of the methods that may be used to achieve these functions. Third, we consider the conclusion, its functions, and the methods that may be used to achieve these functions. Fourth, we focus on outlining the public speech.

THE BODY OF THE SPEECH

Each speech demands a somewhat unique treatment, and no set of rules or principles may be applied without consideration of the uniqueness of this specific speech. Consequently, some general schemes are presented here for organizing the main points in the body of the speech, with the warning that they must be adopted to the needs of the specific speech, speaker, and audience.

Temporal Pattern

Organizing the major issues on the basis of some temporal relationship is a popular organizational pattern. Generally, when we use this pattern we organize the speech into two or three major parts, beginning with the past and working up to the present or the future, or beginning with the present or the future and working back to the past. There are, of course, various ways in which a temporal pattern may be actualized. We might, for example, divide up the major events of our topic and consider each as it occurs or occurred in time. A speech on the development of speech and language in the child might be organized in a temporal pattern, divided something like this:

  I. Babbling Stage
  II. Lallation Stage
  III. Echolalic Stage
  IV. Communication Stage

Here each of the events is considered in temporal sequence beginning with the earliest stage and working up to the final stage—in this case the stage of true communication.

A temporal pattern might also be appropriate in considering the major developments in the history of communication. We might construct a speech outline that looks something like this:

  I. Gutenberg invents movable type.
  II. Bell transmits the first telephone message.
  III. Edison invents the phonograph.
  IV. Marconi sends and receives wireless messages.

Most historical topics lend themselves to organization by temporal patterning. The events leading up to the Civil War, the steps toward a college education, the history of writing, and the like will all yield to temporal patterning.

Spatial Pattern

Similar to temporal patterning is patterning that organizes the main points of a speech on the basis of space. Physical objects generally fit well into organization by spatial patterning. For example, we might give a speech on landmarks in New York City and we might go from south to north, considering first some of the essentials of Manhattan. The base outline for such a speech might look something like this:

  I. Greenwich Village
  II. Murray Hill
  III. Times Square
  IV. Midtown

Similarly the structure of a hospital, school, skyscraper, or perhaps even of a dinosaur would be appropriately described with a spatial pattern of organization.

Problem-Solution/Solution-Problem Pattern

One popular pattern of organization is to present the main ideas in terms of problem and solution. Under this system the speech is divided into two basic parts: one part deals with the problem and one part with the solution. Generally the problem is presented first and the solution second, but under certain conditions the solution may be more appropriately presented first and the problem second.

A visual aid will often help the speaker make clear to the audience the organizational pattern used to structure the speech.

Let us say we are attempting to persuade an audience that teachers should be given higher salaries and increased benefits. Here a problem-solution pattern might be appropriate. We might for example discuss in the first part of the speech some of the problems confronting contemporary education, such as the fact that industry lures away the most highly qualified graduates of the leading universities, that many excellent teachers leave the field after two or three years, and that teaching is currently a low-status occupation in the minds of many undergraduates. In the second part of the speech we might consider the possible solutions—that salaries for teachers must be made competitive with salaries offered by private industry and that the benefits teachers receive must be made at least as attractive as those offered by industry.

The speech might look something like this in outline form.

    I. There are three major problems confronting contemporary education.
        A. Industry lures away the most qualified graduates.
        B. Numerous excellent teachers leave the field after two or three years.
        C. Teaching is currently a low-status occupation.
   II. There are two major solutions to these problems.
        A. Salaries for teachers must be increased.
        B. Benefits for teachers must be made more attractive.

Cause-Effect/Effect-Cause Pattern

Similar to the problem-solution pattern of organization is the cause-effect or effect-cause pattern. Here we divide the speech into two major sections, causes and effects. For example, a speech on the reasons for highway accidents or birth defects might yield to a cause-effect pattern, where we first consider, say, the causes of highway accidents or birth defects and then some of the effects—the number of deaths, the number of accidents, and so on.

Structure-Function Pattern

At times we may wish to consider the structure and the function of, say, a particular organization or perhaps of a particular living organism. Here the obvious pattern would be a division into structure and function, with either one being considered first, again depending on the specifics of the topic, the purpose, and the audience. We might wish to explain the complex nature of a college and might consider the various structures—the major persons (president, deans, department chairpersons, faculty, students) and the various functions of each.

As might be appreciated from this example, the structure-function pattern may be approached in various ways. One way is to divide the speech into two major parts: structure and function. Another way is to identify each unit and consider the structure and functions of each in turn. The two major alternatives would look something like this:

Alternative One
  I. There are five major persons or groups of persons (structures) in a university
    A. President
    B. Deans
    C. Department chairpersons
    D. Faculty
    E. Students
  II. Each performs different functions.
    A. President's functions
    B. Deans' functions
    C. Department chairpersons' functions
    D. Faculty functions
    E. Students' functions

Alternative Two
  I. The President
    A. Structure
    B. Functions
  II. Deans
    A. Structure
    B. Functions
  III. Department Chairpersons
    A. Structure
    B. Functions

    IV. Faculty
       A. Structure
       B. Functions
    V. Students
       A. Structure
       B. Functions

Topical Pattern

Perhaps the most popular pattern of organization is the topical pattern, a pattern that organizes the speech into the major topics without attempting to organize them in terms of time or space or into any of the other patterns already considered. This pattern should not be regarded as a catch-all for topics that do not seem to fit into any of the other patterns, but rather should be regarded as one appropriate to the particular topic being considered. For example, the topical pattern is an obvious one for organizing a speech on the powers of government. Here the divisions are obvious:

    I. The legislative branch is controlled by Congress.
    II. The executive branch is controlled by the President.
    III. The judicial branch is controlled by the courts.

A speech on important cities in the world could be organized into a topical pattern, as could speeches on problems facing the college graduate, great works of literature, the world's major religions, and the like. Each of these topics has several subtopics, or divisions of approximately equal importance; consequently a topical pattern seems most appropriate.

INTRODUCTIONS

The introduction to a speech, like the first day of a class or the first date, is especially important because it sets the tone for what is to follow. The speaker hopes to put the audience into a receptive frame of mind and build up a positive attitude toward the speech and the speaker.

The introduction to a speech, although obviously delivered first, should be constructed last—only after the entire speech, including the conclusion, has been written. In this way you will be in a position to see the entire speech before you and will be better able to determine those elements that should go into introducing this now completed speech.

Although there are many specific purposes an introduction may serve, three general ones are singled out here. First, the introduction should gain the attention of the audience. In many situations this is not a particularly important problem, but in others it is. In a college classroom if a number of students are giving speeches, it is particularly important that the attention of the audience be secured and maintained in the introduction. Similarly the college teacher needs to secure attention at the beginning of his or her lecture lest the class continue to think thoughts and trade stories of the weekend.

Second, the introduction should establish a speaker-audience relationship that is conducive to the achievement of the speech purpose. This relationship is aided if the audience likes the speaker, if they respect the speaker, and if they think the speaker a knowledgeable individual. It is no easy task to instill these attitudes in the audience in the introduction. Unit 25 on credibility elaborates on this important area.

Third, the introduction should orient the audience in some way to what is to follow in the speech. The main points of the speech may be noted here or perhaps a statement of the general conclusion that will be argued or perhaps the way in which the material will be presented.

Notice, for example, how former President Jimmy Carter attempted to establish a relationship with his audience in his July 15, 1979, Address on Energy Problems:

> This is a special night for me. Exactly three years ago, on July 15, 1976, I accepted the nomination of my party to run for President of the United States. I promised to you a President who is not isolated from the people, who feels your pain and shares your dreams and who draws his strength and his wisdom from you.

Former Vice President Spiro Agnew, in his speech criticizing the media's coverage of national and international news, introduced his topic by providing a brief orientation and by demonstrating the significance of the topic and the speech to the listeners.

> Tonight I want to discuss the importance of the television news medium to the American people. No nation depends more on the intelligent judgment of its citizens. No medium has a more profound influence over public opinion. Nowhere in our system are there fewer checks on vast power. So, nowhere should there be more conscientious responsibility exercised than by the news media. The question is, Are we demanding enough of our television news presentations? And are the men of this medium demanding enough of themselves?

In preparing the introduction, be careful to avoid some of the common mistakes that many speakers—both experienced and beginning—make. First, do not apologize. Do not say, for example, "Although I am not an expert . . ." or "I didn't have enough time to do all the reading I would have liked to do, but . . ." Whatever your inadequacies are will be obvious enough; do not emphasize them yourself. Second, do not attempt to be someone you are not. At the same time that you should not apologize, you should not attempt to present yourself as an authority when you are not. Be yourself; highlight your positive qualities. Third, do not promise something to the audience that you will not deliver. Do not promise to tell the audience how they can make a fortune or how to find eternal happiness when you are not going to do so. Last, do not use gimmicks that gain attention but are irrelevant to the nature of the speech or are inconsistent with the mood you want to establish in the speech. Your introduction should gain the attention of the audience but it should do so with means that are integrally related to the speech as a whole. Thus, to yell obscenities or to blow a trumpet will succeed in gaining the attention of your listeners but if these means are not related to the speech as a whole, they will be resented by the audience and will set up a negative barrier between speaker and listener.

CONCLUSIONS

The conclusion is often the most important part of the entire speech, since it is the part that the audience will in many instances remember most clearly. It is the conclusion that will in many cases determine what image of the speaker is left in the minds of the audience members. Particular attention must, therefore, be devoted to this brief but crucial part of the public speech.

Like the introduction, the conclusion may have many specific purposes. Yet, three general ones may be singled out. The first, and perhaps the most obvious, function is to summarize the essentials of the speech. This function is particularly important in an informative speech and less so in persuasive speeches or speeches designed to entertain. In informative speeches, however, it is essential that the speaker wrap up in a convenient summary some of the issues he or she has presented. Eventually, the details that the speaker has spoken will be forgotten; the conclusion and especially the summary will probably be remembered longer.

A second function—most appropriate in persuasive speeches—is that of motivation. In the conclusion the speaker has the opportunity to give the audience one final push in the direction he or she wishes them to take. Whether it is to buy bonds, vote a particular way, or change an attitude in one way or another, the conclusion can be used for a final motivation, a final appeal, a final argument.

The third function of a conclusion is to provide some kind of closure. Often the summary will accomplish this but in many instances it will not be sufficient. The speech should come to a crisp and definite end and the audience should not be hanging on, wondering whether the speaker has finished or whether he or she will continue after a short pause. Some kind of wrap-up, some kind of final statement is helpful in providing this feeling of closure. It is probably best not to say "Thank you" or "It was a pleasure addressing you" or some such trite phrase; these are best left implied.

In a speech delivered at Peking University on August 27, 1979, former Vice President Walter Mondale concluded his speech by summarizing some of the essential points in his speech and providing a clear and definitive closure:

> In a world that hopes to find new energy sources, peace is essential. In a world that aims to eliminate hunger and disparities in wealth, global equilibrium is vital. In a world that is working to eradicate communicable diseases and to safeguard our environment, international cooperation is crucial. To secure that peace, to maintain that equilibrium, to promote that cooperation, the United States is totally committed.

Adlai Stevenson, in a speech on the United States Far Eastern policy, concluded his speech with a summary, a final motivational appeal, and achieved closure by bringing together the various aspects of the speech and relating them to the audience:

> Let this be the American mission in the hydrogen age. Let us stop slandering ourselves and appear before the world once more as we really are—as friends, not as masters; as apostles of principle, not of power; in humility, not arrogance; as champions of peace, not as harbingers of war. For our strength lies, not alone in

our proving grounds and our stockpiles, but in our ideals, our goals, and their universal appeal to all men who are struggling to breathe free.

As with the introduction, be careful to avoid some of the more common faults with conclusions. First (and again) do not apologize—for the time spent on a particular issue or for any shortcomings of your speech or your delivery. Second, do not introduce new material. The conclusion is the place to reemphasize what you have already covered, not to introduce new material. Third, do not drag out the conclusion; end the speech once and end it crisply and finally. Phrases that clue the audience into expecting the speech to end should be used only when the speech is ending. "In conclusion" or "In summary" should be used when you are ready to end the speech and not before.

OUTLINING THE SPEECH

Throughout the discussion of structural patterns, examples were presented in outline form. Here we will review in greater detail the functions, types, and mechanics of the public speech outline.

Functions of Outlines

Obviously, an outline aids in the process of organization. As you outline the speech, you put into clear form the major points of your speech, the major supporting materials, and the transitions. Once these may be easily examined visually, you may see if your assertions are properly coordinate, if your supporting materials do in fact support the assertions they are intended to support, and so on. If you are using a temporal or a spatial organizational pattern, for example, you can quickly examine the outline and readily see if, in fact, this temporal or spatial progression is clear or in need of further clarification, reordering, or qualification of some sort.

Speech outlines provide an efficient way for you to assess the strengths and weaknesses of the speech as it is being constructed. So, for example, let us say you are preparing a speech on censorship and your major points concern sex and violence. With your outline you would be able to see at a glance if your supporting materials are adequately and evenly distributed between the two points rather than discover later that all your examples and statistics concern the violence issue with little relating to the sex issue. The outline will tell you that more material has to be collected on the sex issue or that your speech is almost totally devoted to statistical information and that you need some human interest material, and so on. In short, the outline can guide your collection of information.

The outline, when it is constructed from the beginning of the speech preparation process, provides a means for checking the speech as a whole (or at least as much as you have constructed so far). When you work for a long time on a speech and when each part is constructed over a long period of time, it becomes difficult to see "the forest for the trees." The outline enables you to stand back and examine the entire forest.

Outlines aid in the presentation of the speech—perhaps the only function many speakers at first recognize. The outline is often taken to the podium and referred to by the speaker. In fact, if you are speaking—as you should—extemporaneously you will come to use the outline a great deal in the presentation.

Types of Outlines

Outlines may be extremely detailed or extremely general. In fact, the entire speech may be arranged in outline form—that is, with every item of information arranged not in paragraph form (as it might be in speaking from manuscript) but in outline form. At the other extreme, an outline for a speech on, for example, popular entertainment awards might look something like this:

Popular Entertainment Awards
  I. Oscar
 II. Tony
III. Emmy
 IV. Peabody

In between these extremes there are an infinite number of gradations of completeness of detail. What is best for one speaker might prove totally inadequate for another, and, of course, what will prove adequate for a speaker on one topic may prove inadequate for that same speaker on a different topic.

Since you are now in a learning environment whose object is to make you a more proficient public speaker, your instructor may wish to suggest one type of outline over another. And, of course, just as the type of outline will depend on the specific speaker, the type of outline that proves best for instructional purposes will vary with the instructor. I, for example, prefer that students construct rather detailed outlines, but I recognize that this is for instructional purposes and that once students have learned the art of public speaking, they will adjust the outlining procedures to what fits them best.

The more detail you put into the outline, the easier it will be to examine the parts of the speech for all the qualities and characteristics that were discussed in the previous units. Thus, for example, the speech's balance can only be examined in detail if the outline itself is in detail. The same is true for each of the speech's features. Similarly, it will be easier to see if one item actually supports another item if they are both clearly written out and can be thought about for a moment or two rather than if only key words are written down or, as in the example given above, if all supporting materials are omitted entirely. Consequently, at least in the beginning, outline your speeches in detail and in complete sentences. The usefulness of an instructor's criticism will often depend on the completeness of the outline.

With these factors in mind, then, I would suggest that you do the following, especially in your beginning speeches. Begin constructing the outline as soon as you get the topic clearly in mind. Revise it constantly. Every new idea, every new bit of information will result in some alteration of basic structure. At this point keep the outline brief and perhaps in key words or phrases. Once you feel pretty confident that you are near completion, construct an outline in detail—using complete sentences—and follow the mechanical principles discussed in the next section of this unit. Use this outline to test your organizational structure.

For speaking purposes, however, reduce this outline to its bare bones. It should consist of key words that will aid you in the presentation of the speech and should easily fit on one side of a 3×5 index card. The key word in that advice is *aid*. The outline should *aid* you in the presentation of the speech; it should not be something that you will rely on and read from, thus avoiding direct eye contact with the audience. If the outline is going to aid you in the presentation of the speech, it has to be brief, containing only that information that you will absolutely need for the few minutes that you stand in front of the audience.

Some Mechanics of Outlining

Assuming that the outline you will construct for your early speeches will be relatively complete, here are a few guidelines concerning the mechanics of outlining.

1. Use a Consistent Set of Symbols. The following is the standard, accepted sequence of symbols for outlining:

I.
  A.
    1.
      a.
        (1)
          (a)

Begin the introduction, the body, and the conclusion with Roman numeral I. That is, each of the three major parts should be treated as a complete unit.

2. Use Visual Aspects to Reflect and Reinforce the Organizational Pattern. Use proper and clear indentation. This will help to set off visually coordinate and subordinate relationships.

This:
I. Television caters to the lowest possible intelligence.
  A. Situation Comedies
    1. "Laverne and Shirley"
    2. "Three's Company"
    3. "One Day at a Time"
  B. Soap Operas
    1. "As the World Turns"
    2. "The Doctors"

Not This:
  I. Television caters to the lowest possible intelligence.
A. Situation Comedies
1. "Laverne and Shirley"

3. Use One Discrete Idea per Symbol. If the outline is to reflect the organizational pattern among the various items of information, use just one discrete idea per symbol. Compound sentences are sure giveaways that you have not lim-

447

ited each item to one single idea. Also, be sure that each item is discrete—that is, that it does not overlap with any other item.

This:
I. Education would be improved if teachers were better trained.
II. Education would be improved if students were better motivated.

Not This:
I. Education might be improved if teachers were better trained and if students were better motivated.

Note that in ***This*** items I and II are single ideas, but in ***Not This*** they are combined.

This:
I. Teachers are not adequately prepared to teach.
   A. Teacher education programs are inadequate.
      1. Support for A
      2. Support for A
   B. In-service programs are inadequate.
      1. Support for B
      2. Support for B

Not This:
I. Teachers are not adequately prepared to teach.
   A. Teacher education programs are inadequate.
   B. Course syllabi are dated.

Note that A and B are discrete in ***This*** but overlap in ***Not This*** where B is actually a part of A (one of the inadequacies of teacher education programs is that the course syllabi are dated).

4. Be Brief. This injunction applies more to the outline you take to assist you in the presentation of the speech than to the outline you prepare to test for organizational structure. And yet, each should be brief in relation to the entire speech. If the outline is to assist you in seeing all the various parts of the speech in relation to one another, it should be brief enough so that you can see these relationships at a glance.

5. Use Complete Declarative Sentences. Generally, phrase your ideas in the outline in complete declarative sentences rather than as questions or as phrases. Again, this will further assist you in examining the essential relationships. It is much easier, for example, to see if one item of information supports another if both are phrased in the declarative mode. If one is a question and one is a statement, this will be more difficult.

This:
I. Children should be raised by the state.
   A. All children will be treated equal.
   B. Parents will be released to work.

Not This:
  I. Who should raise children?
 II. Should the state raise children?
     A. Equality for children
     B. Parents will be released for work.

STYLISTIC CONSIDERATIONS

In constructing a speech for a public audience, style is of prime importance. By "style" I mean the selection of words and phrases and their arrangement into sentences. The way in which ideas are phrased will surely influence the way in which they are received as well as the way the audience regards the speaker. Here are several prescriptions and proscriptions that should result in a more effective speech style.

1. USE SIMPLE TERMS AND SENTENCE PATTERNS

Recall that a speech in normal circumstances is only heard once and because of this it is not possible for members of the audience to look up an unfamiliar word or unwind complicated sentence patterns in order to get at the meaning the speaker wishes to convey. On the other hand, overly simple language can turn off the audience and lead them to think that the speaker has nothing of value to communicate. Even more important is that the speaker should never "talk down" to the audience; condescension impedes communication. Simple language and grammatical constructions will result in immediate comprehension but will not insult the audience. Generally, simple, active, declarative sentences are preferred to the more complex, passive sentences because these forms are easier to understand and grasp with just one exposure.

This preference for simple and easily understood constructions should not be taken as a suggestion to use time-worn clichés. Expressions such as "green with envy," "to be in hot water," "pretty as a picture," "the writing on the wall," "the whole ball of wax" and numerous others communicate little information. At the same time they have the effect of drawing attention to themselves and giving the audience the impression that the speaker is unimaginative and uncreative and therefore must resort to these clichés.

2. MIX THE LEVELS OF ABSTRACTION

Most people seem to prefer a mixture of the abstract and the concrete, the specific and the general. By mixing these levels of abstraction we communicate in a much clearer, more interesting, and more meaningful fashion. By mixing the levels of abstraction the speaker can more actively involve the audience in his or her speech. If a speech concentrates solely on low-level abstractions—that is, on concrete terms and sentences—the audience will probably become bored. Similarly, if the speaker only talks in terms of high-order abstractions, using highly abstract and all-inclusive terms, the audience will also become bored.

BOX 26.1
Inaugural Address
Ronald Reagan

Ronald Reagan (1911–   ) delivered his inaugural address on January 20, 1981, in Washington, D.C. The text of the speech is taken from *Vital Speeches of the Day* 47 (Feb. 15, 1981): 258–260.

Thank you. Senator Hatfield, Mr. Chief Justice, Mr. President, Vice President Bush, Vice President Mondale, Senator Baker, Speaker O'Neill, Reverend Moomaw, and my fellow citizens:

To a few of us here today this is a solemn and most momentous occasion. And, yet, in the history of our nation it is a commonplace occurrence.

The orderly transfer of authority as called for in the Constitution routinely takes place as it has for almost two centuries and few of us stop to think how unique we really are.

In the eyes of many in the world, this every-four-year ceremony we accept as normal is nothing less than a miracle.

Mr. President, I want our fellow citizens to know how much you did to carry on this tradition.

By your gracious cooperation in the transition process you have shown a watching world that we are a united people pledged to maintaining a political system which guarantees individual liberty to a greater degree than any other. And I thank you and your people for all your help in maintaining the continuity which is the bulwark of our republic.

The business of our nation goes forward.

These United States are confronted with an economic affliction of great proportions.

We suffer from the longest and one of the worst sustained inflations in our national history. It distorts our economic decisions, penalizes thrift and crushes the struggling young and the fixed-income elderly alike. It threatens to shatter the lives of millions of our people.

Idle industries have cast workers into unemployment, human misery and personal indignity.

Those who do work are denied a fair return for their labor by a tax system which penalizes successful achievement and keeps us from maintaining full productivity.

But great as our tax burden is, it has not kept pace with public spending. For decades we have piled deficit upon deficit, mortgaging our future and our children's future for the temporary convenience of the present.

To continue this long trend is to guarantee tremendous social, cultural, political, and economic upheavals.

You and I, as individuals, can, by borrowing, live beyond our means, but for only a limited period of time. Why then should we think that collectively, as a nation, we are not bound by that same limitation?

We must act today in order to preserve tomorrow. And let there be no misunderstanding—we're going to begin to act beginning today.

The economic ills we suffer have come upon us over several decades. They will not go away in days, weeks or months, but they will go away.

They will go away because we as Americans have the capacity now, as we have had in past, to do whatever needs to be done to preserve this last and greatest bastion of freedom.

In this present crisis, government is not the solution to our problem; government is the problem.

From time to time we've been tempted to believe that society has become too complex to be managed by self-rule, that government by an elite group is superior to government for, by and of the people.

But if no one among us is capable of governing himself, then who among us has the capacity to govern someone else?

All of us together—in and out of government—must bear the burden. The solutions we seek must be equitable with no one group singled out to pay a higher price.

We hear much of special interest groups. Well, our concern must be for a special interest group that has been too long neglected.

It knows no sectional boundaries, or ethnic and racial divisions and it crosses political party lines. It is made up of men and women who raise our food, patrol our streets, man our mines and factories, teach our children, keep our homes and heal us when we're sick.

Professionals, industrialists, shopkeepers, clerks, cabbies and truck drivers. They are, in short, "We the people." This breed called Americans.

Well, this Administration's objective will be a healthy, vigorous, growing economy that provides equal opportunities for all Americans with no barriers born of bigotry or discrimination.

Putting America back to work means putting all Americans back to work. Ending inflation means freeing all Americans from the terror of runaway living costs.

All must share in the productive work of this "new beginning," and all must share in the bounty of a revived economy.

With the idealism and fair play which are the core of our system and our strength, we can have a strong, prosperous America at peace with itself and the world.

So as we begin, let us take inventory.

We are a nation that has a government—not the other way around. And this makes us special among the nations of the earth.

Our Government has no power except that granted it by the people. It is time to check and reverse the growth of government which shows signs of having grown beyond the consent of the governed.

It is my intention to curb the size and influence of the Federal establishment and to demand recognition of the distinction between the powers granted to the Federal Government and those reserved to the states or to the people.

All of us—all of us need to be reminded that the Federal Government did not create the states; the states created the Federal Government.

Now, so there will be no misunderstanding, it's not my intention to do away with government.

It is rather to make it work—work with us, not over us; to stand by our side, not ride on our back. Government can and must provide opportunity, not smother it; foster productivity, not stifle it.

If we look to the answer as to why for so many years we achieved so

BOX 26.1 (*Continued*)

much, prospered as no other people on earth, it was because here in this land we unleashed the energy and individual genius of man to a greater extent than has ever been done before.

Freedom and the dignity of the individual have been more available and assured here than in any other place on earth. The price for this freedom at times has been high, but we have never been unwilling to pay that price.

It is no coincidence that our present troubles parallel and are proportionate to the intervention and intrusion in our lives that result from unnecessary and excessive growth of Government.

It is time for us to realize that we are too great a nation to limit ourselves to small dreams. We're not, as some would have us believe, doomed to an inevitable decline. I do not believe in a fate that will fall on us no matter what we do. I do believe in a fate that will fall on us if we do nothing.

So, with all the creative energy at our command let us begin an era of national renewal. Let us renew our determination, our courage and our strength. And let us renew our faith and our hope. We have every right to dream heroic dreams.

Those who say that we're in a time when there are no heroes—they just don't know where to look. You can see heroes every day going in and out of factory gates. Others, a handful in number, produce enough food to feed all of us and then the world beyond.

You meet heroes across a counter—and they're on both sides of that counter. There are entrepreneurs with faith in themselves and faith in an idea who create new jobs, new wealth and opportunity.

There are individuals and families whose taxes support the Government and whose voluntary gifts support church, charity, culture, art and education. Their patriotism is quiet but deep. Their values sustain our national life.

Now, I have used the words "they" and "their" in speaking of these heroes. I could say "you" and "your" because I'm addressing the heroes of whom I speak—you, the citizens of this blessed land.

Your dreams, your hopes, your goals are going to be the dreams, the hopes and the goals of this Administration, so help me God.

We shall reflect the compassion that is so much a part of your makeup.

How can we love our country and not love our countrymen? And loving them reach out a hand when they fall, heal them when they're sick and provide opportunity to make them self-sufficient so they will be equal in fact and not just in theory?

Can we solve the problems confronting us? Well, the answer is a unequivocal and emphatic yes.

To paraphrase Winston Churchill, I did not take the oath I've just taken with the intention of presiding over the dissolution of the world's strongest economy.

In the days ahead I will propose removing the roadblocks that have slowed our economy and reduced productivity.

Steps will be taken aimed at restoring the balance between the various levels of government. Progress may be slow—measured in inches and feet, not miles—but we will progress.

BOX 26.1 (*Continued*)

It is time to reawaken this industrial giant, to get government back within its means and to lighten our punitive tax burden.

And these will be our first priorities, and on these principles there will be no compromise.

On the eve of our struggle for independence a man who might've been one of the greatest among the Founding Fathers, Dr. Joseph Warren, president of the Massachusetts Congress, said to his fellow Americans, "Our country is in danger, but not to be despaired of. On you depend the fortunes of America. You are to decide the important question upon which rest the happiness and the liberty of millions yet unborn. Act worthy of yourselves."

Well I believe we the Americans of today are ready to act worthy of ourselves, ready to do what must be done to insure happiness and liberty for ourselves, our children and our children's children.

And as we renew ourselves here in our own land we will be seen as having greater strength throughout the world. We will again be the exemplar of freedom and a beacon of hope for those who do not now have freedom.

To those neighbors and allies who share our freedom, we will strengthen our historic ties and assure them of our support and firm commitment.

We will match loyalty with loyalty. We will strive for mutually beneficial relations. We will not use our friendship to impose on their sovereignty, for our own sovereignty is not for sale.

As for the enemies of freedom, those who are potential adversaries, they will be reminded that peace is the highest aspiration of the American people. We will negotiate for it, sacrifice for it; we will not surrender for it—now or ever.

Our forbearance should never be misunderstood. Our reluctance for conflict should not be misjudged as a failure of will.

When action is required to preserve our national security, we will act. We will maintain sufficient strength to prevail if need be, knowing that if we do we have the best chance of never having to use that strength.

Above all we must realize that no arsenal or no weapon in the arsenals of the world is so formidable as the will and moral courage of free men and women.

It is a weapon our adversaries in today's world do not have.

It is a weapon that we as Americans do have.

Let that be understood by those who practice terrorism and prey upon their neighbors.

I am told that tens of thousands of prayer meetings are being held on this day; for that I am deeply grateful. We are a nation under God, and I believe God intended for us to be free. It would be fitting and good, I think, if on each inaugural day in future years it should be declared a day of prayer.

This is the first time in our history that this ceremony has been held, as you've been told, on this West Front of the Capitol.

Standing here, one faces a magnificent vista, opening up on this city's special beauty and history.

At the end of this open mall are those shrines to the giants on whose shoulders we stand.

Directly in front of me, the monument to a monumental man. George

BOX 26.1 (*Continued*)

Washington, father of our country. A man of humility who came to greatness reluctantly. He led America out of revolutionary victory into infant nationhood.

Off to one side, the stately memorial to Thomas Jefferson. The Declaration of Independence flames with his eloquence.

And then beyond the Reflecting Pool, the dignified columns of the Lincoln Memorial. Whoever would understand in his heart the meaning of America will find it in the life of Abraham Lincoln.

Beyond those monuments to heroism is the Potomac River, and on the far shore the sloping hills of Arlington National Cemetery with its row upon row of simple white markers bearing crosses or Stars of David. They add up to only a tiny fraction of the price that has been paid for our freedom.

Each one of those markers is a monument to the kind of hero I spoke of earlier.

Their lives ended in places called Belleau Wood, the Argonne, Omaha Beach, Salerno and halfway around the world on Guadalcanal, Tarawa, Pork Chop Hill, the Chosin Reservoir, and in a hundred rice paddies and jungles of a place called Vietnam.

Under such a marker lies a young man, Martin Treptow, who left his job in a small town barber shop in 1917 to go to France with the famed Rainbow Division.

There, on the Western front, he was killed trying to carry a message between battalions under heavy artillery fire.

We are told that on his body was found a diary.

On the flyleaf under the heading, "My Pledge," he had written these words:

"America must win this war. Therefore I will work, I will save, I will sacrifice, I will endure, I will fight cheerfully and do my utmost, as if the issue of the whole struggle depended on me alone."

The crisis we are facing today does not require of us the kind of sacrifice that Martin Treptow and so many thousands of others were called upon to make.

It does require, however, our best effort, and our willingness to believe in ourselves and to believe in our capacity to perform great deeds; to believe that together with God's help we can and will resolve the problems which now confront us.

And after all, why shouldn't we believe that? We are Americans.

God bless you and thank you. Thank you very much.

For example, in talking about the properties of human language we could say, "Human beings are able to use language that is displaced, metalinguistic, and creative." This is relatively high-level abstraction; there is little here that is concrete. On the other hand, using all low-level abstractions, all concrete terms, we could say, "Human beings are able to talk about yesterday's weather, to identify statements as true or false, and to verbalize such utterances as 'The dog cried when the cat left for Europe.'" Notice that when there is exclusively high or exclusively low levels of abstraction, the language is not only uninteresting but also fails to communicate much of what you want to communicate. In the former case, the abstract terms are relatively meaningless, and in the latter case the specific examples do not provide the general principles of language that we want communicated. A combination seems to work best. Using both high- and low-level abstractions we might say, for example, "Human beings are able to use displaced speech, to talk of what is not here and not now, about yesterday and tomorrow, about the real as well as the unreal, about mermaids and unicorns as well as about men and women. Human beings are able to use metalinguistic speech, speech that refers to itself; we can talk about our talk, correct ourselves, and say, 'This is absurd,' 'This sentence is ungrammatical,' 'This sentence is nonsense.' Human beings are able to use language creatively, to coin new utterances, utterances never said or heard before, such as 'The rock wanted to paint the house red.' " To effectively mix the levels of abstraction takes many more words but effective communication necessitates this combination of the general and the specific, the abstract and the concrete.

3. AVOID OFFENSIVE TERMS AND REFERENCES

The sexist aspect of language has only recently become the center of a great deal of interest. Basically, the masculine pronoun or professions designated by masculine names should not be used generically. Nor should the term *man* be used to refer to human beings. Many, of course, will disagree with this and yet with a bit of reflection we can easily see why these constructions should be avoided. Why should a hypothetical doctor, dentist, or lawyer be referred to with masculine pronouns and references? Similarly why should the hypothetical individual be called *he*? The contentions that this is traditional or even convenient are not satisfactory answers, although these seem the only arguments ever used. It is probably best to use *he and she* or *person* instead of just *he* or *man*. Similarly, terms such as *chairman* should be replaced by *chairperson*. In a similar vein terms that were at one time used to refer to a woman in a specific position (normally originating from a masculine term) should be avoided; for example, *poetess, Negress, Jewess*, and *heroine*.

The sexist aspect of language was singled out primarily because of its widespread usage and because women have for so long been given second-class status that it is clearly time to change. However, we should not assume that women are the only group that we may offend in our use of language. There are many others. The public speaker needs to realize that in his or her audience there will be persons who belong to various minority groups, and these persons should not be offended, not only because this will prevent the speaker from achieving his or her purpose but because no one has the right to insult or to denigrate others because of their sex, age, sexual preference, race, religion, or nationality.

4. USE TRANSITIONAL AND MARKER PHRASES

Listening attentively to a public speech is difficult work, and consequently the speaker should assist the audience in any way he or she can. One of the most effective ways is to use frequent transitional phrases that provide a kind of bridge between one set of ideas and another or between one piece of evidence and another. Phrases such as "Now that we have seen how_____, let us consider how_____" will help to keep the audience on the right track. Even terms such as *first, second, and also, although,* and *however* help the audience to follow the thought patterns of the speaker better.

Much like transitions, markers will help audience comprehension. The speaker should make frequent use of marker terms that will provide signposts to the audience. Numbers and letters are perhaps the most obvious examples, but phrases such as "The second argument is . . ." or "The last example I want to provide . . ." help to focus the audience's thinking on the kind of outline the speaker is using.

BOX 26.2
Sexist Pronouns

A number of proposals have been advanced to eliminate the common gender masculine pronoun. Here are three examples.

Example 1

she, he	tey
her(s), his	ter
her, him	tem
mankind	genkind
manhood	genhood

The professor lectured to ter class on the history of genkind and genhood. Tey talked of ter childhood which had a great influence on tem.

Example 2

she, he	co
her(s), his	cos
her, him	co
herself, himself	coself

The professor lectured to cos class coself. Co talked of cos childhood which had a great influence on co.

Example 3

she, he	ve
her(s), his	vis
her, him	ver

The professor lectured to vis class. Ve talked of vis childhood which had a great influence on ver.

Source: The first example comes from Casey Miller and Kate Swift, "One Small Step for Genkind," *New York Times Magazine,* Apr. 16, 1972, and reprinted in Joseph DeVito, ed., *Language: Concepts and Processes* (Englewood Cliffs, N.J.: Prentice-Hall, 1973). The second and third examples come from Mary Orovan and Vardo One, respectively, and are cited in Donald D. Hook, "Sexism in English Pronouns and Forms of Address," *General Linguistics* 14 (1974): 86–96.

5. USE REPETITION, RESTATEMENT, AND INTERNAL SUMMARIES

Much as transitions and marker phrases help to keep the audience on the same track with the speaker, repetition (repeating something in exactly the same way), restatement (rephrasing an idea or statement), internal summaries (summaries or reviews of subsections of the speech), and previews of what is to come all help the listeners to follow the speaker better.

Speakers often hesitate to include such stylistic elements because they feel it makes the speech seem simple and elementary. The listeners, however, who will hear the speech but once, will surely appreciate these aids to comprehension.

6. USE PERSONALIZED LANGUAGE

Although public speaking is a relatively formal kind of performance, it seems to help if some personalization can be introduced. This is perhaps most clearly seen in the college lecture situation, where the teachers who seem to reach their students are the ones who personalize their courses and lectures, who introduce some of themselves into the discussions. The same is true in public speaking even if you will only face this audience once.

The best guide to what is personalized language is to focus on the language of everyday conversation and note its characteristics. It makes frequent use of personal pronouns, of *I, you, he, she*; it makes use of contractions, simple sentences, and short phrases; it makes use of repetition and restatement. It avoids long, complex, and passive sentences. It avoids the use of the pronoun *one* or phrases such as "the speaker," "the former/the latter" (which are difficult to retrace); and in general those expressions that are more popular and more expected in the language of written prose rather than in the language of everyday communication. This is not to say that the language of a public speech should be common or trite. Quite the contrary! The language of the speech should be as polished as the language of the written essay, but it should be conversational in tone and direct in reference.

SOURCES

Structure and supporting materials are covered thoroughly in Jim D. Hughey and Arlee W. Johnson, *Speech Communication: Foundations and Challenges* (New York: Macmillan, 1975). Organization is clearly handled in Judy L. Haynes, *Organizing a Speech: A Programmed Guide*, 2d ed. (Englewood Cliffs, N.J.: Prentice-Hall, 1981). James C. McCroskey, *An Introduction to Rhetorical Communication*, 3d ed. (Englewood Cliffs, N.J.: Prentice-Hall, 1978), covers both organization and style clearly and with emphasis on experimental support for his conclusions. Style is most thoroughly covered in Jane Blankenship, *A Sense of Style: An Introduction to Style for the Public Speaker* (Belmont, Cal.: Dickenson, 1968).

For the stylistic suggestions I relied heavily on the findings of experimental research as much as was possible, particularly the following: Joseph DeVito, "Some Psycholinguistic Aspects of Active and Passive Sentences," *Quarterly*

Journal of Speech 55 (December 1969): 401–406; "Comprehension Factors in Oral and Written Discourse of Skilled Communicators," *Speech Monographs* 32 (June 1965): 124–128; and, "Relative Ease in Comprehension Yes/No Questions," in *Rhetoric and Communication,* Jane Blankenship and Herman G. Stelzner, eds. (Urbana, Ill.: University of Illinois Press, 1976), pp. 143–154. Considerable insight into language may be obtained from the study of animal communication and of feral children. For both pleasure and profit I would recommend the following two paperbacks: Herbert S. Terrace, *Nim: A Chimpanzee Who Learned Sign Language* (New York: Washington Square Press, 1979), and Roger Shattuck, *The Forbidden Experiment: The Story of the Wild Boy of Aveyron* (New York: Washington Square Press, 1980).

Both organization and style are thoroughly covered in Joseph A. DeVito, *The Elements of Public Speaking* (New York: Harper & Row, 1981) and Paul E. Nelson and Judy C. Pearson, *Confidence in Public Speaking* (Dubuque, Iowa: Wm. C. Brown, 1981).

Experiential Vehicles

26.1 Speech Analysis

This experience is designed to enable you to explore in greater depth some of the properties of a speech—namely, the organizational development and the style.

Carefully read the following speech, "Can't Nobody Here Use This Language?," by Jerry Tarver, and respond to the questions presented below.

1. What organizational pattern is used? Is it effective?
2. What method(s) is used for introducing the speech?
3. What method(s) is used for concluding the speech?
4. Are the introduction and conclusion appropriate? How is "appropriateness" determined?
5. Is the speech stylistically effective? Specifically:
   a. Is the simple rather than the complex term or sentence used? Explain.
   b. Are the levels of abstraction varied? Identify specific instances of high and low levels of abstraction.
   c. Are there any sexist terms or references? Identify specific instances.
   d. Identify any transitional or marker phrases used. Are they helpful?
   e. Is repetition, restatement, or internal summary used?
   f. Is the language personalized? Identify specific instances of such personalization.
   g. Does Tarver follow his own advice?

Can't Nobody Here Use This Language?

Jerry Tarver

The following speech was delivered by Jerry Tarver, Professor at the University of Richmond, to the Connecticut Association of Professional Communicators on February 27, 1979, in Hartford, Connecticut. The text of the speech is taken from *Vital Speeches of the Day* 45 (May 1, 1979): 420–423.

I learned last May you have to be careful in speaking to a group of professional communicators. After I conducted a writer's workshop at the Toronto Conference of the International Association of Business Communicators, Janine Lichacz wrote asking me to speak here tonight and used the communication techniques I had recommended. She even included a footnote citing my lecture. I am susceptible to good communication—and to flattery—so I am pleased to be with you to discuss your topic for the evening, the use of language in the art of speech writing.

I suppose we must begin by shaking our heads woefully over the sad state of language today, whether in formal speeches, casual conversation, or in writing. Most of us in this room no doubt agree with the generally negative tone of *Time* magazine's year-end assessment of 1978, which claims "our language has been besieged by vulgarities." But to preserve our sanity as professionals in communication, most of us would probably join *Time* in optimistically expecting English somehow to survive and even to prosper.

On the negative side, if I may use a vulgarity to criticize vulgarity, I am often moved in my own profession to paraphrase Casey Stengel and ask, "Can't nobody here use this language?"

To generalize about the language ability of students, I would say far too many of them can't express themselves well, and they don't seem to care. The most significant hollow verbalization among students today is not "y'know." It is "needless to say."

I have a respectful appreciation of the rules of the classical rhetoricians, and on occasion I have discussed in class the stylistic device of antithesis. One of my students, quite unconsciously I am sure, gave the technique a try in a speech on physical fitness and said, "A well-rounded body makes for a well-rounded mind." We've come a long way down from *mens sana in corpore sano.*

Faculty members are often worse. Some time back I attended a conference on setting standards for language competence in Virginia's schools. In one presentation a professor from a distinguished university repeatedly used the expression "scribal language." I finally turned to someone to ask what the devil that meant and was told the term was a fancy synonym for 'writing.' I wrote a letter to the professor suggesting a requirement for a report on competence in language should be competence in language. He did not take it well.

One of my colleagues wrote a lengthy document on the proper use of classrooms and stated forthrightly, "It is necessary to employ characteristics of uniqueness where uniqueness is held to be important. The idea of flexibility should be placed in a balanced way with other particular instructional and design needs to achieve a maximized learning atmosphere. In some instances, degrees of flexibility may have to give way to other equally creative and significant dimensions of a classroom environment."

I happen to know what that means, and I will be happy to provide a translation at twenty cents a word. If you want the answer send your dollar to me at the University of Richmond.

A certain church group which supports many colleges throughout the south regularly sends me a publication which purports to be educational. Leaders of this group use up a goodly portion of the alphabet with the impressive degrees they attach to their names and employ this publication to increase the size of the audience for their various pronouncements. The quality of the writing is so gloriously and innocently bad that the entire magazine could easily pass as a satire written by a clever member of a high school debating team. One of the speeches from a couple of months ago contained the striking statement, "Drifting causes a loss of direction." That was one of the major points in the speech, which incidently was delivered at the inauguration of a college president.

On the positive side, *Time* finds our language "enriched by vigorous phrases and terms" from such sources as CB radio and situation comedies. The major bright spots I see are the writing in advertising and on the bathroom wall. Let me quickly add that the *worst* writing also appears in these two places. Some of the most crude and senseless tripe I have encountered has appeared in ads or graffiti. But when they are good, they are very, very good. Both the ad writer and the graffiti artist must work within a small compass. They must be concise. To the point. And each is moved, urgently moved, to communicate. Unfortunately for the motivation of the advertiser, I am one of those people who can enjoy the sizzle and forgo the steak. I don't smoke cigars, and I don't even remember the brand involved, but who can forget the classical commercial in which Edie Adams used to urge, "Why don't you pick one up and smoke it sometime?" I admit I don't have a Texaco credit card, but little I read of modern academic poetry moves me as much as the soothing jingle "You can trust your car to the man who wears the star."

My favorite graffiti is the plaintive sort. A poor soul eloquently crying out to be understood. In the men's room just down from my office, someone in apparent anguish wrote with painstaking care in the grout between the tiles, "What in the hell am I doing here?" Weeks passed before someone undertook a reply. Whether done in a spirit of helpfulness or malice, I cannot say, but finally in different handwriting, there appeared, "If this is an existential question, contact Dr. Hall in the Philosophy Department. If this is a theological question, contact Dr. Alley in the Religion Department. If this is a biological question, take a look."

Years ago I saw a quotation printed on a little gummed paper strip which had been attached to the wall of a men's room off the New Jersey Turnpike. It offered a simple Biblical text and had apparently come to the attention of a tired truck driver. The quotation asked the question, "If God be for us, who can be against us?" No doubt in despair, the truck driver had replied underneath, "The dispatcher."

How can we capture the vitality of the best of graffiti and advertising in our own writing and speaking? Perhaps some of you would agree with a sociologist friend of mine, Dr. James Sartain. Whenever Jim is offered a chance to improve his teaching, he says, "I already know how to teach better than I do." I suspect this is true for most of us. So, we may not be discovering tonight as much as reminding.

But there could be some ground for controversy. Let me first of all attempt to play down the current emphasis on correctness. Grammar—much like spelling—is one of the manual skills of expression. Almost any fool can learn to make a subject agree with a verb according to the standard rules of English.

I think the pseudo objectivity of correctness attracts many followers. But grammatical systems are, after all, themselves arbitrary. We could change the rules if we wanted to. Our failure to alter our grammar to include a sexless pronoun can hardly be blamed on the sanctity of the rules. If you wish to attack the sentence, "He done done it," you can't attack it by claiming it does not follow a rigid set of rules. It just doesn't follow the system most widely taught.

I'm not suggesting you break rules at random. Just don't be too proud of yourself for not using "very unique" or "hopefully, it will rain." And remember George Orwell's advice that you should break any rule rather than "say anything outright barbarous."

I suggest to write and speak our best we need, first, a grasp of the function of language and, second, a sensitivity to the quality of our words.

My desk dictionary includes among its definitions of the word function "The action for which a . . . thing is specially fitted or used or for which a thing exists." The concept of function reminds us that words act upon people.

Let me give you an example of a piece of communication which illustrates function. You may recall in *Catch 22* Lt. Milo Minderbinder at one point instituted an elaborate procedure for going through the chow line. It involved signing a loyalty oath, reciting the pledge of allegiance and singing "The Star-Spangled Banner." But the entire system was destroyed one day when Mayor de Coverly returned from a trip and cut through the red tape with two words: "Gimme eat."

That simple, and quite ungrammatical, phrase shows language in action. Words at work. Expression that eliminates the unnecessary and gets down to cases.

A grasp of function causes a writer to think of results. Impact, Effect. Audience becomes important. Who will read or listen? Why? Function calls for the communicator to examine the reason for the existence of a given communication and to choose words that will be a means of expression and not an end.

Next, as I said, we must be sensitive to quality. I know of no objective way to determine quality. But I agree with Robert Persig who insists in *Zen and the Art of Motorcycle Maintenance* that most people intuitively know quality in language when they encounter it.

Most of us have written material we knew was merely adequate. No errors. All the intended ideas in place. No complaints from the boss or the editor. But deep down inside we knew we had done a pedestrian job.

I use a chill bump test for quality. For poor writing or speaking I get one type of chill bumps. For good language, a better brand of chill bumps. For most of the mediocre stuff in between, no chill bumps at all.

Quality does not mean fancy. When General McAuliffe reportedly answered a Nazi surrender ultimatum with the word "nuts," his language had no less quality than the declaration of the Indian Chief Joseph, "From where the sun now stands, I will fight no more forever." Either of my examples would probably not fare well in a classroom exercise in English composition. But anyone who used such language in that situation would be guilty of ignoring the concept of function.

Only after we agree that we must be concerned about function and quality can we properly turn our attention to rules. I offer the following ten guidelines for the speech writer. Some of the guidelines apply primarily to the language of speeches; some apply to almost any kind of writing. I do not consider my list exhaustive, and I should point out that the items on it are not mutually exclusive.

GUIDELINE NUMBER ONE. Be simple. Tend toward conversational language. Earlier this month I conducted speaker training for a corporation which distributed a speech manuscript containing such expressions as "difficult to ascertain" and "management audits attest." There's nothing wrong with these phrases in print, but I wouldn't say ascertain or attest out loud in front of the Rotary Club. "Find out" and "show" would sound more natural.

GUIDELINE NUMBER TWO. Be expansive. Speeches use more words per square thought than well written essays or reports. The next time you get a speech writing assignment, see if you can't talk your boss into throwing out two-thirds of the content and expanding the remainder into a fully developed expression of a limited topic. I realize gobbledygook is wordy, but I assume none of us will be writing gobbledygook. And I don't know of anyone who has suggested that Martin Luther King's "I Have a Dream" speech suffered from excessive repetition.

GUIDELINE NUMBER THREE. Be concrete. Specific terms limit a listener's chances to misunderstand. Back in November Combined Communications Corporation President Karl Eller gave a speech out in Phoenix in which he used a glass of milk to describe our free enterprise system. He said, "Some farmer bred and raised the cow. Some farmer owned and tended the land it grazed on. He bought special feed from someone. Some farmer milked the cow or cows and sold the milk to someone else who processed it, pasteurized it and packaged it. He sold it to a wholesaler, who sold it to a retailer. And all along the line the produce was either made better or its distribution was simplified and narrowed, and a lot of people had jobs. Wealth was created." I've quoted less than a fifth of Eller's description. I'm convinced nobody left his speech confused.

GUIDELINE NUMBER FOUR. Be vivid. Appeal to the senses. President Carter's speech writers attempted to paint a word picture in the state of the union address when they wrote of the power of nuclear weapons "towering over all this volatile changing world, like a thundercloud in a summer sky." I am reminded of Mark Twain's distinction between the lightning and the lightning bug. The Carter image fails to stir the imagination. But vivid language can be effective.

In demonstrating the point that his company's nuclear plants are safe, Ontario Hydro board Chairman Robert Taylor told members of the Kiwanis Club of Ottawa, "You could sit naked, if you had a mind to, at the boundary fence around the Pickering nuclear station for a year, drink the water and eat the fish from nearby Lake Ontario, and you would pick up a total of five units of radiation. That's less than you would get from natural sources such as rocks, good air and cosmic rays. A single chest x-ray would give you eight times that exposure."

GUIDELINE NUMBER FIVE. Be personal. Use the personal pronoun. Don't be afraid of making a speaker sound egotistical. Ego springs from attitude, not language. A modest speaker can say "I know" and "I did" and "I was" with no problem. But I know a fellow who is so egotistical he can say "Good morning" and seem to take credit for it. Still, it's hard to imagine Caesar saying, "One comes, one sees, one conquers."

GUIDELINE NUMBER SIX. Be smooth. Speech demands uncluttered rhythm. Avoid clauses which interrupt your idea. It's a bit awkward for a speaker to say, "William Safire, former Nixon speech writer," but "former Nixon speech writer William Safire" flows a bit better. If you must add a clause, make a big deal out of it. For example, you might say, "Jogging—which can have a fantastically positive effect on your sex life—may clear up minor sinus problems."

Feel free to use contractions if they help the flow of the speech. In conversation the absence of contractions often becomes a device for emphasis. If you don't use contractions in speaking, you risk overemphasis.

In writing jokes into a speech, be sure to put the "they saids" *before* the quoted material, especially in punch lines. Observe the effect of reading: "Why does a chicken cross the road?" she asked. "To get to the other side," he answered.

GUIDELINE NUMBER SEVEN. Be aggressive. Don't use the loaded language of your enemies. Let me get my prejudice clearly before you. As a consumer, I deeply resent the careless use of the term "consumer advocate." As a breather of air and drinker of water and observer of sunsets, I resent the haphazard application of the term "environmentalist" to anyone who can gather six friends in a living room to organize a Snailshell Defiance. My sympathy goes out to the engineer who finds it all but impossible to explain how fish like warm water without describing the fish as victims of thermal pollution.

I do not assume that American business and industry always have in mind the best interests of consumers, the environment, and fish, but we need to avoid one-sided language if we are to have an honest discussion of the issues. I would prefer to keep away from loaded words or to qualify them with "so-called" or "self-styled."

GUIDELINE NUMBER EIGHT. Be purposeful. Meaning is assigned to words by listeners; your intent is less important than your listener's perception. The controversy over sexism and racism in language can be settled if we remember words are symbols which listeners interpret. I will not use the phrase "girls in the office" because a significant number of people who hear me will react negatively. For the same reason, avoid "a black day" on the market, in favor of a bleak day or a bad day. We need not resort to awkward constructions. You might not want to say "unmanned boat," but this does not mean you must blunder along with "unpeopled boat." What about "a boat with no one aboard?"

GUIDELINE NUMBER NINE. Be eloquent. Use an occasional rhetorical device to enhance your expression of an idea. Indulge at times in a little light alliteration. Balance a pair of phrases: "Ask not what the country can do for General Motors, ask what General Motors can do for the country."

GUIDELINE NUMBER TEN. Be adaptable. Write to suit your speaker. A speech writer for Phillips Petroleum once described his role as being that of a clone. A writer must know the speaker's feelings and the speaker's style. And remember your speaker may need a tersely worded speech one week and a flowery one the next.

My guidelines are far easier to express than to execute. Writing a good speech requires talent, brains, and effort. If you write for others, add to the requirements a self-effacing attitude and a thick skin.

Our language will not be saved by the exhortations of evangelists in the Church of the Fundamental Grammar. It can be saved by writers and speakers with a grasp of function and a sense of quality. We should be proud of your parent organization's contribution; IABC enrolls and nurtures communicators who use language well.

26.2   Introductions and Conclusions

Perhaps the best way to understand the functions served by the introductions and the conclusions of public speeches and the methods by which these functions may be achieved is to examine a number of different introductions and conclusions.

Here we include five introductions and five conclusions from a variety of public speeches—speeches addressed to varied audiences, by very different speakers, at very different times, and with many different purposes. Note the functions each introduction and conclusion serves and the methods used by each speaker.

Introductions

1. Let us ask ourselves, what is education? Above all things, what is our ideal of a thoroughly liberal education?—of that education which, if we could begin life again, we would give ourselves—of that education which, if we could mould the fates to our own will, we would give our children. Well, I know not what may be your conceptions upon this matter, but I will tell you mine, and I hope I shall find that our views are not very discrepant.
   —Thomas Henry Huxley, "A Liberal Education"

2. Five score years ago, a great American, in whose symbolic shadow we stand today, signed the Emancipation Proclamation. This momentous decree came as a great beacon light of hope to millions of Negro slaves, who had been seared in the flames of withering injustice. It came as a joyous daybreak to end the long night of their captivity.

   But one hundred years later, the Negro is still not free. One hundred years later, the life of the Negro is still sadly crippled by the manacles of segregation and the chains of discrimination. One hundred years later, the Negro lives on a lonely island of poverty in the midst of a vast ocean of material prosperity. One hundred years later, the Negro is still languished in the corners of American society and finds himself an exile in his own land. So we have come here today to dramatize a shameful condition.
   —Martin Luther King, Jr., "I Have a Dream"

3. There was a South of slavery and secession—that South is dead. There is a South of union and freedom—that South, thank God, is living, breathing, growing every hour. These words, delivered from the immortal lips of Benjamin H. Hill, at Tammany Hall in 1866, true then, and truer now, I shall make my text tonight.
   —Henry W. Grady, "The New South"

4. Mr. President: When the mariner has been tossed for many days in thick weather, and on an unknown sea, he naturally avails himself of the first pause in the storm, the earliest glance of the sun, to take his latitude, and ascertain how far the elements have driven him from his true course. Let us imitate this prudence, and, before we float farther on the waves of this debate, refer to the point from which we departed, that we may at least be able to conjecture where we now are. I ask for the reading of the resolution before the Senate.
— Daniel Webster, "Second Speech on Foote's Resolution — Reply to Hayne"

5. I doubt if any young woman on this University ever approached a tough assignment with more trepidation than this not-so-young woman is experiencing over this assignment. For a commencement address *is* a tough assignment for the most experienced of speakers. But when the speaker is not experienced, when she is not even a speaker, you can, if you'll put yourselves in her quaking shoes, imagine her state of mind. I find myself experiencing the familiar panic of that recurrent nightmare peculiar to actors in which a ghoulish bevy of directors and fellow players are bustling one onto a strange stage shouting "Hurry! Hurry! You're late!" And one has no idea of what one's part is, or for that matter what the play is. And one arrives before the audience completely speechless and, often as not, completely naked. Things are not quite that crucial for I do seem able to speak and I do appear to be clad.
— Cornelia Otis Skinner, "To Maximize One's Life"

Conclusions

1. If we can stand up to him all Europe may be freed and the life of the world may move forward into broad sunlit uplands; but if we fail, the whole world, including the United States and all that we have known and cared for, will sink into the abyss of a new dark age made more sinister and perhaps more prolonged by the lights of a perverted science.

Let us therefore brace ourselves to our duty and so bear ourselves that if the British Commonwealth and Empire last for a thousand years, men will still say, "This was their finest hour."
— Winston Churchill, "Their Finest Hour"

2. I am endeavoring to show to my countrymen that violent noncooperation only multiplies evil and that as evil can only be sustained by
violence, withdrawal of support of evil requires complete abstention
from violence. Nonviolence implies voluntary submission to the
penalty for noncooperation with evil. I am here, therefore, to invite
and submit cheerfully to the highest penalty that can be inflicted
upon me for what in law is a deliberate crime and what appears to
me to be the highest duty of a citizen. The only course open to you,
the judge, is either to resign your post, and thus dissociate yourself
from evil if you feel that the law you are called upon to administer is
an evil and that in reality I am innocent, or to inflict on me the se-
verest penalty if you believe that the system and the law you are as-
signing to administer are good for the people of this country and that
my activity is therefore injurious to the public weal.
  —Mohandas Gandhi, "Nonviolence"

3. I can conceive of nothing worse than a man-governed world except a
woman-governed world—but I can see the combination of the two
going forward and making civilization more worthy of the name of
civilization based on Christianity, not force. A civilization based on
justice and mercy. I feel men have a greater sense of justice and we
of mercy. They must borrow our mercy and we must use their justice. We are new brooms; let us see that we sweep the right rooms.
  —Lady Astor, "Women and Politics"

4. I am against our participation in this war not only because I hate
war, but because I hate fascism and all totalitarianism, and love democracy. I speak not only for myself, but for my party in summoning
my fellow countrymen to demand that our country be kept out of
war, not as an end in itself, but as a condition to the fulfillment of all
our hopes and dreams for a better life for ourselves and our children,
yes, and all the children of this great land. The extraordinary shifts
and changes in European alliances should but confirm our resolution to stay out of Europe's war, and, ourselves at peace, to seek as
occasion permits, the peace of the world.
  —Norman Thomas, "America and the War"

5. Let me make myself perfectly clear. I do not want any Catholic in the United States of America to vote for me on the 6th of November because I am a Catholic. If any Catholic in this country believes that the welfare, the well-being, the prosperity, the growth and the expansion of the United States is best conserved and best promoted by the election of Hoover, I want him to vote for Hoover and not for me.

But, on the other hand, I have the right to say that any citizen of this country that believes I can promote its welfare, that I am capable of steering the ship of state safely through the next four years and then votes against me because of my religion, he is not a real, pure, genuine American.

—Alfred E. Smith, "Religion and Politics"

26.3   Scrambled Outline

This exercise provides you with an opportunity to work actively with the principles of organization and outlining discussed in the previous units. Your task is to unscramble the following 27 statements, from an outline on "Friendship," and fit them into a coherent and logical outline consisting of an introduction, a body, and a conclusion.

1. We develop an acquaintanceship.
2. Friendship is an interpersonal relationship between two persons that is mutually productive, established and maintained through mutual free choice, and characterized by mutual positive regard.
3. We meet.
4. Without friendships we would not be able to function effectively in our daily lives.
5. Friendship serves to minimize pain.
6. In order to understand friendships, we need to see what a friendship is, the functions it serves, and its stages of development.
7. Friendship is established and maintained through mutual free choice.
8. Friendship is one of the most important of our interpersonal relationships.
9. Friendship is characterized by mutual positive regard.
10. It would be difficult to function effectively without friendships.
11. Friendship is mutually productive.
12. Without friendships our pleasures would not be expanded.
13. Friendships serve a number of significant functions.
14. Friendships serve the function of satisfying our needs.
15. We develop an intimate friendship.
16. Friendships maximize pleasure.
17. Friendship is an interpersonal relationship.
18. Without friendships our pain would not be lessened.
19. Friendships develop through various stages.

20. Friendships do not develop full-blown but rather go through various stages —from the initial meeting, through acquaintance, close friendship, to intimate friendship.
21. We develop a casual friendship.
22. By understanding friendship we will be in a better position to develop and maintain productive and enjoyable friendship relationships.
23. Friendship serves a number of significant functions.
24. Friendships minimize pain.
25. Friendship serves to maximize pleasure.
26. Friendship—an interpersonal communication relationship which is mutually productive, established, and maintained through mutual free choice and characterized by mutual positive regard—serves the functions of satisfying important needs and maximizing pleasure and minimizing pain.
27. We develop a close friendship.

Unit 27

The Speaker-Receiver in Public Communication

THE SPEAKER-RECEIVER IN PUBLIC COMMUNICATION

Audience Analysis and Adaptation
Speaker Apprehension
Delivery
Criticism

LEARNING GOALS

After completing this unit, you should be able to:

1. identify and explain why at least six audience variables should be taken into consideration by the speaker preparing a public speech
2. define *speaker apprehension*
3. identify at least five suggestions for dealing with speaker apprehension
4. identify at least three suggestions listeners might follow to help the speaker deal with apprehension
5. identify the two characteristics that should apply to both the voice and the body actions of the public speaker
6. define *volume, rate, pitch,* and *clarity* as characteristics of effective vocal presentation
7. explain the recommendations made in this unit for the effective use of eye contact, facial expression, gesture, and movement
8. define and explain the nature of *criticism*
9. identify and explain at least three principles to follow in receiving criticism
10. identify and explain at least five principles to follow in giving criticism

In this unit the focus is on the speaker-receiver in public communication, specifically on the factors that need to be considered in analyzing and in adapting one's speech to a specific audience; on speaker apprehension or stage fright; on delivery, the principles for effectively using body actions and voice; and on criticism, the principles to follow in both receiving and in giving criticism in public speaking.

AUDIENCE ANALYSIS AND ADAPTATION

A public speech exists only to be delivered to an audience in order to secure a specific response. Whether that response is increased knowledge, a change in belief, or specific action, the speaker must keep the nature of the audience and the specific response he or she wishes constantly in mind. Preliminary to ensuring that the audience responds as the listener wishes is an understanding of who they are. With such understanding we will be better able to predict the kinds of stimuli (i.e., messages) to which the audience will respond and the ways in which they will respond. If we can predict how an audience will respond to selected messages, we can effectively move them to respond as we wish.

AUDIENCE VARIABLES

Some of the major characteristics that a speaker should consider in his or her attempt to understand the audience are considered here. Recognize that at times we may be unable to secure any information about our intended audience. At times, we are simply asked to speak to a group of "concerned citizens" or to a group of "students." Clearly this is not of much help. But in most instances we can, with some effort, learn significant details about the composition of our audience.

Sex

The sex of the audience is perhaps the most readily apparent characteristic, and at one time it would have been relatively easy to take the sex factor into consideration in composing the speech. Today, however, the sex of members of the audience is a difficult variable to deal with.

At one time, it was possible to talk about women and men as if all women thought or believed alike and as if all men thought or believed alike. Then differences between the sexes could easily be pointed out and adjustments in the speech made. Actually, this was never true, but today it is even more false than it was yesterday. Men as a group and women as a group are extremely heterogeneous. We can no longer speak of "men" or of "women" without recognizing that there is great individual variation within each class. Some women are liberated and others are considered unliberated; some men are liberated and others are considered unliberated.

We should be especially careful that we do not employ the familiar but offensive sexual stereotypes: the woman as housekeeper, the man as provider and protector; the woman as sexually naive and restricted, the man as sexually experienced and free; the woman as a nonprofessional (the secretary, salesperson, or waitress) and the man as professional (the doctor, the lawyer, the scientist).

Age

Age is a peculiar variable especially as it is viewed by students of college age. From my experience in introducing strangers to students and asking them to estimate the age of the stranger, I find that students are notoriously poor judges and will miss estimating correctly by 15 or 20 years. Students view their parents who are in their late thirties or forties as old and high school students who are perhaps two or three years their junior as very young.

Perhaps the most commonly noted characteristic of age difference is the difference in liberal versus conservative attitudes. We tend to think that the young are more liberal than the old and that college students particularly are among the most liberal of all. But I think this is changing. College students seem to be becoming more and more conservative in their attitudes toward capital punishment, foreign involvement, welfare, and various other political, social, and economic issues.

Generally, the young want their rewards immediately; the older seem more capable of delaying rewards. Children, at the extreme, want their rewards without a moment's delay. The amount of delay that people can tolerate seems in part a function of age or, perhaps more correctly, maturity. College students generally want relatively immediate rewards. To freshmen, a college degree seems extremely far off; to a middle-aged person four years seems relatively short.

Freedom is something that is valued very highly by the young, probably because they have not experienced it in all its forms yet. College students want the opportunity to doubt existing values, to question and to evaluate events, people, and objects with their own standards. They want freedom—to do as they wish, to think as they wish, and to live as they wish. They resent parental interference and yet they recognize that they would interfere in probably similar ways with their own children.

They resent the prejudices of their parents and yet seem also to recognize that they have prejudices of their own. Almost without exception, however, they have fewer prejudices than their parents and the students seem more ready to change in light of new information. They seem to have fewer beliefs that they are unwilling to question.

Educational Background

Those of us who have received the benefits of a college education and beyond often forget that the rest of the world has not been through college and has

BOX 27.1
Women's Right to Vote
Susan B. Anthony

At a time when women's rights are so in the news it is instructive to go back in history for one of the early women's liberationists. Susan B. Anthony (1820–1906) pioneered for women's right to vote and was president of the National Woman Suffrage Association. Her efforts helped greatly in the passage of the Nineteenth Amendment, granting women the right to vote.

In this speech, given in 1873, she defends her "illegal" voting. The speech is an excellent example for studying audience analysis and adaptation. It may also prove interesting to compare Anthony's speech with those given by contemporary liberationists.

Friends and fellow citizens:—I stand before you tonight under indictment for the alleged crime of having voted at the last presidential election, without having a lawful right to vote. It shall be my work this evening to prove to you that in thus voting, I not only committed no crime, but, instead, simply exercised my *citizen's rights*, guaranteed to me and all United States citizens by the National Constitution, beyond the power of any State to deny.

The preamble of the Federal Constitution says:

"We, the people of the United States, in order to form a more perfect union, establish justice, insure *domestic* tranquillity, provide for the common defense, promote the general welfare, and secure the blessings of liberty to ourselves and our posterity, do ordain and establish this Constitution for the United States of America."

It was we, the people; not we, the white male citizens; nor yet we, the male citizens; but we, the whole people, who formed the Union. And we formed it, not to give the blessings of liberty, but to secure them; not to the half of ourselves and the half of our posterity, but to the whole people—women as well as men. And it is a downright mockery to talk to women of their enjoyment of the blessings of liberty while they are denied the use of the only means of securing them provided by this democratic-republican government—the ballot.

For any State to make sex a qualification that must ever result in the disfranchisement of one entire half of the people is to pass a bill of attainder, or an *ex post facto* law, and is therefore a violation of the supreme law of the land. By it the blessings of liberty are for ever withheld from women and their female posterity. To them this government has no just powers derived from the consent of the governed. To them this government is not a democracy. It is not a republic. It is an odious aristocracy; a hateful oligarchy of sex; the most hateful aristocracy ever established on the face of the globe; an oligarchy of wealth, where the rich govern the poor. An oligarchy of learning, where the educated govern the ignorant, or even an oligarchy of race, where the Saxon rules the African, might be endured; but this oligarchy of sex, which makes father, brothers, husband, sons, the oligarchs over the mother and sisters, the wife and daughters of every household—which ordains all men sovereigns, all women subjects, carries dissension, discord and rebellion into every home of the nation.

Webster, Worcester and Bouvier all define a citizen to be a person in the United States, entitled to vote and hold office.

The only question left to be settled now is: Are women persons? And I hardly believe any of our opponents will have the hardihood to say they are not. Being persons, then, women are citizens; and no State has a right to make any law, or to enforce any old law, that shall abridge their privileges or immunities. Hence, every discrimination against women in the constitutions and laws of the several States is today null and void, precisely as is every one against Negroes.

not received its benefits. We sometimes forget that the references to philosophers or even to broad areas like sociology, physics, and anthropology may be unknown to an audience that has not been to college. At the same time we must recognize that college degrees do not divide the world into the "haves" and the "have nots." There are many with degrees who are functional idiots and many without degrees who are functional geniuses.

I mention these "obvious" points here because very often we behave as if we did not know them. Perhaps the classic example I witness all too frequently is the teacher who attempts to address beginning students in a particular subject as if they were graduate students, or the teacher who goes to the other extreme and speaks to the students as if every word needs defining and every concept repeated three different ways. Admittedly, it is difficult to adjust our language and our ideas to the educational level of the audience, yet we must attempt it.

Religion and Politics

In many instances the religious and political views of the audience members will not make much of a difference. But when they do make a difference, they really make a difference. Issues such as abortion, censorship, socialized medicine, welfare, immigration, and similar topics would all be greatly influenced by the audience's religious and political beliefs.

We should recognize that in considering politics and religion we must consider not only what political and religious affiliations the audience members have but also the degree to which they are "loyal" members or the degree to which they follow the "party line." This is the most difficult aspect to analyze. While it is relatively easy to discover the most common religion of the audience, it is extremely difficult to discover how they allow that religion to influence their lives, their thoughts, and their behaviors. There are Catholics and Orthodox Jews who are in favor of abortion and there are liberals who argue for rigid censorship. Labels that may legitimately be placed on people will inevitably be inadequate to cover all of their behaviors.

Occupation

The occupation of audience members, like religion and politics, sometimes plays little role, but when it does operate, its role is extremely important. Approximately one-quarter of our lives is spent on our jobs. In many instances the amount of time spent is greater. Teachers, doctors, lawyers, and store owners, for example, often spend a great deal more than one-quarter of their time at their jobs. Consequently, when it comes to issues that relate to one's occupation (even indirectly), we need to take this into consideration. People in different occupations have difficulty communicating with one another. For example, one of the problems I have witnessed is between laborers and teachers. Laborers have difficulty understanding how teachers can get tired from sitting at a desk or from lecturing to a class. Teachers have no such difficulty. On the other hand, teachers feel that they must always be on their job. It does not end when they go home for dinner. At night and on weekends they must grade papers, prepare lectures, make up examinations, work on committees, keep up with the new developments in the field, and of course write articles and books. Many teachers, for these reasons, look with envy on laborers who are finished with their job when they come home at night. On Saturday and Sunday the laborer does not have to worry about preparing for Monday, but the teacher does. The teacher, on the other hand, has difficulty understanding how physically exhausting bricklaying or paperhanging or trucking can be. Similarly, those who are not going to college have difficulty recognizing that the college student's life can be a difficult one. Sitting in class, listening to lectures, and taking notes may seem easy to someone who has never done it.

This is just one example but it should illustrate that it is not easy to empathize with those who work at very different occupations. Perhaps we can at least recognize that most people can easily perceive the difficulties with their own job but have difficulty perceiving the difficulties with the jobs of others. We should also recognize, in a status-conscious society such as ours, that people will inevitably see their job as deserving of higher status than will others. Any teacher who assumes that everyone recognizes the higher status of teaching as compared with, say, firefighting or nursing is in for a rude awakening upon encountering a fireman or a nurse.

Attitudes

We must also take into consideration the audience's attitude toward the topic or subject of the speech, the purpose of the speech, the occasion, and the speaker.

The most common problem with an audience's attitude toward the topic or subject of a speech is that they are generally not interested enough in it to maintain attention. When they are uninterested in the subject, they will probably have no definite feelings about the purpose of the speech. And so this disinterest, while presenting some problems, at least provides the speaker with an audience that is not violently opposed to the purpose of the speech.

Given this disinterest, however, the speaker's first task is to make the subject interesting, to relate it to the needs of the audience. He or she must show the audience why this topic is crucial, why they should listen.

Generally the speaker is best advised to begin where the audience is. If the audience is in favor of his or her position, then he or she may start by stating it and proceed from there. If the audience is against the purpose of the speech, then the speaker must recognize this and proceed to eliminate or lessen their attitudes in some way. The same speech on abortion given to a "right-to-life" group and an adamantly pro-abortion group would be ludicrous.

Most speakers assume, although wrongly, that if an audience is present for a speech that they wish to be there and hence have positive attitudes toward the occasion. These speakers should walk into a college classroom in which the teacher takes attendance and counts it heavily into the grade. The class will be crowded, but to say that the audience is positive toward the occasion would be stretching things. And although the speaker should not overemphasize this, he or she should recognize that it is best to devote some attention to getting the audience to see the occasion as a more positive one than when they walked in. Showing the audience why this topic is important to them, involving them in some way in the proceedings, putting them into a relaxed mood, and similar methods are at the speaker's disposal for altering initially negative attitudes.

Last, and perhaps the most difficult aspect to analyze objectively, is the attitude of the audience toward the speaker as a person. At times, of course, the audience gathers to hear a particular person because of what that person has accomplished. Perhaps the speaker is a famous politician, scientist, or writer. The audience gathers to hear or see that particular person and often the topic of the speech is of secondary importance. But in most cases the attitudes of the members of the audience are neutral or relatively so, and these must be made more positive if the speaker is to have any effect on the audience's thinking. The audience has a right to know why this speaker is speaking on this particular topic. That is, they want to know the speaker's qualifications. Most audiences do not want to hear a man talk about childbirth or a person who has never had children talk about the difficulty in raising children. Similarly we do not want to hear a rich person talk about how to live on a budget or a poor person talk about how to make it big in the stock market. Of course these are extremes that are easily recognized, but most speakers are in the same situation—the audience must recognize the speaker's authority to address his or her subject.

Thus we need to let the audience know that we are qualified to speak on the topic. We need to state our qualifications subtly and with grace and, at the same time, we must not make the audience feel that we are engaging in self-indulgent bragging.

CONTEXT VARIABLES

In addition to analyzing the specific listeners, the speaker has to devote some attention to the specific context in which he or she will speak. Here just a few of the variables that the speaker might focus on are identified: (1) the size of the audience, (2) the physical environment, and (3) the psychological climate. These factors are not totally separate and distinct from those considered in the previous section under "Audience Variables." Those topics considered under "Audience Variables" are relatively stable or static characteristics; they are what are technically called "demographic characteristics." Those factors considered here under "context variables" are more integrally related to the ever-changing nature of the specific context; they are characteristics that are temporary and dynamic (always changing).

Size of the Audience

It is essential to know the size of the audience beforehand. Generally, the larger the audience, the more formal the presentation is expected to be. With a small audience, you may be a great deal more casual and informal. Also, the larger the audience, the more heterogeneous the members are likely to be. Consequently, the broader your supporting materials must be. You will probably have in a large audience more different religions, a greater range of occupations, more different income levels, and so on. Every one of the variables that we considered will probably be more varied in the large audience than in the small audience.

A large audience also presents difficulties with visuals. When I taught psycholinguistics to 30 students, I was able to construct relatively small charts of important concepts. Now, however, in a class of 200, these would be totally inadequate, and so I must use transparencies and slides. The adjustment, of course, is simple, and it is puzzling to me to see other teachers in similar situations holding up charts that no one but those in the first few rows can see and being totally unaware of the fact that the vast majority cannot see what they are pointing to.

The Physical Environment

The physical environment—the room, the auditorium, whether the audience will be sitting or standing, whether it will be outside or inside, and so on—is an important factor. One of the major problems that speakers have that a few minutes of time could solve is that they enter the public speaking environment totally cold. Even if you will be giving your speech in a familiar classroom, you should spend some time in front of the room, seeing the room from the perspective of the speaker before you are ready to speak. When you walk into the room, take a second to stand in the front and survey the entire room—look at the windows, the back wall, the desks, the students. See the room as you will see it as a speaker. This preparation is even more important for rooms that are totally unfamiliar to you, since so much anxiety and uneasiness is the result of the new and unexpected.

Another factor that figures into speech effectiveness is the closeness with which the audience members sit. Whether they are close or far apart will influence the degree of interaction among the listeners and in fact has been found to influence persuasibility. Generally, audiences are easier to persuade if they are sitting close together than if they are spread widely apart. As a teacher I will always exceed the limit on the number of students allowed in my class because I find that with physical closeness it is easier for the students to get to know one another and to interact freely and that this type of interaction makes for a more effective class. If the students are spread out over a large area, they may never interact with one another.

The Psychological Climate

The psychological climate of the audience refers to at least two dimensions. The first is whether the audience is a captive audience or whether they have come willingly to hear you and perhaps even paid an admission price. For your speeches in class, you will probably be facing a captive audience—an audience that has to come to class as part of the requirements of the course. This is helpful since you do not have to worry that on your day to speak, no one will be there (although many will still have this understandable fear). But it is detrimental because you have to face some listeners who would rather be elsewhere. And yet, that is perhaps the way it is in most situations. Teachers face this type of audience all the time.

The other dimension of psychological climate is whether the audience is favorable or unfavorable to the topic and particularly to your purpose. Most often, of course, you are going to find a mixed audience; some will be in favor, some will be neutral, and some will be against your proposition. This diversity is not easy to deal with, and yet it cannot be ignored.

In all cases, it is probably best to secure positive responses in small steps as you go along. Thus, the more you can get your audience to indicate agreement with what you are saying, the more effective you will be. With a favorable audience, you will have an easy task. With a hostile audience, your task will be difficult at best. Thus, for example, with the hostile audience you might try to approach your topic inductively. Give your evidence first, and only after your audience has accepted these several facts and figures relate them to the proposition being advocated. Instead of saying that oil prices should be increased—a proposition that most members will disagree with—you might lead with other arguments that the audience would agree with—for example, the need to conserve energy for the coming years, the need to keep inflation at a reasonable rate, the need to become self-sufficient in energy, and so on. The audience can easily agree with these propositions and will find that the main proposition—that oil prices have to be increased—a bit easier to take when it is prefaced by these more acceptable arguments that have already generated a positive response in the minds of the listeners.

The neutral audience, as can easily be appreciated, needs to be shown that the topic is not one about which they can or should be neutral but one that is of vital importance to them. By relating the topic to those issues they feel are important—by showing its relationship to their job and standard of living, for example—you will be in a better position to have them accept your point of view.

ANALYSIS AND ADAPTATION DURING THE SPEECH

All that has been said has been directed at the preparation stages of the speech. That is, the variables we considered are ones that the speaker should consider as he or she prepares the speech for delivery before an audience. But there is also analysis and adaptation that must be done during the speech, and this is more difficult.

The speaker should constantly be on the lookout for feedback that might help in understanding how the audience members are reacting to the speech. If there are howls of laughter and wild applause at appropriate places, the speaker

As the audience becomes larger, the difficulty of audience analysis and adaptation becomes greater; but it is always an essential part of the public speaker process if a speech is to be effective in achieving its purpose.

can be pretty sure of success. Similarly if half the audience walks out and the other half stays to boo and curse the speaker, he or she can be pretty certain of failure. But what of the speakers who fall between these extremes?

Most beginning speakers should attempt to look for some of the more obvious signals. In a classroom if the students are talking among themselves or if they are sitting with bored looks on their faces or reading the newspapers, some adjustment must be made. I have witnessed teachers lecture to a class in which not one student was paying attention and yet the teacher just continued on as if everything was fine. This teacher, of course, should be fired. But this teacher and thousands of similar ones continue to bore a potentially stimulated audience.

One of the most difficult things to do as a speaker is to see negative reactions as clearly as we see positive reactions. Few of us have difficulty seeing favorable responses, but we need to train ourselves to see the unfavorable responses so that we can adjust what we are saying and turn that unfavorable reaction into a favorable one.

Again, we must remember that being overly concerned with audience re-

BOX 27.2
All For Love
Edward VIII

Edward VIII (1894–1972), perhaps more widely known as the Duke of Windsor, was King of Great Britain from January 20 to December 10, 1936. On December 11, 1936, Edward VIII delivered the following farewell address, abdicating the throne so that he might marry the twice-divorced Wallis Simpson—a marriage that the British hierarchy could not accept.

The speech is a model of effective audience adaptation and style.

At long last I am able to say a few words of my own. I have never wanted to withhold anything, but until now it has not been constitutionally possible for me to speak.

A few hours ago I discharged my last duty as King and Emperor, and now that I have been succeeded by my brother, the Duke of York, my first words must be to declare my allegiance to him. This I do with all my heart.

You all know the reasons which have impelled me to renounce the throne. But I want you to understand that in making up my mind I did not forget the country or the empire, which, as Prince of Wales and lately as King, I have for twenty-five years tried to serve.

But you must believe me when I tell you that I have found it impossible to carry the heavy burden of responsibility and to discharge my duties as King as I would wish to do without the help and support of the woman I love.

And I want you to know that the decision I have made has been mine and mine alone. This was a thing I had to judge entirely for myself. The other person most nearly concerned has tried up to the last to persuade me to take a different course.

I have made this, the most serious decision of my life, only upon the single thought of what would, in the end, be best for all.

This decision has been made less difficult to me by the sure knowledge that my brother, with his long training in the public affairs of this country and with his fine qualities, will be able to take my place forthwith without interruption or injury to the life and progress of the empire. And he has one matchless blessing, enjoyed by so many of you, and not bestowed on me—a happy home with his wife and children.

During these hard days I have been comforted by her Majesty my mother and by my family. The ministers of the crown, and in particular, Mr. Baldwin, the Prime Minister, have always treated me with full consideration. There has never been any constitutional difference between me and them, and between me and Parliament. Bred in the constitutional tradition by my father, I should never have allowed any such issue to arise.

Ever since I was Prince of Wales, and later on when I occupied the throne, I have been treated with the greatest kindness by all classes of the people wherever I have lived or journeyed throughout the empire. For that I am very grateful.

I now quit altogether public affairs and I lay down my burden. It may be some time before I return to my native land, but I shall always follow the

> fortunes of the British race and empire with profound interest, and if at any
> time in the future I can be found of service to his Majesty in a private station,
> I shall not fail.
>   And now, we all have a new King. I wish him and you, his people,
> happiness and prosperity with all my heart. God bless you all! God save the
> King!

sponse can make us too nervous to communicate effectively. And so we need a
judicious rather than an obsessive surveillance of audience feedback.

SPEAKER APPREHENSION

Of all the speaker-related variables, speaker apprehension is perhaps the most
salient. There are numerous terms for the same basic phenomenon. *Stage fright*
is perhaps the most popular and certainly the oldest, but there are others—
speech fright, reticence, shyness, audience sensitivity, unwillingness to communicate,
and *communication apprehension.* Although each theorist defines the concept a
bit differently, all terms refer to a state of fear or anxiety about communication
interaction. The term *speaker apprehension* is used to emphasize that the phenomenon is speaker-centered.

According to a nationwide survey conducted by Bruskin Associates in
1973, speaking in public was ranked as the number-one fear of adult men and
women. (Fear of heights, of insects and bugs, of financial problems, and of deep
water were ranked second, third, fourth, and fifth, respectively.) According to
surveys of college students noted by McCroskey and Wheeless, between 10 and
20 percent suffer "severe, debilitating communication apprehension," while another 20 percent "suffers from communication apprehension to a degree substantial enough to interfere to some extent with their normal functioning."

THE NATURE OF SPEAKER APPREHENSION

Pooling the insights of the various researchers and theorists who have investigated this phenomenon, speaker apprehension may be defined from at least two
perspectives: cognitive and behavioral. That is, speaker apprehension may be
defined in terms of how a person thinks and feels (cognitive) or how a person
behaves (behavioral).

Cognitively, speaker apprehension would be a fear of engaging in communication transactions. That is, persons develop negative feelings and predict negative results as a function of engaging in communication interactions. They feel
that whatever gain would accrue from engaging in communication is clearly out-
weighed by the fear.

Behaviorally, speaker apprehension would be a decrease in the frequency,
the strength, and the likelihood of engaging in communication transactions.
That is, speakers avoid communication situations and, when forced to participate, participate as little as possible.

Speaker apprehension exists on a continuum. Persons are not either apprehensive or not apprehensive; we all experience some degree of apprehension. Some people are extremely apprehensive and become incapacitated in a communication situation. They suffer a great deal in a society oriented, as ours is, around communication and in which success depends on one's ability to communicate effectively. Others are so mildly apprehensive that they appear to experience no fear at all when confronted by communication situations; they actively seek out communication experiences and rarely experience even the slightest apprehension. Most of us lie between these two extremes. We fear some situations more than others. For some of us this apprehension is debilitating and hinders personal effectiveness in dealings with people. Apprehension energizes and makes others of us all the more alert, active, and responsive, and aids us in achieving our goals.

DEALING WITH SPEAKER APPREHENSION

In the public speaking context we are concerned with managing speaker apprehension. Specifically, what does a person with apprehension do? What does one do as a listener-critic in dealing with persons with high apprehension?

It is most important to realize that one cannot *eliminate* speaker apprehension. It may be lessened and it may be controlled, but it probably cannot be totally eliminated. The suggestions offered here will help you to lessen and manage apprehension, not eliminate it. It is also important to realize that these suggestions are addressed to persons with low and moderate levels of apprehension. Persons who experience extremely high levels of speaker apprehension, who are so fearful of the speaking situation that they simply cannot function, should seek professional assistance. Being forced into public speaking situations and being made to go through the motions will not help their speaker apprehension; it might aggravate it.

1. Recognize that stage fright, speaker apprehension, or whatever else it is called, is normal. Everyone experiences some degree of fear in the relatively formal public communication situation in which you are the sole focus and are to be evaluated. Public speaking is perhaps the most anxiety-provoking communication situation; experiencing fear or anxiety is, therefore, not strange or unique. Very likely your instructor experienced speaker apprehension as a student and, perhaps, experiences it even now as a teacher. I have experienced speaker apprehension and, in fact, still do in a variety of situations. In most cases, I think, it actually helps me. It leads me to prepare my lectures very thoroughly and to rehearse a great deal, and it keeps me alert and energized throughout the speaking transaction. Once you recognize—on a gut level—that you are not unique in experiencing speaker apprehension, you will have taken an important first step in managing your own apprehension.

2. Recognize that apprehension is not necessarily detrimental. As noted, fear can energize us and may even get us to work a little more to produce a speech that will be better than it would have been if we had not experienced some apprehension. Gerald Phillips, for example, has noted that "learning proceeds best when the organism is in a state of tension." Phillips cites the results

of studies that followed groups of students with speaker apprehension for one and three years after instruction in dealing with communication apprehension. Almost all the students were able to deal effectively with the originally difficult communication situations, but they still experienced the same level of tension. "Apparently," notes Phillips, "they had learned to manage the tension; they no longer saw it as an impairment, and they went ahead with what they had to do."

3. Prepare and practice thoroughly. Inadequate preparation—not having rehearsed the speech enough, for example, or not having researched it thoroughly and fearing questions you cannot answer—is reasonable cause for anxiety. Much of the fear we experience is a fear of failure. Adequate and even extra preparation will lessen the possibility of failure and the accompanying apprehension.

You should also familiarize yourself with the actual public speaking context. Try, for example, to rehearse in the room in which you will give your speech or stand in front of the room, before the actual presentation, as if you were giving your speech. You will thus acquaint yourself with the context, and this will ease your apprehension.

Practice the speech as you will deliver it. This will help you to remember it better and enable you to iron out any difficulties that may still be present. It will give you greater confidence in your ability to deliver the speech. It will also familiarize you with the speech in all its aspects, and familiarity most effectively fights fear. We fear what we cannot predict; we fear the unexpected. If we know what to expect, we can deal with it more effectively.

4. Physical activity helps. Apprehension is generally eased or lessened by physical activity, by gross body movements as well as by the small movements of the hands, face, and head. If you are apprehensive, you might work into your speech some writing on the blackboard or some demonstration that requires considerable movement. You could use a visual aid: manipulating the aid or showing slides temporarily diverts attention from you and allows you to expend your excess energy.

Obviously, the movement should be integral to the speech. Do not walk around for the sake of walking around; do not use a visual aid just so that you might move about. Integrate such activities into your speech.

Listeners can do a great deal to assist the speakers with their apprehension. I offer here just a few suggestions.

1. Positively reinforce the speaker throughout the speech: a nod of the head, a pleasant smile, and, perhaps most important, an attentive appearance. Resist the temptation to pick up the newspaper or to talk with a friend. Try to make it as easy as possible for the speaker. Obviously, attend those classes when other students are speaking. Speakers often have a particular fear that the audience will not show up ("They know I'm a terrible speaker and so they're not going to come today").

2. If there is a question period after the speeches, ask questions as information-seeking attempts rather than as critical challenges. Instead of saying, for example, "Your criticism of disco music is absurd," you might say "Why do you find the lyrics of disco songs meaningless?" or "What is there about the beat of disco music that you find offensive?" Ask questions in a tone and a manner

that do not make the speaker defensive and that do not signal conflict between you and the speaker.

3. If the speaker fumbles in some way, do not focus on it by putting your head down, covering your eyes, or otherwise nonverbally communicating your intense awareness of the fumble. Instead, continue listening to the content of the speech. Nonverbally, try to communicate to the speaker that you are concerned with what is being said and that the bungling of a sentence is not all that important. In the total scheme of things, of course, it isn't.

DELIVERY

Perhaps the topic of most concern to the beginning public speaker is that of delivery. The speaker seldom worries about organization or even the language of the speech. Instead he or she concentrates on delivery, generally worrying a great deal more than is necessary. Although each speaker must develop a manner of presentation that is suitable to his or her own personality, some general suggestions are offered here. Again we must recognize that these suggestions must be modified in light of the specific audience, specific purpose, and specific topic.

The assumption here is that no one method of delivery, no one speech pattern is right while others are wrong. To be sure, there are patterns to be preferred, but the reasons for the preferences must be based not on arbitrary standards but on legitimate considerations of effectiveness; standards for delivery must be grounded in effectiveness.

GENERAL PRINCIPLES OF DELIVERY

Before discussing the specifics of voice and body action, a number of principles that seem to make delivery more effective should be identified. These are general principles that are not limited or restricted to one style of bodily action or one pattern of speech; rather they are general principles that apply to all aspects and forms of delivery. Delivery is effective, then, when it is characterized by the following principles.

1. Effective delivery does not call attention to itself. When voice or body action calls attention to itself and the audience concentrates on delivery, there is that much attention lost to the speech. Consequently we would judge that kind of delivery ineffective. Whether we concentrate on the voice because it is so melodious or because it is so unclear is irrelevant to this point—both call attention to themselves, draw attention away from the speech, and are therefore ineffective.

2. Effective delivery reinforces the message; effective delivery gives emphasis through vocal and bodily means to what the speaker wishes emphasized. A story of starvation told in a monotone will not emphasize what needs to be emphasized. The voice and the general body movement must reinforce the content, the point of view, and the general perspective of the speech.

3. Effective delivery is appropriate. This concept of appropriateness covers a great deal of territory. Surely the delivery must be appropriate to the speaker; a

speaker cannot assume the delivery mannerisms of another individual without creating some incongruity, some inconsistency. The vocal and the bodily dimension of communication must be your own. Delivery must also be appropriate to the audience, the occasion, and the subject matter of the speech. Delivery that is appropriate to a speech designed to entertain a group of refrigerator salespeople in Duluth may not be appropriate in a speech designed to persuade a group of college men to enlist in the navy. Delivery must be consistent with all the other variables in the public speaking situation; to the extent that it is not, it will call attention to itself in addition to violating the appropriateness principle.

4. Effective delivery is flexible and varied. Listening to a speech is difficult work. It is hard to sit quietly and absorb a great deal of information. One way in which some of the difficulty is relieved is to incorporate a delivery that is flexible and varied. A monotone would surely put the audience to sleep; similarly a motionless body behind a podium hardly helps to keep the audience alert. Not surprisingly, a delivery without flexibility will also function to deaden the speaker; it's almost as if the speaker gets caught up in the monotony and forgets that he or she is attempting to communicate ideas and feelings to an audience.

If you think of your thoughts and what you want to convey to the audience and if you stay relatively loose (but not too loose), you will find that your delivery will vary appropriately with what you are saying and that it will effortlessly reinforce what you want to emphasize.

5. Effective delivery aids instant intelligibility. The objective of the speaker is to make his or her ideas understandable to an audience. Delivery can help comprehension or it can hinder it; it cannot be neutral. A low voice that we have to strain to hear, a sharp decrease in volume at the ends of sentences that forces us to attempt to reconstruct how that last sentence might have ended, slurred enunciation that makes it difficult for us to tell what words the speaker said all obviously hinder intelligibility. If messages are also communicated facially (as they are), then wearing sunglasses during a speech will impair intelligibility, for it will be difficult for the audience to see what the speaker is communicating. The same principle holds true for the speaker who does not maintain eye contact and who looks out the window, at the floor, or at notes.

VOICE

Although many characteristics of the voice may be considered (and certainly many characteristics are significant), only a few can be considered here. We limit our consideration here to those characteristics that the individual can improve (volume, rate, pitch, and clarity) rather than those characteristics that must be dealt with by a trained speech therapist. An appropriate theoretical base for this section was presented in Unit 15, "Paralanguage and Silence."

Volume

Volume is a particularly difficult concept to discuss, since we do not hear ourselves the way others do. In a small classroom, volume seldom presents too many problems, but in a large auditorium volume must be carefully studied.

We need to be aware that the speaker can err in either direction. Generally, we err in the direction of speaking too softly. Perhaps this is due to fear, perhaps to a reticence to take control of the situation; but whatever the reason it should be clear that no speaker will be effective if he or she cannot be heard. The speaker should also recognize that by speaking too loudly he or she makes the audience uncomfortable. Within this relatively normal range that is easy to hear and yet not too piercing, the speaker should vary the volume, speaking certain key words or phrases at a somewhat greater volume and perhaps lowering the voice when the occasion seems to require it. If the speaker has a clear understanding of the topic, the places where the volume should be increased or decreased will suggest themselves.

Rate

Rate refers to the speed with which we speak and also to the pauses we use. A normal speech rate is between 120 and 180 words per minute, and the normal rate within this range is quite varied. The speaker must be careful to avoid either extreme. Speaking at too slow a rate will surely bore the audience, their minds will wander, and it will be almost impossible to get their attention back to the speech. Similarly, speaking at too fast a rate will confuse the audience and they will be unable to follow the ideas presented by the speaker. The rate should be fast enough to keep the interest of the audience but slow enough so that they can follow the speaker's ideas. The rate should be varied so that monotony does not set in. Certain examples may be spoken more rapidly than perhaps an important conclusion. Again, if the speaker understands what he or she is saying, the rates should suggest themselves.

Pauses should be utilized to guide the audience in following the speaker's line of reasoning. The speaker should realize that he or she has gone over the speech a number of times but that the audience is hearing it only once. Consequently, the audience needs time to "digest" significant points and to make important connections.

Pitch

Pitch refers to the highness or lowness of the voice. In the sentence "Are you going to marry that beast?" we can change the meaning of the sentence by varying the pitch of the various words. Compare, for example, the following versions:

Are YOU going to marry that beast?
Are you going to MARRY that beast?
Are you going to marry that BEAST?

Each of these means something quite different.

In everyday conversation we vary our pitch without any conscious awareness. Generally the meaning we wish to convey guides us in raising or lowering our pitch. If public speaking, as many have put it, is enlarged conversation, then we may at times have to exaggerate some of the changes in pitch so that our meaning is extra clear to the audience.

Clarity

Clarity really pertains to articulation and pronunciation rather than to the voice. Clarity of articulation is the production of individual sounds that are free from distortions produced by excessive noise. By clarity of pronunciation we mean the production of words and phrases in the ways considered acceptable for your region.

Do not attempt to imitate the Oxford professor or the street bum; speak in public as you do in private. Generally, be careful to avoid any attempts at overly precise speech. This appears artificial and is insulting to an audience. It in effect says that the speaker is attempting to put something over on them. At the same time the speaker should avoid slovenly speech. The speech of the public speaker should be dignified without being artificial, conversational without being sloppy.

BODY ACTION

The public speaker should give considerable attention to body action and yet not let it become the most important element in the total public speaking process.

Eye Contact

Perhaps the most important aspect of body language is that of eye contact. Intuitively we are apt to rely on the eyes to give us information about another individual; we say we trust the eyes or that the eyes tell the truth while the mouth lies. When a person professes a deep interest in us and yet glances around the room or at the floor, we intuitively begin to doubt the sincerity of what is being said.

Years ago I remember being told that when speaking to a large audience one should focus on something on the back wall, like the clock or the door, and not to worry about looking at the audience. That bit of advice ranks among the dumbest of all things ever said about public speaking. If public speaking is to be effective the speaker must address the audience and that includes looking the audience in the eyes. The audience needs to feel that the speaker is maintaining contact with them and this is best achieved by direct eye contact. Similarly, the speaker needs to have some way of gaining information as to how the speech is going, and he or she can best get this from reading the expressions in the eyes of the audience.

Facial Expression

Second in importance to eye contact is facial expression (not easily separated from eye contact). With the face we again feel intuitively that we can rely on what it tells us. A smile, a frown, a smirk, or a grin can communicate a great deal of information. If the information the speaker communicates with his or her face differs from that communicated by the speaker's verbal messages, the audience will believe the facial messages. Consequently, the speaker must take special care that the messages communicated by the face supplement and complement rather than contradict the messages coming from the mouth.

BOX 27.3
The Murder of Gandhi
Jawaharlal Nehru

Jawaharlal Nehru (1889–1964) became the first prime minister of independent India in 1947. Nehru delivered the following speech on the occasion of the death of Mohandas Gandhi, one of India's most beloved leaders, at the hands of a Hindu nationalist.

This speech is included here because it is one of the best examples of a eulogy—a speech in praise of some individual. Although the speech is about one person, there is still a timelessness and a universality to it.

Friends and comrades, the light has gone out of our lives and there is darkness everywhere. I do not know what to tell you and how to say it. Our beloved leader, Bapu as we called him, the father of the nation, is no more. Perhaps I am wrong to say that. Nevertheless, we will not see him again as we have seen him for these many years. We will not run to him for advice and seek solace from him, and that is a terrible blow, not to me only, but to millions and millions in this country, and it is a little difficult to soften the blow by any other advice that I or anyone else can give you.

The light has gone out, I said, and yet I was wrong. For the light that shone in this country was no ordinary light. The light that has illumined this country for these many years will illumine this country for many more years, and a thousand years later that light will still be seen in this country and the world will see it and it will give solace to innumerable hearts. For that light represented the living truth . . . the eternal truths, reminding us of the right path, drawing us from error, taking this ancient country to freedom.

All this has happened when there was so much more for him to do. We could never think that he was unnecessary or that he had done his task. But now, particularly, when we are faced with so many difficulties, his not being with us is a blow most terrible to bear.

A madman has put an end to his life, for I can only call him mad who did it, and yet there has been enough of poison spread in this country during the past years and months, and this poison has had effect on people's minds. We must face this poison, we must root out this poison, and we must face all the perils that encompass us and face them not madly or badly but rather in the way that our beloved teacher taught us to face them. The first thing to remember now is that no one of us dare misbehave because we are angry. We have to behave like strong and determined people, determined to face all the perils that surround us, determined to carry out the mandate that our great teacher and our great leader has given us, remembering always that if, as I believe, his spirit looks upon us and sees us, nothing would displease his soul so much as to see that we have indulged in any small behavior or any violence.

So we must not do that. But that does not mean that we should be weak, but rather that we should in strength and in unity face all the troubles that are in front of us. We must hold together, and all our petty troubles and difficulties and conflicts must be ended in the face of this great disaster. A great disaster is a symbol to us to remember all the big things of life and forget the small things, of which we have thought too much.

It was proposed by some friends that Mahatmaji's body should be embalmed for a few days to enable millions of people to pay their last homage to him. But it was his wish, repeatedly expressed, that no such thing should happen, that this should not be done, that he was entirely opposed to any embalming of his body.

Tomorrow should be a day of fasting and prayer for all of us. Those who live elsewhere out of Delhi and in other parts of India will no doubt also take such part as they can in this last homage. For them also let this be a day of fasting and prayer. And at the appointed time for cremation, that is, 4:00 P.M. tomorrow afternoon, people should go to the river or to the sea and offer prayers there. And while we pray, the greatest prayer that we can offer is to take a pledge to dedicate ourselves to the truth and to the cause for which this great countryman of ours lived and for which he has died.

Gestures and Movement

The public speaker should rehearse his or her speech using gestures but should not plan the gestures to the point that he or she knows when each gesture will appear. Rather, a rehearsal with gestures should be such that the speaker will feel comfortable using gestures in front of the audience. Put differently, we should be careful not to use gestures that appear studied and artificial but, at the same time, we should practice our speech enough so that we do not feel inhibited in using gestures.

The public speaker should move about a bit but not to the point that he or she becomes difficult to follow. We feel more relaxed when we see a speaker who is relaxed, and one of the best ways to signal relaxation and a feeling of comfort is to move about. Movement should be consonant with the purpose of the speech and with the specifics of the message being communicated. A step forward, for example, may be a convenient way to signal the beginning of a major point and a step back may help to signal the audience to pause for a moment to reflect on what has been said. A walk to the left or to the right helps to keep the entire audience in the purview of the speaker so that no one feels slighted. Again, however, too much or too little movement will hinder the speaker in achieving a naturalness of delivery.

In incorporating any of these delivery suggestions into public speaking behavior, the speaker should keep clearly in mind the two characteristics of effective delivery—naturalness and variety.

CRITICISM

"A critic," noted Channing Pollock, "is a legless man who teaches running." Nobody likes critics, or so it seems. And yet critics and criticism are an essential part of art; they are guides who lead us to see more than we might see if left on our own. They provide us with useful and well-reasoned standards that help us to separate the worthy from the worthless. As Hugh Blair said in his *Lectures on Rhetoric and Belles Lettres,* criticism teaches us "to admire and to blame with judgment, and not to follow the crowd blindly."

Note that Blair says "to admire" as well as "to blame." We often fear and deprecate criticism because we view it as negative evaluation, as fault finding. The term *criticism* comes from the Latin *criticus,* meaning "able to discern," "to judge." There is nothing inherently negative about criticism. And so, keep in mind that we are discussing standards of judgment and evaluation—positive as well as negative, praise as well as blame, applause as well as censure.

Perhaps the major purpose of criticism in the classroom is to improve public speaking. Through criticism you, as a speaker and as a listener-critic, will more effectively learn the principles of public speaking. Feedback seems essential to improvement. By seeing these principles in operation, by dissecting them, and by evaluating their applications through the critical process, you will come to understand and appreciate them better and ultimately internalize them. Through criticism, you will be better able to see what worked and what did not work and what should be retained, enlarged upon, modified, or eliminated.

In a broader sense society as a whole also derives some benefit from the critical evaluation of public speaking. To the extent that criticism improves the quality of public communication and sets higher and higher standards for its communicators, it serves a useful societal function. The current state of most public communication—perhaps seen most clearly in the speeches of our local and national politicians—should convince us that critics should work a bit harder to fulfill this basic function of raising the level of public communication.

RECEIVING AND GIVING CRITICISM

Perhaps the most difficult aspect of the entire course in public speaking, from the point of view of both student-speaker and student-listener, is criticism. How do you give and receive criticism? Inability to deal effectively with this important dimension of public speaking creates an enormous amount of unnecessary and unproductive anxiety.

Criticism is difficult: as an intellectual experience, because so many factors must be taken into account; as a psychological experience, because speaking in public intimately involves one's self-concept. But a few principles of receiving and giving criticism may make this experience easier and more productive for all involved.

Receiving Criticism

You will benefit from criticism if you, as a speaker, learn to control defensiveness, to separate criticism of the speech from criticism of the self, to seek clarification when needed, and to understand the reasons for the criticisms and the suggested changes.

Control Defensiveness. Whenever we are evaluated, especially when negatively, we tend to become defensive, perhaps in an effort to protect ourselves from psychological harm or to preserve our egos or to otherwise save our positive self-concept. But defensiveness seals off effective communication and prevents us from taking in the very information that may prove helpful to our future efforts. After all, we are in a public speaking class to improve our public speaking and not merely to be patted on the back.

Separate Speech Criticism from Self-Criticism. Speech—and, in fact, all aspects of your communication behavior—is so ego-involving that it is difficult (often impossible) to separate it from yourself as a person. But if you are to improve your public speaking performance and yet not be psychologically crushed by negative evaluations, you should recognize that when some aspect of your speech is criticized, your personality or your worth as an individual is not being criticized. Try to externalize critical evaluations so that you view them and analyze them dispassionately.

Seek Clarification. Critics, assuming that what is very clear to them must also be clear to everyone else, often tend to state their comments in vague and general terms. But in many instances the criticism will not be clear. You should not hesitate, when this is the case, to ask for clarification. You should also ask for clarification if you do not see how to apply the criticism to improve your future efforts. Thus, for example, if it is unclear when you are told that your specific purpose was too broad, ask how you might narrow down the specific purpose. Your critics—instructor and fellow students—should welcome such attempts to seek clarification.

Understand Reasons. Try to understand the reasons for the criticism—that is, why certain aspects of the speech or its presentation were criticized and why the suggested alterations would make a more effective speech. Once you understand the *basis* for the criticism you will be in a better position to incorporate suggestions into your future public speaking efforts.

Giving Criticism

The following suggestions should assist you, as a listener, in giving helpful and acceptable criticism.

Say Something Positive. Remember that egos are fragile and that public speaking is extremely personal, especially for the beginning speaker. We all want compliments. We are all like Noel Coward when he said, "I love criticism just as long as it's unqualified praise." Recall that part of your function as a critic is to strengthen the already positive aspects of someone's public speaking performance. Positive criticism is particularly important in itself but is almost essential as a preface to negative comments. In fact, my own practice is to make only positive comments on all first speeches, not to give grades, and in general to use the critical period to build a positive and a supportive atmosphere to strengthen the positive aspects. I reserve the more complex negative criticism for future speeches. There are enough positive characteristics to occupy considerable time, and it is more productive to concentrate on them first.

Be Specific. In any criticism, you should help the speaker improve his or her public speaking efforts. You achieve this by being as specific as you can. To say, "I thought your delivery was bad" or "I thought your examples were good" does not specify what the speaker might do to improve delivery or to capitalize on the examples used. In commenting on delivery, refer to such specifics as eye contact, vocal volume, or whatever else is of consequence.

In giving negative criticism, specify and justify—to the extent that you can —positive alternatives. For example, "I thought the way in which you introduced your statistics was somewhat vague. I wasn't sure where the statistics came from or how recent or reliable they were. It might have been better to say something like 'The 1980 U.S. Census figures show that . . .' In this way we would know that the statistics were recent and the most reliable available."

Be Objective. Objectivity is perhaps the most difficult of all principles of speech criticism; we seem inherently subjective creatures. We see things and respond to them through our unique perceptual apparatus, an apparatus that is made up almost solely of subjective feelings, desires, preferences, prejudices, and the like. In criticizing a speech you should, first of all, acknowledge your own subjectivity, your own biases. Second, try to transcend these as best you can and see the speech as objectively as possible. If, for example, you are strongly in favor of women's right to abortion and you encounter a speech diametrically opposed to your position, you need to take special care not to dismiss the speech because of your own bias. Rather, you need to examine the speech from the point of view of the (detached) critic and evaluate, for example, the validity of the arguments and their suitability to the audience, the language of the speech, the supporting materials, and in fact all the ingredients that went into the preparation and presentation of the speech. Conversely, you need to take special care that you do not evaluate positively a speech simply because it puts forth a position with which you agree. This speech needs to be evaluated for the same factors—the validity of the arguments, the supporting materials, and so on. When evaluating a speech by a speaker you feel strongly about—whether positively or negatively—you must be equally vigilant. A disliked speaker may give an effective, well-constructed, well-delivered speech, whereas a well-liked speaker may give an ineffective, poorly constructed, poorly delivered speech.

The more strongly you feel about the speech purpose or about the speaker, whether positively or negatively, the less likely you are to be objective. In fact, you can never be totally objective. You can only strive to become more aware of your own biases and to limit their influence on your evaluations and criticisms. Keep Matthew Arnold's definition of criticism in mind. Criticism, he noted, is a "disinterested endeavour to learn and propagate the best that is known and thought in the world."

Support the Speaker During the Speech. Criticism is given not only after a speech but during it as well. As listeners in any public speaking effort, you should demonstrate support for the speaker throughout the speech. Listen attentively and otherwise respond actively. When you agree, let the speaker see that you agree by a head nod, a smile, or some other signal. To the public

BOX 27.4
Some Critical Questions

You may find the following questions useful as a checklist on the effectiveness of your own speech and as guidelines for critically evaluating the speeches of others.

A. The Subject
   1. Is the subject a worthwhile one?
   2. Is the subject relevant and interesting to the audience and to the speaker?
   3. Is the subject of benefit to the audience in some way?
B. The Purpose
   4. What is the general purpose of the speech (to inform, to persuade, to secure good will)?
   5. Is the specific purpose sufficiently narrow so that it may be covered in some depth in the time alotted?
   6. Are the general and specific purposes clear to the audience? Is this clarity (or lack of it) appropriate?
C. The Audience, Occasion, Context
   7. Has the speaker taken into consideration the age; sex; education; occupation; and religion and politics of the audience?
   8. Is the speech appropriate to the specific occasion?
   9. Is the speech appropriate to the general context?
D. Research
   10. Is the speech thoroughly researched?
   11. Do the sources appear reliable and up-to-date?
   12. Does the speaker seem to have a thorough understanding of the subject?
E. Subdivisions of the Speech
   13. Are the main subdivisions of the speech appropriate to the topic?
   14. Are these main subdivisions clear to the audience?
   15. Is there an appropriate number of main points in the speech (not too many, not too few)?
   16. Are these subdivisions related to the needs and motives of the audience?
F. Supporting Materials
   17. How is each of the main points supported?
   18. Are the supporting materials appropriate to the speech?
   19. Do the supporting materials amplify what they purport to amplify? Do they prove what they purport to prove?
   20. Are a sufficient variety of supporting materials used?
   21. Are enough supporting materials used so that each main point is clear and forceful?

G. Organization
   22. How is the speech organized? What pattern of organization is used?
   23. Is this pattern of organization appropriate to the speech topic? To the audience?
   24. Is the pattern of organization clear to the audience?
H. Style and Language
   25. Does the language used enable the audience to understand clearly and immediately what the speaker is saying? (For example, are simple rather than complex words used? Concrete rather than abstract words? Personal and informal rather than impersonal and formal language? Simple and active rather than complex and passive sentences?)
   26. Is the language offensive to any person or group of persons?
   27. Are the assertions intended to be persuasive phrased in as convincing a manner as possible?
 I. The Conclusion and Introduction
   28. Does the conclusion effectively summarize the speech? (Are the main points identified again in the conclusion?)
   29. Does the conclusion effectively wrap up the speech and provide some kind of closure?
   30. In a persuasive speech, does the conclusion help to further motivate the audience in the direction the speaker wishes?
   31. Does the introduction gain the attention of the audience?
   32. Does the introduction establish some kind of relationship between the speaker on the one hand and the audience and the topic on the other?
   33. Does the introduction provide an adequate and clear orientation?
J. Delivery
   34. Does the speaker maintain eye contact with the entire audience?
   35. Are there any distractions that will divert attention from the speech?
   36. Can the speaker be easily heard?
   37. Is the volume and rate appropriate to the audience, occasion, and topic?
   38. Are the voice and body action appropriate to the speaker?

speaker new to the experience, nothing seems worse than to look out at an audience and see total indifference written on everyone's face. So, not only is it important to say something positive after the speech, it is also important to demonstrate positiveness during the speech.

SOURCES

On audiences see, for example, Kenneth E. Andersen, *Persuasion: Theory and Practice* (Boston: Allyn & Bacon, 1971), and Paul D. Holtzman, *The Psychology of Speakers' Audiences* (Glenview, Ill.: Scott, Foresman, 1970). On audience analysis see Theodore Clevenger, *Audience Analysis* (Indianapolis: Bobbs-Merrill, 1966), and James W. Gibson and Michael S. Hanna, *Audience Analysis: A Programmed Approach to Receiver Behavior* (Englewood Cliffs, N.J.: Prentice-Hall, 1976).

The area of speaker apprehension owes most to the theoretical and experimental research of James C. McCroskey, and that of reticence to the work of Gerald M. Phillips. Both researchers have contributed significantly to our understanding of apprehension and the entire communication process. For general overviews, I would suggest James C. McCroskey, "Oral Communication Apprehension: A Summary of Recent Theory and Research," *Human Communication Research* 4 (fall 1977): 78–96, and "Classroom Consequences of Communication Apprehension," *Communication Education* 26 (January 1977):27–33, and Gerald M. Phillips, "Reticence: Pathology of the Normal Speaker," *Communication Monographs* 35 (March 1968): 39–49 and "Rhetoritherapy Versus the Medical Model: Dealing with Reticence," *Communication Education* 26 (January 1977):34–43. Another useful survey is contained in James C. McCroskey and Lawrence R. Wheeless, *Introduction to Human Communication* (Boston: Allyn & Bacon, 1976).

Discussions on voice can be found in Joseph A. DeVito, Jill Giattino, and T. D. Schon, *Articulation and Voice: Effective Communication* (Indianapolis: Bobbs-Merrill, 1975).

On criticism and evaluation, see for example, Craig R. Smith, *Speech Criticism* (Chicago: Science Research Associates, 1976). Also see Sidney B. Simon's *Negative Criticism* (Niles, Ill.: Argus Communications, 1978) for an approach to criticism that focuses on what it does to an individual and how to deal with it. On feedback see, for example, Barrie Hopson and Charlotte Hopson's *Intimate Feedback: A Lovers' Guide to Getting in Touch with Each Other* (New York: New American Library, 1976) and B. Aubrey Fisher's *Perspectives on Human Communication* (New York: Macmillan, 1978).

Most of the works on criticism and evaluation are addressed to the professional critic rather than the beginning student concerned with criticizing the speeches of fellow students and most effectively utilizing criticism received. For those who do wish more advanced reading, the following few sources should prove useful: Robert Scott and Bernard Brock, eds., *Methods of Rhetorical Criticism: A Twentieth Century Perspective* (New York: Harper & Row, 1972); Karlyn Kohrs Campbell, *Critiques of Contemporary Rhetoric* (Belmont, Cal.: Wadsworth, 1972); and Lester Thonssen, A. Craig Baird, and Waldo Braden, *Speech Criticism* (New York: Ronald Press, 1970). Dale G. Leathers considers some of the factors involved in verbal and nonverbal feedback responses. See his "The Informational Potential of the Nonverbal and Verbal Components of Feedback Responses," *Southern Speech Communication Journal* 44 (summer 1979): 331–354. For additional insight into the role of criticism in communication, see Karlyn Kohrs Campbell, "The Nature of Criticism in Rhetorical and Communicative Studies," *Central States Speech Journal* 30 (spring 1979): 4–13. For an interesting series of papers on criticism see *Western Journal of Speech Communication* 44 (fall 1980).

Experiential Vehicles

27.1 · Audience Analysis (Class)

Since most of your early speeches will be delivered in this class, it is perhaps best to start with an analysis of the class as your audience.

Take a good look at the class members and complete the following Audience Analysis Form. In most instances you will have no reliable evidence, so just make the best predictions you can.

After the form has been filled out, each of the variables should be discussed with the class as a whole so that accurate and inaccurate predictions may be discovered and so that each member will have an accurate analysis of the audience. It may be helpful to pass around a form with each of the variables listed so that each member can fill in his or her personal information, which can be conveniently tabulated.

AUDIENCE ANALYSIS FORM

1. Sex
   Identify the percentage or number of males and females; also note the most common marital status.

2. Age
   Approximately how many members are in each of these major age groups:

   _____ 17–20, _____ 21–25, _____ 26–30, _____ 31–35, _____ 36+

3. Educational Background
   Since in most college classes the educational backgrounds are very similar, note here if a significant number attended private, religious, or public schools or other colleges or whether some members attended college some years ago. Also note if members have had other educational experiences, such as music, art, or drama instruction, trade instruction, and so forth.

4. Religion and Politics
   Identify the major religious and political preferences of the class members as well as how strongly they identify with these religious and political groups.

5. Occupation/Occupational Goals
   Note the major present occupations of the class members, either part-time or full-time, as well as the professional goals of the members.

6. Attitudes
   Try to predict what the attitudes of this audience would be to the following speeches. On what specific factors do you base your predictions?

   a. speech in favor of antiabortion legislation
   b. speech against school busing to achieve racial balance
   c. speech in favor of strong censorship laws
   d. speech in favor of increasingly high college admissions requirements for new entering students
   e. speech against the current welfare system
   f. speech in favor of socialized medicine

   What kinds of speech adaptations would you make in light of this audience analysis? Be as specific as possible.

27.2   Analyzing a Mass Audience

The purpose of this experience is to familiarize you with some of the essential steps in analyzing a mass audience on the basis of relatively little evidence and in adapting various speeches to this audience.

   The class should be broken up into small groups of five or six members. Each group will be given a different magazine, and its task is to analyze the audience (i.e., the readers or subscribers) of that particular magazine in terms of the variables noted on the following analysis form and discussed in this unit. The only information the groups will have about their audience is that they are avid readers of the given magazine. Pay particular attention to the type of articles published in the magazine, the advertisements, the photographs or illustrations, the editorial statement, the price of the magazine, and so on.

   Appropriate magazines for analysis are: *Gentlemen's Quarterly, Movie Life, Ms., Playboy, Playgirl, Scientific American, Field and Stream, Family Circle, Good House-keeping, Reader's Digest, Book Digest, National Geographic.* Magazines differing widely from one another are the most appropriate ones for this experience.

   To complete the analysis, try to assess the attitude of the audience to the speeches identified in the "Attitudes" category and indicate the kinds of adaptations you would make in light of the findings of your audience analysis.

   Each group should then share their insights with the rest of the class.

AUDIENCE ANALYSIS FORM

Record here your analysis of the readers of the specific magazines assigned in terms of percentages.

1. Sex

   _____ males, _____ females

2. Age

_____ below 18, _____ 19–25, _____ 26–35, _____ 36 +

3. Educational Background
   (Note the highest level reached.)

_____ elementary school, _____ high school, _____ college, _____ graduate school

4. Religion and Politics

_____ Protestant, _____ Catholic, _____ Jew, _____ Atheist, _____ other

_____ democrat, _____ republican, _____ socialist, _____ liberal, _____ conservative, _____ communist, _____ other

5. Occupations/Occupational Goals
   (Identify the major occupations or occupational goals of the audience members.)

6. Attitudes
   Try to predict what the attitudes of this audience would be to the same speeches noted in exercise 27.1, that is:

   a. abortion
   b. school busing
   c. censorship
   d. increasingly high college admissions requirements
   e. current welfare system
   f. socialized medicine

Part Eight

Mass Communication

Unit 28

Preliminaries to Mass Communication

PRELIMINARIES TO MASS COMMUNICATION

LEARNING GOALS

After completing this unit, you should be able to:

1. define *mass communication*
2. explain the one-way process view of mass communication
3. explain the two-way selection process
4. explain the relationship between technology and the need for media
5. explain the nature of the audiences to which the media appeal
6. explain the social nature of the mass media
7. identify and explain the major forms of mass communication and the major functions each serves
8. explain the uses and gratifications approach to mass media

The topic of mass communication is introduced in this unit. First, mass communication is defined and distinguished from other forms of communication. Second, the various forms of mass communication are explored in terms of their structures and functions. Third, the audiences of mass communication are examined. Taken together these topics will provide the essential preliminaries for increasing our understanding of and our ability to effectively deal with the mass media.

A DEFINITION OF MASS COMMUNICATION

As the term implies, mass communication is a form of communication, a special kind of communication. At a very general level two characteristics of this form of communication may be considered definitional. First, mass communication is communication addressed to the masses, to an extremely large audience, an audience that is largely and generally rather poorly defined. Second, mass communication is communication mediated by audio and/or visual transmitters. Mass communication is perhaps most easily and most logically defined by its forms: television, radio, newspapers, magazines, films, books, and tapes. Mass communication is indeed all around us.

Charles Wright, in his *Mass Communication*, notes, in a somewhat more extensive definitional approach, that mass communication depends on three variables: the nature of the audience, the nature of the communication experience, and the nature of the communicator. First, the mass communication audience is a relatively large one. Second, the audience is a heterogeneous one composed of people from varied social groups and with varied and different characteristics. Third, the audience is an anonymous one; the audience member and the communicator are generally not personally known to each other. These last two characteristics need to be considered at greater length.

The mass communication experience is a public one; everyone has access to it. Unlike a talk at a bar or a classroom lecture, mass communications may be received by anyone. The communication is also rapid; the messages are sent to an audience as soon as they are received by the communicators. This characteristic of speed has a number of qualifications, however. A novel may take years to write and a television series years to put together. And yet once they are completed, there is little time lost in the transmission of the message. This rapid nature of mass communication refers most specifically to the broadcasting of news items and events. We can see fires, robberies, political rallies, and speeches while they are in progress and this, to use Marshall McLuhan's term, has turned us into a "global village" where world events are common knowledge. The communication experience is transient; the message is meant to be consumed once and it is gone. It is much like human speech in its transient, evanescent character. Although video and cassette tapes and libraries have preserved many of our mass communications and have enabled us to see television shows and read messages again and again, the general nature of mass communication seems to be transient.

The nature of the communicator is that of a complex organization that goes to great expense to construct and transmit the communication messages. Television programs are put together by enormous teams of people. Even this book, although written by one person, was put together by an entire staff of people. An editor signed up the book; a designer was needed to select the typefaces and design the pages. Photographers were needed to take the pictures. Typesetters and printers were needed to compose and print the actual pages. Proofreaders and editors were needed to see that typographical and grammatical errors did not remain. A production editor coordinated the various efforts of the entire staff. People were needed to design the advertisements, and salespeople were needed to sell it. Bookstores had to stock it, and teachers had to order it for you to have it now. A book such as you are now reading might cost the publishers $35,000 to produce. Although this seems like a great deal, recall that it took millions to produce *Cleopatra* or *Bluebird*, and how many even remember these films? Although mass communications cost a great deal to produce, they cost the receiver or consumer very little, at least in direct cost. Books are perhaps the most expensive media products, because the price of a book must meet the entire cost of production. It costs us nothing to watch a television program or to listen to a radio show because the consumer pays for the shows indirectly by purchasing the advertisers' products. The advertiser assumes the direct cost of the communications through the purchase of "air time" for commercials.

Rivers, Peterson, and Jensen, in their *The Mass Media and Modern Society*, offer five general characteristics of the process nature of mass communication; these should help to further clarify the nature of mass communication.

1. Mass communication is essentially one-way, going from source or sources to receivers, whereas in interpersonal communication, on the other hand, communication goes from source to receiver and then from receiver back to source and continues to alternate between the parties involved. In mass communication the messages flow from the media to the receivers but not back again, except in the form of letters to the editor, audience ratings, box office receipts, and the like. It is true, as Nicholas Johnson says, that we can talk back to our television sets, but we can only do so indirectly and with considerable delay, at least with network television. This special kind of message (feedback) is discussed at length in Unit 30.

2. There is a two-way selection process involved. The first part of this selection process refers to the media selecting that portion of the total population that it will attempt to make its audience. For example, the media might attempt to gain unmarried women in their twenties and thirties as their principal audience, and so will direct their messages to this particular group of people. The second part of this selection process refers to the selection, from all the media available, of that particular subsection of media to which that individual will at-

tend. Some will read *Photoplay*, others will read *Ms.*, others will read *Time*, still others will read *Playboy*, and so on.

3. As technology advances, the need for different media decreases. Consider, for example, what it would take to transmit a handwritten note to a large audience across the country. Thousands of people would have to be involved, or someone would have to march across country and deliver the note to each person in turn. But with advanced technology the situation changes dramatically. One television station can reach millions at the same time, a photograph can be reproduced in the offices of every major newspaper in the country in a matter of minutes, one newspaper can be distributed throughout the country within one day's time. Put differently, relatively few media are needed to reach audiences of millions.

4. Because of the vast number of people receiving mass messages, it is impossible for the media to adapt to each person, even generally. It is necessary for the message to be directed to some "mythical modal point at which the largest number of people cluster," as Rivers, Peterson, and Jensen put it. In this way the media attempt to secure the largest number of possible receivers as their audience.

5. Mass media are social institutions that are influenced by the social environment in which they function. Conversely, the media in turn influence the social environment. There is, in other words, a transactional relationship between the media and the society; each influences the other. Thus, for example, the media influence the economic conditions of the society, but they are also influenced by the economic conditions as well. And the same transactional relationship holds for the political and educational dimensions.

FORMS OF MASS COMMUNICATION

Of the numerous forms of mass communication, seven are singled out for consideration: television, radio, newspapers, magazines, films, books, and records-tapes-cassettes.

TELEVISION

Without a doubt television is the most pervasive and the most popular of all the mass media in this country and throughout a large part of the world. Although there are many nations in which television is not as popular or as widespread as in the United States, the televisionless world is shrinking rapidly and will soon be gone completely.

It is reported that the average television set is on between 5 and 6 hours per day. This is a total of 1825 to 2190 hours per year or between 76 and 91 complete days per year. Each week this comes to 35 to 42 hours, which is approximately the amount of time people work or sleep. It is, in short, a significant and vital part of the American way of life. Although we might argue over whether it would be for the better or for the worse, we would have to agree that American life without television would be drastically different.

Although there are only 721 television stations in the United States (com-

Based on the British television program, "Till Death Us Do Part," "All in the Family,"
first televised in 1971, became popular largely through its use of taboo language and its
candid treatment of such topics as abortion, religious and ethnic prejudices, homosexuality, menopause, and swinging. Alex McNeil, in his *Total Television* (New York: Penguin,
1980), says that it is "perhaps the single most influential program in the history of
television."

pared with 4357 AM stations and 2448 FM stations), Nielsen estimates that of
the 70 million homes in the United States in 1976, 98 percent are television
homes, 81 percent are color television homes, and 48 percent have two or more
sets.

Over the past 10 or 15 years television has changed drastically, and during
the next 10 or 15 years it will change a great deal more. Cable TV, originally
designed to provide improved reception in poor reception areas, now operates to
provide more specialized programming. X-rated movies, counterculture stations
and programs, and programs directed at small groups would have been impossible without cable television. Satellite television is now an important part of television and will in the next several years increase in influence. Intelsat or Early
Bird goes back only to 1965, but today the entire world is connected through
satellite television, bringing to reality a "global village." Perhaps the development of most interest to most people is the video recorder, which provides the
viewer with control over the television rather than the television having control

BOX 28.1
30 Years of Top Television Shows

1950

Texaco Star Theatre
Fireside Theatre
Your Show of Shows
Philco Television Playhouse
The Colgate Comedy Hour
Gillette Cavalcade of Sports
Arthur Godfrey's Talent Scouts
I Remember Mama
Robert Montgomery Presents
Martin Kane, Private Eye

1960

Gunsmoke
Wagon Train
Have Gun, Will Travel
The Andy Griffith Show
The Real McCoys
Rawhide
Candid Camera
The Untouchables
The Price Is Right
The Jack Benny Program

1970

Marcus Welby, M.D.
The Flip Wilson Show
Here's Lucy
Ironside
Gunsmoke
ABC Movie of the Week
Hawaii Five-O
Medical Center
Bonanza
The F.B.I.

1980

60 Minutes
Three's Company

That's Incredible
M*A*S*H
Alice
Dallas
Flo
The Jeffersons
Dukes of Hazzard
One Day at a Time

Source: The 1950–1970 ratings are based on A. C. Nielsen Company surveys as reported in Alex McNeil, *Total Television: A Comprehensive Guide to Programming from 1948 to 1980* (Baltimore, Md.: Penguin Books, 1980). The 1980 listing was supplied by A. C. Nielsen Company.

over the viewer. Since the video recorders can tape shows at pre-set times even when the viewer is not at home, the viewer can watch shows at any time and can watch them repeatedly. With enough video recorders, reruns of popular movies would be virtually ignored, since most viewers would have already recorded *The Godfather, Jaws,* or *Gone With the Wind.* The fact that the viewer may edit out advertisements has created considerable difficulty for the advertising industry. Surely in the not too distant future television sets will come equipped with video recorders built right into the set, much like cassette players are built into stereo systems and memories are built into calculators and typewriters. Video disc players are now available and should soon become as popular as the video tape recorders.

Television is a particularly good example of what Marshall McLuhan called a "cool" medium. A "cool" medium is one that requires the audience to supply a great deal of information; a fuzzy television picture requires that the viewer fill in the missing information, and this requires active participation by the audience. A "hot" medium, on the other hand, requires little audience participation; an example would be a cinemascope movie. The distinction McLuhan drew was actually a perceptual one. The television screen presents its pictures by transmitting an enormous number of small dots of light. The central nervous system has to organize these into meaningful wholes, hence television requires active participation. McLuhan did not leave the issue of hot and cool here, however. Rather, he extended its implications to account for, for example, the tendency of the television generation to get involved actively in social issues. People raised on hot media did not feel the need to become so involved. Academically, the television generation finds lectures, however logically presented, boring; they want to become actively involved in the educational process and resent functioning solely as receptacles into which teachers pour their knowledge. Obviously not everyone agrees with McLuhan. But his theories certainly are interesting and provocative. And, as Tom Wolfe said, "What if he is right?"

RADIO

Before the advent of television radio was the dominant mass communication system. Much like families who now gather to watch the hit television shows, families used to gather to listen to the hit radio shows—"Jack Benny," "Charlie McCarthy," "The Shadow," "The Lone Ranger"—shows we remember from trivia quizzes and from stories told by those in their forties, fifties, and sixties.

Television has surely usurped the dominant role of radio, and because of this radio has had to redirect its focus. Instead of appealing to the large audience that television has permanently won over, radio has concentrated on the smaller audiences and attempts to cater to these more specialized interests—for example, opera and symphony music lovers, news enthusiasts, country and western, disco, or rock and roll fans, and so on. At the same time, radio remains dominant in those situations in which sufficient visual attention cannot be given to the media, and it serves as a kind of background noise while resting on the beach, working in the office, or driving to school. Here television cannot compete and so radio seems to be relatively secure—at least it seemed that way before the coming of tape decks and cassette players. These may eventually take over those functions radio now serves. They seem to have done this with a significant portion of the young already. And the reason for this, I think, is the lack of originality of radio. With only few exceptions radio functions to play recorded music and to a lesser extent report some news, though in a less well-researched and less carefully presented manner than even the poorest television station. Because of this lack of originality, one's own tapes and cassettes are often preferred.

Radio does apparently play an important part for youngsters who have few close interpersonal relationships. In a study of sixth-grade boys and girls, it was found that those having few close interpersonal relationships listened to radio a great deal more than did those who had greater interpersonal relationships. Further, those with few interpersonal relationships listened more for informational reasons and less for entertainment. Interestingly enough, there were no differences between those with few and those with many interpersonal relationships in their use of other media; television viewing, magazine reading, and movie attendance was the same for both groups.

Today radio represents a curious mixture of immediacy and prepackaged presentations much like television. Some radio programs are "live," but many—and these seem to be increasing—are prepackaged tapes containing music and talk, into which the local stations insert their taped commercials at appropriate times. And so what sounds like a live radio show may actually have been taped weeks earlier. The same tape may be played on hundreds of different stations at different times. This system saves a great deal of money and thus makes advertising less expensive. Hence radio advertising, although lacking the impact of television commercials, is still attractive to advertisers; for the number of people it reaches, it is relatively inexpensive.

NEWSPAPERS

Although newspapers are clearly a form of mass communication, they are less "mass" than, say, radio or television. Today, almost everyone watches television, even the highly educated who at one time resisted, and similarly almost everyone listens to the radio at least at some time. But not everyone reads newspapers. Newspapers are read by the more educated and by older people. Generally, people between the ages of 21 and 35 rely little on newspapers.

Newspapers serve two general functions. First, and perhaps most obvious, they are sources of information, about what is happening throughout the world and locally. Older and more educated readers use newspapers for this function. Part of this news is presented to persuade us to a particular point of view—a function that is clearly not limited to the editorial page. Some news deals with important political, economic, and social issues; some deals with "unimportant" gossip about TV and Hollywood stars, advice to the lovelorn, and human interest stories about lost dogs, stray cats, and kindly old people; and some tries to persuade us to buy everything from stocks and bonds to underwear and cologne and meat and potatoes. The second major function is to entertain, and it is for this function that the young and the less-educated generally use newspapers—whether that entertainment is in the arts, in sports, or in comics.

Newspapers may be classified in terms of the size of the audience they reach. First, there are general newspapers, such as *The New York Times* or the *Washington Post*. These papers are addressed to the largest segment of the population. Second, there are the local newspapers, the neighborhood weeklies or small-city dailies. Third, there are the specialized papers, which might better be called magazines, such as *Variety*, *Billboard*, and *Women's Wear Daily*. These papers are addressed to a specialized audience, and although they rely on their news value, it is news in the very specialized sense of trade information or gossip. The same seems true of the *Wall Street Journal*, which has a very large but very specialized audience. Fourth, there are publications such as the *Star* and the *National Enquirer*, which provide news but of a very limited and specialized sort—the kind that concerns itself with miraculous cures for all sorts of diseases, quick-weight-loss diets, how to earn $50,000 a year without leaving your living room, and, of course, news of movie, television, and sports personalities. Although these publications use a newspaper format and deal in a type of news, they are in many ways similar to weekly or monthly magazines. They seem to represent an attempt to combine the popular appeal elements of both newspapers and magazines into one easy-to-read paper.

Many newspapers are today faced with declining readership. When this happens advertisers put their money elsewhere. This loss of revenue forces the newspaper to cut back on various features or coverage, which further reduces their readership, which further cuts down their advertising revenues. The end result of this spiral is the closing of the paper—an event that is not uncommon today. Among the reasons people have given for their declining readership is that television news serves their needs in an easier and more efficient way; newspapers contain too much politics and too much crime, and newspapers are not personalized enough to serve their individual needs. The *New York Times* has attempted to increase readership by offering special weekday supplements to appeal to different specific interests. Supplements on sports, science, living, home, and entertainment are each offered once a week. Other papers are attempting to gain back lost readers and to secure new readers by similar methods.

This declining readership should not lead you to assume that newspapers

BOX 28.2
The 10 Daily Newspapers with Highest Circulation

New York Daily News	1,554,604
Los Angeles Times	1,024,322
The New York Times	914,938
Chicago Tribune	789,767
Chicago Sun-Times	657,275
New York Post	654,314
Detroit News	630,573
Detroit Free Press	601,721
Washington Post	601,417
Boston Globe	491,682

Source: Audit Bureau of Circulations FAS-FAX Report, March 31, 1980. Reported in *The World Almanac and Book of Facts 1981*, p. 411.

are not influential. They are. It has been estimated that something over 60 million copies of daily newspapers are sold each day. That represents a lot of news, a lot of advertisements, and, in general, a lot of influence.

MAGAZINES

Much that applies to newspapers also applies to magazines. Magazines are both general and specialized. The general magazines would include *Reader's Digest*, *TV Guide*, and *Family Circle*. The specialized magazines would include all of those that appeal to a specific and relatively small audience. For example, *Science* appeals to that relatively small group of persons concerned with sophisticated scientific developments. *Scientific American* appeals to a similar audience but one that is somewhat less specialized, almost to the general but educated reader interested in science. *Gentlemen's Quarterly* appeals to fashion-conscious men, much as *Vogue* appeals to fashion-conscious women. *Sports Illustrated, Modern Bride, Stereo Review, Road and Track, Field and Stream*, and similar magazines, as their titles imply, likewise appeal to fairly specialized interests and audiences.

Some magazines are disposed of very quickly. *Time, Newsweek, TV Guide*, and similar magazines are treated much as newspapers. Others, however, are treated more as books and are retained for long periods of time. *National Geographic, Gourmet, Architectural Digest*, and the like are retained for their visual appeal as well as for the relatively permanent nature of their articles.

Magazines are now very big business and, in fact, most of the larger magazines are owned and controlled by major corporations. Time Inc., for example, owns *Time, Life, Fortune, Sports Illustrated, People*, and *Money*. The Hearst Corporation owns *Good Housekeeping, Cosmopolitan, Harper's Bazaar, Popular Mechanics*, and *House Beautiful*. The Johnson Publishing Corporation owns *Ebony, Jet*, and

BOX 28.3
The 10 Magazines with Highest Circulation

TV Guide	18,870,730
Reader's Digest	18,193,255
National Geographic	10,560,885
Better Homes and Gardens	8,057,386
Woman's Day	7,574,478
Family Circle	7,366,482
McCall's	6,256,183
Playboy	5,746,536
Ladies' Home Journal	5,403,015
Good Housekeeping	5,138,948

Source: Audit Bureau of Circulations FAS-FAX Report, June 30, 1980. Reported in *The World Almanac and Book of Facts 1981*, p. 412.

Tan, and Condé Nast owns *Glamour, Vogue, House and Garden*, and *Mademoiselle*. Thus, although there are numerous different magazines, they are actually controlled by relatively few corporations, and the points of view—on significant political, social, and economic issues—are likewise relatively few.

FILMS

Films represent a paradox. On the one hand, television severely cuts into the profits of the movie industry, leading to the closing of numerous theaters throughout the country and to a drop in the percentage of entertainment income spent on the movies. On the other hand, films are today better than ever. Contrary to what so many people would say—namely, that they will never make films as good as those made years ago—it seems to me that the best films are being made now. The twenties, thirties, forties, and fifties have nothing to offer to compare with *Midnight Cowboy, In Cold Blood, The Godfather, Zorba the Greek, Apocalypse Now, West Side Story, Gypsy, The Hustler, A Clockwork Orange, Star Wars, Seven Beauties, The Deer Hunter, They Shoot Horses Don't They?, 2001: A Space Odyssey, Bonnie and Clyde, Taxi Driver, The Empire Strikes Back, Rocky*, and numerous others. True there are *Casablanca, Lost Weekend, Gentleman's Agreement, Gone With the Wind*, and *The Grapes of Wrath*, so perhaps it is impossible to argue for or against such a proposition. What should be obvious is that some of the most creative writing, the most expert photography, and the most ingenious music is being directed into contemporary film.

Today, films are youth-oriented and constitute one of the most convenient places for the social activities of today's teenagers. They are relatively inexpensive and easily accessible to the young. At the same time they afford the young a judicious mixture of the company of peers and yet an opportunity to maintain sufficient privacy.

BOX 28.4
The 20 Largest-Grossing Films

Star Wars (20th Century Fox, 1977)	$175,685,000
Jaws (Universal, 1975)	133,435,000
The Empire Strikes Back (20th Century Fox, 1980)	120,000,000
Grease (Paramount, 1978)	96,300,000
The Exorcist (Warner Brothers, 1973)	88,500,000
The Godfather (Paramount, 1972)	86,275,000
Superman (Warners, 1978)	82,500,000
The Sound of Music (20th Century Fox, 1965)	79,748,000
The Sting (Universal, 1973)	78,963,000
Close Encounters of the Third Kind (Columbia, 1977)	77,000,000
Gone With the Wind (MGM, 1939)	76,700,000
Saturday Night Fever (Paramount, 1977)	74,100,000
National Lampoon Animal House (Universal, 1978)	74,000,000
Smokey and the Bandit (Universal, 1977)	61,055,000
Kramer vs. Kramer (Columbia, 1979)	60,528,000
One Flew Over the Cuckoo's Nest (Universal, 1975)	59,000,000
Star Trek (Paramount, 1979)	56,000,000
American Graffiti (Universal, 1973)	55,886,000
Jaws II (Universal, 1978)	55,608,000
Rocky (United Artists, 1976)	54,000,000
Every Which Way But Loose (Warners, 1978)	51,800,000

Source: These figures are based on rental fees and are taken from *Variety* (January 14, 1981), pp. 28ff. Because these films are periodically rereleased, the figures may change radically from month to month. Figures for "gross receipts"—the amount of money taken in at the box office—are often reported in the popular press and would be much higher than rental fees, which represent the amount of money the distributor gets from the movie theaters renting the films. At the time of this writing *The Empire Strikes Back* is still playing in many first-run theaters and so its figure should change drastically. Industry predictions are that *Empire* will become the all-time largest grossing film. *Superman II* and *Raiders of the Lost Ark* are currently breaking records and will assume positions probably in the top five.

Because of the widespread popularity of television, films are attempting to do what commercial television cannot do, and perhaps the most obvious direction is in the making and showing of pornographic films. Throughout the major cities of the United States and even in the smaller, more conservative communities, the pornographic film has become extremely popular, and as the films gain even a pseudorespectability they will be shown in theaters that normally cater to *The Sound of Music* set. Eventually, of course, they will be seen on television on regular channels while they are now restricted to cable TV.

Although we often think of film as synonymous with entertainment, there are many films that serve numerous other functions, and in fact even the entertainment film does more than "just entertain." Films like *Apocalypse Now* and

The Deer Hunter showed us how horrible war really is, *Norma Rae* showed us how unskilled workers are often exploited, and *Rocky* and *Rocky II* tried to demonstrate that the "American Dream" can be a reality. But there are other films that function primarily to influence and persuade. Agee, Ault, and Emery, in their *Introduction to Mass Communications*, have this to say:

> Film is probably the most powerful propaganda medium yet devised. As a consequence, its potential for aiding or injuring civilization is enormous. In addition to supplying a verbal message through dialog, narration, or subtitles, the film provides an instantaneous, accompanying visual message—supplying the viewer with a picture to bulwark what has been learned through language. Thus, the imagination need not conjure a mental image to accompany the words; the viewer leaves the theater complete with a concept and its substantiation. If a picture is worth 1,000 words, a picture together with three or four carefully chosen words is worth 10,000 words.

The film of information is being used with considerable success in schools and business organizations. Concepts such as nonverbal communication, conference and public speaking techniques, and anatomical and physiological aspects of speech and hearing—to name just a few of those in the area of communication—are so much easier to teach with the help of films. That these films also make for greater efficiency and enjoyment seems almost universally agreed.

BOOKS

Of all the mass media, books are perhaps the most elitist. They are read by the intelligentsia of the mass communication audience, and this is true even when we add the popular pornographic pocket books to this list. Generally, people who read books earn higher incomes, have attained a higher level of education, and live in the city rather than in rural areas.

Books are both entertainment and education; they offer a historical record of the past, guidance for the present, and direction for the future. Approximately 30,000 trade books (nontexts) are issued each year; approximately 5 percent (only 1500) will sell over 5000 copies. The vast majority will fail to secure an audience and to make money.

Television is currently having some impact on book sales and book reading and in the years to come will probably have a great deal more influence. For example, some time ago Irwin Shaw's *Rich Man, Poor Man* was shown on television over a period of weeks. It proved an excellent and popular way of getting books to the general public. Its success led to the bestsellers series and to the dramatization of Alex Haley's *Roots*. *Book Digest's* current popularity seems to be due to its ability to appeal to a large group of people who want to read books but who are unwilling to invest the time required; here they have convenient summaries of the bestsellers.

RECORDS/TAPES/CASSETTES

Although not generally discussed much in works on mass communication, records, tapes, and cassettes are becoming more and more important in entertain-

515

BOX 28.5
Books: Some Records

Best-selling book: *The World Almanac and Book of Facts* (1868 to present) has sold 38,000,000 copies.

Fastest-selling book: *Guinness Book of World Records* (first published in 1955) has sold 34,000,000.

Top-selling male author: Erle Stanley Gardner has sold 304,000,000 copies of his books.

Top-selling female author: Agatha Christie has sold 300,000,000 copies of her books.

Most-printed books: *Bible*, 2,500,000,000; *Quotations from the Works of Mao Tse-tung*, 800,000,000; *The Truth That Leads to Eternal Life* (Jehovah's Witnesses), 84,000,000; *The American Spelling Book*, by Noah Webster, 75,000,000.

Best-selling novel: Jacqueline Susann's *Valley of the Dolls* (1966) has sold 20,856,000 copies.

Most-stolen book: *Guinness Book of World Records* is reportedly the most stolen book from the public libraries in Great Britain.

Largest dictionary: *The Oxford English Dictionary* contains 414,825 word listings and 1,827,306 illustrative quotations.

Largest encyclopedia: *Great Standard Encyclopedia* of Yung-lo ta tien, written by over 2,000 Chinese scholars, from 1403 to 1408, contained 22,937 manuscript books, of which 370 survive.

Source: Guinness Book of World Records, edited by Norris McWhirter (New York: Bantam, 1978).

ment and in education. Stereo records account for at least as much and probably more of the spending of college students than do books. Currently, approximately 600 million records and tapes are sold each year and account for over $2 billion in sales. The amount of money involved in this business was dramatically illustrated in the famous payola scandals of some years ago, in which promotors paid huge sums of money to disc jockeys to play their songs. A song given extensive play by an important disc jockey could mean thousands and even millions of dollars in profit for the recording company and the artist and a boost to the artist's career that would be difficult to calculate in purely financial terms. Many publishers of books are now becoming interested in the use of cassette tapes to supplement and even replace the traditional methods of presenting information.

Like film, records are designed primarily to entertain but at the same time also function to influence attitudes and values. This function is seen most clearly during times of political and social turmoil. The Vietnam War, for example, spawned numerous records directed at influencing attitudes and behaviors. Joan Baez and Buffy Sainte-Marie, for example, had considerable impact during this time, particularly with the college student. Today, there do not seem to be

BOX 28.6
Records: Some Records

The most-successful record artist: Bing Crosby sold over 300,-
000,000 records and recorded approximately 2,600 singles and
125 albums.

The most-successful recording group: The Beatles sold approximately 200,000,000 records—100,000,000 singles and 100,-
000,000 albums.

The first gold record: Enrico Caruso, *Vesti la Giubba* from *I Pagliacci*
(1902).

The most-recorded songs: *Yesterday*, written by Paul McCartney and
John Lennon, was recorded approximately 1,186 times; *Tie a Yel-
low Ribbon Round the Old Oak Tree*, written by Irwin Levine and L.
Russell Brown, was recorded approximately 1,000 times.

Biggest-selling song: *White Christmas* sold over 125,000,000.

The loudest popular group: The Who is reportedly the loudest popular group; at 50 yards from the sound system, a sound of 120 deci-
bels is produced.

The singer making the most recordings: Lata Mangeshker of India recorded some 25,000 songs in 20 Indian languages.

The most gold records: For an individual, the gold record was earned
by Elvis Presley (37), and for a group by the Beatles (42).

Best-selling album: *Saturday Night Fever*, as of mid-1978, sold over
12,000,000.

Longest best-selling album: Johnny Mathis' *Johnny's Greatest Hits*
stayed on the best-seller charts for 490 weeks (over 9 years).

Source: Guinness Book of World Records, edited by Norris McWhirter (New York:Bantam,
1978).

comparable persuasive agents. Perhaps it is because we are not engaged in a
war. Our major problems are financial, and it would seem a bit out of place for
record stars, many of whom are earning millions of dollars a year, to complain
about inflation and unemployment.

THE AUDIENCES OF MASS COMMUNICATION

The title to this section is "The Audiences of Mass Communication" because
there is really no single audience, only many different and diverse mass communication audiences. Obviously, the audience must be regarded as the single
most important element in any conception of mass communication. Marshall
McLuhan sees the audience as the center of numerous attacks by the different

media, rather like the diagram in Figure 28.1. McLuhan refers to this as a media implosion: the media are directed toward the audience and bombard the audience with all sorts of sensory stimulation.

THE MOTIVATIONS OF AUDIENCES: USES AND GRATIFICATIONS

In any given situation we may reasonably ask why an audience chooses to select a particular medium. Wilbur Schramm, in his *Men, Messages, and Media*, proposes a formula:

$$\frac{\text{Promise of reward}}{\text{Effort required}} = \text{Probability of selection}$$

Under the promise of reward Schramm includes both immediate and delayed rewards. The rewards would focus basically on the satisfaction of the needs of the audience—that is, we attend to a particular mass communication because it satisfies some need. The specific nature of these needs is covered

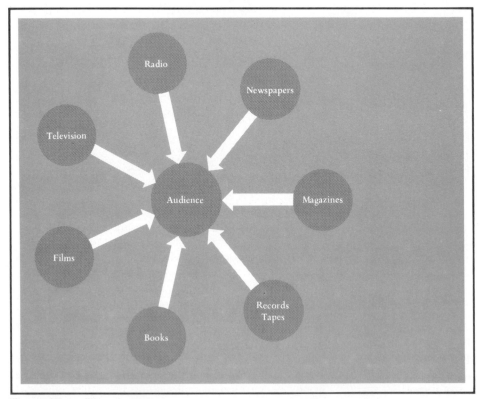

Figure 28.1   The mass media.

from a somewhat different perspective in our discussion of the functions of mass communication. The effort required for attending to mass communications may be looked at in terms of the availability of the media and the ease with which we may use the media. We must also consider such factors as the expense involved and the time investment it would take to satisfy these needs. For example, there is less effort required—less expense, less time lost, extreme ease in using the media—in watching television than in going to a movie, and there is less effort in going to a movie than there is in going to a play. When we divide the *effort required* into the *promise of reward*, we obtain the *probability of selection* of a particular mass communication medium.

This approach to media has come to be referred to as the *uses-and-gratifications approach*. It assumes that the people's interaction with the media can best be understood (1) by the uses they put the media to and (2) by the gratifications they derive from the media. This represents a distinct move away from the concentration on what the media do to people (a concentration on media effects). Typical gratifications are escape from everyday worries, relieving of loneliness, emotional support, the acquisition of information helpful in dealing with the outside world, social contact, and numerous other benefits covered more formally in the discussion of the functions of mass communication. The main assumption of the uses-and-gratifications approach is that audience members actively and consciously link themselves to certain media for certain purposes—that is, to obtain certain gratifications. The media are seen in this approach as competing with other sources (largely interpersonal) to serve the needs of the audience.

THE SUBGROUPS OF AUDIENCES

John Merrill defines three basic subgroups of audiences. The *illiterates* constitute the largest group, perhaps some 60 percent of the mass communication audience. Some of these are functionally illiterate, while others are merely attitudinally illiterate—that is, even though they are able to read they choose not to. These people rely on the picture media (television, films, etc.) rather than on the print media (newspapers, books, etc.). They are passive rather than active members of society. They are oriented to fulfilling their own needs rather than to concentrating on ideas. Economically they constitute the poorer classes.

The *pragmatists* constitute about 30 percent of the total mass audience. Unlike the illiterates the pragmatists are active rather than passive members; they are doers rather than watchers. They expose themselves to numerous different media; they watch television and go to the movies, but they also read newspapers, magazines, and books. They are ambitious and status-conscious; they seek information so that they can advance in business or in the eyes of their peers. These people are more concerned with material attainments than with ideas, and so they are the major audience the advertiser seeks.

The *intellectuals* constitute the remaining 10 percent of the entire audience. The term *intellectual* should not be taken to mean intelligent, although many of this group would normally be labeled intelligent. These people are concerned with issues, ideas, aesthetics, and philosophy rather than with material things and, as with the illiterates, the advertisers have little to work with here. Intellectuals do not care much for mass communications because they cater to the lower levels of society. This group seeks mental rather than physical or material stimulation.

We might also, along with John Merrill, distinguish between the general public audience and the specific or specialized audience. The *general public audience* includes just about everyone, and the *specialized audience* includes individuals who have something in common and who, because of this commonality, select the same media to read, listen to, or watch. The medium of television, for example, appeals to the general public, since there is something on television for everyone, but it is the specialized audiences that are appealed to by "Over Easy," "Julia Child," and "Popeye." Both audiences are heterogeneous, but the general audience is obviously more so.

Throughout this unit, the importance of the audience in mass communications was stressed. The various media survive (and usually in considerable luxury) largely because they can deliver to advertisers potential buyers for their products. This should not be taken to imply that the media serve only this function of holding the buyers' attention until an advertiser can grab their wallets. The media serve a number of other important functions as well. They entertain, educate, persuade, and perform various other functions, on which we focus in the next unit.

SOURCES

For overviews of the mass communication process I would recommend a number of general works. Perhaps the best introduction to the area is Wilbur Schramm's *Men, Messages, and Media: A Look at Human Communication* (New York: Harper & Row, 1973). Another excellent overview is Melvin L. DeFleur's *Theories of Mass Communication*, 3d ed. (New York: David McKay, 1975). Two books of readings that are particularly useful are Wilbur Schramm, ed., *Mass Communications: A Book of Readings*, 2d ed. (Urbana, Ill.: University of Illinois Press, 1960), and Wilbur Schramm and D. F. Roberts, eds., *The Process and Effects of Mass Communication*, rev. ed. (Urbana, Ill.: University of Illinois Press, 1971). For information on the audiences of mass communication, see Schramm's *Men, Messages, and Media*, cited above; and John C. Merrill and Ralph L. Lowenstein, *Media, Messages, and Men: New Perspectives in Communication* (New York: David McKay, 1971); and William L. Rivers, Theodore Peterson, and Jay W. Jensen, *The Mass Media and Modern Society*, 2d ed. (San Francisco: Rinehart Press, 1971). An excellent anthology devoted to television is Horace Newcomb, ed., *Television: The Critical View* (New York: Oxford University Press, 1976). The study of radio and interpersonal relationships was conducted by Joseph R. Dominick, "The Portable Friend: Peer Group Membership and Radio Usage," *Journal of Broadcasting* 18 (spring 1974): 161–170. An excellent overview of mass communication is provided by Joseph M. Foley," Mass Communication Theory and Research: An Overview," in Dan Nimmo, ed., *Communication Yearbook 3* (New Brunswick, New Jersey: Transaction Books, 1979), pp. 263–270. For an interesting analysis of the differences between the audiences of books and television see Howard Gardner, "Reprogramming the Media Researchers," *Psychology Today* 13 (January 1980): 6–14. For an in-depth analysis of one particular type of audience see Bruce A. Austin, "Portrait of a Cult Film Audience: The Rocky Horror Picture Show," *Journal of Communication* 31 (spring 1981): 43–54.

Experiential Vehicles

28.1   Models of Mass Communication

The purpose of this exercise is to further sensitize you to the essential elements and processes involved in the mass communication act. The class should be divided into groups of five or six members. Each group should then select one of the mass communication situations listed below and construct a diagrammatic model of the elements and processes involved. That is, each group should retrace (in the form of a model) the essential elements and processes that were prerequisites or prior steps to one of the behaviors listed below. In other words, identify those things that had to be done before one could watch a film or TV commercial, read a magazine article, listen to the car radio, and so on.

Be sure to include, as a minimum, *source, encoder, channel, noise, decoder, receiver, feedback, message, context*, and *effect*. Note that in mass communication situations there will be several sources, messages, effects, and so on.

1. watching a movie
2. watching a TV commercial
3. reading a magazine article on offshore oil
4. listening to the top 40 on a car radio
5. reading the morning newspaper's account of yesterday's bank robbery
6. listening to a new record album

28.2   Creating an Advertisement

The purpose of the following exercise is to highlight a few of the many factors that must be taken into consideration in constructing a persuasive advertisement. The advertisements may be constructed individually or by groups of five or six persons. In either case the completed advertisements should be shared with the entire class.

Create an advertisement for a new product—for example, a caffeine-free tea or a nicotine- and tar-free cigarette. Create your advertisement for a full-page ad in general interest magazines, such as *Time, Family Circle, Life*. Draw this advertisement or use pictures cut from magazines. In constructing this ad, keep the following questions in mind.

1. What will you name the product? Why?
2. How will the package be designed? Shape? Color? Type of construction?
3. What kind of advertising copy will you use? That is, what will the ad say?
4. Will you create a catch phrase, like, for example, "It's the real thing" or "Come to Marlboro Country"? What is the advantage of such phrases? What will your catch phrase be?
5. Will you use a noted personality in the ad? Who? Why? Would this personality differ if you were appealing to special interest groups reading, for example, *Vogue, Sports Illustrated, Rolling Stone?* Explain.
6. What objects (if any) will you include in the ad? That is, do you want the product to become associated with certain objects? For example, ads for expensive liquors are often set in drawing rooms, club rooms, and elegant dining rooms amid other symbols of status.
7. What general image will you attempt to create for the product?
8. What media would you select to advertise the product most effectively? That is, if you were an advertiser with a limited budget, where would you put your money? If you select radio or television, when would the ads appear? On what programs? If you select newspapers, which ones would you use? If billboards, where would they be most effective?

Unit 29

The Functions of Mass Communication

THE FUNCTIONS OF MASS COMMUNICATION

Entertain
Reinforce
Change or Persuade
Educate
Confer Status
Activate
Narcotize
Create Ties of Union
Ethicize
   29.1 Television and Values

LEARNING GOALS

After completing this unit, you should be able to:

1. identify and explain at least six functions of mass communication
2. provide at least one example of how the media perform each of the functions identified
3. explain the distinction between functional and dysfunctional effects of the media
4. define the narcotizing and the ethicizing functions of the media

The popularity and pervasive influence of the mass media can only be maintained by its serving significant functions. Nine of the most important functions are to entertain, to reinforce, to change or persuade, to educate, to confer status, to activate, to narcotize, to create ties of union, and to ethicize.

I purposely offer such an extensive list of functions—rather than following the standard practice of discussing three or four functions—in order to sensitize you to the numerous ways in which the mass media impinge on our everyday lives. These nine functions are not all equal in importance, nor does each mass communication event necessarily serve all these functions. Rather, all nine functions are significant to an understanding of mass communication, and each mass media event possesses the potential for serving any or all of these functions.

As will become obvious throughout the discussion, these functions often overlap and interact with each other. It is doubtful, for example, that a communication could change an individual's attitudes or behaviors without also educating or focusing attention. These functions of the media are also the reasons why people attend to the media.

ENTERTAIN

If you were to ask the typical television or film viewer why he or she watched television or went to the movies, the answer would probably involve something about being entertained. Similarly, if you asked typical people why mass media exist, they would say something about the media being designed to entertain. And it is true that the media design their programs to entertain. In reality, of course, they are attempting to entertain in order to secure the attention of as large a group as possible so that they may in turn sell this attention to advertisers. This seems to be the major reason why mass communications exist. They exist so that they may sell viewers to advertisers. In societies where the state supports the media, the process is different. In our society, however, if the media did not entertain, they would no longer have viewers or readers and would quickly be out of business. At least this is true for the most part. Certainly, many books are published that are not primarily for entertainment—dictionaries, reference books, textbooks, and the like are not designed primarily to entertain. Yet take a close look at your current textbooks. Notice all the features designed to entertain—the colors used, the fancy typefaces, the pictures. All these features and more are designed to secure the attention of an audience so that a publisher may in turn sell that attention to instructors or to a school system.

REINFORCE

It is difficult in any situation to convert someone from one attitudinal extreme to another, and the media, with all the resources and power at their disposal, are no exception. For the most part the media rarely achieve conversion, but they do function to reinforce or make stronger our beliefs, attitudes, values, and opinions. Democrats will expose themselves to democratic persuasion and will emerge reinforced from the experience. Similarly, religious people will expose themselves to messages in line with their beliefs and will emerge reinforced or stronger in their convictions.

The problem the media face in achieving something beyond reinforcement, of course, is that we are the ones who choose the messages to which we will attend, and we generally do not choose to expose ourselves to messages that may contradict our existing belief structure.

This reinforcement view applies to situations in which people are relatively polarized in their beliefs, values, and opinions. The media will achieve some conversions with those who are in the middle on any individual dimension. Thus, those who are torn between the Republicans and the Democrats may well find themselves converted to one side or the other on the basis of the media's messages.

Even those communications we think are changing attitudes are often only reinforcing existing ones. For example, it had long been assumed that "All in the Family" was changing attitudes toward prejudice and stereotyping. The entire program was assumed by many to be a satire on prejudice. Archie, in particular, was assumed to be close to an idiot who was constantly being put down by his daughter and son-in-law. But the studies that have been done on this show and similar shows indicate that this is not the case. For example, Neil Vidmar and Milton Rokeach, in their study "Archie Bunker's Bigotry," found that the show reinforces rather than reduces racial and ethnic prejudice. "The data," note Vidmar and Rokeach, "seem to support those who have argued that the program is not uniformly seen as satire and those who have argued that it exploits or appeals to bigotry."

Another aspect of this function is that we actively search out the reinforcement that the media provide. Thus, people who continue to smoke, although they may have nagging doubts and feelings that they should quit, may well seek out cigaret advertisements in the newspapers and magazines. These advertisements will reinforce their behavior by telling them, in effect, that their behavior is just fine; cigarets are low in tar and nicotine and in the process they are getting all this pleasure. Who could resist?

CHANGE OR PERSUADE

While the media do not function primarily to change our behavior or to persuade us, they do perform this function at times and in certain situations. Changes or conversions seldom occur with extremists, but they do occur with the middle-of-the-roaders.

BOX 29.1
The Advertising Code of American Business

1. *Truth* . . . Advertising shall tell the truth, and shall reveal significant facts, the concealment of which would mislead the public.
2. *Responsibility* . . . Advertising agencies and advertisers shall be willing to provide substantiation of claims made.
3. *Taste and Decency* . . . Advertising shall be free of statements, illustrations or implications which are offensive to good taste or public decency.
4. *Disparagement* . . . Advertising shall offer merchandise or service on its merits, and refrain from attacking competitors unfairly or disparaging their products, services or methods of doing business.
5. *Bait Advertising* . . . Advertising shall offer only merchandise or services which are readily available for purchase at the advertised price.
6. *Guarantees and Warranties* . . . Advertising of guarantees and warranties shall be explicit. Advertising of any guarantee or warranty shall clearly and conspicuously disclose its nature and extent, the manner in which the guarantor or warrantor will perform and the identity of the guarantor or warrantor.
7. *Price Claims* . . . Advertising shall avoid price or savings claims which are false or misleading, or which do not offer provable bargains or savings.
8. *Unprovable Claims* . . . Advertising shall avoid the use of exaggerated or unprovable claims.
9. *Testimonials* . . . Advertising containing testimonials shall be limited to those of competent witnesses who are reflecting a real and honest choice.

Source: Developed and initially distributed by: the Advertising Federation of America; the Advertising Association of the West; the Association of Better Business Bureau, Inc. Reproduced by permission of the American Advertising Federation.

Minor behavior changes, however, are frequent. The changes in our toilet-paper-buying behavior may well be greatly or even totally influenced by the media; but except to toilet paper manufacturers, few people care about which toilet paper is used. Similarly, we may choose stuffing instead of potatoes, Revlon instead of Hazel Bishop, or L'Oreal instead of Toni, but in the total scheme of things these decisions matter little. Political preferences, religious attitudes, social commitments, and the like, however, are not so easily changed.

However, once an attitude is formed or a behavior pattern is established, the media function to canalize it—to channel it in specific directions. For example, once the pattern of paying $30 to $40 for a pair of jeans is established, the media can relatively easily function to channel that behavior, that value, to Vanderbilt, Calvin Klein, Sasson, or in fact to any jean with a high price tag, preferably a tag that can be easily seen, as it can on all the popular best-selling jeans.

BOX 29.2
Women in Advertising

The following excerpt is taken from the report Advertising and Women: A Report on Advertising Portraying or Directed to Women, *prepared by a Consultive Panel of the National Advertising Review Board.*

What the Panel Recommends

The Panel offers no hard and fast rules for dealing with advertising appealing to or portraying women. The scene is changing too rapidly. Accordingly, we have not attempted to compile a list of current ads that the Panel thinks merit praise or criticism.

Recognizing that principles are more enduring than specific cases, the Panel has distilled its many months of study into a checklist of questions for advertisers and agency personnel to consider when creating or approving an advertisement. We realize that there will probably be differences of opinion about some of the items on this checklist, but we believe that whatever discussion may be stimulated by the controversial ones will be helpful in clarifying the issues.

Checklist: Destructive Portrayals

- Am I implying in my promotional campaign that creative, athletic, and mind-enriching toys and games are not for girls as much as for boys? Does my ad, for example, imply that dolls are for girls and chemistry sets are for boys, and that neither could ever become interested in the other category?
- Are sexual stereotypes perpetuated in my ad? That is, does it portray women as weak, silly, and overemotional? Or does it picture both sexes as intelligent, physically able, and attractive?
- Are the women portrayed in my ad stupid? For example, am I reinforcing the "dumb blonde" cliché? Does my ad portray women who are unable to balance their checkbooks? Women who are unable to manage a household without the help of outside experts, particularly male ones?
- Does my ad use belittling language? For example, "gal Friday" or "lady professor"? Or "her kitchen" but "his car"? Or "women's chatter" but "men's discussions"?
- Does my ad make use of contemptuous phrases? Such as "the weaker sex," "the little woman," "the ball and chain," or "the war department"?
- Do my ads consistently show women waiting on men? Even in occupational situations, for example, are women nurses or secretaries serving coffee, etc., to male bosses or colleagues? And never vice versa?

BOX 29.2 (*Continued*)

- Is there a gratuitous message in my ads that a woman's most important role in life is a supportive one, to cater to and coddle man and children? Is it a "big deal" when the reverse is shown, that is, very unusual and special—something for which the woman must show gratitude?
- Do my ads portray women as more neurotic than men? For example, as ecstatically happy over household cleanliness or deeply depressed because of their failure to achieve near perfection in household tasks?

(A note is needed here, perhaps. It is not the Panel's intention to suggest that women never be portrayed in the traditional role of homemaker and mother. We suggest instead that the role of homemaker be depicted not in a grotesque or stereotyped manner, but be treated with the same degree of respect accorded to other important occupations.)

- Do my ads feature women who appear to be basically unpleasant? For example, women nagging their husbands or children? Women being condescending to other women? Women being envious or arousing envy? Women playing the "one-upmanship" game (with a sly wink at the camera)?

- Do my ads portray women in situations that tend to confirm the view that women are the property of men or are less important than men?

- Is there double entendre in my ads? Particularly about sex or women's bodies?

Checklist: Negative Appeals

- Do my ads try to arouse or play upon stereotyped insecurities? Are women shown as fearful of not being attractive to men or to other women, fearful of not being able to keep their husbands or lovers, fearful of an in-law's disapproval, or, for example, of not being able to cope with a husband's boss coming for dinner?

- Does my copy promise unrealistic psychological rewards for using the product? For example, that a perfume can lead to instant romance?

- Does my ad blatantly or subtly suggest that the product possesses supernatural powers? If believed literally, is the advertiser unfairly taking advantage of ignorance? Even if understood as hyperbole, does it insult the intelligence of women?

BOX 29.2 (*Continued*)

Checklist: Constructive Portrayals

- Are the attitudes and behavior of the women in my ads suitable models for my own daughter to copy? Will I be happy if my own female children grow up to act and react the way the women in my ads act and react?
- Do my ads reflect the fact that girls may aspire to careers in business and the professions? Do they show, for example, female doctors and female executives? Some women with both male and female assistants?
- Do my ads portray women and men (and children) sharing in the chores of family living? For example, grocery shopping, doing laundry, cooking (not just outdoor barbecuing), washing dishes, cleaning house, taking care of children, mowing the lawn, and other house and yard work?
- Do the women in my ads make decisions (or help make them) about the purchase of high-priced items and major family investments? Do they take an informed interest, for example, in insurance and financial matters?
- Do my ads portray women actually driving cars and showing an intelligent interest in mechanical features, not just in the color and upholstery?
- Are two-income families portrayed in my ads? For example, husband and wife leaving home or returning from work together?
- Are the women in my ads doing creative or exciting things? Older women, too? In social and occupational environments? For example, making a speech, in a laboratory, or approving an ad?

Checklist: Positive Appeals

- Is the product presented as a means for a woman to enhance her own self-esteem, to be a beautiful human being, to realize her full potential?
- Does my advertisement promise women realistic rewards for using the product? Does it assume intelligence on the part of women?

Source: From *Advertising and Women: A Report on Advertising Portraying or Directed to Women* by a Consultive Panel of the National Advertising Review Board, 1975. Reprinted by permission of the National Advertising Review Board.

EDUCATE

When we think of education we generally think of a formal school situation, with a teacher in front of the classroom and the students taking notes, hoping to get down on paper what will eventually appear on an examination. But most of the information we have has been attained not from the schoolroom but from the media. We have learned music, politics, film, art, sociology, psychology, economics, and a host of other subjects from the media and not from high school or college classrooms. We learn about other places and other times much more effectively from seeing a good movie than from reading a history textbook.

One type of education is to teach the viewers the values, opinions, and rules that society judges to be proper and just. That is, part of the educational function of the media is directed at socializing the audience. They do this in stories, in discussions, in articles, in comics, in advertisements and commercials. In all these situations, the values of the society are expressed in an almost unspoken manner. We are taught how to dress for different occasions, the proper way to eat, what a proper meal should consist of, how to hold a discussion or conversation, how to respond to people of different national and racial groups, how to behave in strange places, and so on.

One of the nice things about learning from the media is that it is less "painful" than learning in schools (at least in too many cases). One of the not so nice things about education from the media is that it is slanted; it is education with a bias that is carefully hidden. For example, during the oil crisis we were educated to the great profits OPEC was making but were left relatively ignorant concerning the profits of the oil companies. The education the media concerns itself with is the education that will return a profit. The media support those issues or slant their education so that an audience is delivered to the advertiser who in turns supports the media. And so while it is comforting to have "60 Minutes" in prime time, it is there primarily (perhaps only) because it delivers an audience that the network can sell to the advertiser at a substantial profit.

CONFER STATUS

If you were to list the 100 most important people in the world, they would undoubtedly be people who have been given a great deal of mass media exposure. Without such exposure, the people would not in fact be important, at least not in the popular mind. Paul Lazarsfeld and Robert Merton, in their famous "Mass Communication, Popular Taste, and Organized Social Action," put it this way: "If you really matter, you will be at the focus of mass attention and, if you are at the focus of mass attention, then surely you must really matter." Conversely, of course, if you do not get mass attention, then you do not matter, and if you do not matter, then you do not get mass attention.

Consider the guests on a show like "Tonight" (Johnny Carson). They actually get paid very little, at least in comparison with what they would normally get for performing. Yet, they get mass exposure that is perhaps more financially rewarding than getting their normally high salaries. In effect, they are made national personalities from this type of exposure.

The media can also confer status (or perhaps in this case, "focus attention" is a better phrase) on issues and problems. The media in effect tell us what is

Dolly Parton is an excellent example of the influence of television in conferring (or enlarging) status. Her national and even international fame was due in great part to television shows like Johnny Carson's which proved an ideal medium for capturing Parton's personality, humor, and talent. Her television fame led to an even more productive record and concert career and to films.

and what is not important. Wilbur Schramm in *Men, Messages, and Media* explains this function well:

> A reasonable hypothesis is that the most powerful effect of the mass media on public knowledge—comparable even to the effect of the realism with which it can present distant events and places—is the ability of the media to focus public attention on certain problems, persons, or issues at a given time. This may be an effect controlled in part by people who are able to use the media skillfully, but it is clearly important. It feeds the conversation that goes on interpersonally. It stimulates other viewing, listening, or reading. It encourages reporters to dig deeper and commentators to interpret a problem in great depth.

Notice the things we think are important. They are in fact the very things on which the media concentrate. The obvious question is whether they are important and the media, therefore, concentrates on them, or whether the media concentrates on them and they, therefore, become important. What does seem clear is that the media surely do lead us to focus attention on what they focus attention on.

ACTIVATE

From the advertiser's point of view, the most important function is to activate — to move to action. Put simply, the media function to get the viewer to buy the bread, to use Gillette, to choose Brut and not Canoe, and in general to make all the decisions we think so trivial but that advertisers and manufacturers consider important. The advertisers' objective is to get us to buy their product and not someone else's, as well as to buy their product instead of nothing. Room deodorizers, for example, should be a substitute for cleanliness though it is never put in these terms. If we did not buy what advertisers want us to buy, they would no longer pay for the time or space to advertise, and we would no longer have the variety of media we now have.

NARCOTIZE

One of the most interesting and the most overlooked functions of the media is the narcotizing function. This refers to the media's function of providing the receiver with information that is in turn confused, by the receiver, with doing something about something. The individual is drugged into inactivity as if under the influence of a narcotic. As Lazarsfeld and Merton explain it:

> The individual reads accounts of issues and problems and may even discuss alternative lines of action. But this rather intellectualized, rather remote connection with organized social action is not activated. The interested and informed citizen can congratulate himself on his lofty state of interest and information and neglect to see that he has abstained from decision and action. In short, he takes his secondary contact with the world of political reality—his reading and listening and thinking—as a vicarious performance. He comes to mistake *knowing* about problems of the day with *doing* something about them.

Lazarsfeld and Merton term this *dysfunctional* rather than functional "on the assumption that it is not in the interest of modern complex society to have large masses of the population politically apathetic and inert." And with five or six hours of television viewing each day, there is little wonder that knowledge of problems and issues is confused with or is a substitute for action.

CREATE TIES OF UNION

One of the functions of mass communication that few people ever think of is the ability of the media to make us feel like a member of a group. Consider the lone television viewer, sitting in his or her apartment watching television while eating a TV dinner. The television programs make this lone soul feel a part of some larger group. Whether the individual is watching members of his or her own racial group, or those who think or worship as he or she does, the viewer is made to feel a part of this larger and, by virtue of the media coverage, important group of people. These ties of union, however, are artificial; the viewers are not joined with others; they only think that some connection is established between them and the actors on the small screen.

Many viewers develop what are called "parasocial" relationships with media personalities and even with dramatic characters and will see these people or characters as friends and advisers. As a result of this perceived relationship, viewers may wave to an actor whom they see on the street as if they are friends, write to a television doctor or lawyer for medical or legal advice, and send warning letters to their "friends" who are about to be murdered on the latest soap opera. As can be expected, these parasocial relationships are more important to those who spend a great deal of time with the media and who have few interpersonal relationships.

The media, however, also function to establish the opposite of union and relationships—namely, what is referred to as privatization, a tendency for an individual to retreat from social groups into a world of his or her own. Some theorists have proposed that the tremendous quantities of information almost forced upon us by the media may overwhelm us and make us feel inadequate to deal with it. The wars, the inflation, the crime rate, the robberies, the deterioration in housing, the unemployment make some people feel so inadequate, so helpless in dealing with or changing such issues that they retreat into their own private worlds to concentrate on matters that they can control. In many cases, this takes the form of concentrating on the trivial, on issues and problems that are really insignificant in the total scheme of things—about the problems of getting the apartment painted, about which pair of designer jeans to buy, about what restaurant to go to for dinner.

ETHICIZE

By making public certain deviations from the norms, the media arouse people to change the situation. They provide viewers with a collective ethic or ethical system. For example, without the media coverage of Watergate, it seems unlikely that there would have been such a public outcry over the events that eventually led Richard Nixon to resign.

> In mass society [note Lazarsfeld and Merton, writing some 15 years before Watergate], this function of public exposure is institutionalized in the mass media of communication. Press, radio, and television expose fairly well known deviations to public view, and as a rule, this exposure forces some degree of public action against what has been privately tolerated. The mass media may, for example, introduce severe strains on polite ethnic discrimination by calling public attention to these practices that are at odds with the norm of nondiscrimination. At times, the media may organize exposure activities into a "crusade."

In evaluating and analyzing these general functions of the media we should keep in mind at least three related issues. First, each time we turn on the television, read a newspaper, or listen to a radio, we do so for a *unique* reason. Each and every mass communication event serves a unique function, a function at least a little bit different from every previous function. Second, every mass communication event serves a different function for each individual viewer-reader-listener. The same television program may serve to entertain one person, to educate another, and to narcotize still another. Third, we should recognize that the functions served by any mass communication event for any individual will be different from one time to the next. Where a particular record once served to entertain, it may now function to socialize or to create ties of union.

Earlier it was pointed out that the narcotizing function of the media is a dysfunctional one in the sense that it is detrimental to the social system; it hinders rather than fosters development and needed change. Actually, all nine functions may be viewed from a functional-dysfunctional perspective. For example, the media as entertainment are generally viewed as functional or positive; the media provide viewers with convenient, inexpensive entertainment much needed after a day's work. On the other hand, the steady and constant flow of entertainment may prove dysfunctional in its discouraging people to engage in interpersonal communication, to study, to learn, to work, and so on. The media's conferral of status is functional if those gaining the status prove deserving and socially productive but dysfunctional if they prove undeserving and socially unproductive. Each of the nine functions, then, should be seen as neither positive or negative but as functional or dysfunctional to a certain degree. Even the most noble purpose may have some dysfunctional aspects, and even the most negative may have some functional aspects.

Each of the nine functions should also be viewed in terms of their being manifest or latent. Robert Merton introduced these terms in his influential *Social Theory and Social Structure* in 1957. Manifest functions are those that the media intend; they are purposeful functions. Latent functions, on the other hand, are unintended; these are functions that the media accomplish but did not intend to. For example, an advertisement may have as its manifest function the selling of a certain soap, but it may also influence our attitudes toward the role of women in society. By portraying only women in soap advertisements, the ad is teaching us values and attitudes concerning women, and this is its latent function. You would be hard-pressed to identify a mass media message that did not have both manifest and latent functions.

SOURCES

On the functions of mass communication see Charles R. Wright, *Mass Communication: A Sociological Perspective*, 2d ed. (New York: Random House, 1975); Paul F. Lazarsfeld and Robert K. Merton, "Mass Communication, Popular Taste, and Organized Social Action," in Lyman Bryson, ed., *The Communication of Ideas* (New York: Harper & Row, 1951), pp. 95–118, and reprinted in Wilbur Schramm and D. F. Roberts, eds., *The Process and Effects of Mass Communication*, rev. ed. (Urbana, Ill.: University of Illinois Press, 1971), pp. 554–578; and Wilbur Schramm, *Men, Messages, and Media: A Look at Human Communication* (New York: Harper & Row, 1973). I relied on all three of these excellent works.

For a somewhat different perspective see Frank E. X. Dance and Carl E. Larson, *The Functions of Human Communication: A Theoretical Approach* (New York: Holt, Rinehart and Winston, 1976). For the study on "All in the Family" cited in the text and a review of previous studies in this area see Neil Vidmar and Milton Rokeach, "Archie Bunker's Bigotry: A Study in Selective Perception and Exposure," *Journal of Communication* 24 (winter 1974): 36–47. On the reasons why people attend to the media see John C. Merrill and Ralph L. Lowenstein, *Media, Messages, and Men: New Perspectives in Communication* (New York: David McKay, 1971), and Bradley S. Greenberg, "Mass Communication and Social Behavior," in Gerhard J. Hanneman and William J. McEwen, eds., *Communication and Behavior* (Boston: Addison-Wesley, 1975), pp. 268–284. For a provocative discussion of media influences on cognitive processes, see Gavriel Salomon, *Interaction of Media, Cognition, and Learning* (San Francisco: Jossey Bass, 1979). On media advertising and ethics see Quentin J. Schultze, "Professionalism in Advertising: The Origin of Ethical Codes," *Journal of Communication* 31 (spring 1981): 64–71.

Experiential Vehicle

29.1 Television and Values

Listed below are eight values that were found to be significant among college students in a Daniel Yankelovich survey and reported in Barry Tarshis, *The "Average American" Book* (New York: Atheneum/SMI, 1979). The percentage figures represent the proportion of the respondents who identified the value as "very important."

1. self-fulfillment, 87 percent   _____

2. education, 76 percent   _____

3. family, 68 percent   _____

4. hard work, 43 percent   _____

5. having children, 31 percent   _____

6. religion, 28 percent   _____

7. money, 20 percent   _____

8. patriotism, 19 percent   _____

Examine the list of values and next to each value identify one, two, or three television characters who best seem to exemplify that value. After you have identified at least one character for each value, the entire class should pool their results and discuss them, considering some or all of the following questions. It may facilitate discussion if the values are written on the blackboard and some of the more frequently named characters were listed next to the value. Do not read any further until you have identified the several characters requested above.

1. Are there any sex differences? That is, do male and female characters exemplify the same or different values? What are the implications of these similarities or differences for television serving an educational function? reinforcing function? persuasive function?
2. Are there differences based on age, race, religion, or nationality? Again, what are the implications of these similarities or differences?
3. What type of character would you like to see achieve some prominence on television? For example, at the least identify the sex, race, nationality, reli-

gion, occupation, affectional preference, age, intelligence level, marital status, and general physical condition of the character you would like to see on television. What values would you like to see this character embody? What media functions would you particularly like to influence?

4. What type of character would you like to see less of on television? Identify specific characters. Why?

5. Are the characters in the movies similar to those on TV? Explain the reasons for the differences (if any).

6. Television characters seem not to have achieved the kind of prominence that many characters in novels and dramas have. For example, Scarlett O'Hara, Huck Finn, Willie Loman, George and Martha, and so many others have achieved a level of prominence that television characters rarely, if ever, achieve. What factors might account for these differences in universal and lasting fame? One possible exception that comes quickly to mind is Archie Bunker. Are there other "exceptions"?

Unit 30

The Flow of Mass Communication

THE FLOW OF MASS COMMUNICATION

LEARNING GOALS

After completing this unit, you should be able to:

1. explain the two-step and the multistep flow-of-communication hypotheses
2. explain the concept of diffusion of information
3. identify some of the essential characteristics of opinion leaders
4. define *gatekeeping*
5. provide examples of the gatekeeping process
6. identify at least four characteristics of mass media feedback
7. identify some of the issues relating to the depiction of sex and violence on television

In this final unit, the interaction of audience and mass media is explored. Specifically, we examine the ways in which the media have an effect on their audiences and the ways in which audiences have an effect on the media. In addition, the issues of violence and sex—perhaps the two most controversial media issues—are explored in terms of their possible effects on individuals and on society in general and the questions which these issues raise for freedom of communication.

FROM MEDIA TO AUDIENCE

THE FLOW OF MASS COMMUNICATION

Perhaps the issue in mass communication creating the most interest in the popular mind is the way in which mass communication has an effect on people's thoughts and behaviors. One obvious explanation of this is that people read the newspapers or watch television or listen to the radio and are persuaded by what they read, see, and/or hear and, as a result, change their thoughts and behaviors. This explanation, which postulates a rather direct relationship between the media and the individual, might be referred to as a one-step flow model; the messages go only one step, from media to reader-viewer-listener. But this explanation is too simple and perhaps not as accurate as we would want.

A somewhat more sophisticated proposal was presented by Paul Lazarsfeld, Bernard Berelson, and Helen Gaudet in their *The People's Choice.* In this study of the voters in the 1940 presidential election these Columbia University researchers found that people were influenced more by other people and less by the mass media (then primarily newspapers and radio). Those who did the influencing were termed opinion leaders. Mass communications, the researchers proposed, do not affect the people directly. Instead of this one-step process, they proposed a two-step process, in which messages from the mass communications influence opinion leaders and these opinion leaders then influence the general population in more interpersonal situations. Elihu Katz, in his 1957 "The Two-Step Flow of Communication: An Up-to-Date Report on an Hypothesis," concluded that "most opinion leaders are primarily affected not by the communication media but by still other people."

As Wilbur Schramm has noted, the two-step flow concept, although useful and revealing, is perhaps a bit too simple. For one thing it is not always true; much of our information comes right from the media, whether television, newspapers, or magazines. As the media become more and more a part of our everyday life, they grow as our initial source for information on a variety of issues.

Second, the concept of an opinion leader must be looked at in terms of degree and not in either-or terms. Some opinion leaders are more opinion leaders than others. Some are leaders of leaders, whereas others are leaders only of followers. Some leaders therefore get their information from the media, while others get their information from other leaders.

Third, and perhaps most important, is that the flow of communication seems more reasonably characterized as a reciprocal process rather than a step process. That is, there seems more of a back and forth process from the media to people to the media to people and so on. We may hear about something on television, then talk to a friend about it, then hear about it again on the evening news, then read about it in the morning newspaper, and then talk about it with friends at work. This especially seems true today, with media so much a part of our lives. It also seems logical in terms of the finding that people who expose themselves to one medium will often expose themselves to other media as well. Inevitably the same issues and news items will be covered in the different media, and we must further assume that interpersonal interaction occurs in between.

In short, a multistep flow model of mass communication seems much more accurate in describing what happens in opinion and attitude formation. Some people get their information and their opinions directly from the media; others get them from interpersonal interactions; still others get them from a combination of sources.

THE DIFFUSION OF INFORMATION

Closely related to the flow of communication is the concept of the diffusion and adoption of innovations. *Diffusion* refers to the new information, the innovation, or the new process as it passes through the society at large or through the relevant social system. The innovation may be of any type—for example, contact lenses, calculators, electric typewriters, food processors, behavioral objectives in teaching, experiential learning, multimedia instruction. *Adoption* refers to individuals' positive reactions to the innovation and its incorporation into their habitual behavior patterns. In the process of adoption McEwen (in Hanneman and McEwen) identifies three general stages:

1. *Information acquisition* —the information relevant to the innovation is secured and understood (for example, a teacher learns about a new approach to teach mass communication).
2. *Information evaluation* —the information relevant to the innovation is evaluated as good or bad or anywhere in between these extremes (for example, the teacher recognizes that the new method is more effective than the old).
3. *Adoption or rejection* —the innovation is either adopted or rejected by the individual (for example, the teacher begins to teach mass communication by this new method).

Obviously all people do not choose to adopt or reject the innovation at the same time. Researchers in the area of information diffusion generally distinguish five types of adopters (Figure 30.1).

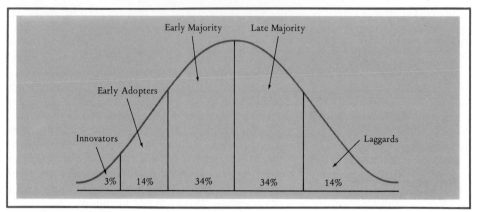

Figure 30.1   The five types of adopters as represented in the population.

1. **Innovators.** These are the first to adopt the innovation and constitute less than 3 percent of the total population. The innovators are not necessarily the originators of the new idea; rather, they are the ones who introduce the idea on a reasonably broad scale.

2. **Early Adopters.** These people adopt the innovation next and make up about 14 percent of the total population. Sometimes called "the influentials," these people legitimize the idea and make it acceptable to people in general.

3. **Early Majority.** These adopt the innovation next and constitute about 34 percent. This group follows the influentials and further legitimize the innovation.

4. **Late Majority.** This group also constitutes about 34 percent of the total population and are next-to-last in adopting the innovation. People in this group may follow either the influentials or the early majority.

5. **Laggards.** This group is the last to adopt the innovation and constitutes about 14 percent of the total population. People in this group may take the lead from people in any of the previous three groups.

These five groups constitute almost 100 percent of the population. The remaining portion are referred to as "diehards," and these are people who never adopt the innovation. These are the cooks who never use the blender or the food processor, the teachers who refuse to use audiovisual materials in their teaching, the doctors who refuse to use newly discovered medication, and so on. There are some instances in which there are no diehards. For example, teachers may wish to continue using a particular textbook, but when it goes out of print, they are forced to change and join the group of laggards.

It has been found that early as opposed to late adopters—the innovators as compared with the laggards—generally are younger, are of a higher socioeconomic status, have more specialized occupations, are more empathic, are less dogmatic, are most oriented toward change, make more use of available information, are closer to the actual agents of change, have a more cosmopolitan orientation, and are generally opinion leaders.

OPINION LEADERS

Throughout the discussions of the flow of communication and the diffusion of information, the concept of the opinion leader was noted. We need to elaborate here on this important person. The opinion leader is different from the people who are influenced in a number of important ways, ways that clearly distinguish this person from others. Opinion leaders have been found to have more formal education, to have greater wealth, to be of higher social status, and to have greater exposure to mass communications than those they influence. They also participate in social activities to a greater extent and are more innovative, cosmopolitan, competent, and accessible than those they influence.

Possessing these characteristics does not ensure that someone will become an opinion leader, and yet, when opinion leaders are studied, they are found to possess these characteristics. If you look at the people to whom you turn for opinion leadership, you will probably find that they possess a good number of the characteristics noted. We would hardly turn to someone who was less competent, who had less formal education, and who was less innovative (to name just a few characteristics) than ourselves for opinion leadership. These characteristics, it should be emphasized, are all relative. The opinion leader does not possess these characteristics in an absolute sense but rather possesses them to a greater extent than the individual who is influenced. Thus, for example, a graduate student in economics might be looked to by some people for opinion leadership concerning inflation and taxes. The graduate student possesses more formal education and more competence than those seeking such information. But that same graduate student would hardly be looked to for this opinion leadership by the graduate faculty in economics of Harvard or Yale.

Much as opinion leaders differ from the people they influence, they also differ from one another. Some opinion leaders, for example, are cosmopolitan, whereas others are local. The cosmopolitan leader is concerned with national and international issues. Today, as I write this, the cosmopolitan leader would be concerned with such issues as the killings of children in Atlanta, the possible Russian invasion of Poland, the powers of the C.I.A., Indira Gandhi's renewed influence, and the Palestinian issue. The local opinion leader, on the other hand, is concerned with issues that are more immediate, more localized. The issues with which a local opinion leader would be concerned today would depend on where that leader was. If in New York this leader might be concerned with rent increases, fuel costs, Yankee Stadium, and millions of possible issues that are less than national or international in scope. These issues, it should be emphasized, are not necessarily unimportant; rather, they are simply of concern to less people than the issues the cosmopolitan leader deals with. The cosmopolitan leader is generally restricted to one field of expertise, whereas the local leader is generally more broadly based, extending through several different and diverse fields of knowledge. A cosmopolitan leader might, for example, be restricted to economic issues, to Central American affairs, or to Soviet-American relations. A local opinion leader is looked to for guidance and information on a broad variety of issues. Robert Merton introduced the terms *monomorphism* and *polymorphism* to highlight this distinction. The terms are, in a way, self-explanatory. *Monomorphism* refers to the tendency to serve as a leader for one topic (for example, national politics, contemporary fiction, carpentry); monomorphism generally characterizes cosmopolitan leaders. *Polymorphism,* on the other hand, refers to the tendency for a leader to serve as a leader for a number of different topics; polymorphism generally characterizes local opinion leaders.

GATEKEEPING AND GATEKEEPERS

In the passage of a message from the source of mass media to the actual individual viewer or listener there intervenes what is referred to as a gatekeeper. The term *gatekeeping* was originally used by Kurt Lewin in his *Human Relations* (1947) to refer to (1) the process by which a message passes through various gates as well as to (2) the people or groups that allowed the message to pass (gatekeepers). Gatekeepers may be individual persons or a group of persons through which a message passes in going from sender to receiver. A gatekeeper's main function is to filter the messages that an individual receives. Teachers are perfect examples of gatekeepers. Teachers read the various books in an area of study, read various journal articles, listen to convention papers, talk among themselves about developments in the field, and conduct their own research in the field. From all this information they pass some of it on to the students and, at the same time, prevent other information from getting through to the students. In the passage of the information from researchers to students, the teacher in effect filters what he or she knows about an area of study. A cameraperson is another clear example of a gatekeeper. From all that he or she can possibly photograph, certain areas are selected for photographing and then are shown to the viewers. Editors of magazines and publishing houses are gatekeepers; they allow certain information to get through and not other information.

Everyone functions to some extent as a gatekeeper. For example, of all the messages that come to you during the day, you select certain of these to be passed on to, say, your parents, your friends, your teachers, and so on. In passing them on, you may modify them in any number of ways for any number of reasons. Other messages may not be passed on at all; these may be messages that are too insignificant to repeat or those that are too personal and become your secrets. In mass media discussions the term *gatekeeping* is used to refer to individuals or groups operating in relatively formal communication systems (for example, newspapers, television stations, education) whose gatekeeping activities have significant social implications. These gatekeepers are generally from the "preferred" social class—they tend to be highly educated and come from the "right" schools, have high income, and are generally white males.

The gatekeeper, then, limits the messages that we receive. The teacher, for example, limits the information the students receive. Without the teacher, however, the students would learn a great deal less. The teacher expands the informational awareness of the students through his or her distillation of the material, organization of the information, and analysis of the findings and results of study. That is, without gatekeepers we would not get half the information we now receive.

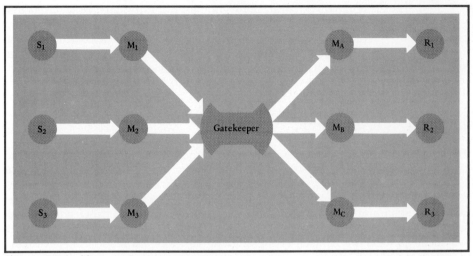

Figure 30.2   The gatekeeping process.

We might diagram the gatekeeping process as in Figure 30.2. Note that the messages (M_1, M_2, M_3) received by the gatekeeper come from various different sources (S_1, S_2, S_3), so one of the functions the gatekeeper serves is to select the messages to be communicated and reject the ones that will not be allowed to pass. The gatekeeper then transmits numerous messages (M_A, M_B, M_C) to different receivers (R_1, R_2, R_3) and, it should be noted, may transmit certain messages to some receivers and other messages to other receivers. Teachers, for example, do not pass on the same messages to different classes: advanced courses get very different messages from elementary courses. Perhaps the most important aspect to note about this process is that the messages received by the gatekeeper (M_1, M_2, M_3) are not the same as the messages the gatekeeper sends (M_A, M_B, M_C); the extent to which they differ is the measure of the gatekeeper's changes.

FROM AUDIENCE TO MEDIA: FEEDBACK

Letters to the editor of a newspaper or magazine, sales of a novel or textbook, Nielsen ratings for "Taxi" or "The Incredible Hulk," sales for Charmin toilet tissue and Lipton tea, book reviews appearing in professional journals or in the daily newspapers, receipts for *Superman II* and *The Empire Strikes Back*, subscriptions to *Cosmopolitan* and *Penthouse*, and numerous other responses to the mass media are mass communication feedback. As already noted, feedback is information that is fed back to the source from the receiver and which in turn tells the source something about how his or her messages are being received. In interpersonal communication, this feedback is immediate and can result in an almost instantaneous adjustment of the message by the source. In mass communication, the feedback is of quite a different nature.

Ray Hiebert, Donald Ungurait, and Thomas Bohn in their *Mass Media* distinguish six characteristics of feedback in mass communication. These six characteristics will enable us to distinguish feedback in mass communication from feedback in interpersonal, small group, or public speaking situations and at the same time will help to define the nature of mass communication in more specific detail.

REPRESENTATIVE

Because the audiences of mass communication are so large and so scattered throughout a huge area, it is impossible to secure feedback from all viewers or listeners. Instead a sample is selected, which ideally is representative of the entire audience. This sample, it should be noted, is extremely small in comparison with the total number in the real audience. In order to record this feedback television sets are equipped with electronic devices that record the programs watched, as with the Nielsen ratings; telephone calls are made to secure reactions; or perhaps a studio audience is given a questionnaire to fill out. In all these cases, the individuals from whom feedback is sought are ideally supposed to represent the entire audience. Before this textbook was published, it was reviewed by a number of different communication teachers. These reviewers, it was assumed, were representative of the entire audience of communication teachers, and what the reviews had to say was assumed to be representative of what this larger audience would say had they been asked. Similarly the students who read and commented on earlier versions of this book were considered representative of the college student audience throughout the country.

INDIRECT

In interpersonal communication, the feedback from a receiver goes directly to the source, at least usually. In some interpersonal communication situations, the receiver may talk with a third party about a conversation he or she had with the source, and the source may then hear about this person's reactions from still another person. The feedback here would be indirect. In most interpersonal situations, however, the feedback is direct. As a source you can read the feedback from the receiver—you can see the puzzled looks or the smiles, you can hear the words of agreement, the questions, or the disagreements—without the intervention of a third party. With mass communication, however, the situation is different. Consider your responses to an editorial in *The New York Times*. You may send a letter to the paper, but the editor will probably only read your letter if it gets published in the paper through some third party. Or the editor may be given summary statistics; for example, of the 250 letters received on Tuesday's editorial on domestic affairs, 200 expressed disagreement, 30 expressed agreement, and 20 asked for further clarification. Similarly our responses to M*A*S*H do not go directly to the stars or the producer but are filtered through some third party—a program director, an agent, or some such paid intermediary.

DELAYED

Perhaps the most important characteristic of mass communication feedback is its delayed nature. Mass communication feedback is almost always delayed, perhaps by days, perhaps by weeks, perhaps by months or even years. Surveys, censuses, and the like take enormous amounts of time to complete, so the results are never immediate. Sales records for a new product or a new advertising campaign may take months to compile. Generally, the more detailed the analysis or feedback, the more delayed it will be.

Because of this delayed nature, mass communication feedback results not in immediate changes in the messages of the media, as in interpersonal communication, but rather in long-range changes or alterations.

Recently, however, *The New York Times* (November 21, 1980) reported the remarkable success of Warner Amex Cable Communications in winning franchises for cable television. The main reason for their success has been Qube, which has already been put into operation in Columbus, Ohio, and which will surely become popular in other cities as well. Unlike other media systems Qube enables the cable television audience to participate immediately in various television programs. For example, viewers may give immediate feedback on television political polls, may participate in quiz shows, and in some cases even order shopping by means of a small keypad that permits them to communicate their responses without delay to the media.

Feedback to the media in general is still largely delayed. But these recent developments in interactive technology force us to qualify this characteristic and lead us to predict that, at least with cable television, the feedback will become less and less delayed over the next decade.

INSTITUTIONALIZED

Because of the difficulty in securing accurate and reliable feedback from the mass media audience, it is necessary to engage sophisticated research organizations in the task. A. C. Nielsen's organization for obtaining feedback on the number of viewers watching various television programs is perhaps the most well-known example. The various public opinion polls such as Gallup, Harris, and Roper are also conducted by relatively complex organizations and are representative of the institutionalized nature of feedback-obtaining organizations.

QUANTITATIVE

Mass communication feedback involves so much data from so many different people that it must be put into quantitative form if it is to be useful in redirecting the messages of the source. If Oldsmobile wishes to advertise its new cars in various publications, it must know the type of audience that reads the particular magazine under consideration. It needs to know, for example, the economic status of the readers—their median income, the number earning, say, over $30,000 per year, the number owning their own homes; their locations—the part of the country in which they live and whether they are urban or rural residents; their educational levels—the number who are high-school and college graduates and the number who are currently attending school; the sex breakdown—the number of men and the number of women. It needs to know these data and many more before it invests $30,000, $40,000, $50,000, or more for a single page in a popular magazine. Data such as these would be impossible to handle were they not in quantitative form. Book reviews, on the other hand, would be an example of qualitative feedback. If a publisher wished to buy the paperback rights to a book, it might first, however, want these reviews put in quantitative form—specifically, it will wish to know how many reviews were favorable and how many were unfavorable.

CUMULATIVE

Feedback in mass communication may be cumulative or noncumulative. An example of noncumulative feedback might be the reaction of an audience to a particular segment of a comedy series, say "WKRP in Cincinnati." This is helpful to the program directors and to everyone concerned with the show, yet it is not as important as cumulative feedback, which would entail responses from a large number of people over a long period of time—say, an entire season. Thus, the responses to the Jefferson family while they were on "All in the Family" that

Your opinion really does count.

BOX 30.1
The 10 Largest U.S. Advertisers

Procter and Gamble Co.	$614 million
General Foods Corporation	393 million
Sears, Roebuck & Co.	379 million
General Motors Corporation	323 million
Philip Morris	291 million
K-Mart	287 million
R. J. Reynolds Industries	258 million
Warner-Lambert Co.	220 million
AT & T	219 million
Ford Motor Co.	215 million

Source: Based on figures reported in *Advertising Age* (September 11, 1980); expenditures are for the year 1979.

were relevant to the producers were the cumulative feedback. In other words, one would need to be sure that the Jefferson family were well received over a long period of time before the time and money to create a new series were invested. The Ropers on "Three's Company" proved themselves popular for quite some time before they were launched into their own series. Similarly, before a new detective series is launched, the audiences' cumulative feedback toward detective series would be secured. Generally, cumulative feedback results in influencing long-range decisions, whereas noncumulative feedback will result in influencing short-range decisions.

VIOLENCE AND SEX: SOME MEDIA ISSUES

While granting that there are considerable individual differences, it seems reasonable to postulate that there is one basic ruling criterion for determining what gets on the television screen, produced at the major film studios, and into the magazines and newspapers. And that ruling criterion is the number of viewers-readers-listeners that the medium can deliver to the advertiser or to the box office. With only few exceptions, the networks, film studios, and magazines and newspapers present those messages that will draw an audience and do not present those that will not draw an audience. Federal and local laws have led to some minor modifications; yet, for all practical purposes, this seems the general rule followed.

It should also be clear, from looking through our newspapers, from seeing recent films, and from watching television that violence and sex deliver the audience and hence will not only remain but will increase in frequency and degree of vividness. This relationship seems fairly easy to postulate and to document; whatever brings in a profit is increased to bring in a bigger profit. But most people are not concerned with the profit that a television station or newspaper makes. Rather people are concerned with the effects of violence and sex on the audience. Thousands of studies have been conducted on these issues, and it would be impossible to summarize even a small portion of them here. What is important is to raise some crucial issues concerning effects and to increase our awareness of how the media operate and influence our attitudes and opinions and ultimately our behaviors.

Perhaps the practical issues need to be raised first. What constitutes violence? When is sex obscene? In *Miller* v. *California* the Supreme Court in a 5-to-4 vote concluded that something should be judged obscene or nonobscene on the basis of "(1) whether the average person, applying contemporary community standards, would find that the work taken as a whole appeals to the prurient interest; (2) whether the work depicts or describes in a patently offensive way, sexual conduct specifically defined by the applicable state law; and (3) whether the work taken as a whole lacks serious literary, artistic, political, or scientific value."

Because of the difficulty in formulating clear and unambiguous guidelines, and the resultant general statements such as the one formulated by the Supreme Court, the question of what constitutes obscenity has not been answered to everyone's satisfaction and still arouses considerable controversy. Even if we could determine what constitutes obscenity, we would still not be able to answer the more important questions pertaining to its effect and what, if anything, should be done about it. Thus, even if we could determine that certain sex acts are obscene, it would not necessarily follow that these acts lead to obscene behavior in viewers.

For years the questions about sex on television have been phrased in a manner that invited negative responses: Does the depiction of sex lead to a breakdown in moral behavior? Does the depiction of sex encourage young people to experiment before they can understand the consequences of their behavior? Does sexual behavior on the screen lead to promiscuous behavior? But note that we might also state the questions from a different perspective: Does the portrayal of sex teach people how to relate to one another more effectively? Do depictions of rape educate viewers about how to fight off rape attacks, lead to a greater willingness to talk about rape experiences, and encourage greater understanding of the victim of rape as well as of the rapist? Do depictions of sexual behavior help to relieve guilt feelings that inhibit effective and honest sexual relationships?

Similar issues have been raised in regard to violence. What constitutes violence is just as difficult to define as obscenity and, again, even if we had a workable definition, it would still not be possible to answer the other and more meaningful questions. Does the depiction of violence lead to actual violence? Does the portrayal of violence lead people to suppress their violent behavior? Is the vicarious experience of violence enough to dissipate violent tendencies? Do depictions of violence teach viewers how to avoid violence, to defend themselves against violence, and to understand the causes of violence? Does the depiction of violence lead to abnormal fear?

George Gerbner and his associates, for example, have contended that people who watch a great deal of violence in the media develop "paranoid reactions" and that they respond to the world as it is depicted in the media rather than as it really is. This "paranoid effect" has been much debated and is not universally accepted. In fact, in an exploration of this effect in Great Britain, no evidence for it was found, and it was suggested that even in the United States this effect may not exist.

Even if we could determine some of the effects of obscenity and violence, we would still have to weigh the advantages and disadvantages of censorship against the losses to be derived from restrictions on our basic constitutional rights of free speech. Is it worth restricting our rights to free speech to prevent a movie from being made or shown or to have a television show canceled?

Although violence and sex are used as examples, it should not be thought that these are the only instances in which negative effects on the audiences may be expected. For example, as we noted earlier it has been found that the prejudice of Archie Bunker does not—in the minds of many viewers—poke fun at prejudice but actually reinforces the prejudice of others. Should Archie Bunker, therefore, be taken off the air? *Roots* depicted the cruelty and violence done to blacks by both whites and blacks. Should *Roots* have been taken off the air? There is obviously no end to the questions that might be asked or to the types of programs about which they might be asked. We might even ask the very same questions about the news, situation comedies, and even cartoons.

In this final unit an attempt has been made to explain the flow of media messages, from the media to the audience and from the audience to the media. Some of the media issues relating to the depiction of sex and violence in television and film were discussed in an attempt to further clarify the transactional relationship existing between media and audience. Especially today, we are in large part products of the media; the media influence us in hundreds of ways. They influence our attitudes, our beliefs, our values, what we know, what we think is important or unimportant, our level of satisfaction or dissatisfaction, and so on. And, of course, the audience (we) influence the media; the media exist as they do largely as a result of their audience's responses. The ways in which we respond to the media—buying or not buying the advertised products, viewing one program rather than another, seeing one movie and not another—largely determine the nature of the media.

One of our priorities, it seems, should be to influence the media in ways that are productive and beneficial to us and to the society as a whole. Although not an easy task, it is certainly worth the effort. After all, what is the alternative?

SOURCES

For the discussion of gatekeeping and feedback I relied heavily on the work of Ray Eldon Hiebert, Donald F. Ungurait, and Thomas W. Bohn, *Mass Media: An Introduction to Modern Communication* (New York: David McKay, 1974). For the two-step hypothesis see Paul F. Lazarsfeld, Bernard Berelson, and Helen Gaudet, *The People's Choice* (New York: Duell, Sloan and Pearce, 1944) and Elihu Katz, "The Two-Step Flow of Communication: An Up-to-Date Report on an Hypothesis," *Public Opinion Quarterly* 21 (spring 1957): 61–78. For the diffusion of information discussion see E. M. Rogers and F. F. Shoemaker, *Communication of Innovations: A Cross-Cultural Approach* (New York: Free Press, 1971). Nan Lin, in *The Study of Human Communication* (Indianapolis: Bobbs-Merrill, 1973), also provides an excellent summary of this area.

A great deal has been written on the violence issue. See, for example, the exchange between David M. Blank and George Gerbner in *Journal of Broadcasting* 21 (1977): 273–305 and J. M. Wober, "Televised Violence and Paranoid Perception: The View from Great Britain," *Public Opinion Quarterly* 42 (fall 1978): 315–321. A summary of ongoing research is presented by George Gerbner, Larry Gross, Michael Morgan, and Nancy Signorielli, "The 'Mainstreaming' of America: Violence Profile No. 11," *Journal of Communication* 30 (summer 1980): 10–29. A useful collection of articles relevant to the issues raised throughout the discussions of mass communications is Gerhard J. Hanneman and William J. McEwen, eds., *Communication and Behavior* (Boston: Addison-Wesley, 1975).

Experiential Vehicle

30.1 Character Development on the Small Screen

The class should be divided into groups of five, six, or seven individuals. Each group should examine the list of characters presented below and attempt to identify at least one strength and one weakness in each of these characters. Record these conclusions in the appropriate spaces. After all groups have completed the identification of these characteristics, the groups should pool their insights and consider some or all of the following questions.

1. Do male and female characters possess different strengths and weaknesses? If so, in what ways are these characters different?
2. What are or might be the effects of these differences on viewers' perceptions of themselves? On viewers' perceptions of significant others? Put more generally, are these characters influential? Do they influence you? Which ones? In what ways? Are your friends, parents, siblings, or intimates influenced by these characters? Which ones? In what ways?
3. Do young and old characters possess different strengths and weaknesses? Explain. What are the implications of these differences?

Character	Strength	Weakness
Hawkeye, "M*A*S*H"		
Jennifer, "WKRP in Cincinnati"		
Billie, "Lou Grant"		
Jack, "Three's Company"		
Tom, "Eight Is Enough"		
Mary, "Soap"		
Ralph, "Greatest American Hero"		
Bo, "Dukes of Hazzard"		
Benson, "Benson"		
J.R., "Dallas"		
Vera, "Alice"		

Roarke, "Fantasy Island"   _____   _____

Flo, "Flo"   _____   _____

Jennifer, "Hart to Hart"   _____   _____

Chrissy, "Three's Company"   _____   _____

Glossary

Listed here are definitions of the technical terms of communicology—the words that are peculiar or unique to this discipline. These definitions should make new or difficult terms a bit easier to understand. For the most part the words included here are used in this text. Also included, however, are terms that, although not used here, may be used in the conduct of a course in communication.

Abstraction A general concept derived from a class of objects; a part representation of some whole.

Abstraction process The process by which a general concept is derived from specifics; the process by which some (never all) characteristics of an object, person, or event are perceived by the senses or included in some term, phrase, or sentence.

Accent The stress or emphasis that is placed on a syllable when pronounced.

Accommodation A state of cold-war conflict; a condition in which the parties, although still in conflict, agree not to battle; a state in which the conflicting individuals have adjusted to each other's position and in which interpersonal communication may take place though real cooperation is absent.

Action language Movements of the body—for example, the way one walks, runs, sits.

Adaptors Nonverbal behaviors that, when emitted in private or in public without being seen, serve some kind of need and occur in their entirety—for example, scratching one's head until the itch is eliminated.

Adjustment, principle of The principle of verbal interaction that claims that communication may take place only to the extent that the parties communicating share the same system of signals.

Affect displays Movements of the facial area that convey emotional meaning —for example, anger, fear, and surprise.

Allness The assumption that all can be known or is known about a given person, issue, object, or event.

Ambiguity The condition in which a word or phrase may be interpreted as having more than one meaning.

Arbitrariness The feature of human language that refers to the fact that there is no real or inherent relationship between the form of a word and its meaning. If we do not know anything of a particular language, we could not examine the form of a word and thereby discover its meaning.

Argot A kind of *sublanguage;* cant and jargon of a particular class, generally an underworld or criminal class, which is difficult and sometimes impossible for outsiders to understand.

Attention The process of responding to a stimulus or stimuli.

Attitude A predisposition to respond for or against an object.

Attraction The state or process by which one individual is drawn to another, by having a highly positive evaluation of that other person.

Authoritarian leader A group leader who determines the group policies or makes decisions without consulting or securing agreement from group members.

Balance A state of psychological comfort in which all the attitude objects in our minds are related as we would want them to be or as we would psychologically expect them to be.

Batons Body movements that accent or emphasize a specific word or phrase.

Belief Confidence in the existence or truth of something; conviction.

Bit of information The amount of information that is necessary to divide the possible alternatives in half. If, for example, you are trying to guess which number will be chosen from 1 to 8, and you are told that it will not be 1, 2, 3, or 4, then one bit of information has been communicated, since it reduced the number of alternatives by half.

Blindering A misevaluation in which a label prevents us from seeing as much of the object as we might see; a process of concentrating on the verbal level while neglecting the nonverbal levels; a form of *intensional orientation.*

Body English Popularly, *tactile communication.*

Body language A form of nonverbal communication in which messages are communicated by gesture, posture, spatial relations, and so forth; all aspects of nonverbal communication.

Brainstorming A technique for generating ideas among people.

Bypassing A misevaluation caused when the same word is used but each of the individuals gives it different meaning.

Cant A kind of *sublanguage;* the conversational language of a special group, which is generally understood only by members of the subculture.

Censorship Legal restrictions imposed on one's right to produce, distribute, or receive various communications.

Certainty An attitude of closed-mindedness that creates a defensiveness among communication participants; opposed to *provisionalism.*

Channel The vehicle or medium through which signals are sent.

Channel capacity The maximum amount of information that a communication system can handle at any given time.

Cliché An expression that is overused and calls attention to itself; a description of a man as "tall, dark, and handsome" would be a cliché.

Closed-mindedness An unwillingness to receive certain communication messages.

Code A set of symbols used to translate a message from one form to another.

Codifiability The ease with which certain concepts may be expressed in a given language.

Cognitive complexity The state of having numerous different concepts for describing people.

Cohesiveness The property of togetherness. Applied to group communication situations, it refers to the mutual attractiveness among members; a measure of the extent to which individual members of a group work together as a group.

COIK Acronym for "clear only if known," referring to messages that are unintelligible for anyone who does not already know what the messages refer to.

Communication (1) The process or act of communicating; (2) the actual message or messages sent and received; and (3) the study of the processes involved in the sending and receiving of messages. (The term *communicology* (q.v.) is suggested for the third definition.)

Communication gap The inability to communicate on a meaningful level because of some difference between the parties—for example, age, sex, political orientation, religion.

Communication network The pathways of messages; the organizational structure through which messages are sent and received.

Communicology The study of communication and particularly that subsection concerned with human communication.

Competence *Language competence* is a speaker's ability to use the language; a knowledge of the elements and rules of the language. *Communication competence* refers to the rules of the more social or interpersonal dimensions of communication and is often used to refer to those qualities that make for effectiveness in interpersonal communication. See *performance*.

Competition An interpersonal process in which persons strive to attain something and at the same time to prevent others from attaining it.

Conditioning An approach to the control of behavior in which the learning or unlearning of behaviors is dependent on their consequences.

Conflict An extreme form of competition in which a person attempts to bring his or her rival to surrender; a situation in which one person's behaviors are directed at preventing or interfering with or harming another individual.

Connotation The feeling or emotional aspect of meaning, generally viewed as consisting of the evaluative (for example, good-bad), potency (strong-weak), and activity (fast-slow) dimensions; the associations of a term. See *denotation*.

Consonance A psychological state of comfort created by having two elements (for example, cognitions or beliefs), one of which follows from the other.

For example, consonance would exist for the following two cognitions: (1) X is healthy, (2) I engage in X.

Context of communication   The physical, psychological, social, and temporal environment in which communication takes place.

Cooperation   An interpersonal process by which individuals work together for a common end; the pooling efforts to produce a mutually desired outcome.

Cosmopolitan leader   An opinion leader who is concerned with national and international (as opposed to local) issues. See *local leader.*

Credibility   The degree to which a receiver perceives the speaker to be believable. See *ethos.*

Credibility gap   A tendency between or among people to disbelieve each other and to doubt the honesty and integrity of each other; the difference between the image a person tries to convey (highly positive) and the image a receiver perceives (usually less positive), which is often taken as a measure of the extent to which the public image is disbelieved.

Culture   The knowledge concerning the appropriate and inappropriate patterns of thoughts and behaviors of a group.

Date   An extensional device used to emphasize the notion of constant change and symbolized by a subscript: for example, John Smith$_{1972}$ is not John Smith$_{1982}$.

Decoder   That which takes a message in one form (for example, sound waves) and translates it into another code (for example, nerve impulses) from which meaning can be formulated. In human communication, the decoder is the auditory mechanism; in electronic communication the decoder is, for example, the telephone earpiece. See *encoder.*

Decoding   The process of extracting a message from a code—for example, translating speech sounds into nerve impulses. See *encoding.*

Delayed reactions   Reactions that are consciously delayed while the situation is analyzed; a symbol reaction.

Democratic leader   A group leader who stimulates self-direction and self-actualization of the group members.

Denotation   Referential meaning; the objective or descriptive meaning of a word. See *connotation.*

Derived credibility   See *intrinsic credibility.*

Determinism, principle of   The principle of verbal interaction that holds that all verbalizations are to some extent purposeful, that there is a reason for every verbalization.

Dialect   A specific variant of a language used by persons from a specific area or social class; dialects may differ from the "standard" language in phonology, semantics, or syntax, but they are intelligible to other speakers of the language.

Differential probability hypothesis   The theory that high-frequency behaviors may be used to reinforce low-frequency behaviors.

Digital communication   Communication signals that are discrete rather than continuous; opposed to *analogic communication.*

Directive function of communication   Communication intended to persuade; communication that serves to direct the receiver's thoughts or behaviors.

Disconfirmation   The process by which one ignores or denies the right of the individual even to define himself or herself.

Discreteness   The feature of human language that refers to the fact that the sounds of language (that is, the phonemes) are discrete categories of sound. Any given sound is either one particular phoneme of the language or another; it cannot be partly one phoneme and partly another.

Displaced speech   Speech used to refer to that which is not present or in the immediate perceptual field.

Dissonance   A psychological state of discomfort created by having two elements (for example, cognitions and beliefs), one of which would not follow, given the other. Two such elements might be "X is harmful" and "I engage in X." These two elements represent dissonance, since given one of them, the other would not follow. See *consonance.*

Dogmatism   Closed-mindedness in dealing with communications.

Duality of patterning   The feature of language that refers to the fact that language consists of two levels: the level of individual sounds (phonemic) and the level of individual meaningful units or morphemes (morphemic). Duality of patterning makes it possible for a language to consist of relatively few phonemes (about 45), which can be combined in various different ways or patterns to form an extremely large number of morphemes.

Dyadic communication   Two-person communication.

Dyadic consciousness   An awareness of an interpersonal relationship or pairing of two individuals; distinguished from situations in which two individuals are together but do not perceive themselves as being a unit or twosome.

Dynamic judgments   Perceptual judgments that refer to those characteristics of another person that change relatively rapidly. See *static judgments.*

Dysfunctional effects of mass communication   Effects of the media that are not in the interest of society.

Ectomorphy   The skinny dimension of body build.

Ego states   More or less stable patterns of feelings that correspond to patterns of behaviors; in *transactional analysis* (three such ego states are defined: *Parent ego state, Adult ego state,* and *Child ego state*).

Elementalism   The process of dividing verbally what cannot be divided nonverbally—for example, speaking of body and mind as separate and distinct entities.

Emblematic movements   *Elements* used to illustrate a verbal statement, either repeating or substituting for a word or phrase.

Emblems   Nonverbal behaviors that directly translate words or phrases—for example, the signs for O.K. and peace.

Emotive function of communication Communication that tells us something about the speaker as opposed to the external world or serves some personal need of the speaker.

Empathy The feeling of another person's feeling; feeling or perceiving something as does another person.

Encoder Something that takes a message in one form (for example, nerve impulses) and translates it into another form (for example, sound waves). In human communication the encoder is the speaking mechanism; in electronic communication the encoder is, for example, the telephone mouthpiece. See *decoder*.

Encoding The process of putting a message into a code, for example, translating nerve impulses into speech sounds. See *decoding*.

Endomorphy The fatty dimension of body build.

Entropy A measure of the extent of disorganization or randomness in a system. Entropy is a measure of the degree of uncertainty that a destination has about the messages to be communicated by a source. Entropy is high if the number of possible messages is high and low if the number of possible messages is low.

E-Prime A form of the language that omits the verb *to be* except when used as an auxiliary or in statements of existence. Designed to eliminate the tendency toward *projection*, or assuming that characteristics that one attributes to a person (for example, "Pat is brave") are actually in that person instead of in the observer's perception of that person.

Equality An attitude that recognizes that each individual in a communication interaction is equal, that no one is superior to any other; encourages *supportiveness*; opposed to *superiority*.

Etc. An extensional device used to emphasize the notion of infinite complexity; since one can never know all about anything, any statement about the world or event must end with an explicit or implicit *etc.*

Ethicizing function of communication The media's function of providing viewers with a collective ethic or ethical system.

Ethics The branch of philosophy that deals with the rightness or wrongness of actions; the study of moral values.

Ethos The aspect of persuasiveness that depends on the audience's perception of the character of the speaker; to Aristotle *ethos* or ethical proof depended upon the speaker's perceived good will, knowledge, and moral character. *Ethos* is more commonly referred to as *speaker credibility*.

Evaluation A process whereby a value is placed on some person, object, or event.

Experiential limitation The limit of an individual's ability to communicate, as set by the nature and extent of his or her experiences.

Extemporaneous speech A speech that is thoroughly prepared and organized in detail and in which certain aspects of style are predetermined.

Extensional devices Those linguistic devices proposed by Alfred Korzybski for keeping language as a more accurate means for talking about the world. The extensional devices include the *etc.*, *date*, and *index*, the working devices; the *hyphen* and *quotes*, the safety devices.

Extensional orientation A point of view in which the primary consideration is given to the world of experience and only secondary consideration is given to the labels. See *intensional orientation*.

Extrinsic credibility The credibility or believability that the communicator is seen to possess before the actual communication begins; the communicator's initial credibility. See *intrinsic credibility*.

Fact-inference confusion A misevaluation in which one makes an inference, regards it as a fact, and acts upon it as if it were a fact.

Factual statement A statement made by the observer after observation, and limited to the observed. See *inferential statement*.

Faith A type of attitude or belief that is primarily emotional.

Fear appeal The appeal to fear to persuade an individual or group of individuals to believe or to act in a certain way.

Feedback Information that is fed back to the source. Feedback may come from the source's own messages (as when we hear what we are saying) or from the receiver(s) in the form of applause, yawning, puzzled looks, questions, letters to the editor of a newspaper, increased or decreased subscriptions to a magazine, and so forth. See *negative feedback*, *positive feedback*.

Field of experience The sum total of an individual's experiences, which influences his or her ability to communicate. In some views of communication, two people can only communicate to the extent that their fields of experience overlap.

Frozen evaluation See *static evaluation*.

Game A simulation of some situation with rules governing the behaviors of the participants and with some payoff for winning; in *transactional analysis*, *game* refers to a series of ulterior transactions that lead to a payoff; in TA, *game* also refers to a basically dishonest kind of transaction where participants hide their true feelings.

General Semantics The study of the relationships among language, thought, and behavior.

Gatekeeping The process of filtering messages from source to receiver. In this process some messages are allowed to pass through and others are changed or not allowed to pass at all.

Ghostwriting The procedure by which one writes or prepares messages for someone else and the identity of the real author is kept hidden.

Grammar The set of rules of syntax, semantics, and phonology. Prescriptive grammar deals with how educated speakers ought to speak; descriptive grammar deals with the knowledge (competence) speakers have of their language.

Group A collection of individuals related to each other with some common purpose and with some structure among them.

Heterophily The degree of difference between individuals. See *homophily*.

High-order abstraction A very general or abstract term or statement; an inference made on the basis of another inference. See *level of abstraction*.

Homophily The degree of similarity between individuals. See *heterophily*.

Honorific Expressing high regard or respect. In some languages certain pronouns of address are honorific and are used to address those of high status. In English such expressions as "Dr.," "Professor," and "the Honorable" are honorific.

Hyphen An *extensional device* used to illustrate that what may be separated verbally may not be separable on the event or nonverbal level; although one may talk about body and mind as if they were separable, in reality they are better referred to as body-mind.

Iconic signals Signals that bear real or nonarbitrary relationships to their referents; opposed to *arbitrariness*.

Identification In general semantics, a misevaluation whereby two or more items are considered as identical; according to Kenneth Burke, a process of becoming similar to another individual; a process of aligning one's interests to those of another. Burke sees identification as a necessary process for persuasion.

Ideographs Bodily movements that sketch the path or direction of a thought.

Idiolect An individual's personalized variation of the language.

Illustrators Nonverbal behaviors that accompany and literally illustrate the verbal messages—for example, upward movements that accompany the verbalizations "It's up there."

Immanent reference, principle of The principle of verbal interaction that holds that all verbalizations make some reference to the present, to the specific context, to the speaker, and to the receivers.

Impromptu speech A speech that is given without any direct prior preparation.

Index An *extensional device* used to emphasize the notion of nonidentity (no two things are the same) and symbolized by a subscript—for example, politician$_1$ is not politician$_2$.

Indiscrimination A misevaluation that is caused by categorizing people or events or objects into a particular class and responding to specific members only as members of the class: a failure to recognize that each individual is an individual and is unique; a failure to apply the *index*.

Inferential statement A statement that can be made by anyone, is not limited to the observed, and can be made at any time. See *factual statement*.

Information That which reduces uncertainty. See *bit of information*.

Initial credibility See *extrinsic credibility*.

Intensional orientation A point of view in which primary consideration is given to the way in which things are labeled and only secondary consideration (if any) to the world of experience. See *extensional orientation.*

Interaction diagrams Diagrams used to record the number of messages sent from one person to another.

Interaction process analysis A content analysis method that classifies messages into four general categories: social emotional positive, social emotional negative, attempted answers, and questions.

Interchangeability The feature of language that makes possible the reversal of roles between senders and receivers of messages. Because of interchangeability all adult members of a speech community may serve as both senders and receivers; people may produce any linguistic message they can understand.

Interpersonal communication Communication between or among persons, generally distinguished from mass communication and from public communication. Often, intrapersonal communication, dyadic communication, and small group communication in general.

Interpersonal conflict A conflict between two persons; a conflict within an individual caused by his or her relationships with other people.

Intimate distance The closest proxemic distance, ranging from touching to 6 to 18 inches.

Intrapersonal communication Communication with oneself.

Intrinsic credibility The credibility or believability that a listener perceives a communicator to possess based on what takes place during the actual communication encounter. See *extrinsic credibility.*

Jargon A kind of *sublanguage;* the language of any special group, often a professional class, which is unintelligible to individuals not belonging to the group; the "shop talk" of the group.

Kinesics The study of the communicative dimension of face and body movements.

Laissez-faire leader A group leader who allows the group to develop and progress or make mistakes on its own.

Language The rules of *syntax, semantics,* and *phonology;* a potentially self-reflexive structured system of symbols that catalogs the objects, events, and relations in the world. A *language* is an infinite set of grammatical sentences generated by the grammar of any language—for example, English, Italian, Bantu, Chinese.

Learnability The feature of language that refers to the fact that any normal human being is capable of learning any language as a first language. Learnability is dependent on and follows from language being traditionally or culturally transmitted.

Level of abstraction The relative distance of a term or statement from the actual perception; a low-order abstraction would be a description of the perception, whereas a high-order abstraction would consist of inferences about inferences about descriptions of a perception.

Linguistic determinism A theory that holds that language determines what we do, say, and think and in fact limits what we are able to do, say, and think.

Linguistic relativity A theory that argues that the language we speak influences what we perceive and think. Since different languages catalog the world differently, speakers of different languages will see the world differently.

Linguistics The study of language; the study of the system of rules by which meanings are paired with sounds.

Listening An active process of receiving aural stimuli.

Local leader An opinion leader who is concerned with local rather than national or international issues. See *cosmopolitan leader*.

Loving An interpersonal process in which one feels a closeness, a caring, a warmth, and an excitement for another person.

Low-order abstraction A description of what is perceived. See *level of abstraction*.

Macroscopic approach to communication The focus on broad and general aspects of communication.

Manuscript speech A speech designed to be read from a script verbatim.

Mass communication Communication addressed to an extremely large audience, mediated by audio and/or visual transmitters, and processed by gatekeepers before transmission.

Mere exposure hypothesis The theory that holds that repeated or prolonged exposure to a stimulus may result in attitude change toward the stimulus object, generally in the direction of increased positiveness.

Mesomorphy The muscular dimension of body build.

Message Any signal or combination of signals that serve as *stimuli* for a receiver.

Metacommunication Communication about communication.

Metalanguage Language used to talk about language.

Microscopic approach to communication The focus on minute and specific aspects of communication.

Model A physical representation of an object or process.

Monomorphism The tendency to serve as a leader for one topic; generally characterizes cosmopolitan leaders. See *polymorphism*.

Multiordinality In general semantics, a condition whereby a term may exist on different levels of abstraction.

Multivalued orientation A point of view that emphasizes that there are many sides (rather than only one or two sides) to any issue.

Narcotizing function of communication The media's function of providing receivers with information the knowledge of which is, in turn, confused by receivers with doing something about something.

Negative feedback Feedback that serves a corrective function by informing the source that his or her message is not being received in the way intended. Negative feedback serves to redirect the source's behavior. Looks of boredom, shouts of disagreement, and letters critical of newspaper policy would be examples of negative feedback.

Negative reinforcement The strengthening of a particular response by removing an aversive stimulus. See *positive reinforcement.*

Neutrality A response pattern lacking in personal involvement; encourages *defensiveness;* opposed to *empathy.*

Noise Anything that distorts the message intended by the source. Noise may be viewed as anything that interferes with the receiver's receiving the message as the source intended the message to be received. Noise is present in a communication system to the extent that the message received is not the message sent. Noise may originate in any of the components of the communication act—for example, in the source as a lisp, in the channel as static, in the receiver as a hearing loss, in written communication as blurred type. Noise is always present in any communication system, and its effects may be reduced (but never eliminated completely) by increasing the strength of the signal or the amount of redundancy, for example.

Nonallness An attitude or point of view in which it is recognized that one can never know all about anything and that what we know or say or hear is only a part of what there is to know, say, or hear.

Nonelementalism See *elementalism.*

Object adaptors Nonverbal behaviors (see *adaptors*) that make use of some kind of prop that itself does not serve any instrumental function, for example, scratching your head with a pencil or chewing on your necklace.

Object language Language used to communicate about objects, events, and relations in the world; the structure of the object language is described in a *metalanguage;* the display of physical objects—for example, flower arranging and the colors of the clothes we wear.

Object level The nonverbal level of sense perception, which we abstract from the event level; the level on which we live our lives.

Objective abstracting A form or type of abstracting in which we group individual units into a class of which they are all members, as, for example, all chapters being grouped into a book.

Obstinate audience A view of the audience, particularly the public and mass communication audience, as critical, selective, and active.

Olfactory communication Communication by smell.

Openness See *productivity.*

Operant A response emitted without a clearly identifiable prior stimulus; a bit of behavior controlled by its consequences.

Operant conditioning A process whereby reinforcement is contingent upon a particular response with the effect that the response is strengthened, or a process whereby punishment is contingent upon a particular response with the effect that the response is weakened. See *negative reinforcement, positive reinforcement.*

Opinion A tentative conclusion concerning some object, person, or event.

Paralanguage The vocal (but nonverbal) aspect of speech. Paralanguage consists of voice qualities (for example, pitch range, resonance, tempo), vocal characterizers (for example, laughing or crying, yelling or whispering), vocal qualifiers (for example, intensity, pitch height), and vocal segregates (for example, *uh-uh,* meaning "no," or *sh,* meaning "silence").

Perception The process of becoming aware of objects and events from the senses.

Performance The actual utterances that a speaker speaks and a hearer hears. See *competence.*

Performative A statement whose utterance is itself an action; includes such verbal acts as voting, delivering verdicts, apologizing, and cursing.

Personal distance The second-closest proxemic distance, ranging from 1.5 feet to 4 feet.

Persuasion The process of influencing attitudes and behavior.

Phatic communion Communication that is primarily social; communication designed to open the channels of communication rather than to communicate something about the external world; "Hello," and "How are you?" in everyday interaction are common examples.

Phonology The area of linguistics concerned with sound.

Pictics The study of the pictorial code of communication.

Pictographs Bodily movements that draw pictures in the air of the general shape of the thing being talked about.

Pitch The highness or lowness of the vocal tone.

Polarization A form of fallacious reasoning by which only the two extremes are considered; also referred to as "black-or-white" and "either-or" thinking.

Polymorphism The tendency to serve as a leader for a number of different topics; generally characterizes local opinion leaders.

Positive feedback *Feedback* that supports or reinforces behavior along the lines it is already proceeding in—for example, applause during a speech.

Positive reinforcement The strengthening of a particular response by making a reward contingent upon it. The process may be visualized in three stages: (1) a response is emitted—for example, a child says "daddy"; (2) a reward is given—for example, a smile or candy or touching; (3) the response, "daddy," is strengthened—that is, it is more likely to occur under similar circumstances. See *negative reinforcement*.

Prevarication The feature of human language that makes lying possible. This feature depends on and is a function of displacement, openness or productivity, and semanticity.

Primacy effect The condition by which what comes first exerts greater influence than what follows. See *recency effect*.

Problem orientation A focus on a problem and its possible solutions rather than on controlling the group processes; encourages *supportiveness*; opposed to *control*.

Process Ongoing activity; nonstatic; communication is referred to as a process to emphasize that it is always changing, always in motion.

Productivity The feature of language that makes possible the creation and understanding of novel utterances. With human language we can talk about matters that have never been talked about before, and similarly we can understand utterances that we have never heard before. Also referred to as *openness*.

Projection A psychological process whereby we attribute characteristics or feelings of our own to others; often used to refer to the process whereby we attribute our own faults to others.

Provisionalism An attitude of open-mindedness that leads to the creation of *supportiveness*; opposed to *certainty*.

Proxemics The study of the communicative function of space; the study of how people unconsciously structure their space—the distance between people in their interactions, the organization of space in homes and offices and even the design of cities.

Public communication Communication in which the source is one person and the receiver is an audience of many persons.

Public distance The farthest proxemic distance, ranging from 12 to over 25 feet.

Public speaking Communication that occurs when a speaker delivers a relatively prepared, continuous address in a specific setting to a large audience that provides little immediate feedback.

Punctuation of communication The breaking up of continuous communication sequences into short sequences with identifiable beginnings and endings or stimuli and responses.

Punishment Noxious or aversive stimulation.

Pygmalion The condition in which one makes a prediction and then proceeds to fulfill it; a type of self-fulfilling prophecy but one that refers to others and to our evaluation of others rather than to ourselves.

Quotes An *extensional device* used to emphasize that a word or phrase is being used in a special sense and should therefore be given special attention.

Rapid fading The evanescent or nonpermanent quality of speech signals.

Rate The speed with which we speak, generally measured in words per minute.

Receiver Any person or thing that takes in messages. Receivers may be individuals listening or reading a message, a group of persons hearing a speech, a scattered television audience, or a machine that stores information.

Recency effect The condition in which what comes last (that is, most recently) exerts greater influence than what comes first. See *primacy effect.*

Recurrence, principle of The principle of verbal interaction that holds that individuals will repeat many times and in many different ways who they are, how they see themselves, and, in general, what they think is important and significant.

Redundancy The quality of a message that makes it totally predictable and therefore lacking in information. A message of zero redundancy would be completely unpredictable; a message of 100 percent redundancy would be completely predictable. All human languages contain some degree of redundancy built into them, generally estimated to be about 50 percent.

Reflexiveness The feature of language that refers to the fact that human language can be used to refer to itself; that is, we can talk about our talk and create a *metalanguage*, a language for talking about language. See *self-reflexiveness.*

Regulators Nonverbal behaviors that regulate, monitor, or control the communications of another person.

Reinforcement The strengthening of a particular response. See *positive reinforcement, negative reinforcement.*

Reinforcement/Packaging, Principle of The principle of verbal interaction that holds that in most interactions, messages are transmitted simultaneously through a number of different channels that normally reinforce each other; messages come in packages.

Rejection A response to an individual that rejects or denies the validity of an individual's self-view.

Relational abstracting A form or type of abstracting in which relationships among items are abstracted and represented in some kind of formula or equation or diagram; for example, the formula $a^2 = b^2 + c^2$ expressing the relationship among the sides of a right triangle is the result of relational abstracting.

Reliability The degree of agreement that can be obtained from a number of different observers; the degree to which an instrument or observers will yield the same results on repeated observations.

Response Any bit of overt or covert behavior.

Rhythmic movements Body movements that depict or visually imitate the rhythm or pacing of an event.

Role The part an individual plays in a group; an individual's function or expected behavior.

Self-acceptance Being satisfied with ourselves, with our virtues and vices, abilities and limitations.

Self-adaptors Nonverbal behaviors (see *adaptors*) that serve some personal need—for example, autoerotic activity.

Self-concept An individual's self-evaluation; an individual's self-appraisal.

Self-disclosure The process of revealing something significant about ourselves to another individual or to a group, which would not normally be known by them.

Self-fulfilling prophecy The situation in which we make a prediction or prophecy and fulfill it ourselves—for example, expecting a class to be boring and then fulfilling this expectation by perceiving it as boring.

Self-reflexive abstracting A form or type of abstracting in which the abstraction is of itself, as when, for example, we think about our thinking, love our love, or fear our fear.

Self-reflexiveness The property of being able to refer back to itself; for example, language is self-reflexive because it can be used to refer to itself. See *reflexiveness*.

Semantic differential A device for measuring connotative meaning consisting of 7-point, bipolar scales; generally three dimensions of meaning are measured: evaluation, potency, and activity.

Semantic reaction A total reaction; a reaction of the organism-as-a-whole; a reaction that is determined by what the whole situation means to an individual.

Semantic space The connotative meaning of a term viewed as existing in a three-dimensional space consisting of evaluative, potency, and activity dimensions.

Semanticity The feature of human language that refers to the fact that some words have denotations in the objective world. All human languages possess semanticity, but not all words have denotations (for example, *of*, *the*, and *is* do not have objective referents in the real world).

Semantics The area of language study concerned with meaning.

Semantogenic Caused by semantics or labels; used most widely in reference to a problem or disorder whose origin may be found in the labels. For example, stuttering has been called semantogenic; because some particular behavior was labeled "stuttering," according to the semantogenic theory, that behavior became stuttering.

Sequential communication Communication in which messages are passed from A to B, B to C, C to D, and so on; linear communication.

Sexist language Language derogatory to one sex, generally women.

Shyness The condition of discomfort and uneasiness in interpersonal situations.

Sign Something that stands for something else and that bears a natural, nonarbitrary relationship to it—for example, dark clouds as a sign of rain. See *symbol*.

Sign language Gesture language that is highly codified—for example, a hitch-hiker's gesture.

Signal and noise, relativity of The principle of verbal interaction that holds that what is signal (meaningful) and what is noise (interference) is relative to the communication analyst, the communication participants, and the communication context.

Signal reaction A conditioned response to a signal; a response to some signal that is immediate rather than delayed. See *symbol reaction.*

Silence The absence of vocal communication; often misunderstood to refer to the absence of any and all communication.

Slang The language used by special groups, which is not considered proper by the general society; the language made up of the *argot, cant,* and *jargon* of various subcultures, known by the general public.

Small group communication Communication among a collection of individuals, few enough in number so that all members may interact with relative ease as both senders and receivers, who are related to each other by some common purpose and with some degree of organization or structure among them.

Social distance The third proxemic distance, ranging from 4 to 12 feet; the distance at which business is usually conducted.

Social kinesics The area of *kinesics* concerned with the role and meanings of different body movements.

Somatotype Body type measured in terms of the degree to which one is fat, muscular, and skinny.

Source Any person or thing that creates messages. A source may be an individual speaking, writing, or gesturing or a computer solving a problem.

Spatial movements Body movements that depict spatial movements—for example, rapid hand motions to depict the passing of a speeding car.

Specialization The feature of human language that refers to the characteristic of human language serving no purpose other than that of communication. Human language (unlike a dog's panting, for example) does not serve any biological function; it is a specialized system.

Specialized communication system A communication system that serves no other function than that of communication; human language is a specialized system.

Speech Messages utilizing a vocal-auditory channel.

Speech community A group of persons using the same language.

Spontaneity The communication pattern in which one verbalizes what one is thinking without attempting to develop strategies for control; encourages *supportiveness;* opposed to *strategy.*

Stability The principle of perception that refers to the fact that our perceptions of things and people are relatively consistent with our previous conceptions.

Static evaluation An orientation that fails to recognize that the world is characterized by constant change; an attitude that sees people and events as fixed rather than as constantly changing.

Static judgments Perceptual judgments that refer to those characteristics of another person that are relatively unchanging—for example, race, occupation, age, and nationality. See *dynamic judgments.*

Status The relative level one occupies in a hierarchy; status always involves a comparison, and thus one's status is only relative to the status of another. In our culture occupation, financial position, age, and educational level are significant determinants of status.

Stereotype In communication, refers to a fixed impression of a group of people through which we then perceive specific individuals; stereotypes are most often negative (Martians are stupid, uneducated, and dirty) but may also be positive (Venusians are scientific, industrious, and helpful).

Stimulus Any external or internal change that impinges on or arouses an organism.

Stimulus-response models of communication Models of communication that assume that the process of communication is a linear one, beginning with a stimulus that then leads to a response.

Strategy The use of some plan for control of other members of a communication interaction which guides one's own communications; encourages *defensiveness;* opposed to *spontaneity.*

Structural differential A model of the abstraction process consisting of an *event level,* an *object level,* and *first, second, third,* and further *verbal levels.*

Subjectivity The principle of perception that refers to the fact that one's perceptions are not objective but rather are influenced by one's wants and needs and one's expectations and predictions of the perceiver.

Sublanguage A variation from the general language used by a particular subculture; *argot, cant,* and *jargon* are particular kinds of sublanguages.

Superiority A point of view or attitude that assumes that others are not equal to oneself; encourages *defensiveness;* opposed to *equality.*

Supportiveness An attitude of an individual or an atmosphere in a group that is characterized by openness, the absence of fear, and a genuine feeling of equality; messages evidencing *description, problem orientation, spontaneity, empathy, equality,* and *provisionalism* are assumed to lead to supportiveness. See *defensiveness.*

Symbol Something that stands for something else but that bears no natural relationship to it—for example, purple as a symbol of mourning. Words are symbols in that they bear no natural relationship to the meaning they symbolize. See *sign.*

Symbol reaction A reaction that is made with some delay. See *signal reaction.*

Symmetrical relationship A relation between two or more persons in which one person's behavior serves as a stimulus for the same type of behavior in the other person(s). Examples of such relationships include situations in which anger in one person encourages or serves as a stimulus for anger in another person or in which a critical comment by the person leads the other person to respond in like manner.

Syntax   The area of language study concerned with the rules for combining words into sentences

Taboo   Forbidden; culturally censored. Taboo language is that which is frowned upon by "polite society." Themes and specific words may be considered taboo, for example, death, sex, certain forms of illness, and various words denoting sexual activities and excretory functions.

Tactile communication   Communication by touch; communication received by the skin.

Territoriality   A possessive or ownershiplike reaction to an area of space or to particular objects.

Theory   A general statement or principle applicable to a number of related phenomena.

Third verbal level   The level of inferences about inferences.

Time-binders   A class of life that survives by passing information on from one generation to another, thus making knowledge cumulative; human beings.

Total feedback   The quality of speech that refers to one's ability to receive all the communications that one sends.

Traditional transmission   The feature of language that refers to the fact that human languages (at least in their outer surface form) are learned. Unlike various forms of animal language, which are innate, human languages are transmitted traditionally or culturally. This feature of language does not deny the possibility that certain aspects of language may be innate. Also referred to as *cultural transmission*.

Transactional   The relationship among elements in which each influences and is influenced by each other element; communication is a transactional process since no element is independent of any other element.

Transactions   The patterns of interaction between people; in *transactional analysis* three types of transactions are defined: *complementary, crossed,* and *ulterior*.

Trust   Faith in the behavior of another person; confidence in another person that leads us to feel that whatever we risk will not be lost.

Two-step flow of communication   A hypothesis that states that the influence of the media occurs in two steps: (1) the media influence opinion leaders, and (2) the opinion leaders influence the general population through interpersonal communication.

Two-valued orientation   A point of view in which events are seen or questions are evaluated in terms of two values—for example, right or wrong, good or bad. Often referred to as the fallacy of black-or-white and *polarization*.

Undelayed reaction   A reaction that is immediate; a signal response; a reaction made without any conscious deliberation.

Universal language A language understood by all people and that all people have the ability to use.

Universal of communication A feature of communication that is common to all communication acts.

Universal of language A feature of language that is common to all known languages.

Value Relative worth of an object; a quality that makes something desirable or undesirable; ideals or customs about which we have emotional responses, whether positive or negative.

Variable A quantity that can increase or decrease; something that can have different values.

Vocal qualifiers Aspects of *paralanguage*, specifically, intensity, pitch height, and extent of vocalizations.

Vocal segregates Aspects of *paralanguage*, specifically such vocalizations as *uh-uh, uh-huh, sh,* and pauses.

Voice qualities Aspects of *paralanguage*, specifically, pitch range, vocal lip control, glottis control, pitch control, articulation control, rhythm control, resonance, and tempo.

Volume The relative loudness of the voice.

Word association A method for measuring connotative meaning; a way of measuring the meaningfulness of words; a projective technique in which associations to stimulus words are analyzed in terms of their psychological significance.

Index of Names

Index of Subjects